APPLYING MATHEMATICS
in Daily Living

Albert P. Shulte
Director, Mathematics
Oakland Schools
Pontiac, Michigan

Harriet Haynes
Mathematics Staff Developer
School District 19
Brooklyn, New York

Stuart A. Choate
Coordinator of Mathematics
and Computer Education
Midland Public Schools
Midland, Michigan

CONTENTS OF THE TEACHER'S EDITION

GLENCOE PUBLISHING COMPANY
Mission Hills, California

To Develop Essential Mathematics Skills and Problem-Solving Abilities...

Teacher's Edition

1 A developmental text that **enables students to succeed**

2 A Teacher's Edition that gives you **abundant teaching helps** and makes classroom management easy

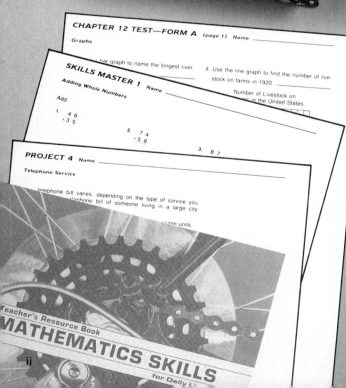

CHAPTER 12 TEST—FORM A (page 1) Name _____

Graphs

___ bar graph to name the longest river

2. Use the line graph to find the number of livestock on farms in 1920

Number of Livestock on ___ in the United States

SKILLS MASTER 1 Name _____

Adding Whole Numbers

Add

1. 4 6
  + 3 5

2. 7 4
  + 5 8

3. 8 7

PROJECT 4 Name _____

Telephone Service

__ telephone bill varies, depending on the type of service you
__ __ telephone bill of someone living in a large city

___ units

Teacher's Resource Book

MATHEMATICS SKILLS
for Daily Li___

3 Tests

4 Skills Masters

5 Projects...bound into a complete Resource Book of reproducible master

Use either textbook for a full-year's course. Or

To Provide Skills Reinforcement Through Practical Applications...

1 A motivating text that **helps students apply math**

2 **Computing Skills Refresher** built into the student's text

APPLYING MATHEMATICS in Daily Living

Teacher's Edition

3 A comprehensive Teacher's Edition with **all the help you want**

4 Tests

5 Applications...bound into a Teacher's Resource Book

use both books together for a two-year sequence.

CHAPTER 8 TEST—FORM A (page 1) Name _____

Managing Money

1. Find each amount of cash on hand.

Day	Item	Income	Expense	Cash on hand
	Balance			$65.25
Thurs.	Groceries		$32.60	
	Gasoline			
Fri.				

APPLICATION 2 Name _____

Grade Point Average

In many schools a grade point average (GPA) is computed for each student. Usually an A is worth 4 honor points per credit; a B, 3; a C, 2; a D, 1; and an F, 0.

To find a **grade point average**, do the following:

Computer disks— a software supplement for the text

Teacher's Resource Book
APPLYING MATHEMATICS in Daily Living

Ten Chapters Develop Practical Skills, Problem-Solving Ability, and Applications

1.11 | ESTIMATING PRODUCTS

Sometimes it is helpful to estimate a product.

Example 1: During a typical week, the Carlsons spend $87 for groceries. Estimate how much they spend in 52 weeks by rounding each number to the nearest ten.

ESTIMATE: **Think:**

$87	about	**$90**	**$90**
52	about	**50**	**×50**

Using Data and Making Estimates (Chapter 1)

2.5 | READING LINE GRAPHS

Line graphs make it easy to see change. The graph below shows the amount of rainfall El Paso, Texas, received each month.

Normal Monthly Rainfall in El Paso, Texas

July has the most rain, about 1.5 inches.

The scale cannot be

Using Graphs (Chapter 2)

3.4 | USING FORMULAS

A formula is a rule or a principle written as a mathematical sentence.

Principle:
To find the distance an object travels, multiply its rate of speed by the time it travels.

Formula:

Equations and Formulas (Chapter 3)

4.3 | PROPORTIONS

Wilma has driven 252 miles since last filling her car's 12-gallon gas tank. She has used 9 gallons. Can she make her next exit 70 miles away?

252 miles on   ? miles on
9 gallons   3 gallons

Wilma used equivalent ratios to make a quick calculation.

$$\frac{252}{9} \xleftarrow{\text{distance}} \frac{m}{3}$$

Ratio, Proportion, and Percent (Chapter 4)

5.5 | THE METRIC SYSTEM

Zurich	221 km
Munich	225 km
Copenhagen	1013 km

The system of measurement that includes feet, inches, yards, pounds, gallons, quarts, degrees Fahrenheit, and so on, is called the **customary system.**

Another system, called the **metric system,** is used in most countries of the world. It is easier to use than the customary system.

Comparisons

Measurement (Chapter 5)

6.6 | TRIANGLES

John D. Cunningham   Jack Corn/Corn's Photo Service

Remember that the area of a parallelogram is the product of the base and the height.

Perimeter, Area, and Volume (Chapter 6)

Ample Problem Solving In Every Chapter!

...Including Consumer Mathematics!

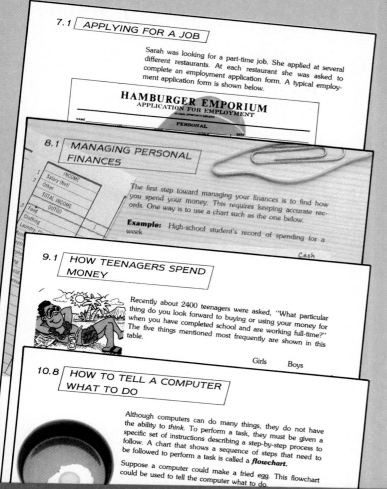

7.1 APPLYING FOR A JOB

Sarah was looking for a part-time job. She applied at several different restaurants. At each restaurant she was asked to complete an employment application form. A typical employment application form is shown below.

HAMBURGER EMPORIUM
APPLICATION FOR EMPLOYMENT
AN EQUAL OPPORTUNITY EMPLOYER

NAME _____ PERSONAL _____ DATE _____

8.1 MANAGING PERSONAL FINANCES

INCOME
1 Salary (Net)
2 Other
TOTAL INCOME
OUTGO
3 Food
Clothing
Laundry

The first step toward managing your finances is to find how you spend your money. This requires keeping accurate records. One way is to use a chart such as the one below.

Example: High-school student's record of spending for a week

Cash

9.1 HOW TEENAGERS SPEND MONEY

Recently about 2400 teenagers were asked, "What particular thing do you look forward to buying or using your money for when you have completed school and are working full-time?" The five things mentioned most frequently are shown in this table.

Girls   Boys

10.8 HOW TO TELL A COMPUTER WHAT TO DO

Although computers can do many things, they do not have the ability to *think*. To perform a task, they must be given a specific set of instructions describing a step-by-step process to follow. A chart that shows a sequence of steps that need to be followed to perform a task is called a *flowchart*.

Suppose a computer could make a fried egg. This flowchart could be used to tell the computer what to do.

Earning Money
(Chapter 7)

Managing Money
(Chapter 8)

Using Money
(Chapter 9)

Probability and Computer Literacy
(Chapter 10)

Plus! A Complete COMPUTING SKILLS REFRESHER

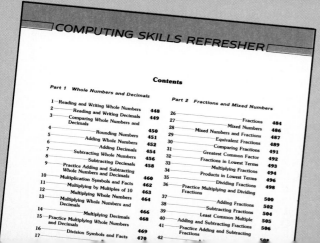

COMPUTING SKILLS REFRESHER

A comprehensive aid to help develop skills. Can be used to provide review before or during coverage of the 10 chapters. (Teacher's Edition provides Daily Lesson-Plan Guide for both approaches and more.)

APPLYING MATHEMATICS IN DAILY LIVING
is more than a
Consumer Mathematics book!

Contents

Computing Skills Refresher and Skills Refresher Quizzes for Review of Fundamental Operations

PART 1: Whole Numbers and Decimals

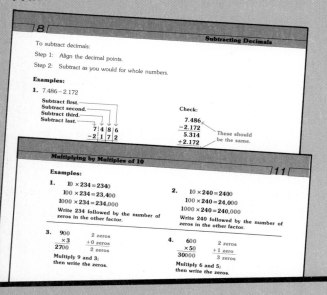

]8[

Subtracting Decimals

To subtract decimals:

Step 1: Align the decimal points.

Step 2: Subtract as you would for whole numbers.

Examples:

1. $7.486 - 2.172$

Subtract first.
Subtract second.
Subtract third.
Subtract last.

$$7 \ 4 \ 8 \ 6$$
$$-2 \ 1 \ 7 \ 2$$

Check:
$$7.486$$
$$-2.172$$
$$5.314$$
$$+2.172$$
These should be the same.

Multiplying by Multiples of 10

]11[

Examples:

1. $10 \times 234 = 2340$
$100 \times 234 = 23,400$
$1000 \times 234 = 234,000$
Write 234 followed by the number of zeros in the other factor.

2. $10 \times 240 = 2400$
$100 \times 240 = 24,000$
$1000 \times 240 = 240,000$
Write 240 followed by the number of zeros in the other factor.

3. $\begin{array}{r}900 \\ \times 3 \\ \hline 2700\end{array}$ $\quad \begin{array}{l}2\ zeros \\ +0\ zeros \\ \hline 2\ zeros\end{array}$
Multiply 9 and 3; then write the zeros.

4. $\begin{array}{r}600 \\ \times 50 \\ \hline 30000\end{array}$ $\quad \begin{array}{l}2\ zeros \\ +1\ zero \\ \hline 3\ zeros\end{array}$
Multiply 6 and 5; then write the zeros.

PART 2: Fractions and Mixed Numbers

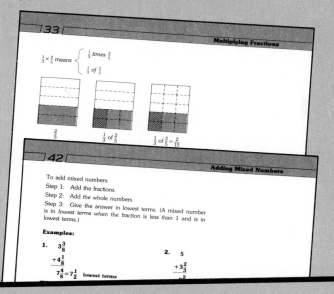

]33[

Multiplying Fractions

$\frac{1}{3} \times \frac{2}{5}$ means $\begin{cases} \frac{1}{3} \text{ times } \frac{2}{5} \\ \frac{1}{3} \text{ of } \frac{2}{5} \end{cases}$

$\frac{2}{5}$ $\qquad$ $\frac{1}{3}$ of $\frac{2}{5}$ $\qquad$ $\frac{1}{3}$ of $\frac{2}{5} = \frac{2}{15}$

]42[

Adding Mixed Numbers

To add mixed numbers:

Step 1: Add the fractions.

Step 2: Add the whole numbers.

Step 3: Give the answer in lowest terms. (A mixed number is in *lowest terms* when the fraction is less than 1 and is in lowest terms.)

Examples:

1. $\begin{array}{r}3\frac{3}{8} \\ +4\frac{1}{8} \\ \hline 7\frac{4}{8} = 7\frac{1}{2}\end{array}$ lowest terms

2. $\begin{array}{r}5 \\ +3\frac{2}{3} \\ \hline \end{array}$

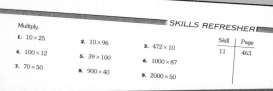

SKILLS REFRESHER

Multiply.

1. 10×25

2. 10×96

3. 472×10

4. 100×12

5. 39×100

6. 1000×87

7. 70×50

8. 900×40

9. 2000×50

Skill	Page
11	463

Skills Refresher Quizzes—at least two per chapter—help the student anticipate computing skills needed in upcoming sections of the text. The quizzes are keyed to specific skill sections of the Computing Skills Refresher.

CALCULATOR SKILLS—10 Lessons Tied to the Book's Content

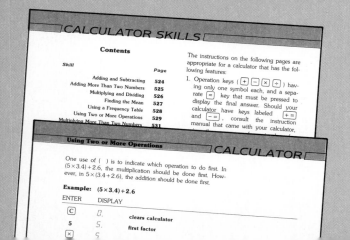

CALCULATOR SKILLS

Contents

The instructions on the following pages are appropriate for a calculator that has the following features:

1. Operation keys ($+$ $-$ $\times$ $\div$) having only one symbol each, and a separate $=$ key that must be pressed to display the final answer. Should your calculator have keys labeled $+=$ and $-=$, consult the instruction manual that came with your calculator,

Using Two or More Operations

CALCULATOR

One use of ( ) is to indicate which operation to do first. In $(5 \times 3.4) + 2.6$, the multiplication should be done first. However, in $5 \times (3.4 + 2.6)$, the addition should be done first.

Example: $(5 \times 3.4) + 2.6$

ENTER	DISPLAY	
C	0.	clears calculator
5	5.	first factor
×	5.	

Instruction and practice in the use of a hand-held calculator. Located at the back of the book (pp. 523-536), these lessons can be used at any time—or together as a separate unit.

Special Features that Create Interest and Encourage Problem Solving

CAREER

Building Trades Apprentice

To become a carpenter, an electrician, a bricklayer, or other skilled worker, you need special training. The training period is called an *apprenticeship*. Some apprentices get all their training on the job. Others have to go to some classes.

Here are some problems an apprentice may have to solve with a formula.

> Information to make students aware of mathematics-related careers and the importance of mathematics in jobs. One per chapter.

CONSUMER TOPIC

Formulas for Shopping

Many problems involving money are solved with a rule that can be written as a formula.

At the store:

How would you find the cost of 3 stereo tapes at $8 apiece? You would multiply 3 by 8 and get $24. You are using this rule:

To find the cost, multiply the number of items by the price

> Topics that highlight interesting aspects of consumerism, to help students become more knowledgeable consumers. One per chapter.

MUSICAL INTERLUDE

The music below is written in $\frac{4}{4}$ time. The table at the right shows the note values for music written in $\frac{4}{4}$ time.

All music is separated into *measures*. Each measure is separated from the next measure by a vertical line called a *bar line*. When music is written in $\frac{4}{4}$ time, there are four counts to each measure.

Symbol	Name	Note value
o	whole note	4 counts
♩	half note	2 counts
♩	quarter note	1 count
♪	eighth note	$\frac{1}{2}$ count

> A variety of optional features, including activities, challenging problems, discussion questions, games, puzzles—that frequently require nonroutine problem solving. Several in each chapter.

MATH FROM THE 1870'S

The following problems appeared in a math book that was published in 1877. Can you do them?

The Bettmann Archive

1. A field 100 rods long and 30 rods wide contains how many acres? (1 acre = 160 square rods)

2. Upon how many acres of ground can the entire population of the globe stand, supposing that 25000 persons can stand upon one acre

COMPLETE REVIEW AND EVALUATION

PREVIEW TEST

1. What town is located in region B-4?

2. In which region is Carthage located?

Graph and label each point.

3. (6,4), (5,5), (0,3), (0,0)

4.
x	6	3	4	5	$2\frac{1}{2}$	0
y	6	0	$2\frac{1}{2}$	2	4	1

From the line graph, in which ten-year period did the

5. decrease?

6. increase most rapidly?

Refer to the bar graph for exercises 7–8.

Photographer's Guide to People in Motion

Swimming
Walking
Running
Bicycling
Skating

8. _____ is more than twice as fast as running

CHAPTER REVIEW

Refer to the map for exercises 1–2.

1. In which region is each of these?
   a. Old Faithful Geyser
   b. The Thunderer
   c. Lewis Lake
   d. North Entrance

2. Which regions do not have camping areas (indicated by ⌂)?

Graph and label each point for exercises 3–4.

3. (0,2), (6,4), (2,5), (4,1)

4.
x	5	3	6	$4\frac{1}{2}$	7	2
y	0	7	6	4	5	$3\frac{1}{2}$

Refer to the line graph for exercises 5–7.

6. In which year was the average admission price about $2.05?

CHAPTER TEST

Refer to the map for exercises 1–2.

1. In which region is Wrangell located?

2. Which city is located in region A-2?

Graph and label each point for exercises 3–4.

3. (6,3), (1,5), (3,3), (2,0)

4.
x	4	0	6	$2\frac{1}{2}$	5	2
y	1	3	8	5	$5\frac{1}{2}$	1

5. Make a line graph of the table below.

Stopping Distance of a Car	
Speed (km/h)	Distance (m)
30	12
45	20
65	36
80	49
100	80

6. Below are (in pounds some anim graph.
Kangaroo
Kodiak bear
Gorilla
Siberian tige

7. In a pictograph, the

8. Out of every 100 people, _____ prefer to watch a comedy or

CUMULATIVE REVIEW

Refer to the bus schedule.

1. At what time does bus 4413 leave Omaha?

2. At what time does bus 4416 reach Omaha?

3. At what time is there a bus from Ashland to Lincoln?

4. Which buses make flag stops?

	OMAH
READ DOWN	
503 4413 608 1157	
2 30	8 15 4 00 12 45
	1
	8 55
	3 9 10
3 40	9 30 5 10 1 55

†—Flag stop.   AM—

Use sets A and B to find each mode, median, mean, and

Set A:
10	9	8
10	8	11
12	11	10
11	10	

Set B:
3	1	2
5	9	1
3	10	9
9	10	10

5. mode (or modes) of set A
6. mode (or mode
7. median of set A
8. median of set B
9. mean of set A

32, 29, 31, 32, 37, 41, 33, 32, 37, 35, 38, 40, 32, 41

13. Make

...and there's more review and evaluation in the teacher's materials (turn the page).

All Kinds of Teaching Help for You!

A COMPREHENSIVE TEACHER'S EDITION

1 **Manual** of teaching information...
- Overview of student text
- Detailed, Daily Lesson-Plan Guide for three suggested courses.
- Notes to the teacher, including suggestions for teaching each section. An Error-Analysis approach for the sections in the Computing Skills Refresher pinpoints typical computational errors that students may make.
- Correlation of the Teacher's Resource Book to the student text

- Performance Objectives—reproducible for optional classroom use

2 Full-size Student Textbook with annotations...
- Answers
- References suggesting uses of the **Applications** in the Teacher's Resource Book and of the lessons in the **Computer Supplement.**
- Correlations of the tests in the student book to student sections. Facilitates use of these tests as in-book diagnostic aids.

TEACHER'S RESOURCE BOOK

A complete, versatile set of reproducible masters (includes answer key)

CHAPTER 8 TEST—FORM B (page 2) Name _____

Reconcile the following accounts:

6. Bank balance: $255.32
Check-register balance: $270.77
Outstanding checks: $16.48, $25.42, $17.65
Outstanding deposits: $75.00

7. Bank balance: $188.18
Check-register balance: $119.33
Outstanding checks: $29.35, $42.50
Service charge: $3.00

−	Bank balance Outstanding checks	Check-register balance
+	Outstanding deposits Corrected balance	− Service charges
		Corrected balance

−	Bank balance Outstanding checks	Check-register balance
+	Outstanding deposits Corrected balance	− Service charges
		Corrected balance

Complete the chart for simple interest.

Principal   Rate   Term   Interest   Amount

CUMULATIVE TEST 2 (page 1) Name _____

Chapters 3–4

Tell if each sentence is true, false, or open.

1. $12 \div 4 = 8 - 5$ _____
2. $3 \times w = 30$ _____
3. $19 + 6 = 5 \times 4$ _____
4. $15 - 7 = x + 2$ _____

Find each answer when y is replaced with 7.

If line 37 (taxable income) is—   And you are— At least   But less than   Single   Married filing jointly

Married filing sepa-   Head of a house-   Your tax is—

COMPUTING SKILLS TEST 1—FORM A (page 1) Name _____

Name the value of each underlined digit. (*Example:* 5**6**4 *Answer:* 6 tens)

1. 4**0**31 _____
2. 751,6**4**3 _____
3. 8.**2** _____
4. 6.3**4**87 _____

Write in words.

5. 702,600 _____
6. 8,000,231,007 _____
7. 13.082 _____
8. 4.521 _____

TESTS

- **Chapter Tests**—two versions for each chapter. Can be used as pretests and posttests—or as two forms of posttests.
- **Cumulative Tests**—one test for every two chapters.
- **Computing Skills Tests**—two tests; two forms of each test. Can be used as pretests and/or posttests.

APPLICATIONS

- A unique, flexible resource of additional applications
- Many are consumer-oriented
- Enrichment activities, hands-on projects, discovery lessons, simulations, computer programs...

APPLICATION 42 Name _____

How Record Albums Are Priced

One reason why record albums are fairly expensive is that they are sold several times before reaching a consumer. For example, the record company that produces an album may sell it to a wholesaler, who in turn may sell it to a retailer, who in turn may sell it to a rackjobber, who in turn sells it to the consumer. (A rackjobber provides albums to a number of stores in a given area.)

The following percent of markup are often used to determine the retail price (the price you pay) for an album:

Transaction   Percent of

And a Separate Computer Supplement!

Round as indicated.

12. 85 (nearest ten)

Retailer to consumer   15%

APPLYING MATHEMATICS

in Daily Living

TEACHER'S MANUAL

Contents

Send all inquiries to:
Glencoe Publishing Company
15319 Chatsworth Street, P.O. Box 9509
Mission Hills, California 91345-9509

Printed in the United States of America

ISBN 0-8445-1865-4 (Student Text)
ISBN 0-8445-1866-2 (Teacher's Edition)

7 8 9 10 11 12   93 92 91 90 89 88

GLENCOE PUBLISHING COMPANY
Mission Hills, California

Introduction to Teacher's Edition, Teacher's Resource Book, and Computer Supplement

The Teacher's Edition for APPLYING MATHE-MATICS IN DAILY LIVING contains an annotated student's text and a bound-in teacher's manual.

Annotated Student's Text The full-size student's pages are overprinted with the following teacher's information:

☐ **Answers** to exercises are overprinted on the student's pages.

☐ **Correlations of Test Items** to sections in the chapter are given in a chart printed with each Preview Test and Chapter Test. See pages 9 and 50 for sample correlations. (Correlations for the Chapter Reviews and the Cumulative Reviews are printed in the student's text.)

☐ **Correlations of Applications From the Teacher's Resource Book (TRB)** key appropriate sections from the text to Applications in the Teacher's Resource Book. See page T3 for a description of the Applications, and see the bottom of page 13 for a sample correlation. A complete correlation chart appears on pages T42–T43.

☐ **Correlations of the Computer Supplement** key appropriate sections from the text to specific lessons on one of three computer disks. See the bottom of page 285 for a sample correlation. A description of the Computer Supplement and a complete correlation chart appear on page T3.

Manual Special teacher's pages are bound with the annotated student's text. These pages include the following:

☐ **Overview of Student's Text,** page T4, is a brief summary of the organization and the special features of the text.

☐ **Daily Lesson-Plan Guide,** pages T5–T17, suggests exercise assignments—both oral and written—for three possible courses of study (based on a 170-day school year). The lesson plans integrate the sections from the text, the skill sections from the *Computing Skills Refresher,* the Skills Refresher quizzes, the special topics and features, the Calculator skills, the tests and reviews, and the Applications.

☐ **Notes to the Teacher,** pages T18–T41, provides an overview of each chapter and suggestions for teaching each section. It also provides an overview of the *Computing Skills Refresher* and an error-analysis approach to help the teacher pinpoint typical computational errors that students may make. Included is a chart that correlates the items from the Computing Skills Tests (in the TRB) to the appropriate skills in the *Computing Skills Refresher.*

☐ **Correlation of the Teacher's Resource Book to the Text,** pages T42–T43, provides a list of all tests and a chart that keys the Applications to sections of the text.

☐ **Performance Objectives,** pages T44–T48, for the entire text are given in a separate list that may be reproduced for classroom use.

The **Teacher's Resource Book (TRB)** contains the following components, all in reproducible-master form:

☐ **Tests** consist of three types: Chapter Tests, Cumulative Tests, and Computing Skills Tests. For each Chapter Test, two versions, Form A and Form B, are included. Depending on the teacher's preference, one form could be used as a pretest and the other as a posttest, or perhaps one form could be used as an alternate posttest. Cumulative Tests are provided for every two chapters. These tests cover the same material as the Cumulative Reviews that appear in the text following every even-numbered chapter.

There are two forms for each of the two Computing Skills Tests. Computing Skills Tests 1 and 2 cover Parts 1 and 2, respectively, of the *Computing Skills Refresher*. The teacher may want to administer the tests at the beginning of the year to ascertain the computational needs of the students. The tests could also be used as pretests and/or posttests in conjunction with the *Computing Skills Refresher*.

A complete list of the tests appears on page T42. Answers for the tests may be found on pages 135–140 in the TRB.

☐ **Applications** cover a variety of practical topics and in many cases are consumer oriented. The Applications are extensions of the material in the chapter and consist of enrichment activities, hands-on projects, discovery lessons, simulations, and computer programs. Also included are forms (such as a tax form and blank checks) that can be used directly with exercises in the text. The Applications are correlated to the text by annotations that appear at the bottom of appropriate pages (in the Teacher's Edition). A complete correlation chart appears on pages T42–T43. Answers for the Applications may be found on pages 140–144 in the TRB.

The optional **Computer Supplement,** entitled *Applying Mathematics Skills,* consists of three disks and a teacher's manual. Complete instructions for each disk are included in the teacher's manual and also appear on the screen for the student. Disks 1 and 3 are tutorials that focus on interesting consumer topics from Chapters 7–9. Disk 2 is a game simulation on personal financial planning. The simulation gives students practice in managing money in such areas as paying bills, shopping for and selling items, buying insurance, and using a checking and a savings account. Variables, such as sudden sales, income fluctuations, and property losses, add interest and make it important for students to develop strategies and make prudent decisions. The goal is to earn the most "finance points."

There are four lessons on each of Disks 1 and 3, and each lesson consists of three or four problem sets. The problems are introduced with animated sequences and displays that are randomly generated from a pool of problem settings. The numbers used in the problems are also randomly generated; hence, there is an unlimited supply of problems available. Students are permitted to proceed to another problem set after successfully completing two problems.

On Disks 1 and 3, the following two options can be accessed as often as necessary to aid students in the problem-solving process:

1. Use the on-screen calculator to perform computations.
2. Request help.

The on-screen calculator is a unique feature of the Computer Supplement. The calculator that appears on the screen is an arithmetic-function calculator that uses the computer keyboard for input. Students may access help when needed. Each problem has its own built-in sequence of help routines. The help is given in the form of leading questions, hints, or analyses of the data. If help is still needed after all of the help routines for a problem have been exhausted, a detailed solution is shown.

The following correlation chart keys the Computer Supplement to the text. Individual annotations appear at the bottom of appropriate pages in the Teacher's Edition.

	Use after text page
Disk 1	
Lesson 1—Salary	285
Lesson 2—Commission	289
Lesson 3—Pay Periods	293
Lesson 4—Net Pay	297
Disk 2 (Simulation on Personal Finances)	331
Disk 3	
Lesson 1—Buying on Credit	342
Lesson 2—Layaway and Credit Cards	352
Lesson 3—Purchases and Sales Tax	375
Lesson 4—Discount	379

☐ **Answers,** which may be reproduced for students, are provided for all the odd-numbered exercises in the student's text.

Overview of Student's Text

APPLYING MATHEMATICS IN DAILY LIVING provides a fresh approach to a comprehensive course in general mathematics. The content—a blend of practical applications and basic computational skills—is relevant to today's students. The very flexible organization of the text gives the teacher such options as concentrating the review of computational skills before the application of those skills or interspersing the review of computation among other topics. Flexibility is also built into the abundant practice exercises and the special features of the text.

The book is organized into three sections: the ten chapters, the *Computing Skills Refresher,* and the *Calculator Skills.* The ten chapters develop practical, usable skills with an emphasis on consumer mathematics. A large amount of problem solving and basic computation is embedded in each chapter.

The *Computing Skills Refresher,* pages 447–522, provides review sections covering the four fundamental operations (addition, subtraction, multiplication, and division) of whole numbers, decimals, fractions, and mixed numbers. See pages T5–T17 for suggested lesson plans showing three ways to integrate the *Computing Skills Refresher* with the ten chapters.

The *Calculator Skills* provide instruction and practice in the use of a hand-held calculator. Each Calculator Skills lesson can be used with an appropriate section in the text. Annotations in the student's text key the ten Calculator Skills lessons to text pages 13, 16, 19, 23, 30, 97, 251, 334, 338, and 418. Of course, at the teacher's discretion the Calculator Skills lessons can be used at any time—even together as a separate unit.

Each of the ten chapters has the following consistent organization:

☐ **Preview Test** This test can be used at the beginning of a chapter to determine student familiarity with the various topics. At least one test item is included for each performance objective. The teacher may use the test scores to decide whether certain topics can be omitted or covered more quickly and to pinpoint topics that may need extra attention or practice as they are developed.

☐ **Skills Refresher** At least two Skills Refresher quizzes occur in each chapter. These brief quizzes anticipate basic computing skills that the student will need in the next section or two. A student who does not do well on a particular Skills Refresher quiz can use the appropriate skill section or sections of the *Computing Skills Refresher* for remedial work before proceeding in the chapter.

☐ **Career** One Career feature is included per chapter, and coverage is optional. Each Career feature is devoted to one or more careers.

☐ **Consumer Topic** One Consumer Topic feature is included per chapter, and coverage is optional. These features highlight interesting topics and will help students become more-knowledgeable consumers in today's complex society.

☐ **Other Special Features** A variety of optional full-page or partial-page features are included with each chapter. These features may consist of games, activities, discussion questions, puzzles, challenging problems, or interesting mathematical information. Often, nonroutine problem solving is required to complete a feature. Each chapter's features are listed with the chapter in the Table of Contents.

☐ **Chapter Review** The Chapter Review is used to review all the topics within a chapter. Reference numbers key the exercises to the related sections.

☐ **Chapter Test** This test covers the same objectives as the Preview Test. The Chapter Test can be used for grading purposes, as a student self-test, or as a diagnostic test to determine if further teaching is needed.

☐ **Cumulative Review** Following every even-numbered chapter is a review of the two preceding chapters. The exercises are grouped by sections, so that these reviews are usable even if parts of a preceding chapter have been omitted. Reference numbers key the exercises to the related sections.

☐ **Selected Answers** Answers to all the odd-numbered exercises are in the Teacher's Resource Book.

Daily Lesson-Plan Guide

This guide presents suggested daily lesson plans for three possible courses of study. These suggestions are only samples, however, and the teacher should feel free to utilize the flexibility of the textbook and the supplementary materials to meet the needs of the students.

The entries that appear in red are included in the Teacher's Resource Book (TRB).

Course A concentrates extensive refresher work with computing skills at the beginning of the year. Chapter 6 and Sections 10.1–10.5 are omitted.

Course B distributes extensive refresher work with computing skills among the sections of Chapters 1–4. Sections 6.5–6.11 and 10.1–10.5 are omitted.

Course C is set up so that refresher work with computing skills can be individualized by using the *Skills Refresher* quizzes as suggested on page T4.

Before deciding which course is best suited for a certain class, the teacher may wish to administer the Computing Skills Tests 1 and 2—Form A or Form B—as pretests. These tests are in the Teacher's Resource Book on pages 51–66. These tests will also help the teacher decide how much time should be allotted to the special topics—*Career, Consumer Topic, Calculator* skills, and other special features—in the textbook and to the *Application* activities in the Teacher's Resource Book.

Lesson	Course A	Course B	Course C
1	**Skill 1,** p. 448 *Orally:* 1–20 **Skill 2,** p. 449 *Written:* 1–19	**Skill 1,** p. 448 *Orally:* 1–20 **Skill 2,** p. 449 *Written:* 1–19	Preview Test, p. 9 (See p. T4.)
2	**Skill 3,** p. 450 *Orally:* 1–9 **Skill 4,** p. 451 *Written:* 1–29 odds	**Skill 3,** p. 450 *Orally:* 1–9 **Skill 4,** p. 451 *Written:* 1–29 odds	**Sec 1.1,** pp. 10–13 *Orally:* 1–8 *Written:* 13–45 odds Skills Refresher, p. 13
3	**Skill 5,** pp. 452–453 *Written:* 1–47 odds	**Sec 1.1,** pp. 10–13 *Orally:* 1–8 *Written:* 9–37 odds	Calculator skill, p. 524 Cross-Number Puzzle, p. 14 Application 1, TRB pp. 67–68
4	**Skill 6,** pp. 454–455 *Written:* 1–45 odds	Application 1, TRB pp. 67–68 Calculator skill, p. 524	**Sec 1.2,** pp. 15–16 *Orally:* 1–2 *Written:* 7–14 Skills Refresher, p. 16 Calculator skill, p. 525
5	**Skill 7,** pp. 456–457 *Written:* 1–55 odds	**Sec 1.2,** pp. 15–16 *Orally:* 1–2 *Written:* 3–11 Calculator skill, p. 525	**Sec 1.3,** pp. 17–19 *Orally:* 1–5 *Written:* 12–32 Skills Refresher, p. 19 Calculator skill, p. 526
6	**Skill 8,** pp. 458–459 *Written:* 1–61 odds	**Skill 5,** pp. 452–453 *Written:* 15–47 odds **Skill 6,** pp. 454–455 *Written:* 15–45 odds	**Sec 1.4,** pp. 20–23 *Orally:* 1–4 *Written:* 15–35 Skills Refresher, p. 23 Calculator skill, p. 527

Lesson	Course A	Course B	Course C
7	**Skill 9,** pp. 460–461 *Written:* 1–53 odds	**Skill 7,** pp. 456–457 *Written:* 21–45 odds **Skill 8,** pp. 458–459 *Written:* 21–61 odds	**Sec 1.5,** p. 24 *Written:* 1–15 Taking the Census, p. 25
8	**Skill 9,** pp. 460–461 *Written:* 55–103 odds	**Sec 1.3,** pp. 17–19 *Written:* 1–25 Calculator skill, p. 526	**Sec. 1.6,** pp. 26–28 *Orally:* 1–4 *Written:* 5–18
9	**Skill 10,** p. 462 *Orally:* 1–60 **Skill 11,** p. 463 *Written:* 1–39 odds	**Sec 1.4,** pp. 20–23 *Orally:* 1–4 *Written:* 5–28 Calculator skill, p. 527	**Sec 1.7,** pp. 29–30 *Written:* 1–10 Skills Refresher, p. 30 Calculator skill, p. 528 Application 2, TRB p. 69
10	**Skill 12,** pp. 464–465 *Written:* 1–51 odds	**Sec 1.5,** p. 24 *Orally:* 1–3 *Written:* 4–15 Taking the Census, p. 25	**Sec 1.8,** pp. 31–33 *Orally:* 1–4 *Written:* 5–24 Skills Refresher, p. 33
11	**Skill 13,** pp. 466–467 *Written:* 1–49 odds	**Sec 1.6,** pp. 26–28 *Written:* 1–16	Consumer Topic, p. 34 Application 3, TRB p. 70
12	**Skill 14,** p. 468 *Written:* 1–26	**Skill 9,** pp. 460–461 *Written:* 31–53 odds, 73–103 odds	**Sec 1.9,** pp. 35–37 *Orally:* 1–12 *Written:* 13–42
13	**Skill 15,** p. 469 *Written:* 1–51 odds	**Skill 10,** p. 462 *Orally:* 1–60 **Skill 11,** p. 463 *Written:* 1–39 odds	**Sec 1.10,** pp. 38–40 *Orally:* 1–12 *Written:* 13–42
14	**Skill 16,** p. 470 *Orally:* 1–55 **Skill 17,** p. 471 *Written:* 1–39 odds	**Skill 12,** pp. 464–465 *Written:* 1–51 odds **Skill 13,** pp. 466–467 *Written:* 1–35 odds	**Sec 1.11,** pp. 41–43 *Written:* 1–41 odds Skills Refresher, p. 43 Application 4, TRB p. 71
15	**Skill 18,** pp. 472–473 *Written:* 1–59 odds	**Sec 1.7,** pp. 29–30 *Written:* 1–10 **Sec 1.8,** pp. 31–33 *Written:* 1–19	**Sec 1.12,** pp. 44–46 *Orally:* 1–12 *Written:* 16–40 Career, p. 47
16	**Skill 19,** pp. 474–475 *Written:* 1–23 odds, 41–51 odds	Skills Refresher, p. 33 Consumer Topic, p. 34 Application 3, TRB p. 70	Application 5, TRB pp. 72–73 Application 6, TRB p. 74
17	**Skill 20,** pp. 476–477 *Written:* 9–27 odds, 33–51 odds	**Skill 14,** p. 468 *Written:* 1–25 odds **Skill 16,** p. 470 *Written:* 1–45 odds	Chapter Review, pp. 48–49
18	**Skill 21,** p. 478 *Orally:* 1–12 *Written:* 13–35 odds	**Skill 17,** p. 471 *Written:* 1–35 odds **Skill 18,** pp. 472–473 *Written:* 1–39 odds	Chapter 1 Test—Form A or Form B—TRB pp. 1–2 or pp. 3–4
19	**Skill 22,** p. 479 *Orally:* 1–8 *Written:* 9–28	**Skill 19,** pp. 474–475 *Written:* 1–23 odds, 41–51 odds	Preview Test, p. 51
20	**Skill 23,** pp. 480–481 *Written:* 1–47 odds	**Skill 20,** pp. 476–477 *Written:* 9–27 odds, 33–51 odds	**Sec 2.1,** pp. 52–55 *Orally:* 1–18 *Written:* 25–46 Numbers on the Map, p. 56

Lesson	Course A	Course B	Course C
21	**Skill 24,** p. 482 *Written:* 1–59 odds	**Sec 1.9,** pp. 35–37 *Orally:* 1–12 *Written:* 17–42	**Sec 2.2,** pp. 57–58 *Written:* 1–28 Skills Refresher, p. 58 Application 7, TRB p. 75
22	**Skill 25,** p. 483 *Orally:* 1–6 *Written:* 7–24	**Sec 1.10,** pp. 38–40 *Orally:* 1–12 *Written:* 17–42	**Sec 2.3,** pp. 60–61 *Written:* 1–20 Graph Pictures, pp. 62–63
23	Computing Skills Test 1—Form A or Form B—TRB pp. 51–54 or pp. 55–58 (May require 2 days.)	**Skill 21,** p. 478 *Orally:* 1–12 *Written:* 13–36	**Sec 2.4,** pp. 64–66 *Orally:* 1–8 *Written:* 9–18 Skills Refresher, p. 66
24	**Skill 26,** pp. 484–485 *Orally:* 1–38 *Written:* 39–56	**Skill 22,** p. 479 *Orally:* 1–8 *Written:* 9–27 odds	**Sec 2.5,** pp. 67–69 *Written:* 1–28 Skills Refresher, p. 69
25	**Skill 27,** p. 486 *Orally:* 1–6, 15–22 *Written:* 7–14 **Skill 28,** pp. 487–488 *Written:* 1–63 odds	**Skill 23,** pp. 480–481 *Written:* 1–47 odds	**Sec 2.6,** pp. 70–73 *Orally:* 1–4 *Written:* 5–16 Skills Refresher, p. 73
26	**Skill 29,** pp. 489–490 *Orally:* 1–8 *Written:* 9–39 odds **Skill 30,** p. 491 *Written:* 1–12	**Sec 1.11,** pp. 41–43 *Orally:* 1–12 *Written:* 17–41	Consumer Topic, pp. 74–75 Application 8, TRB p. 76
27	**Skill 31,** p. 492 *Written:* 1–8 **Skill 32,** p. 493 *Written:* 1–15	**Sec. 1.12,** pp. 44–46 *Orally:* 1–12 *Written:* 16–40	**Sec 2.7,** pp. 76–77 *Orally:* 1–4 *Written:* 5–19
28	**Skill 33,** pp. 494–495 *Written:* 1–37 odds	Career, p. 47 Application 6, TRB p. 74	Application 9, TRB p. 77
29	**Skill 34,** pp. 496–497 *Written:* 1–51 odds	Chapter Review, pp. 48–49	**Sec 2.8,** pp. 78–81 *Written:* 1–32
30	**Skill 35,** pp. 498–499 *Orally:* 1–10 *Written:* 11–49 odds	Chapter 1 Test—Form A or Form B—TRB pp. 1–2 or pp. 3–4	Application 10, TRB pp. 78–79
31	**Skill 36,** pp. 500–501 *Written:* 1–49 odds	**Skill 24,** p. 482 *Written:* 1–59 odds	**Sec 2.9,** pp. 82–84 *Written:* 1–32
32	**Skill 36,** pp. 500–501 *Written:* 51–99 odds	**Skill 25,** p. 483 *Written:* 1–24	Career, p. 85 Application 11, TRB p. 80
33	**Skill 37,** pp. 502–503 *Written:* 1–53 odds	Computing Skills Test 1—Form A or Form B—TRB pp. 51–54 or pp. 55–58 (May require 2 days.)	Chapter Review, pp. 86–87
34	**Skill 38,** p. 504 *Orally:* 1–6 *Written:* 7–30	**Sec 2.1,** pp. 52–55 *Orally:* 1–18 *Written:* 25–44	Chapter 2 Test—Form A or Form B—TRB pp. 5–6 or pp. 7–8

Lesson	Course A	Course B	Course C
35	**Skill 39,** p. 505 *Orally:* 1–12 **Skill 40,** pp. 506–507 *Written:* 1–39 odds	**Sec 2.2,** pp. 57–58 *Orally:* 1–4 *Written:* 5–25	Cumulative Review: Chapters 1–2, pp. 89–92 *Written:* 1–36
36	**Skill 41,** pp. 508–509 *Written:* 1–49 odds	Gone Fishing, p. 59 Application 7, TRB p. 75	Cumulative Review: Chapters 1–2, pp. 89–92 *Written:* 37–54
37	**Skill 41,** pp. 508–509 *Written:* 51–99 odds	**Skill 26,** pp. 484–485 *Orally:* 1–38 *Written:* 39–56	Cumulative Test 1: Chapters 1–2, TRB pp. 41–42
38	**Skill 42,** pp. 510–511 *Written:* 1–29 odds	**Skill 27,** p. 486 *Orally:* 1–6, 15–22 *Written:* 7–14 **Skill 28,** pp. 487–488 *Written:* 1–63 odds	Preview Test, p. 93
39	**Skill 42,** pp. 510–511 *Written:* 31–45 odds	**Sec 2.3,** pp. 60–61 *Written:* 1–18 Graph Pictures, pp. 62–63	**Sec 3.1,** pp. 94–95 *Orally:* 1–14 *Written:* 15–30
40	**Skill 43,** pp. 512–513 *Written:* 1–29 odds	**Skill 29,** pp. 489–490 *Written:* 1–39 odds **Skill 30,** p. 491 *Written:* 1–12	**Sec 3.2,** pp. 96–97 *Orally:* 1–24 *Written:* 25–42 Calculator skill, pp. 529–530
41	**Skill 43,** pp. 512–513 *Written:* 31–51 odds	**Sec 2.4,** pp. 64–66 *Orally:* 1–8 *Written:* 9–16	**Sec 3.3,** pp. 98–99 *Written:* 1–45 odds Ingenious Genie, p. 100
42	**Skill 44,** pp. 514–515 *Written:* 1–27 odds	**Skill 31,** p. 492 *Written:* 1–8 **Skill 32,** p. 493 *Written:* 1–15	**Sec 3.4,** pp. 101–103 *Orally:* 1–2 *Written:* 3–20 Skills Refresher, p. 103
43	**Skill 44,** pp. 514–515 *Written:* 29–55 odds	**Skill 33,** pp. 494–495 *Written:* 1–37 odds	**Sec 3.5,** pp. 104–107 *Written:* 1–45 Skills Refresher, p. 107 Application 12, TRB p. 81
44	**Skill 45,** pp. 516–517 *Written:* 1–35 odds	**Skill 34,** pp. 496–497 *Written:* 1–51 odds	**Sec 3.6,** pp. 108–111 *Orally:* 1–6 *Written:* 19–42
45	**Skill 45,** pp. 516–517 *Written:* 37–71 odds	**Sec 2.5,** pp. 67–69 *Written:* 1–26	Application 13, TRB pp. 82–83
46	**Skill 45,** pp. 516–517 *Written:* 73–96	**Sec 2.6,** pp. 70–73 *Orally:* 1–4 *Written:* 5–16 Skills Refresher, p. 73	**Sec 3.7,** pp. 112–115 *Orally:* 1–10 *Written:* 15–45 Skills Refresher, p. 116
47	**Skill 45,** pp. 516–517 *Written:* 97–120	Consumer Topic, pp. 74–75 Application 8, TRB p. 76	Cross-Number Puzzle, p. 116 Application 14, TRB p. 84
48	**Skill 46,** pp. 518–519 *Written:* 1–27	**Skill 35,** pp. 498–499 *Orally:* 1–10 *Written:* 11–49 odds	**Sec 3.8,** pp. 117–119 *Written:* 5–45 odds Application 15, TRB p. 85

Lesson	Course A	Course B	Course C
49	**Skill 47,** p. 520 *Written:* 1–23	**Skill 36,** pp. 500–501 *Written:* 1–99 odds	**Sec 3.9,** pp. 120–123 *Written:* 1–49 odds
50	**Skill 48,** pp. 521–522 *Orally:* 1–9 *Written:* 11–47 odds	**Sec 2.7,** pp. 76–77 *Orally:* 1–4 *Written:* 5–17	**Sec 3.10,** pp. 124–128 *Written:* 1–31 odds Career, p. 129 Consumer Topic, p. 130
51	Computing Skills Test 2—Form A or Form B—TRB pp. 59–62 or pp. 63–66 (May require 2 days.)	**Sec 2.8,** pp. 78–81 *Orally:* 1–10 *Written:* 11–30	Day for a Date, p. 131 Application 16, TRB pp. 86–87 Application 17, TRB p. 88
52	**Sec 1.1,** pp. 10–13 *Orally:* 1–8 *Written:* 9–37 odds Calculator skill, p. 524	**Skill 37,** pp. 502–503 *Written:* 1–53 odds	Chapter Review, pp. 132–133
53	**Sec 1.2,** pp. 15–16 *Written:* 1–11 Calculator skill, p. 525	**Skill 38,** p. 504 *Orally:* 1–6 *Written:* 7–30	Chapter 3 Test—Form A or Form B—TRB pp. 9–10 or pp. 11–12
54	**Sec 1.3,** pp. 17–19 *Orally:* 1–5 *Written:* 6–25 Calculator skill, p. 526	**Sec 2.9,** pp. 82–84 *Orally:* 1–6 *Written:* 7–30	Preview Test, p. 135
55	**Sec 1.4,** pp. 20–23 *Written:* 1–28 Calculator skill, p. 527	Career, p. 85 Application 11, TRB p. 80	**Sec 4.1,** pp. 136–138 *Orally:* 1–14 *Written:* 17–28
56	**Sec 1.5,** p. 24 *Orally:* 1–3 *Written:* 4–15 Taking the Census, p. 25	Chapter Review, pp. 86–87	**Sec 4.2,** pp. 139–141 *Orally:* 1–4 *Written:* 9–37 Skills Refresher, p. 141 Graphing Equivalent Ratios, p. 142
57	**Sec 1.6,** pp. 26–28 *Orally:* 1–4 *Written:* 5–16	Chapter 2 Test—Form A or Form B—TRB pp. 5–6 or pp. 7–8	**Sec 4.3,** pp. 143–145 *Orally:* 1–9 *Written:* 13–33
58	**Sec 1.7,** pp. 29–30 *Written:* 1–10 Calculator skill, p. 528	Cumulative Review: Chapters 1–2, pp. 89–92 *Written:* 1–36	**Sec 4.4,** pp. 146–149 *Orally:* 1–11 *Written:* 14–35
59	**Sec 1.8,** pp. 31–33 *Orally:* 1–4 *Written:* 5–19	Cumulative Review: Chapters 1–2, pp. 89–92 *Written:* 37–54	Application 18, TRB p. 89 Application 19, TRB p. 90
60	**Sec 1.9,** pp. 35–37 *Orally:* 1–12 *Written:* 17–42	Cumulative Test: Chapters 1–2, TRB pp. 41–42	**Sec 4.5,** pp. 150–153 *Written:* 1–20 Application 20, TRB p. 91
61	**Sec 1.10,** pp. 38–40 *Orally:* 1–12 *Written:* 17–42	**Sec 3.1,** pp. 94–95 *Orally:* 1–14 *Written:* 15–27	**Sec 4.6,** pp. 154–158 *Orally:* 1–18 *Written:* 19–32

Lesson	Course A	Course B	Course C
62	**Sec 1.11,** pp. 41–43 *Orally:* 1–12 *Written:* 17–41	**Sec 3.2,** pp. 96–97 *Orally:* 1–24 *Written:* 25–40 Calculator skill, pp. 529–530	Career, p. 159 Application 21, TRB pp. 92–93 Application 22, TRB pp. 94–95
63	**Sec 1.12,** pp. 44–46 *Orally:* 1–12 *Written:* 16–40	**Sec 3.3,** pp. 98–99 *Written:* 1–41 odds Ingenious Genie, p. 100	**Sec 4.7,** pp. 160–162 *Orally:* 1–2 *Written:* 6–44
64	Career, p. 47 Application 6, TRB p. 74	**Sec 3.4,** pp. 101–103 *Orally:* 1–2 *Written:* 3–18 Skills Refresher, p. 103	**Sec 4.8,** pp. 163–167 *Orally:* 1–6 *Written:* 9–37 odds Skills Refresher, p. 167
65	Chapter Review, pp. 48–49	**Sec 3.5,** pp. 104–107 *Written:* 1–43 odds	Application 23, TRB p. 96 Application 24, TRB p. 97
66	Chapter 1 Test—Form A or Form B—TRB pp. 1–2 or pp. 3–4	Skills Refresher, p. 107 Application 12, TRB p. 81	**Sec 4.9,** pp. 168–170 *Orally:* 1–12 *Written:* 17–55 odds Consumer Topic, p. 171
67	**Sec 2.1,** pp. 52–55 *Orally:* 1–18 *Written:* 19–45 odds	**Sec 3.6,** pp. 108–111 *Orally:* 1–6 *Written:* 11–41 odds	**Sec 4.10,** pp. 172–175 *Orally:* 1–18 *Written:* 22–45
68	**Sec 2.2,** pp. 57–58 *Written:* 1–22 Skills Refresher, p. 58	**Sec 3.7,** pp. 112–115 *Orally:* 1–10 *Written:* 13–43	Chapter Review, pp. 176–177
69	**Sec 2.3,** pp. 60–61 *Orally:* 1–7 *Written:* 8–16 Graph Pictures, pp. 62–63	Cross-Number Puzzle, p. 116 Skills Refresher, p. 116	Chapter 4 Test—Form A or Form B—TRB pp. 13–14 or pp. 15–16
70	**Sec 2.4,** pp. 64–66 *Orally:* 1–8 *Written:* 9–15 Skills Refresher, p. 66	**Skill 39,** p. 505 *Orally:* 1–12 **Skill 40,** pp. 506–507 *Written:* 1–39 odds	Cumulative Review: Chapters 3–4, pp. 179–182 *Written:* 1–59 odds
71	**Sec 2.5,** pp. 67–69 *Written:* 1–20 Skills Refresher, p. 69	**Skill 41,** pp. 508–509 *Written:* 1–49 odds	Cumulative Review: Chapters 3–4, pp. 179–182 *Written:* 61–109 odds
72	**Sec 2.6,** pp. 70–73 *Written:* 1–13 Skills Refresher, p. 73	**Skill 41,** pp. 508–509 *Written:* 51–99 odds	Cumulative Test 2: Chapters 3–4, TRB pp. 43–44
73	**Sec 2.7,** pp. 76–77 *Orally:* 1–4 *Written:* 5–15	**Sec 3.8,** pp. 117–119 *Written:* 7–43 odds Application 15, TRB p. 85	Preview Test, p. 183
74	**Sec 2.8,** pp. 78–81 *Orally:* 1–10 *Written:* 11–27	**Sec 3.9,** pp. 120–123 *Orally:* 1–6 *Written:* 9–47 odds	**Sec 5.1,** pp. 184–186 *Orally:* 1–30 *Written:* 31–52 It's About Time, p. 187 Application 25, TRB p. 98
75	**Sec 2.9,** pp. 82–84 *Orally:* 1–6 *Written:* 7–27 Career, p. 85	**Skill 42,** pp. 510–511 *Written:* 1–45 odds	**Sec 5.2,** pp. 188–190 *Orally:* 1–14 *Written:* 15–25

Lesson	Course A	Course B	Course C
76	Chapter Review, pp. 86–87	**Skill 43,** pp. 512–513 *Written:* 1–51 odds	**Sec 5.3,** pp. 191–193 *Written:* 1–24 Skills Refresher, p. 194 Application 26, TRB pp. 99–100
77	Chapter 2 Test—Form A or Form B—TRB pp. 5–6 or pp. 7–8	**Sec 3.10,** pp. 124–128 *Orally:* 1–6 *Written:* 9–27 odds Career, p. 129	**Sec 5.4,** pp. 195–196 *Orally:* 1–6 *Written:* 7–25 Career, p. 197
78	**Sec 3.1,** pp. 94–95 *Orally:* 1–14 *Written:* 15–24	Consumer Topic, p. 130 Application 17, TRB p. 88	**Sec 5.5,** pp. 198–201 *Orally:* 1–16 *Written:* 21–40 Skills Refresher, p. 201
79	**Sec 3.2,** pp. 96–97 *Orally:* 1–24 *Written:* 25–38 Calculator skill, pp. 529–530	Chapter Review, pp. 132–133	**Sec 5.6,** pp. 202–203 *Orally:* 1–10 *Written:* 11–27
80	**Sec 3.3,** pp. 98–99 *Orally:* 1–6 *Written:* 7–39 odds Ingenious Genie, p. 100	Chapter 3, Test—Form A or Form B—TRB pp. 9–10 or pp. 11–12	**Sec 5.7,** pp. 204–207 *Orally:* 1–10 *Written:* 11–43 odds
81	**Sec 3.4,** pp. 101–103 *Written:* 1–16 Skills Refresher, p. 103	**Sec 4.1,** pp. 136–138 *Orally:* 1–14 *Written:* 15–26	**Sec 5.8,** pp. 208–210 *Orally:* 1–14 *Written:* 15–44
82	**Sec 3.5,** pp. 104–107 *Orally:* 1–6 *Written:* 7–41 odds Skills Refresher, p. 107	**Sec 4.2,** pp. 139–141 *Orally:* 1–4 *Written:* 7–35 Skills Refresher, p. 141	**Sec 5.9,** pp. 211–213 *Orally:* 1–8 *Written:* 9–32 Consumer Topic, p. 214
83	**Sec 3.6,** pp. 108–111 *Orally:* 1–6 *Written:* 7–39 odds	**Sec 4.3,** pp. 143–145 *Orally:* 1–9 *Written:* 12–31	Line Art, p. 215 Application 27, TRB p. 101
84	**Sec 3.7,** pp. 112–115 *Orally:* 1–10 *Written:* 11–41 odds	**Sec 4.4,** pp. 146–149 *Orally:* 1–11 *Written:* 12–31 Application 18, TRB p. 89	**Sec 5.10,** pp. 216–217 *Orally:* 1–12 *Written:* 13–24
85	Cross-Number Puzzle, p. 116 Skills Refresher, p. 116	**Skill 44,** pp. 514–515 *Written:* 1–55 odds	Application 28, TRB pp. 102–103
86	**Sec 3.8,** pp. 117–119 *Written:* 1–41 odds	**Skill 45,** pp. 516–517 *Written:* 1–71 odds	**Sec 5.11,** pp. 218–221 *Orally:* 1–14 *Written:* 15–23
87	**Sec 3.9,** pp. 120–123 *Orally:* 1–6 *Written:* 7–45 odds	**Skill 45,** pp. 516–517 *Written:* 73–119 odds	Application 29, TRB pp. 104–105 Application 30, TRB p. 106
88	**Sec 3.10,** pp. 124–128 *Orally:* 1–6 *Written:* 7–28	**Sec 4.5,** pp. 150–153 *Orally:* 1–7 *Written:* 8–19	Chapter Review, pp. 222–223

Lesson	Course A	Course B	Course C
89	Career, p. 129 Consumer Topic, p. 130	**Sec 4.6,** pp. 154–158 *Orally:* 1–18 *Written:* 19–32 Career, p. 159	Chapter 5 Test—Form A or Form B—TRB pp. 17–18 or pp. 19–20
90	Chapter Review, pp. 132–133	**Skill 46,** pp. 518–519 *Written:* 1–27	Preview Test, p. 225
91	Chapter 3 Test—Form A or Form B—TRB pp. 9–10 or pp. 11–12	**Skill 47,** p. 520 *Written:* 1–23 odds **Skill 48,** pp. 521–522 *Orally:* 1–9 *Written:* 11–47 odds	**Sec 6.1,** pp. 226–228 *Orally:* 1–12 *Written:* 13–28 Skills Refresher, p. 228 Application 31, TRB p. 107
92	**Sec 4.1,** pp. 136–138 *Orally:* 1–14 *Written:* 15–24	Computing Skills Test 2—Form A or Form B—TRB pp. 59–62 or pp. 63–66 (May require 2 days.)	**Sec 6.2,** pp. 229–232 *Orally:* 1–14 *Written:* 15–37 odds
93	**Sec 4.2,** pp. 139–141 *Written:* 1–33 Skills Refresher, p. 141	**Sec 4.7,** pp. 160–162 *Written:* 1–40 Application 23, TRB p. 96	**Sec 6.3,** pp. 233–236 *Orally:* 1–12 *Written:* 13–41 odds, 42–44
94	**Sec 4.3,** pp. 143–145 *Orally:* 1–9 *Written:* 10–29	**Sec 4.8,** pp. 163–167 *Orally:* 1–6 *Written:* 9–35 odds Skills Refresher, p. 167	**Sec 6.4,** pp. 237–239 *Written:* 1–35 odds Career, p. 240 Patterns With Squares, p. 241
95	**Sec 4.4,** pp. 146–149 *Orally:* 1–11 *Written:* 12–29 Application 18, TRB p. 89	**Sec 4.9,** pp. 168–170 *Orally:* 1–12 *Written:* 15–53 odds Consumer Topic, p. 171	**Sec 6.5,** pp. 242–244 *Orally:* 1–6 *Written:* 7–27 Skills Refresher, p. 244
96	**Sec 4.5,** pp. 150–153 *Orally:* 1–7 *Written:* 8–18	**Sec 4.10,** pp. 172–175 *Orally:* 1–18 *Written:* 22–43	**Sec 6.6,** pp. 245–247 *Orally:* 1–8 *Written:* 9–30 The Number Pi, p. 248
97	**Sec 4.6,** pp. 154–158 *Orally:* 1–18 *Written:* 19–30 Career, p. 159	Chapter Review, pp. 176–177	Application 32, TRB p. 108 Application 33, TRB p. 109
98	**Sec 4.7,** pp. 160–162 *Orally:* 1–2 *Written:* 3–36 Application 23, TRB p. 96	Chapter 4 Test—Form A or Form B—TRB pp. 13–14 or pp. 15–16	**Sec 6.7,** pp. 249–251 *Orally:* 1–10 *Written:* 11–39 odds Application 34, TRB p. 110
99	**Sec 4.8,** pp. 163–167 *Orally:* 1–6 *Written:* 7–33 odds Skills Refresher, p. 167	Cumulative Review: Chapters 3–4, pp. 179–182 *Written:* 1–59 odds	**Sec 6.8,** pp. 252–254 *Written:* 1–37 odds Skills Refresher, p. 254 Calculator skill, p. 531 Application 35, TRB p. 111
100	**Sec 4.9,** pp. 168–170 *Orally:* 1–12 *Written:* 13–51 odds Consumer Topic, p. 171	Cumulative Review: Chapters 3–4, pp. 179–182 *Written:* 61–109 odds	**Sec 6.9,** pp. 255–258 *Orally:* 1–4 *Written:* 5–25
101	**Sec 4.10,** pp. 172–175 *Orally:* 1–18 *Written:* 19–41	Cumulative Test 2: Chapters 3–4, TRB pp. 43–44	Slicing Cubes, p. 259 Application 36, TRB pp. 112–113

Lesson	Course A	Course B	Course C
102	Chapter Review, pp. 176–177	**Sec 5.1,** pp. 184–186 *Orally:* 1–30 *Written:* 31–52 It's About Time, p. 187	**Sec 6.10,** pp. 260–262 *Written:* 1–25 odds Surface Area, p. 263 Platonic Solids, p. 264
103	Chapter 4 Test—Form A or Form B—TRB pp. 13–14 or pp. 15–16	**Sec 5.2,** pp. 188–190 *Orally:* 1–14 *Written:* 15–25	**Sec 6.11,** pp. 265–267 *Written:* 1–18 Consumer Topic, p. 268 Volume Projects, p. 269
104	Cumulative Review: Chapters 3–4, pp. 179–182 *Written:* 1–59 odds	**Sec 5.3,** pp. 191–193 *Orally:* 1–6 *Written:* 7–23	Chapter Review, pp. 270–271
105	Cumulative Review: Chapters 3–4, pp. 179–182 *Written:* 61–109 odds	Measuring on the Job, p. 194 Skills Refresher, p. 194 Application 26, TRB pp. 99–100	Chapter 6 Test—Form A or Form B—TRB pp. 21–22 or pp. 23–24
106	Cumulative Test 2: Chapters 3–4, TRB pp. 43–44	**Sec 5.4,** pp. 195–196 *Orally:* 1–6 *Written:* 7–24 Career, p. 197	Cumulative Review: Chapters 5–6, pp. 273–276 *Written:* 1–51 odds
107	**Sec 5.1,** pp. 184–186 *Orally:* 1–30 *Written:* 31–52 It's About Time, p. 187	**Sec 5.5,** pp. 198–201 *Orally:* 1–16 *Written:* 21–38 Skills Refresher, p. 201	Cumulative Review: Chapters 5–6, pp. 273–276 *Written:* 53–81 odds
108	**Sec 5.2,** pp. 188–190 *Orally:* 1–14 *Written:* 15–24	**Sec 5.6,** pp. 202–203 *Orally:* 1–10 *Written:* 11–25	Cumulative Test 3: Chapters 5–6, TRB pp. 45–46
109	**Sec 5.3,** pp. 191–193 *Orally:* 1–6 *Written:* 7–22	**Sec 5.7,** pp. 204–207 *Orally:* 1–10 *Written:* 11–43 odds	Preview Test, p. 277
110	Measuring on the Job, p. 194 Skills Refresher, p. 194 Application 26, TRB pp. 99–100	**Sec 5.8,** pp. 208–210 *Orally:* 1–14 *Written:* 15–43	**Sec 7.1,** pp. 278–279 *Orally:* 1–4 Skills Refresher, p. 279 Application 37, TRB p. 114
111	**Sec 5.4,** pp. 195–196 *Orally:* 1–6 *Written:* 7–23 Career, p. 197	**Sec 5.9,** pp. 211–213 *Orally:* 1–8 *Written:* 9–30 Consumer Topic, p. 214	**Sec 7.2,** pp. 280–282 *Written:* 1–20 Skills Refresher, p. 282 Consumer Topic, p. 283
112	**Sec 5.5,** pp. 198–201 *Orally:* 1–16 *Written:* 17–36 Skills Refresher, p. 201	Line Art, p. 215 Application 27, TRB p. 101	**Sec 7.3,** pp. 284–285 *Written:* 1–17
113	**Sec 5.6,** pp. 202–203 *Orally:* 1–10 *Written:* 11–24	**Sec 5.10,** pp. 216–217 *Orally:* 1–12 *Written:* 13–22 How Warm Is It?, p. 217	**Sec 7.4,** pp. 286–287 *Written:* 1–12 **Sec 7.5,** pp. 288–289 *Written:* 1–7
114	**Sec 5.7,** pp. 204–207 *Orally:* 1–10 *Written:* 11–41 odds	**Sec 5.11,** pp. 218–221 *Orally:* 1–14 *Written:* 15–23	**Sec 7.6,** pp. 290–291 *Written:* 1–9 Skills Refresher, p. 291 Choosing a Job, pp. 292–293

Lesson	Course A	Course B	Course C
115	**Sec 5.8,** pp. 208–210 *Orally:* 1–14 *Written:* 15–42	Chapter Review, pp. 222–223	**Sec 7.7,** pp. 294–297 *Written:* 1–12 Social Security, pp. 298–299
116	**Sec 5.9,** pp. 211–213 *Orally:* 1–8 *Written:* 9–28	Chapter 5 Test—Form A or Form B—TRB pp. 17–18 or pp. 19–20	**Sec 7.8,** pp. 300–305 *Orally:* 1–4 *Written:* 5–16
117	Consumer Topic, p. 214 Line Art, p. 215 Application 27, TRB p. 101	**Sec 6.1,** pp. 226–228 *Orally:* 1–12 *Written:* 13–26 Skills Refresher, p. 228	Tax Rate Schedules, p. 306 Career, p. 307 Application 38, TRB p. 115
118	**Sec 5.10,** pp. 216–217 *Orally:* 1–12 *Written:* 13–20 How Warm Is It?, p. 217	**Sec 6.2,** pp. 229–232 *Orally:* 1–14 *Written:* 15–33 odds	Chapter Review, pp. 308–309
119	**Sec 5.11,** pp. 218–221 *Orally:* 1–14 *Written:* 15–23	**Sec 6.3,** pp. 233–236 *Orally:* 1–12 *Written:* 19–43 odds	Chapter 7 Test—Form A or Form B—TRB pp. 25–26 or pp. 27–28
120	Chapter Review, pp. 222–223	**Sec 6.4,** pp. 237–239 *Written:* 1–35 odds Career, p. 240	Preview Test, p. 311
121	Chapter 5 Test—Form A or Form B—TRB pp. 17–18 or pp. 19–20	**Sec 7.1,** pp. 278–279 *Orally:* 1–4 Skills Refresher, p. 279 Application 37, TRB p. 114	**Sec 8.1,** pp. 312–315 *Orally:* 1–4 *Written:* 5–14 Skills Refresher, p. 315
122	**Sec 7.1,** pp. 278–279 *Orally:* 1–4 Skills Refresher, p. 279 Application 37, TRB p. 114	**Sec 7.2,** pp. 280–282 *Written:* 1–18 Skills Refresher, p. 282 Consumer Topic, p. 283	**Sec 8.2,** pp. 316–319 *Orally:* 1–4 *Written:* 5–18
123	**Sec 7.2,** pp. 280–282 *Written:* 1–17 Skills Refresher, p. 282 Consumer Topic, p. 283	**Sec 7.3,** pp. 284–285 *Written:* 1–16	**Sec 8.3,** pp. 320–323 *Orally:* 1–6 *Written:* 7–17
124	**Sec 7.3,** pp. 284–285 *Written:* 1–15	**Sec 7.4,** pp. 286–287 *Written:* 1–11 **Sec 7.5,** pp. 288–289 *Written:* 1–6	**Sec 8.4,** pp. 324–327 *Orally:* 1–2 *Written:* 3–10
125	**Sec 7.4,** pp. 286–287 *Written:* 1–10 **Sec 7.5,** pp. 288–289 *Written:* 1–5	**Sec 7.6,** pp. 290–291 *Written:* 1–8 Skills Refresher, p. 291 Choosing a Job, pp. 292–293	**Sec 8.5,** pp. 328–331 *Orally:* 1–4 *Written:* 7–12
126	**Sec 7.6,** pp. 290–291 *Written:* 1–7 Skills Refresher, p. 291 Choosing a Job, pp. 292–293	**Sec 7.7,** pp. 294–297 *Written:* 1–11 Social Security, pp. 298–299	Application 39, TRB pp. 116–120
127	**Sec 7.7,** pp. 294–297 *Written:* 1–10 Social Security, pp. 298–299	**Sec 7.8,** pp. 300–305 *Written:* 1–15 Tax Rate Schedules, p. 306	**Sec 8.6,** pp. 332–334 *Written:* 1–17 Calculator skill, pp. 532–533

Lesson	Course A	Course B	Course C
128	**Sec 7.8,** pp. 300–305 *Written:* 1–14	Career, p. 307 Application 38, TRB p. 115	**Sec 8.7,** pp. 335–336 *Written:* 1–12
129	Tax Rate Schedules, p. 306 Career, p. 307 Application 38, TRB p. 115	Chapter Review, pp. 308–309	**Sec 8.8,** pp. 337–338 *Written:* 1–10 Calculator skill, p. 534
130	Chapter Review, pp. 308–309	Chapter 7 Test—Form A or Form B—TRB pp. 25–26 or pp. 27–28	**Sec 8.9,** pp. 339–342 *Written:* 1–22 Skills Refresher, p. 342
131	Chapter 7 Test—Form A or Form B—TRB pp. 25–26 or pp. 27–28	**Sec 8.1,** pp. 312–315 *Orally:* 1–4 *Written:* 5–12 Skills Refresher, p. 315	**Sec 8.10,** pp. 343–346 *Orally:* 1–8 *Written:* 11–24 That'll Be 5 Clams, p. 347 Career, p. 348
132	**Sec 8.1,** pp. 312–315 *Written:* 1–11 Skills Refresher, p. 315	**Sec 8.2,** pp. 316–319 *Written:* 1–17	**Sec 8.11,** pp. 349–352 *Written:* 1–10 Consumer Topic, p. 353
133	**Sec 8.2,** pp. 316–319 *Written:* 1–16	**Sec 8.3,** pp. 320–323 *Written:* 1–16	Chapter Review, pp. 354–355
134	**Sec 8.3,** pp. 320–323 *Orally:* 1–6 *Written:* 7–14	**Sec 8.4,** pp. 324–327 *Orally:* 1–2 *Written:* 3–10	Chapter 8 Test—Form A or Form B—TRB pp. 29–30 or pp. 31–32
135	**Sec 8.4,** pp. 324–327 *Orally:* 1–2 *Written:* 3–10	**Sec 8.5,** pp. 328–331 *Orally:* 1–4 *Written:* 7–12	Cumulative Review: Chapters 7–8, pp. 357–360 *Written:* 1–13
136	**Sec 8.5,** pp. 328–331 *Orally:* 1–4 *Written:* 7–12	Application 39, TRB pp. 116–120	Cumulative Review: Chapters 7–8, pp. 357–360 *Written:* 14–37
137	Application 39, TRB pp. 116–120	**Sec 8.6,** pp. 332–334 *Written:* 1–16 Calculator skill, pp. 532–533	Cumulative Test 4: Chapters 7–8, TRB pp. 47–48
138	**Sec 8.6,** pp. 332–334 *Written:* 1–16 Calculator skill, pp. 532–533	**Sec 8.7,** pp. 335–336 *Written:* 1–10	Preview Test, p. 361
139	**Sec 8.7,** pp. 335–336 *Written:* 1–8	**Sec 8.8,** pp. 337–338 *Written:* 1–11 Calculator skill, p. 534	**Sec 9.1,** pp. 362–363 *Written:* 1–20 Skills Refresher, p. 363
140	**Sec 8.8,** pp. 337–338 *Written:* 1–10 Calculator skill, p. 534	**Sec 8.9,** pp. 339–342 *Written:* 1–21 Skills Refresher, p. 342	**Sec 9.2,** pp. 364–366 *Orally:* 1–6 *Written:* 7–26
141	**Sec 8.9,** pp. 339–342 *Orally:* 1–4 *Written:* 5–20 Skills Refresher, p. 342	**Sec 8.10,** pp. 343–346 *Orally:* 1–8 *Written:* 11–22 Career, p. 348	Application 40, TRB pp. 121–122
142	**Sec 8.10,** pp. 343–346 *Orally:* 1–8 *Written:* 9–19 Career, p. 348	**Sec 8.11,** pp. 349–352 *Orally:* 1–2 *Written:* 3–8 Consumer Topic, p. 353	**Sec 9.3,** pp. 367–370 *Orally:* 1–2 *Written:* 3–34 For Pizza Freaks Only, p. 371

Lesson	Course A	Course B	Course C
143	**Sec 8.11,** pp. 349–352 *Orally:* 1–2 *Written:* 3–7 Consumer Topic, p. 353	Chapter Review, pp. 354–355	**Sec 9.4,** pp. 372–375 *Written:* 1–25 Application 41, TRB pp. 123–124
144	Chapter Review, pp. 354–355	Chapter 8 Test—Form A or Form B—TRB pp. 29–30 or pp. 31–32	**Sec 9.5,** pp. 376–379 *Written:* 1–16 Skills Refresher, p. 379
145	Chapter 8 Test—Form A or Form B—TRB pp. 29–30 or pp. 31–32	Cumulative Review: Chapters 7–8, pp. 357–360 *Written:* 1–13	**Sec 9.6,** pp. 380–383 *Written:* 1–14 Scoring in Bowling, pp. 384–385 Application 42, TRB p. 125
146	Cumulative Review: Chapters 7–8, pp. 357–360 *Written:* 1–13	Cumulative Review: Chapters 7–8, pp. 357–360 *Written:* 14–37	**Sec 9.7,** pp. 386–389 *Written:* 1–18 Application 43, TRB p. 126
147	Cumulative Review: Chapters 7–8, pp. 357–360 *Written:* 14–37	Cumulative Test 4: Chapters 7–8, TRB pp. 47–48	**Sec 9.8,** pp. 390–393 *Written:* 1–20 Consumer Topic, p. 394 Career, p. 395
148	Cumulative Test 4: Chapters 7–8, TRB pp. 47–48	**Sec 9.1,** pp. 362–363 *Written:* 1–18 Skills Refresher, p. 363	**Sec 9.9,** pp. 396–399 *Written:* 1–22
149	**Sec 9.1,** pp. 362–363 *Orally:* 1–4 *Written:* 5–16 Skills Refresher, p. 363	**Sec 9.2,** pp. 364–366 *Orally:* 1–6 *Written:* 9–26	Application 44, TRB pp. 127–128
150	**Sec 9.2,** pp. 364–366 *Orally:* 1–6 *Written:* 7–20	**Sec 9.3,** pp. 367–370 *Written:* 1–30 For Pizza Freaks Only, p. 371	**Sec 9.10,** pp. 400–403 *Orally:* 1–18
151	**Sec 9.3,** pp. 367–370 *Orally:* 1–2 *Written:* 3–30	**Sec 9.4,** pp. 372–375 *Orally:* 1–4 *Written:* 5–24	Chapter Review, pp. 404–405
152	**Sec 9.4,** pp. 372–375 *Orally:* 1–4 *Written:* 5–22	**Sec 9.5,** pp. 376–379 *Written:* 1–15 Skills Refresher, p. 379	Chapter 9 Test—Form A or Form B—TRB pp. 33–34 or pp. 35–36
153	**Sec 9.5,** pp. 376–379 *Written:* 1–14 Skills Refresher, p. 379	**Sec 9.6,** pp. 380–383 *Written:* 1–12 Scoring in Bowling, pp. 384–385	Preview Test, p. 407
154	**Sec 9.6,** pp. 380–383 *Written:* 1–10 Scoring in Bowling, pp. 384–385	**Sec 9.7,** pp. 386–389 *Written:* 1–16 Application 43, TRB p. 126	**Sec 10.1,** pp. 408–410 *Orally:* 1–6 *Written:* 7–38
155	**Sec 9.7,** pp. 386–389 *Written:* 1–11 Application 43, TRB p. 126	**Sec 9.8,** pp. 390–393 *Written:* 1–18	**Sec 10.2,** pp. 411–412 *Orally:* 1–4 *Written:* 5–20
156	**Sec 9.8,** pp. 390–393 *Written:* 1–16	Consumer Topic, p. 394 Career, p. 395	**Sec 10.3,** pp. 413–415 *Written:* 1–37 Skills Refresher, p. 415

Lesson	Course A	Course B	Course C
157	Consumer Topic, p. 394 Career, p. 395	**Sec 9.9,** pp. 396–399 *Written:* 1–21	**Sec 10.4,** pp. 416–418 *Written:* 1–39 Skills Refresher, p. 418
158	**Sec 9.9,** pp. 396–399 *Written:* 1–20	**Sec 9.10,** pp. 400–403 *Orally:* 1–16	Know Your Chances, p. 419 Calculator skill, pp. 535–536
159	**Sec 9.10,** pp. 400–403 *Orally:* 1–14	Chapter Review, pp. 404–405	**Sec 10.5,** pp. 420–421 *Written:* 1–17 Application 45, TRB p. 129 Application 46, TRB p. 130
160	Chapter Review, pp. 404–405	Chapter 9 Test—Form A or Form B—TRB pp. 33–34 or pp. 35–36	**Sec 10.6,** pp. 422–424 *Written:* 1–12
161	Chapter 9 Test—Form A or Form B—TRB pp. 33–34 or pp. 35–36	**Sec 10.6,** pp. 422–424 *Written:* 1–11	**Sec 10.7,** pp. 425–427 *Written:* 1–10
162	**Sec 10.6,** pp. 422–424 *Written:* 1–10	**Sec 10.7,** pp. 425–427 *Written:* 1–10	**Sec 10.8,** pp. 428–431 *Orally:* 1–3 *Written:* 4–10 Skills Refresher, p. 431
163	**Sec 10.7,** pp. 425–427 *Written:* 1–10	**Sec 10.8,** pp. 428–431 *Written:* 1–10 Skills Refresher, p. 431	**Sec 10.9,** pp. 432–434 *Orally:* 1–6 *Written:* 7–22
164	**Sec 10.8,** pp. 428–431 *Written:* 4–10 Skills Refresher, p. 431	**Sec 10.9,** pp. 432–434 *Orally:* 1–6 *Written:* 7–21	**Sec 10.10,** pp. 435–437 *Written:* 1–10 Career, p. 438
165	**Sec 10.9,** pp. 432–434 *Orally:* 1–6 *Written:* 7–20	**Sec 10.10,** pp. 435–437 *Written:* 1–10 Career, p. 438	Guess the Computer's Number, p. 439 Application 47, TRB p. 131 Application 48, TRB p. 132
166	**Sec 10.10,** pp. 435–437 *Written:* 1–10 Career, p. 438	Application 49, TRB p. 133 Application 50, TRB p. 134	Application 49, TRB p. 133 Application 50, TRB p. 134
167	Chapter Review, pp. 440–441	Chapter Review, pp. 440–441	Chapter Review, pp. 440–441
168	Chapter 10 Test—Form A or Form B—TRB pp. 37–38 or pp. 39–40 (Omit items 1–11.)	Chapter 10 Test—Form A or Form B—TRB pp. 37–38 or pp. 39–40 (Omit items 1–11.)	Chapter 10 Test—Form A or Form B—TRB pp. 37–38 or pp. 39–40
169	Cumulative Review: Chapters 9–10, pp. 443–446 *Written:* 1–17 odds, 34–43	Cumulative Review: Chapters 9–10, pp. 443–446 *Written:* 1–17 odds, 34–43	Cumulative Review: Chapters 9–10, pp. 443–446 *Written:* 1–43 odds
170	Cumulative Test 5: Chapters 9–10, TRB pp. 49–50 (Omit items 11–15.)	Cumulative Test 5: Chapters 9–10, TRB pp. 49–50 (Omit items 11–15.)	Cumulative Test 5: Chapters 9–10, TRB pp. 49–50

Notes to the Teacher

Chapter 1   Using Data and Making Estimates
Pages 9–50

Overview   The first part of this chapter deals with descriptive statistics. Students learn how to read tables to find information. They learn how to find the mean, the median, the mode, and the range of a set of data. Frequency tables are introduced as a way of organizing raw data, and students learn how to use frequency tables to find the mean, the median, and the mode.

The work with the mean and with frequency tables provides a good deal of computational practice. You may wish to allow students to use calculators in these lessons.

The last part of Chapter 1 deals with estimation in addition, subtraction, and multiplication, and division of whole numbers and decimals. Students will use estimation in problem solving.

The *Skills Refreshers* in this chapter review the following skills for whole numbers and decimals: writing word names, comparing, adding, subtracting, multiplying, dividing, rounding, and finding quotients to the nearest tenth.

1.1   For the train schedule used with exercises 17–22, page 11, point out that a vertical line means that a particular train does not stop at the designated station.

For exercise 27, point out that the table could be read in two ways: with Ames as the row and Des Moines as the column, or vice versa. For the exercises that refer to the distance table on the right on page 12, make sure students understand that the city listed farther up and to the left must be the column and that the city listed farther down and to the right must be the row. Otherwise, there will not be an intersection for the two cities.

Skills Refresher, page 13, is the first of a recurring feature (at least two per chapter). This brief quiz tests for skills that students will need in the next few sections. Practice exercises in the *Computing Skills Refresher* can be assigned to students who do not do well on the *Skills Refresher*.

A chart is provided with each *Skills Refresher* that lists skill numbers and the pages in the *Computing Skills Refresher* where the skills are taught.

Calculator skill, page 524, may be used after page 13. Annotations for use of *Calculator* skill lessons appear with appropriate sections in both the student's text and in the Teacher's Edition.

Application 1 in the Teacher's Resource Book, *Catalog Orders,* may be used at this time. Annotations for use of the *Application* activities appear with appropriate sections in the Teacher's Edition.

Cross-Number Puzzle, page 14, is the first of a variety of special features. The special features may be games, puzzles, or topics of general interest. These features are optional, but most students will find them of interest.

1.2   Point out to students that the mode is the only measure of central tendency that can be used with data that are not numbers.

You might mention that an alternative definition of "no mode" is sometimes given as follows: It is considered that there is no mode if each item is listed the same number of times (even if each is listed more than once).

1.3   Point out that when there is an odd number of scores, the median will be one of the scores. When there is an even number of scores, the median may or may not be one of the scores. The median will be one of the scores if the two middle scores are the same. It will not be one of the scores if the two middle scores are different.

Point out that students can list numbers in order from largest to smallest or from smallest to largest.

Skills Refresher, page 19, reviews division of whole numbers. Students will use this skill in Section 1.4, when they find the mean of a set of numbers.

1.4   Point out in Example 2, page 20, that the mean can be a whole number or a mixed number. If students use a calculator to find the mean of a set of numbers, you may want to tell them to round some answers to the nearest tenth or hundredth.

Use *Get a Kick out of This,* page 23, to bring out the idea that if the mean for a specific number of scores is given, the total number of points can be found by multiplying the mean by the number of scores.

Skills Refresher, page 23, reviews subtraction, which is used in Section 1.5, and multiplication, used in Section 1.7.

1.5 The range is used to describe the spread of a distribution. Exercises 1–3 can be done orally.

Taking the Census, page 25, shows students how gathering information through polls can help predict changes.

1.6 Make sure students understand that the mode is the score or scores that occur with the greatest frequency—and not the frequency of those scores. (In the example at the top of page 27, some students may erroneously think that the mode is 10.)

When the sum of the frequencies is odd, the median can be found by adding 1 to the sum, dividing by 2, then counting down this number of scores from the top. When the sum is even, divide the sum by 2. Count down this number of scores. Average this score with the *next* score in the frequency table.

1.7 You may want to allow students to use calculators when they do this section. *Calculator skill*, page 528, shows how to use a calculator to find the mean from a frequency table. If the calculators do not have a memory key, students can write the products on a piece of paper, add the products, then divide by the sum of the frequencies.

Application 2 in the Teacher's Resource Book, *Grade Point Average*, may be used to extend this section.

1.8 This section begins by providing practice for students in finding the mean, the median, and the mode of a set of numbers. The first four exercises can be done orally.

Exercises 17–24 show students certain differences in the way the three averages describe a distribution. The mean is based on all of the scores and can be affected by extreme scores. The median is not affected by extreme scores. It can be a more useful average if extreme scores are not an important consideration (such as in averages of income or home values). The mode is useful to know when one needs to know the most frequent score or most popular item.

Application 3 in the Teacher's Resource Book, *Collecting, Organizing, and Summarizing Data*, may be used to extend this section.

Consumer Topic *What's Average?* page 34, is the first of a recurring optional *Consumer Topic* feature (one per chapter). This *Consumer Topic* shows students that they should read carefully when they see the word "average." The mean, the median, and the mode are all averages.

1.9 Sections 1.9 through 1.12 follow a similar pattern. Students are asked to estimate a calculation by first rounding to a particular place value and then carrying out the calculations with the rounded numbers.

Three types of exercises are included in each section: exercises involving selecting the best estimate from three choices, exercises involving estimating and checking the answers by finding the exact calculation, and application exercises. If students have access to calculators, all the exercises may be assigned. Otherwise, you may want to select exercises carefully to avoid overlong and tedious assignments.

Skill in estimating, both to get an approximate answer and to determine if a calculated answer is reasonable, is extremely important. Encourage students to use estimation as a tool in all computational work.

Estimating sums is covered in this section.

1.10 This section covers estimating differences.

1.11 This section covers estimating products.

Application 4 in the Teacher's Resource Book, *Estimating the Number of Words on a Page*, may be used to extend this section.

1.12 This section covers estimating quotients.

Applications 5–6 in the Teacher's Resource Book, *Checking Estimates With a Calculator* and *Estimation Activities*, may be used to extend this section.

Career *Sales and Marketing*, page 47, is the first of a recurring optional *Career* feature (one per chapter). In exercise 2, point out that the interval 4:00–5 would include 5:00 and that the interval 5–6 would not include 5:00. Time is continuous, so the next interval begins as the last one ends.

Overview   The graphs and tables in this chapter are based on factual information. Students are taught how to read maps, bar graphs, line graphs, pictographs, and circle graphs in separate lessons. Lessons on graphing ordered pairs and on making bar graphs and line graphs are included. A lesson is included on reading schematics.

The *Skills Refreshers* in this chapter review (a) changing decimals to fractions and fractions to decimals, (b) reducing fractions to lowest terms, (c) adding and subtracting fractions, and (d) multiplying by multiples of 10, 100, and 1000.

2.1   Make sure students fully understand the symbol-to-region correspondence that is necessary for reading a map. Exercises 1–6 may be done orally to help reinforce this concept.

Numbers on the Map, page 56, provides computational practice for students. Point out that in Example 2 "$\frac{1}{2}$" is read as "half" instead of "one half."

2.2   Most students have been introduced to coordinate graphing in earlier courses. Review the use of the coordinate axes and the "over-up" procedure for locating points. Only nonnegative coordinates are used in this section.

Application 7 in the Teacher's Resource Book, *Ordered Pairs on a Globe,* may be used to extend this section.

Gone Fishing, page 59, is a variation of the game Battleship. This activity, while optional, is fun for students and provides additional practice with graphing.

2.3   This section links Section 2.1 to Section 2.6, where students learn to draw line graphs. Exercises 1–7 may be done orally to emphasize that the x-axis and the y-axis may have different scale values. Next, you might want to have students do one of exercises 13–18 so that they can understand the need for different scale values on each axis.

Graph Pictures, pages 62–63, is an optional feature. You may want to challenge students to design their own pictures on graph paper. Have students list the ordered pairs they use, as in the example and the exercises.

2.4   Students should have initial success in reading bar graphs, since numerals are included on the bars. Point out that the bars of each bar graph are of equal width. The lengths of the bars show the relative sizes of the numbers they represent.

If students have difficulty answering exercises 13–14, point out that one bar graph is organized by country and the other by type of medal.

2.5   The second graph on page 67 has three scales instead of two. Students should read the scale on the left for degrees Celsius. Each horizontal line represents 5°C on this scale. Students should read the scale on the right for degrees Fahrenheit. Each horizontal line represents 9°F on this scale.

Point out that to answer exercise 8, *either* scale (Celsius or Fahrenheit) can be used, but the same scale should be used when finding the range for each city.

2.6   The number scale on a bar graph should begin at zero. Before making a bar graph or a line graph, students should determine the largest number needed on the scale. From that they can determine a convenient value for each unit on the number scale.

Application 8 in the Teacher's Resource Book, *Getting a Pulse on Line Graphs,* may be used to extend this section.

Consumer Topic   *Misleading Graphs,* pages 74–75, shows how two graphs can convey exactly the same information, but one graph can be more dramatic in appearance because of the way in which the graph has been drawn.

2.7   In the graphs for this section, students will have to estimate fractional parts of symbols. You can expect the answers to some of the exercises to vary somewhat.

Application 9 in the Teacher's Resource Book, *Graphs and Grams,* may be used to extend this section.

2.8   When a graph is used to compare parts of a whole, a circle (as in the examples) or a rectangle (as in exercises 28–32) can be used to represent the whole, or 100%. Each section is usually labeled with a percent. The sum of the percents should equal 100%.

Application 10 in the Teacher's Resource Book, *Making a Circle Graph,* may be used to extend this section.

2.9 Schematics are included in many different kinds of kits, from models to toys to replacement parts for a car or household items. Schematics are useful in clarifying written instructions.

Application 11 in the Teacher's Resource Book, *Using a Nomograph,* may be used to extend this section.

Career *Factory Technician,* page 85, shows schematics that a worker in a factory might encounter. You might want to show students the following three-dimensional views of the top, front, and side views of the solid object:

view from left   view from right

Chapter 3   Equations and Formulas
Pages 93–134

Overview Basic algebraic topics are introduced in this chapter, such as simplifying phrases, solving open sentences, and using formulas to solve word problems. The major objective of this chapter is to prepare students to use formulas. Additionally, the chapter includes considerable computational work with whole numbers and decimals, as well as some work with fractions, which occur near the end of the chapter.

The Skills Refreshers in this chapter review (a) adding and subtracting whole numbers and decimals, (b) multiplying and dividing whole numbers and decimals, (c) changing fractions to mixed numbers, and (d) multiplying whole numbers by fractions.

3.1 Because it is important for students to be able to distinguish between true, false, and open mathematical sentences, this section lays the foundation for working with equations and formulas, both of which occur later in the chapter. After they complete exercises 1–14, encourage the students to make up their own true, false, and open sentences, both English and mathematical. These can then be read to the class and identified.

3.2 Two uses of parentheses are pointed out in this section, namely, to indicate which operation is to be performed first and to indicate multiplication. A concept that students may have difficulty remembering is that $5x$ means $5(x)$ and xy means $x(y)$. Point out that in exercises 29–36, both uses of parentheses appear in each problem.

3.3 In this section, the standard rule concerning the order of operations is introduced. In an effort to assist students in remembering the correct order, you may wish to use the mnemonic "**P**lease, **m**y **d**ear **A**unt **S**ally" or any other mnemonic of your choice. Such a mnemonic can be used to emphasize a three-step approach. (First do the operations inside the **p**arentheses. Then, from left to right, do the **m**ultiplication and **d**ivision. Finally, from left to right, do the **a**ddition and **s**ubtraction.)

Students may find *Ingenious Genie,* page 100, both interesting and challenging and may be amused by exercise 3 in *Puzzle = 13,628,160* on the same page.

3.4 Because the major goal of this chapter is to prepare students to use formulas, this is a most important section. Formulas are introduced here and appear extensively throughout the rest of the chapter. Students will sometimes try to solve the problems by just multiplying or dividing the given numbers rather than by substituting into the formula. To discourage this, you may wish to have selected students explain their solutions of the exercises to the class.

3.5 While the analogy of a balance is used to introduce a method of solving equations using addition or subtraction, it is not used in the exercises. Some students may wish to use the problem-solving strategy of drawing a diagram to help them visualize the operation.

Note that exercises 1–24 involve whole numbers, whereas exercises 25–30 introduce equations with decimals. Word problems involving the use of a formula appear in the exercises of this section. Because these are troublesome for some students, assign these according to individual or class ability.

Students should think of the check as a necessary step in solving an equation.

Application 12 in the Teacher's Resource

Book, *Stopping Distance,* may be used to extend this section.

3.6 This section can be approached in much the same way as the previous section, except that it involves multiplication and division. Emphasize that students are to interpret $\frac{1700}{2}$ as 1700 divided by 2, not as 1700 halves. Note that equations with decimals are presented in the later exercises.

Slippery Sam, page 111, may more easily be solved if the students draw a diagram.

Application 13 in the Teacher's Resource Book, *Lightning and Thunder,* may be used to extend this section.

3.7 Since order of operations was introduced in Section 3.3, point out that the "reverse order" is employed in solving two-step equations. Remind the students that in the check, however, they are to follow the usual order.

Application 14 in the Teacher's Resource Book, *Magnifying Power,* may be used to extend this section.

The *Cross-Number Puzzle* on page 116 can be used as a second day's assignment for additional drill and practice.

3.8 The procedures for solving equations with fractional solutions are the same as for those with whole-number solutions. The skills necessary for solving and checking the equation in Example 1 were reviewed in the *Skills Refreshers* in Chapter 3. Finding the solution in Example 2 involves dividing a decimal by a whole number, which was illustrated in the example on page 110.

Application 15 in the Teacher's Resource Book, *Hear the Music,* may be used to extend this section.

3.9 In this section, all the equations contain fractions and decimals. Remind the students that the same procedures used in whole-number equations are used here. The multiplication of a fraction and a whole number, necessary for checking the solutions, was reviewed in the *Skills Refresher* on page 116.

3.10 Point out that an advantage of using a formula is that any variable in the formula can be expressed in terms of the other variables. On page 124, the same formula is used to find the number of tickets in Example 1 and to find the price per ticket in Example 2. Emphasize the meaning of t^2 in exercises 17–19.

Applications 16–17 in the Teacher's Resource Book, *Air Conditioning* and *Skid Marks and Speed,* may be used to extend this section.

Career *Building Trades Apprentice,* page 129, illustrates the practical application of formulas in various trades. Students should find the formula used in exercise 4 especially challenging.

Consumer Topic *Formulas for Shopping,* page 130, explains the use of formulas to solve common household problems.

Point out to students that the formula used in *Day for a Date,* page 131, does not by itself give the day of the week. Rather it provides a number (*W*) to be divided by 7, the *remainder* of which indicates the day of the week. Because of its length and the order of operations involved, the formula is a difficult one.

Chapter 4   Ratio, Proportion, and Percent
Pages 135–178

Overview This chapter concentrates on the meaning of ratio, the writing and solving of proportions, and percents. Other important topics include similarity, scale drawings, enlargements and reductions, and estimating.

Chapter 4 provides a good deal of computational practice with equivalent fractions; multiplication of whole numbers and decimals; division of whole numbers, resulting in whole number or decimal quotients; and rounding numbers.

The *Skills Refreshers* in this chapter review (a) comparing fractions and (b) division of whole numbers and decimals by 10, 100, and 1000.

4.1 The concept of ratio is defined in this section. Encourage students to use the three forms of naming a ratio.

Exercises 1–18 give students practice in writing ratios represented by pictures. Emphasize that each ratio will make one of these three comparisons: a comparison of a part to the whole, of the whole to a part, or of a part to a part. It is essential that students understand the importance of the order of comparison in a ratio. Point out to students that they should be aware of this concept as they do the exercises.

4.2 Equivalent ratios are introduced first, with the use of diagrams. Such visual aids enable students to relate the concrete to the abstract. You might want to make special mention of the diagram at the top of page 140. Point out that the first rectangle is divided into 4 parts, the second rectangle into 8 parts, and the third rectangle into 12 parts. Mention that the second rectangle has twice as many parts as the first and that the third rectangle has three times as many parts as the first. But the *same amount of area* is shaded in each rectangle.

Graphing Equivalent Ratios, page 142, reviews graphing on a coordinate plane. Guide students to conclude from exercises 1–7 that the graph of a set of equivalent ratios using the ordered pair (denominator, numerator) is a line.

For exercises 9–11, students' measurements may vary slightly. Any slight error in measurement will cause the graph to be other than a line. For exercise 11, point out that to express a ratio as a decimal, the numerator must be divided by the denominator. From these exercises, students should conclude that the ratio of the circumference of a circle to its diameter is 3.14, or π.

4.3 Solving a proportion is an important skill, necessary for successfully completing this chapter. Emphasize that the cross products in a true proportion are equal and that proportions are solved by finding the value that makes the cross products equal. You might want to mention that the solution to a proportion does not have to be a whole number.

4.4 This section presents the possibility of using different pairs of equivalent ratios to solve a proportion. If $\frac{a}{b} = \frac{c}{d}$, then these three proportions are also true because they yield the same cross products:

$$\frac{b}{a} = \frac{d}{c}, \quad \frac{a}{c} = \frac{b}{d}, \quad \frac{c}{a} = \frac{d}{b}.$$

Advise students that any one of the four proportions could be used to solve a problem. Point out, however, that the first ratio of each proportion determines how the second ratio is written.

You might want to do exercises 1–11 orally. Have students check to see if they have a true proportion. Ask students to write other true proportions, using the numbers in exercises 1–11. Have one student choose the first ratio of the proportion and let another student complete the proportion by using the appropriate ratio. This practice should help students set up the proportions needed in exercises 12–35. Emphasize that every student will not necessarily choose the same proportion, but all should have the same solution.

Applications 18–19 in the Teacher's Resource Book, *Property Tax* and *Estimating Fish Population,* may be used to extend this section.

4.5 Make sure students understand the term *corresponding sides.* You might want to mention that in similar figures, corresponding angles also have the same measure.

After students can identify the corresponding sides of similar figures, introduce the relationship between similarity and proportion. Show that cross products can be used to solve a proportion in which each ratio represents a pair of corresponding sides.

Application 20 in the Teacher's Resource Book, *Indirect Measurement,* may be used to extend this section.

4.6 Emphasize that when an enlargement (or reduction) is made, the enlargement (or reduction) scale is always written as a ratio of the new figure to the old figure.

Review measuring to the nearest $\frac{1}{4}$ inch before doing Example 3 on page 156. After you discuss Example 3, you may want to point out that the problem could have been solved by using this proportion: $\frac{1}{880} = \frac{2\frac{1}{4}}{x}$. Point out that $2\frac{1}{4} \times 880$ is actually the cross product of this proportion.

For exercises 29–32, mention that the length (or the width) of a room should be measured from the *inside* walls, not the outside walls.

Applications 21–22 in the Teacher's Resource Book, *Decorating and Furnishing an Apartment* and *Which Way and How Fast?* may be used to extend this section.

Career *Public–Service Jobs,* page 159, gives examples of using mathematics on the job.

4.7 In this section equivalent ratios are used to develop the meaning of *percent,* and students learn how to write a ratio as a percent. Point out that one of the ratios in these proportions will always have a denominator of 100. Proportions are solved by using the cross-product method introduced in earlier sections.

You may want to provide additional examples, like Example 5, to show students how to write a percent as a ratio in lowest terms.

Application 23 in the Teacher's Resource Book, *Percent-a-lator*, may be·used to extend this section.

4.8 Each problem in this section can be classified according to one of the following types: Type 1—Find the percent; Type 2—Find the part; Type 3—Find the total. Stress, however, that all three types can be solved using the proportion $\frac{part}{total} = \frac{number\ of\ percent}{100}$.

Skills Refresher, page 167, reviews the concept of dividing by 10, 100, and 1000. This concept will be used in the next two sections.

Application 24 in the Teacher's Resource Book, *Using Percent,* may be used to extend this section.

4.9 In this section, students learn how to change a percent to a decimal, and vice versa. Show students the long way to do these problems before introducing the shortcut. When you discuss Example 2, emphasize that multiplying by $\frac{100}{100}$ is the same as multiplying by 1. Point out that the purpose of using $\frac{100}{100}$ is to enable us to rename 0.06 as a fraction with a denominator of 100.

You might want to first introduce Example 3, using the proportion $\frac{x}{75} = \frac{36}{100}$. Then show students the multiplication method. Point out that both methods give the same answer, but the second method is a shortcut. Check that students place the decimal point correctly in the product.

You may want to show students how to use a calculator to do exercises 25–48.

Consumer Topic *Budgets,* page 171, presents information in a form often found in periodicals. For an additional activity, have students estimate the percents for an unlabeled, subdivided circle.

4.10 Estimation is an important skill that requires practice. Example 1 and exercises 1–18 require mental computation. Notice that the percents used are all multiples of 5. Students should

not have much difficulty mentally computing with such numbers to obtain *exact* results. Example 2 shows how a similar procedure is used to *estimate* results when the given percents are not multiples of 5. The procedure involves rounding each percent to the nearest 5%. Exercises 19–45 require estimating results.

Chapter 5   Measurement

Pages 183–224

Overview   This chapter explores both the customary system and the metric system of measuring length, weight, capacity, and temperature. Additionally, the measurement of time and angles is covered. While there is conversion between units of the same system, there is none between different systems, with the exception of temperatures. Metric usage and spellings were determined by consulting SI (International System of Units) recommendations and those of the National Council of Teachers of Mathematics.

This chapter provides numerous opportunities for students to assume an active role in the learning process. The more measuring instruments you can provide for a hands-on experience, the more interesting and exciting the lessons will be. In addition to protractors to be used in measuring angles, a list of measuring instruments might include the following:

	Customary System	Metric System
length	inch ruler yardstick tape measure	cm ruler meterstick metric tape
weight	scale with ounces and pounds	balance gram weights kg scale
capacity	teaspoon tablespoon measuring cup	liter container mL spoon
temperature	Fahrenheit thermometer	Celsius thermometer

The *Skills Refreshers* in this chapter review (a) changing improper fractions to mixed numbers and mixed numbers to improper fractions, (b) multiplying whole numbers by fractions or mixed numbers, and (c) multiplying and dividing by 10, 100, and 1000.

5.1 Be sure that students understand the difference between units of measure and instruments of measure. They will need to make this distinction in order to complete exercises 1–20. For exercises 1–10, allow answers to be either customary *or* metric units of measure. The answers in the Teacher's Edition are given in customary units, followed by metric units in parentheses. Exercises 31–46 will require the use of a dictionary or an encyclopedia and will provide students with an opportunity to improve their reference skills while learning about some specialized measuring instruments.

Application 25 in the Teacher's Resource Book, *Using Measurement to Solve Outdoor Problems,* may be used to extend this section.

It's About Time makes reference to the *Guinness Book of World Records,* which provides many more examples of "oldest" and "longest" than are listed on page 187. An extra assignment might be to have the students use the *Guinness Book of World Records* to list any records given in hours that they find interesting. Then have them convert their findings into days by dividing by 24.

5.2 An interesting fact to be realized from this section is that several of our present-day units of measure evolved from ancient measurements. You might point out that while we have retained the name of the unit, modern civilization requires a standard unit of measure. Have the students try to imagine what the exploration of outer space or the advancement of computer science might be like if the concept of a foot or an inch varied from person to person.

After the students have identified the measuring instruments in the *Photo Puzzle* on page 190, have them give an example of what might be measured with each one.

5.3 To help students measure accurately, it is best to work on measuring first to the nearest inch, then to the nearest $\frac{1}{2}$ inch, and so forth, as is done in exercises 1–12. To assist students in completing exercises 13–20, you may wish to use a transparent ruler on an overhead projector. A review of equivalent fractions in which the denominator is a power of 2 may be helpful.

Application 26 in the Teacher's Resource Book, *Using a Map,* may be used to extend this section.

Measuring on the Job, page 194, provides a practical application of estimating and measuring lengths. Point out that there are times when an estimated measurement is sufficient and times when an exact measurement is required. You may want to allow students to work in pairs or in small groups.

5.4 Note that students are to find equivalent lengths within the same system by the ratio and proportion method. Remind students that cross-multiplication of the numbers in a proportion will result in equivalent products. Take some time to practice setting up proportions properly, especially when a variable is used.

Career *Machinist,* page 197, may appeal especially to students with a penchant for industrial arts. You may want to have students discuss how they have used tolerance in industrial arts classes or in some of their outside work. Completion of the table on page 197 requires addition and subtraction of decimals and fractions.

5.5 A presentation of some background on the metric system may help students better understand its importance and its application here. Such information is readily available in most encyclopedias and in many government publications. While several prefixes are presented on page 198, point out that the most commonly used are *kilo-, centi-,* and *milli-.* One of the advantages of using the metric system is that the same prefixes are used whether one is measuring length, weight, or capacity. Exercises 1–16 are designed to help students relate metric measurement to familiar objects.

Skills Refresher, page 201, reviews skills that will help students make the conversions in Section 5.6.

5.6 Conversions within the metric system are done by the proportion method (as on page 195).

Note that when five or more digits are written in metric measurement, spaces are used instead of commas.

Once students have mastered this technique for converting from one metric unit to another, you may want to show them a shortcut that demonstrates the advantage of using the metric system. For example, to change from kilometers to meters, count the number of lines from *kilo-* to *meter,* using the chart on page 198. *Meter* is 3 lines **down** from *kilo-,* so move the decimal point in the given measure 3 places to the **right** (32 km = 32 000 m). If you go **up** the chart, move the decimal point to the **left** one place for every line (143 cm = 1.43 m).

5.7 This section covers measuring mass in the metric system and weight in the customary system. The proportion method from previous sections is used to change from one unit of weight or mass to another. Note that students are not asked to change measurements from one system to another.

Finding Weights, page 207, allows students to apply logical reasoning skills.

5.8 Both customary and metric units of capacity are presented in this section. If measuring instruments are available, this section lends itself well to hands-on experience. If metric models are not available, remember that a cube with a side of 10 centimeters holds 1 liter and that a cube with a side of 1 centimeter holds 1 milliliter. You may wish to point out that this relationship between units of length and units of capacity is unique to the metric system.

5.9 Caution students to be aware of A.M. and P.M. designation when determining length of time, as in Example 4. Point out that in the U.S. armed forces and in European countries, the day is not divided into A.M. and P.M. Instead, a 24-hour clock is used, so that 6 P.M. is referred to as "1800 hours." The 24-hour clock is a part of SI.

Exercises 27–32 involve practical applications of finding a length of time.

Application 27 in the Teacher's Resource Book, *Flying Time,* may be used to extend this section.

Consumer Topic *Harvesting a Garden,* page 214, demonstrates how the measure of time,

weight, and cost can be related. Remind students to convert the cents to decimals before multiplying.

Line Art, page 215, is fun for students. Some students may enjoy making these designs by using colored string and nails on a board.

5.10 There is an occasional need to change temperature from degrees Fahrenheit to degrees Celsius, or conversely. The easiest way is to use a nomograph, such as the one on page 216. More-advanced students may be given the formulas $C = \frac{5}{9}(F - 32)$ and $F = \frac{9}{5}C + 32$ for making conversions.

Completing exercises 1–12 will enable students to become more familiar with the comparison of degrees Fahrenheit and degrees Celsius.

Exercises 21–24 involve working with positive and negative temperature readings.

Application 28 in the Teacher's Resource Book, *Temperature,* may be used to extend this section.

5.11 In this section, students are shown how to measure and how to draw angles. Students are sometimes confused by the two scales on a protractor. Emphasize that they should first determine if the angle is less than or greater than 90° before deciding which scale to use. If possible, demonstrate how to measure and how to draw an angle with a transparent protractor on an overhead projector.

Applications 29–30 in the Teacher's Resource Book, *Making Square Corners* and *What's the Angle?* may be used to extend this section.

Chapter 6　Perimeter, Area, and Volume　　*Pages 225–272*

Overview This chapter introduces students to various plane and solid figures. Students work with formulas for finding perimeter, area, circumference, and volume.

The exercises in this chapter give students practice solving proportions and computing with whole numbers, fractions, and decimals. The chapter is replete with special topics that students should enjoy.

The *Skills Refreshers* review operations with fractions, mixed numbers, and decimals. They also review proportions and exponents.

6.1 This section introduces polygons and draws special attention to four kinds of quadrilaterals. You might want to point out that the sides of a polygon must meet at the vertices. Since the sides of a polygon cannot cross, figures like the following are not polygons:

 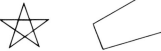

Exercises 17–20 are very important. These exercises encourage students to draw conclusions and state properties about particular quadrilaterals. Exercises 21–26 involve drawing polygons with certain properties.

Application 31 in the Teacher's Resource Book, *Tessellations*, may be used to extend this section.

6.2 This section explains the concept of perimeter. You might want to stress the idea that perimeter is the distance around a figure. You may need to remind students that units, such as meters, must be included in their answers.

The answer for exercise 36 assumes that the frame is beveled and that some of it is wasted. However, if the frame is flat, it can be cut according to the diagram below. The answer would then be $91\frac{1}{2}$ inches.

21	18	27	24	$1\frac{1}{2}$
$1\frac{1}{2}$ 18	21	24	27	

6.3 This section is an introduction to area. Students may have difficulty understanding that area is a measure of square units of surface. Use the diagram in Example 1 on page 233 to help emphasize this point. Then introduce the shortcut of multiplying the number of rows by the number of squares in each row—which is the basis of the formula for finding the area of a rectangle. Remind students that a square is a rectangle whose length and width are the same. Therefore, to find the area of a square, they can use the formula $A = s \times s$, or s^2.

Remind students that the proper square units need to be included with their answers. Point out

that the units of measure (for length and width) must be the same before they use either formula.

6.4 Equivalent areas can be found by setting up and solving a correct proportion. Remind students that more than one proportion can be used to solve a problem. Emphasize that 1 yd$^2 = 9$ ft^2 and 1 ft$^2 = 144$ in^2. The two drawings on pages 237–238 are presented to help students remember these facts.

Exercises 26–29 on pages 238–239 are practical applications of working with equivalent ratios. You might want to review the meaning of various metric prefixes before assigning exercises 31–33.

The problems in *Math From the 1870's*, page 239, are written exactly as they appeared in *Robinson's Progressive Practical Arithmetic for Common Schools and Academies* (copyright 1858, 1863, and 1877). Students may enjoy discussing various aspects of the problems.

Career *Farmer*, page 240, introduces students to some of the expenses and earnings that are involved in running a farm.

Patterns With Squares, page 241, is an activity that involves area relationships.

6.5 This section introduces the formula for finding the area of a parallelogram. You may want to point out that either pair of opposite sides could be used as the bases in a parallelogram. Emphasize that the height is the length of any segment forming right angles with both bases. Point out that the height of a parallelogram between the chosen bases is unique because the distance between two parallel lines is constant.

It is advisable to introduce the area of a parallelogram by first finding the area of the rectangle that can be formed from the parallelogram. This will give students a better understanding of how the formula for the area of a parallelogram is derived.

6.6 Visual aids are helpful for showing that any parallelogram can be divided into two identical triangles and that any two identical triangles can be combined into a parallelogram. Exercise 2 on page 246 would be a good in-class activity. After students visualize the relationship between a parallelogram and two identical triangles, introduce the formula for finding the area of a triangle.

For exercise 29 on page 247, mention that in a right triangle, one of the legs functions as the base, while the other leg functions as the altitude drawn to the base.

Applications 32–33 in the Teacher's Resource Book, *Area of a Triangle Through Paper Folding* and *Angles of a Triangle*, may be used to extend this section.

The Number Pi, page 248, provides a concrete approach for finding the value of pi.

6.7 You might want to measure the circumference and the diameter of several objects to show that $C \div d = \pi$. Once students understand that $C \div d = \pi$, it will naturally follow that $C = \pi d$. You might want to talk about the need for approximating π as $\frac{22}{7}$, or 3.14.

For exercises 19–26, emphasize that the length of a *diameter* is given and that students are to use *3.14* for π. For exercises 27–34, the length of a *radius* is given and students are to use $\frac{22}{7}$ for π.

Application 34 in the Teacher's Resource Book, *How Fast Are You Going?* may be used to extend this section.

6.8 If you approach the development for the area of a circle slowly, students should be able to understand why $3r^2$ is a reasonable approximation for the area of a circle.

In the second part of the example on page 252, the base of the red triangle is $r + r$, or $2r$, and the height of the triangle is r. Therefore, the area of the red triangle is $\frac{1}{2}(2r)(r)$, or r^2.

Before you assign exercises 37–38, you may want to discuss a procedure for finding the "wasted part."

Application 35 in the Teacher's Resource Book, *Find the Center*, may be used to extend this section.

6.9 Students may need to familiarize themselves with three-dimensional figures before they are able to understand volume. You may want to have students construct or draw some rectangular solids. Point out that all rectangular solids have six faces, each a rectangle. The sides of the rectangle are called edges and each rectangular solid has twelve edges. Make sure that students understand that a cube is a rectangular solid whose faces are squares.

Point out that in Example 1 on page 255, it is not necessary to count the number of cubes in the bottom layer to find the total. Encourage students to draw the conclusion that the formula for the area of a rectangle can be used. Measuring with cubes is used to develop the formula $V = Bh$. Stress that B represents the number of cubes in one layer of the base. In the formula $V = \ell wh$, page 256, ℓw replaces B.

Application 36 in the Teacher's Resource Book, *Squares and Boxes*, may be used to extend this section.

Slicing Cubes, page 259, gives students additional practice visualizing spatial relationships.

6.10 Make sure that students understand that $1 \text{ yd}^3 = 27 \text{ ft}^3$ before you discuss the examples. Remind students that different proportions can be used to solve a given problem and that order is important when setting up ratios.

When you discuss *Surface Area*, page 263, use a visual aid so that students can see which edges have the same length and which faces have the same area. Emphasize that surface area is the sum of the areas of all six faces.

Platonic Solids, page 264, should arouse student interest. You may find it helpful to have students make an equilateral triangle, a square, and a regular pentagon out of cardboard and then trace the patterns for the platonic solids from these figures.

6.11 Students should have an easy time grasping the development of the formula for the volume of a cylinder. It is similar to the development of the formula for the volume of a rectangular solid. Emphasize that the base of a cylinder is a circle. You might want to review the formula for the area of a circle and the meaning of r^2. Remind students that both $\frac{22}{7}$ and 3.14 can be used as approximations for π.

For exercises 17–18 on page 267, you may want to suggest that students first find the volume using the outer radius and then find the volume using the inner radius.

Consumer Topic *Comparing Volumes*, page 268, is an informative consumer education lesson. You may want to have students visit stores or look in their home to find any packaging that may be deceiving to the buyer.

Volume Projects, page 269, will probably have to be seen to be believed. Students will determine the volume of a pyramid in relation to the volume of a rectangular solid and the volume of a cone in relation to the volume of a cylinder.

Chapter 7   Earning Money
Pages 277–310

Overview   In this chapter, students are introduced to a variety of methods that can be used to pay employees. Payment for overtime is figured, as is payment for piecework. Commissions and tips are discussed as a part of weekly earnings.

Types of deductions are discussed, as is figuring income taxes.

You may want to allow students to use calculators when they do the exercises in this chapter.

The *Skills Refreshers* in this chapter review (a) changing percents to decimals, (b) multiplying decimals, (c) adding decimals, and (d) subtracting decimals.

7.1   The employment application form shown on page 278 is similar to many forms used by employers. *Application 37* in the Teacher's Resource Book contains an employment application form similar to the one shown on page 278. You might want to make a copy for each student and have them fill it out. Emphasize that handwriting must be legible and all information accurate. Point out that it is a good idea to keep a permanent record of all work experience. Dates, addresses, and phone numbers are usually required on application forms. Some application forms may also ask about volunteer work done.

7.2   As an alternative method for solving Example 1, you may want to explain that the sale price is $100\% - 20\%$, or 80%, of the regular price. Hence, the sale price is $0.8 \times \$12.99$, or $\$10.39$.

You may want to show students how to use the % key on certain calculators to do exercises 1–8.

regular price $15.99;   20% off

Enter	Display	
C	0.	clears calculator
15.99	15.99	regular price
−	15.99	
20	20.	
%	12.792	sale price

On some calculators, the = key may have to be pressed after the % key.

Consumer Topic   When you discuss *Universal Product Code,* page 283, you might mention that some items do not have a UPC because they are priced by weight.

7.3   You might mention that some people are paid triple time if they work on holidays. There is sometimes a restriction on receiving double-time or triple-time pay: The person usually has to work the day before and the day after the holiday. Otherwise, he or she will receive straight pay.

Some employers offer **compensation time** (time off with pay) as an alternative to overtime pay.

7.4   Some employers pay by the piecework plan to give workers an incentive to produce more work.

7.5   You might mention that commission is similar to piecework. Commission depends on the number of items sold, piecework on the number of items produced.

Example 3 is an example of a graduated commission—the rate of commission increases as the amount of sales increases.

7.6   Point out that people in service occupations depend greatly on tips as a part of their incomes. So, wherever appropriate, good service should be rewarded with good tips.

Many students will probably benefit from a discussion of *Choosing a Job,* pages 292–293. If any students are already working, you might ask them about the kind of work they are doing and if they have any points to consider besides those mentioned in the book. (For example, sometimes meals are provided or store discounts are available.)

7.7 You might point out that some deductions are required by law. Other deductions are voluntary on the part of the employee. Some companies offer optional health or life insurance. Sometimes employees can order products through the company, and the cost is deducted from the paycheck. You may want to mention that *F.I.C.A.* stands for "Federal Insurance Contributions Act."

Tell students that there is a zero-column included in the table for figuring taxes to be withheld. You might mention that some people like to claim fewer withholding allowances than they are allowed. A larger amount of taxes is then withheld from each paycheck. Some people prefer this because it could mean a tax refund for them at the end of the year.

Exercise 7 is for a single person with 2 withholding allowances. Point out that this may be a single person with a dependent child. However, a person can claim a second withholding allowance for being over 65 or for being blind.

When you do the special topic *Social Security,* pages 298–299, you may want students to find out the kinds of restrictions on who may receive benefits and on how much a person may receive.

In Example 2, make sure students understand that any amount earned *over* the wage base is not taxed for social security.

7.8 You might wish to obtain other tax forms from your local IRS office. Not all single people can use form 1040EZ. Another form must be used if there are dependent children or if the filer wishes to itemize deductions.

You might mention that the most common error made on tax returns is not copying the correct entry from the tax tables. Other common mistakes include not adding or subtracting correctly and not figuring the correct amount of medical deductions.

After students complete exercises 1–12, you may want them to find the *amount* of refund or balance due.

Application 38 in the Teacher's Resource Book contains income tax form 1040EZ. You might want to make four copies for each student to use with exercises 13–16.

Tax Rate Schedules, page 306, shows a method that can be used for computing taxes when a person cannot use the tax tables. One such case occurs when a person uses income averaging.

Career *Tax Consultant,* page 307, shows students how a tax consultant can help people pay the least amount of taxes allowable by law. Point out that people should keep accurate records so that a tax consultant can determine which deductions can be legally made.

Chapter 8   Managing Money
Pages 311–356

Overview The goal of this chapter is to help students become wise consumers. Students get some experience with budgeting and managing personal finances, maintaining and balancing a checking account, and computing the cost of credit purchases. Student interest should be high in this chapter because the topics are relevant and applicable.

This chapter also reviews many basic math skills. You may want to allow students to use calculators to do some of the basic computations.

The *Skills Refreshers* in this chapter review (a) reducing fractions to lowest terms, (b) dividing whole numbers with decimal quotients, (c) finding products in lowest terms, and (d) changing decimals to percents.

8.1 Advise students that keeping track of expenses and income is basic to good money management. The exercises in this section should give students a better understanding of how income and expenses affect cash on hand.

Have students keep records of their own weekly expenses and income for one month. Encourage students to review their spending habits and to make adjustments, if necessary.

Talk It Over, page 315, introduces students to fixed and variable expenses and the problem of income not meeting expenses.

8.2 Mention that since individuals spend their money in different ways, each person's budget is separated into different categories. Point out that the total amount of money that will be separated into categories is *net income,* not gross income.

Remind students that a percent is a ratio that compares a number to 100. So in each exercise, one of the ratios in the proportion will have a denominator of 100. Students can check their work in exercises 15–18 by adding the percents to see if the sum is 100%.

Talk It Over, page 319, allows students to discuss the importance of written records, the variables that could affect the percent of income spent on each category, and the importance of maintaining a regular savings plan.

8.3 Advise students that making a workable budget requires a good deal of thought and is based on past financial history and anticipated needs. The questions at the top of page 320 suggest topics that need to be considered.

It might be necessary to review both the proportion method and the multiplication method of finding a percent of a number. For exercises 9–12, students can check their work by making sure that the sum of the amounts is equal to the total (net) income.

Talk It Over, page 323, poses questions relating to budgets. You may want to have students discuss these questions with their family.

8.4 This section teaches students how to properly maintain a checking account. Point out that it is important to correctly fill out the following information on a check: the date; the name of the person or organization to whom the check will be made; the amount of the check, written in numerals and in words; the memo; and the signature.

Advise students that a signed check authorizes the bank to deduct money from the account. Stress the importance of filling in the check register at the time a deposit is made or a check is written. You might want to discuss with students the advantages of using a checking account rather than paying cash.

Application 39, pages 3–4 in the Teacher's Resource Book, contains forms that you may want to duplicate. If you make two copies of page 3

and four copies of page 4 (for each student), students will have six blank checks and eight blank check registers to use with exercises 3–10.

8.5 Point out to students that using a monthly bank statement enables a person to compare the balance of a checking account (as recorded in the check register) with the balance in the bank's records (as shown in the bank statement).

Application 39, page 5 in the Teacher's Resource Book, contains a form students can use to reconcile a bank statement. Eight copies (for each student) of this form can be used for exercises 5–12.

Application 39 in the Teachers' Resource Book, *Balancing a Checking Account,* may be used to extend this section.

8.6 In this section, students learn to compute simple interest by using the formula $i = prt$. Remind students to use the formula $A = p + i$ to add the simple interest to the principal to determine the total amount due at the end of a term.

8.7 Stress the difference between simple interest and compound interest. Point out that compound interest is the interest earned on the sum of the original principal and the accumulated interest. Mention that the formula for simple interest, $i = prt$, is used to find the interest for a given period. Also, make sure students understand the different compounding periods. (Notice that a compounding period usually is given as a fraction, but an equivalent decimal is used in computation.)

8.8 Students should quickly appreciate the convenience of using a compound-interest table. Make sure students have ample practice with the table before they begin the exercises.

8.9 An understanding of the cost of credit and knowing how it is determined are important consumer skills. Point out that the cost of credit increases as the amount of money borrowed increases or as the length of time to repay the loan increases.

In this section, students are given a formula to compute the cost of credit. Make sure students understand what each variable in the formula represents.

Make special mention of the note at the bottom of page 340. Encourage students to always ask questions (even seek professional advice) before signing any kind of contract or agreement.

8.10 Remind students that lending institutions require customers to pay interest on loans. Most consumers are interested in installment loans. These loans are usually repaid in relatively small payments each month. The Truth-in-Lending Law requires the lender to inform the customer of the actual cost of credit—the annual percentage rate. Point out that the annual percentage rate is not the same as simple interest applied to single-payment loans. This section introduces a formula to use for computing the annual percentage rate.

That'll Be 5 Clams, page 347, provides a brief history of the development of economic systems —from a system of bartering to a system using money.

Career *Credit Union Officer,* page 348, introduces students to a volunteer position in which a workable knowledge of financing and banking would be helpful.

8.11 One way to compute finance charges is to use an average daily balance. Point out that if a bill is paid in full on time, no finance charge is added. If a balance is carried over from a previous month, then a finance charge is applied on *all* new purchases (from the date of the purchase) as well as on the old balance. However, the earlier a customer makes a late monthly payment, the smaller the finance charge. Since the process of determining a finance charge is complex, do several examples in class for students.

Consumer Topic *Borrowing Money,* page 353, shows that the cost of credit can vary, depending on the arrangements of a loan.

Chapter 9   Using Money

Pages 361–406

Overview This chapter presents a variety of topics, including renting an apartment, doing comparison shopping, eating economically, buying and financing a new car, and using car and health insurance. Student interest should be high in this chapter. Most students should be able to make personal contributions when the topics are discussed.

Many basic computational skills are reviewed in this chapter. You may want to allow the use of calculators in cases where computations become burdensome.

The *Skills Refreshers* in this chapter review (a) comparing whole numbers and decimals, (b) rounding decimals, (c) dividing whole numbers with decimal quotients, and (d) multiplying whole numbers and decimals.

9.1 Students should find this survey interesting to analyze. Mention that the sum of the percents for each sex is not 100% because only the five things mentioned most frequently are listed. You may want to conduct a similar survey with your class or classes.

9.2 The idea of renting an apartment of their own is very appealing to young adults. This section points out some of the financial responsibilities that occur even before a person actually moves into an apartment (the move-in cost). Remind students that there are additional costs that usually are not included in rent, such as insurance, utilities, decorating, and so on. In Sections 9.3 and 9.4 students will learn about food costs.

Discuss with students the advantages and the disadvantages of renting an apartment rather than living at home. Ask students what kind of arrangements and agreements they would make with someone before sharing an apartment.

Application 40 in the Teacher's Resource Book, *Cost of Electricity,* may be used to extend this section.

9.3 In this section, students learn how to find the unit price of an item. Review the division and rounding process with students. You may suggest that students take along a calculator when they are shopping, for quick and accurate calculations. Point out that even if stores list unit prices, it is still desirable to be able to check prices quickly and accurately. Make sure students understand why comparisons of unit prices for the items in exercises 21–24 cannot be made until the quantities being compared are expressed in the same unit.

Talk It Over, page 370, suggests that consumers consider factors in addition to the unit price when making a selection. Students should find the information generated from exercise 2 interesting. You may want to point out that prices vary from store to store. You may also want to discuss the advantages and the disadvantages of shopping at "no frills" grocery stores.

For Pizza Freaks Only, page 371, allows students to compute the area of a pizza using the formula for the area of a circle. Students are also given opportunities to make a comparison to determine the better buy.

9.4 This section presents four common ways for a person to plan a meal. Point out that convenience foods differ in quality, preparation and clean-up time, and price. Carry-out meals and restaurant food differ in quality, price, and nutritional value.

When you discuss Example 2, emphasize that the tip is not paid on sales tax. Students who work in a restaurant may offer to share some personal experiences concerning tipping.

You may want to have students prepare a menu for a family dinner. Then have students find the cost of serving that meal, using each of the approaches discussed in this section.

Application 41 in the Teachers' Resource Book, *Counting Calories,* may be used to extend this section.

9.5 This section should make students aware of how costly it is to try to keep up with changing styles. After students learn how to compute the wearing cost of an article of clothing, they should be able to make better choices when shopping. If you permit students to use a calculator, you may want to refer to Section 7.2 in the Notes to the Teacher on how to use the % key to solve discount problems.

As an outside project, have students research different types of fabrics. Suggest that students compare cost, care, quality, and durability of the different fabrics.

9.6 Leisure activities can provide students with physical exercise as well as recreation. Remind students to include in their budgets the cost of participating in leisure activities.

You may suggest that students bring in brochures from different athletic or tape clubs and discuss different membership plans.

Application 42 in the Teacher's Resource

Book, *How Record Albums Are Priced,* may be used to extend this section.

Scoring in Bowling, pages 384–385, provides a good review of addition of whole numbers and teaches students how to keep score in bowling. You may want to arrange a field trip to a local bowling alley so that students can apply these skills.

9.7 This section alerts students to several facts that any new-car buyer should know. Stress the importance of researching car prices and option costs in such magazines as *Consumer Reports.* Point out that a consumer should shop around before making any final decision. Dealer markup will vary from one dealer to the next. There are other factors that affect the price of a car, such as the state of the economy, the popularity of the car, and the time of the year.

Ask students to research how the trade-in value of an old car should be negotiated into the selling price of a new car. You may also want to discuss the advantages and the disadvantages of purchasing a used car rather than a new car.

Application 43 in the Teacher's Resource Book, *Automobile Depreciation,* may be used to extend this section.

9.8 You may want to offer the following advice to your students about financing the purchase of a new car: First, negotiate the best selling price of the car with a salesperson. Then, shop around for the best rate of interest on a loan. Remind students to take note of the annual percentage rate (a topic covered in Section 8.10). The interest paid on the car loan adds significantly to the price of the car.

Consumer Topic *Car Maintenance and Repairs,* page 394, shows students that they can save a considerable amount of money by doing basic car repairs and maintenance themselves.

Career *Travel Agent,* page 395, gives students some information about an interesting and exciting career. You may want to invite a travel agent to class to discuss the daily responsibilities of a travel agent. You may also want to discuss the advantages and the disadvantages of using a travel agent to plan a trip.

9.9 This section introduces some types of car-insurance coverage available to a consumer.

Make sure students understand the terms used in the section before they begin the exercises.

The rates for car insurance vary from company to company. Comparison shopping is advisable. Emphasize the importance of the driver-rating factor in determining insurance premiums. Insurance companies gather statistics on accidents and on the people that are involved in these accidents. The driver-rating factors are determined from these statistics. People are then grouped into categories by age, sex, geographical location, and so forth. People who fall into a category that has been determined to be a high risk have a higher driver-rating factor than people who do not. As a result, people with a higher driver-rating factor must pay higher insurance premiums. Also mention that if a car is driven by several people, the highest driver-rating factor of all the drivers is usually used to determine the premium.

Make sure students are able to read the table on page 396 correctly. You may want to do the following examples before assigning exercises 9–22: What is the base rate for liability insurance with   (a) 25,000/50,000/100,000 limits? ($46) (b) 50,000/100,000/25,000 limits? ($48.20) (c) 50,000/200,000/100,000 limits? ($53)

Ask students to research what types of car-insurance coverages, if any, are mandatory in their state. You may want an insurance agent to speak to the class on the different types of available insurance coverages.

Application 44 in the Teacher's Resource Book, *Traffic Lights,* may be used to extend this section.

9.10 This section should alert students to the necessity of having health insurance. Emphasize the difference between basic medical insurance and major medical insurance. Point out that even with insurance, the patient usually must pay some portion of the expenses.

Ask students to investigate and to report on the type of medical coverage their family has. Make special mention of Health Maintenance Organizations (HMOs). Discuss the advantages and the disadvantages of belonging to medical-care groups like HMOs.

Chapter 10 Probability and Computer Literacy *Pages 407–442*

Overview This chapter covers two topics—probability (Sections 10.1–10.5) and computer literacy (Sections 10.6–10.10). Basic probability concepts are presented without overemphasizing advanced vocabulary. Students learn how to determine outcomes, find probabilities, and make predictions.

The computer-literacy sections provide an introduction to computers that all students should find interesting. Students will learn what a computer can and cannot do and will learn to read and write a simple flowchart. Students will also be introduced to some symbols and instructions in the BASIC language and will learn how to determine the output of a simple program written in BASIC. It is not necessary, nor is it the intent, for students to use a computer when they study these sections. (Students will interact with a computer when they do *Applications 47–50* in the Teacher's Resource Book.)

The *Skills Refreshers* in this chapter review (a) changing a fraction to a decimal, (b) multiplying fractions and decimals, and (c) evaluating expressions.

10.1 Point out that when the Wheel of Luck on page 408 is spun, the pointer has an equally likely chance of landing on any one of the twelve sections. Use an example like the one below to expose students to a situation that does not have equally likely outcomes.

Since the circle is not separated into three sections of the same size, the outcomes are not equally likely.

Point out that the formula at the bottom of page 408 can be used only when the outcomes are equally likely. Make sure students understand that the notation p( ) means ''the probability of.'' You may want to mention that an **event** is a collection of outcomes, that there are 5 outcomes in event C on the Wheel of Luck, and that p(C) means ''the probability of event C.''

Mention that a probability of $\frac{5}{12}$ does not mean

that you will get 5 C's in every 12 spins. It merely means that you will *most likely* get 5 C's in every 12 spins.

Exercise 38, page 410, and exercise 20, page 412 (Section 10.2), introduce students to the idea of dependent events.

10.2 Students should have little difficulty understanding probabilities of 0 and 1. Emphasize that the probability of an outcome must be 0, 1, or between 0 and 1.

Some students may erroneously think that there are only 3 possible outcomes in exercise 13. You may need to explain that there are 3 *kinds of sandwiches* (events)—corned beef, bologna, and salami—but that there are 8 outcomes of corned beef, 6 of bologna, and 1 of salami.

Use exercises 16–19 to bring out the idea that the sum of the probabilities of an event happening and of that event not happening is 1.

10.3 Advise students that using a sample space makes it easy to see all of the possible outcomes in an experiment. This, in turn, makes it easy to determine probabilities. Mention that the sample space at the top of page 414 and the one on page 415 are called *tree diagrams*.

Invite a life-science teacher to class to show students how sample spaces are used for simple combinations of genes for some trait or traits in plants or animals.

Skills Refresher, page 415, reviews writing a fraction as a decimal—a skill that is used extensively in the next section.

10.4 Ask students to suggest a situation where they have seen probability given as a percent, for example, "There is a 25% chance that it will rain today." Advise students that a probability given as a fraction can be changed to a percent by using one of the two methods shown on page 416.

Skills Refresher, page 418, reviews computational skills needed for making predictions (Section 10.5).

Consumer Topic *Know Your Chances,* page 419, gives examples of the use of probability in various aspects of daily life.

10.5 Discuss with students situations in which predictions are made, such as elections, weather forecasting, and so forth. In this section, students learn how to predict the number of times an out-come (or event) will occur when an experiment is repeated a relatively large number of times. Explain that such predictions are based on probabilities.

When you discuss the top of page 420, point out that a prediction of "getting 5 four times" means that you will *most likely* get 5 on four of the twenty-four rolls. Emphasize that a probability tells what is most likely to happen and not necessarily what will actually happen.

Applications 45–46 in the Teacher's Resource Book, *Experimenting (Coin Flipping)* and *Experimenting (Cereal Simulation),* may be used to extend this section.

10.6 This section discusses the functions of a computer and the major components of computer hardware. Make sure that students familiarize themselves with all the terms in this section. Stress the difference between a calculator and a computer.

You may suggest that students do some research to find out the differences between the various brands and types of home computers.

10.7 This section gives examples of the diversified uses of computers. Point out that our society is becoming more and more computer oriented, which makes it essential for a person to be computer literate. Have students research an area and determine how computers make procedures run more efficiently.

You may want to discuss how a person's right to privacy can be violated by misuse of personal information stored in data banks. Another topic for discussion would be, what, if anything, should be done about computer hackers (people who illegally gain access to a computer system by breaking the security code)?

10.8 Advise students that a flowchart is part of the necessary planning done before actually writing a computer program. A flowchart helps computer programmers develop a logical sequence of instructions to use when solving a problem. Emphasize that a flowchart is made up of symbols and that each symbol represents a specific type of statement.

10.9 You may want to mention that BASIC is only one of many computer languages. This section introduces students to some of the symbols and instructions used in the BASIC language. Emphasize similarities and differences between math symbols and BASIC symbols. You may want to review the rule for order of operations (Section 3.3, pages 98–99) before beginning this section.

10.10 This section introduces students to some programs written in BASIC. Point out that multiples of 10 are usually used for line numbers for consistency and to enable the insertion of new lines without affecting other line numbers.

Tell students that there are many other computer languages, such as COBOL, PASCAL, and ASSEMBLER. You might ask students to research some of these languages. Ask students to find out why one language may be more effectively used in a particular field than another language.

Applications 47–50 in the Teacher's Resource Book, *Using a Computer to Make a Frequency Table, Using a Computer to Find the Median, Using a Computer to Estimate a Budget,* and *Using a Computer to Find Compound Interest,* may be used to extend this section.

Career *Computer Specialist,* page 438, presents various opportunities for students who have a desire to enter the computer field.

Guess the Computer's Number, page 439, is a game that encourages students to develop strategies at guessing a 3-digit number. Make sure students understand the rules. Encourage students to guess in some orderly fashion and to eliminate as many incorrect digits as early as possible.

Computing Skills Refresher

Pages 448–522

Overview The *Computing Skills Refresher* covers addition, subtraction, multiplication, and division with whole numbers and decimals in Part 1, and with fractions and mixed numbers in Part 2. Each computational skill is presented in a section that can usually be covered in one lesson. Each section contains numerous exercises, and care should be taken to make sure that assignments are not overly long or tedious. The Daily Lesson-Plan Guide on pages T5–T17 suggests possible exercise assignments for each skill section.

Encourage students to get in the habit of checking their own work. Some of the exercises in Part 1 can be used to practice working with calculators, especially checking answers.

The table on page T41 keys the items from the Computing Skills Tests (in the TRB) to the appropriate skills in the *Computing Skills Refresher.* Computing Skills Test 1 and Test 2—Form A and Form B—are included in the Teacher's Resource Book, pages 51–66. Since each form of a test covers identical skills, the table can be used with either Form A or Form B. This table should be helpful to teachers who wish to individualize computational instruction based on the skills with which students need refresher work.

The following notes provide an error-analysis approach to help the teacher pinpoint typical computational errors that students may make in each skill section:

Skill 1 Some students may have difficulty expressing large numbers in oral and written form. Stress that it is important to read one period at a time. Make sure students understand the different periods and the place values within each period. Refer to the table at the top of page 448 to develop these concepts.

Students may make the following errors when reading or writing whole numbers:

942,031 *nine hundred thousand, forty-two thousand, thirty-one*

Individual place values rather than periods are named. (exercise 9)

234,234,000 *two hundred thirty-four million, two hundred thirty-four*

Period names are omitted. (exercise 11)

Skill 2 Students may make the following error when reading or writing decimals:

4.06 *four and six tenths*

Since the *tens* position is two places to the left of the decimal point, the *tenths* position must be two places to the right of the decimal point. (exercise 6)

Skill 3 Many students confuse the symbols $<$ and $>$. Stress that the "closed" end of the symbol must always point to the smaller number. Also point out that a sentence is read from left to right. So, when a student is choosing the symbol, emphasize that the number on the left is being compared with the number on the right.

Students may make the following error when comparing decimals:

22.5<22.47 The decimal points are omitted
because   and place value is ignored.
225<2247   (exercise 13)

Skill 4 Remind students that to round to a specific place value, they should always look at the digit to the right of that place value.

Students may make the following errors when rounding whole numbers and decimals:

7609 rounded   When a number is rounded
to the nearest   to a specific place value, the
1000 is 8609.   remaining digits are not re-
                  placed with 0's. (exercise 11)

16.98 rounded   The value of the digit to the
to the nearest   left of the place being
tenth is 16.1.   rounded to does not get in-
                  creased. (exercise 24)

Skill 5 Suggest that students write exercises 41–48 vertically before adding.

Students may make the following errors when adding whole numbers:

```
 1
 3 2   A number is          8 1   10 was not
+2 6   renamed             +  9   renamed as 0
 6 8   unnecessarily.       8 1 0 ones and 1 ten.
       (exercise 1)               (exercise 3)
```

Skill 6 Suggest that students rewrite exercises 26–31 and exercises 42–45 vertically before adding. Stress that the decimal points in the addends must be aligned before adding. Make sure students do not confuse adding and multiplying decimals. (They may place the decimal point in a sum by using the rule for placing the decimal point in a product.)

Skill 7 Suggest that students write exercises 51–56 vertically before subtracting. If necessary, demonstrate the renaming process, using manipulative aids. Show students how 1 ten can be exchanged for 10 ones, 1 hundred for 10 tens, and so forth. Be aware that some students may disregard order of subtraction and always subtract the smaller digit from the larger digit. For example:

```
  632
-  46
  614
```

Students may make the following errors when subtracting whole numbers:

```
 12    Part of the      3 10 10  Renaming is
 8 2   renaming is      5 0 0    done by using
-1 9   not recorded.   -1 2 6    2 hundreds as
 7 3   (exercise 6)     2 8 4    10 tens and
                                 10 ones.
                                 (exercise 26)
```

Skill 8 Emphasize that to subtract decimals, the decimal points must be aligned. Stress the importance of writing 0's when the minuend has fewer digits after the decimal point than the subtrahend, or vice versa. (The 0's aid in renaming and help students subtract in the correct place-value positions.)

Skill 9 This section provides more practice with addition and subtraction of whole numbers and decimals.

Skill 10 This section reviews basic multiplication facts. It is essential that students master these facts before proceeding. However, you may wish to allow those students who are having great difficulty in memorizing the facts to use a multiplication table.

Skill 11 Multiplying by multiples of 10 is an important topic, especially for estimation. Students should easily grasp the shortcut approach developed in this section. Use Example 4 to point out that a product may have more 0's than the sum of the number of 0's in each factor. This happens when the product of two nonzero numbers contains a 0.

Skill 12 Students may make the following errors when multiplying whole numbers:

```
  2                      2
 9 3   The remain-      9 3   The remain-
× 7    der digit is    × 7    der digit is
6 3 1  not added.      7 7 1  added before
       (exercise 22)          multiplying.
```

In Examples 5 and 6, point out that since multiplication is commutative and associative, numbers can be multiplied in any order and with any grouping. However, once two numbers are multiplied, neither can be used again as a factor. For example, some students may find the product

$5 \times 12 \times 8$ (exercise 49) in either of these two ways:

$5 \times 12 + 5 \times 8$ or $5 \times 12 + 5 \times 8 + 12 \times 8$
$60 \;+\; 40$ $60 \;+\; 40 \;+\; 96$
$\quad 100$ 196

Skill 13   Point out that when a number is multiplied by a power of 10 greater than 1, the product will be larger than that number (as in exercise 25: $100 \times 0.7 = 70$). However, when a number is multiplied by a power of 10 less than 1, the product will be smaller than that number (as in exercise 27: $6 \times 0.1 = 0.6$).

Skill 14   Students may make the following errors in placing the decimal point in the product:

$\begin{array}{r} 8.37 \\ \times\,0.42 \\ \hline 351.54 \end{array}$ The decimal point in the product is aligned with the decimal points in the factors. (exercise 10)	$\begin{array}{r} 4.17 \\ \times\,2.8 \\ \hline 116.76 \end{array}$ Digits to the left of the decimal point are counted. (exercise 11)

Skill 15   This section provides more practice with multiplying whole numbers and decimals.

Skill 16   This section reviews basic division facts. It is essential that students master these facts before proceeding.

Skill 17   The divisions in this section all involve one-digit divisors and one-digit quotients. Emphasize that the remainder must always be less than the divisor. You may want to use manipulative aids to demonstrate that if an obtained remainder is larger than the divisor, the quotient can be increased until the remainder is less than the divisor.

Skills 18–19   Skill 18 covers division with one-digit divisors. Skill 19 covers division with two-digit and three-digit divisors.

Students may make the following errors when dividing:

$\begin{array}{r} 7\;1 \\ 5)\overline{3505} \\ 35 \\ \hline 5 \\ 5 \\ \hline 0 \end{array}$ The necessary 0 is not recorded in the quotient. (Skill 18, exercise 21)	$\begin{array}{r} 12 \\ 4)\overline{68} \\ 4 \\ \hline 8 \\ 8 \\ \hline 0 \end{array}$ The student fails to subtract before "bringing down" the next digit. (Skill 18, exercise 38)

Skill 20   Students may make the following errors when dividing a decimal by a whole number:

$\begin{array}{r} 3 \\ 3)\overline{0.9} \end{array}$ The decimal point in the quotient is not written. (exercise 1)	$\begin{array}{r} 0.50 \\ 92)\overline{46.46} \\ 46\;0 \\ \hline 46 \\ 46 \\ \hline 0 \end{array}$ No 0 is written in the dividend, so the division process stops. (exercise 29)

Skill 21   You may want to do a few examples using the long-division process and then do the same examples using the shortcut method developed in this section.

Students may make the following errors when they divide by a power of 10:

$752 \div 10 = 7520$ The decimal point is moved to the right instead of to the left. (exercise 13)	$7.46 \div 100 = 0.746$ Since there are not enough decimal places to the left of the decimal point, the decimal point is only moved one place. (exercise 21)

Skill 22   Students may make the following errors when they divide by a decimal:

$\begin{array}{r} 0.05 \\ 0.07)\overline{0.35} \end{array}$ The decimal point in the divisor is completely ignored. (exercise 13)	$\begin{array}{r} 8 \\ 0.08)\overline{0.064} \end{array}$ The decimal point in both the divisor and the dividend is moved so that both are whole numbers. (exercise 14)

Skill 23   Review rounding decimals to the nearest tenth and to the nearest hundredth (Skill 4). Then emphasize the following rule: When rounding a quotient to a given place value, divide until you find the quotient to one more place than you are rounding to. Then round.

Students may make the following errors when rounding a quotient to a specific place value: Round each quotient to the nearest tenth.

$\begin{array}{r} 15.7 \\ 4)\overline{63.0} \\ 4 \\ \hline 23 \\ 20 \\ \hline 3\;0 \\ 2\;8 \\ \hline 2 \end{array}$ The division is carried out to the *specified place*, but the quotient is not rounded. (exercise 22)	$\begin{array}{r} 6.3 \rightarrow 6.4 \\ 3.4)\overline{21.532} \\ 20\;4 \\ \hline 1\;13 \\ 1\;02 \\ \hline 11 \end{array}$ The quotient is rounded up because the remainder is greater than 5. (exercise 17)

Skill 24 This lesson provides more practice with division of whole numbers and decimals.

Skill 25 Make sure students understand the term *factor*. Then emphasize the definition of *exponent*. You may want to point out that Example 4 shows *powers of 10*.

Skill 26 Use the two examples at the top of page 484 to reacquaint students with these two interpretations of fractions: the geometric interpretation (tell how much of a figure is shaded) and the set interpretation (tell how much of a set is different from the rest). When using a fraction to tell how much of a figure is shaded, emphasize that the figure must be separated into parts of the same size. If such emphasis is not made, students may only focus attention on "how many parts are shaded." Such thinking could result in errors like the following in later sections:

Complete. Compare. Subtract.

$\frac{2}{3} = \frac{\boxed{2}}{6}$ $\frac{4}{10} > \frac{3}{5}$ $\frac{3}{4} - \frac{1}{2} = \frac{2}{4}$

Skill 27 Review that fractions like $\frac{4}{4}$ and $\frac{6}{6}$ are names for 1. Emphasize that a mixed number is a short way of naming the sum of a whole number and a fraction.

Skill 28 Students may make the following errors when changing a mixed number to a fraction, and vice versa:

$4\frac{3}{5} = \frac{17}{5}$ $\frac{23}{7} = 3\frac{1}{2}$

The *denominator* is added to the product of the whole number and the *numerator*: $(4 \times 3) + 5 = 17$. (exercise 2)

Since $7\overline{)23}$ $\ \ \frac{3 \ R2}{}$, the denominator of the fraction must be 2. (exercise 48)

Skill 29 Mention that multiplying (or dividing) the numerator and the denominator of a fraction by the same nonzero number does not change the value of the fraction because the fraction is actually being multiplied by (or divided by) 1.

Students may make the following errors when finding equivalent fractions:

$\frac{2}{3} \neq \frac{8}{12}$

Cross products are found by multiplying the two numerators and the two denominators: $16 \neq 36$. (exercise 1)

$\frac{3}{5} = \frac{\boxed{2}}{10}$

Since $10 \div 5 = 2$, the numerator must be 2. (exercise 30)

Skill 30 Some students use $<$ and $>$ incorrectly, even though they know the meaning of *is less than* and *is greater than*.

Students may make the following errors when comparing fractions:

$\frac{1}{2} < \frac{1}{3}$

Fractions are compared by comparing the denominators. (exercise 1)

$\frac{4}{7} > \frac{3}{2}$

Fractions are compared by comparing the numerators. (exercise 13)

Skill 31 Make sure students understand the difference between factors and multiples of a number. Students that have difficulty with multiplication facts may find a table helpful.

Skill 32 Emphasize that dividing the numerator and the denominator of a fraction by the same nonzero number does not change the value of the fraction.

Students may make the following errors when changing a fraction to lowest terms:

$\begin{array}{c} 18 \div 9 \\ 18 \\ \overline{24} = \frac{2}{3} \\ 24 \div 8 \end{array}$ The numerator and the denominator are divided by different numbers. (exercise 7)

$\begin{array}{c} 12 \div 4 \\ \frac{12}{28} = \frac{3}{28} \\ \\ \frac{12}{28} = \frac{12}{7} \\ 28 \div 4 \end{array}$ Only the numerator or only the denominator is divided by some number. (exercise 15)

Skill 33 Students may make the following errors when multiplying fractions and whole numbers:

$\frac{5}{2} \times \frac{5}{2} = \frac{25}{2}$

When fractions have the same denominator, the numerators are multiplied, but the denominators remain the same. (exercise 13)

$\frac{8}{2} \times \frac{3}{2} = \frac{16}{6}$ (or $\frac{6}{16}$)

The numerators and the denominators are cross multiplied. (exercise 14)

$5 \times \frac{1}{4} = \frac{21}{4}$

The rule for changing a mixed number to a fraction is applied. (exercise 18)

$7 \times \frac{2}{5} = \frac{14}{35}$

Both the numerator and the denominator of the fraction are multiplied by the whole number. (exercise 19)

Skill 34 Point out to students that completely reducing (or canceling) fractions before multiplying gives a product in lowest terms.

Students may make the following errors when reducing fractions before multiplying:

$$\overset{1}{\underset{}{\cancel{3}}} \times \frac{\overset{4}{\cancel{12}}}{7} = \frac{4}{112}$$

The numerators are "reduced." (exercise 5)

$$\frac{4}{\underset{3}{\cancel{15}}} \times \frac{9}{\underset{2}{\cancel{10}}} = \frac{36}{6}$$

The denominators are "reduced."(exercise 11)

Skill 35 You may want to develop Example 8 by first using the following example: $0 \div 2 = 0$ because $0 \times 2 = 0$. But $2 \div 0$ is not possible because $? \times 0 = 2$ has no solution. Students often confuse $a \div 0$ and $0 \div a$ $(a \neq 0)$.

Students may make the following errors when dividing fractions:

$\frac{1}{4} \div \frac{3}{5} = \frac{1}{4} \times \frac{3}{5} = \frac{3}{20}$

The division problem is rewritten in terms of multiplication, but the divisor is not inverted. (exercise 11)

$\frac{3}{5} \div \frac{1}{4} = \frac{5}{3} \times \frac{1}{4} = \frac{5}{12}$

The dividend is inverted, instead of the divisor. (exercise 12)

Skill 36 This section provides more practice with multiplying and dividing fractions.

Skill 37 Students may make the following error when adding fractions with the same denominators:

$\frac{3}{5} + \frac{4}{5} = \frac{7}{10}$ Both the numerators and the denominators are added. (exercise 6)

Skill 38 Students may make the following error when subtracting fractions with the same denominators:

$\frac{4}{5} - \frac{2}{5} = 2$ Both the numerators and the denominators are subtracted. Since the difference of the denominators is always 0, the denominator is disregarded. (exercise 2)

Skill 39 Make sure students understand the difference between multiples and factors of a num-

ber. Point out that although two numbers can have more than one common multiple, students should be able to identify the least common multiple.

Skill 40 You may want to use diagrams to develop the concept of adding and subtracting fractions with different denominators.

Students may make the following errors when adding or subtracting fractions that have different denominators:

$\frac{2}{3} + \frac{3}{4} = \frac{5}{7}$ (exercise 1)

$\frac{7}{15} - \frac{3}{10} = \frac{4}{5}$ (exercise 25)

Both the numerators and the denominators are added (subtracted).

$\frac{2}{5} + \frac{1}{3} = \frac{2}{15} + \frac{1}{15} = \frac{3}{15}$ (exercise 4)

$\frac{3}{5} - \frac{2}{7} = \frac{3}{35} - \frac{2}{35} = \frac{1}{35}$ (exercise 32)

Fractions are rewritten with the same denominator, but the numerators are not changed to make equivalent fractions.

Skill 41 This section provides more practice adding and subtracting fractions with the same denominators or with different denominators.

Skill 42 You may want to encourage students to estimate the answer before actually doing any computation.

Students may make the following error when adding mixed numbers:

$$\begin{array}{r} 4\frac{1}{8} \\ + 3\frac{1}{4} \\ \hline \end{array} \quad \begin{array}{r} \frac{1}{8} \\ + \frac{2}{8} \\ \hline \frac{3}{8} \end{array}$$

Only the fractions are rewritten when finding common denominators, so adding the whole numbers is overlooked. (exercise 13)

Skill 43 Students may make the following errors when subtracting mixed numbers:

$$\begin{array}{r} 9\frac{1}{6} \\ - 2\frac{5}{6} \\ \hline 7\frac{4}{6}, \text{ or } 7\frac{2}{3} \end{array}$$

The smaller fraction is subtracted from the larger fraction. (exercise 24)

$$\begin{array}{r} 11\frac{1}{5} \\ - 7\frac{3}{5} \\ \hline \end{array} \rightarrow \begin{array}{r} 11\frac{6}{5} \\ - 7\frac{3}{5} \\ \hline 4\frac{3}{5} \end{array}$$

When renaming the mixed number, the fraction is increased by 1 but the whole number is not reduced by 1.(exercise 25)

Skill 44 Students may make the following errors when multiplying mixed numbers:

$$3\tfrac{2}{3} \times 5\tfrac{4}{5} = 15\tfrac{8}{15} \qquad 5\tfrac{3}{4} \times \tfrac{1}{8} = 5\tfrac{3}{32}$$

The whole numbers and the fractions are multiplied separately. (exercise 7)

The fractions are multiplied and the whole number is carried into the product. (exercise 11)

Students may make the following errors when dividing mixed numbers:

$$\cancel{4}\tfrac{1}{2} \div \cancel{2}\tfrac{1}{2} = \qquad 6\tfrac{2}{5} \div 3\tfrac{4}{5} = 2\tfrac{1}{2}$$
$$2 \div 1 = 2$$

The whole numbers are canceled with the fractions. (exercise 29)

The whole numbers and the fractions are divided separately. (exercise 30)

$5\tfrac{1}{5} \div \tfrac{4}{5} = 5\tfrac{1}{4}$ The fractions are divided and the whole number is carried into the quotient. (exercise 41)

Skill 45 This section provides more practice with adding, subtracting, multiplying, and dividing mixed numbers.

Skill 46 Students may make the following error when changing a fraction to a decimal:

$$\tfrac{9}{2} = 9\overline{)2}^{\,0.\overline{2}}$$ The denominator is divided by the numerator. (exercise 5)

Skill 47 Students may make the following error when changing a mixed number to a decimal:

$$12\tfrac{3}{10} = \tfrac{15}{10} = 10\overline{)15}^{\,1.5}$$ The whole number is added to the numerator. Then the sum is divided by the denominator. (exercise 3)

Skill 48 Students may make the following errors when changing a decimal to a fraction:

$$0.03 = \tfrac{3}{10} \qquad 5.7 = 5\tfrac{7}{100}$$

The place value held by the zero is not recognized. (exercise 5)

The number of digits in the number is used to determine the number of 0's in the denominator. (exercise 31)

Correlation of Computing Skills Test Items to the Computing Skills Refresher

Test 1—Form A or Form B	Test Items	Skill
	1–2, 5–6	1
	3–4, 7–8	2
	9–11	3
	12–15	4
	16–19, 24–25	5
	20–23, 26–27	6
	28–33	7
	34–41	8
	42–45	10
	46–47	11
	48–53, 58	12
	54, 59–60	13
	55–57, 61	14
	62–64	16
	65–66	17
	67–70	18
	71–73	19
	74–76	20
	77–78	21
	79–81	22
	82–83	23
	84–87	25

Test 2—Form A or Form B	Test Items	Skill
	1–7	26
	8–11	27
	12–17	28
	18–21	29
	22–24	30
	25–26	31
	27–29	32
	30	33
	31–35	34
	36–41	35
	42–46	37
	47–50	38
	51–53	39
	54–62	40
	63–66	42
	67–70	43
	71–77	44
	79–81	46
	82–84	47
	85–87	48

Correlation of Teacher's Resource Book to Text

Test	Resource Manual page
Chapter 1 Test—Form A	1
Chapter 1 Test—Form B	3
Chapter 2 Test—Form A	5
Chapter 2 Test—Form B	7
Chapter 3 Test—Form A	9
Chapter 3 Test—Form B	11
Chapter 4 Test—Form A	13
Chapter 4 Test—Form B	15
Chapter 5 Test—Form A	17
Chapter 5 Test—Form B	19
Chapter 6 Test—Form A	21
Chapter 6 Test—Form B	23
Chapter 7 Test—Form A	25
Chapter 7 Test—Form B	27
Chapter 8 Test—Form A	29
Chapter 8 Test—Form B	31
Chapter 9 Test—Form A	33
Chapter 9 Test—Form B	35
Chapter 10 Test—Form A	37
Chapter 10 Test—Form B	39
Cumulative Test 1—Chapters 1–2	41
Cumulative Test 2—Chapters 3–4	43
Cumulative Test 3—Chapters 5–6	45
Cumulative Test 4—Chapters 7–8	47
Cumulative Test 5—Chapters 9–10	49
Computing Skills Test 1—Form A	51
Computing Skills Test 1—Form B	55
Computing Skills Test 2—Form A	59
Computing Skills Test 2—Form B	63

Application	Resource Manual page	Use after text page
1—Catalog Orders	67	13
2—Grade Point Average	69	30
3—Collecting, Organizing, and Summarizing Data	70	33
4—Estimating the Number of Words on a Page	71	43
5—Checking Estimates With a Calculator	72	46
6—Estimation Activities	74	46
7—Ordered Pairs on a Globe	75	58
8—Getting a Pulse on Line Graphs	76	73

Performance Objectives

This list of course goals includes objectives for each section of APPLYING MATHEMATICS IN DAILY LIVING.

Chapter 1

The student can do the following:

1.1 ☐ Read and interpret tables.

1.2 ☐ Find the mode of a set of numbers.

1.3 ☐ Find the median of a set of numbers.

1.4 ☐ Find the mean of a set of numbers.

1.5 ☐ Find the range of a set of numbers and express the range in two ways.

1.6 ☐ Make a frequency table for a set of numbers. Use a frequency table to find the mode and the median of a set of numbers.

1.7 ☐ Use a frequency table to find the mean of a set of numbers.

1.8 ☐ Find the mean, the median, and the mode of a set of numbers. Determine how the mean, the median, and the mode are affected by extreme numbers.

1.9 ☐ Estimate the sum of two or more numbers.

1.10 ☐ Estimate the difference of two numbers.

1.11 ☐ Estimate the product of two numbers.

1.12 ☐ Estimate the quotient of two numbers.

Chapter 2

The student can do the following:

2.1 ☐ Use coordinate names for regions on a map to locate specific areas or places.

2.2 ☐ Use coordinates to graph a point or to identify a point.

2.3 ☐ Graph a set of points, given a table of their coordinates. Choose an appropriate scale for a graph.

2.4 ☐ Read and interpret bar graphs.

2.5 ☐ Read and interpret line graphs.

2.6 ☐ Make a bar graph (vertical or horizontal) or a line graph based on a table of information.

2.7 ☐ Read and interpret pictographs.

2.8 ☐ Read and interpret circle graphs.

2.9 ☐ Read and interpret simple schematics.

Chapter 3

The student can do the following:

3.1 ☐ Identify a sentence (English or mathematical) as true, false, or open. Find solutions to an open sentence by trial and error.

3.2 ☐ Simplify expressions containing parentheses.

3.3 ☐ Simplify expressions by using the rule for the order of operations.

3.4 ☐ Use a formula to solve a problem by substituting known values in the formula and then simplifying the expression.

3.5 ☐ Solve one-step equations involving addition or subtraction.

3.6 ☐ Solve one-step equations involving multiplication or division.

3.7 ☐ Solve two-step equations involving addition or subtraction *and* multiplication or division.

3.8 ☐ Solve equations for which the solution must be expressed as a fraction or as a decimal.

3.9 ☐ Solve equations in which the coefficient of the variable is a fraction.

3.10 ☐ Apply formulas to solve verbal problems.

Chapter 4

The student can do the following:

4.1 ☐ Write ratios to represent comparisons expressed in diagrams or statements.

4.2 ☐ Find ratios equivalent to a given ratio, using diagrams or computation. Express a given ratio in lowest terms.

4.3 ☐ Use cross products to solve proportions.

4.4 ☐ Solve problems by writing appropriate proportions and solving the proportions.

4.5 ☐ Identify similar figures. Use proportions to determine the lengths of corresponding sides of similar figures.

4.6 ☐ Recognize a figure as an enlargement (or reduction) of a given figure and determine the ratio of enlargement (or reduction) for the given pair. Use the scale of a drawing to determine the real measurement represented in the drawing.

4.7 ☐ Write ratios as percents and percents as ratios.

4.8 ☐ Use proportions to solve the three types of percent problems: finding the percent, finding the part, and finding the total.

4.9 ☐ Write a percent as a decimal and a decimal as a percent. Use the decimal form of a percent to solve problems by multiplication.

4.10 ☐ Estimate percentages, using tenths, halves of tenths, and multiples of tenths.

Chapter 5

The student can do the following:

5.1 ☐ Select appropriate units of measure or measuring instruments for given situations.

5.2 ☐ Use ancient units of measure. Compare ancient units of measure with standard units of measure.

5.3 ☐ Use a ruler to obtain an accurate measurement. Use a ruler to draw segments of given lengths.

5.4 ☐ Convert from one customary unit of length to another.

5.5 ☐ Define metric prefixes and use metric units of length.

5.6 ☐ Convert from one metric unit of length to another.

5.7 ☐ Convert from one customary (or metric) unit of weight to another.

5.8 ☐ Convert from one customary (or metric) unit of capacity to another.

5.9 ☐ Convert from one unit of time to another. Determine the length of time between two given times.

5.10 ☐ Use Fahrenheit and Celsius scales to change a temperature reading from one scale to the other.

5.11 ☐ Use a protractor to measure angles and to draw angles.

Chapter 6

The student can do the following:

6.1 ☐ Identify types of polygons. Identify polygons when given certain properties.

6.2 ☐ Find the perimeters of polygons.

6.3 ☐ Find the areas of rectangles and squares.

6.4 ☐ Change a given area to an equivalent area in the same system.

6.5 ☐ Use a formula to find the areas of parallelograms.

6.6 ☐ Use a formula to find the areas of triangles.

6.7 ☐ Use a formula to find the circumferences of circles.

6.8 ☐ Use a formula to find the areas of circles.

6.9 ☐ Find the volumes of rectangular solids, using either of two formulas.

6.10 ☐ Change a given volume to an equivalent volume in the same system.

6.11 ☐ Use a formula to find the volumes of cylinders.

Chapter 7

The student can do the following:

7.1 ☐ Correctly fill out a job application. Apply job-interviewing techniques and strategies.

7.2 ☐ Find the sale price of an item, given the percent of discount. Read and interpret a tax table. Make change in as few bills and coins as possible.

7.3 ☐ Compute weekly earnings (including overtime pay) based on an hourly rate.

7.4 ☐ Compute earnings based on a piecework or bonus system.

7.5 ☐ Compute earnings based on commission.

7.6 ☐ Compute earnings based on tips.

7.7 ☐ Read a tax table to determine federal income-tax withholdings. Determine net pay, given all deductions.

7.8 ☐ Use a taxable-income table to determine whether a refund or a balance is due.

Chapter 8

The student can do the following:

8.1 ☐ Keep a record of expenses and income to determine the amount of cash on hand.

8.2 ☐ Compute the percent of income spent on each budget category, given the cash amount.

8.3 ☐ Compute the amount of income to be spent in each budget category, given the percent.

8.4 ☐ Correctly write out a check and fill in a check record.

8.5 ☐ Reconcile a checking account.

8.6 ☐ Use a formula to compute the total amount of money due (or interest earned) at the end of a term.

8.7 ☐ Compute compound interest on a semi-annual, quarterly, annual, or daily basis.

8.8 ☐ Use a compound-interest table to help find compound interest.

8.9 ☐ Use a formula to compute the cost of credit.

8.10 ☐ Use a formula to compute the annual percentage rate for a monthly payment plan.

8.11 ☐ Use an average daily balance to compute finance charges; then determine the new balance of the account.

Chapter 9

The student can do the following:

9.1 ☐ Use survey results to solve problems about how teenagers plan to spend money.

9.2 ☐ Compute the move-in cost of renting an apartment. Determine whether a person can or cannot afford to rent an apartment.

9.3 ☐ Compute the unit price of an item. Use unit prices to determine which of two items is the better buy.

9.4 ☐ Choose the most (or least) economical way to eat a meal. Find the total cost of a restaurant meal, including tax and tip, by exact calculation and by estimating.

9.5 ☐ Compute the wearing cost of an article of clothing. Determine which of two articles of clothing is the better buy.

9.6 ☐ Compute the cost of participating in leisure activities.

9.7 ☐ Compute the sticker price and the invoice price of a new car.

9.8 ☐ Compute the amount of down payment required on a car loan and the amount of interest to be paid on the loan.

9.9 ☐ Determine the type of insurance coverage that applies in a given situation. Compute the premiums for insurance coverages, using the table provided.

9.10 ☐ Determine the amount of a medical bill that will be covered under a given insurance plan.

Chapter 10

The student can do the following:

10.1 ☐ Find mathematical probabilities.

10.2 ☐ Recognize situations with probabilities of 0 or 1.

10.3 ☐ Use a sample space to find probabilities.

10.4 ☐ Express probabilities as percents.

10.5 ☐ Use probabilities to predict results.

10.6 ☐ Recognize the four main functions of a computer. Identify the main components of computer hardware.

10.7 ☐ Recognize some of the uses and misuses of computers.

10.8 ☐ Place a set of given steps in the proper order in a flowchart. Write a flowchart for a simple step-by-step procedure.

10.9 ☐ Understand the meaning of certain BASIC symbols and instructions.

10.10 ☐ Determine the output of a simple computer program written in the BASIC language.

Computing Skills Refresher

Part 1
Whole Numbers and Decimals

The student can do the following:

1 ☐ Determine the value of any digit of a whole number. Express a whole number in words, and vice versa.

2 ☐ Determine the value of any digit of a decimal. Express a decimal in words, and vice versa.

3 ☐ Compare whole numbers and decimals, using the less-than ($<$) and greater-than ($>$) symbols.

4 ☐ Round a whole number or a decimal to a specified place.

5 ☐ Add two or more whole numbers.

6 ☐ Add two or more decimals. Add decimals and whole numbers.

7 ☐ Subtract two whole numbers. Check subtraction by adding.

8 ☐ Subtract one decimal from another decimal. Subtract a whole number from a decimal, and vice versa.

9 ☐ Practice adding and subtracting whole numbers and decimals.

10 ☐ Recognize several common ways of indicating the operation of multiplication. Review the basic multiplication facts for the whole numbers 0 through 9.

11 ☐ Use a shortcut to multiply a whole number by a power of ten or by a multiple of ten.

12 ☐ Multiply two or more whole numbers.

13 ☐ Multiply a whole number and a decimal. Use a shortcut to multiply a decimal by a power of ten.

14 ☐ Multiply two or more decimals.

15 ☐ Practice multiplying two whole numbers, two decimals, or a whole number and a decimal.

16 ☐ Recognize several common ways of indicating the operation of division. Review the basic division facts for the whole numbers 0 through 9. Check division by multiplying.

17 ☐ Divide a two-digit number by a one-digit number where the quotients are from 0 through 9. Check division by multiplying and then adding the remainder.

18 ☐ Divide a whole number by a one-digit divisor (remainders possible).

19 ☐ Divide a whole number by a two-digit or three-digit divisor (remainders possible).

20 ☐ Divide a decimal by a whole number. Express the quotient of a whole-number divisor and a whole-number dividend as a decimal.

21 ☐ Use a shortcut to divide by a power of ten.

22 ☐ Divide a whole number or a decimal by a decimal.

23 ☐ Round a decimal quotient to a specified place.

24 ☐ Practice dividing two whole numbers, a whole number and a decimal, or two decimals.

25 ☐ Read powers of numbers and evaluate expressions containing powers.

Part 2

Fractions and Mixed Numbers

The student can do the following:

26 ☐ Write a fraction to represent the portion of a figure or a set that is being considered. Read fractions and express them in words.

27 ☐ Interpret mixed numbers as sums or by using models. Express mixed numbers in words.

28 ☐ Change a mixed number to a fraction, and vice versa.

29 ☐ Find fractions equivalent to a given fraction. Use cross products to determine if two fractions are equivalent.

30 ☐ Use cross products to compare two fractions.

31 ☐ Find the greatest common factor of two whole numbers.

32 ☐ Reduce fractions to lowest terms.

33 ☐ Express the product of two or more fractions or the product of one or more whole numbers and one or more fractions in lowest terms.

34 ☐ Find the product of fractions in lowest terms by first dividing the numerators and the denominators by their greatest common factors.

35 ☐ Find the reciprocal of a given number. Divide fractions by multiplying the dividend by the reciprocal of the divisor.

36 ☐ Practice multiplying and dividing fractions and whole numbers.

37 ☐ Add two or more fractions having the same denominator.

38 ☐ Subtract two fractions having the same denominator.

39 ☐ Find the least common multiple of two or more numbers.

40 ☐ Add or subtract fractions that have different denominators.

41 ☐ Practice adding and subtracting fractions with the same or with different denominators.

42 ☐ Add two or more mixed numbers, mixed numbers and whole numbers, or mixed numbers and fractions.

43 ☐ Subtract a mixed number, a fraction, or a whole number from a mixed number. Subtract a mixed number or a fraction from a whole number.

44 ☐ Multiply and divide with mixed numbers.

45 ☐ Practice the four basic operations with mixed numbers.

46 ☐ Change a fraction to a terminating or a repeating decimal.

47 ☐ Change a mixed number to a terminating or a repeating decimal.

48 ☐ Change a decimal to a fraction or a mixed number.

APPLYING MATHEMATICS
in Daily Living

Albert P. Shulte

Director, Mathematics
Oakland Schools
Pontiac, Michigan

Harriet Haynes

Mathematics Staff Developer
School District 19
Brooklyn, New York

Stuart A. Choate

Coordinator of Mathematics
and Computer Education
Midland Public Schools
Midland, Michigan

GLENCOE PUBLISHING COMPANY
Mission Hills, California

Send all inquiries to:
Glencoe Publishing Company
15319 Chatsworth Street, P.O. Box 9509
Mission Hills, California 91345-9509

Printed in the United States of America

ISBN 0-8445-1865-4 (Student Text)
ISBN 0-8445-1866-2 (Teacher's Edition)

7 8 9 10 11 12   93 92 91 90 89 88

Contents

D. Giussolli/FPG

Paul Light/Lightwave

Grant Heilman

William J. Weber/John D. Cunningham

Brent Jones

Bryce Flynn/Picture Group

Artstreet

Michael Phillip Manheim/Marilyn Gartman Photo Agency

Computing Skills Refresher

Calculator Skills

MEN'S SHIRT PATTERN

Body measurements

Chest (inches)	34–36	38–40	42–44	46–48
Size	Small	Medium	Large	X-Large

View 1 Shirt	Fabric required (yards)			
35"/36" width	$2\frac{7}{8}$	$2\frac{7}{8}$	3	$3\frac{1}{8}$
42"/44" width	$2\frac{1}{2}$	$2\frac{1}{2}$	$2\frac{5}{8}$	$2\frac{7}{8}$
58"/60" width	$1\frac{5}{8}$	$1\frac{5}{8}$	$1\frac{5}{8}$	2

1. How much fabric is needed for a large shirt if 35-inch-wide fabric is used? 3 yards

2. How much fabric is needed to make a shirt for a man with a 36-inch chest if 44-inch-wide fabric is used? $2\frac{1}{2}$ yards

Use this set of numbers for exercises 3–7.

3, 5, 5, 5, 6, 6, 9, 11, 14, 16

3. Find the mode. 5

4. Find the median. 6

5. Find the mean. 8

6. Find the range. 16-3 or 13

7. Make a frequency table. See table at right.

8. Find the mean score from the frequency table at the right. 88

Score	Frequency
100	3
90	2
80	5

7.

	F
3	1
5	3
6	2
9	1
11	1
14	1
16	1

9. Find the mode, the median, and the mean of the following set of numbers:

3.4, 2.7, 0.3, 9.1, 8.2, 5.6, 6.2, 10.1, 4.2, 8.2

mode: 8.2; median: 5.9; mean: 5.8

Estimate the answer by rounding each number to the nearest ten. Then find the exact answer.

Estimates for exercises 10–17 are given first.

10. $57 + 64$
120; 121

11. $93 + 18 + 62$
170; 173

12. $78 - 29$
50; 49

13. $155 - 47$
110; 108

Estimate the answer by rounding each number to the nearest hundred. Then find the exact answer.

14. 127×287
30,000; 36,449

15. 615×407
240,000; 250,305

16. $812 \div 203$
4; 4

17. $1764 \div 294$
6; 6

Information is often presented in tables. Here is part of a sales-tax table. Listed beside it are some of the facts the table reveals. (Of course, taxes are not the same in each state or city.)

Cost of purchase	Sales tax	
$0.00–0.15	$0.00	← **Purchases of up to 15¢ are not taxed.**
0.16–0.24	0.01	
0.25–0.49	0.02	
0.50–0.74	0.03	
0.75–0.99	0.04	← **An item priced 79¢ costs 79¢ + 4¢, or 83¢.**
1.00–1.15	0.05	
1.16–1.24	0.06	
1.25–1.49	0.07	
1.50–1.74	0.08	← **A purchase of $1.67 is taxed 8¢.**
1.75–1.99	0.09	
		← **If the pattern continues, a purchase of $2.00 is taxed 10¢.**

EXERCISES

Use the tax table above for exercises 1–16.

Find what the tax would be for each of these purchases.

1. 17¢
1¢

2. 26¢
2¢

3. 9¢
0¢

4. 66¢
3¢

5. $0.49
2¢

6. $1.00
5¢

7. $1.30
7¢

8. $1.82
9¢

Find the total cost, including tax, for each of these purchases.

9. 48¢
50¢

10. 58¢
61¢

11. 74¢
77¢

12. 75¢
79¢

13. $1.18
$1.24

14. $1.38
$1.45

15. $1.89
$1.98

16. $2.00
$2.10

CHICAGO—SPRINGFIELD—ST. LOUIS

Read Down				(Local Time)					Read Up
305	303	307	301	Train Number	300	308	302	304	306
The State House				Train Name	The State House				
Daily	Su thru Fr	Sa and Su	Mo thru Fr	Frequency of Operation	Mo thru Sa	Su only	Mo thru Sa	Mo thru Fr	Sa and Su
6 15 p	5 10 p	8 10 a	8 10 a	Dp CHICAGO, IL (Union Sta.) Ar	9 50 a	12 20 p	12 24 p	9 24 p	10 05 p
6 58 p	5 53 p	8 53 a	8 53 a	.... Joliet	9 03 a	11 33 a	11 35 a	8 35 p	9 14 p
7 50 p		9 44 a		.... Pontiac	8 05 a	10 35 a			8 20 p
8 35 p	7 13 p	10 24 a	10 13 a	.... Bloomington	7 35 a	10 05 a	10 17 a	7 17 p	7 49 p
9 02 p		10 53 a		.... Lincoln	7 00 a	9 30 a			7 06 p
9 35 p	8 10 p	11 30 a	11 10 a	.... SPRINGFIELD	6 30 a	9 00 a	9 16 a	6 16 p	6 37 p
10 11 p		12 06 p		.... Carlinville	5 48 a	8 18 a			5 56 p
10 51 p	9 16 p	12 43 p	12 16 p	.... Alton, IL	5 18 a	7 48 a	8 10 a	5 10 p	5 24 p
11 50 p	10 09 p	1 40 p	1 09 p	Ar .... ST. LOUIS, MO .. Dp	4 30 a	7 00 a	7 25 a	4 25 p	4 30 p

Train 305 stops at Alton, Ill., at 10:51 at night.

Train 306 leaves St. Louis at 4:30 in the afternoon.

Use the train schedule above for exercises 17–22.

17. At what time does train 304 reach Chicago? 9:24 P.M.

18. At what time does train 301 reach Bloomington? 10:13 A.M.

19. Which train arrives in St. Louis at 11:50 P.M. daily? 305

20. Which trains could you take from Carlinville to Chicago? 300, 308, 306

21. At what time would you leave St. Louis on a Sunday morning? 7:00 A.M.

22. At what time would you leave Lincoln for Alton on Wednesday? 9:02 A.M.

Refer to the table of calorie needs.

23. How many calories does a 14-year-old boy need each day? 3100

24. How many calories does a 17-year-old girl need each day? 2400

25. Who needs more calories, a 15-year-old girl or a 60-year-old woman? 15-year-old girl

26. A 46-year-old man who does heavy work needs 1500 calories a day more than the number of calories shown in the table. How many calories a day does such a man need? 4500

Daily Calorie Needs
(for people of average weight)

	Age	Calories
Boys	13–15	3100
	16–19	3600
Girls	13–15	2600
	16–19	2400
Men	25–44	3200
	45–64	3000
	65+	2550
Women	25–44	2300
	45–64	2200
	65+	1800

On most highway maps distances between small towns are printed near the roads between the towns, but distances between cities are often shown in tables like these. (The distances are for the most direct routes. The colored rows and columns illustrate the examples below.)

	Ames	Boone	Burlington	Cedar Rapids	Clinton	Council Bluffs	Davenport	Des Moines	Dubuque
Ames		15	185	101	183	164	178	27	173
Boone	15		55	116	198	149	193	42	188
Burlington	185	55		101	114	279	78	157	150
Cedar Rapids	101	116	112		82	249	78	110	72
Charles City	120	131	219	243	200	196	196	133	135
Clinton	183	198	114	82		75	36	192	62
Council Bluffs	164	149	279	249	331		303	135	321
Davenport	178	193	78	178	36	303		174	72
Des Moines	27	42	157	110	192	135	174		182
Dubuque	193	188	150	72	62	321	72	180	
Fort Dodge	61	50	246	162	244	151	239	88	198
Fort Madison	190	205	21	106	129	284	99	164	165
Iowa City	118	133	77	24	87	249	78	110	83
Keokuk	199	214	46	116	154	294	124	174	175
Marshalltown	38	53	162	68	150	182	145	47	140
Mason City	98	106	248	147	229	248	225	125	164
Muscatine	153	168	50	59	64	275	28	149	100
Newton	51	66	143	84	166	166	143	31	156
Oskaloosa	86	101	99	91	161	180	123	60	157
Ottumwa	111	126	74	100	160	205	125	85	166
Sioux City	169	154	345	270	352	98	347	186	317
Spencer	153	141	338	249	331	158	327	180	266
Waterloo	93	109	168	67	149	237	145	102	93

Newton	Norton	Oakley	Olathe	Ottawa	Parsons	Pittsburg	Pratt	Russell	Salina	Scott City	Sedan	Sharon Springs
242												
238	84											
162	320	358										
131	310	338	32									
156	394	395	131	102								
182	420	419	115	111	36							
91	202	198	253	221	209	236						
130	114	114	246	224	286	311	90					
63	179	186	174	151	219	245	118	73				
209	130	46	355	323	365	390	164	142	194			
123	364	360	179	150	68	103	175	252	186	331		
286	138	53	411	389	442	467	241	164	237	77	408	
181	63	144	263	253	332	363	163	73	118	198	304	198
336	103	98	423	413	492	518	297	214	281	143	459	65
263	203	119	410	380	388	415	179	216	260	80	354	65
144	260	298	60	50	145	161	231	184	113	306	165	349
255	169	84	401	369	411	436	210	188	240	47	377	31
223	263	346	77	98	200	190	306	260	188	382	244	398
57	295	295	220	188	141	177	98	186	121	262	79	339
26	267	264	188	156	132	159	77	155	89	235	98	312
68	309	306	209	177	117	153	119	197	131	276	56	354
103	343	342	102	70	62	87	177	233	166	312	82	389

Example 1: Charles City and Dubuque are 135 miles apart.

Example 2: Parsons and Sedan are 68 miles apart.

Find the distance between the cities.

27. Ames, Des Moines 27 miles

28. Waterloo, Davenport 145 miles

29. Iowa City, Council Bluffs 249 miles

30. Mason City, Clinton 229 miles

31. Salina, Norton 179 miles

32. Sedan, Oakley 360 miles

33. Oakley, Olathe 358 miles

34. Pratt, Russell 90 miles

35. How far is it to Davenport from Des Moines by way of Marshalltown? How much shorter is the direct route?
192 miles; 18 miles

36. How far is it from Pittsburg to Salina by way of Parsons? How much longer is this than the direct route?
255 miles; 10 miles

37. Is it farther from Pratt to Salina through Newton or through Russell? How much farther? Russell; 9 miles

38. Is it farther from Clinton to Des Moines through Oskaloosa or through Marshalltown? How much farther?
Oskaloosa; 24 miles

The table below shows results of road tests on four models of 1984 cars.

mi/h means miles per hour.	RENAULT ENCORE LS	FORD ESCORT L	PLYMOUTH HORIZON	CHEVROLET CHEVETTE CS
ACCELERATION				
0–30 mi/h (seconds)	7.3	5.5	4.7	6.7
Passing: 45–65 mi/h (seconds)	12.9	11.8	7.9	13.5
FUEL ECONOMY				
EPA estimates, city/highway (mi/g)	28/37	27/37	26/36	30/42
195-mile test trip (mi/g)	32	32	28	32
BRAKING				
From 60 mi/h with no wheels locked (feet)	185	170	185	195
ENGINE AND TRANSMISSION				
Acceleration				
Engine drivability				

mi/g means miles per gallon.

See below for meaning of symbols.

◉ Excellent; ◐ Very good; ○ Good; ◑ Fair; ● Poor

©1984 Consumers Union of United States, Inc., Mt. Vernon, N.Y. Reprinted by permission from *Consumer Reports*, March 1984.

39. How long did it take the Plymouth Horizon to accelerate from 0 mi/h to 30 mi/h? 4.7 seconds

40. Which car took 12.9 seconds to accelerate from 45 mi/h to 65 mi/h? Renault Encore LS

41. What is the EPA-estimated city mi/g for the Ford Escort L? 27 mi/g

42. What is the EPA-estimated highway mi/g for the Chevrolet Chevette CS? 42 mi/g

43. Which car did not get 32 mi/g on the 195-mile test trip? Plymouth Horizon

44. Which car took the greatest distance to stop when the brakes were applied at 60 mi/h? Chevrolet Chevette CS

45. Which two cars were rated "Fair" for acceleration? Renault Encore LS and Chevrolet Chevette CS

46. What rating was given to the Renault Encore LS for engine drivability? Excellent

CALCULATOR SKILL on page 524 may be used at this time.

1. five thousand two hundred eighty-three
2. four hundred twenty-two thousand, seven hundred

3. three million, seven hundred one thousand, twenty-six

Write in words.
4. five and six hundredths

			Skill	Page
1. 5283	**2.** 422,700	**3.** 3,701,026	1	448

5. seven hundred twenty-five thousandths

4. 5.06	**5.** 0.725	**6.** 1.2345	2	449

6. one and two thousand three hundred forty-five ten-thousandths

Application 1 may be used at this time. **13**

CROSS—NUMBER PUZZLE

1. 1	**2.** 9	**3.** 8	▓	**4.** 1	**5.** 1	**6.** 9	**7.** 9
8. 2	0	▓	**9.** 1	6	**10.** 8	**11.** 8	2
12. 0	▓	**13.** 1	3	8	0	**14.** 1	**15.** 6
▓	**16.** 3	4	8	▓	**17.** 4	0	**18.** 7
19. 9	2	0	▓	▓	**20.** 6	4	**21.** 5
▓	**22.** 3	0	**23.** 4	▓	**24.** 1	3	2	▓
25. 1	▓	**26.** 1	5	**27.** 2	6	8	**28.** 8
29. 4	**30.** 9	▓	**31.** 6	2	0	**32.** 1	0
33. 4	3	**34.** 8	▓	**35.** 1	▓	**36.** 4	6	0

Copy this pattern on grid paper. Fill in the squares by using the clues for numbers to be written *across* the page or the clues for numbers to be written *down* the page. (In this puzzle, the *across* clues are harder than the *down* clues.)

Here is what the corner of the puzzle should look like after you fill in **1.** Across and **1.** Down.

(Final 0's to the right of the decimal point are not written in the puzzle.)

Across

1. $87{,}654 - 87{,}456$
4. $20 \div 20$
5. $198.9 + 0.1$
8. $\frac{1}{4} \times 80$
9. 14×12
11. $78\frac{5}{8} + 3\frac{3}{8}$
12. 7599×0
13. $13{,}799.98 + 1.02$
15. $4\frac{1}{2} \times 1\frac{1}{3}$
16. $355.4 - 7.4$
17. $4 \times 101\frac{3}{4}$
19. $922\frac{1}{2} - 2\frac{1}{2}$
20. $322.5 \div 0.5$
22. $\frac{4560}{15}$
24. $\frac{1}{3} \times 396$
25. $\frac{5}{12} + \frac{1}{3} + \frac{1}{4}$
26. $3817 \div 0.25$
28. 2^3
29. 7^2
31. $\frac{49}{310} = \frac{98}{?}$
32. $1000 \div 100$
33. $6(24 + 49)$
35. $\frac{3}{4} \div \frac{3}{4}$
36. $46 \times 20 \times 0.5$

Down

1. $115.3 + 4.7$
2. 45×2
3. $100 - 92$
4. $856.7 - 688.7$
5. $8 \div 8$
6. 7×14
7. $3704 \div 4$
9. 34.5×4
10. 201×4
13. $15{,}000 - 999$
14. $1750 + 8888$
16. $299 + 15 + 9$
18. $739.4 + 2.6$
19. $\frac{135}{15}$
21. $5\frac{1}{2} - \frac{1}{2}$
23. $4241 - 3785$
24. $1760 \div 11$
25. $4 \times 3 \times 12$
27. $(11 \times 11) + 100$
28. 40×20
30. $48.7 + 44.3$
32. $9 + 11 - 4$
34. $2 \times 2 \times 2$
36. $3\frac{1}{4} + \frac{3}{4}$

1.2 | THE MODE

To raise some money, the Pep Club plans to sell school T-shirts. The T-shirts come in the sizes listed below. Do you think the Pep Club should order the same number of each size?

small   medium   large   extra large

To know which size should be their best seller, the Pep Club needs to know the size that is worn by *the most* students.

The item that occurs most often in a list is the **mode.**

3, 4, 4, 5, 6, 6, 6, 7, 7 — The mode is 6.

2, 1, 7, 7, 1, 1, 3, 5, 1 — The mode is 1.

There may be more than one mode.

7, 7, 8, 9, 12, 12, 12, 15, 21, 23, 23, 29, 29, 29, 35, 37
The modes are 12 and 29.

If each item in a list occurs only once, there is no mode.

3, 8, 10, 11, 15, 30, 50

There is no mode.

Mary Elenz Tranter

EXERCISES

1. Which of these mean the same thing?

   a. The most common test score is 82.
   b. The highest test score is 82.
   c. The mode of the test scores is 82.
   d. The test score that occurs most frequently is 82.

2. You are given this list of scores: 0, 1, 1, 3, 3, 3, 3, 9, 9, 10. Which of these scores is the mode or modes?

   a. 4   b. 3   c. 1 and 9   d. 10

Find the mode or modes.

3. 3, 4, 5, 5, 5, 5, 6, 6, 7 5

4. 9, 9, 9, 8, 8, 7, 6, 5, 4 9

5. 23, 34, 23, 49, 62, 9, 49, 71
23 and 49

6. 12, 15, 22, 54, 15, 18, 94, 54
15 and 54

7. 2, 4, 6, 8, 10, 12, 14, 16 no mode

8. 2, $2\frac{1}{2}$, 3, $3\frac{1}{2}$, 4, $4\frac{1}{2}$, 5, $5\frac{1}{2}$ no mode

9. 28, 18, 15, 12, 18, 15, 19, 20, 28, 20, 28 28

10. 41, 16, 24, 12, 16, 30, 24, 41, 17, 16, 21 16

11. 1.7, 1.4, 1.4, 1.6, 1.5, 1.7, 1.4, 1.6, 1.3, 1.6, 1.3, 1.3 1.3, 1.4, and 1.6

12. 2.5, 3.6, 1.9, 4.2, 2.5, 4.3, 8.6, 2.8, 3.1, 4.2, 2.8 2.5, 2.8, and 4.2

13. The mode can be found for a list of items that are not numbers. Shown below is a list of student math grades.

Which grade is the mode?

C, A, B, B, D, C, B, F, A, B, D, B, C, C, A, A B

14. Which letter occurs most often in this question? t

CALCULATOR SKILL on page 525 may be used at this time.

SKILLS REFRESHER

Write < or > for each ●.

		Skill	Page
1. 98 > 89	**2.** 7026 < 7030	3	450
3. 0.9 > 0.88	**4.** 42.68 > 4.268		

Add.

				Skill	Page
5. 347 +251 598	**6.** 657 +574 1231	**7.** 5723 + 948 6671	**8.** 27 131 94 + 80 332	5	452

9. 199 + 8 + 46 + 77 + 804 1134

16

1.3 | THE MEDIAN |

On many highways the *median* is a strip down the *middle* that separates the lanes of traffic.

The **median** of a set of numbers is the middle number *when the numbers are listed in order.*

Example 1:

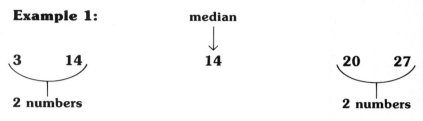

John D. Cunningham

An even number of scores has no middle number. To find the median in such a case, do the following:

• Add the two middle scores.

• Then divide by 2.

Example 2:

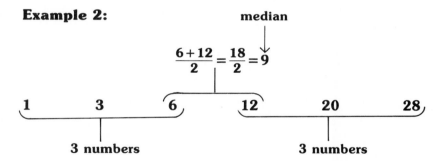

In the preceding examples, the numbers are listed from smallest to largest. It would be just as easy to find the median if the numbers were listed from largest to smallest.

Example 3:

Given these numbers, →15 12   7 16 2 1   7   3   9

list them in this order →1   2   3   7 ⌐7⌐ 9 12 15 16

      or this order →16 15 12   9 ⌐7⌐ 7   3   2   1

to find the median. ————————→ **median**

EXERCISES

True or false?

1. The median of a set of numbers may be one of the numbers. True

2. The median of a set of numbers must be one of the numbers. False

3. The median of 7, 6, 1, 3, 5, 4, and 2 is 3. False

4. The median of 1, 2, 3, 4, 5, 6, and 7 is 4. True

5. The median of 3, 3, 3, 5, 5, and 5 is 4. True

Find the median in exercises 6–17.

6. 52, 66, 74, 82, 97 74

7. 46, 58, 62, 76, 85 62

8. 30, 121, 7, 12, 59, 3, 20 20

9. 91, 32, 49, 6, 11, 73, 18 32

10. 7, 11, 18, 26, 30, 71 22

11. 3, 19, 20, 26, 32, 47 23

12. 19, 8, 36, 25, 50, 14 22

13. 23, 12, 1, 27, 23, 30 23

14. 1.1, 4.9, 6.2, 7.4, 9.6, 11.5, 16.2, 23.1, 27.7, 27.9, 30.2 11.5

15. 3.2, 5.7, 11.2, 6.8, 1.6, 22.5, 20.6, 8.3, 10.4, 7.1, 6.9 7.1

16. Heights of students (in centimeters):

    160, 162, 155, 163, 176, 160, 166, 172, 180, 158, 165, 172 164

17. Hourly rates paid to students:

    $4.06, $3.90, $4.30, $5.00, $3.91, $4.15, $3.85 $4.06

Use these NCAA Championship Game Scores (recent years).

Marquette	67	Kentucky	94	Michigan State	75		
N. Carolina	59	Duke	88	Indiana State	64		
Louisville	59	Indiana	63	N. Carolina State	54	Georgetown	84
UCLA	54	N. Carolina	50	Houston	52	Houston	75

18. Find the median of the 7 winning scores. 67

19. Find the median of the 7 losing scores. 59

20. Find the median of all 14 scores. 63.5

Median Age of Americans (in years)

Year	Male	Female	Total population
1950	29.8	30.5	30.2
1960	28.7	30.3	29.5
1970	26.8	29.3	28.0
1980	28.8	31.3	30.0

Source: U.S. Bureau of the Census, *Statistical Abstract of the United States,*
1980 and *1981*

21. What was the median age of females in 1980? 31.3

22. What was the median age of the total population in 1960? 29.5

23. In 1950, half the males were 29.8 years old or older.

24. In 1970, half the females were 29.3 years old or younger.

25. During which year was the median age of females 30.3? 1960

26. During which year was the median age of males the lowest? 1970

27. During which year was the median age of the total population the highest? 1950

28. From 1970 to 1980, the median age of females increased by 2 years.

29. From 1960 to 1970, the median age of males decreased by 1.9 years.

30. During which year was the median age of males and the median age of females most nearly the same? 1950

31. In 1970, more than half the total population was too young to have been alive when Pearl Harbor was attacked. Did the attack take place before or after 1942? before

32. In 1820, the median age of all Americans was only 16.7 years. By 1920, it had increased by 8.6 years. What was the median age of all Americans in 1920? 25.3

CALCULATOR SKILL on page 526 may be used at this time.

Divide.

				Skill	Page
1. $3\overline{)156}$ 52	**2.** $7\overline{)763}$ 109	**3.** $1012 \div 4$ 253	**4.** $\frac{356}{9}$ $39\frac{5}{9}$	18	472
5. $24\overline{)72}$ 3	**6.** $18\overline{)324}$ 18	**7.** $4520 \div 30$ $150\frac{2}{3}$	**8.** $\frac{822}{12}$ $68\frac{1}{2}$	19	474

19

1.4 THE MEAN

Don Lansu

Jamie and Benjamin bowled 3 games each. The results are shown below.

Name	Game 1	Game 2	Game 3
Jamie	125	182	113
Benjamin	110	158	167

To determine who bowled better, we could find each bowler's *average* score.

To find the average of a set of numbers, do the following:

• Add the numbers.

• Divide the sum by how many numbers there are.

$$\begin{array}{r} 125 \\ 182 \\ +113 \\ \hline 420 \end{array}$$

$$\begin{array}{r} 140 \\ 3\overline{)420} \end{array} \longleftarrow \begin{array}{l}\textbf{Jamie's} \\ \textbf{average}\end{array}$$

$$\begin{array}{r} 110 \\ 158 \\ +167 \\ \hline 435 \end{array}$$

$$\begin{array}{r} 145 \\ 3\overline{)435} \end{array} \longleftarrow \begin{array}{l}\textbf{Benjamin's} \\ \textbf{average}\end{array}$$

An average, like each of those above, is called the **mean.** How much higher was Benjamin's mean score than Jamie's?

5 pins higher

Example 1: What is the mean number of letters in the words of this question?

letters in ⟶ 4   2 3   4   6   2 7 2 3   5   2 4   8
each word

Add to find the total number of letters. ⟶ 52

Count the number of words. ⟶ 13

$52 \div 13 = 4 \longleftarrow$ mean number of letters per word

Example 2: Marge bowled 6 games and had 828 total pins. Al bowled 8 games and had 1089 total pins. Whose mean score was higher?

$$\begin{array}{r} 138 \\ 6\overline{)828} \end{array} \qquad \begin{array}{r} 136\frac{1}{8} \\ 8\overline{)1089} \end{array}$$

Marge's mean score was higher.

EXERCISES

1. To find the mean of 2, 4, 6, and 8, add the numbers and divide by __4__.

2. You take 5 tests and score 440 total points. Your mean score is __88__.

3. You score 80 on each of 3 tests. Your mean score is __80__.

4. The mean of 10 equal scores is 37. What is each score? __37__

Find the mean.

5. 7, 3, 2, 4   4

6. 5, 3, 8, 8   6

7. 15, 17, 8, 5, 0   9

8. 16, 13, 9, 8, 29   15

9. 5231, 7000, 1293, 304   3457

10. 6000, 4377, 526, 2597   3375

11. 62, 7, 23, 12, 21, 1   21

12. 74, 18, 3, 31, 0, 48   29

13. 28, 69 $48\frac{1}{2}$

14. 16, 41 $28\frac{1}{2}$

15. 17, 32, 4, 12, 19, 75, 42 $28\frac{5}{7}$

16. 15, 6, 52, 12, 19, 31, 4 $19\frac{6}{7}$

17. 320, 401, 624, 218 $390\frac{3}{4}$

18. 603, 128, 434, 300 $366\frac{1}{4}$

19. John Glazeski is a construction worker. His income depends on the weather. The first six months of last year he earned $720, $842, $1212, $1675, $2900, and $3757. What was his mean monthly income? $1851

20. Linda Jaffe is a commissioned salesperson. Her income varies from week to week. In seven weeks she earned $410, $580, $640, $620, $530, $490, and $755. What was her mean weekly income? $575

21. Saree Halevy rushed for 54 yards in 9 carries. Luisa Cruz rushed for 90 yards in 18 carries.

   a. Whose mean yards per carry was greater?   Saree Halevy

   b. What is the difference between the means?   1 yard

22. Willie Mays hit 660 home runs in 22 seasons. Hank Aaron hit 755 home runs in 23 seasons.

a. Willie Mays hit an average of __30__ home runs per season.

b. Who hit more home runs per season, Willie Mays or Hank Aaron?

Many teachers determine student grades or scores by finding the mean of each student's test scores or assignment scores. Find the mean of each student's scores.

	Student	Scores	
23.	Paul	82, 94, 86, 79, 83, 92	86
24.	Gertrude	93, 87, 83, 90, 84, 85	87
25.	Shawn	83, 76, 72, 80, 74, 68, 75, 80, 96, 96	80
26.	Juanita	73, 83, 77, 79, 73, 69, 78, 84, 99, 85	80
27.	Igor	91, 83, 87, 79, 81, 85, 82, 80	$83\frac{1}{2}$
28.	Chung	84, 92, 87, 83, 79, 88, 93, 86	$86\frac{1}{2}$

Refer to the table below.

Tennis player	Letters in first name	Letters in last name	Letters in full name
Tracy Austin	5	6	11
Andrea Jaeger	6	6	12
Martina Navratilova	7	11	18
Jimmy Connors	5	7	12
Ivan Lendl	4	5	9
John McEnroe	4	7	11

29. Complete the table with the number of letters in each name.

30. Find the mean number of letters per first name. $5\frac{1}{6}$

31. Find the mean number of letters per last name. 7

32. Find the mean number of letters per full name. $12\frac{1}{6}$

22

Some typical sports statistics are given below. Find the average (mean) asked for in each exercise.

33. Soccer: goalie's goals-against average 3

game	1	2	3	4	5	6	7
goals against	3	5	2	5	0	2	4

34. Basketball: player's points-per-game average 20

game	1	2	3	4	5	6
points scored	12	20	32	24	18	14

35. Football: team's punt-return average 28

punt	1	2	3	4	5	6	7
yards returned	33	24	41	25	36	12	25

GET A KICK OUT OF THIS

George Blanda, who still played in the National Football League at age 48, is football's all-time leading scorer. During his 26-season career, he averaged 77 points per season. How many points did he score during his career? 2002

CALCULATOR SKILL on page 527 may be used at this time.

SKILLS REFRESHER

Subtract.

							Skill	Page

1. 658
−236
422

2. 371
−158
213

3. 423
−379
44

Skill 7 Page 456

4. 79.5
−31.2
48.3

5. 84.1
−53.6
30.5

6. 45.42
− 3.59
41.83

Skill 8 Page 458

Multiply.

7. 21×7 147

8. 9×36 324

9. 43×12 516

Skill 12 Page 464

10. 23×3.7 85.1

11. 271×0.6 162.6

12. 5.34×6 32.04

Skill 13 Page 466

23

1.5 | THE RANGE

Connie and P. C. Peri

The numerals on the cards are scores awarded in a school diving competition. The **range** of the scores may be given in either of the following two ways:

9.5—5.0 or **4.5**

Name the highest and lowest scores. **Give the difference between the highest and lowest scores.**

EXERCISES

1. To find the range of a set of numbers, you need to know

a. any two of the numbers   b. the median
c. the largest and smallest numbers   d. the mean

Give the range of each set of numbers in two ways.

2. 1, 5, 5, 7, 8, 9, 9, 13, 15 15-1; 14   **3.** 2, 5, 7, 8, 15, 15, 18 18-2; 16

4. 37, 27, 26, 25, 23, 19, 18 37-18; 19   **5.** 23, 22, 22, 21, 16, 14, 8 23-8; 15

6. 26, 5, 38, 21, 40, 39, 18, 6 40-5; 35   **7.** 15, 26, 20, 50, 34, 42, 12, 49
50-12; 38

8. 6, 12, 0, 18, 1, 92, 13, 12, 92, 80   **9.** 42, 13, 76, 84, 69, 2, 35, 20, 2, 15
92-0; 92   84-2; 82

10. 2.3, 2.8, 3.0, 3.6, 4.8, 5.1   **11.** 1.6, 2.0, 3.8, 4.1, 4.7, 5.3
5.1-2.3; 2.8   5.3-1.6; 3.7

12. 7.5, 4.1, 9.9, 2.0, 5.7, 0.6, 4.1   **13.** 3.3, 0.4, 5.0, 8.2, 9.5, 3.3, 6.5
9.9-0.6; 9.3   9.5-0.4; 9.1

14. 6.42, 6.39, 7.01, 6.88, 6.40   **15.** 5.08, 5.12, 5.99, 6.12, 6.09
7.01-6.39; 0.62   6.12-5.08; 1.04

Do you know what these words mean?

census   *poll*   *data*   *statistics*

census   a count of people

poll   a survey to get facts (or opinions)

data   facts

statistics   data involving numbers

Our government takes a **census** every ten years. In addition to counting people, our government takes a **poll** to gather **data** on such things as housing and education. The **statistics** are often organized into tables. This makes the information easy to read and helps us to detect trends and make predictions.

The statistics used in the following problems were published by the United States Bureau of the Census:

Connie and P. C. Peri

1. *Housing:*   In 1970, there were 1,775,000 people living in Arizona. In 1980, there were 2,718,000 people living in Arizona. Find the increase in population. How has this changed housing needs? 943,000; Needs have increased.

2. *Education:*   In 1960, there were about 4,258,000 babies born in the United States. In 1980, about 3,598,000 babies were born. Most people enter junior high school about twelve years after birth. How will the need for junior-high-school teachers in 1992 compare with the need in 1972? Need will be less in 1992 than in 1972.

3. *Environment:*   In 1970, Americans used an average of 372.18 billion gallons of water a day. It is expected that by the year 2000 Americans will use 66.15 billion *fewer* gallons of water a day. (This decrease will be due, in part, to recycling.) How much water a day are Americans expected to use in the year 2000? 306.03 billion gallons

4. *Health care:*   In 1980, the population of North Dakota was 653,000. There were about 800 doctors in North Dakota. In South Dakota, there were about 700 doctors for a population of 690,000. Which state had better health care in terms of having fewer people per doctor? North Dakota

Bryce Flynn/Picture Group

In many cities workers are urged to save gasoline by using car pools to get to work. As a check, one company recorded how many people arrived in each car on one working day. The record is given below.

2	4	2	3	5	1	3	1	1	6	2	4	1
2	1	7	4	1	5	2	3	2	1	4	2	5
2	4	6	1	4	2	4	3	6	4	1	4	2

Can you tell at a glance how many cars had 2 people? To make it easier to interpret the data, you could make a *frequency table* like the one below. No

List the numbers in order.

Use tally marks to count how many times each number occurs.

Record how many times each number occurs.

Number of people in each car	Tally	Frequency
1	ⅢⅠ ⅢⅠ	9
2	ⅢⅠ ⅢⅠ	10
3	ⅢⅠ	4
4	ⅢⅠ ⅢⅠ	9
5	ⅢⅠ	3
6	ⅢⅠ	3
7	Ⅰ	1

A **frequency table** shows how many times each number occurs. It should be easy to see that there were 10 cars with 2 people. How many cars had 4 people? 9

You can use a frequency table to find the mode and the median.

To find the median, first add the frequencies. The sum of the frequencies is 39, so the median is the 20th number.

	Number of people in each car	Frequency
2 occurs the most times, so the *mode* is 2. →	1	9 ⎱ **19 numbers**
	2	10 ⎰
	3	4 ← **The 20th number is**
	4	9 **one of the four 3's,**
	5	3 **so the *median* is 3.**
	6	3
	7	1
		39 ← **sum of the frequencies**

EXERCISES

1. A __frequency table__ shows how many times each number occurs.

2. The (mean, median, <u>mode</u>) is the number that occurs with the greatest frequency.

3. If 35 numbers are listed in order, the median is the (<u>17th</u>, 18th, 19th) number.

4. If 40 numbers are listed in order, the median is the average of the __20th__ and __21st__ numbers.

Find the mode (or modes) and the median.

5. Math Test Results

Score	Frequency
100	4
90	9
80	5
70	3
60	4

5. mode: 90
   median: 90

6. mode: 260
   median: 270

6. Daily Water Use

Gallons	Frequency
230	5
260	6
270	5
300	4
310	5
600	5

Copy and complete the frequency table for each set of numbers.

7. Shoe size of 44 students:
7, 6, 5, 7, 12, 9, 7, 6, 8, 6, 4, 5, 6, 7,
7, 6, 7, 5, 9, 7, 6, 8, 6, 8, 7, 6, 7, 5,
7, 9, 6, 7, 5, 7, 6, 4, 11, 7, 6, 10, 11,
7, 6, 10

Shoe size	Tally	Frequency
4		2
5		5
6		12
7		14

8-3; 9-3; 10-2; 11-2; 12-1

8. Quiz scores of 40 students:
5, 5, 4, 9, 4, 1, 7, 7, 7, 5, 3, 4, 5, 6,
6, 9, 8, 2, 3, 2, 1, 6, 6, 8, 5, 4, 0, 2,
8, 10, 5, 5, 3, 4, 4, 6, 3, 6, 5, 7

Quiz score	Tally	Frequency
10		1
9		2
8		3

7-4; 6-6; 5-8; 4-6; 3-4; 2-3; 1-2; 0-1

Make a frequency table for each set of numbers.

9. Numbers of brothers and sisters of 43 students:
3, 1, 0, 8, 1, 2, 0, 4, 1, 1, 2, 7, 0, 2, 1, 2, 3, 0, 1, 2, 1,
2, 2, 3, 0, 2, 3, 1, 2, 0, 7, 2, 0, 1, 3, 1, 1, 5, 2, 1, 3, 0,
1

10. Numbers of hours slept last night of 42 students:
7, 7, 5, 10, 9, 8, 8, 8, 6, 9, 9, 6, 7, 6, 7, 4, 8, 9, 9, 7,
7, 7, 5, 6, 11, 10, 8, 8, 9, 7, 10, 8, 9, 7, 7, 8, 8, 9, 8,
9, 8, 8

11. Daily high temperatures (in degrees Fahrenheit):
64, 66, 62, 68, 66, 62, 60, 62, 64, 60, 58, 52, 48, 46,
48, 46, 48, 52, 56, 60, 62, 62, 62, 57, 56, 56, 58, 56,
54, 48, 48

12. Daily stream depths (in inches) of the Shallow River:
18, 20, 22, 20, 22, 24, 25, 23, 24, 23, 21, 22, 23, 21,
22, 20, 20, 22, 23, 26, 26, 27, 29, 30, 30, 29, 28, 29,
25, 26

9.	F
0	8
1	13
2	11
3	6
4	1
5	1
7	2
8	1

10.	F
4	1
5	2
6	4
7	10
8	12
9	9
10	3
11	1

11.	F
46	2
48	5
52	2
54	1
56	4
57	1
58	2
60	3
62	6
64	2
66	2
68	1

12.	F
18	1
20	4
21	2
22	5
23	4
24	2
25	2
26	3
27	1
28	1
29	3
30	2

Find the mode (or modes) and the median from the frequency table you made for each of these exercises. The mode is given first, followed by the median.

13. exercise 7 7; 7   **14.** exercise 8 5; 5   **15.** exercise 9 1; 2

16. exercise 10 8; 8 **17.** exercise 11   **18.** exercise 12 22; 23
62; 58

28 students in Mr. Engelbrecht's class took a test. The results are given below.

100, 90, 90, 80, 80, 80, 60, 100, 100, 50, 70, 90, 80, 90, 60, 70, 70, 70, 100, 70, 60, 70, 80, 90, 80, 100, 80, 80

To find the mean you could add the scores and divide by 28. However, since many scores are repeated, it might be easier to use a frequency table.

James H. Pickerell

Score	Frequency	Score × Frequency
100	5	$100 \times 5 = 500$
90	5	$90 \times 5 = 450$
80	8	$80 \times 8 = 640$
70	6	$70 \times 6 = 420$
60	3	$60 \times 3 = 180$
50	1	$50 \times 1 = 50$
	28	2240

To find the mean, do the following:

a. Multiply each score by its frequency.

b. Add the products.

$$28\overline{)2240}^{\,80}$$

c. Divide by the sum of the frequencies.

The **mean** is 80.

EXERCISES

Find the mean from each frequency table in exercises 1–4.

1.   Math Quiz Results   8

Score	Frequency
10	4
9	5
8	2
7	5
6	4

2.   Science Quiz Results   7

Score	Frequency
12	5
10	3
8	2
6	4
4	9
2	1

3.

Concert Tickets Sold		$17
Price ($)	Frequency	
50	1	
25	4	
20	14	
15	16	
12	15	

4.

Daily Salaries at BMS Company		$50
Salary ($)	Frequency	
80	1	
64	5	
56	10	
48	15	
40	4	
32	5	

Make a frequency table for each set of numbers. Then find the mean.
Frequency tables are not given.

5. Normal number of days with precipitation each month (Wilmington, Delaware):

11, 10, 11, 11, 12, 10, 9, 10, 8, 8, 10, 10   10

6. Normal number of days with precipitation each month (Cleveland, Ohio):

16, 15, 16, 13, 13, 11, 10, 10, 10, 11, 15, 16   13

7. Driver's education test scores:

75, 85, 90, 70, 80, 65, 85, 75, 95, 55, 80, 85, 70, 90, 75, 85, 80, 70, 95, 75, 100, 70, 85, 90, 50, 95, 75, 85, 100, 75, 80, 65, 80, 90, 85, 75   80

8. Weekly price per pound of frying chicken (in cents):

72, 72, 68, 72, 72, 68, 68, 66, 68, 66, 60, 58, 58, 58, 60, 66, 62, 60, 64, 66, 68, 68, 70, 72, 74, 76, 74, 76, 74, 72, 72, 70, 68, 68, 70, 72   68

9. In exercise 1, the mean is (less than, equal to, greater than) the median.

10. In exercise 2, the mean is (less than, equal to, greater than) the median.

CALCULATOR SKILL on page 528 may be used at this time.

SKILLS REFRESHER

Add.

		Skill	Page
1. $3.45 + 7.21 + 4.5 + 2.36 + 5.72$ 23.24	**2.** 3.61 +4.27 7.88	6	454
3. $6.8 + 9.04 + 3.26 + 50.07$ 69.17			

Divide.

4. $8\overline{)76.8}$ 9.6   **5.** $7\overline{)52.85}$ 7.55   **6.** $11\overline{)148.72}$ 13.52   **7.** $12\overline{)948.96}$ 79.08

	Skill	Page
	20	476

30   *Application 2 may be used at this time.*

1.8 | MORE ABOUT AVERAGES

This table shows the normal amount of precipitation each month in Mobile, Alabama.

Month	Inches
January	4.71
February	4.76
March	7.07
April	5.59
May	4.53
June	6.09
July	8.86
August	6.93
September	6.59
October	2.55
November	3.39
December	5.89

Werner Stoy/FPG

To find the mode, the median, and the mean, do the following:

a. List the numbers in order.

b. *Mode:* Since no number occurs more than once, there is no mode.

c. *Median:* Add the two middle numbers and divide by 2. The median monthly precipitation is 5.74 inches.

d. *Mean:* Add the numbers and divide by 12. The mean monthly precipitation is 5.58 inches.

```
8.86
7.07
6.93
6.59
6.09
5.89 ⎫      5.89      5.74
5.59 ⎭    + 5.59    2)11.48
4.76       11.48     10
4.71                  1 4
4.53                  1 4
3.39                   08
2.55       5.58         8
66.96   12)66.96        0
            60
             6 9
             6 0
               96
               96
                0
```

31

EXERCISES

Refer to the example on page 31 for exercises 1–4.

1. Why is there no mode? No number occurs more than once.

2. During how many months is there more than 5.74 inches of precipitation? 6

3. During how many months is there less than 5.74 inches of precipitation? 6

4. In finding the mean, why was 66.96 divided by 12? because there were 12 numbers

Find the mode (or modes), the median, and the mean in exercises 5–14.

5. 3.2, 7.1, 5.9, 12.2, 4.7, 9.5, 5.9, 7.1 5.9 and 7.1; 6.5; 6.95

6. 6.7, 5.1, 10.9, 3.5, 8.8, 5.1, 12.6, 8.8, 4.2 5.1 and 8.8; 6.7; 7.3

7. 2.41, 3.45, 6.42, 4.91, 9.28, 1.07, 3.45, 5.89 3.45; 4.18; 4.61

8. 4.32, 8.95, 2.36, 5.80, 3.55, 6.56, 8.95, 7.91 8.95; 6.18; 6.05

9. 12.65, 9.41, 6.57, 12.65, 13.81, 15.23 12.65; 12.65; 11.72

10. 18.47, 20.16, 15.61, 9.85, 13.90, 15.61 15.61; 15.61; 15.6

11. 132.81, 164.26, 153.79, 121.28, 146.13, 121.21, 170.2
no mode; 146.13; 144.24

12. 181.43, 179.2, 160.02, 177.2, 186.3, 160.09, 190
no mode; 179.2; 176.32

13. 1.21, 2.25, 4, 2.9, 2.80, 1.60, 1.2, 3.23, 1.03, 2.99, 3.6, 3, 1.2, 2.08, 3.32, 5, 5, 2.25, 1.31 1.2, 2.25, 5; 2.8; 2.63

14. 2, 1.03, 0.85, 0.62, 2.53, 2.35, 1, 0.7, 6.0, 1.8, 6.06, 2, 0.6, 2.53, 1.6, 0.85, 2, 1.3 2; 1.7; 1.99

15. Bulldozer operators in 8 cities work at the following hourly rates (in dollars). Find the median and the mean.
9.97, 11.48, 8.65, 12.08, 9.95, 11.02, 7.70, 9.55
9.96; 10.05

16. A certain record album sells for the following prices (in dollars) at 9 stores. Find the mode and the mean.
9.98, 10.99, 8.88, 7.09, 9.98, 9.49, 6.99, 8.88, 9.98
9.98; 9.14

Runk/Schoenberger/Grant Heilman

Use these math scores for exercises 17–19.

94 86 92 12 100 99 91 99 83

17. Find the mode, the median, and the mean.   mode: 99; median: 92;
mean: 84
18. The teacher decides to discard the lowest score (12).
Find the mode, the median, and the mean of the remaining 8 scores.   mode: 99; median: 93; mean: 93

19. Compare your answers for exercises 17–18. Which
seems to be affected most by a very low score—the
mode, the median, or the mean?   the mean

Use these yearly salaries of 12 employees at a small company for exercises 20–22.

| $12,000 | $25,000 | $14,000 | $12,000 | $11,500 | $22,000 |
| $18,000 | $154,500 | $22,000 | $12,000 | $12,000 | $21,000 |

20. Find the mode, the median, and the mean.   mode: $12,000; median: $16,000;
mean: $28,000
21. Suppose you discard the $154,500 salary. Find the
mode, the median, and the mean of the remaining 11
salaries.   mode: $12,000; median: $14,000; mean: $16,500

22. Compare your answers for exercises 20–21. Which
seems to be affected most by a very high salary—the
mode, the median, or the mean?   the mean

23. A manager of a shoe store would like to know which
shoe size is her best seller. Which shoe size should she
find—the mean, the median, or the mode?   the mode

24. In a gymnastics meet, 4 judges score each gymnast. The
highest and lowest scores are discarded. The mean of the 2
middle scores is found. This gives the *final score*. The
final score is really the (mode, median, mean) of the 4
original scores.

SKILLS REFRESHER

Round.

		Skill	Page
1. 52 (nearest 10) 50	**2.** 897 (nearest 10) 900	4	451
3. 508 (nearest 100) 500	**4.** 2252 (nearest 100) 2300		
5. $4.51 (nearest dollar) $5	**6.** $0.89 (nearest dollar) $1		
7. 3.09 (nearest tenth) 3.1	**8.** 0.705 (nearest tenth) 0.7		

Application 3 may be used at this time.   **33**

The *mean* is the average of a set of numbers. The term "average" is sometimes used to refer to the *mode* or to the *median*. Such use of the term "average" could lead to confusion.

Read the ad at the left. Then study the examples below. In each example, the mode, the median, or the mean is $10—but the sets of numbers are quite different.

Example A

	Hourly income	Frequency
	$13	6
	12	7
mode median	10	22
	8	6
	5	4

mean: $\frac{450}{45} = 10$

Example B

	Hourly income	Frequency
	$50	2
	26	3
	13	8
	11	8
median ⟶	4	8
mode ⟶	3	16

mean: $\frac{450}{45} = 10$

Example C

	Hourly income	Frequency
	$16	2
	11	7
mode ⟶	10	8
median ⟶	6	7
	5	7
	4	7
	3	7

mean: $\frac{315}{45} = 7$

Each statement below describes one of the examples. Write A, B, or C to tell which example is described.

1. The mean, median, and mode all are $10 per hour.   A

2. Both the mean and the median are less than $10 per hour.   C

3. Almost half the people earn $10 per hour.   A

4. No person earns $10 per hour.   B

5. The mode does not occur much more often than other amounts.   C

6. About half the people earn $4 or less per hour.   B

1.9 | ESTIMATING SUMS

Sometimes it is not necessary to find an *exact* answer. An answer that is "in the ball park" will do. Other times, you may want to check to make sure that an answer you obtain is at least *reasonable*. For these purposes, **estimates** can be very handy.

Example 1: You want to buy the orange juice and the cereal, and you have only $5. To see if you have enough money, estimate the total cost by rounding each amount to the nearest tenth of a dollar.

$2.19 $1.94

Brent Jones

ESTIMATE: **Think:**

$2.19   about   **$2.**20

$1.94   about   **$1.**90

$1.10

\+ 3.00

$4.10

You have enough money to buy the milk and cereal.

Example 2: You do the following computation on a calculator:
552 + 946 + 314 = 4512.
To see if the answer is reasonable, estimate the sum by rounding each addend to the nearest hundred.

ESTIMATE: **Think:**

552	about	**600**
946	about	**900**
+314	about	**300**
		1800

According to the estimate, the sum should be about 1800. Consequently, the calculator answer (4512) is wrong. (It is what you would get by accidently entering 314 as 3014.) You could use the calculator again to find the correct sum (1812).

EXERCISES

Select the *best estimate* for each sum.

1. $0.29 + $0.29   a. $0.40   b. $0.50   c. $0.60

2. 127 + 486   a. 600   b. 700   c. 500

3. 7.8 + 3.3   a. 10   b. 11   c. 12

4. $1.39 + $2.19   a. $3.40   b. $3.00   c. $3.60

5. 673 + 384   a. 900   b. 1000   c. 1100

6. $1.29 + $3.19   a. $4.00   b. $5.00   c. $3.00

7. $0.87 + $3.91   a. $4.00   b. $5.00   c. $6.00

8. $2.25 + $7.98   a. $9.00   b. $10.00   c. $11.00

9. $1.07 + $6.79 + $3.46   a. $10.00   b. $11.00   c. $12.00

10. $0.28 + $0.44 + $0.59   a. $1.10   b. $1.20   c. $1.30

11. 187 + 243 + 368   a. 700   b. 800   c. 900

12. 6.3 + 4.7 + 8.1   a. 18   b. 19   c. 20

Estimates for exercises 13-36 are given first.

Estimate the sum by rounding each addend to the nearest tenth of a dollar. Then find the exact sum.

Example: **$7.12**   **Estimate:**   **$10.90**
              + 3.79   **Exact sum:**   **$10.91**

16. $19.30; $19.29

13. $2.71
     + 1.28
       $4.00; $3.99

14. $3.43
     + 4.58
       $8.00; $8.01

15. $7.04
     + 8.39
       $15.40; $15.43

16. $12.34
     + 6.95

17. $0.39
       0.19
     + 0.53
       $1.10; $1.11

18. $1.28
       0.43
     + 0.16
       $1.90; $1.87

19. $0.93
       0.78
       0.36
     + 0.23
       $2.30; $2.30

20. $0.37
       0.86
       1.29
     + 2.15
       $4.80; $4.67

Estimate the sum by rounding each addend to the nearest hundred. Then find the exact sum.

24. 8700; 8707

21.   508
     + 187
       700; 695

22.   281
     + 176
       500; 457

23.   955
     + 749
       1700; 1704

24.   6078
     + 2629

36

25.
```
   4666
 +1999
```
6700; 6665

26.
```
  387
  247
 +112
```
700; 746

27.
```
  257
  398
 +156
```
900; 811

28.
```
  5705
   990
 +3457
```
10,200; 10,152

Estimate the sum by rounding each addend to the nearest whole number. Then find the exact sum.

29.
```
  6.8
 +3.4
```
10; 10.2

30.
```
  2.6
 +8.4
```
11; 11

31.
```
  6.8
  7.1
 +3.5
```
18; 17.4

32.
```
  22.4
   0.8
 +52.5
```
76; 75.7

33.
```
  1.70
  4.49
 +6.25
```
12; 12.44

34.
```
   3.98
  11.63
 + 0.89
```
17; 16.5

35.
```
  28.38
   2.78
 + 1.30
```
32; 32.46

36.
```
  8.099
  9.547
 +0.387
```
18; 18.033

37. At a restaurant, you pay the bill for yourself and two friends. The checks are for $3.49, $4.78, and $6.10. Estimate the total bill by rounding each addend to the nearest dollar. $14

38. You do the following computation on a calculator:
$187 + 621 + 385 + 178 = 1371$.
Estimate the sum to see if your answer is reasonable. Round each addend to the nearest hundred. 1400

39. On a trip, you record the numbers of gallons of gasoline you bought: 11.2 gallons, 10.6 gallons, 9.8 gallons, and 9.3 gallons. Estimate the total amount of gasoline you bought by rounding each addend to the nearest gallon. 41

40. At a store, you select four items costing $0.39, $0.41, $0.28, and $0.69. Estimate the total cost by rounding each addend to the nearest tenth of a dollar. $1.80

41. The Sluggers played five games before crowds of 315, 408, 278, 359, and 222 fans. Find a "ball park" figure for the total attendance by rounding each addend to the nearest hundred. 1600

42. A taxi driver received the following amounts in tips one morning: $2.25, $0.80, $1.75, and $1.15. Estimate her total tips by rounding each addend to the nearest dollar. $6

Berg & Associates

1.10 ESTIMATING DIFFERENCES

You can use the ideas for estimating sums to estimate differences.

Example 1: Your car's odometer readings before and after a trip are shown below. Estimate the distance you drove by rounding each number to the nearest hundred.

Before	**After**
7298.0	7922.0

ESTIMATE: **Think:**

$$\begin{array}{rcr} \mathbf{7922} & \text{about} & \mathbf{7900} \\ \underline{\mathbf{-7298}} & \text{about} & \underline{\mathbf{7300}} \\ & & \mathbf{600} \end{array}$$

You drove about 600 miles.

Example 2: The total bill at a grocery store is \$13.73. You give a cashier a \$20 bill and you receive \$5.27 in change. You are not sure that the amount of change is correct. So you estimate the difference by rounding \$13.73 to the nearest dollar.

ESTIMATE: **Think:**

$$\begin{array}{rcr} \mathbf{\$20.00} & & \mathbf{\$20} \\ \underline{\mathbf{-\ \ 13.73}} & \text{about} & \underline{\mathbf{14}} \\ & & \mathbf{\$6} \end{array}$$

The amount of change is incorrect. You should receive \$6.27.

EXERCISES

Choose the *best estimate* for each difference.

1. 798 − 235 a. 400 b. 500 c. 600

2. 19.8 − 3.5 a. 15 b. 16 c. 17

3. \$10.00 − \$5.98 a. \$4.00 b. \$5.00 c. \$6.00

4. $5.00 − $0.29   a. $4.70   b. $4.80   c. $4.00

5. 8391 − 8123   a. 100   b. 200   c. 300

6. $1.00 − $0.41   a. $0.40   b. $0.50   c. $0.60

7. 908 − 173   a. 600   b. 700   c. 800

8. $20.00 − $11.98   a. $8.00   b. $9.00   c. $10.00

9. 28.7 − 7.8   a. 20   b. 21   c. 22

10. 93 − 64   a. 20   b. 30   c. 40

11. 818 − 525   a. 200   b. 300   c. 400

12. 14,815 − 14,670   a. 100   b. 200   c. 400

Estimates for exercises 13-36 are given first.
Estimate the difference by rounding each number to the nearest hundred. Then find the exact difference.

13.
   478
− 123
400; 355

14.
   913
− 281
600; 632

15.
   804
− 555
200; 249

16.
   974
− 89
900; 885

17.
   1282
− 1125
200; 157

18.
   6852
− 6201
700; 651

19.
   1381
− 1128
300; 253

20.
   20,450
− 18,505
2000; 1945

Estimate the difference by rounding each amount to the nearest dollar. Then find the exact difference.

21.
   $28.85
−   3.89
$25; $24.96

22.
   $1.74
− 0.89
$1; $0.85

23.
   $12.05
−   3.15
$9; $8.90

24.
   $62.48
−   0.98
$61; $61.50

25.
   $44.31
− 13.87
$30; $30.44

26.
   $16.00
−   8.63
$7; $7.37

27.
   $27.84
− 14.28
$14; $13.56

28.
   $99.55
− 12.09
$88; $87.46

Estimate the difference by rounding the amount being subtracted to the nearest tenth of a dollar. Then find the exact difference.

29.
   $2.00
−   0.49
$1.50; $1.51

30.
   $1.00
−   0.63
$0.40; $0.37

31.
   $5.00
−   2.57
$2.40; $2.43

32.
   $10.00
−   3.98
$6.00; $6.02

33.
   $10.00
−   7.87
$2.10; $2.13

34.
   $3.00
−   0.37
$2.60; $2.63

35.
   $25.00
− 11.77
$13.20; $13.23

36.
   $25.00
− 16.52
$8.50; $8.48

37. You buy $27.73 worth of groceries, but you have coupons that give a total discount of $1.75. Estimate how much the groceries will cost. Round each amount to the nearest dollar. $26

38. You do the following computation on a calculator: $783 - 377 = 306$. Estimate the difference to see if your answer is reasonable. Round each number to the nearest hundred. 400, so calculator answer is not reasonable

39. A salesperson earned $925 in March and $1038 in April. Estimate how much more the salesperson earned in April by rounding each amount to the nearest 100 dollars. $100

40. Carlos has $78. He would like to buy a stereo that sells for $237. Estimate how much more he needs by rounding each amount to the nearest 10 dollars. $160

41. Your bill at a restaurant is $13.76. You give the cashier $20.00. Estimate how much change you should get by rounding each amount to the nearest dollar. $6

42. A home computer that regularly sells for $289.98 is on sale for $199.99. Estimate the amount of reduction by rounding each amount to the nearest dollar. $90

Roger Sandler/Picture Group

1.11 ESTIMATING PRODUCTS

Sometimes it is helpful to estimate a product.

Example 1: During a typical week, the Carlsons spend $87 for groceries. Estimate how much they spend in 52 weeks by rounding each number to the nearest ten.

ESTIMATE: **Think:**

$87	about	**$90**	$90
52	about	50	×50
			$4500

They spend about $4500 in 52 weeks.

Example 2: You do the following computation on a calculator: $287 \times 643 = 184{,}541$. Estimate the product to see if your answer is reasonable. Round each factor to the nearest hundred.

ESTIMATE: **Think:**

287	about	**300**	300
643	about	**600**	× 600
			180,000

The estimate makes your answer seem reasonable.

Example 3: You are being sent to buy 3 hamburgers that cost $1.74 each. Estimate how much money you need by rounding $1.74 to the nearest dollar.

ESTIMATE: **Think:**

$1.74	about	**$2**
		×3
		$6

You need about $6.

EXERCISES

Pick the *best estimate* for each product.

1. $0.98 × 4   a. $3.60   b. <u>$4.00</u>   c. $5.00

2. 44 × 51   a. 200   b. <u>2000</u>   c. 20,000

Mary Elenz Tranter

3. 592×383 <u>a.</u> 240,000   b. 24,000   c. 2400

4. $12 \times \$1.19$ a. \$10.00   <u>b.</u> \$12.00   c. \$20.00

5. $\$6.95 \times 4$ a. \$24.00   b. \$2.80   <u>c.</u> \$28.00

6. 88×68 a. 630   <u>b.</u> 6300   c. 63,000

7. $\$54.95 \times 7$ a. \$300   <u>b.</u> \$350   c. \$3000

8. 759×195 a. 1600   b. 16,000   <u>c.</u> 160,000

9. 97×97 a. 8100   <u>b.</u> 10,000   c. 1000

10. $\$1.98 \times 12$ <u>a.</u> \$24.00   b. \$20.00   c. \$30.00

11. $\$27.98 \times 24$ <u>a.</u> \$600   b. \$400   c. \$900

12. 186×493 a. 8000   <u>b.</u> 80,000   c. 100,000

Estimates for exercises 13-36 are given first.

Estimate the product by rounding each factor to the nearest ten. Then find the exact product.

13. 12 $\times 37$ 400; 444	**14.** 71 $\times 49$ 3500; 3479	**15.** 56 $\times 84$ 4800; 4704	**16.** 90 $\times 89$ 8100; 8010
17. 59 $\times 59$ 3600; 3481	**18.** 98 $\times 47$ 5000; 4606	**19.** 94 $\times 98$ 9000; 9212	**20.** 99 $\times 13$ 1000; 1287

Estimate the product by rounding each factor to the nearest hundred. Then find the exact product.

21. 215 $\times 536$ 100,000; 115,240	**22.** 627 $\times 181$ 120,000; 113,487	**23.** 356 $\times 429$ 160,000; 152,724	**24.** 555 $\times 349$ 180,000; 193,695
25. 723 $\times 610$ 420,000; 441,030	**26.** 841 $\times 207$ 160,000; 174,087	**27.** 920 $\times 375$ 360,000; 345,000	**28.** 229 $\times 973$ 200,000; 222,817

Estimate the product by rounding each amount of money to the nearest dollar. Then find the exact product.

29. \$1.76 $\times 4$ \$8; \$7.04	**30.** \$2.14 $\times 5$ \$10; \$10.70	**31.** \$9.27 $\times 8$ \$72; \$74.16	**32.** \$6.09 $\times 8$ \$48; \$48.72
33. \$6.79 $\times 3$ \$21; \$20.37	**34.** \$4.89 $\times 7$ \$35; \$34.23	**35.** \$8.25 $\times 6$ \$48; \$49.50	**36.** \$9.95 $\times 4$ \$40; \$39.80

37. At a concert, balcony tickets sell for $9.75 each. Estimate the cost of 4 balcony tickets by rounding the ticket price to the nearest dollar. $40

38. There are 12 rows of parking spaces in a lot. Each row has 28 parking spaces. Estimate how many cars can be parked by rounding each factor to the nearest ten. 300

39. Carpeting sells for $18 a square yard, and you need 32 square yards. Estimate the total cost by rounding each factor to the nearest ten. $600

40. You do the following computation on a calculator: $398 \times 465 = 185{,}070$. Check your answer by estimating. Round each factor to the nearest hundred. 200,000

41. Ground beef sells for $1.55 per pound. Estimate the cost of 3 pounds by rounding the price per pound to the nearest tenth of a dollar. $4.80

SKILLS REFRESHER

Find each quotient to the nearest tenth.

			Skill	Page
1. $178 \div 19$ 9.4	**2.** $227\overline{)780}$ 3.4	**3.** $6\overline{)75.08}$ 12.5	23	480
4. $83 \div 3.6$ 23.1	**5.** $37.9\overline{)126}$ 3.3	**6.** $15.4\overline{)300}$ 19.5		

Application 4 may be used at this time.

43

In this section, you will learn how to estimate quotients.

Example 1: You do the following computation on a calculator: 8704 ÷ 32 = 272. Check to see if your answer is reasonable by estimating the quotient. Round 8704 to the nearest thousand and round 32 to the nearest ten.

ESTIMATE: **Think:**

8704	about	**9000**
32	about	**30**

$$\begin{array}{r} 300 \\ 30\overline{)9000} \end{array} \quad \text{or} \quad \frac{900\not0}{3\not0} = 300$$

The estimate makes your answer seem reasonable.

Example 2: A farmer spends $237.96 for seed corn to plant 18.5 acres. Estimate how much he spends on seed corn per acre. Round $237.96 to the nearest ten dollars and round 18.5 to the nearest ten.

Steve Woit/Picture Group

ESTIMATE: **Think:**

$237.96 about **$240**
18.5   about   **20**

$$\begin{array}{r} 12 \\ 20\overline{)240} \end{array} \quad \text{or} \quad \frac{24\cancel{0}}{2\cancel{0}} = 12$$

The farmer spends about $12 per acre for seed corn.

EXERCISES

Choose the *best estimate* for each quotient.

1. $6315 \div 71$ a. 90   b. 900   c. 9000
2. $1423 \div 21$ a. 700   b. 70   c. 7000
3. $163 \div 19$ a. 8   b. 80   c. 90
4. $357 \div 41$ a. 90   b. 80   c. 9
5. $199 \div 11.2$ a. 20   b. 10   c. 100
6. $397 \div 18.6$ a. 200   b. 20   c. 40
7. $9.95 \div 9$ a. $0.10   b. $10   c. $1

8. $19.95 ÷ 5   a. $5   b. $6   c. $4

9. $44.98 ÷ 9   a. $4   b. $5   c. $6

10. 3195 ÷ 319   a. 10   b. 100   c. 8

11. 8098 ÷ 905   a. 90   b. 100   c. 9

12. 6291 ÷ 713   a. 9   b. 90   c. 100

For exercises 13–24, estimate the quotient by rounding each number to the nearest ten. Then find the exact quotient to the nearest tenth.

Example: $21\overline{)78}$ **Estimate:** **4**   **To nearest tenth:** **3.7**

13. $18\overline{)78}$ 4; 4.3

14. $39\overline{)124}$ 3; 3.2

15. $63\overline{)423}$ 7; 6.7

16. $81\overline{)244}$ 3; 3.0

17. $76\overline{)396}$ 5; 5.2

18. $31\overline{)152}$ 5; 4.9

19. $12.6\overline{)195}$ 20; 15.5

20. $18.3\overline{)158}$ 8; 8.6

21. $27.9\overline{)304}$ 10; 10.9

22. $48.2\overline{)397}$ 8; 8.2

23. $33.5\overline{)237}$ 8; 7.1

24. $86.4\overline{)182}$ 2; 2.1

Estimate the quotient by rounding each number to the nearest hundred. Then find the exact quotient to the nearest tenth.

25. $187\overline{)758}$ 4; 4.1

26. $314\overline{)927}$ 3; 3.0

27. $164\overline{)831}$ 4; 5.1

28. $216\overline{)398}$ 2; 1.8

29. $98\overline{)794}$ 8; 8.1

30. $104\overline{)998}$ 10; 9.6

31. $731\overline{)3542}$ 5; 4.8

32. $484\overline{)2521}$ 5; 5.2

33. $634\overline{)3620}$ 6; 5.7

34. $814\overline{)1560}$ 2; 1.9

35. $193\overline{)1185}$ 6; 6.1

36. $580\overline{)2430}$ 4; 4.2

37. On a trip, you travel 198 miles in 3 hours 54 minutes. Estimate the average speed for the trip. Round 198 to the nearest ten and 3 hours 54 minutes to the nearest hour. 50 mi/h

38. Ron rode his motorcycle 267 miles on 3 gallons of gasoline. Estimate how many miles per gallon he was able to get by rounding 267 to the nearest ten. 90 mi/g

39. You do the following computation on a calculator: 196.5 ÷ 39.3 = 50. Estimate the quotient to see if your answer is reasonable. Round 196.5 to the nearest hundred and round 39.3 to the nearest ten. 5; calculator answer is not reasonable

40. A classroom has a volume of 6025 cubic feet. Estimate how many *cubic yards* this is (27 cubic feet = 1 cubic yard). Round 27 to the nearest ten and round 6025 to the nearest hundred. 200 cubic yards

Peter Glass/Glass Eye Photography

The mathematics in this chapter is useful in jobs like these:

1. *Automobile salesperson:* Sometimes the ability to perform quick estimates can help make a sale. Suppose a customer wants to buy a car with the options listed below. Estimate the total cost by rounding each amount to the nearest hundred dollars. $10,400

base price	$9084	air conditioning	$697
vinyl top	$278	AM–FM radio/tape player	$315

2. *Store manager:* A store manager made this tally of how many people entered her store during each hour one evening.

Hour	Tally	Frequency
4:00–5	╫╫ ╫╫ ╫╫ ╫╫ I	21
5–6	╫╫ II	7
6–7	╫╫ ╫╫ III	13
7–8	╫╫ ╫╫ IIII	14
8–9	╫╫ ╫╫ ╫╫ IIII	19
9–10	╫╫ ╫╫ I	11

Copy and complete the frequency table. Suppose the manager would like to hire an extra salesperson for the busiest 3-hour period. Which 3-hour period should she choose?
6:00-9:00

3. *Market researcher:* A market researcher recorded the reactions of 50 people after they tasted a new brand of pizza. The people were asked to respond (on a scale of 1 to 5) to the statement shown at the left.

Then the market researcher used the data from the survey to make the frequency table below. Find the *mean* rating.
(4) Above average

Compare the taste of this pizza with that of others you have eaten. (Check one box.)

☐ (5) Excellent

☐ (4) Above average

☐ (3) Average

☐ (2) Below average

☐ (1) Poor

Rating	Frequency
5	20
4	16
3	10
2	2
1	2

47

The table shows the chilling effect of wind. When there is a temperature of 50°F and the wind speed is 20 mi/h, your body loses heat as fast as on a calm day at 32°F.

1.1

1. What is the windchill when there is a thermometer reading of 20°F and the wind speed is 10 mi/h? 4°F

2. How strong a wind gives a windchill of 18°F when there is a thermometer reading of 40°F? 20 mi/h

3. If the temperature is 0°F and the wind speed is 15 mi/h, what temperature must you dress for? -32°F

4. At 30°F, a wind speed greater than 25 mi/h gives the effect of below-zero temperatures.

Windchill Chart

Wind speed (mi/h)	Thermometer reading (°F)					
	50	40	30	20	10	0
	Windchill (°F)					
calm	50	40	30	20	10	0
5	48	37	27	16	6	⁻5
10	40	28	16	4	⁻9	⁻24
15	36	22	9	⁻5	⁻18	⁻32
20	32	18	4	⁻10	⁻25	⁻39
25	30	16	0	⁻15	⁻29	⁻44
30	28	13	⁻2	⁻18	⁻33	⁻48
35	27	11	⁻4	⁻20	⁻35	⁻51
40	26	10	⁻6	⁻21	⁻37	⁻53

degrees above zero   degrees below zero

Use these sets of numbers for exercises 5–12.

A: 4, 4, 7, 11, 15, 5, 17, 21, 21, 21, 26, 30

B: 8, 13, 15, 15, 6, 10, 13, 8, 12, 8, 13

5. mode (or modes) of set A 21

6. mode (or modes) of set B 8 and 13   1.2

7. median of set A 16

8. median of set B 12   1.3

9. mean of set A $15\frac{1}{6}$

10. mean of set B 11   1.4

11. range of set A 30-4 or 26

12. range of set B 15-6 or 9   1.5

13. Make a frequency table for set A above. See table at right.

14. Make a frequency table for set B above.   1.6

15. Find the mode and median scores from the frequency table at the right. mode: 80; median: 80

Score	Frequency
100	4
90	6
80	9
70	4

13.

	F
4	2
5	1
7	1
11	1
15	1
17	1
21	3
26	1
30	1

14.

	F
6	1
8	3
10	1
12	1
13	3
15	2

Find the mean.   1.7

16.   Math Quiz Results   8   **17.**   English Test Results   88

Score	Frequency
10	6
9	5
8	3
7	1
6	4
0	1

Score	Frequency
97	7
92	7
87	2
82	6
75	2
61	1

Find the mode (or modes), the median, and the mean.   1.8

18. 15.31, 12.72, 10.16, 15.31, 9.72, 13.21, 10.16 modes: 10.16 and 15.31;
median: 12.72; mean: 12.37

19. 7.6, 8.9, 3.2, 6.2, 4.7, 8.2, 7.5, 10.6, 6.1   mode: none; median: 7.5;
mean: 7

Estimates for exercises 20-35 are given first.

Estimate the sum by rounding each addend to the nearest hundred. Then find   1.9
the exact sum.

20. $139 + 176$ 300; 315   **21.** $399 + 405$ 800; 804

22. $465 + 990$ 1500; 1455   **23.** $218 + 555 + 87$ 900; 860

Estimate the difference by rounding each amount to the nearest dollar. Then   1.10
find the exact difference.

24. $\$1.79 - \$0.82$ $1; $0.97   **25.** $\$8.06 - \$5.80$ $2; $2.26

26. $\$37.25 - \$19.99$ $17; $17.26   **27.** $\$55.00 - \$34.75$ $20; $20.25

Estimate the product by rounding each factor to the nearest ten. Then find the   1.11
exact product.

28. 39×21 800; 819   **29.** 25×24 600; 600

30. 72×42 2800; 3024   **31.** 97×53 5000; 5141

Estimate the quotient by rounding each number to the nearest ten. Then find   1.12
the exact quotient to the nearest tenth.

32. $29\overline{)88}$ 3; 3.0   **33.** $42\overline{)204}$ 5; 4.9

34. $19.2\overline{)161}$ 8; 8.4   **35.** $32.5\overline{)148}$ 5; 4.6

CHAPTER REVIEW

MOTORCYCLE SPECIFICATIONS

Model	Gears	Wheel-base (in.)	Weight (lb)	Price
A	1	32	89	$444
B	4	38	100	610
C	4	38	95	575
D	1	37	90	529
E	4	44	98	649

1. Which motorcycle model has a 38-inch wheelbase and weighs less than 100 pounds? C

2. Which motorcycle model has 4 gears and the highest price? E

Use this set of numbers for exercises 3–7.

3, 4, 4, 5, 6, 8, 12, 12, 12, 14

3. Find the mode. 12

4. Find the median. 7

5. Find the mean. 8

6. Find the range.
14-3 or 11

7. Make a frequency table.
See table at right.

7.

	F
3	1
4	2
5	1
6	1
8	1
12	3
14	1

8. Find the mean score from the frequency table at the right. 92

Score	Frequency
95	6
90	3
88	3

9. Find the mode, the median, and the mean of the following set of numbers:

3.27, 5.43, 6.95, 2.73, 3.27, 6.95, 4.21, 3.27 mode: 3.27;
median: 3.74; mean: 4.51

Estimate the answer by rounding each number to the nearest ten. Then find the exact answer. Estimates for exercises 10-17 are given first.

10. 48+62
110; 110

11. 19+84+45
150; 148

12. 91−22
70; 69

13. 172−48
120; 124

Estimate the answer by rounding each number to the nearest hundred. Then find the exact answer.

14. 389×427
160,000; 166,103

15. 107×88
10,000; 9416

16. 1236÷309
4; 4

17. 780÷195
4; 4

1. What town is located in region B-4?

     Lomax

2. In which region is Carthage located?

     D-4

Graph and label each point.

See students' graphs.

3. (6,4), (5,5), (0,3), (0,0)

4.

x	6	3	4	5	$2\frac{1}{2}$	0
y	6	0	$2\frac{1}{2}$	2	4	1

Correlation

Items	Sec
1–2	2.1
3	2.2
4	2.3
5–6	2.5
7–8	2.4
9	2.7
10	2.8
11	2.9

From the line graph, in which ten-year period did the number of cranes

5. decrease?

     1930–1940

6. increase most rapidly?

     1960–1970

Use with exercises 5–6.

Whooping Cranes in the United States

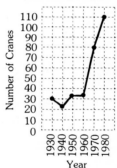

Refer to the bar graph for exercises 7–8.

Photographer's Guide to People in Motion

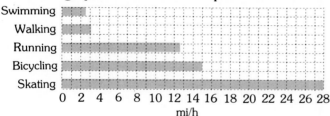

7. Which is faster, swimming or <u>walking</u>?

8. <u>Skating</u> is more than twice as fast as running.

9. In a pictograph the symbol 🍎 stands for 20 apples. How many symbols would be needed to stand for 50 apples? $2\frac{1}{2}$

10. The circle graph shows that 26 out of every 100 cars in use are under 3 years old.

11. According to the schematic, the hollow ball fits into the spout.

Use with exercise 10.

Ages of Cars in Use

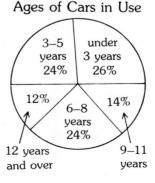

Use with exercise 11.

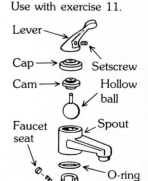

51

Part of a map of the state of New Mexico is shown on page 53. To find the town of Pecos, you could do the following:

Step 1: Look for Pecos in the Index of Cities and Towns. (The index is alphabetical, like a dictionary.) You should find this entry: Pecos   C-4

Step 2: Follow *across* the band labeled C and *down* the band labeled 4. The region where the bands cross is region C-4 on this map. It includes Pecos, as well as other towns and cities. Search in this region to find Pecos.

Navajo Dam is circled near the top of the map. How could you tell someone where to find the dam on this map? The dam is in the bands labeled A (at the left of the map) and 1 (at the top of the map). So the dam is in region A-1 on this map.

EXERCISES

Refer to the map on page 53.

1. The name of each region is made up of a ___ and a ___. letter; number

2. What other towns besides Pecos are shown in region C-4?
   Glorietta, Gallinas, El Pueblo

3. What towns would be labeled B-1 in the complete index?
   Blanco Trading Post, Counselor

4. How many *regions* are named B-4 on this map? one

5. How many names does any one region of the map have? one

6. Is there any reason why the region containing Pecos should be labeled C-4 on other maps of New Mexico? No

Locate each town on the map on page 53 by using the Index of Cities and Towns. Then tell in which region you found it.

7. Abo   E-3   8. Ambrosia Lake C-1   9. Gallina B-2   10. Abiquiu   B-3

11. Pojoaque B-3   12. Punta de Agua E-3   13. Galisteo C-3   14. Placitas   C-3

15. Algodones C-3   16. Questa   A-4   17. Frijoles C-3   18. Alameda D-2

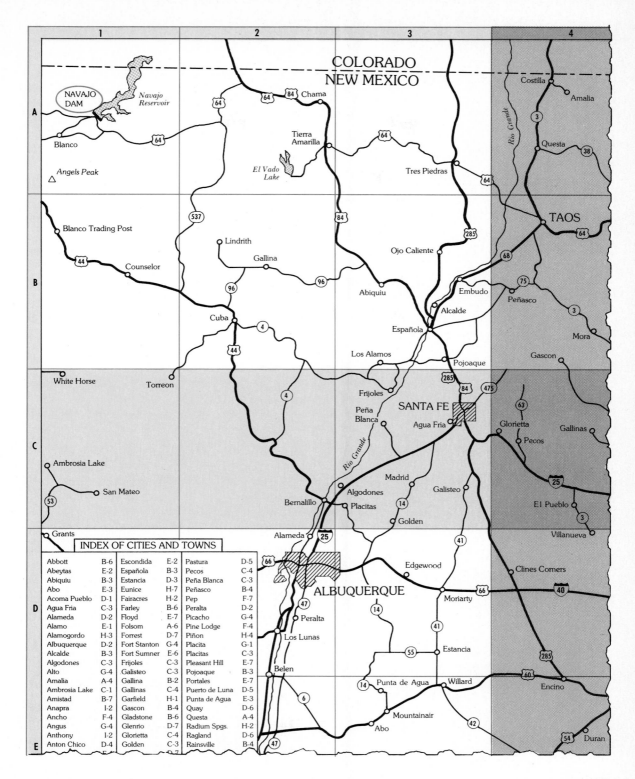

INDEX OF CITIES AND TOWNS

In which region of the map on page 53 can each place be found? (These places are not in the part of the index shown.)

19. Cuba B-2 **20.** Grants D-1 **21.** Los Alamos B-3

22. Santa Fe C-3 **23.** El Vado Lake A-2 **24.** Angels Peak A-1

In which region of the map on page 55 is each of these located?

25. The White House F-5 **26.** The Washington Monument G-5

27. The Capitol G-6 **28.** The Lincoln Memorial G-5

29. Washington National Airport H-5 **30.** Arlington National Cemetery G-4

31. The Pentagon G-5 **32.** The Smithsonian Institution G-5

33. The intersection of U.S. Highway 1 and Glebe Road H-5 **34.** The intersection of Interstate Highway 295 and Interstate Highway 495 J-6

35. Chevy Chase, Maryland D-4 **36.** Lake Barcroft, Virginia H-2

37. Alaska Avenue C-5 **38.** American University E-4

Use the map on page 55 to find what river or creek runs through the region listed.

39. J-7 **40.** I-2 **41.** F-7 **42.** I-5
Henson Creek   Holmes Run   Anacostia River   Potomac River

Gene Ahrens/FPG

Refer to the map on page 55.

43. In which region does Pennsylvania Avenue cross the Anacostia River? G-7

44. In which region does Military Road cross Rock Creek Park? D-5

45. Locate the Capital Beltway south of Washington. Name the regions that it goes through. J2-J7, I7-I8

46. Locate the Capital Beltway north of Washington. Name the regions that it goes through. B2-B8

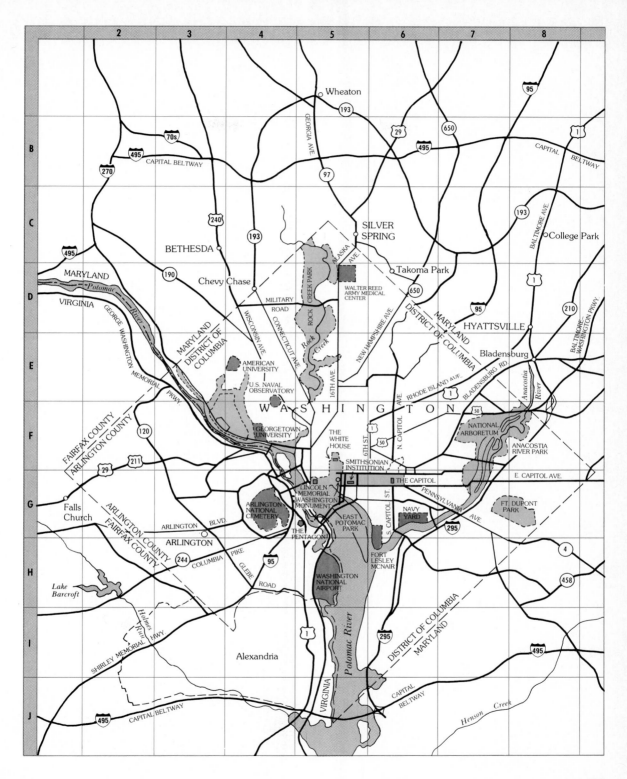

55

Have you ever heard of Three Forks, West Virginia, or Seven Stars, Pennsylvania? There are many place-names that are made up partly or entirely of numbers. Some of them are listed below. But you will have to do some figuring, and then spell out your results, to find out what they are!

Example 1: $(18 \div 3) - 1$ Points, Alabama $\longrightarrow$ Five Points, Alabama

Example 2: $\frac{1}{12-10}$ Acre, New York $\longrightarrow$ Half Acre, New York

1. $9 + 13 - 18$ Oaks, N.C.
Four Oaks, N.C.

2. $(4 \times 7) + 1$ Palms, Calif.
Twentynine Palms, Calif.

3. $(90 \div 9)$ Sleep, Wyo.
Ten Sleep, Wyo.

4. $15 \times 2 \div 10$ Rivers, Mass.
Three Rivers, Mass.

5. $6 \times 2 \div 4$ Lakes, Wis.
Three Lakes, Wis.

6. $(32 \div 16) \times 11$ Mile Village, Alaska
Twenty-two Mile Village, Alaska

7. $1.7 + 2.3$ Points, Ga.
Four Points, Ga.

8. $(48 - 6) \div 3$ Mile Point, Mich.
Fourteen Mile Point, Mich.

9. $(9 \times 8) + 15 - 3$, Pa.
Eightyfour, Pa.

10. $(3 + 1) \times 2$ Mile, Ala.
Eight Mile, Ala.

11. $91 \div 13$ Fountains, Va.
Seven Fountains, Va.

12. $(999 + 1)$ sticks, Ky.
Thousandsticks, Ky.

13. $(5 + 3 - 6)$ dot, Mont.
Twodot, Mont.

14. $3.7 + 7.3$ Mile Corner, Ariz.
Eleven Mile Corner, Ariz.

15. $5 \times 5 \times 2$ Lakes, Minn.
Fifty Lakes, Minn.

16. $(110 \div 11)$ killer Ferry, Okla.
Tenkiller Ferry, Okla.

17. $0 + 2$ Buttes, Colo.
Two Buttes, Colo.

18. $(36 + 15) \div 51$ Tree Peak, N.Mex.
One Tree Peak, N. Mex.

19. $105 \div 21$ Islands, Maine
Five Islands, Maine

20. 0.25×100 Miles Wash, Utah
Twentyfive Miles Wash, Utah

21. 1.5×2 Creek, Idaho
Three Creek, Idaho

22. (2.5×4) sas River, La.
Tensas River, La.

23. $(5 + 1) \times 2$ Mile, Ind.
Twelve Mile, Ind.

24. $(52 \div 13) + 3$ Sisters, Tex.
Seven Sisters, Tex.

25. $(9 \times 10) - 2$, Ky.
Eighty Eight, Ky.

26. $22 - 15 + 2$ Mile Falls, Wash.
Nine Mile Falls, Wash.

27. 12×8, S.C.
Ninety Six, S.C.

28. $12 - 5 + 3$ Mile, Tenn.
Ten Mile, Tenn.

29. $9.6 - 3.6$ Mile Lake, La.
Six Mile Lake, La.

30. $1 \times 4 \times 250$ Spring Creek, Nev.
Thousand Spring Creek, Nev.

31. $\frac{1}{51-49}$ Day, Ill.
Half Day, Ill.

32. $\frac{1}{16.2 \div 8.1}$ Moon Bay, Calif.
Half Moon Bay, Calif.

33. 2×51 River, Mo.
Hundred and Two River, Mo.

34. $(1 + 4) \times 5 - 10$ Mile Falls, N.H.
Fifteen Mile Falls, N.H.

35. $(64 \div 4) + 1$, Ohio
Seventeen, Ohio

36. $5598 + 4402$ Islands, Fla.
Ten Thousand Islands, Fla.

37. $(21 - 7) \times 4$, Ark.
Fiftysix, Ark.

38. $(17 + 3) \times 2$ Fort, Pa.
Forty Fort, Pa.

39. $22.4 - 19.4$ Bridges, N.J.
Three Bridges, N.J.

40. $(32 - 7) \times 4$, W.Va.
Hundred, W.Va.

41. $(174 \div 29)$ es, Oreg.
Sixes, Oreg.

42. $5(28 \div 2)$ mile River, Alaska
Seventymile River, Alaska

On the map on page 53, B-3 names a region that includes several towns and cities. But in a theater, B3 names a region that contains only *one* seat.

Points on a plane are also named so that each name refers to exactly *one* point. Instead of a letter and a number, the name consists of two numbers, called the **coordinates** of the point.

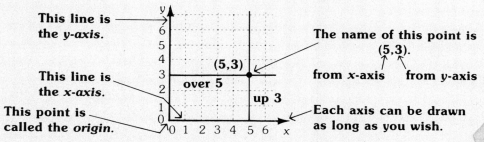

This line is the *y-axis*.

This line is the *x-axis*.

This point is called the *origin*.

The name of this point is (5,3).

from *x*-axis   from *y*-axis

Each axis can be drawn as long as you wish.

Since both coordinates of a point are numbers, let us agree upon an order for giving the two numbers.

The number on the *x*-axis is *first*; **The number on the *y*-axis is *last*:**
it tells how far *over* the point is. **it tells how far *up* the point is.**

(x,y)

So the coordinates are always given in the order (x,y).

EXERCISES

1. How would you locate the point (3,5)? Is the point (3,5) the same as the point (5,3)? 3 units over, 5 units up; No

2. What are the coordinates of the origin? (0,0)

Ed Hoppe Photography

3. If the first coordinate of a point is 0, where is the point located? on the y-axis

4. How many **axes** (plural of *axis*) are used to locate points in a plane?   2

On graph paper, draw axes like those shown on page 57. Make the axes 12 units long. Then draw a dot for each of these points and label each point with its coordinates.
See students' graphs.

5. (4,8)   **6.** (5,10)   **7.** (6,0)   **8.** (9,0)

9. (0,7)   **10.** (0,3)   **11.** (12,2)   **12.** (10,1)

13. (4,4)   **14.** (11,11)   **15.** (8,10)   **16.** (9,12)

What are the coordinates of each point?

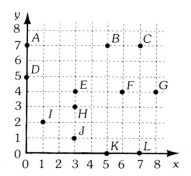

17. A (0,7)   **18.** B(5,7)   **19.** C(7,7)

20. D (0,5)   **21.** E(3,4)   **22.** F (6,4)

23. G (8,4)   **24.** H(3,3)   **25.** I (1,2)

26. J (3,1)   **27.** K(5,0)   **28.** L (7,0)

SKILLS REFRESHER

Write in words.

				Skill	Page
1. $\frac{1}{2}$	**2.** $\frac{2}{3}$	**3.** $\frac{4}{5}$	**4.** $\frac{3}{7}$	26	484
one half	two thirds	four fifths	three sevenths		

Change each decimal to a fraction.

				Skill	Page
5. 0.3	**6.** 0.13	**7.** 0.5	**8.** 0.25	48	521
$\frac{3}{10}$	$\frac{13}{100}$	$\frac{5}{10}$, or $\frac{1}{2}$	$\frac{25}{100}$, or $\frac{1}{4}$		

Change each fraction to a decimal.

				Skill	Page
9. $\frac{7}{10}$ 0.7	**10.** $\frac{1}{2}$ 0.5	**11.** $\frac{3}{4}$ 0.75	**12.** $\frac{1}{5}$ 0.2	46	518

Players: Two (The instructions are the same for both players.)

Materials for each player: Graph paper, pencil

Mark off two sets of axes, each 10 units by 10 units, on graph paper.

One graph is your *sea*, and the other is your *map*. Do not let the other player see your *sea*. (Place a hand or a book in front of it.)

There are fish in the sea, and each fish covers a certain number of points.

shark: 5 points   swordfish: 4 points   tuna: 3 points

mackerel: 2 points   sardine: 1 point

Place one fish of each kind anywhere in your sea. Do this by circling vertical, horizontal, or diagonal rows. (See example.)

Example of a Sea:

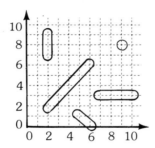

Charles Gupton/Southern Light

To play: Take turns fishing by giving the coordinates of a point. The object is to catch all the fish in the other player's sea. (A fish is caught when all its points have been named.)

When you fish, the other player must say "hit" or "miss" to tell you whether or not you hit a fish. Mark your hits (X) and misses (O) on your map so that you can plan your next move.

Mark the other player's hits on your sea. Do not tell the other player what kind of fish is hit. But if a hit catches a fish, you should say "hit and caught."

The first player to catch all the fish in the other player's sea wins.

GRAPHING POINTS FROM
TABLES

Sometimes a list of coordinates is given in table form.

Coordinates: (0,0), (4,1), (6,3), (8,4), (12,3), (14,1)

Table:

x	0	4	6	8	12	14
y	0	1	3	4	3	1

You can see why, if you were graphing these points, it might
be easier to keep track of the coordinates by using the table.
Here are two graphs of these coordinates.

Graph A:

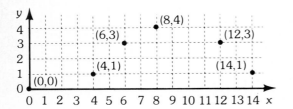

Graph B:

**Every mark on
the axes does
not have to be
labeled.**

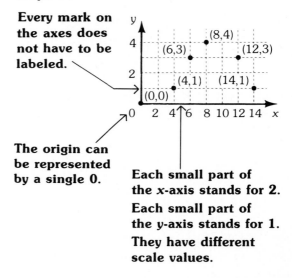

**The origin can
be represented
by a single 0.**

**Each small part of
the x-axis stands for 2.**

**Each small part of
the y-axis stands for 1.**

**They have different
scale values.**

Suppose the list included coordinates like $(6,3\frac{1}{2})$, (10,2.5), and
(3,2). How could you graph these points?

$3\frac{1}{2}$ **is midway
between 3 (un-
labeled) and 4.**

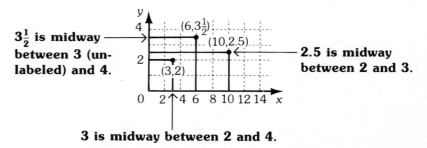

**2.5 is midway
between 2 and 3.**

3 is midway between 2 and 4.

EXERCISES

Use Graphs A and B on page 60 to answer these questions.

1. In Graph A, does each small part of the x-axis stand for 1? Yes

2. In Graph A, does each small part of the y-axis stand for 1? Yes

3. In Graph B, does each small part of the x-axis stand for 1? No

4. In Graph B, does each small part of the y-axis stand for 1? Yes

5. Does the x-axis of a graph have to have the same scale value as the y-axis? No

6. Tell how to locate point (9,2) on Graph B.
9 is midway between 8 and 10; 9 units right, 2 units up

7. Tell how to locate point $(8,1\frac{1}{2})$ on Graph B.
$1\frac{1}{2}$ is midway between 1 (not labeled) and 2; 8 units right, $1\frac{1}{2}$ units up

8. Write the coordinates in exercise 9 in (x,y) form.
(1,0), (2,5), (3,3), (4,4), (5,1), (6,2)

Make a separate graph for each table. (In exercises 13–18, it may be convenient to use different scale values on the axes.)
See students' graphs.

9.

x	1	2	3	4	5	6
y	0	5	3	4	1	2

10.

x	1	2	3	4	5	6
y	4	0	3	5	2	1

11.

x	2	4	6	8	10	12
y	9	7	5	3	1	0

12.

x	1	3	5	7	9	11
y	10	8	6	4	2	0

13.

x	0	5	11	18	26	35
y	1	2	3	4	5	6

14.

x	1	4	9	16	25	36
y	1	2	3	4	5	6

15.

x	1	2	3	4	5	6
y	4	8	12	16	24	28

16.

x	1	2	3	4	5	6
y	5	10	15	20	25	30

17.

x	0	5	10	15	20	25
y	0	10	30	70	85	125

18.

x	3	6	9	12	18	21
y	12	24	60	96	66	84

19.

x	2	0	$4\frac{1}{2}$	$3\frac{1}{2}$
y	$3\frac{1}{2}$	$\frac{1}{2}$	6	$3\frac{1}{2}$

20.

x	1.5	0	0.5	4.5
y	2	3.5	7	2.5

Graph paper can be used for playing games, drawing patterns and designs, and even drawing pictures.

Graph the points in table 1 below and then connect them in order. Next, using the same axes, do the same for table 2, table 3, and so on. (Of course the points could also be given as (0,6), (1,10), (3,10), and so forth.)

1.
x	0	1	3	4	3	2	2	3	3	1	1	0
y	6	10	10	8	8	7	6	6	5	4	1	0

2.
x	2	3	3	4	5	6	6	8	8	9
y	7	7	6	5	5	6	5	4	1	0

3.
x	2	3	3	4	5	6	6	7
y	0	1	2	3	3	2	1	0

4.
x	1	2	2	3	3
y	0	1	3	4	5

5.
x	5	6	7	6	6	7	7
y	8	8	7	7	6	6	7

6.
x	5	6	7	7	8
y	3	4	3	1	0

7.
x	9	9	6	5	4
y	7	10	9	8	8

8.
x	3	4
y	4	3

9.
x	6	6
y	5	4

This creature is the result!

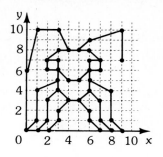

Try these!

1. For this picture you need graph paper 10 squares wide and 15 squares high. Graph each set of points and connect them in order. `sailboat`

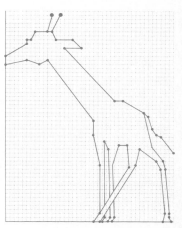

$(0,0)$, $(1,\frac{1}{2})$, $(2,0)$, $(3,\frac{1}{2})$, $(4,0)$, $(5,\frac{1}{2})$, $(6,0)$, $(7,\frac{1}{2})$, $(8,0)$, $(9,\frac{1}{2})$, $(10,0)$

$(4,0)$, $(2,3)$, $(5,2)$, $(10,3)$, $(9,\frac{1}{2})$

$(5,2)$, $(5,3)$, $(2,4)$, $(4,14)$, $(10,4)$, $(5,3)$, $(4,14)$, $(3,15)$, $(1,14)$, $(4,14)$

2. For this picture you need graph paper 40 squares wide and 52 squares high. Graph each set of points and connect them in order. `giraffe`

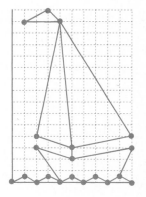

$(0,39)$, $(0,41)$, $(5,44)$, $(5,45)$, $(6,45)$, $(7,47)$, $(11,47)$, $(12,45)$, $(16,45)$, $(18,43)$, $(14,43)$, $(26,30)$, $(28,30)$, $(33,27)$, $(35,18\frac{1}{2})$, $(37\frac{1}{2},15)$, $(38,13)$, $(39,2)$, $(39,1)$, $(39\frac{1}{2},0)$, $(37\frac{1}{2},0)$, $(38,2)$, $(37,13)$, $(36,15)$, $(32,18)$, $(31,14)$, $(22\frac{1}{2},0)$, $(21,0)$, $(22\frac{1}{2},2)$, $(29\frac{1}{2},13\frac{1}{2})$, $(29,19)$, $(27,19)$, $(25\frac{1}{2},14\frac{1}{2})$, $(26,1)$, $(25\frac{1}{2},0)$, $(24\frac{1}{2},0)$, $(25,1)$, $(24\frac{1}{2},18)$, $(23\frac{1}{2},20)$, $(23\frac{1}{2},1)$, $(23,0)$, $(22\frac{1}{2},0)$, $(22\frac{1}{2},14)$, $(21,21\frac{1}{2})$, $(21,25)$, $(10,40)$, $(8,39)$, $(5,40)$, $(0,39)$

$(33,27)$, $(34,26)$, $(35,23)$, $(36,21\frac{1}{2})$, $(37,21)$, $(40,17)$

$(11,51)$, $(10,47)$ Make a large dot at $(11,51)$.

$(13,51)$, $(11,47)$ Make a large dot at $(13,51)$.

2.4 READING BAR GRAPHS

A **bar graph** is used to compare amounts. The graph below shows the number of motorcycles registered in the United States every tenth year since 1920.

Motorcycle Registrations in the United States (to the nearest thousand)

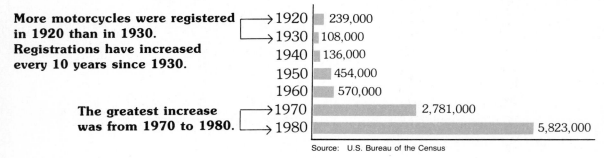

More motorcycles were registered in 1920 than in 1930. Registrations have increased every 10 years since 1930.

The greatest increase was from 1970 to 1980.

1920	239,000
1930	108,000
1940	136,000
1950	454,000
1960	570,000
1970	2,781,000
1980	5,823,000

Source: U.S. Bureau of the Census

By the use of different kinds of bars, as shown below, more than one comparison can be shown on a bar graph.

This graph shows how many homes out of every 1000 had black-and-white television sets and how many had color sets.

Homes (out of Every 1000) With Television Sets

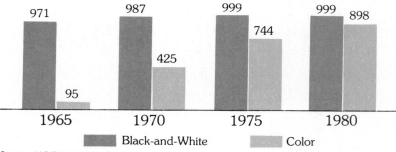

Black-and-White   Color

Source: U.S Bureau of the Census

Another way to show more than one comparison is to make the parts of each bar different in some way.

Average Television Viewing Time (per week)

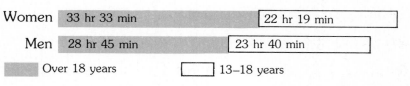

| Women | 33 hr 33 min | 22 hr 19 min |
| Men | 28 hr 45 min | 23 hr 40 min |

Over 18 years   13–18 years

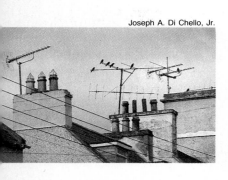

Joseph A. Di Chello, Jr.

EXERCISES

Use the first graph on page 64 to answer these questions.

1. How many motorcycles were registered in 1950? In 1970?
454,000; 2,781,000

2. How do you know that the numbers after the bars do not tell the exact number of motorcycles registered? graph
label (to the nearest thousand)

3. How could you compare the number
of motorcycles registered in two different years if no numbers were listed after the bars? Compare the lengths
of the bars.

Cameramasters

Use the second graph on page 64 to answer these questions.

4. How many homes out of every 1000
had black-and-white television sets in
1965? In 1975? 971; 999

5. How many homes out of every 1000
had color television sets in 1970? In
1980? 425; 898

6. Out of every 1000 homes, the number
with black-and-white TV and the number with color TV both increased from
1965 to 1980. Which increased more?
the number with color TV

7. Do you think that either the number
of black-and-white or the number of
color television sets will ever reach
1000? (Give the reasons for your
answer.) Answers may vary.

8. For any year, how could you find out
how many homes out of every 1000
had no color TV? by subtracting
the number with color TV from
1000

9. women over 18 years, women
13-18 years, men over 18 years,
men 13-18 years

Use the third graph on page 64 to answer these questions.

9. Describe the four groups of people
represented by the graph. See answer
above.

10. Which group watched the most TV
per week? women over 18 years

11. In the group aged 13–18 years, who
watched more TV? men

12. What is the average amount of time a
20-year-old male watches TV in a
week? 28 hr 45 min

65

These two graphs show the same information. Use them to do exercises 13–18.

Graph A: Olympic Games Medal Winners, 1896–1984

Graph B: Olympic Games Medal Winners, 1896–1984

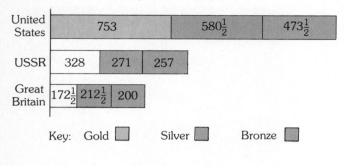

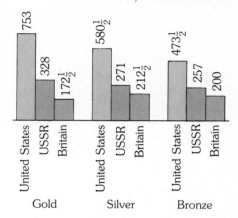

Key: Gold ☐   Silver ▨   Bronze ▨

13. Which graph is better for comparing the *total* number of medals won by each country? Graph A

14. Which graph is better for comparing the number of silver medals won by each country? Graph B

15. Find the total number of medals won by the USSR. 856

16. How many more gold medals has the United States won than the USSR? 425

17. How many more bronze medals has the USSR won than Great Britain? 57

18. Which two countries are more nearly the same in the total number of medals won? USSR and Great Britain

---

SKILLS REFRESHER

Reduce to lowest terms.

				Skill	Page
				32	493

1. $\frac{2}{4}$ $\frac{1}{2}$ **2.** $\frac{6}{10}$ $\frac{3}{5}$ **3.** $\frac{9}{12}$ $\frac{3}{4}$ **4.** $\frac{16}{20}$ $\frac{4}{5}$ 32   493

Find each sum in lowest terms.

5. $\frac{2}{7}+\frac{3}{7}$ $\frac{5}{7}$ **6.** $\frac{2}{4}+\frac{1}{4}$ $\frac{3}{4}$ **7.** $\frac{3}{8}+\frac{3}{8}$ $\frac{3}{4}$ **8.** $\frac{1}{2}+\frac{1}{2}$ 1   37   502

Find each difference in lowest terms.

9. $\frac{3}{4}-\frac{2}{4}$ $\frac{1}{4}$ **10.** $\frac{5}{9}-\frac{1}{9}$ $\frac{4}{9}$ **11.** $\frac{7}{12}-\frac{5}{12}$ $\frac{1}{6}$ **12.** $\frac{3}{10}-\frac{3}{10}$ 0   38   504

Line graphs make it easy to see change. The graph below shows the amount of rainfall El Paso, Texas, received each month.

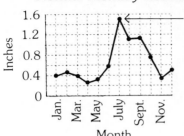

Normal Monthly Rainfall in El Paso, Texas

July has the most rain, about 1.5 inches.

The scale cannot be read exactly—so you must *estimate* each amount.

Source: U.S. National Oceanic and Atmospheric Adm.

Lewis H. Ellsworth/FPG

Changes in several things can be compared by showing more than one line on the same graph. The graph below compares the normal high temperatures of two cities.

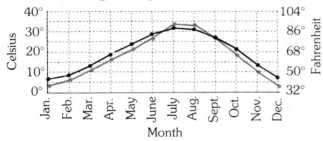

Normal High Temperature for the Month

——— Washington, D.C.

——— Salt Lake City, Utah

Source: U.S. National Oceanic and Atmospheric Adm.

EXERCISES

Refer to the graph of rainfall in El Paso.

1. About how much rain does El Paso have in July? In May? 1.5 in.; 0.3 in.

2. During which month does El Paso have the least rain? April

3. What is the difference between the amount of rainfall in July and the amount of rainfall in March? 1.1 in.

4. Which is the wettest month from May through November? July

5. Which is the wettest month from November through May? December

Refer to the graph of normal high temperatures on page 67.

6. Which city has lower normal winter temperatures? Salt Lake City

7. Which city has higher normal summer temperatures? Salt Lake City

8. Which city has a greater range in normal temperatures over a year's time? Salt Lake City

Marvin L. Dembinsky, Jr.

9. The normal high temperature in Washington in April is about __19__ °C.

10. The normal high temperature in Salt Lake City in June is about __82__ °F.

Refer to the graph of cable television subscribers. The lower part of the scale is not needed. A break or ∿ shows that it is left off.

11. About how many people subscribed to cable television in 1975? In 1981? 9.8; 18.3

12. About how many more people subscribed to cable television in 1983 than in 1979? 11 million

13. Between which two years did the number of cable television subscribers increase the most? 1981 and 1983

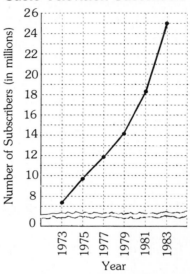

Cable Television Subscribers

Source: Television Digest, Inc., *Statistical Abstract of the United States, 1983–1984*

Refer to the graph of median weekly wages.

14. What was the approximate median weekly earnings of males and females in 1977? In 1981? males: $250, females: $156; males: $347, females: $224

15. From 1976 to 1982, which group had the greater change in median weekly earnings? About how much was the change? males; $140

16. In which year was the difference between male and female median weekly earnings the greatest? 1982

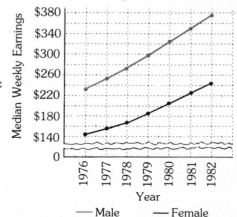

Median Weekly Earnings of Full-Time Workers

— Male   — Female

Source: U.S. Bureau of Labor Statistics, *Statistical Abstract of the United States, 1983–1984*

68

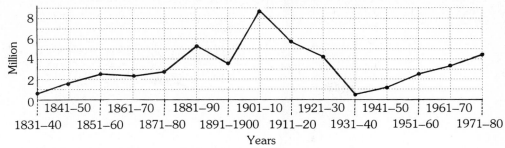

Immigrants Entering the United States   1831–1980

Source: U.S. Immigration and Naturalization Service

17. In which period did fewer immigrants enter the United States, 1961–1970 or 1861–1870? 1861-1870

18. In which period did more immigrants enter the United States, 1841–1850 or 1941–1950? 1841-1850

19. During which 10-year period did the greatest number of immigrants enter the United States? 1901-1910

20. From 1901 to 1940, the number of immigrants entering the United States (rose sharply, stayed about the same, dropped sharply) during each 10-year period.

About how many million immigrants entered the United States during each of these periods? Answers for exercises 21-28 may vary.

21. 1931–1940 0.5   **22.** 1951–1960 2.5   **23.** 1881–1890 5.2

24. 1971–1980 4.4   **25.** 1831–1840 0.6   **26.** 1871–1880 2.8

27. About how many immigrants entered the United States from 1961 to 1980? 7.7 million

28. About how many more immigrants entered the United States from 1841 to 1850 than from 1941 to 1950? 0.5 million

SKILLS REFRESHER

Find each sum in lowest terms.

1. $\frac{1}{2}+\frac{3}{10}$ $\frac{4}{5}$ **2.** $\frac{2}{3}+\frac{5}{8}$ $1\frac{7}{24}$ **3.** $\frac{5}{6}+\frac{1}{4}$ $1\frac{1}{12}$ **4.** $\frac{6}{8}+\frac{3}{4}$ $1\frac{1}{2}$

Skill	Page
40	506

Find each difference in lowest terms.

5. $\frac{2}{3}-\frac{1}{2}$ $\frac{1}{6}$ **6.** $\frac{2}{3}-\frac{1}{6}$ $\frac{1}{2}$ **7.** $\frac{7}{8}-\frac{7}{10}$ $\frac{7}{40}$ **8.** $\frac{9}{10}-\frac{11}{15}$ $\frac{1}{6}$

Blair Seitz/FPG

You can make bar graphs from the information in the tables below. Think of the numbers in each table as a set of ordered pairs.

Motor-Vehicle Deaths

Year	Number of deaths
1960	38,137
1965	49,163
1970	54,633
1975	45,853
1980	52,600

Number of People Speaking Principal Languages of the World

Language	Number of people
Arabic	151,000,000
English	391,000,000
Hindustani	245,000,000
Mandarin (Chinese)	713,000,000
Russian	270,000,000
Spanish	251,000,000

The graph on the left is a *vertical* bar graph because the bars are vertical. The graph on the right is a *horizontal* bar graph because the bars are horizontal.

Motor-Vehicle Deaths

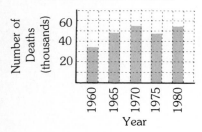

Number of People Speaking Principal Languages of the World

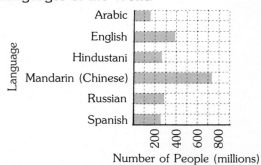

Your teacher asked you to record the temperature at 6 A.M. on five consecutive days. You recorded the following information:

Day	Mon.	Tues.	Wed.	Thurs.	Fri.
Temperature (°C)	8°	10°	0°	1°	5°

You can show the change in the temperature on a line graph.

Step 1: Draw the scales.

Step 2: Look at the table to choose convenient values for each scale.

Step 3: Graph the ordered pairs.

Step 4: Connect the points.

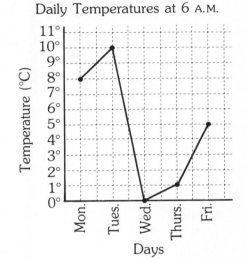

Daily Temperatures at 6 A.M.

EXERCISES

Look at the bar graphs on the bottom of page 70.

1. What do the lengths of the bars in the vertical graph show? numbers of motor-vehicle deaths in thousands

2. How was the length of each bar determined? by using the information in the table of motor-vehicle deaths

3. In the horizontal graph, what do the lengths of the bars show? number of people (in millions) who speak each language

4. Which language is spoken by the most people? Mandarin (Chinese)

5. Make a vertical bar graph from the information in the following table: See students' graphs.

National Parks in the United States

Year	1920	1930	1940	1950	1960	1970	1980
Number	19	28	33	34	37	43	48

See students' graphs for exercises 6-12.

6. Make a horizontal bar graph from the information in the following table:

Magazine	Circulation
Reader's Digest	17,926,542
TV Guide	17,670,543
National Geographic Magazine	10,861,186
Sports Illustrated	2,284,800
Newsweek	2,848,399
Better Homes & Gardens	8,059,717
Seventeen	1,480,236
Good Housekeeping	5,425,790

Make a vertical bar graph from the information in each table below.

7.

Country	Number of operational nuclear reactors
United States	81
Great Britain	32
Japan	25
France	32
Canada	12

8.

Country	Number of daily newspapers
Brazil	299
India	929
West Germany	412
Mexico	325
USSR	686
United States	1829
Turkey	493

Make a separate line graph for each table in exercises 9–12.

9.

Number of units	2	4	6	8	10	12
Price per unit	\$1.20	1.10	1.00	0.85	0.70	0.55

10.

Gallons	0	1	2	3	4
Liters	0	3.8	7.6	11.4	15.1

11.

x	40	50	60	70	80	90	100
y	0	10	15	20	25	30	35

12. The faster you drive, the farther your car travels after you "hit the brakes." This table shows how much farther (on dry pavement).

Driving speed (mi/h)	5	10	15	20	30	40	50	55	60	70
Braking distance (feet)	2	5	12	20	45	80	125	152	180	245

Match each table with the correct line graph below.

13. c

x	0	1	2	3
y	0	2	4	6

14. b

x	0	2	4	6
y	0	1	2	3

15. d

x	0	2	4	6
y	0	4	6	8

16. a

x	0	2	4	6
y	0	1	4	9

a.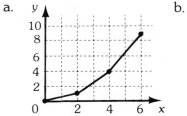

b.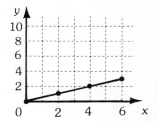

c.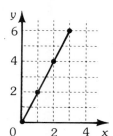

d.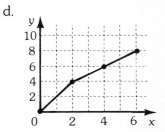

Even though a person knows how to read graphs, a cleverly drawn graph can create an incorrect impression.

Suppose you are the circulation manager for a national magazine. The magazine is published once a month. The following table shows the number of copies sold each month:

Month	Circulation
January	182,165
February	185,765
March	188,348
April	190,221
May	193,054
June	196,436

Month	Circulation
July	198,315
August	201,872
September	204,601
October	208,743
November	212,565
December	215,006

You made a graph to show companies that might advertise in the magazine how circulation has been growing.

Graph A:

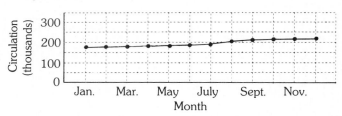

This graph doesn't look very impressive.

After several attempts you make a new graph.

Graph B:

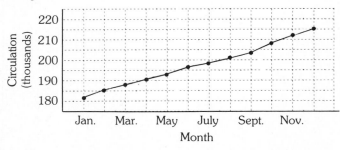

The new graph appears to show that the circulation is growing very rapidly!

"Are you sure the boss hasn't noticed?"

Graphs used in advertisements are designed to make a quick, dramatic impression. Be on the lookout for graphs that create an incorrect impression.

Look at these examples. What has been done in each case to make the second graph look "better" than the first graph?

1. Increase in Land Values, Swampville Estates

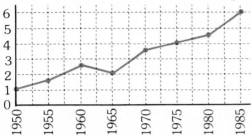 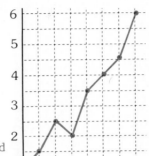

1. The vertical scale was stretched and the horizontal scale condensed to make the line rise more sharply.

2. The scale was changed to begin at 40 to give the impression that Megabucks has several times the sales that the others have.

2. Sales Comparison, Megabucks Advertising Corp.

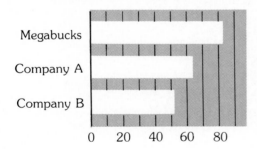 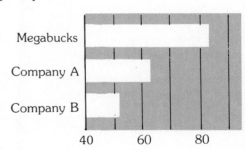

3. The Five-Year Profit Picture, Fly-by-Night Investment Firm

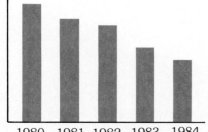 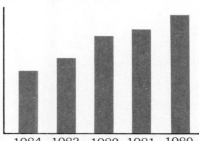

3. The order was changed to make a left-to-right reading give an incorrect impression of increased profit.

In a **pictograph,** a symbol is used to represent a number of objects. The symbol chosen usually gives a clue as to the kind of information that is graphed.

EXERCISES

Refer to the graph at the right.

1. Explain why this graph could be considered a bar graph. Each line of letters could be considered a bar.

2. How many pieces of first-class mail does each small segment of the horizontal scale stand for? 10 billion

3. About how many pieces of first-class mail were handled in 1950? 25 billion

4. Can you tell from the graph whether or not the amount of first-class mail handled went up *every year* from 1970 to 1980? No

Pieces of First-Class Mail
Handled by U.S. Postal Service

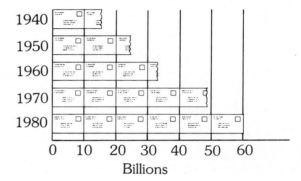

Instead of a numerical scale, a symbol can be used to stand for a number of pieces of mail. The graph below is a pictograph.

5. How many pieces of first-class mail does each 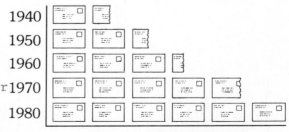 represent? 10 billion

6. Is it as easy to tell from the bottom graph as it is from the top graph about how many pieces of first-class mail were handled in 1970? Why or why not? No; lack of scale makes estimating harder

7. Is it as easy to tell from the bottom graph as it is from the top graph whether more first-class mail was handled in 1960 than in 1980? Yes

8. How many pieces of first-class mail were handled in 1980? 60 billion

Pieces of First-Class Mail
Handled by U.S. Postal Service

Key: Each ⬜ represents 10 billion pieces of first-class mail.

9. About how many more pieces of first-class mail were handled in 1980 than in 1970? 12 billion

Refer to the graph at the right.

Answers for exercises 16-17 may vary.

10. For each year shown, the life expectancies of _men_ and of _women_ are compared.

11. The graph could be considered a (line, bar)) graph.

12. Was men's life expectancy as great as women's in any year shown? No

13. Did men's life expectancy increase as much as women's from 1920 to 1980? No

14. When did men's life expectancy first go over 60 years? 1940

15. When did women's life expectancy first go over 60 years? Over 70 years? 1930; 1950

16. About what was men's life expectancy in 1980? In 1920? 70; 53

17. About what was women's life expectancy in 1950? In 1980? 73; 78

18. In which year was the life expectancy for men and women most nearly the same? 1920

19. If the same number of female and male babies were born, would you expect to find more women over 65 or more men over 65? women

Life Expectancy at Birth in the United States

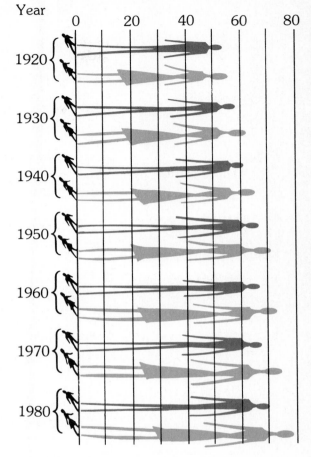

Source: U.S. National Center for Health Statistics

FISHY PICTOGRAPHS

Sometimes drawings of three-dimensional objects of different sizes are used in pictographs. Comparisons are very difficult to make from such drawings.

For example, could you guess that the elephant stands for 5000 species of mammals? How many species of fishes do you think the fish stands for? There are about 20,000 species of fishes.

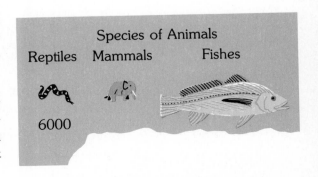

Application 9 may be used at this time.   **77**

Lambert Studios

Sources of Air Pollution

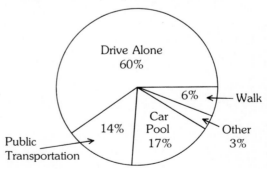

Transportation
60.4%

Garbage Disposal 2.8%

Heating 5.6%

14.0% Industry
17.2%

Generating Electricity

Source: U.S. Public Health Service

A *circle graph* is used to compare parts of a whole. This circle graph shows how different sources of air pollution compare with one another and with the total air pollution.

The interior of the circle stands for the total air pollution, or 100% of the air pollution. This graph shows that 2.8%, or 2.8 parts out of every 100 parts, of air pollution results from garbage disposal (probably by burning).

A quick glance at the graph shows that garbage disposal is the smallest source and transportation is the largest source of air pollution.

Means of Transportation to Work

Drive Alone
60%

6% ← Walk

Public
Transportation

14%

Car
Pool
17%

Other
3%

This graph shows the results of a survey of how people get to work. The interior of the graph represents all the people, or 100% of the people, in the survey.

If 100 people were surveyed, then 14 of them took public transportation.

Suppose 1000 people were surveyed. We know that 1000 is *10 times* as great as 100. So *10 × 14*, or 140, people took public transportation.

Here is how some percents relate to the size of a graph.

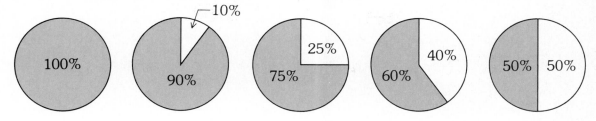

EXERCISES

1. What is the sum of the percents in a circle graph? 100%

2. Suppose a circle graph shows that 28% of those people surveyed enjoy jogging. Thus, _28_ out of every _100_ people surveyed enjoy jogging.

Refer to the top graph on page 78.

3. Which source accounts for 17.2% of all air pollution? industry

4. Which source accounts for more than half of all air pollution? transportation

5. How many tons of air pollution out of every 100 tons are due to heating? 5.6

6. How would a part representing 28% look compared with the part shown for generating electricity? twice as large

Refer to the bottom graph on page 78.

7. How many people out of every 100 drive alone to work? 60

8. Suppose 1000 people were surveyed. How many of them walk to work? 60

9. Suppose 1000 people were surveyed. How many more people drive alone than travel in a car pool? 430

10. What are some ways that people get to work that would be classified as *other*? riding a bicycle or motorcycle, taking a taxi

The graph shows a typical comparison of the costs of operating a one-year-old car.

11. How many cents of every dollar go for maintenance of the car? 6¢

12. How many cents of every dollar go for insurance? 8¢

13. How many dollars of every $100 go for parking fees, tolls, and garage rent? $9

14. How many dollars of every $100 are accounted for by depreciation? $45

15. What does $12 of every $100 go for? taxes

16. What does $20 of every $100 go for? gas and oil

17. If the total operating costs are $100, how much is spent for taxes? $12

18. If the total operating costs are $100, how much is spent for insurance? $8

19. If the total operating costs are $1000, how much is spent for taxes? $120

20. If the total operating costs are $1000, how much is spent for insurance? $80

Costs of Operating a Car

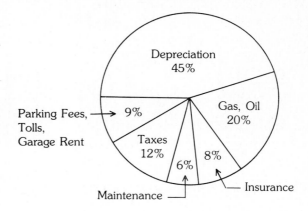

The two graphs below compare the sources of energy used to produce electricity in 1970 with the sources of energy used to produce electricity in 1980. Use the graphs for exercises 21–27.

Electric Energy Production, by Source of Energy

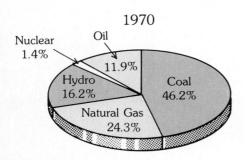

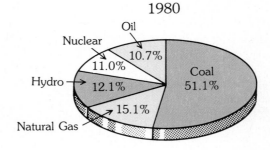

21. In 1970, which source of energy provided the most electricity? The least? coal; nuclear

22. In 1980, which source of energy provided the most electricity? The least? coal; oil

23. From 1970 to 1980, which sources of energy decreased in use? oil, hydro, and natural gas

24. From 1970 to 1980, which sources of energy increased in use? nuclear and coal

25. In 1980, of every 100 kilowatt-hours of electricity produced, how many kilowatt-hours were produced using oil? 10.7

26. In 1980, of every 100 kilowatt-hours of electricity produced, how many kilowatt-hours were produced using natural gas? 15.1

27. In 1980, about half of the electricity was produced using __coal__.

Use the graph below for exercises 28–32.

Age Distribution in the United States

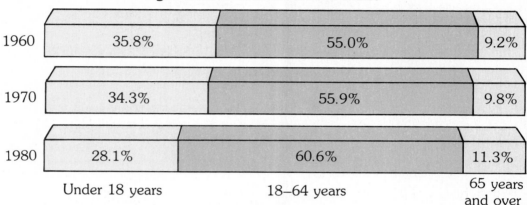

	Under 18 years	18–64 years	65 years and over
1960	35.8%	55.0%	9.2%
1970	34.3%	55.9%	9.8%
1980	28.1%	60.6%	11.3%

28. In 1960, which age group represented the largest share of the population?
18-64 years

29. From 1970 to 1980, which age group had the greatest change?
under 18 years

30. In 1960, how many people out of every 100 were under 18 years old? From 18 to 64 years old? 65 years or older? 35.8; 55; 9.2

31. In 1970, how many people out of every 1000 were under 18 years old? From 18 to 64 years old? 65 years or older? 343; 559; 98

32. In 1980, how many people out of every 10,000 were under 18 years old? From 18 to 64 years old? 65 years or older? 2810; 6060; 1130

Jacqueline Durand

Application 10 may be used at this time.   **81**

Have you ever taken a clock or a watch apart? It isn't hard to do! But when you tried to put it back together again, you may have wished you had a diagram to show where each part came from.

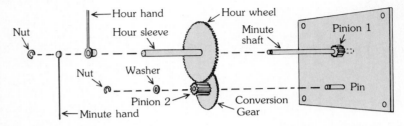

A diagram that shows how the parts of a system fit together is called a **schematic.**

Here is a schematic for assembling some parts of a model airplane. The numbers tell the order of assembling the parts and the arrows show where they go.

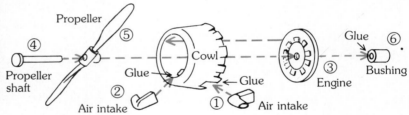

Howard L. Luray/FPG

EXERCISES

Refer to the schematics above.

1. Which parts of the clock go on the minute shaft? hour wheel, hour sleeve, hour hand, minute hand, and nut

2. Which parts go on the pin below the minute shaft? conversion gear, pinion 2, washer, and nut

3. Does the conversion gear go on the pin before the hour wheel goes on the minute shaft, or after? before

4. Which parts of the model airplane are put together first? air intakes and cowl

5. Which parts does the propeller shaft go through? propeller, cowl, engine, and bushing

6. To which parts of the plane is glue applied? cowl and bushing

Refer to the schematic below, which shows how to install the drive unit for a bicycle speedometer.

7. In what order are the fork and the fender brackets put on the axle? *fork, then fender brackets*

8. In what order are the fork and the drive unit put on the axle? *drive unit, then fork*

9. How many washers are shown? *3*

10. How many fender brackets are shown? *2*

11. Which part of the wheel does the axle go through? *cone*

12. What goes on the axle last? *nut*

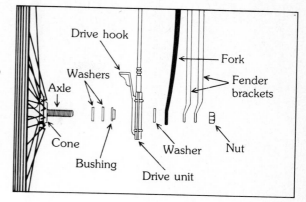

Instructions for macrame and other types of knotting often use schematics. The ones shown here are for some popular necktie knots, as tied by a right-handed person.

Four-in-Hand

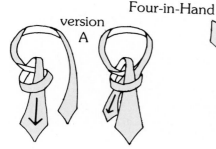

version A

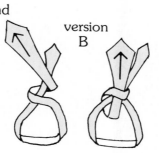

version B

Half-Windsor

13. How can you tell the back of the tie from the front in these schematics? *The back is white.*

14. How do the schematics show which end of the tie is held still and which is moved to make the knot? *The arrow indicates motion.*

15. Which knots are shown from the wearer's point of view? Which are shown from the point of view of a person looking at the wearer? *four-in-hand version B, half-windsor; four-in-hand version A*

16. On which side of the wearer is the narrow end of the tie placed to start each knot, the right or the left? *left*

17. On which side would a left-handed person probably want to start the narrow end of the tie? Why? *right; so the wide end can be moved with the left hand*

18. Tie each knot in a necktie or a piece of cloth around your own neck. Which schematics were easiest to use? (Does point of view make a difference?) *Answers may vary.*

19. Which knot is started by tying a loop in the wide end of the tie? *four-in-hand version A*

20. To start each knot, which end of the tie should be longer, the wide end or the narrow end? *wide end*

The schematic below shows how two switches may be wired to control the same light. Each switch is actually always up or down—there is no middle position. The light is on only when the wires form a closed path from the power source, through the light, and back to the power source. Complete the chart.

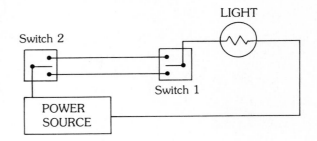

	Switch 1	Switch 2	Light
21.	up	up	on
22.	up	down	off
23.	down	down	on
24.	down	up	off

The schematic shows an electric train system. A train leaves the passenger station going clockwise. It passes the water tower and then returns to the station as soon as possible without going in reverse.

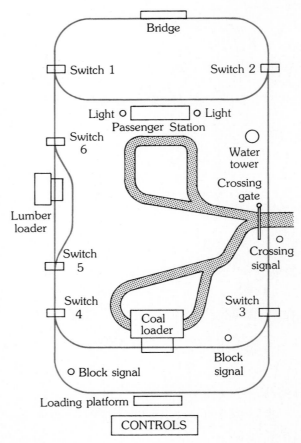

25. How many switches does the train pass? 8 (6 different)

26. How many times does the train have a choice of paths? 4

27. Can the train go to both the coal loader and the lumber loader on this trip? Yes

28. Can the train go to both the coal loader and the loading platform on this trip? No

29. Must the train pass the crossing signal on this trip? Yes

30. Must the train pass a block signal on this trip? Yes

31. How many switches does the train pass twice? 2

32. How many times does the train cross the bridge? 2

84   *Application 11* may be used at this time.

James H. Pickerell

Machine operators and repairers, assemblers, inspectors, and so on, form a large and important part of industry. There are millions of such workers throughout the country, and reading schematics is a needed skill for many of them.

The dashed lines in the schematic below indicate edges that cannot be seen from that particular view.

Part No. 275,
Machine 38

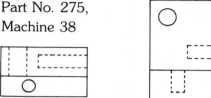

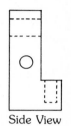

Top View   Front View   Side View

How many holes are there in the piece?   3
How many of them are drilled from the front?   1
From a side? 1 From the bottom? 0 From the top? 1
Do any of the holes go all the way through the piece?
Which ones? Yes; the one drilled from the front

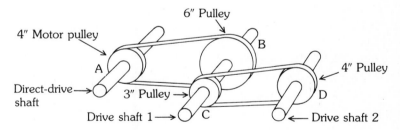

6″ Pulley

4″ Motor pulley

B

A

4″ Pulley

Direct-drive → shaft

3″ Pulley →

D

Drive shaft 1 →   C

Drive shaft 2

How many pulleys are involved in this setup?   4
How many belts? 2 How many shafts? 3
Which pulley "drives" the other pulleys? motor pulley

For which of these purposes can a pulley system be used? a, b, c, and d

a. to transfer power from one place to another

b. to turn several shafts at different rates

c. to transfer power around obstacles

d. to use one motor to drive several machines

85

Refer to the map for exercises 1–2.

1. In which region is each of these?
   a. Old Faithful Geyser   B-1
   b. The Thunderer   A-3
   c. Lewis Lake   C-2
   d. North Entrance   A-2

2. Which regions do not have camping areas (indicated by 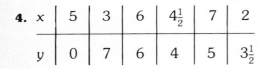)?
   C-1 and C-3

Graph and label each point for exercises 3–4. See students' graphs.

3. (0,2), (6,4), (2,5), (4,1)

4.

x	5	3	6	$4\frac{1}{2}$	7	2
y	0	7	6	4	5	$3\frac{1}{2}$

Refer to the line graph for exercises 5–7. Answers for exercises 5 and 7 may vary.

5. In 1960, the average admission price was about _____.   65¢

6. In which year was the average admission price about $2.05?   1975

7. About how much did the average admission price increase from 1975 to 1980?   65¢
   See students' graphs for exercises 8-9.

8. Make a line graph from this table of cooking times for turkeys.

Weight (lb)	8	10	12	14	16
Cooking time (hr)	$3\frac{1}{2}$	4	$4\frac{1}{2}$	5	$5\frac{1}{2}$

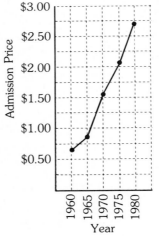

Average Admission Prices at Motion Picture Theaters

2.1

2.2

2.3

2.5

2.6

9. Make a bar graph to show the given information.

Average Annual Snowfall (inches)

Juneau, Alaska	106
Buffalo, New York	94
Denver, Colorado	60
Sault St. Marie, Michigan	112
Burlington, Vermont	79

10. Which sport had the least change in the number of spectators from 1975 to 1980? basketball

11. Which sport had the greatest change in the number of spectators from 1970 to 1980? baseball

12. About how much was the total attendance at professional baseball games for the three years shown? 103 million
(Answers may vary.)

13. If the bar graph were a pictograph in which a symbol stood for five million people, how many symbols would be needed for football in 1970? For baseball in 1975? 2; 6

14. Out of every 100 tons of residential solid waste, how many tons are organic materials? 19

15. More than half of all residential solid waste is _paper_.

16. How many lenses are shown in the schematic? How many prisms? 3; 2

17. Name the parts of the binoculars in the order in which light passes through them to reach the eye. See answer at right.

Use with exercises 10–13.   2.6

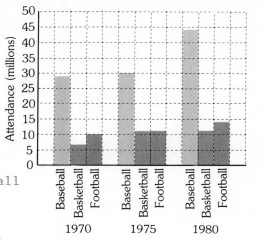

Spectator Attendance at Professional Sports

    2.4

Use with exercises 14–15.

Residential Solid Waste

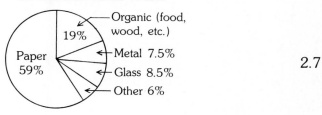

Paper 59%
19%
Organic (food, wood, etc.)
Metal 7.5%
Glass 8.5%
Other 6%

    2.7

Use with exercises 16–17.

Lenses & Prisms in Binoculars

    2.8

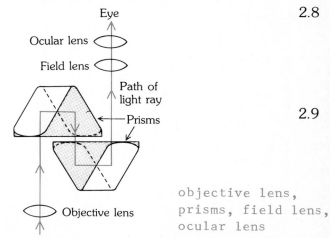

Eye
Ocular lens
Field lens
Path of light ray
Prisms
Objective lens

    2.9

objective lens, prisms, field lens, ocular lens

CHAPTER TEST

Refer to the map for exercises 1–2.

1. In which region is Wrangell located?
C-2

2. Which city is located in region A-2?
Juneau

Graph and label each point for exercises 3–4.
See students' graphs for exercises 3-6.

3. (6,3), (1,5), (3,3), (2,0)

4.

x	4	0	6	$2\frac{1}{2}$	5	2
y	1	3	8	5	$4\frac{1}{2}$	$\frac{1}{2}$

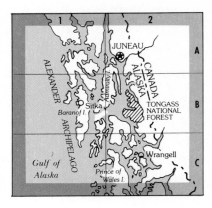

Correlation

Items	Sec
1–2	2.1
3	2.2
4	2.3
5–6	2.6
7	2.7
8–9	2.8
10–11	2.9

5. Make a line graph of the table below.

Stopping Distance of a Car

Speed (km/h)	Distance (m)
30	12
45	20
65	36
80	49
100	80

6. Below are the normal weights (in pounds) of adult males of some animals. Make a bar graph.

Kangaroo	160
Kodiak bear	1100
Gorilla	400
Siberian tiger	580

7. In a pictograph, the symbol ⬚$ stands for $500. How many symbols would be needed for $250? For $3500? $\frac{1}{2}$; 7

8. Out of every 100 people, __30__ prefer to watch a comedy on television.

9. Out of every 1000 people, __250__ prefer to watch a drama on television.

10. How many washers are needed for the faucet?   2

11. Which two parts are pressed together when the water faucet is turned off? washer on valve and seating

Use with exercises 8–9.

Television Programs Preferred

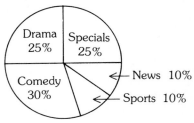

Use with exercises 10–11.

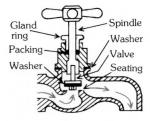

Refer to the bus schedule.

BUS SCHEDULE
OMAHA-LINCOLN

1.1

READ DOWN						READ UP		
503	**4413**	**505**	**1157**	◄—— Bus ——►		**504**	**4416**	**4418**
2 30	8 15	4 00	12 45	Lv **Omaha, Nebr.** Ar	11 40	**5 15**	**8 45**
	8 30			Lv 110th & "I" St. Lv		**5 00**	**8 30**
	f			Lv Millard Lv	f		
	f			Lv Gretna....... Lv	f		
	8 55			Lv Ashland Lv	10 55		
	f			Lv Greenwood ... Lv	f		
	f			Lv Waverly...... Lv	f		
3 40	9 30	5 10	1 55	Ar **Lincoln, Nebr.** Lv	10 25	**4 00**	**7 30**

f—Flag stop. AM—Light Face. **PM—Bold Face.**

1. At what time does bus 4413 leave Omaha? 8:15 A.M.

2. At what time does bus 4416 reach Omaha? 5:15 P.M.

3. At what time is there a bus from Ashland to Lincoln? 8:55 A.M.

4. Which buses make flag stops? 4413 and 504

Use sets A and B to find each mode, median, mean, and range for exercises 5–12.

Set A:

10	9	8
10	8	11
12	11	10
11	10	

Set B:

3	1	2
5	9	1
3	10	9
9	10	10

5. mode (or modes) of set A   10

6. mode (or modes) of set B   9, 10

1.2

7. median of set A   10

8. median of set B   7

1.3

9. mean of set A   10

10. mean of set B   6

1.4

11. range of set A   12-8 or 4

12. range of set B   10-1 or 9

1.5

Use this set of numbers for exercises 13–15.

32, 29, 31, 32, 37, 41, 33, 32, 37, 35, 38, 40, 32, 41

13. Make a frequency table. See answer at right.

14. Use the frequency table to find the median and the mode (or modes). median: 34; mode: 32

15. Use the frequency table to find the mean. 35

16. The normal monthly high temperatures (in degrees Fahrenheit) for Cincinnati are given. Find the mean, the median, and the mode monthly high temperatures.
39.7, 42.7, 51.8, 65.0, 74.4, 83.2, 86.5, 85.8, 79.7, 68.8, 53.2, 42.0 mean: 64.4; median: 66.9; no mode

13.

	F
29	1
31	1
32	4
33	1
35	1
37	2
38	1
40	1
41	2

1.6

1.7

1.8

Estimate the sum by rounding each addend to the nearest hundred. Then find the exact sum.

17. $229 + 187$ 400; 416

18. $305 + 589$ 900; 894

19. $170 + 665$ 900; 835

20. $555 + 76 + 128$ 800; 759

21. You buy four items that sell for $4.84, $3.19, $6.79, and $1.98. Estimate the total cost of the items. Round each amount to the nearest tenth of a dollar. $16.80

Estimate the difference by rounding each amount to the nearest dollar. Then find the exact difference.

22. $3.69 − $0.73 $3; $2.96

23. $8.07 − $3.70 $4; $4.37

24. $42.16 − $27.99 $14; $14.17

25. $61.00 − $26.29 $35; $34.71

26. You do the following computation on a calculator: $807 − 299 = 508$. Estimate the difference to see if your answer is reasonable. Round each number to the nearest hundred.   500; calculator answer is reasonable

Estimate the product by rounding each factor to the nearest ten. Then find the exact product.

27. 32×49 1500; 1568

28. 15×53 1000; 795

29. 31×82 2400; 2542

30. 42×88 3600; 3696

31. A company sold 183 computers at $399 each. Estimate the total sales by rounding each number to the nearest hundred. $80,000

Estimate the quotient by rounding each number to the nearest ten. Then find the exact quotient to the nearest tenth.

32. $18\overline{)79}$ 4; 4.4

33. $31\overline{)208}$ 7; 6.7

34. $24.8\overline{)297}$ 15; 12.0

35. $19.4\overline{)183}$ 9; 9.4

36. A worker is paid $417 for working 41 hours. Estimate the hourly wage. Round $417 to the nearest hundred and 41 to the nearest ten. $10

Refer to the map for exercises 37–38.

37. In which region is each of these?

   a. White Center C-2

   b. Seattle-Tacoma International Airport C-3

   c. Mercer Island B-3

   d. The U.S. Naval Reservation B-1

38. What state park is in region B–1?
Blake Island State Park

39. Graph and label each point.

(3,0), (1,4), (5,5), (4,1), (0,2)
See students' graphs.

40. Graph and label each point.

x	2	3	$4\frac{1}{2}$	6	0	3
y	4	3	1	$2\frac{1}{2}$	5	0

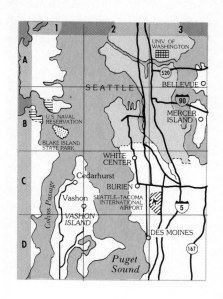

Refer to the bar graph for exercises 41–43.

41. In 1980, which party candidate got the most votes? Republican

42. About how many votes did the Democratic candidate get in 1964? 43 million
(Answers may vary.)

43. In which year did a candidate win by the most votes? 1972

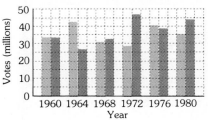

Votes Cast for Major-Party Presidential Candidates

Refer to the line graph for exercises 44–46.

44. For which years is game attendance shown? 1960, 1965, 1970, 1975, and 1980

45. How many people attended college football games in 1980? 36 million

46. About how many more people attended college football games in 1975 than professional football games? 21 million
(Answers may vary.)

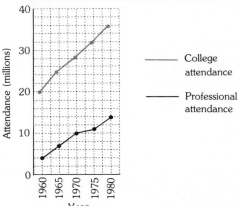

Attendance at Football Games

47. Make a bar graph to show the given information.

2.6

Length of U.S. Bridges, in Feet

Golden Gate	4200
Mackinac Straits	3800
Transbay	2310
George Washington	3500
Tacoma Narrows II	2800
Verrazano Narrows	4260

See students' graphs for exercises 47-48.

48. Make a line graph to show the given information.

Thousands of Miles of Interstate Highway Open to Traffic

Year	1960	1965	1970	1975	1980
Miles (in thousands)	10	21	32	37	40

49. In a pictograph, the symbol ☎ stands for 1000 telephones. How many symbols are needed to represent 5000 telephones? 15,500 telephones? $5; 15\frac{1}{2}$

2.7

Use of Corrective Eye Lenses Among Persons 17–24 Years Old

Refer to the circle graph for exercises 50–51.

2.8

50. Out of every 100 persons 17 to 24 years old, how many do not wear corrective eye lenses? 61

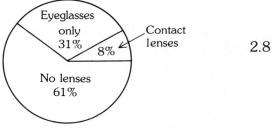

Source: U.S. National Center for Health Statistics

51. How many people out of every 100 in this age group wear contact lenses? 8

Refer to the schematic of a lamp.

2.9

52. Which two parts are connected by the wire? plug and socket

53. When the lamp is put together, what covers the socket? socket shell

54. Which two parts does the coupling connect? lamp base and socket shell

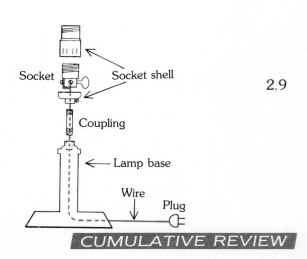

CUMULATIVE REVIEW

Tell if each sentence is true, false, or open.

Correlation

Items	Sec
1–4	3.1
5–7	3.2
8–10	3.3
11–12	3.4
13–14	3.5
15–16	3.6
17–18	3.7
19–20	3.8
21	3.9
22–23	3.10

1. $3+5=2+6$ **2.** $x+8=10$ **3.** $63=7\times8$ **4.** $5n=20$

True   Open   False   Open

Find each answer when x is replaced with 6.

5. $3x$ 18   **6.** $2(x-3)$ 6   **7.** $x(5-3)$ 12

Find each answer.

8. $12+8-4$ 16   **9.** $9+18\div3$ 15   **10.** $3(4)-2(5)$ 2

Use the given formula to solve.

11. A car travels at a rate of 50 miles an hour for 4 hours. What distance does it go? $(d=rt)$

200 mi

12. A rectangle is 5 feet wide and 8 feet long. Find its perimeter. $(P=2\ell+2w)$ 26 ft

Solve and check.

13. $w-8=10$ 18   **14.** $14=x+6$ 8   **15.** $3n=18$ 6

16. $9=\frac{z}{5}$ 45   **17.** $3a+2=14$ 4   **18.** $2=\frac{x}{3}-4$ 18

19. $4y=7$ $\frac{7}{4}$ **20.** $7=5b+4$ $\frac{3}{5}$ **21.** $\frac{4}{5}n=20$ 25

Use the given formula.

22. $w=\frac{11}{2}h-220$
w: weight (pounds)
h: height (inches)

If the formula is used, what is the weight of someone who is 5 feet 8 inches (68 inches) tall?

154 lb

23. $P=tn-c$
P: profit   t: price per ticket
n: number of tickets
c: daily cost

A theater charges $2 per ticket. The daily cost of running the theater is $300. How many tickets must be sold each day to make a profit of $200? 250 tickets

3.1 | OPEN SENTENCES

In both English and mathematics, a sentence can be true, false, or open.

Examples:

| | | Mathematical |
English sentences		sentences

1. George Washington was the first president of the United States. ←— **True** —→ $3 + 7 = 10$

2. Chicago is in Kentucky. ←— **False** —→ $11 - 2 = 4$

┌ **pronoun**

3. She was the first woman to fly solo over the Atlantic. ←— **Open** —→ $x - 4 = 18$
(neither true nor false)

┌ **variable**

The pronoun can be replaced with a name.

The variable can be replaced with a number.

4. Amelia Earhart was the first woman to fly solo over the Atlantic. ←— **True** —→ $22 - 4 = 18$

5. Billie Jean King was the first woman to fly solo over the Atlantic. ←— **False** —→ $10 - 4 = 18$

EXERCISES

1. An __open__ sentence is neither true nor false.

2. A variable can be replaced with a __number__.

Tell if each sentence is true, false, or open.

3. Lake Erie is one of the Great Lakes. True

4. He flew a kite to discover electricity. Open

5. Babe Ruth hit many home runs. True

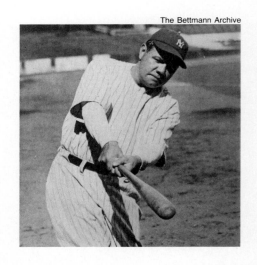

The Bettmann Archive

6. Australia is the largest continent.   False

7. One meter is shorter than one yard.   False

8. It is red and white on the outside and gray on the inside.   Open

9. $7 \times 9 = 63$ True   **10.** $5 + x = 8$ Open   **11.** $6 + 13 = 13 + 6$ True

12. $48 \div 8 = 2 \times 6$ False   **13.** $2 \times a = 12$ Open   **14.** $24 = 4 + y$ Open

Copy and complete the chart.

Open sentence	Variable	Replace variable with 3.	Replace variable with 5.
Example: $n + 5 = 8$	n	$3 + 5 = 8$; True	$5 + 5 = 8$; False
15. $4 + x = 9$	x	4 + 3 = 9; False	4 + 5 = 9; True
16. $8 = 13 - a$	a	8 = 13 - 3; False	8 = 13 - 5; True
17. $12 = 4 \times c$	c	12 = 4 x 3; True	12 = 4 x 5; False
18. $w - 2 = 3$	w	3 - 2 = 3; False	5 - 2 = 3; True
19. $10 = p + 7$	p	10 = 3 + 7; True	10 = 5 + 7; False
20. $5 \times b = 15$	b	5 x 3 = 15; True	5 x 5 = 15; False

Find a replacement to make each sentence true.

21. He is President of the United States right now.   current president

22. It is known as the King of Beasts.   lion

23. It is the smallest state in the United States.   Rhode Island

24. It is a river running through Egypt.   Nile, or any other river in Egypt

25. $4 \times y = 16$ 4   **26.** $15 = a + 7$ 8   **27.** $9 = n - 2$ 11

28. $b = 3 \times 4$ 12   **29.** $7 + x = 10$ 3   **30.** $4 \times w = 24$ 6

3.2 PARENTHESES

One use of parentheses ( ) is to indicate which operation to do first.

Example 1: Find each answer.

a. **(2+3)×4**

      5×4   **Add first.**

      20   **Then multiply.**

b. **2+(3×4)**

      2+12   **Multiply first.**

      14   **Then add.**

A second use of parentheses is to indicate multiplication.

Example 2: Find each answer.

a. 4(7) means 4×7.

    4(7)=28

b. **2(7−3)**

    2(4)   **Subtract first.**

    8   **Then multiply.**

When there is a variable, parentheses are sometimes left out.

Example 3: Replace x with 2 and y with 6. Then find each answer.

a. $5x$ means $5(x)$ or $5 \times x$.

    5(2)   **Replace x.**

    10   **Multiply.**

b. xy means $x(y)$ or $x \times y$.

    2(6)   **Replace x and y.**

    12   **Multiply.**

NOTE: You cannot omit the parentheses when the expression consists only of numbers. $4(7)=28$, but 47 is forty-seven.

EXERCISES

1. In which of these should you multiply first? b and c

   a. $5(4+7)$ b. $8+(3 \times 2)$ c. $(9 \times 8) \div 6$ d. $6(11-9)$

2. Which *two* of the following mean $5 \times x$? a and d

   a. $5(x)$ b. $5 \div x$ c. $\dfrac{5}{x}$ d. $5x$

Place ( ) in each so that the answer is 32.

3. 4 (8)

4. (6 − 2) × 8

5. 2 (1 6)

6. 4 + (4 × 7)

Find each answer.

7. $(2+3) \times 4$ 20

8. $2+(3 \times 4)$ 14

9. 2(7) 14

10. 3(4) 12

11. $5+(2 \times 3)$ 11

12. $(4+1) \times 2$ 10

13. $(7-2) \times 3$ 15

14. $7-(2 \times 3)$ 1

15. $(8-4) \div 2$ 2

16. $6-(4 \div 2)$ 4

17. 2(5+3) 16

18. 3(6−4) 6

19. 4(7+5) 48

20. 5(6+7) 65

21. $7-(3+2)$ 2

22. $(7-3)+2$ 6

23. $12-(4+5)$ 3

24. $(12-4)+5$ 13

Replace n with 2 and x with 5. Then find each answer.

25. $5n$ 10

26. $4x$ 20

27. nx 10

28. xn 10

29. $5(n+2)$ 20

30. $3(n+4)$ 18

31. $4(x-3)$ 8

32. $2(x+4)$ 18

33. $x(5-3)$ 10

34. $n(4+1)$ 10

35. $3(n+x)$ 21

36. $4(x-n)$ 12

Substitute 7 for c in each open sentence. Then tell if the new sentence is true or false.

Examples:

a. $4c=28$

$4(7)=28$ **Replace c with 7.**

$28=28$ **Multiply.**

True

b. $(c-2)+3=4$

$(7-2)+3=4$ **Replace c with 7.**

$5+3=4$ **Subtract first.**

$8=4$ **Then add.**

False

37. $3c=21$ True

38. $4c=11$ False

39. $2(c-2)=7$ False

40. $3(9-c)=6$ True

41. $(c-3)+5=9$ True

42. $(c-5)+3=5$ True

CALCULATOR SKILL on pages 529–530 may be used at this time.

What is the answer to $2+3\times4$?

There are no parentheses to tell what to do first.

If you add first,

$$2+3\times4$$
$$5\times4$$
$$\mathbf{20}$$

You get different answers!

If you multiply first,

$$2+3\times4$$
$$2+12$$
$$\mathbf{14}$$

When there are no parentheses, the following rule applies:

Order of operations:
First multiply and divide in order from left to right.
Then add and subtract in order from left to right.

Then everyone will get the same answer.

14 is the right answer for $2+3\times4$ above.

Example 1: Find each answer.

a. $9-4+2$
$$5+2 \quad \text{Add or subtract}$$
$$7 \quad\;\; \text{from left to right.}$$

b. $12-9\div3$
$$12-3 \quad \text{Divide first.}$$
$$9 \quad\;\; \text{Then subtract.}$$

Example 2: Substitute 8 for x and 6 for y. Then find each answer.

a. $2x+3$
$$2(8)+3 \quad \text{Replace } x \text{ with 8.}$$
$$16+3 \quad \text{Multiply first.}$$
$$19 \quad\;\; \text{Then add.}$$

b. $\dfrac{y}{2}-1$
$$\dfrac{6}{2}-1 \quad \text{Replace } y \text{ with 6.}$$
$$3-1 \quad \text{Divide first.}$$
$$2 \quad\;\; \text{Then subtract.}$$

EXERCISES

Tell what should be done first to find each answer.

1. $2+3\times4$ Multiply

2. $9-4+2$ Subtract

3. $12-9\div3$ Divide

4. $\frac{12}{3}\times2$ Divide

5. $8+2\times3$ Multiply

6. $8-2(3)$ Multiply

Find each answer.

7. $18-7+5$ 16

8. $23-2+4$ 25

9. $5\times4+7$ 27

10. $3+6\times4$ 27

11. $16\div2\times4$ 32

12. $12\div2\times3$ 18

13. $8+\frac{12}{4}$ 11

14. $\frac{15}{3}+2$ 7

15. $8-3(2)$ 2

16. $10-2(3)$ 4

17. $4(5)+8$ 28

18. $5(2)+3$ 13

19. $5(4)-2$ 18

20. $2(5)-3$ 7

21. $8-4-2$ 2

22. $9-5-3$ 1

23. $2(3)+4\div2$ 8

24. $8\div2+3(2)$ 10

Substitute 8 for x and 6 for y. Then find each answer.

25. $2x+1$ 17

26. $5+3y$ 23

27. $5y-7$ 23

28. $4x-5$ 27

29. $\frac{y}{3}+9$ 11

30. $5+\frac{x}{2}$ 9

31. $2x+3y$ 34

32. $4y-x$ 16

33. $xy+2$ 50

34. $50-xy$ 2

35. $9-\frac{24}{x}$ 6

36. $\frac{18}{y}-3$ 0

Substitute 5 for n in each open sentence. Then tell if the new sentence is true or false.

37. $3n+2=17$ True

38. $4n+2=27$ False

39. $6n-4=34$ False

40. $5n-3=22$ True

41. $21=3(n+2)$ True

42. $16=4(n-1)$ True

43. $25=2n+3n$ True

44. $25=4n-2n$ False

45. $65\div n=2n$ False

I will grant any wish if you bring me a 5!

But, alas, you have only a 3. Luckily, you can change your number each time you come to a blue expression passage. Use your number to evaluate the expression and continue on with the new value.

Example: You have a 3. You come to $4x - 5$. $4(3) - 5 = 12 - 5 = 7$. You continue with a 7.

Can you find a path that gets you to the gate with a 5?

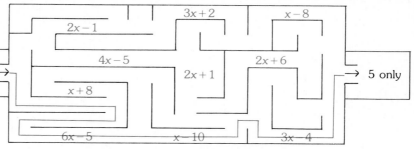

Start with 3. → 5 only

$2x - 1$ $3x + 2$ $x - 8$ $4x - 5$ $2x + 1$ $2x + 6$ $x + 8$ $6x - 5$ $x - 10$ $3x - 4$

If you started with a 2, a 4, or a 5, you could also reach the end with a 5. Can you find those paths? Typical solutions are given above and below. Other solutions are possible.

PUZZLE = 13,628,160

Start with 2.

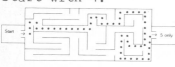

Start with 4.

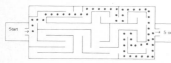

Start with 5.

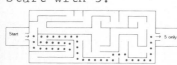

Give each letter of the alphabet the value of its position: a is 1, b is 2, and so on up to z is 26. Since writing no symbol between letters means to multiply, you can find the "value" of a word.

Example: $and = 1(14)(4)$
$= 14(4)$
$= 56$ The value of *and* is 56.

1. Find the value of each of these:

up 336   for 1620   bean 140   money 341,250

Answers for exercises 2-3 will vary.

2. Find the value of your first name.

3. Who has the most "value-able" name in the class?

4. Check to see if the title "Puzzle = 13,628,160" is correct.

Title is correct.

3.4 USING FORMULAS

A formula is a rule or a principle written as a mathematical sentence.

Principle:
To find the distance an object travels, multiply its rate of speed by the time it travels.

Formula:

$$d = rt$$

distance   rate   time

Example 1: How far will a car go in 3 hours at 50 miles per hour (mi/h)?

$d = rt$	**Write the formula.**
$d = 50(3)$	**Substitute the given values.** **The rate r is 50. The time t is 3.**
$d = 150$	**Multiply.**

The car will go 150 miles.

Example 2: A person's *approximate* normal blood pressure can be found by dividing the person's age by 2 and adding 110.

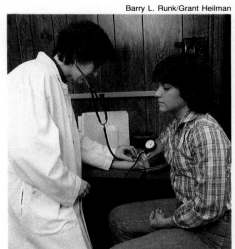

Barry L. Runk/Grant Heilman

blood pressure   age

$$P = \frac{a}{2} + 110$$

Find the blood pressure of an average 16-year-old.

$P = \frac{a}{2} + 110$	**Write the formula.**
$P = \frac{16}{2} + 110$	**Substitute the given values.** **The age a is 16.**
$P = 8 + 110$	**Divide first.**
$P = 118$	**Then add.**

A 16-year-old's blood pressure is about 118.

EXERCISES

1. A formula is a rule or a principle written as a ___mathematical sentence___.

2. Tell what each formula is used for.

    a. $d = rt$ finding distance for a given rate and time

    b. $P = \frac{a}{2} + 110$ finding blood pressure for a given age

Use the formula $P = \frac{a}{2} + 110$. Find the blood pressure P for a person with a given age a.

3. 14 years old 117

4. 24 years old 122

5. 30 years old 125

6. 60 years old 140

Use the formula $d = rt$. Find the distance d for the given rate r and time t.

7. Car: 40 miles per hour
           2 hours 80 mi

8. Car: 70 kilometers per hour
           3 hours 210 km

9. Jet: 600 miles per hour
        4 hours 2400 mi

10. Turtle: 5 centimeters per minute
             10 minutes 50 cm

Use the formula $x = ab + c$. Find x for each a, b, and c.

Example: a is 5, b is 4, and c is 9.

$x = ab + c$ **Write the formula.**
$x = 5(4) + 9$ **Substitute.**
$x = 20 + 9$ **Multiply.**
$x = 29$ **Add.**

	a	b	c	
11.	2	9	7	25
12.	4	5	8	28
13.	3	9	1	28
14.	6	7	14	56

Use the formula $d = 1100t$ to find the distance to a storm.

$d = 1100t$
d: distance (in feet)
t: time (in seconds)

15. You hear thunder 3 seconds after you see lightning. How far away is the storm? 3300 ft

16. How far away is the storm if there are 5 seconds between the lightning and the thunder? 5500 ft

Charles R. Potter/FPG

Find how far each car can go.

$d = mg$
d: distance (in miles)
m: miles per gallon   **g:** number of gallons

17. How far can a car go on 16 gallons of gas if it gets 21 miles per gallon? 336 mi

18. A car gets 18 miles per gallon. How far can it go on 15 gallons? 270 mi

Use the formula for the perimeter of a rectangle.

$P = 2\ell + 2w$
P: perimeter   **ℓ:** length   **w:** width

19. Find the perimeter of a room 12 feet wide and 18 feet long. 60 ft

20. How much fence is needed to enclose a lot that is 9 meters wide and 15 meters long? 48 m

---

SKILLS REFRESHER

Add.

						Skill	Page
1.	24 +39 63	**2.**	327 +408 735	**3.**	7.50 +6.27 13.77	**4.** 14.95 + 6.26 21.21	5 6	452 454

Subtract.

						Skill	Page
5.	32 −19 13	**6.**	519 −324 195	**7.**	8.25 −1.99 6.26	**8.** 34.25 − 9.08 25.17	7 8	456 458

3.5 EQUATIONS WITH ADDITION OR SUBTRACTION

A mathematical sentence containing an equal sign (=) is called an **equation.**

Example 1: Solve $n+4=7$.

To solve an equation means to find the number or numbers that can replace the variable and make the sentence true. When solving an equation, you must keep it in "balance."

$n+4=7$

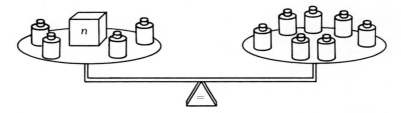

There are 4 weights on the side with n. To find n, remove these 4 weights. To keep the balance, you must also remove 4 weights from the other side.

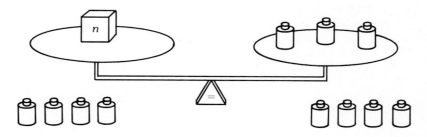

The solution can be written like this.

$$n+4=\ \ \ 7 \quad \text{Write the equation.}$$
$$\underline{-4 \quad -4} \quad \text{Subtract 4 from each side.}$$
$$n\ \ =\ \ 3$$

It is always a good idea to check.

Check: $n+4=7$ **Write the equation.**

        $3+4=7$ **Replace n with 3.**

           $7=7$ ✔ **(It checks.)**

Example 2: Solve $23 = x + 17$.

$$
\begin{array}{ll}
23 = x + 17 & \text{Notice 17 is added to } x. \\
& \text{To } \textit{undo} \text{ this, subtract 17.} \\
\underline{-17 \quad -17} & \text{Subtract 17 from each side.} \\
6 = x &
\end{array}
$$

Check: $23 = x + 17$
$23 = 6 + 17$
$23 = 23$ ✔

Example 3: Solve $y - 8 = 12$.

		Notice 8 is subtracted from y.
This step does	$y - 8 = 12$	To *undo* this, add 8.
not have to be ⟶	$\underline{+8 \quad +8}$	Add 8 to each side.
written.	$y = 20$	

Check: $y - 8 = 12$
$20 - 8 = 12$
$12 = 12$ ✔

EXERCISES

What number should be added to or subtracted from each side?

1. $x + 9 = 13$ Subtract 9. **2.** $16 = y - 8$ Add 8. **3.** $w - 9 = 4$ Add 9.

4. $a + 2 = 27$ Subtract 2. **5.** $19 = b + 2$ Subtract 2. **6.** $8 + t = 18$ Subtract 8.

Solve and check each equation.

7. $x + 15 = 22$ 7 **8.** $8 = y + 6$ 2 **9.** $a - 9 = 4$ 13

10. $w - 4 = 11$ 15 **11.** $36 = x + 16$ 20 **12.** $b - 14 = 14$ 28

13. $27 = n - 13$ 40 **14.** $p - 22 = 48$ 70 **15.** $34 = n + 11$ 23

16. $56 = d + 25$ 31 **17.** $c - 56 = 4$ 60 **18.** $85 = z + 83$ 2

Solve and check each equation.

19. $w - 156 = 39$ 195   **20.** $234 = c + 83$ 151

21. $x + 32 = 142$ 110   **22.** $29 = s - 189$ 218

23. $145 = m - 399$ 544   **24.** $a + 279 = 486$ 207

Equations with decimals can be solved the same way.

Example:
$$8.4 = x - 5.5$$
$$\underline{+5.5 \quad\quad +5.5} \quad \textbf{Add 5.5 to each side.}$$
$$13.9 = x$$

Solve and check.

25. $7.9 = y + 2.8$ 5.1   **26.** $c + 2.5 = 7.7$ 5.2

27. $p - 6.50 = 9.95$ 16.45   **28.** $7.66 = b - 2.33$ 9.99

29. $w + 3.55 = 7.00$ 3.45   **30.** $8.45 = x + 4.55$ 3.90

For each exercise, substitute the given values into the formula. Then solve for the remaining variable.

Example: $a = b + c$, a is 28, c is 13.

$$a = b + c \quad \textbf{Write the formula.}$$
$$28 = b + 13 \quad \textbf{Substitute the given values.}$$
$$\underline{-13 \quad\quad -13} \quad \textbf{Subtract 13 from each side.}$$
$$15 = b \quad \textbf{So } b \textbf{ is 15.}$$

	$a = b + c$				$x = y - z$	
	a	b	c		x	y	z
31.	93	17	76	**35.**	6	14	8
32.	49	37	12	**36.**	54	76	22
33.	37	28	9	**37.**	87	111	24
34.	10.25	7.40	2.85	**38.**	10.25	12.50	2.25

106

Use the given formula to solve.

retail price = wholesale price + markup

$$p = w + m$$

39. A salesclerk must put a $3 markup on a sweater that costs $12 wholesale. What should the retail price be? $15

40. A jacket has a retail price of $32. The store's markup is $11. What is the wholesale price? $21

41. A tennis racket has a retail price of $26 and a wholesale price of $18. What is the markup? $8

sale price = regular price − discount (markdown)

$$s = p - d$$

42. An album that regularly sells for $8.98 is marked down by $2.49. What is the sale price? $6.49

43. A rug is on sale for $42.50. The discount from the regular price is $12.60. Find the regular price. $55.10

amount = principal + interest

$$a = p + i$$

44. An account opened two years ago with a principal of $240 now has an amount of $291.68. Find the interest. $51.68

Write an equation and solve.

45. If you add 15 to x, you get 34. What is x? x + 15 = 34
          x = 19

46. If you subtract 18 from y, you get 26. What is y? y - 18 = 26
          y = 44

SKILLS REFRESHER

Multiply.

				Skill	Page
1. 24 × 17	**2.** 4.5 × 3.2	**3.** 12(254)	**4.** 6.7(1.25)	12	464
408	14.40	3048	8.375	14	468

Divide.

				Skill	Page
5. 96 ÷ 8	**6.** 312 ÷ 13	**7.** $\frac{135}{9}$	**8.** $\frac{560}{35}$	18	472
12	24	15	16	19	474

A plane flies 1700 kilometers from Chicago to Denver in 2 hours. What is its average rate of speed?

To solve this, use the formula $d = rt$.

$d = rt$ **Write the formula.**

The distance d is 1700 kilometers. The time t is 2 hours.

$1700 = r(2)$ **Substitute the given values into the formula.**

In writing the product of a variable and a number, write the number first.

$1700 = 2r$ **Change the order of the multiplication.**

Now solve the equation.

Example 1: Solve $1700 = 2r$.

Notice r is multiplied by 2.

$1700 = 2r$ **To undo this, divide by 2.**

$\dfrac{1700}{2} = \dfrac{2r}{2}$ **Divide each side by 2.**

$850 = r$

The plane's speed is 850 kilometers per hour (km/h).

Check: $1700 = 2r$

$1700 = 2(850)$

$1700 = 1700$ ✔

Example 2: Solve $\frac{a}{3} = 15$.

$\frac{a}{3} = 15$ **Notice a is divided by 3.**
To *undo* this, multiply by 3.

$3\left(\frac{a}{3}\right) = 3(15)$ **Multiply each side by 3.**

$a = 45$

Check: $\frac{a}{3} = 15$

$\frac{45}{3} = 15$

$15 = 15$ ✔

EXERCISES

By what number should each side be multiplied or divided?

1. $4y = 96$ Divide by 4.   **2.** $36 = 12b$ Divide by 12.   **3.** $14 = \frac{x}{4}$ Multiply by 4.

4. $\frac{c}{9} = 7$ Multiply by 9.   **5.** $23 = \frac{w}{6}$ Multiply by 6.   **6.** $5t = 65$ Divide by 5.

Solve and check each equation.

7. $3x = 18$ 6   **8.** $4a = 96$ 24   **9.** $50 = 10w$ 5   **10.** $2y = 128$ 64

11. $\frac{b}{4} = 10$ 40   **12.** $17 = \frac{y}{3}$ 51   **13.** $6d = 126$ 21   **14.** $245 = 7p$ 35

15. $17m = 289$ 17   **16.** $256 = 16n$ 16   **17.** $8 = \frac{a}{24}$ 192   **18.** $\frac{x}{13} = 9$ 117

For each exercise, substitute the given values into the formula. Then solve for the remaining variable.

$a = bc$

	a	b	c
19.	92	4	23
20.	104	8	13
21.	126	9	14

$\frac{x}{y} = z$

	x	y	z
22.	102	6	17
23.	84	7	12
24.	133	19	7

Equations with decimals can be solved in the same way.

Example: $3x = 1.74$

$$\frac{3x}{3} = \frac{1.74}{3} \longleftarrow \quad 3\overline{)1.74}$$

$$x = 0.58$$

$$\begin{array}{r} 0.58 \\ 3\overline{)1.74} \\ \underline{1\,5} \\ 24 \\ \underline{24} \\ 0 \end{array}$$

Solve and check each equation.

25. $3y = 4.23$ 1.41

26. $4n = 9.60$ 2.40

27. $8.46 = 6w$ 1.41

28. $24.95 = 5p$ 4.99

29. $\frac{a}{4} = 12.50$ 50

30. $4.75 = \frac{b}{12}$ 57

Use the given formula to solve.

distance = rate × time
$$d = rt$$

31. If a car goes 168 miles in 4 hours, what is its average rate of speed? $42\ mi/h$

32. A car can keep up a rate of 76 km/h on a certain road. How much time will a 304-kilometer trip take? $4\ hr$

machine's output = machine's rate × running time
$$M = r \times t$$

33. A machine produces metal parts at the rate of 16 per minute. How long will it take the machine to produce 400 parts? $25\ min$

34. A postage meter can stamp and seal envelopes at the rate of 8 per second. How long will it take to do 2400 envelopes? Give the answer in minutes. $5\ min$

A light plane will glide about 1 mile for every 500 feet of altitude.

distance (in miles) $\searrow d = \dfrac{a}{500} \longleftarrow$ **altitude (in feet)**

35. How far will a plane glide for an altitude of 6000 feet? $12\ mi$

36. A plane has an engine failure 15 miles from the closest airport. How high would it have to be in order to glide safely to the airport? $7500\ ft$

Brent Jones

total wages = hourly pay × time
$$W = p \times t$$

37. For an 8-hour day, Denise's wages were $98.00. What was her hourly rate? $12.25

38. At $4 an hour, how many hours would you have to work to make $50? 12.5 hr

Write an equation and solve.

39. 7 times a number *n* is 105. Find the number. $7n = 105$; $n = 15$

40. If you divide *y* by 6, you get 14. What is *y*? $\frac{y}{6} = 14$, $y = 84$

41. A number *b* divided by 12 is 9. Find the number. $\frac{b}{12} = 9$; $b = 108$

42. The product of 4 and a number *a* is 396. Find *a*. $4a = 396$; $a = 99$

SLIPPERY SAM

A frog fell into a 20-foot well. It started climbing up the wall to escape. It climbed 5 feet the first day, but slipped back 4 feet during the night. Each day it climbed up 5 feet and slipped back 4 during the night. How many days will it take the frog to climb out of the well? (HINT: The answer is not 20.) 16 days

Mary Elenz Tranter

Example 1: Solve $3x - 2 = 19$.

If x in $3x - 2$ is replaced with a number, you should *first* multiply by 3 and then subtract 2. To solve the equation, you should undo these operations in the *reverse* order.

$$3x - 2 = 19 \quad \text{First } undo \text{ ``subtract 2.''}$$
$$\underline{+2 \quad +2} \quad \textbf{Add 2 to each side.}$$
$$3x \quad = 21 \quad \text{Then } undo \text{ ``multiply by 3.''}$$

$$\frac{3x}{3} = \frac{21}{3} \quad \textbf{Divide each side by 3.}$$

$$x = 7$$

Check: $3x - 2 = 19$ **Notice that in the**
$\quad\quad 3(7) - 2 = 19$ **check the opera-**
$\quad\quad 21 - 2 = 19$ **tions are done in**
$\quad\quad 19 = 19$ ✔   **the usual order.**

Example 2: Solve $8 = \frac{c}{4} + 5$.

$$8 = \frac{c}{4} + 5$$
$$\underline{-5 \quad\quad -5} \quad \textbf{Subtract 5 from each side.}$$
$$3 = \frac{c}{4}$$

$$4(3) = 4\left(\frac{c}{4}\right) \quad \textbf{Multiply each side by 4.}$$

$$12 = c$$

Check: $8 = \frac{c}{4} + 5$

$$8 = \frac{12}{4} + 5$$
$$8 = 3 + 5$$
$$8 = 8 \quad ✔$$

112

Example 3: You have 80 feet of fence to enclose a rectangular garden. If you make it 14 feet wide, how long will it be?

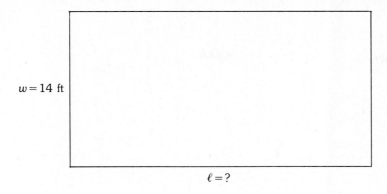

$w = 14$ ft

$\ell = ?$

Perimeter $= 80$ ft

$P = 2\ell + 2w$ **Write the formula.**

$80 = 2\ell + 2(14)$ **Substitute the given values.**

$80 = 2\ell + 28$

$\underline{-28 \qquad -28}$ **Subtract 28 from each side.**

$52 = 2\ell$

$\dfrac{52}{2} = \dfrac{2\ell}{2}$ **Divide each side by 2.**

$26 = \ell$

The garden will be 26 feet long.

EXERCISES

Tell (a) what number you would add or subtract and (b) by what number you would then multiply or divide.

1. $6x + 5 = 17$ Subtract 5; divide by 6.

2. $5y - 7 = 13$ Add 7; divide by 5.

3. $\frac{w}{4} - 2 = 9$ Add 2; multiply by 4.

4. $\frac{h}{2} + 8 = 12$ Subtract 8; multiply by 2.

5. $16 = 3a - 2$ Add 2; divide by 3.

6. $17 = 2t + 3$ Subtract 3; divide by 2.

7. $20 = \frac{c}{9} + 6$ Subtract 6; multiply by 9.

8. $2 = \frac{m}{7} - 8$ Add 8; multiply by 7.

9. $40 = 2w + 2(9)$ Subtract 18; divide by 2.

10. $4p + 2(6) = 32$ Subtract 12; divide by 4.

113

Solve and check each equation.

11. $2x + 3 = 21$ 9

12. $5b + 4 = 19$ 3

13. $4a - 6 = 22$ 7

14. $3w - 9 = 6$ 5

15. $35 = 8t - 5$ 5

16. $20 = 6z + 2$ 3

17. $5 = \frac{w}{3} - 7$ 36

18. $14 = \frac{s}{5} + 6$ 40

19. $14 = \frac{n}{4} + 10$ 16

20. $16 = \frac{t}{7} - 3$ 133

21. $\frac{m}{13} - 2 = 8$ 130

22. $\frac{r}{9} + 4 = 10$ 54

23. $2d - 9 = 19$ 14

24. $12x + 12 = 12$ 0

25. $48 = 4x + 3(4)$ 9

26. $31 = 3m + 2(8)$ 5

27. $5x - 17 = 68$ 17

28. $\frac{n}{6} + 13 = 55$ 252

For each exercise, substitute the given values into the formula. Then solve for the remaining variable.

	$ab + c = d$					$w = xy - z$			
	a	b	c	d		w	x	y	z
29.	5	12	7	_67_	**34.**	17	3	_7_	4
30.	3	_8_	4	28	**35.**	_17_	4	8	15
31.	6	_3_	8	26	**36.**	25	_9_	4	11
32.	2	7	_26_	40	**37.**	22	5	_6_	8
33.	_4_	2	5	13	**38.**	_11_	2	9	7

Use the given formula to solve.

perimeter = twice length + twice width
$$P = 2\ell + 2w$$

39. The perimeter of a rectangle is 48 feet. The width is 10 feet. Find the length.
14 ft

40. Mike put a fence around his rectangular backyard. He used 36 meters of fence. If his yard is 7 meters wide, how long is it? 11 m

blood pressure   age

$$P = \frac{a}{2} + 110$$

41. Find about how old a person is if that person's blood pressure is 122. *24 years*

42. Theresa's blood pressure is 134. According to the formula, how old is she? *48 years*

For any container filled with equal-weight objects:

full weight	=	**weight of each object**	×	**number of objects**	+	**weight of empty container**

$$W = wn + c$$

43. Metal parts weighing 3 kilograms apiece are packed in a crate that weighs 14 kilograms empty. A shipping clerk finds the full crate weighs 80 kilograms. How many parts are in the crate? *22 parts*

44. Suppose an apple weighs 54 grams and an empty basket weighs 250 grams. How many apples are in a full basket that weighs 1600 grams?

25 apples

Betty Davis/FPG

For any area cut into pieces of the same size:

whole area = area of each piece × number of pieces

$$A = an$$

odd-shaped piece
16 in²

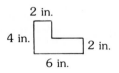
2 in.
4 in.
2 in.
6 in.

steel sheet
192 in²

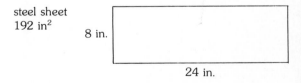
8 in.
24 in.

45. A sheet-metal worker is cutting copies of an odd-shaped piece from a steel sheet. The piece has an area of 16 square inches. The whole sheet has an area of 192 square inches. How many pieces should there be? *12 pieces*

46. Make a drawing that shows the arrangement of pieces on the sheet to verify your answer for exercise 45.
Typical answers:

 or

Copy the puzzle onto graph paper. Use the equations to complete it.

1. 1	**2.** 2		**3.** 9		**4.** 3 · **5.** 6
6. 3 · 5			**7.** 9	**8.** 4		**9.** 5
10. 2		**11.** 1 · 9			**12.** 4 · 0
	13. 6 · 7			**14.** 3 · 2	
15. 5 · 4			**16.** 1 · 6		**17.** 4
18. 7		**19.** 2 · 2			**20.** 2 · 6
21. 6 · **22.** 3			**23.** 5		**24.** 4 · 0

Across

1. $3x = 36$

3. $40 = 4a + 4$

4. $40 = b + 4$

6. $2x - 3 = 67$

7. $n + 6 = 100$

9. $17 = 4b - 3$

10. $7m + 6 = 20$

11. $40 = 2y + 2$

12. $6t = 240$

13. $w + 3 = 70$

14. $4 = \frac{n}{8}$

15. $30 = \frac{x}{2} + 3$

16. $2b - 16 = 16$

17. $30 = 7x + 2$

18. $30 = 4x + 2$

19. $\frac{c}{2} = 11$

20. $r - 6 = 20$

21. $\frac{a}{7} = 9$

23. $17 = 4b - 3$

24. $100 = 2y + 20$

Down

1. $\frac{n}{12} = 11$

2. $100 = 4p$

3. $w + 1 = 1000$

4. $30 = 8t + 6$

5. $\frac{z}{13} = 50$

8. $20 = 6y - 4$

11. $2d + 3 = 37$

12. $\frac{w}{6} + 3 = 10$

13. $\frac{m}{8} = 8$

14. $75 = 2d + 3$

15. $36 = \frac{x}{16}$

16. $1000 = 8a$

17. $\frac{r}{2} + 20 = 250$

19. $13 = 5x + 3$

20. $3d + 3 = 75$

22. $4q + 4 = 16$

Write as mixed numbers.

				Skill	Page
1. $\frac{24}{5}$ $4\frac{4}{5}$	**2.** $\frac{37}{8}$ $4\frac{5}{8}$	**3.** $\frac{21}{9}$ $2\frac{1}{3}$	**4.** $\frac{26}{8}$ $3\frac{1}{4}$	28	487

Multiply.

				Skill	Page
5. $3\left(\frac{5}{3}\right)$ 5	**6.** $6\left(\frac{5}{6}\right)$ 5	**7.** $4\left(\frac{5}{2}\right)$ 10	**8.** $8\left(\frac{7}{4}\right)$ 14	33	494

3.8 EQUATIONS WITH FRACTIONAL SOLUTIONS

Most of the equations you have solved so far have had whole-number solutions. When solving problems, many equations have fraction or decimal solutions.

Example 1: Solve $5a + 4 = 13$.

$$5a + 4 = 13$$
$$\underline{-4-4} \quad \text{Subtract 4 from each side.}$$
$$5a = 9$$

$$\frac{5a}{5} = \frac{9}{5} \quad \text{Divide each side by 5.}$$

$$a = \frac{9}{5}, \text{ or } 1.8$$

Richard Wood/Taurus

The check can be done with either fractions or decimals.

Check by using fractions:
$$5a + 4 = 13$$
$$5\left(\frac{9}{5}\right) + 4 = 13$$
$$\frac{45}{5} + 4 = 13$$
$$9 + 4 = 13$$
$$13 = 13 \quad \checkmark$$

Check by using decimals:
$$5a + 4 = 13$$
$$5(1.8) + 4 = 13$$
$$9.0 + 4 = 13$$
$$9 + 4 = 13$$
$$13 = 13 \quad \checkmark$$

Example 2: Solve $3x + 1.65 = 6$.

Notice that the decimal point and 0's are included for the subtraction.

$$3x + 1.65 = 6.00$$
$$\underline{-1.65-1.65} \quad \text{Subtract 1.65 from each side.}$$
$$3x = 4.35$$

$$\frac{3x}{3} = \frac{4.35}{3} \quad \text{Divide each side by 3.}$$

$$x = 1.45$$

Check:
$$3x + 1.65 = 6$$
$$3(1.45) + 1.65 = 6$$
$$4.35 + 1.65 = 6$$
$$6.00 = 6 \quad \checkmark$$

EXERCISES

Solve and check each one-step equation.

1. $4x = 9$ $\frac{9}{4}$

2. $8n = 13$ $\frac{13}{8}$

3. $14 = 3y$ $\frac{14}{3}$

4. $7 = 9b$ $\frac{7}{9}$

5. $w + 2.9 = 3.8$ 0.9

6. $3.2 = c - 4.6$ 7.8

7. $5.50 = p - 4.45$ 9.95

8. $x + 3.45 = 6.75$ 3.30

9. $n + 2.67 = 9.1$ 6.43

Solve and check each equation.

10. $5x - 12 = 16$ $\frac{28}{5}$

11. $25 = 3y - 8$ 11

12. $7n + 4 = 12$ $\frac{8}{7}$

13. $15 = 5w + 11$ $\frac{4}{5}$

14. $21 = 3b + 1$ $\frac{20}{3}$

15. $7r + 8 = 10$ $\frac{2}{7}$

16. $5 = 5a - 2$ $\frac{7}{5}$

17. $4p + 3 = 12$ $\frac{9}{4}$

18. $5x + 11 = 15$ $\frac{4}{5}$

19. $24n - 6 = 0$ $\frac{1}{4}$

20. $3z - 1.1 = 1.3$ 0.8

21. $3r + 2.1 = 6.3$ 1.4

22. $2.45 = 4b - 2.47$ 1.23

23. $2.26 = 2y - 6.12$ 4.19

24. $7 = 2n - 2.8$ 4.9

25. $10 = 3c + 1.9$ 2.7

26. $20 = 6x + 5.6$ 2.4

27. $20 = 4w - 2.4$ 5.6

28. $3a + 2.14 = 7$ 1.62

29. $2b - 2.8 = 7$ 4.9

30. $19.5 = 13n - 11.7$ 2.4

For each exercise, substitute the given values into the formula. Then solve for the remaining variable.

	$r = st + v$				$cd - e = f$		
	r	s	t	v	c	d	e	f

	r	s	t	v		c	d	e	f
31.	_77.6_	8	9.2	4	**35.**	2	3.5	4	_3_
32.	19.4	_4.1_	4	3	**36.**	_2.8_	3	2.4	6
33.	5	3	_1.2_	1.4	**37.**	5	_2.4_	2	10
34.	28	2	8	_12_	**38.**	2	_5.6_	1.3	9.9

118

Use the given formula to solve.

39. How long will it take a car to go 216 kilometers at a rate of 48 km/h? $(d=rt)$ 4.5 hr

$$d=mg$$

d: **distance**   *m:* **miles per gallon**   *g:* **number of gallons**

40. A car gets 20 miles to the gallon. How many gallons will it take for a 90-mile trip? 4.5 gal

41. Nora drove 87 miles on 5 gallons of gasoline. How many miles per gallon does her car get? 17.4 mi/g

42. A rectangle has a perimeter of 81 meters. If it is 14 meters wide, how long is it? $(P=2\ell+2w)$ 26.5 m

total cost = cost per unit × number of units + additional charge
$$C=cn+a$$

43. A record club charges $8 per record plus a total of $7.30 for shipping and handling. How many records did Rosa get if her total cost was $55.30? 6 records

44. Rick bought 5 T-shirts. The tax on his purchase was $1.43. If his total cost was $30.18, what was the price of each T-shirt? $5.75

$$\frac{\text{total}}{\text{time}} = \frac{\text{time}}{\text{per unit}} \times \frac{\text{number}}{\text{of units}} + \frac{\text{additional}}{\text{time}}$$
$$T=tn+a$$

45. It takes 7 minutes to jog around a track. You need a total of 2 minutes to change clothes. How many laps can you make if you have exactly half an hour? 4 laps

46. A machine-tool operator knows her machine can produce a finished part in 8 seconds. She can load and prepare her machine in 28 seconds. How many parts can she expect to make in 5 minutes (300 seconds)? 34 parts

The Bettmann Archive

Application 15 may be used at this time.

3.9 EQUATIONS CONTAINING FRACTIONS

Example 1: Solve $\frac{2}{3}x = 18$.

In the equation, x is multiplied by $\frac{2}{3}$. To do that, multiply x by 2 and then divide the result by 3. To find the value of x, undo the operations in reverse order.

$$\frac{2}{3}x = 18$$

$$3\left(\frac{2}{3}\right)x = 3(18) \quad \textbf{Multiply each side by 3.}$$

$$2x = 54$$

$$\frac{2x}{2} = \frac{54}{2} \quad \textbf{Divide each side by 2.}$$

$$x = 27$$

Check:
$$\frac{2}{3}x = 18$$
$$\frac{2}{3}(27) = 18$$
$$\frac{54}{3} = 18$$
$$18 = 18 \quad \checkmark$$

Example 2: Solve $17 = \frac{5}{8}y - 3$.

$$17 = \frac{5}{8}y - 3$$

$$\underline{+\ 3 \qquad\quad +3} \quad \textbf{First add 3.}$$

$$20 = \frac{5}{8}y$$

$$8(20) = 8\left(\frac{5}{8}y\right) \quad \textbf{Then multiply by 8.}$$

$$160 = 5y$$

$$\frac{160}{5} = \frac{5y}{5} \quad \textbf{Finally divide by 5.}$$

$$32 = y$$

Check:
$$17 = \frac{5}{8}y - 3$$
$$17 = \frac{5}{8}(32) - 3$$
$$17 = \frac{160}{8} - 3$$
$$17 = 20 - 3$$
$$17 = 17 \quad \checkmark$$

EXERCISES

Tell (a) by what number you would multiply each side and (b) by what number you would then divide each side.

1. $\frac{2}{3}x = 18$ Multiply by 3; divide by 2.

2. $\frac{3}{4}n = 30$ Multiply by 4; divide by 3.

3. $16 = \frac{4}{5}a$ Multiply by 5; divide by 4.

4. $\frac{7}{2}w = 42$ Multiply by 2; divide by 7.

5. $\frac{8}{3}t = 56$ Multiply by 3; divide by 8.

6. $45 = \frac{5}{7}r$ Multiply by 7; divide by 5.

120

Solve and check each equation.

7. $\frac{2}{3}x = 24$ 36

8. $27 = \frac{3}{4}b$ 36

9. $28 = r\left(\frac{4}{3}\right)$ 21

10. $\frac{2}{9}n = 14$ 63

11. $56 = \frac{4}{13}c$ 182

12. $\frac{9}{5}z = 72$ 40

13. $\frac{7}{3}t = 105$ 45

14. $32 = r\left(\frac{4}{7}\right)$ 56

15. $4 = \frac{3}{4}x - 5$ 12

16. $37 = \frac{7}{3}w + 2$ 15

17. $12 = \frac{2}{3}z + 2$ 15

18. $13 = \frac{4}{5}a - 3$ 20

19. $\frac{5}{4}c - 3 = 17$ 16

20. $\frac{3}{4}w + 4 = 10$ 8

21. $\frac{4}{9}m + 22 = 34$ 27

22. $\frac{8}{3}d - 3 = 45$ 18

23. $\frac{3}{4}x = 1.5$ 2

24. $\frac{2}{3}n = 7.2$ 10.8

25. $3.72 = \frac{4}{5}b$ 4.65

26. $5.43 = \frac{3}{11}c$ 19.91

27. $4.2 = \frac{2}{5}x + 2.4$ 4.5

28. $13.8 = \frac{4}{3}a - 2.6$ 12.3

29. $\frac{4}{5}n - 17.5 = 3.7$ 26.5

30. $8x + 15 = 19.4$ 0.55

Use the given formula to solve.

total cost	=	number (of units)	×	cost per unit

$$C = np$$

31. If $\frac{3}{5}$ pound of hamburger costs 87¢, what is the cost per pound? $1.45

32. A $2\frac{1}{2}$-ounce bottle of perfume costs $15. Find the cost per ounce. (Use $\frac{5}{2}$ for $2\frac{1}{2}$.) $6

33. A car went a distance of 39 miles in $\frac{3}{4}$ hour. Find its rate of speed. $(d = rt)$
52 mi/h

34. Suppose a snail moves at a rate of $\frac{2}{3}$ inch per hour. How long will it take to crawl a distance of 16 inches? $(d = rt)$
24 hr

121

This photograph has the shape of the golden rectangle. Do you find the shape to be a pleasing one?

35. Many people believe a rectangle has the most pleasing shape when the width is $\frac{5}{8}$ of the length ($w = \frac{5}{8}\ell$). Such a rectangle is called a golden rectangle. If a window 90 centimeters wide is a golden rectangle, how long is it?

144 cm

36. An electroplater's instructions call for this solution: The amount of copper equals $\frac{4}{7}$ of the amount of nickel. ($C = \frac{4}{7}N$). For 76 grams of copper, how much nickel should be used? 133 g

A person's height (h) in inches and weight (w) in pounds are approximately related by this formula:

$$w = \frac{11}{2}h - 220$$

37. About how tall is a 154-pound person? 68 in.

38. 90 in.; for extremely overweight or underweight people

38. According to the formula, what is the height of someone who weighs 275 pounds? For what kind of people do you suppose the formula gives the least-correct answers? See answer at left.

122

$$F = \frac{9}{5}C + 32$$

F: temperature (in degrees Fahrenheit)
C: temperature (in degrees Celsius)

Find the Fahrenheit equivalent for each temperature in degrees Celsius.

39. 0°C 32°F   **40.** 10°C 50°F   **41.** 25°C 77°F   **42.** 100°C 212°F

Find the Celsius equivalent for each temperature in degrees Fahrenheit.

43. 77°F 25°C   **44.** 32°F 0°C   **45.** 95°F 35°C   **46.** 98.6°F 37°C

Use the given rule or principle to write a formula. (Choose your own letters.) Then use the formula to solve the problems.

distance = **number of gallons** × **miles per gallon**

47. A car gets 19 miles per gallon. How far will it go on 20 gallons? 380 mi

48. Suppose the odometer of your car shows you went 300 miles since you last filled the gasoline tank. If it takes $12\frac{1}{2}$ gallons to fill the tank now, how many miles per gallon do you get? (Use $\frac{25}{2}$ for $12\frac{1}{2}$.) 24 mi/g

total weight = **weight per unit** × **number of units**

49. Gasoline weighs about 0.7 kilogram per liter. How many liters are in a tank containing 84 kilograms of gasoline? 120 liters

50. To find how much wire was left in a coil of wire without unrolling it, an electrician weighed the coil. It weighed 186 ounces. If the wire weighs $1\frac{1}{2}$ ounces per foot, how many feet of wire were in the coil? 124 ft

Cameramasters

Joseph A. Di Chello, Jr.

Example 1: The prom committee decided to raise money by giving a rock concert. They charged $6 a ticket and their expenses were $500. How many tickets do they have to sell to make a $850 profit?

Here is a rule that can be used:

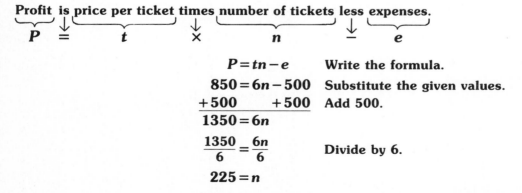

Profit is price per ticket times number of tickets less expenses.

$$P = t \times n - e$$

$P = tn - e$	**Write the formula.**
$850 = 6n - 500$	**Substitute the given values.**
$\underline{+500 \qquad +500}$	**Add 500.**
$1350 = 6n$	
$\dfrac{1350}{6} = \dfrac{6n}{6}$	**Divide by 6.**
$225 = n$	

They need to sell 225 tickets to make a $850 profit.

Example 2: Suppose only 200 people are expected to attend the concert. How much should each ticket cost to keep the profit at $850?

$$P = tn - e \qquad \text{Write the formula.}$$

$$850 = t(200) - 500 \qquad \text{Substitute the given values.}$$

$$850 = 200t - 500 \qquad \text{Change the order of the multiplication.}$$

$$\underline{+500 = \qquad +500} \qquad \text{Add 500.}$$

$$1350 = 200t$$

$$\frac{1350}{200} = \frac{200t}{200} \qquad \text{Divide by 200.}$$

$$6.75 = t$$

Each ticket would have to cost $6.75 to make the same profit.

EXERCISES

Use the following problem and formula:

Problem: A movie theater charges $3 for all tickets. It costs $510 a day to run the theater. How many tickets must be sold each day to make a daily profit of $150?

Formula: $P = tn - e$

© 1984 Dave Wade/Lightwave

1. Which variable has the value $3? t

2. Which variable has the value $510? e

3. Which variable has the value $150? P

4. Which variable is to be found? n

5. Solve the problem. 220 tickets

6. Suppose the theater has 400 seats. If the theater is filled every night, how much could the manager charge per ticket and still have the same profit and expenses? $1.65

Use the given formula to solve.

7. At a rate of 75 kilometers per hour, how long will it take a car to go 450 kilometers? $(d=rt)$ 6 hr

8. A gallon of paint covers about 240 square feet. You are to paint a fence that is 8 feet high. What length of fence can you expect to paint with 1 gallon of paint? 30 ft

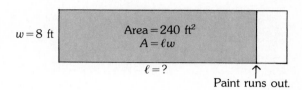

batting average   hits

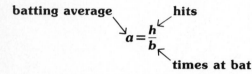

times at bat

9. Suppose you make 8 hits in 20 times at bat. What is your batting average?
0.4 or 0.400

10. How many hits did someone whose batting average is 0.450 get in 40 times at bat? 18 hits

A cricket will chirp faster as the temperature goes up.
approximate formula

$$T=\frac{c}{4}+37$$

T: **temperature (°F)**   *c:* **chirps per minute**

11. How fast will a cricket chirp at 80°F?
172 chirps/min

12. Find the temperature when the cricket chirps 120 times a minute. 67°F

An ant will run faster as the temperature goes up.
approximate formula

$$T=11s+39$$

T: **temperature (°F)**   *s:* **speed (inches per minute)**

13. Find the temperature when an ant moves at 4 inches per minute. 83°F

14. How fast is the ant at 72°F? 3 in./min

15. If a cricket chirps 96 times a minute, how fast does an ant run? (HINT: Use two formulas.) 2 in./min

$$P = bn - e$$
P: profit   **b:** price per bracelet
n: number of bracelets   **e:** expenses

16. Lydia decided to earn some money by making and selling bracelets. She spent $43 on supplies to make 24 bracelets. For what price should she sell them to make a profit of $65? $4.50

The longer an object falls, the farther it goes.

$$d = 16t^2$$
d: distance (feet)   **t:** time (seconds)
t^2 means $t \times t$.

17. Jean dropped a stone into a well. It hit bottom in 2 seconds. How deep is the well? 64 ft

18. A life raft dropped from a helicopter hit the water in 6 seconds. How high was the helicopter? 576 ft

19. A rock falls 400 feet into a canyon. Estimate the time it will fall. Try values for t. 5 sec

Diana H. Olson/Marilyn Gartman Photo Agency

The faster a car is moving, the farther it takes to stop.

stopping distance on dry concrete road *after* the brakes are applied

$$d = 0.04s^2$$
d: distance (ft)   **s:** speed (mi/h)
s^2 means $s \times s$.

20. How many feet does it take to stop at 55 miles per hour? 121 ft

21. Find the stopping distance at 70 miles per hour. 196 ft

22. The skid marks left by a stopping car measured 81 feet. Estimate the speed it was going when it started to brake. Try values for s. 45 mi/h

23. Light travels 300,000 kilometers per second. How many seconds does it take light to get from the sun to the earth, 150 million kilometers away? $(d=rt)$ 500 sec

24. How many minutes does it take the sun's light to reach the earth? (Use your answer to exercise 23.) $8\frac{1}{3}$ min

Here are two important electrical formulas.

$E = IR$ $W = EI$

E: (volts) **amount of *pressure* pushing the electricity through the wire**

I: (amps) ***rate* of flow of the current**

R: (ohms) ***resistance* of the wire to the flow of current**

W: (watts) **unit of *power***

Switch on your brain and be bright about choosing the right formula for each of these.

25. How many ohms of resistance does a copper wire have if 5 amps of current flows through it at 110 volts? 22 ohms

26. Find the number of amps used by a light bulb with a resistance of 50 ohms on a 110-volt line. 2.2 amps

27. How many amps does a 60-watt bulb use on a 120-volt line? 0.5 amp

28. How many ohms of resistance does a 60-watt bulb have on a 120-volt line? (HINT: Use both formulas.) 240 ohms

Use the given rule to write your own formula. Then use it to solve the problems.

For the rpm (revolutions per minute) of two gears A and B:

$$\frac{\text{number of}}{\text{teeth in } A} \times \frac{\text{rpm}}{\text{of } A} = \frac{\text{number of}}{\text{teeth in } B} \times \frac{\text{rpm}}{\text{of } b}$$

29. If B rotates at a rate of 50 rpm, how fast will A turn? 80 rpm

30. If A rotates at 120 rpm, how fast will B turn? 75 rpm

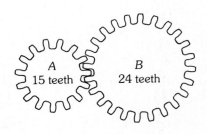

Total wages equal pay per hour times the number of hours.

31. At $5.80 an hour, how much would you earn in 8 hours? $46.40

32. If your wages were $52.50 for a 7-hour day, what is your hourly rate? $7.50/hr

To become a carpenter, an electrician, a bricklayer, or other skilled worker, you need special training. The training period is called an *apprenticeship*. Some apprentices get all their training on the job. Others have to go to some classes.

Here are some problems an apprentice may have to solve with a formula.

1. *Electrician's apprentice:* Find the watt rating of an electric motor that is rated $\frac{1}{2}$ horsepower.

   373 watts

   $$H = \frac{W}{746}$$

   H: horsepower
   W: watts

2. *Bricklayer's apprentice:* Find the number of common bricks it takes to build a wall 12 feet long, 8 feet high, and 18 inches wide. 2880 bricks

   For a wall of common brick:
   $$N = 20 \times \ell \times w \times h$$

   N: number of bricks
   ℓ: length (feet)
   w: width (feet)
   h: height (feet)

3. *Carpenter's apprentice:* A roof is being built over a span of 30 feet. How many feet should be in the rise if the pitch is to be $\frac{1}{6}$? 5 ft

   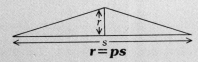

   $$r = ps$$

   r: rise (feet)
   s: span (feet)
   p: pitch (amount of slope)

4. *Pipe fitter's apprentice:* How many inches of expansion must be allowed for when laying 300 feet of brass pipe for water that will vary in temperature from 180°F to 40°F?

   5.2416 in.

   For a brass pipe:
   $$E = 0.0001248L(T - t)$$

   E: expansion (inches)
   L: length (feet)
   T: high temperature
   t: low temperature

Mary Elenz Tranter

Many problems involving money are solved with a rule that can be written as a formula.

At the store:

How would you find the cost of 3 stereo tapes at $8 apiece? You would multiply 3 by 8 and get $24. You are using this rule:

To find the cost, multiply the number of items by the price per item.

This rule can be written as a formula:

$$\text{cost} \quad \underset{\text{of items}}{\overset{\text{number}}{\downarrow}} \quad \underset{\text{per item}}{\overset{\text{price}}{\downarrow}}$$
$$c = np$$

Since there is usually a sales tax, the formula gets a little more complicated. Write this rule as a formula:

To find the cost, multiply the number of items by the price per item, and then add the sales tax. $c = np + t$

Kenji Kerins

In the home:

Suppose you want to find the cost of carpeting a room. Room sizes are usually given in feet. Carpet prices are usually given per square yard. You need three rules. Write all three as formulas:

To find area in square feet, multiply the length (in feet) by the width (in feet). $a = lw$

To find area in square yards, divide the area in square feet by 9. $A = a \div 9$

To find the cost, multiply the number of square yards by the price per square yard. $c = np$

Try these problems.

1. Find the cost of 6 pairs of stockings at $1.98 a pair with a sales tax of $0.58. $12.46

2. Find the cost of carpeting a room 18 feet long and 14 feet wide if the carpet costs $12.50 a square yard. $350

The formula below can be used to determine the day of the week on which any date falls. Once W is found, follow the directions given after Example 3.

$$W = d + 2m + [(3m + 3) \div 5] + y + \left[\frac{y}{4}\right] - \left[\frac{y}{100}\right] + \left[\frac{y}{400}\right] + 2$$

d: day of the month (from 1 to 31)

m: month (March is 3, April is 4, and so on up to December is 12. January is 13 and February is 14.)

y: year (For dates in January or February, use the previous year.)

Example 1: For February 29, 1980, *d* is 29, *m* is 14, and *y* is 1979.

Example 2: For July 4, 1776, *d* is 4, *m* is 7, and *y* is 1776.

The brackets [ ] or $\left[\ \right]$ mean do the division inside them, discard any remainder, and use only the whole-number part of the quotient.

Example 3: For March the part $+[(3m + 3) \div 5] +$ looks like this:

$+[(3(3) + 3) \div 5] +$

$+[(9 + 3) \div 5] +$

$+[12 \div 5] +$

$+\left[2\frac{2}{5}\right] +$

$+2 +$

When you work out each part and then add and subtract from left to right, you will know what W is. Divide W by 7. The remainder will tell you the day of the week. 0 is Saturday, 1 is Sunday, 2 is Monday, and so on up to 6 is Friday.

Answers will vary for exercises 2-3.

1. See if the formula works for today's date.

2. On which day of the week were you born?

3. On which day of the week will Christmas fall this year?

4. On which day of the week will New Year's Eve fall in 1999?
Friday

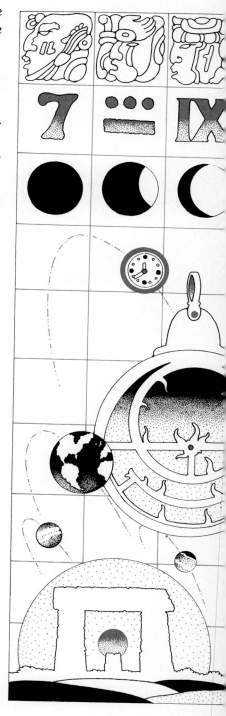

CHAPTER REVIEW

Tell whether each sentence is true, false, or open. 3.1

1. $4 \times 7 = 16 + 4$ False

2. $18 = 4b$ Open

3. $2w - 7 = 15$ Open

4. $6 + 12 = 6 \times 3$ True

Find each answer. 3.2

5. $(2 + 9) - 5$ 6

6. $8 - (4 + 3)$ 1

7. $(4 \times 3) + 5$ 17

8. $8 + (20 \div 4)$ 13

Find each answer when y is replaced with 4.

9. $3y$ 12   **10.** $6y$ 24   **11.** $2(y + 5)$ 18   **12.** $4(y - 1)$ 12

Find each answer. 3.3

13. $14 - 9 + 5$ 10

14. $20 + 2 - 8$ 14

15. $2(8) - 3(4)$ 4

16. $8 \div 4 + 2(3)$ 8

Find each answer when x is replaced with 7.

17. $3x + 1$ 22   **18.** $2x - 9$ 5   **19.** $4(x - 5)$ 8   **20.** $3(x + 3)$ 30

Use the given formula. 3.4

21. $P = \frac{a}{2} + 110$

Find the blood pressure of a person who is 30 years old. 125

22.

$$\overset{\text{wages}}{\nearrow} W = pt \overset{\text{time}}{\nwarrow}$$
$$\underset{\text{hourly pay}}{\uparrow}$$

Suppose you worked 38 hours a week at \$5 an hour. What would your week's wages be? \$190

Solve and check. 3.5

23. $a + 18 = 25$ 7   **24.** $b - 13 = 22$ 35   **25.** $36 = x - 10$ 46

26. $y + 9 = 46$ 37   **27.** $4.5 = p + 3.2$ 1.3   **28.** $6.5 = c - 2.6$ 9.1

Solve and check. 3.6

29. $6n = 78$ 13   **30.** $36 = 9p$ 4   **31.** $\frac{x}{5} = 12$ 60

32. $17 = \frac{w}{8}$ 136   **33.** $105 = 7y$ 15   **34.** $11r = 132$ 12

35. If a plane flies a distance of 1740 miles in 3 hours, what is its average rate of speed? $(d = rt)$ 580 mi/h

Solve and check. 3.7

36. $2a - 3 = 7$ 5   **37.** $25 = 3b + 4$ 7   **38.** $\frac{x}{6} - 5 = 3$ 48

39. $14 = \frac{y}{2} + 9$ 10   **40.** $40 = 4w + 4$ 9   **41.** $3t + 2 = 35$ 11

42. If 22 meters of fence is used to enclose a rectangular lot 4 meters wide, how long will the lot be? $(P = 2\ell + 2w)$ 7 m

Solve and check. 3.8

43. $3x = 11$ $\frac{11}{3}$ **44.** $13 = 2y$ $\frac{13}{2}$ **45.** $10 = 4n + 7$ $\frac{3}{4}$

46. $3m - 2 = 3$ $\frac{5}{3}$ **47.** $2z - 4 = 5$ $\frac{9}{2}$ **48.** $11 = 5w - 8$ $\frac{19}{5}$

49. $15 = \frac{3}{7}x$ 35   **50.** $\frac{2}{9}y = 4$ 18   **51.** $\frac{3}{2}c + 1 = 10$ 6   3.9

52. $\frac{2}{9}n + 2 = 4$ 9   **53.** $12 = \frac{3}{4}a - 3$ 20   **54.** $20 = \frac{7}{3}p - 1$ 9

Use the given formula. 3.10

$$a = \frac{h}{b} \qquad \begin{array}{l} \textbf{\textit{a}: batting average} \\ \textbf{\textit{h}: hits} \quad \textbf{\textit{b}: times at bat} \end{array}$$

55. Sarah got 9 hits in 25 times at bat. What is her batting average? 0.360

56. If your average was 0.250 for 36 times at bat, how many hits did you get? 9 hits

$$F = \frac{9}{5}C + 32$$

57. Find the Fahrenheit reading for 30°C. 86°F

58. What is the Celsius reading for 68°F? 20°C

Tell whether each sentence is true, false, or open.

Correlation

Items	Sec
1–3	3.1
4–6	3.2
7–9	3.3
10–11	3.4
12–13	3.5
14–15	3.6
16–17	3.7
18–19	3.8
20	3.9
21–22	3.10

1. $7 + n = 18$ Open

2. $3 \times 5 = 11 + 4$ True

3. $4 + 18 = 2 \times 12$ False

Find each answer when n is replaced with 3.

4. $2n$ 6

5. $5(n + 2)$ 25

6. $n(6 - 4)$ 6

Find each answer.

7. $16 - 9 + 5$ 12

8. $35 \div 5 + 2$ 9

9. $3(6) - 15 \div 3$ 13

Use the given formula to solve.

10. What distance will a car go in 3 hours at 55 mi/h? $(d = rt)$ 165 mi

11. Find the perimeter of a rectangle 8 meters wide and 14 meters long. $(P = 2\ell + 2w)$ 44 m

Solve and check.

12. $x + 13 = 29$ 16

13. $8 = y - 27$ 35

14. $4n = 68$ 17

15. $12 = \frac{w}{3}$ 36

16. $4a - 3 = 17$ 5

17. $3 = \frac{b}{4} - 9$ 48

18. $3n = 7$ $\frac{7}{3}$

19. $10 = 5x + 6$ $\frac{4}{5}$

20. $\frac{3}{5}t = 18$ 30

Use the given formula.

21. $d = mg$
d: distance   m: miles per gallon
g: number of gallons
A car went 276 miles on 12 gallons of gasoline. How many miles per gallon did it get? 23 mi/g

22. $C = pn + a$
C: total cost   n: number of items
p: price per item   a: additional charge
Allen ordered 5 shirts from a catalog. Shipping and handling was $2. If the total cost was $47, what was the price of each shirt? $9

Give the ratio of circles to triangles.

1. ○ ○ △ △ △ △ △ $\frac{2}{5}$ 2. ○ △ △ ○ ○ ○ △ $\frac{4}{3}$

Find an equivalent ratio in lowest terms.

3. $\frac{4}{6}$ $\frac{2}{3}$ 4. $\frac{20}{8}$ $\frac{5}{2}$ 5. $\frac{18}{42}$ $\frac{3}{7}$

Use cross products to solve each proportion.

6. $\frac{2}{3} = \frac{8}{x}$ 12   7. $\frac{8}{a} = \frac{10}{35}$ 28   8. $\frac{18}{10} = \frac{n}{25}$ 45

Solve this problem by using a proportion.

9. If a car can go 90 miles on 4
gallons of gas, how far can it go
on 10 gallons? 225 miles

Use the similar figures at the right.

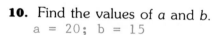

10. Find the values of a and b.
a = 20; b = 15

A map has a scale of 1 inch = 32 miles. Find the real distance for each map distance.

11. 10 inches 320 miles   12. $2\frac{1}{2}$ inches 80 miles

Write each percent as a ratio in lowest terms.

13. 32% $\frac{8}{25}$ 14. 53% $\frac{53}{100}$

Write each ratio as a percent.

15. 3:12 25%   16. 12 out of 15 80%

Solve this problem by using a proportion.

17. If 38 out of 50 people use Brand X, what percent use
Brand X? 76%

Estimate the answer. Then find the exact answer by multiplying.
Estimates are given first and may vary.
18. 19% of 51 10; 9.69   19. 32% of 78 24; 24.96

135

Grant Heilman

If you were asked how the team is doing, you might say "They won 6 out of 10 games."

When you say "6 out of 10," you are using a *ratio*.

A **ratio** is the comparison of two numbers by division.

The ratio "6 out of 10" can be written in 3 ways:

$$\frac{6}{10} \qquad 6 \text{ to } 10 \qquad 6:10$$

Example 1:

The ratio of squares to triangles is $\frac{5}{8}$, or 5 to 8, or 5:8.

The ratio of triangles to squares is $\frac{8}{5}$, or 8 to 5, or 8:5.

Example 2:

The ratio of green parts to all parts is $\frac{4}{9}$.

The ratio of white parts to green parts is $\frac{5}{4}$.

The ratio of all parts to white parts is $\frac{9}{5}$.

EXERCISES

1. The ratio of circles to all figures is _3_ to _7_.

2. The ratio of circles to squares is _3_ to _4_.

3. The ratio of squares to all figures is _4_ to _7_.

4. The ratio of squares to circles is _4_ to _3_.

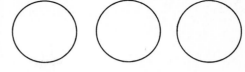

Give each ratio as a fraction.

5. shaded squares to all squares $\frac{7}{16}$

6. unshaded squares to all squares $\frac{9}{16}$

7. all squares to unshaded squares $\frac{16}{9}$

8. shaded squares to unshaded squares $\frac{7}{9}$

Use with exercises 5–8.

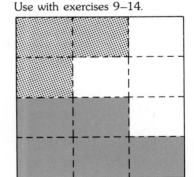

9. green parts to all parts $\frac{5}{12}$

10. gray parts to all parts $\frac{3}{12}$

11. white parts to gray parts $\frac{4}{3}$

12. green parts to white parts $\frac{5}{4}$

13. green parts to gray parts $\frac{5}{3}$

14. all parts to white parts $\frac{12}{4}$

Use with exercises 9–14.

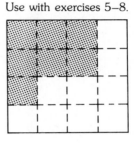

Make a drawing to show each ratio.
Drawings for exercises 15-18 will vary.

15. The ratio of circles to squares is $\frac{6}{5}$. ○○○○○○ ☐☐☐☐☐

16. The ratio of shaded parts to all parts is 5 to 8.

17. 7 out of 15 parts are shaded.

18. The ratio of triangles to circles is 4:7. △△△△○○○○○○○

Give each ratio as a fraction.

19. A room is 17 feet long and 12 feet wide. What is the ratio of length to width? $\dfrac{17}{12}$

20. A woman weighs 125 pounds. Her husband weighs 184. What is the ratio of her weight to his? $\dfrac{125}{184}$

21. What is the ratio of air intake during rest to air intake during vigorous activity? See the pictures below. $\dfrac{8}{100}$

22. What is the ratio of stars to stripes in the American flag? $\dfrac{50}{13}$

8 liters per minute

100 liters per minute

23. A bricklayer mixes mortar with 3 parts cement, 10 parts sand, and 1 part lime. What is the ratio of sand to cement? $\dfrac{10}{3}$

24. A chemical technician analyzed a sample and found 6 parts carbon, 2 parts sulfur, and 10 parts hydrogen. What is the ratio of carbon to hydrogen? $\dfrac{6}{10}$

The distance a car travels from the time a driver realizes he must stop until he actually hits the brakes is called the *reaction distance*. At 40 mi/h, for example, the reaction distance is about 44 feet. See the graph. Write each ratio.

Answers to exercises 25-28 may vary.

25. reaction distance at 20 mi/h to that at 40 mi/h $\dfrac{22}{44}$

26. reaction distance at 60 mi/h to that at 40 mi/h $\dfrac{66}{44}$

27. reaction distance at 70 mi/h to that at 50 mi/h $\dfrac{77}{55}$

28. reaction distance at 20 mi/h to that at 50 mi/h $\dfrac{22}{55}$

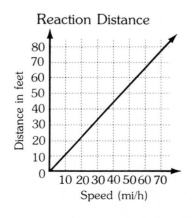

Reaction Distance

Distance in feet

Speed (mi/h)

The ratio $\frac{4}{10}$ can be shown with a diagram.

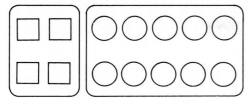

For 4 squares, there are 10 circles.

These give the same comparison.

But each row can be grouped separately.

For every 2 squares, there are 5 circles.

This shows the ratio $\frac{2}{5}$.

$\frac{4}{10}$ and $\frac{2}{5}$ are called **equivalent ratios** because they are different ratios for comparing the same objects.

Notice that $\dfrac{4}{10} = \dfrac{4 \div 2}{10 \div 2} = \dfrac{2}{5}$.

Example 1: Find an equivalent ratio for $\frac{16}{24}$ in **lowest terms.**

Equivalent ratios can be found by dividing the numerator and the denominator of a fraction by the same number (except zero).

$$\frac{16}{24} = \frac{16 \div 8}{24 \div 8} = \frac{2}{3}$$

Example 2: Find two ratios equivalent to $\frac{3}{4}$.

Equivalent ratios can be found by multiplying the numerator and the denominator of a fraction by the same number (except zero).

$$\frac{3}{4} = \frac{3 \times 2}{4 \times 2} = \frac{6}{8} \qquad \frac{3}{4} = \frac{3 \times 3}{4 \times 3} = \frac{9}{12}$$

Example 3: Show $\frac{3}{4} = \frac{6}{8} = \frac{9}{12}$ with a diagram.

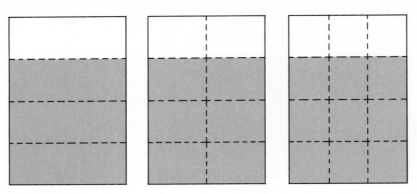

The three rectangles are the same size and have the *same amount* shaded. The first has 3 out of 4 parts shaded, the second has 6 out of 8 parts shaded, and the third has 9 out of 12 parts shaded. Since the *same amount* is shaded in each rectangle, $\frac{3}{4} = \frac{6}{8} = \frac{9}{12}$.

EXERCISES

Give the equivalent ratios of black figures to red figures shown by each diagram.

1. ○ ☆ ☆ ☆
○ ☆ ☆ ☆ $\quad \frac{2}{6} = \frac{1}{3}$

2. △ △ □ □ □
△ △ □ □ □ $\quad \frac{6}{4} = \frac{3}{2}$

3. □ □ ○ ○ ○
□ □ ○ ○ ○
□ □ ○ ○ ○ $\quad \frac{9}{6} = \frac{3}{2}$

4. □ △ △ △ △
□ △ △ △ △
□ △ △ △ △ $\quad \frac{3}{12} = \frac{1}{4}$

Show by multiplying or dividing that the ratios in each pair are equivalent.

Example: $\frac{4}{6}, \frac{32}{48} \quad \frac{4}{6} = \frac{4 \times 8}{6 \times 8} = \frac{32}{48}$
$\qquad \frac{12 \div 6}{18 \div 6} = \frac{2}{3}$

5. $\frac{3}{7}, \frac{9}{21} \quad \frac{3 \times 3}{7 \times 3} = \frac{9}{21}$

6. $\frac{4}{5}, \frac{8}{10} \quad \frac{4 \times 2}{5 \times 2} = \frac{8}{10}$

7. $\frac{20}{12}, \frac{5}{3} \quad \frac{20 \div 4}{12 \div 4} = \frac{5}{3}$

8. $\frac{12}{18}, \frac{2}{3}$

9. $\frac{8}{3}, \frac{32}{12} \quad \frac{8 \times 4}{3 \times 4} = \frac{32}{12}$

10. $\frac{5}{3}, \frac{25}{15} \quad \frac{5 \times 5}{3 \times 5} = \frac{25}{15}$

11. $\frac{20}{24}, \frac{5}{6} \quad \frac{20 \div 4}{24 \div 4} = \frac{5}{6}$

12. $\frac{7}{12}, \frac{21}{36} \quad \frac{7 \times 3}{12 \times 3} = \frac{21}{36}$

140

Give any two ratios equivalent to each ratio below.

Example: $\dfrac{4}{6}$ $\dfrac{4}{6}=\dfrac{4\div2}{6\div2}=\dfrac{2}{3}$, $\dfrac{4}{6}=\dfrac{4\times3}{6\times3}=\dfrac{12}{18}$

Answers for exercises 13-17 may vary.

13. $\dfrac{2}{6}$ $\dfrac{1}{3}$; $\dfrac{4}{12}$ **14.** $\dfrac{8}{6}$ $\dfrac{4}{3}$; $\dfrac{16}{12}$ **15.** $\dfrac{2}{5}$ $\dfrac{4}{10}$; $\dfrac{6}{15}$ **16.** $\dfrac{6}{7}$ $\dfrac{12}{14}$; $\dfrac{18}{21}$ **17.** $\dfrac{4}{3}$ $\dfrac{8}{6}$; $\dfrac{12}{9}$

Find an equivalent ratio in lowest terms.

18. $\dfrac{8}{10}$ $\dfrac{4}{5}$ **19.** $\dfrac{4}{12}$ $\dfrac{1}{3}$ **20.** $\dfrac{20}{36}$ $\dfrac{5}{9}$ **21.** $\dfrac{39}{21}$ $\dfrac{13}{7}$ **22.** $\dfrac{28}{18}$ $\dfrac{14}{9}$

23. $\dfrac{20}{28}$ $\dfrac{5}{7}$ **24.** $\dfrac{20}{4}$ $\dfrac{5}{1}$ **25.** $\dfrac{12}{42}$ $\dfrac{2}{7}$ **26.** $\dfrac{35}{14}$ $\dfrac{5}{2}$ **27.** $\dfrac{54}{27}$ $\dfrac{2}{1}$

Draw a diagram to show that the ratios in each pair are equivalent.

Diagrams for exercises 28-31 may vary.

28. $\dfrac{3}{7}, \dfrac{6}{14}$ **29.** $\dfrac{4}{5}, \dfrac{8}{10}$ **30.** $\dfrac{8}{12}, \dfrac{2}{3}$ **31.** $\dfrac{1}{4}, \dfrac{3}{12}$

Write each ratio in lowest terms.

Example: 2 feet to 6 inches

$$\dfrac{2\text{ feet}}{6\text{ inches}}=\dfrac{24\text{ inches}}{6\text{ inches}}=\dfrac{24}{6}=\dfrac{24\div6}{6\div6}=\dfrac{4}{1}$$

32. 4 yards to 2 feet $\dfrac{6}{1}$

33. 3 hours to 5 minutes $\dfrac{36}{1}$

34. 2 hours to 20 minutes $\dfrac{6}{1}$

35. 75 centimeters to 2 meters $\dfrac{3}{8}$

36. 450 grams to 2 kilograms $\dfrac{9}{40}$

37. 8 inches to 3 feet $\dfrac{2}{9}$

SKILLS REFRESHER

Replace ● with $<$, $>$, or $=$.

1. $\dfrac{3}{5}\overset{>}{●}\dfrac{4}{7}$ **2.** $\dfrac{8}{2}\overset{=}{●}\dfrac{16}{4}$ **3.** $\dfrac{9}{11}\overset{<}{●}\dfrac{9}{10}$

4. $\dfrac{2}{9}\overset{<}{●}\dfrac{1}{3}$ **5.** $\dfrac{1}{8}\overset{>}{●}\dfrac{1}{9}$ **6.** $\dfrac{7}{7}\overset{=}{●}\dfrac{6}{6}$

Skill	Page
30	491

A ratio can be graphed by plotting the ordered pair (denominator, numerator).

Example: Graph $\frac{1}{3}$ and $\frac{2}{6}$.

The ordered pair for $\frac{1}{3}$ is $(3,1)$.

The ordered pair for $\frac{2}{6}$ is $(6,2)$.

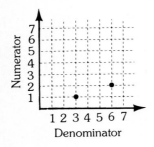

Graph each set of equivalent ratios on the same grid. Connect the points of each set. See graph at left.

1. $\left\{\dfrac{1}{3}, \dfrac{2}{6}, \dfrac{3}{9}, \dfrac{4}{12}, \dfrac{5}{15}\right\}$

2. $\left\{\dfrac{1}{2}, \dfrac{2}{4}, \dfrac{3}{6}, \dfrac{4}{8}, \dfrac{5}{10}, \dfrac{6}{12}\right\}$

3. $\left\{\dfrac{3}{4}, \dfrac{6}{8}, \dfrac{9}{12}, \dfrac{12}{16}\right\}$

4. $\left\{\dfrac{1}{1}, \dfrac{2}{2}, \dfrac{3}{3}, \dfrac{4}{4}, \dfrac{8}{8}, \dfrac{12}{12}\right\}$

5. $\left\{\dfrac{3}{2}, \dfrac{6}{4}, \dfrac{9}{6}, \dfrac{12}{8}, \dfrac{15}{10}\right\}$

6. $\left\{\dfrac{2}{1}, \dfrac{4}{2}, \dfrac{6}{3}, \dfrac{8}{4}, \dfrac{10}{5}, \dfrac{12}{6}\right\}$

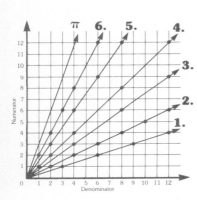

7. What does the graph of a set of equivalent ratios look like? a straight line

8. If the graph were larger, how many more equivalent ratios could you find for each set? infinitely many more

There is a relationship between the diameter and the circumference of circular objects.

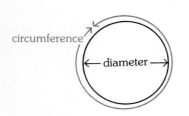

As an experiment, use a tape measure to find the diameter and the circumference of 6 circular objects, such as tin cans or rolls of tape.

Find and graph each ratio $\dfrac{\text{circumference}}{\text{diameter}}$, using the ordered pair (diameter, circumference).

9. Are the points for the six ratios in a straight line? Yes

10. Are the ratios for the six objects equivalent ratios? Yes

11. Express any of those ratios as a decimal to the nearest hundredth. 3.14 (Answers may vary depending on measurements.)

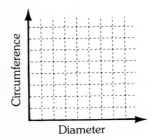

4.3 | PROPORTIONS

Wilma has driven 252 miles since last filling her car's 12-gallon gas tank. She has used 9 gallons. Can she make her next exit 70 miles away?

252 miles on   ? miles on
9 gallons   3 gallons

Wilma used equivalent ratios to make a quick calculation.

$$\frac{252}{9} \quad \longleftarrow \text{ distance } \longrightarrow \quad \frac{m}{3}$$
$$\quad\quad \longleftarrow \text{ gallons } \longrightarrow$$

Since $\frac{252}{9} = \frac{252 \div 3}{9 \div 3} = \frac{84}{3}$, m must be 84.

She can go another 84 miles, so she can reach her next exit.

The sentence $\frac{252}{9} = \frac{m}{3}$ is called a *proportion*.

A **proportion** is a sentence stating that two ratios are equivalent.

The following property of proportions is useful for solving problems:

In a proportion, the cross products are equal.

$$\frac{2}{3} = \frac{4}{6}$$

12   **12**

The cross products are both 12.

$$\frac{3}{5} = \frac{6}{10}$$

30   **30**

The cross products are both 30.

Example 1: Solve $\frac{252}{9} = \frac{m}{3}$.

$$\frac{252}{9} = \frac{m}{3}$$

$252 \times 3 = 9 \times m$ **Take the cross products.**

$756 = 9m$

$\dfrac{756}{9} = \dfrac{9m}{9}$ **Divide each side by 9.**

$84 = m$

Example 2: Solve $\frac{4}{5} = \frac{6}{x}$.

$$\frac{4}{5} \rlap{\diagup}{=} \frac{6}{x}$$

$4 \times x = 5 \times 6$ **Take the cross products.**

$4x = 30$

$\dfrac{4x}{4} = \dfrac{30}{4}$ **Divide each side by 4.**

$x = 7\dfrac{1}{2}$, **or 7.5**

EXERCISES

Use cross products to tell whether each sentence is true.

1. $\dfrac{4}{6} = \dfrac{8}{10}$ False

2. $\dfrac{2}{3} = \dfrac{5}{6}$ False

3. $\dfrac{16}{4} = \dfrac{4}{1}$ True

4. $\dfrac{5}{3} = \dfrac{20}{12}$ True

5. $\dfrac{4}{4} = \dfrac{7}{7}$ True

6. $\dfrac{11}{9} = \dfrac{6}{4}$ False

7. $\dfrac{7}{1} = \dfrac{8}{1}$ False

8. $\dfrac{4}{7} = \dfrac{8}{10}$ False

9. $\dfrac{10}{18} = \dfrac{5}{9}$ True

Use cross products to solve each proportion.

10. $\dfrac{2}{5} = \dfrac{n}{20}$ 8

11. $\dfrac{3}{7} = \dfrac{x}{21}$ 9

12. $\dfrac{6}{9} = \dfrac{26}{y}$ 39

13. $\dfrac{4}{7} = \dfrac{20}{a}$ 35

14. $\dfrac{12}{15} = \dfrac{16}{b}$ 20

15. $\dfrac{4}{5} = \dfrac{12}{c}$ 15

16. $\dfrac{21}{r} = \dfrac{6}{8}$ 28

17. $\dfrac{20}{a} = \dfrac{8}{12}$ 30

18. $\dfrac{m}{16} = \dfrac{27}{72}$ 6

19. $\dfrac{n}{51} = \dfrac{25}{17}$ 75

20. $\dfrac{x}{15} = \dfrac{3}{2}$ $22\dfrac{1}{2}$

21. $\dfrac{2}{5} = \dfrac{7}{m}$ $17\dfrac{1}{2}$

22. $\dfrac{4}{9} = \dfrac{w}{12}$ $5\dfrac{1}{3}$

23. $\dfrac{45}{n} = \dfrac{10}{8}$ 36

24. $\dfrac{3}{x} = \dfrac{5}{100}$ 60

25. $\dfrac{c}{10} = \dfrac{56}{16}$ 35

26. $\dfrac{75}{25} = \dfrac{45}{a}$ 15

27. $\dfrac{20}{85} = \dfrac{32}{w}$ 136

Jim Badgett/Photo Trends

Use proportions to solve.

28. $\dfrac{6}{10}$ ⟵ games won ⟶ $\dfrac{w}{15}$
⟵ games played ⟶

A basketball team won 6 out of its first 10 games. At this pace, how many games will the team win in 15 games?
9 games

29. $\dfrac{126}{7}$ ⟵ distance ⟶ $\dfrac{d}{4}$
⟵ gallons ⟶

A car can go 126 miles on 7 gallons of gas. How far can it go on 4 gallons? 72 miles

30. $\dfrac{6}{32}$ ⟵ pages ⟶ $\dfrac{15}{t}$
⟵ time ⟶

A secretary typed 6 pages in 32 minutes. How long will 15 pages take?
80 minutes

31. $\dfrac{4}{6}$ ⟵ flour ⟶ $\dfrac{6}{e}$
⟵ eggs ⟶

A recipe calls for 4 cups of flour and 6 eggs. How many eggs are needed for 6 cups of flour? 9 eggs

32. $\dfrac{3}{18}$ ⟵ minutes ⟶ $\dfrac{m}{24}$
⟵ hours ⟶

A clock loses 3 minutes every 18 hours. How much time will it lose in 24 hours? 4 minutes

33. $\dfrac{3}{16}$ ⟵ hours worked ⟶ $\dfrac{h}{80}$
⟵ money earned ⟶

John earns $16 for 3 hours of work. How many hours must he work in order to earn $80? 15 hours

4.4 | SOLVING PROBLEMS WITH PROPORTIONS

Regulation pool tables are made in different sizes, but the length and the width have the same ratio. A pool table 88 inches long will be 44 inches wide.

Example 1: If a pool table is 76 inches long, how wide is it?

You can use either of the following proportions to solve the problem. You can write ratios to compare:

first table	to	second table	or	lengths	to	widths

$$\frac{88 \leftarrow \text{lengths} \rightarrow 76}{44 \leftarrow \text{widths} \rightarrow w} \qquad \frac{88 \leftarrow \text{first table} \rightarrow 44}{76 \leftarrow \text{second table} \rightarrow w}$$

$$\frac{88}{44} = \frac{76}{w} \qquad\qquad \frac{88}{76} = \frac{44}{w}$$

$88 \times w = 44 \times 76$ **cross products** $\qquad 88 \times w = 76 \times 44$

$\qquad 88w = 3344 \qquad\qquad\qquad\qquad\qquad 88w = 3344$

$\qquad \dfrac{88w}{88} = \dfrac{3344}{88}$ **Divide by 88.** $\qquad \dfrac{88w}{88} = \dfrac{3344}{88}$

$\qquad\qquad w = 38 \qquad\qquad\qquad\qquad\qquad\qquad w = 38$

The width is 38 inches.   The width is 38 inches.

Example 2: It costs $3 to ship a 5-pound package. What will it cost to ship a 20-pound package?

There is more than one correct proportion. You could compare:

first package	to	second package	or	costs	to	weights

$$\frac{3 \leftarrow \text{costs} \rightarrow c}{5 \leftarrow \text{weights} \rightarrow 20} \qquad \frac{3 \leftarrow \text{first package} \rightarrow 5}{c \leftarrow \text{second package} \rightarrow 20}$$

Suppose you choose the second.

$$\frac{3}{c} = \frac{5}{20}$$

$60 = 5c$ **Take the cross products.**

$12 = c$ **Divide each side by 5.**

It will cost $12 to ship a 20-pound package.

EXERCISES

Copy and complete the table.

			Ratio	Ratio	True proportion
Example:	22 miles, 2 gal	77 miles, 7 gal	$\frac{22}{2}$	$\frac{77}{7}$	$\frac{22}{2} = \frac{77}{7}$
1.	21 km, 3 liters	119 km, 17 liters	$\frac{21}{119}$	$\frac{3}{17}$	$\frac{21}{119} = \frac{3}{17}$
2.	21 km, 3 liters	119 km, 17 liters	$\frac{21}{3}$	$\frac{119}{17}$	$\frac{21}{3} = \frac{119}{17}$
3.	6 m long, 4 m wide	15 m long, 10 m wide	$\frac{4}{10}$	$\frac{6}{15}$	$\frac{4}{10} = \frac{6}{15}$
4.	300 g, 14 cm	450 g, 21 cm	$\frac{300}{14}$	$\frac{450}{21}$	$\frac{300}{14} = \frac{450}{21}$
5.	8 baskets, 36 shots	6 baskets, 27 shots	$\frac{6}{27}$	$\frac{8}{36}$	$\frac{6}{27} = \frac{8}{36}$
6.	4 hr, 20 min	6 hr, 30 min	$\frac{20}{30}$	$\frac{4}{6}$	$\frac{20}{30} = \frac{4}{6}$
7.	12 oz, 72¢	7 oz, 42¢	$\frac{7}{42}$	$\frac{12}{72}$	$\frac{7}{42} = \frac{12}{72}$
8.	80 km, 50 miles	30 km, x miles	$\frac{80}{30}$	$\frac{50}{x}$	$\frac{80}{30} = \frac{50}{x}$
9.	20 knots, 23 mi/h	25 knots, y mi/h	$\frac{23}{y}$	$\frac{20}{25}$	$\frac{23}{y} = \frac{20}{25}$
10.	10.5 zips, 16.5 zaps	7 zips, 11 zaps	$\frac{7}{11}$	$\frac{10.5}{16.5}$	$\frac{7}{11} = \frac{10.5}{16.5}$
11.	9 ft wide, 15 ft long	21 ft wide, 35 ft long	$\frac{9}{21}$	$\frac{15}{35}$	$\frac{9}{21} = \frac{15}{35}$

Solve each problem by using a proportion.

12. If it costs $6 to ship a 10-pound package, what does it cost to ship a 25-pound package? $15

13. A car went 64 km on 8 liters of gas. How much gas would it take to go 320 km? 40 liters

14. A 14-kilogram weight stretches a spring 6 centimeters. How far will a 35-kilogram weight stretch the spring?
15 cm

15. A recipe that serves 6 requires 2 quarts of water. If a cook is preparing for 15 people, how much water should be used? 5 qt

16. A 28-inch bicycle wheel has a circumference of 88 inches. What is the circumference of a 21-inch wheel?
66 in.

17. 12 feet of brass pipe weighs 26 pounds. How much does 30 feet of the same pipe weigh? 65 lb

18. A printer wants to reduce a photograph 10 inches wide by 8 inches tall to a size 4 inches wide. How tall will it be? $3\frac{1}{5}$ in.

19. Nora made $17 for 4 hours of work. How much could she make if she worked 10 hours? $42.50

20. A snowmobile needs a fuel mixture of 2 quarts of oil for every 5 gallons of gas. How much oil is needed for 3 gallons of gas? $1\frac{1}{5}$ qt

21. There are 180 calories in 3 ounces of veal. How many calories are in 5 ounces of veal? 300 calories

22. If a 3-kilogram weight stretches a spring 5 centimeters, how much weight will stretch it 7 centimeters? 4.2 kg

23. Ken paid $6.65 for 5 gallons of gas. At that rate, what would it cost him to fill his 18-gallon gas tank? $23.94

Paul Light/Lightwave

24. Mrs. Rockow won an election by a 5 to 2 margin. Her opponent got 2800 votes. How many votes did Mrs. Rockow get? 7000 votes

25. If property taxes are assessed at $2.24 per $100, what is the tax on a $72,900 house? $1632.96

26. An engine is turning at the rate of 8400 revolutions every 7 minutes. How many revolutions does it turn in 10 minutes? 12,000 revolutions

27. Wanda Witch worked 12 wonderful whammies with 20 wand waves. How many waves would she need for 15 whammies? 25 waves

At 30 mi/h a car is traveling 44 feet per second.

28. How many feet per second does a car travel at 45 mi/h? 66 ft/sec

29. How many mi/h is 22 feet per second? 15 mi/h

Use 62 mi/h and 100 km/h as the same speed.

30. Find the km/h equivalent of 93 mi/h. 150 km/h

31. Find the mi/h equivalent of 70 km/h. $43\frac{2}{5}$ mi/h

A certain pulley will lift 12 kilograms when the rope is pulled with a force of 3 kilograms.

32. If you pulled the rope with a force of 20 kilograms, how much weight could you lift? 80 kg

33. How hard does a garage mechanic have to pull to lift a 180-kilogram auto engine with the pulley? with a force of 45 kilograms

Boat speeds are usually given in knots instead of mi/h. 20 knots is the same as 23 mi/h.

34. A boat's top speed is 35 knots. How many mi/h is that? $40\frac{1}{4}$ mi/h

35. What is the speed in knots of a boat going 46 mi/h? 40 knots

Applications 18–19 may be used at this time.

Photos by Leonard Lee Rue III/Photri

When you get a picture enlarged, you expect it to look like the original. You wouldn't want the picture made 3 times as tall but only 2 times as wide. Everything would look tall and skinny. You expect everything to keep the same shape.

Similar figures have the same shape but may have different sizes.

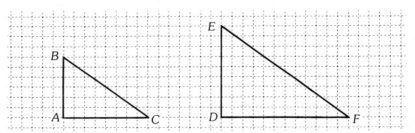

Triangle *ABC* and triangle *DEF* are similar.

Take the ratios of corresponding sides.

$$\frac{AB}{DE} = \frac{6}{9} = \frac{2}{3} \qquad \frac{AC}{DF} = \frac{8}{12} = \frac{2}{3} \qquad \frac{BC}{EF} = \frac{10}{15} = \frac{2}{3}$$

All three ratios are equal!

In similar figures, the ratios of corresponding sides are equal.

150

Example 1: The triangles are similar. Find x.

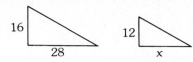

Since the ratios of corresponding sides are equal, a proportion can be set up.

$$\frac{16}{12} = \frac{28}{x}$$

$16x = 336$ **Take the cross products.**

$x = 21$ **Divide by 16.**

Example 2: The figures are similar. Find the missing values.

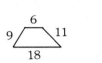

Set up a proportion for each missing value.

$$\frac{6}{10} = \frac{9}{a} \qquad \frac{6}{10} = \frac{18}{b} \qquad \frac{6}{10} = \frac{11}{c}$$

$6a = 90 \qquad\qquad 6b = 180 \qquad\qquad 6c = 110$

$a = 15 \qquad\qquad b = 30 \qquad\qquad c = 18\frac{1}{3}$

EXERCISES

Choose the figure in each row that is similar to the red figure.

1.   a.   b.   c.   d.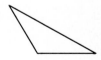

2.   a.   b.   c.   d.

3.   a.   b.   c.    d.

To measure slanted sides, mark off the units of the grid on the edge of a sheet of paper, and use that as a ruler. Copy and complete the table.

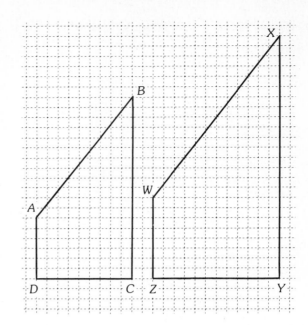

	Ratios of corresponding sides	Ratios in lowest terms
4. $\frac{AD}{WZ}$	$\frac{6}{8}$	$\frac{3}{4}$
5. $\frac{CD}{YZ}$	$\frac{9}{12}$	$\frac{3}{4}$
6. $\frac{BC}{XY}$	$\frac{18}{24}$	$\frac{3}{4}$
7. $\frac{AB}{WX}$	$\frac{15}{20}$	$\frac{3}{4}$

Find the missing values for each pair of similar figures.

8.

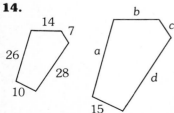

$x = 25$

9.

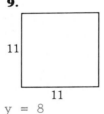

$y = 8$

10.

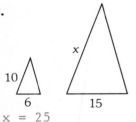

$c = 27; \ a = 22\frac{1}{2}$

11.

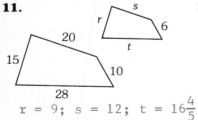

$r = 9; \ s = 12; \ t = 16\frac{4}{5}$

12.

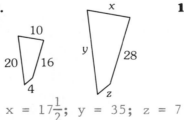

$x = 17\frac{1}{2}; \ y = 35; \ z = 7$

13.

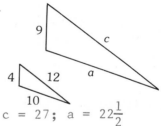

$w = 64; \ x = 24; \ y = 48; \ z = 32$

14.

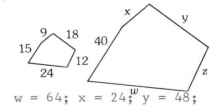

$a = 39; \ b = 21; \ c = 10\frac{1}{2}; \ d = 42$

15.

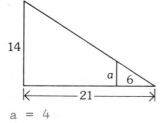

$a = 4$

16.

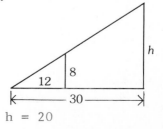

$h = 20$

152

Use a proportion to solve each problem.

17.

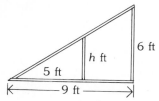

A carpenter is cutting a vertical brace for a roof. How long should the brace be? $3\frac{1}{3}$ ft

18.

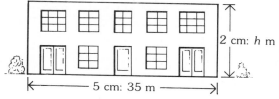

A drawing of a building measures 5 centimeters wide and 2 centimeters tall. The actual building measures 35 meters wide along the ground. Find the height h for the actual building. 14 m

Mary Elenz Tranter

19.

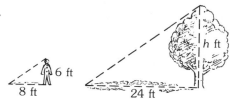

A tree's shadow is 24 feet long. The 6-foot-tall orchard owner has a shadow 8 feet long. How tall is the tree? 18 ft

20.

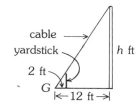

A pole is braced with a cable. Dave held a yardstick perpendicular to the ground and found that one end just touched the cable when the other end was 2 feet from G. How tall is the pole? 18 ft

Application 20 may be used at this time.   **153**

If you looked at an insect through a microscope, you would see an **enlargement** of the insect.

original   enlargement

Photos by Lambert Studios

If you measured both pictures, you would find that each measurement in the enlargement is 5 times as large as the corresponding measurement in the original.

The new picture is an enlargement by a factor of 5.

It is also convenient to use ratios:

The ratio of the enlargement to the original is

5 to 1   or   **5:1**   or $\frac{5}{1}$

Note that in the ratio, the *new* figure always comes *first,* or is the numerator. The *original* figure always comes *second*, or is the denominator.

Example 1: Make a 3 to 2 enlargement of the rectangle.

The ratio of the new figure to the original figure is to be 3:2. (The new figure will be $\frac{3}{2}$, or $1\frac{1}{2}$ times, the size of the original figure.)

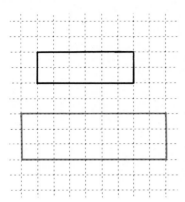

The new figure, the enlargement, is drawn with 3 units for every 2 units in the original.

The enlargement scale is 3 units to 2 units.

It is just as easy to make a **reduction,** a smaller new figure.

Example 2: Make a 1:3 reduction of the figure.

The ratio of the new figure to the original figure is to be 1:3. (The new figure will be $\frac{1}{3}$ the size of the original figure.)

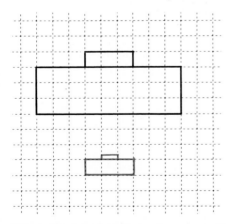

The new figure is drawn with only 1 unit for every 3 units in the original.

The reduction scale is 1 unit to 3 units.

Notice that where the original figure has a length of 1 unit, the new figure has a length of $\frac{1}{3}$ unit.

Example 3: Find the distance from Los Angeles to Detroit.

Scale: 1 inch = 880 miles

Each inch on the map represents 880 miles.

Step 1: Measure.

From the Los Angeles dot to the Detroit dot is $2\frac{1}{4}$ inches.

Step 2: Multiply.

$$2\frac{1}{4} \times 880 = \frac{9}{4} \times 880 = \frac{7920}{4} = 1980$$

The distance from Los Angeles to Detroit is 1980 miles.

EXERCISES

Tell whether each new figure is an enlargement or a reduction. Then give the scale for each pair of figures.

1.

original   new

enlargement; 2:1

2.

original   new

reduction; 3:5

3.

original   new

reduction; 2:3

4.

original   new

enlargement; 3:1

156

5.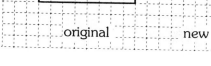

original · new

reduction; 1:4

6.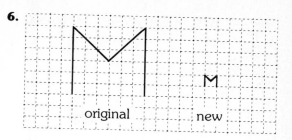

original · new

reduction; 1:6

For each ratio, tell whether the new figure will be an enlargement, a reduction, or an identical copy.

7. 2 to 5 reduction   **8.** 3 to 1 enlargement   **9.** 2:3 reduction

10. 4:4 idential copy   **11.** $\frac{6}{2}$ enlargement   **12.** $\frac{1}{100}$ reduction

13. 7:8 reduction   **14.** $\frac{6}{10}$ reduction   **15.** $\frac{9}{5}$ enlargement

16. 3:2 enlargement   **17.** 5 to 5 identical copy   **18.** 7 to 11 reduction

Copy and complete the table. Use the map on page 156.

	Map distance to nearest $\frac{1}{4}$ inch	Real distance in miles
19. Chicago to Los Angeles	2	1760
20. Houston to Detroit	$1\frac{1}{4}$	1100
21. New York to Miami	$1\frac{1}{4}$	1100
22. Los Angeles to Boston	3	2640
23. Seattle to San Francisco	$\frac{3}{4}$	660
24. Boston to Chicago	1	880
25. Denver to Houston	1	880
26. Chicago to Seattle	2	1760
27. Los Angeles to New York	$2\frac{3}{4}$	2420
28. Denver to Boston	2	1760

Use the floor plan to find each measurement.

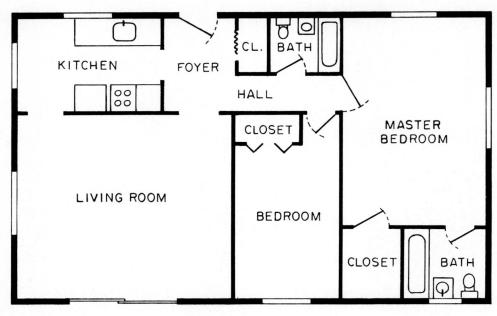

Scale: 1 inch = 8 feet

Example: Find the length of the house.

$$\frac{1}{8} \begin{matrix} \longleftarrow \text{scale length (inches)} \longrightarrow \\ \longleftarrow \text{real length (feet)} \longrightarrow \end{matrix} \frac{5}{h}$$

Take the cross products.

$$\frac{1}{8} = \frac{5}{h}$$

$$h = 40$$

The length of the house is 40 feet.

Answers for exercises 29–32 may vary.

29. Find the length of the kitchen. Find the width. 12 ft; 8 ft

30. Find the length of the living room. Find the width. 18 ft; 16 ft

31. Find the length of the master bedroom. Find the width. 18 ft; 12 ft

32. Find the width of the foyer. 6 ft

Applications 21–22 may be used at this time.

Many workers do not make a product, but they perform a service for the public. The problems a public-service worker may run into are often about money.

Some problems are given below. They can be solved with proportions, but other methods may work as well. Can you solve them?

Laimute E. Druskis/Taurus

Al Stephenson/Corn's Photo Service

Norman Prince

1. *Supermarket cashier:* What should be charged for 2 cans of soup marked 3 for $1.29? 86¢

2. *Bookkeeper:* A company's income for the first 3 months of the year was $45,380. Estimate the income for the year. $181,520

3. *Cabdriver:* Some city taxi companies charge "rate and a half" for fares to the suburbs. What should be charged for a suburban fare when the taxi meter shows $5.40? $8.10

159

James H. Pickerell

A **percent** is a ratio of some number to 100.

The symbol for percent is %. Percent means "out of 100," "per 100," or "hundredths."

Player	Baskets made	Total attempts
Alvin	6	10
Bernice	16	25
Cas	10	15

To find who has the best record, you can find a percent for each player.

Example 1: Alvin made 6 out of 10. That is the same as how many out of 100?

6 ⟶ 6/10 $\frac{6}{10} = \frac{a}{100}$ ⟵ how many out of 10 ⟶ out of 100

$$600 = 10a$$
$$60 = a$$

If he continued to make baskets at the same rate, he would make 60 out of 100 attempts. His rate is 60%.

Example 2: Find the percents for Bernice and Cas.

$$\frac{16}{25} = \frac{b}{100} \qquad\qquad \frac{10}{15} = \frac{c}{100}$$

$1600 = 25b$ **Take the cross products.** $1000 = 15c$

$64 = b$ **Divide.** $66\frac{2}{3} = c$

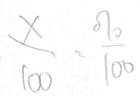

Bernice made 64% of her attempts. At that rate she would average 64 per 100.

Cas's rate is $66\frac{2}{3}$%. At that rate Cas would average $66\frac{2}{3}$ baskets in each 100 tries.

When the records are given as percents, it is easy to see that Cas's rate of $66\frac{2}{3}$% is the best record.

160

Example 3: Write the ratio $\frac{5}{8}$ as a percent.

$\frac{5}{8} = \frac{x}{100}$ **Think: 5 out of 8 is what out of 100?**

$500 = 8x$ **Take the cross products.**

$62\frac{4}{8} = x$ **Divide by 8.**

So $\frac{5}{8} = 62\frac{1}{2}\%$, or 62.5%.

Example 4: Show 25% on a diagram.

$25\% = \frac{25}{100}$

Therefore, shade 25 out of the 100 squares.

Example 5: Write 56% as a ratio in lowest terms.

$56\% = \frac{56}{100} = \frac{56 \div 4}{100 \div 4} = \frac{14}{25}$

EXERCISES

1. If $60\% = \frac{n}{100}$, then $n = \underline{60}$.

2. 30% means $\underline{30}$ out of 100 or 3 out of $\underline{10}$.

Copy and shade each figure to show the given percent.
Possible answers for exercises 3-8 are given.

3.

40%

4.

60%

5.

50%

6.

75%

7.

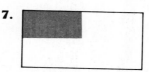

25%

8.

20%

Write each percent as a ratio in lowest terms.

9. 50% $\frac{1}{2}$ **10.** 75% $\frac{3}{4}$ **11.** 20% $\frac{1}{5}$ **12.** 15% $\frac{3}{20}$

13. 95% $\frac{19}{20}$ **14.** 12% $\frac{3}{25}$ **15.** 37% $\frac{37}{100}$ **16.** 49% $\frac{49}{100}$

Write each ratio as a percent.

17. $\frac{3}{10}$ 30%   **18.** $\frac{1}{20}$ 5%   **19.** 3:5 60%   **20.** 1 out of 5 20%

21. $\frac{1}{3}$ $33\frac{1}{3}\%$ **22.** $\frac{4}{6}$ $66\frac{2}{3}\%$ **23.** 4 out of 25 16%   **24.** 17:20 85%

25. $\frac{4}{9}$ $44\frac{4}{9}\%$ **26.** $\frac{7}{16}$ $43\frac{3}{4}\%$ **27.** 65:125 52%   **28.** 66 out of 120 55%

Find the percent of games each team won.

	Team	Wins	Total games	Percent
29.	Central H.S.	14	20	70%
30.	East H.S.	18	27	$66\frac{2}{3}\%$
31.	West H.S.	19	25	76%

32. Which team won the largest percent of its games? West H.S.

Find the percent of commission each salesperson is getting.

		Commission	Total sales	Percent
33.	Ann	$16	$80	20%
34.	Mitch	$18	$96	$18\frac{3}{4}\%$
35.	Carla	$15	$60	25%

36. Who received the highest commission percent? Carla

Find the percent of defective parts.

	Machine	Defective	Total parts	Percent
37.	A	21	300	7%
38.	B	18	225	8%
39.	C	27	450	6%

40. Which machine has the smallest percent of defective parts? C

Find the percent of interest each bank pays.

	Bank	Interest for 1 year	Principal	Percent
41.	First Natl.	$9	$150	6%
42.	City Natl.	$4.40	$80	$5\frac{1}{2}\%$
43.	Farmer's	$23	$400	$5\frac{3}{4}\%$

44. Which bank pays the highest percent of interest? First Natl.

SOLVING PROBLEMS WITH PERCENT

One way to solve a percent problem is to use a proportion:

$$\frac{\textbf{part}}{\textbf{total}} = \frac{\textbf{number of percent}}{\textbf{100}}$$

Type 1: Find the percent.

14 is what percent of 20?

$\dfrac{\textbf{14}}{\textbf{20}} = \dfrac{\textbf{x}}{\textbf{100}}$ **Think: 14 out of 20 is how many out of 100?**

$\textbf{1400} = \textbf{20x}$

$\textbf{70} = \textbf{x}$

Answer: 14 out of 20 is 70%.
          70% of 20 is 14.

Type 2: Find the part.

What is 20% of 45?

$\dfrac{\textbf{x}}{\textbf{45}} = \dfrac{\textbf{20}}{\textbf{100}}$ **Think: How many out of 45 is 20 out of 100?**

$\textbf{100x} = \textbf{900}$

$\textbf{x} = \textbf{9}$

Answer: 9 out of 45 is 20%.
          20% of 45 is 9.

Type 3: Find the total.

15% of what number is 12?

$\dfrac{\textbf{12}}{\textbf{x}} = \dfrac{\textbf{15}}{\textbf{100}}$ **Think: 12 out of how many is 15 out of 100?**

$\textbf{1200} = \textbf{15x}$

$\textbf{80} = \textbf{x}$

Answer: 12 out of 80 is 15%.
          15% of 80 is 12.

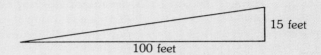

15 feet

100 feet

A road that rises 15 feet in a level distance of 100 feet is said to have a 15% *grade*, or a slope of 15%.

Example 1: What is the percent grade of a road that rises 6 feet in *every* 25 feet?

In this problem you are looking for a percent.

$$\frac{6}{25} = \frac{x}{100}$$ **Think: 6 out of 25 is how many out of 100?**

$$600 = 25x$$ **Take the cross products.**

$$24 = x$$ **Divide.**

The road has a 24% grade.

Example 2: If a state has a 4% sales tax, how much tax is charged on a $305 purchase?

In this problem you are looking for a part.

$$\frac{x}{305} = \frac{4}{100}$$ **Think: How many out of 305 is 4 out of 100?**

$$100x = 1220$$ **Take the cross products.**

$$x = 12.20$$ **Divide.**

If the sales tax is 4%, $12.20 tax is charged on a $305 purchase.

164

Example 3: Beverly opened a 5% savings account. How much should she deposit to earn $12 interest in one year?

In this problem you are looking for a total.

$\dfrac{12}{x} = \dfrac{5}{100}$ **Think: 12 out of what is 5 out of 100?**

$1200 = 5x$ **Take the cross products.**

$240 = x$ **Divide.**

She would have to deposit $240 to earn $12 interest.

EXERCISES

Copy and complete the tables by solving the proportions.

	Part	Whole	Percent			Part	Whole	Percent
1.	1	4	25%		**6.**	20	125	16%
2.	52	80	65%		**7.**	21	60	35%
3.	18	30	60%		**8.**	30	120	25%
4.	4	10	40%		**9.**	19	25	76%
5.	27	75	36%		**10.**	36	80	45%

165

Use proportions to solve these problems.

11. 25% of what number is 6? 24

12. What is 60% of 50? 30

13. 45 is what percent of 75? 60%

14. What is 80% of 40? 32

15. 40% of what number is 10? 25

16. 8 is what percent of 25? 32%

17. 44 is what percent of 50? 88%

18. 15% of what number is 90? 600

19. 20% of what number is 80? 400

20. What is 40% of 25? 10

Solve each type-1 problem.

21. You make 12 baskets out of 15 shots. Find your percent. 80%

22. A magazine sold for 60¢ a copy. Then the cost went up 3¢. What was the percent of increase? 5%

23. On his English test, Jim got 36 of the 40 questions correct. What was his percent? 90%

24. Ann made $21 in commission on a $175 sale. What is her commission percent? 12%

25. A car manages to climb just 14 feet in a distance of 40 feet. What is the maximum percent grade it can climb? 35%

26. Suppose you bought a $250 item on the installment plan. If the total of your monthly payments comes to $45 more than that, what percent finance charges are you paying? 18%

Solve each type-2 problem.

27. If 70% is passing, how many questions do you have to get right on a 30-question test to get a passing grade? 21

28. A $65 bicycle is on sale at 20% off. Find the savings. $13

29. For winter protection a car's radiator should contain 40% antifreeze. If the radiator holds 15 quarts, how many quarts of antifreeze should be used?
6 qt

30. Suppose inflation is running at 8% a year. How much more will you have to pay for a $75 item if you wait a year to buy it? $6

Solve each type-3 problem.

31. How much would you have to deposit in a 6% savings account to earn $27 interest in a year? $450

32. Meg gave her brother this puzzle: "I got 12 hits playing ball. That was 40% of my number of times at bat." How many times was she at bat? 30

33. A curb ramp is to be built for use by handicapped persons who must use wheelchairs. How much level distance is needed for a ramp up to a 6-inch curb if the grade is to be 8%? 75 in.

34. If the 84 people who preferred Brand X in a poll represented 60% of the total, how many people were polled? 140

Solve these problems, using proportions.

35. If the down payment on a $2000 motorcycle is 25%, how much money must you pay down? $500

36. Mr. Jones sold his car for $5700. That was 75% of the original cost. What was the original cost? $7600

37. In the election for class president, Katie got 98 of the 175 votes cast. What percent of the votes did she get? 56%

38. How much money would you save buying a $40 watch at 15% off? $6

SKILLS REFRESHER

				Skill	Page
Divide each number by 10. Write the answer as a decimal.

1. 7 0.7 **2.** 23 2.3 **3.** 3.1 0.31 **4.** 0.23 0.023 | 21 | 478 |

Divide each number by 100. Write the answer as a decimal.

5. 9 0.09 **6.** 75 0.75 **7.** 12.6 0.126 **8.** 0.45 0.0045

Divide each number by 1000. Write the answer as a decimal.

9. 3 0.003 **10.** 19 0.019 **11.** 51.2 0.0512 **12.** 0.72 0.00072

4.9 | PERCENTS IN DECIMAL FORM

A percent can be written as a fraction with a denominator of 100. That makes it easy to change a percent to a decimal or to change a decimal to a percent.

Example 1: Change each percent to a decimal.

$$35\% = \frac{35}{100} = 0.35$$

$$12\frac{1}{2}\% = 12.5\% = \frac{12.5}{100} = 0.125$$

$$103\% = \frac{103}{100} = 1.03$$

Another way would be to use a shortcut. Move the decimal point two places to the *left* and omit the %.

$$35\% = 0.35$$
$$12.5\% = 0.125$$
$$103\% = 1.03$$

Example 2: Change each decimal to a percent.

$$0.06 = \frac{0.06}{1} \times \frac{100}{100} = \frac{6}{100} = 6\%$$

$$0.378 = \frac{0.378}{1} \times \frac{100}{100} = \frac{37.8}{100} = 37.8\%$$

$$1.53 = \frac{1.53}{1} \times \frac{100}{100} = \frac{153}{100} = 153\%$$

Another way would be to use a shortcut. Move the decimal point two places to the *right* and write the %.

$$0.06 = 6\%$$
$$0.378 = 37.8\%$$
$$1.53 = 153\%$$

Example 3: Find 36% of 75. Solve by multiplying.

$$36\% = \frac{36}{100} = 0.36$$

Then $0.36 \times 75 = 27.00$, or 27.

EXERCISES

Change each percent to a decimal.

1. 16% 0.16

2. 79% 0.79

3. 56% 0.56

4. 102% 1.02

5. 0.2% 0.002

6. 206% 2.06

7. 15.5% 0.155

8. 3% 0.03

9. 5% 0.05

10. 26.4% 0.264

11. $16\frac{1}{2}$% 0.165

12. $29\frac{1}{2}$% 0.295

Change each decimal to a percent.

13. 0.42 42%

14. 0.56 56%

15. 0.91 91%

16. 3.7 370%

17. 0.029 2.9%

18. 0.4 40%

19. 0.05 5%

20. 0.375 37.5%

21. 0.415 41.5%

22. 0.08 8%

23. 0.293 29.3%

24. 0.038 3.8%

Find each answer by multiplying.

25. 25% of 36 9

26. 60% of 35 21

27. 14% of 50 7

28. 15% of 40 6

29. 40% of 18 7.2

30. 30% of 24 7.2

31. 85% of 64 54.4

32. 18% of 40 7.2

33. 32% of 275 88

34. 48% of 325 156

35. 22% of 382 84.04

36. 28% of 270 75.6

37. 40% of 12.50 5

38. 60% of 14.80 8.88

39. 5% of 14.80 0.74

40. 100% of 39.5 39.5

41. 2.8% of 75 2.1

42. 150% of 80 120

43. 10.5% of 120 12.6

44. 35.7% of 98 34.986

45. 106% of 106 112.36

46. 9.75% of 50.80 4.953

47. 225% of 160.44 360.99

48. $8\frac{1}{2}$% of 85.06 7.2301

Solve each problem by multiplication.

49. A shipper expects 12% of a fresh fruit shipment to spoil before it is sold. How many cases can he expect to lose out of a 2100-case shipment? *252 cases*

50. You pay an 18% carrying charge if you buy a $70 coat on credit. How much is the carrying charge? $12.60

51. A town has 5300 registered voters. If the turnout for an election was 42%, how many people voted? *2226 people*

52. How much would you save if you bought a $250 TV at 15% off? $37.50

Use multiplication for the first step of each problem.

53. Ted bought an old car for $160. He repaired it, intending to sell it for 80% more than he paid for it. What is his intended selling price? $288

54. Some new cars depreciate 25% during the first year of ownership. If you buy a new car for $8400, what will it be worth one year later? $6300

55. According to the tax rate schedule, Monica's income tax is $608 plus 19% of $1550. What is her total tax? $902.50

56. Suppose you earn a salary of $650 a month plus 18% commission. Your sales for last month were $2575. What were your total earnings for the month? $1113.50

An average person's budget usually shows what part of his or her income will be spent on different things. Suppose you divided your income according to the graph below.

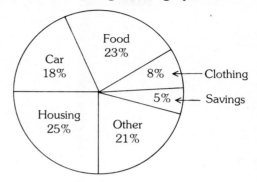

If your take-home pay was $1500 a month,

1. What would housing cost you? $375

2. How much would you spend on food? $345

3. How much would you spend on your car? $270

4. What would you spend on clothing? $120

5. How much would you save? $75

6. What would you have left for medical and dental expenses, education, insurance, entertainment, etc.? $315

Governments and companies use budgets, too. Sometimes they show how their income will be spent. Other budgets show where their income is coming from. In 1981, the United States received nearly 627 billion dollars in federal budget receipts.

About how many billions were collected from each of the following? Answers for exercises 7-12 may vary.

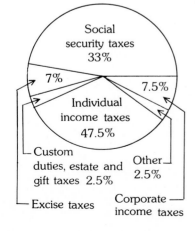

7. Individual income taxes 298

8. Corporate income taxes 47

9. Social security 207

10. Excise taxes 44

11. Customs, duties, estate, and gift taxes 16

12. Other sources 16

171

How much is the price reduced?

Refer to Example 1b. below.

You could solve this proportion:

$$\frac{x}{210} = \frac{30}{100}$$

You could solve this equation:

$x = 30\%$ of 210

Or you might solve the problem by doing only mental computation. Remember that 10% means $\frac{10}{100}$, or $\frac{1}{10}$.

To find $\frac{1}{10}$ of a number, or divide a number by 10, simply move the decimal point one place to the left.

Example 1: Find each result by mental computation.

a. Find 10% of 43.

    Think: 10% of $43 = \frac{1}{10} \times 43 = 4.3$

b. Find 30% of 210.

Think: 30% of $210 = 3 \times (10\%$ of $210)$ since $30\% = 3 \times 10\%$

$$= 3 \times \left(\frac{1}{10} \times 210 \right)$$

$$= 3 \times 21$$

$$= 63$$

c. Find 15% of 48.

Think: **15% of 48 = 10% of 48 + 5% of 48**   **since 15% = 10% + 5%**

$$= \frac{1}{10} \times 48 + \frac{1}{2} \text{ of } \left(\frac{1}{10} \times 48 \right) \quad \textbf{since } 5\% = \tfrac{1}{2} \textbf{ of } 10\%$$

$$= 4.8 + \frac{1}{2} \times 4.8$$

$$= 4.8 + 2.4$$

$$= 7.2$$

You can also use mental computation to estimate results.

Example 2:   Estimate each result by rounding the percent to the nearest 5%.

a. Estimate 38% of 79.

> **Think:**   **38% is about 40%.**
>   **79 is about 80.**

40% of 80 = 4 × (10% of 80)   **since 40% = 4 × 10%**

$$= 4 \times \left(\frac{1}{10} \times 80 \right)$$

$$= 4 \times 8$$

$$= 32$$

38% of 79 is about 32.

b. Estimate 26% of 82.

> **Think:**   **26% is about 25%.**
>   **82 is about 80.**

25% of 80 = 10% of 80 + 10% of 80 + 5% of 80   **since 25% = 10% + 10% + 5%**

$$= \frac{1}{10} \times 80 + \frac{1}{10} \times 80 + \frac{1}{2} \text{ of } \left(\frac{1}{10} \times 80 \right) \quad \textbf{since } 5\% = \tfrac{1}{2} \textbf{ of } 10\%$$

$$= 8 + 8 + \frac{1}{2} \times 8$$

$$= 8 + 8 + 4$$

$$= 20$$

26% of 82 is about 20.

c. Estimate $14\frac{3}{4}\%$ of 198.75.

$\qquad$ **Think:** $14\frac{3}{4}\%$ **is about 15%.**

$\qquad$ **198.75 is about 200.**

15% of 200 = 10% of 200 + 5% of 200 $\quad$ **since 15% = 10% + 5%**

$$= \frac{1}{10} \times 200 + \frac{1}{2} \text{ of } \left(\frac{1}{10} \times 200\right)$$

$$= 20 + \frac{1}{2} \times 20$$

$$= 20 + 10$$

$$= 30$$

$14\frac{3}{4}\%$ of 198.75 is about 30.

EXERCISES

Find each result by mental computation.

1. 10% of 90 $\quad$ 9
2. 10% of 40 $\quad$ 4
3. 10% of 48 $\quad$ 4.8

4. 10% of 63 $\quad$ 6.3
5. 20% of 60 $\quad$ 12
6. 20% of 80 $\quad$ 16

7. 20% of 46 $\quad$ 9.2
8. 20% of 74 $\quad$ 14.8
9. 15% of 80 $\quad$ 12

10. 15% of 60 $\quad$ 9
11. 30% of 160 $\quad$ 48
12. 25% of 180 $\quad$ 45

13. 25% of 280 $\quad$ 70
14. 30% of 320 $\quad$ 96
15. 5% of 120 $\quad$ 6

16. 35% of 80 $\quad$ 28
17. 35% of 60 $\quad$ 21
18. 5% of 160 $\quad$ 8

Estimate each result by rounding the percent to the nearest 5%.
Estimates for exercises 19-30 may vary.

19. 11% of 59 $\quad$ 6
20. 9% of 81 $\quad$ 8
21. 19% of 52 $\quad$ 10

22. 16% of 40 $\quad$ 6
23. 21% of 148 $\quad$ 30
24. 4% of 21 $\quad$ 1

25. 24% of 282 $\quad$ 70
26. 11% of 128 $\quad$ 13
27. 6% of 78 $\quad$ 4

28. $9\frac{1}{2}\%$ of 240 $\quad$ 24
29. 31% of 49.95 $\quad$ 15
30. 21% of 99.50 $\quad$ 20

Copy and complete the table.

	Regular price	Discount %	Estimated reduction	Estimated sale price
31.	$19.99	11%	$2	$18
32.	$129.95	21%	$26	$104
33.	$299.50	$9\frac{1}{2}$%	$30	$270
34.	$24.95	19%	$5	$20
35.	$59.49	24%	$15	$45
36.	$88.95	32%	$27	$63
37.	$197.00	14%	$30	$170
38.	$10.95	$5\frac{3}{4}$%	$0.55	$10.45

Solve each problem by estimating.

39. About how much will a $14.95 tennis racket cost at 15% off? about $12.75

40. About how much will a $97.50 coat cost at 22% off? about $80

41. Estimate the cost of a $49.50 item with a 5% sales tax. about $52

42. Mrs. Parker earned $24,800 last year. She got an 11% raise. About how much will she earn this year? about $27,500

43. A $5\frac{1}{2}$% savings account is opened with $759. About how much will be in the account 1 year from now? about $800

44. This year there are 394 students in the freshman class. Enrollment for next year will increase by 6%. Estimate the number of students that the freshman class will have. about 420 students

45. A farmer harvested 862 bushels of wheat last year. This year's yield is expected to be 15% greater. About how many bushels can be expected this year? about 1000 bushels

Give each ratio as a fraction.

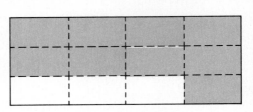

4.1

1. red parts to all parts $\frac{5}{12}$

2. all parts to white parts $\frac{12}{3}$

3. blue parts to red parts $\frac{4}{5}$

4. A room is 8 feet long and 7 feet wide. What is the ratio of width to length? $\frac{7}{8}$

5. There are 17 girls and 15 boys in a class. What is the ratio of boys to girls? $\frac{15}{17}$

Find an equivalent ratio in lowest terms.

4.2

6. $\frac{9}{15}$ $\frac{3}{5}$

7. $\frac{12}{36}$ $\frac{1}{3}$

8. $\frac{10}{8}$ $\frac{5}{4}$

9. $\frac{35}{20}$ $\frac{7}{4}$

10. $\frac{63}{54}$ $\frac{7}{6}$

11. $\frac{27}{81}$ $\frac{1}{3}$

Use cross products to tell whether or not these ratios are equivalent.

4.3

12. $\frac{6}{14} = \frac{9}{21}$ Yes

13. $\frac{7}{7} = \frac{10}{10}$ Yes

14. $\frac{20}{25} = \frac{28}{37}$ No

Use cross products to solve each proportion.

15. $\frac{2}{5} = \frac{4}{x}$ 10

16. $\frac{3}{8} = \frac{x}{24}$ 9

17. $\frac{10}{x} = \frac{6}{21}$ 35

18. $\frac{x}{45} = \frac{8}{18}$ 20

19. $\frac{20}{15} = \frac{x}{18}$ 24

20. $\frac{15}{6} = \frac{85}{x}$ 34

Solve each problem by using a proportion.

4.4

21. A car traveled 80 miles on 3 gallons of gas. How much gas will be needed to travel 400 miles? 15 gal

22. If you walked a distance of 4 blocks in 7 minutes, how long would it take to walk 10 blocks at the same rate? $17\frac{1}{2}$ min

23. Find the missing values for this pair of similar figures.

4.5

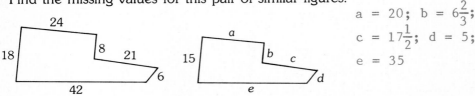

$a = 20;\ b = 6\frac{2}{3};$
$c = 17\frac{1}{2};\ d = 5;$
$e = 35$

Copy and complete the chart. Use the scale drawing of the building at the right.

4.6

Measurement	Drawing (cm)	Real (m)
24. Total length	5	15
25. Total height	2	6
26. Distance between doorways	1.5	4.5
27. Width of each window	0.5	1.5

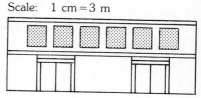

Scale: 1 cm = 3 m

Write each percent as a ratio in lowest terms.

4.7

28. 25% $\frac{1}{4}$ **29.** 60% $\frac{3}{5}$ **30.** 18% $\frac{9}{50}$ **31.** 84% $\frac{21}{25}$

Write each ratio as a percent.

32. $\frac{9}{36}$ 25%   **33.** 14:25 56%   **34.** 6 out of 40   **35.** $\frac{57}{75}$ 76%
                                            15%

Use a proportion to solve each problem.

4.8

36. What is 40% of 65? 26   **37.** 48 is what percent of 200? 24%

38. 15% of what number is 105? 700   **39.** What is 75% of 24? 18

40. A team won 9 of the 15 games it played. What percent of its games did the team win? 60%

41. If 70% is passing, how many correct answers would you have to get to pass a test that has 40 problems? 28

Change each percent to a decimal.

4.9

42. 53% 0.53   **43.** 4% 0.04   **44.** 23.3% 0.233   **45.** 0.07% 0.0007

Change each decimal to a percent.

46. 0.67 67%   **47.** 2.8 280%   **48.** 0.09 9%   **49.** 0.08 8%

Find each answer by multiplying.

50. 12% of 75 9   **51.** 6% of 18   **52.** 16% of 47   **53.** 23% of 126 28.98
                      1.08   7.52

Estimate each result. Estimates for exercises 54-57 may vary.

4.10

                                                    32
54. 46% of 80 36   **55.** 16% of 41 6   **56.** 21% of 159   **57.** 11% of 19.88 2

CHAPTER REVIEW

CHAPTER TEST

Give the ratio of circles to squares.

1. ○○○□□□□ $\frac{3}{4}$

2. ○○□□○○○ $\frac{5}{2}$

Find an equivalent ratio in lowest terms.

3. $\frac{4}{8}$ $\frac{1}{2}$

4. $\frac{10}{15}$ $\frac{2}{3}$

5. $\frac{20}{15}$ $\frac{4}{3}$

Use cross products to solve each proportion.

6. $\frac{3}{4} = \frac{x}{12}$ 9

7. $\frac{4}{14} = \frac{6}{a}$ 21

8. $\frac{n}{6} = \frac{24}{9}$ 16

Solve this problem by using a proportion.

9. A 14-lb weight stretches a spring 4 inches. What weight will stretch it 10 inches? 35 lb

Use the similar figures at the right.

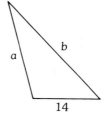

10. Find the values of a and b.
a = 21; b = 28

A map has a scale of 1 inch = 24 miles. Find the real distance for each map distance.

11. 4 inches 96 mi

12. $1\frac{3}{4}$ inches 42 mi

Write each percent as a ratio in lowest terms.

13. 35% $\frac{7}{20}$

14. 67% $\frac{67}{100}$

Write each ratio as a percent.

15. $\frac{2}{5}$ 40%

16. 6 out of 20 30%

Solve this problem by using a proportion.

17. A $40 coat is reduced 20%. How much money will you save? $8

Estimate the answer. Then find the exact answer by multiplying.
Estimates are given first and may vary.

18. 31% of 49 15; 15.19

19. 79% of 62 48; 48.98

CUMULATIVE REVIEW

Tell whether each sentence is true, false, or open.

3.1

1. $4+n=24$ Open   **2.** $6\times2=10+2$ True   **3.** $8+7=3\times4$ False

Find each answer.

3.2

4. $8+(12-4)$ 16   **5.** $3(7-2)$ 15   **6.** $(4\times6)-5$ 19

7. $9+(15\div5)$ 12   **8.** $(5+4)\div3$ 3   **9.** $(5+3)\times2$ 16

Find each answer when n is replaced with 5.

10. $2n$ 10   **11.** $6n$ 30   **12.** $3(6-n)$ 3

13. $3(n-3)$ 6   **14.** $n(7+4)$ 55   **15.** $2(4+n)$ 18

Find each answer.

3.3

16. $12-5+2$ 9   **17.** $8(3)+4$ 28   **18.** $24\div6\times2$ 8

19. $5(4)-12$ 8   **20.** $18\div3+3(2)$ 12   **21.** $2(4)+20\div4$ 13

Find each answer when x is replaced with 8.

22. $2x-5$ 11   **23.** $7-\frac{16}{x}$ 5   **24.** $6+\frac{x}{8}$ 7

25. $3(x-2)$ 18   **26.** $4(x+2)$ 40   **27.** $3x+4$ 28

Use the given formula to solve.

3.4

28. How many miles will a plane go in 4 hours at a rate of 340 miles per hour? $(d=rt)$ 1360 mi

29. How many meters of fencing will be needed to enclose a lot 12 meters long and 7 meters wide? $(P=2\ell+2w)$ 38 m

30. What will the blood pressure of a 32-year-old person be? $(P=\frac{a}{2}+110)$ 126

Solve and check.

3.5

31. $x+18=32$ 14   **32.** $y-12=50$ 62   **33.** $57=n-23$ 80

34. $b+14=28$ 14   **35.** $39=a+36$ 3   **36.** $9=w-42$ 51

Solve and check.

37. $6x=78$ 13   **38.** $2x=115$ 57.5   **39.** $\frac{x}{6}=31$ 186   **40.** $17=\frac{w}{9}$ 153

Solve and check.

41. $17=3y+2$ 5   **42.** $4m-3=29$ 8   **43.** $12=\frac{x}{5}-8$ 100   **44.** $\frac{w}{7}+4=10$ 42

Solve and check.

45. $4x=9$ $\frac{9}{4}$ **46.** $8y=4$ $\frac{1}{2}$ **47.** $3m-5=3$ $\frac{8}{3}$ **48.** $19=5c+3.5$ 3.1

Solve and check.

49. $6=\frac{2}{3}x$ 9   **50.** $\frac{4}{9}y=12$ 27   **51.** $18=\frac{5}{2}b+3$ 6   **52.** $2.1=\frac{3}{4}a-3$ 6.8

Use the given formula to solve.

$d=mg$

d: distance   **m: miles per gallon**   **g: number of gallons**

53. Ellen knows her car gets 27 miles per gallon on the highway. How much gas will she need to drive a distance of 486 miles? 18 gal

54. If a car went 378 miles on 14 gallons of gas, how many miles per gallon did it get? 27 mi/gal

$P=\frac{a}{2}+110$

P: blood pressure   **a: age**

55. Find the approximate normal blood pressure of a person who is 48 years old. 134

56. About how old is a person whose blood pressure is 145? 70

$F=\frac{9}{5}C+32$

57. Find the Celsius equivalent for 77°F. 25°C

58. Find the Fahrenheit equivalent for 10°C. 50°F

$P=2\ell+2w$

P: perimeter   **ℓ: length**   **w: width**

59. The perimeter of a room is 40 feet. If the length of the room is 12 feet, what is the width? 8 ft

Give each ratio as a fraction.

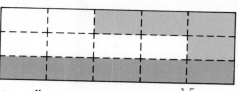

60. blue parts to all parts $\frac{4}{15}$

61. green parts to white parts $\frac{5}{6}$

62. green parts to blue parts $\frac{5}{4}$

63. all parts to white parts $\frac{15}{6}$

4.1

For each ratio give an equivalent one in lowest terms.

4.2

64. $\frac{2}{8}$ $\frac{1}{4}$ **65.** $\frac{6}{10}$ $\frac{3}{5}$ **66.** $\frac{18}{15}$ $\frac{6}{5}$ **67.** $\frac{35}{14}$ $\frac{5}{2}$

Use cross products to solve each proportion.

4.3

68. $\frac{3}{7} = \frac{x}{35}$ 15 **69.** $\frac{6}{5} = \frac{24}{m}$ 20 **70.** $\frac{10}{w} = \frac{12}{18}$ 15 **71.** $\frac{n}{54} = \frac{4}{18}$ 12

Solve each problem by using a proportion.

4.4

72. An 18-pound weight stretches a spring 4 inches. How far will a 45-pound weight stretch the spring? 10 in.

73. If it cost $7 to ship a 15-pound package, what will a 42-pound package cost at the same rate? $19.60

74. If 4 rolls of wallpaper cover a wall 10 feet long, how many rolls will be needed for a wall 15 feet long? 6 rolls

Use the similar figures at the right.

4.5

75. Find the missing values.

$a = 12$; $b = 9$; $c = 7\frac{1}{5}$; $d = 21\frac{3}{5}$

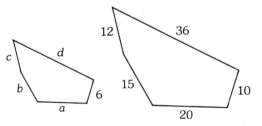

Find the real distance for each map distance.

4.6

Scale: 1 inch = 48 miles

76. 2 inches 96 mi **77.** $1\frac{3}{4}$ inches 84 mi **78.** $2\frac{3}{8}$ inches 114 mi

Scale: 1 cm = 28 km

79. 4 cm 112 km **80.** 2.5 cm 70 km **81.** 6.3 cm 176.4 km

Copy and complete the chart. Use the scale drawing of a sailboat at the right.   4.6

Measurement	Drawing (inches)	Real (feet)
82. Total length of boat	$1\frac{3}{4}$	21
83. Height of mast	$1\frac{3}{4}$	21
84. Length of boom	1	12
85. Depth of keel below bottom of boat	$\frac{1}{4}$	3
86. Height on mast at which jib is attached	$1\frac{1}{2}$	18

mast →

Scale:
1 inch = 12 feet

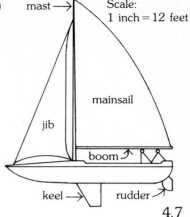

mainsail

jib

boom →

keel →   rudder →

Write each ratio as a percent.

87. $\frac{14}{35}$ 40%   **88.** 13:52 25%   **89.** 8 to 40 20% **90.** $\frac{52}{80}$ 65%

4.7

Write each percent as a ratio in lowest terms.

91. 70% $\frac{7}{10}$ **92.** 45% $\frac{9}{20}$ **93.** 96% $\frac{24}{25}$ **94.** 2% $\frac{1}{50}$

Solve each problem by using a proportion.   4.8

95. 15% of what number is 24?   160   **96.** 180 is what percent of 400?   45%

97. What is 20% of 65?   13   **98.** 16% of what number is 12?   75

Solve each problem by using a proportion.

99. Evan borrowed $700 from a bank at 9% interest. How much money must he pay in interest? $63

100. Peggy sold 32 of the 40 magazines she had to sell. What percent did she sell?   80%

Find by multiplying.   4.9

101. 28% of 50   14   **102.** 77% of 250   192.5   **103.** 30% of 87   26.1

Find each result by mental computation.   4.10

104. 10% of 240   24   **105.** 45% of 300   135   **106.** 15% of 100   15

Estimate each result.
Estimates for exercises 107-109 may vary.
107. 29% of 149   45   **108.** 12% of 39.95   4   **109.** 19% of 19.98   4

CUMULATIVE REVIEW

Choose the correct answer.

Correlation

Items	Sec
1	5.1
2	5.2
3–4	5.3
5–6	5.4
7–8	5.5
9–10	5.6
11–12	5.7
13–14	5.8
15–17	5.9
18	5.10
19–20	5.11

1. The (meter, <u>thumb width</u>) is not a standard unit of measure.

2. The (yard, <u>cubit</u>) is an ancient unit that is the distance from the elbow to the end of the middle finger.

Measure each segment to the nearest $\frac{1}{2}$ inch.

3. ———————————— $1\frac{1}{2}$ in. **4.** ————————————————— 2 in.

Complete the following:

5. 3 yards is <u>108</u> inches. **6.** 144 inches is <u>12</u> feet.

Measure each segment to the nearest centimeter.

7. ———————————— 4 cm **8.** ————————— 2 cm

Complete the following:

9. 2000 mm is <u>200</u> cm. **10.** 20 km is —— m. $\quad$ 20 000 **11.** $\frac{1}{2}$ lb is <u>8</u> oz.

12. 4000 g is <u>4</u> kg. **13.** 15 gal is <u>60</u> qt. **14.** 3500 mL is <u>3.5</u> liters.

Add or subtract.

15.
$$\begin{array}{r} 8 \text{ hr } 28 \text{ min} \\ +2 \text{ hr } 42 \text{ min} \\ \hline 11 \text{ hr } 10 \text{ min} \end{array}$$

16.
$$\begin{array}{r} 8 \text{ hr } 5 \text{ min} \\ -2 \text{ hr } 23 \text{ min} \\ \hline 5 \text{ hr } 42 \text{ min} \end{array}$$

17.
$$\begin{array}{r} 1 \text{ hr } 46 \text{ min} \\ +9 \text{ hr } 30 \text{ min} \\ \hline 11 \text{ hr } 16 \text{ min} \end{array}$$

18. What is the freezing temperature of water on the Celsius scale? 0°C

Use a protractor to draw an angle for each measurement.
See students' drawings.

19. 53° **20.** 107°

UNITS OF MEASURE

Measurements are used to describe such things as length, weight, volume, area, and time. Measurements like those below are seen often.

$3\frac{1}{2}$ inches   140 pounds   12 seconds

12.2 gallons   78 centimeters   95 grams

Many different measuring instruments are used to make measurements. Some of them are shown here.

Don Renner/Photo Trends

Often, more than one measuring instrument can be used to measure the same thing. A person's height can be measured with both a ruler and a tape measure.

Also, more than one unit of measure can be used to measure the same thing. Possible units of measure for your height include the inch, the foot, and the centimeter.

Suppose the two people in the cartoon use their feet as units of measure. If they both measure the length of a room, their measurements will certainly not agree.

So that a measurement will mean the same thing to everyone, people have agreed upon a constant size for each unit. Such units are called **standard units of measure.**

EXERCISES

Name a unit of measure that could be used to find each of the following. More than one answer is usually possible.
Possible answers given for exercises 1-10.

1. your weight `pound (kilogram)`

2. the weight of a locomotive `ton (kilogram)`

3. the time it takes to broil a steak `minute`

4. your age `year`

5. the weight of an aspirin tablet `milligram`

6. the height of the Sears Tower `foot (meter)`

7. the length of a bus `foot (meter)`

8. room temperature `degree Fahrenheit (degree Celsius)`

9. the distance from Chicago to Miami `mile (kilometer)`

10. the amount of gasoline in a car's tank `gallon (liter)`

What measuring instrument would you use to find each of the following?

11. the length of a room `yardstick (meterstick)`

12. waist size `tape measure`

13. water temperature `thermometer`

14. the time it takes to run 100 meters `stopwatch`

15. your weight `scale`

16. tire pressure `air-pressure gauge`

17. the distance from one city to another odometer

18. the amount of flour needed to bake a cake measuring cup

19. the amount of oil in a car's crankcase dipstick

20. spark-plug gap gap gauge

Which do you think are standard units of measure?

21. yard Yes

22. truckload No

23. smidgen No

24. kilometer Yes

25. gram Yes

26. quart Yes

27. pinch of salt No

28. scoop of ice cream No

29. liter Yes

30. pat of butter No

Look up the following standard units in a dictionary. Give a definition for each.

31. rod $5\frac{1}{2}$ yd

32. light-year distance light travels in 1 year

33. hand 4 inches

34. hogshead 63 gallons

35. furlong 200 yd

36. peck 8 quarts

37. knot 1 nautical mile per hour

38. parsec 19.2 trillion miles

39. nautical mile 6076.115 ft

40. Mach number ratio of speed of object to speed of sound in surrounding atmosphere

Look up the following words in a dictionary or an encyclopedia and give a definition for each.

41. micrometer caliper instrument that measures small linear distances

42. pluviometer rain gauge

43. sphygmomanometer instrument that measures blood pressures

44. theodolite instrument that measures angles

45. tachometer instrument that measures speed of rotation

46. ammeter instrument that measures electric current

Tell which measuring instrument in exercises 41–46 would probably be most useful for each person below.

47. nurse sphygmomanometer

48. forest ranger pluviometer

49. race-car driver tachometer

50. electrician ammeter

51. surveyor theodolite

52. machinist micrometer caliper

"Young man, don't talk back to me! You're only four hundred years old!"

The cartoon shown above is actually misleading. According to the *Guinness Book of World Records,* the world's oldest tortoise lived to be 152 years old. Of course, there are claims of tortoises living much longer. But these claims often stretch the truth.

For humans, the claims of great age are even harder to believe. Recently a man who claimed to be 168 died in Russia. However, such claims are almost impossible to prove. The oldest person whose age has been proved beyond a doubt lived to be 115, in Japan.

The Guinness book lists these age records:

oldest dog: 29 years 5 months

oldest cat: 36 years

oldest tree: 4900 years

Besides age records, there are many other records involving time. Who knows—maybe you'll break one someday!

longest shower bath: 336 hours

longest solo singing: 153 hours

longest marriage: 80 years

The pictures below show some ancient units of measure.

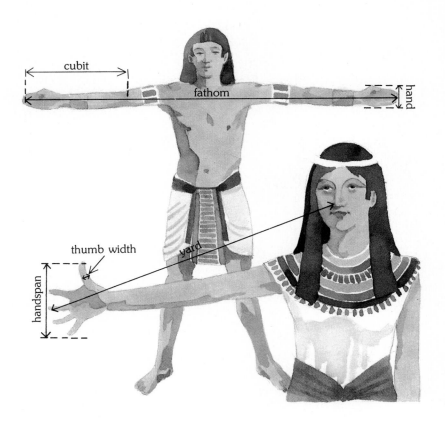

yard: about 3 feet

fathom: about 6 feet

hand: about 4 inches

cubit: about 18 inches

handspan: about 8 inches

thumb width: about an inch

Since people were not the same size, different people would use the same unit, like cubit, and give different measurements for the same length. To eliminate such confusion, people agreed to use standard units like inch, foot, and meter.

EXERCISES

Refer to the ancient units on page 188.

1. Which unit is the distance from the tip of the nose to the tips of the fingers of an outstretched arm? yard

2. Which unit is the distance from the elbow to the tip of the middle finger? cubit

3. Which unit is the distance between fingertips of outstretched arms? fathom

4. 1 fathom is about __6__ feet.

5. 1 foot is about __3__ hands.

6. 1 handspan is about __8__ inches.

7. 1 cubit is about __18__ inches.

8. Which unit is about an inch? thumb width

9. A boater says a lake is 3 fathoms deep. How many feet is that? 18 ft

10. A horse trainer says a horse is 18 hands high. How many inches is that? 72 in.

Which word in the list best completes each sentence?

yards	cubits	hands
handspans	thumb widths	fathoms

11. The length of a caterpillar is about 2 thumb widths

12. The depth of a pool for high diving is about 2 fathoms

13. The length of a yardstick is about 2 cubits

14. The height of a man is about 2 yards

Find each measurement, using the units suggested.
Answers for exercises 15-25 will vary.

15. width of this book in thumb widths (HINT: Using both thumbs is quicker.)

16. length of your desk in handspans

17. width of your desk in hands

18. length of your foot in hands

Find the length, in inches, of each unit.

19. your cubit   **20.** your yard   **21.** your foot

22. your hand   **23.** your handspan   **24.** your thumb width

25. Make a list of all the answers that your class gave for exercise 20. Use that list to find the following:

     a. mode   b. median   c. mean   d. range

PHOTO PUZZLE

From left to right in each row: clock, dry measuring cups, scale, liquid measuring cup, hourglass, thermometer/hygrometer; slide rule, compass, triangular scale, protractor, measuring spoons; meat thermometer, slide rule, tire gauge, sewing gauge; yardstick

How many measuring instruments in the photograph can you name?

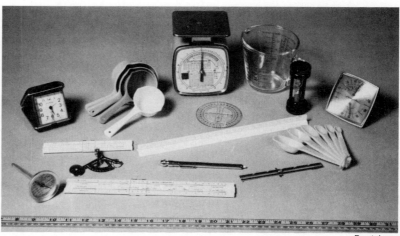

Brent Jones

5.3 | *MEASURING LENGTH*

The length of the pen is found by using four different rulers, as shown below. As the unit becomes smaller, the measurement becomes more precise.

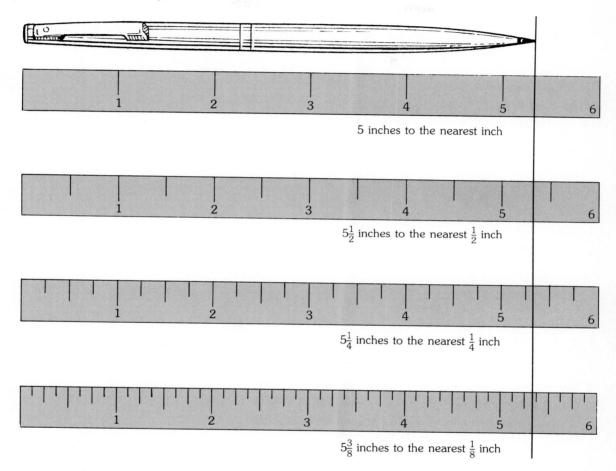

5 inches to the nearest inch

$5\frac{1}{2}$ inches to the nearest $\frac{1}{2}$ inch

$5\frac{1}{4}$ inches to the nearest $\frac{1}{4}$ inch

$5\frac{3}{8}$ inches to the nearest $\frac{1}{8}$ inch

With most rulers you can measure to the nearest $\frac{1}{16}$ inch, which is close enough for everyday purposes. However, a technical worker might use special measuring instruments to measure to the nearest $\frac{1}{1000}$ inch.

Just because a ruler is marked in $\frac{1}{16}$-inch units, you do not have to make all measurements to the nearest $\frac{1}{16}$ inch. You can also make measurements to the nearest $\frac{1}{8}$ inch, $\frac{1}{4}$ inch, or some other larger unit.

Grant Heilman

Example:

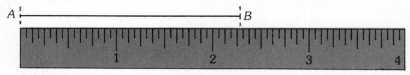

Length *AB* is 2 inches to the nearest inch.

$2\frac{1}{2}$ inches to the nearest $\frac{1}{2}$ inch.

$2\frac{1}{4}$ inches to the nearest $\frac{1}{4}$ inch.

The length seems to be halfway between $2\frac{4}{16}$ and $2\frac{5}{16}$. We always choose the larger measure.

$2\frac{2}{8}$ inches to the nearest $\frac{1}{8}$ inch.

$\longrightarrow 2\frac{5}{16}$ inches to the nearest $\frac{1}{16}$ inch.

EXERCISES

Use the ruler below. Find the length of each segment to the nearest inch.

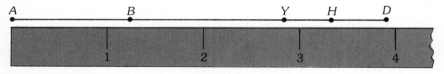

1. $\overline{AB}$ 1 in.

2. $\overline{AD}$ 4 in.

3. $\overline{AY}$ 3 in.

4. $\overline{AH}$ 3 in.

5. Can the same segment have measurements of $2\frac{1}{2}$ inches and $2\frac{1}{4}$ inches? How? Yes; See example above.

6. Can two segments both have measurements of 3 inches, to the nearest inch, and still not have exactly the same length? Find an example above. Yes; $\overline{AY}$ and $\overline{AH}$

7. Make a 4-inch ruler out of paper. Mark it in $\frac{1}{2}$-inch units. Then measure each object below to the nearest $\frac{1}{2}$ inch. Answers are given below.

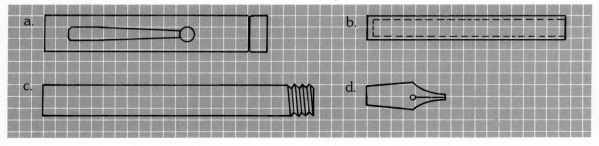

a. $2\frac{1}{2}$ in. b. 2 in. c. 3 in. d. 1 in.

8. Mark the ruler in exercise 7 in $\frac{1}{4}$-inch units. Use it to measure each object in exercise 7 to the nearest $\frac{1}{4}$ inch.   a. $2\frac{1}{4}$ in.   b. 2 in.

9. Use a ruler marked in $\frac{1}{16}$-inch units to measure each seg- c. $2\frac{3}{4}$ in.   d. $\frac{3}{4}$ in.
ment below to the nearest $\frac{1}{2}$ inch.

$2\frac{1}{2}$ in.

a. —————————— $1\frac{1}{2}$ in.   b. _____

c. ——————— $\frac{1}{2}$ in.   d. ————————————— 2 in.

10. Repeat exercise 9 to the nearest $\frac{1}{4}$ inch.   10. a. $1\frac{1}{4}$ in.   b. $2\frac{3}{4}$ in.   c. $\frac{3}{4}$ in.

11. Repeat exercise 9 to the nearest $\frac{1}{8}$ inch.   d. $1\frac{3}{4}$ in.   11. a. $1\frac{3}{8}$ in.

12. Repeat exercise 9 to the nearest $\frac{1}{16}$ inch.   b. $2\frac{5}{8}$ in.   c. $\frac{5}{8}$ in.   d. $1\frac{7}{8}$ in.

12. a. $1\frac{5}{16}$ in.   b. $2\frac{10}{16}$ in.   c. $\frac{11}{16}$ in.   d. $1\frac{14}{16}$ in.

Using the magnified view, give the length of each segment. (In cases where there is more than one answer, give all of them. For example, $AI = \frac{8}{16} = \frac{4}{8} = \frac{2}{4} = \frac{1}{2}$ inch.)

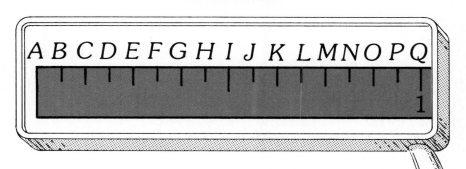

13. $\overline{AD}$ $\frac{3}{16}$ in.   **14.** $\overline{AF}$ $\frac{5}{16}$ in.   **15.** $\overline{AH}$ $\frac{7}{16}$ in. $\frac{10}{16} = \frac{5}{8}$ in.
16. $\overline{AK}$

17. $\overline{AN}$ $\frac{13}{16}$ in.   **18.** $\overline{AP}$ $\frac{15}{16}$ in.   **19.** $\overline{HI}$ $\frac{1}{16}$ in.   **20.** $\overline{EI}$

$\frac{4}{16} = \frac{2}{8} = \frac{1}{4}$ in.

Draw a segment of the given length.
See students' drawings.

21. $4\frac{5}{16}$ inches   **22.** $3\frac{5}{8}$ inches   **23.** $10\frac{12}{16}$ inches   **24.** $2\frac{7}{16}$ inches

MEASURING ON THE JOB

Answers for exercises 1-8 will vary.

Suppose you are a painter hired to paint your classroom. You might make a list like the one below.

	Estimate	Actual length
1. length of longer wall	____	____
2. length of shorter wall	____	____
3. height of ceiling	____	____
4. height of door(s)	____	____
5. width of door(s)	____	____

For your classroom, first estimate each measurement above. Then use a yardstick or a tape measure to check your estimates. Record all these estimates and measurements in a table like that above.

Make a list of the measurements you would need to make if you were employed to do each job. Then estimate each measurement for your classroom. Check your measurements by actually measuring.

6. carpet the floor   **7.** install ceiling tiles
8. install window blinds

Mary Elenz Tranter

SKILLS REFRESHER

Change to mixed numbers.

				Skill	Page
1. $\frac{3}{2}$ $1\frac{1}{2}$	**2.** $\frac{5}{3}$ $1\frac{2}{3}$	**3.** $\frac{32}{6}$ $5\frac{1}{3}$	**4.** $\frac{54}{12}$ $4\frac{1}{2}$	28	487

Change to fractions.

5. $1\frac{1}{2}$ $\frac{3}{2}$	**6.** $2\frac{1}{3}$ $\frac{7}{3}$	**7.** $2\frac{3}{4}$ $\frac{11}{4}$	**8.** $4\frac{3}{16}$ $\frac{67}{16}$

Multiply.

9. $12 \times \frac{1}{3}$ 4	**10.** $12 \times \frac{3}{4}$ 9	**11.** $36 \times 1\frac{1}{2}$ 54	**12.** $7\frac{3}{4} \times 12$ 93	44	514

194

5.4 EQUIVALENT LENGTHS

Measurements like *12 inches* and *1 foot* both name the same length. Such lengths are called **equivalent lengths.** The following table is helpful in finding equivalent lengths:

12 inches (in.) = 1 foot (ft)

3 feet (ft) = 1 yard (yd)

36 inches = 1 yard

5280 feet = 1 mile (mi)

Notice how proportions are used in the examples below.

Example 1: Change 15 feet to inches.

12 inches = 1 foot ← **Be sure to list the units**
? inches = 15 feet ← **in the same order.**

$$\frac{12}{n} = \frac{1}{15}$$ **Let *n* stand for the number of inches.**

$12 \times 15 = n \times 1$ **Find the cross products.**

$180 = n$ **Multiply.**

15 feet = 180 inches

Example 2: Change 54 inches to feet.

12 inches = 1 foot
54 inches = *n* feet

$$\frac{12}{54} = \frac{1}{n}$$

$12 \times n = 54 \times 1$

$12n = 54$

$$\frac{12n}{12} = \frac{54}{12}$$ **Divide.**

$$n = 4\frac{6}{12}$$

$$n = 4\frac{1}{2}$$

54 inches = $4\frac{1}{2}$ feet

Example 3: Change $1\frac{1}{2}$ yards to inches.

36 inches = 1 yard
n inches = $1\frac{1}{2}$ yards

$$\frac{36}{n} = \frac{1}{1\frac{1}{2}}$$

$$36 \times 1\frac{1}{2} = n \times 1$$

$$\frac{\overset{18}{\cancel{36}}}{1} \times \frac{3}{\underset{1}{\cancel{2}}} = n$$

$$\frac{54}{1} = n$$

$1\frac{1}{2}$ yards = 54 inches

EXERCISES

1. There are __12__ inches in 1 foot.

2. There are __3__ feet in 1 yard.

3. There are __36__ inches in 1 yard.

4. There are __5280__ feet in 1 mile.

5. Which is longer, 2 feet or 25 inches? 25 in.

6. Which is shorter, 5 yards or 175 inches? 175 in.

Change each measurement.

7. 7 feet to inches 84 in.

8. 3 yards to inches 108 in.

9. $2\frac{1}{2}$ feet to inches 30 in.

10. $4\frac{1}{2}$ yards to inches 162 in.

11. 5 miles to feet 26,400 ft

12. 38 yards to inches 1368 in.

13. 108 inches to feet 9 ft

14. 108 inches to yards 3 yd

15. $\frac{1}{2}$ mile to feet 2640 ft

16. 2 miles to feet 10,560 ft

17. $3\frac{3}{4}$ yards to inches 135 in.

18. $7\frac{3}{4}$ feet to inches 93 in.

19. 80 inches to feet $6\frac{2}{3}$ ft

20. 90 inches to yards $2\frac{1}{2}$ yd

21. $1\frac{1}{2}$ miles to feet 7920 ft

22. $\frac{3}{4}$ mile to feet 3960 ft

23. A 4-foot-high window is $2\frac{1}{2}$ feet above the floor. Curtains come in standard lengths of 72, 78, 84, 90, and 96 inches. Which length should be bought if the curtains are to hang from the top of the window to the floor? 78 in.

24. An 82-inch plank is to be cut into 1-foot lengths. How long a piece of wood will be left? 10 in.

25. A patio that is 15 feet long by 9 feet wide adjoins a house, as shown. A fence is to be built on the three outer sides. If the fencing sells for $23 per yard, how much will the fencing cost? $253

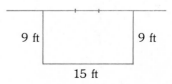

Norma Morrison

Barry L. Runk/Grant Heilman

When making machine parts, a machinist must be aware of tolerances. *Tolerance* is the acceptable amount of variance from a given dimension. For example, a gear might be designed to have the following thickness:

1 ± 0.01 inches

The tolerance is ± 0.01 inch. The symbol $\pm$ is read "plus or minus." So the thickness of the gear might be anywhere from $1 - 0.01$ inch to $1 + 0.01$ inches. Any thickness between 0.99 inch and 1.01 inches is acceptable.

Sometimes a dimension is given as $1.5 + 0.01$ inches or as $3 - 0.02$ inches. In such cases the tolerance is allowed in *only one direction*. For $1.5 + 0.01$ inches, the length could be anywhere between 1.5 inches and 1.51 inches. For $3 - 0.02$ inches, the length could be anywhere between 2.98 inches and 3 inches.

Example: A metal gear is designed to have a diameter of 0.57 inch with a tolerance of ± 0.005 inch. Find the acceptable upper and lower limits for the diameter.

The upper limit is $0.57 + 0.005$ inch, or 0.575 inch.
The lower limit is $0.57 - 0.005$ inch, or 0.565 inch.

Copy and fill in the table.

	Designed length	Tolerance	Upper limit	Lower limit
1.	0.22 inch	± 0.01 inch	0.23 in.	0.21 in.
2.	0.83 inch	± 0.005 inch	0.835 in.	0.825 in.
3.	$7\frac{1}{2}$ inches	$\pm \frac{1}{4}$ inch	$7\frac{3}{4}$ in.	$7\frac{1}{4}$ in.
4.	8 inches	$\pm \frac{1}{16}$ inch	$8\frac{1}{16}$ in.	$7\frac{15}{16}$ in.
5.	2 inches	$+ 0.05$ inch	2.05 in.	2 in.
6.	10 inches	$- \frac{1}{16}$ inch	10 in.	$9\frac{15}{16}$ in.

197

Photri

The system of measurement that includes feet, inches, yards, pounds, gallons, quarts, degrees Fahrenheit, and so on, is called the **customary system.**

Another system, called the **metric system,** is used in most countries of the world. It is easier to use than the customary system.

Comparisons

1 meter is about 1.1 yards.

2.5 centimeters is about 1 inch.

1 kilometer is about 0.6 mile.

The metric system is used to measure length, weight, capacity, and temperature. In this section, however, we will use only metric units of length. The basic unit of length is the **meter.** Look at the table below. Each unit is 10 times larger than the next smaller unit.

Prefix	Meaning	Unit	Symbol	
kilo-	thousand	kilometer	km	1000 meters
hecto-	hundred	hectometer	hm	100 meters
deka-	ten	dekameter	dam	10 meters
		meter	m	1 meter
deci-	tenth	decimeter	dm	0.1 meter
centi-	hundredth	centimeter	cm	0.01 meter
milli-	thousandth	millimeter	mm	0.001 meter

The units listed in red are used most often.

The ruler shown in the following example is marked in millimeters and in centimeters. The smaller units are millimeters. The larger units are centimeters.

Example:

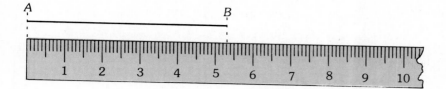

Length *AB* is 5 centimeters to the nearest centimeter.

52 millimeters to the nearest millimeter.

Length *AB* is 5 centimeters to the nearest centimeter. 53 millimeters to the nearest millimeter.

A measurement like 53 millimeters can also be expressed as 5.3 centimeters.

EXERCISES

1. The prefix *milli-* means (0.1, 0.01, 0.001).

2. The prefix *kilo-* means (10, 100, 1000).

3. Which is longer, a millimeter or a centimeter? centimeter

4. Which is shorter, a meter or a kilometer? meter

5. Which metric unit is about a yard? meter

6. Which metric unit is about 0.6 mile? kilometer

Name the metric unit that would be best for finding each measurement.

7. the thickness of a penny millimeter

8. the length of the Mississippi River kilometer

9. the length of a whale meter

10. the height of a person centimeter or decimeter

On a TV game show, four people made the following statements. Which of statements 11–14 could be true?

11. "I caught a fish that was 3 kilometers long." No

12. "I live in a house that is 300 millimeters wide." No

13. "My waist measurement is 75 centimeters." Yes

14. "My foot is 10 meters long." No

15. Which is longer, the 100-meter dash or the 100-yard dash? 100-meter dash

16. If a lake is 10 kilometers away, is the distance more or less than 10 miles? less

Use the ruler below. Find the length of each segment to the nearest centimeter.

17. $\overline{AB}$ 3 cm   **18.** $\overline{AD}$ 10 cm   **19.** $\overline{AY}$ 7 cm   **20.** $\overline{AH}$
8 cm

Use the ruler above. Find the length of each segment to the nearest millimeter.

21. $\overline{AH}$ 84 mm   **22.** $\overline{AY}$ 72 mm   **23.** $\overline{AD}$ 100 mm   **24.** $\overline{AB}$
33 mm

Find the length of each object below to the nearest centimeter and to the nearest millimeter. Answers are given below. (Millimeter measurements may vary.)

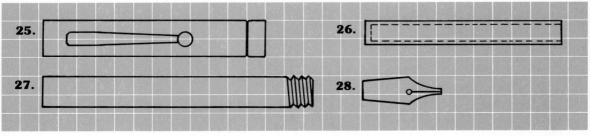

25. 6 cm; 59 mm   26. 5 cm; 52 mm   27. 7 cm; 72 cm   28. 2 cm; 21 mm

200

Draw a segment of each length.
See students' drawings.

29. 4 cm   **30.** 16 cm   **31.** 48 mm

32. 88 mm   **33.** 40 mm   **34.** 160 mm

35. 10 cm   **36.** 25 cm   **37.** 7.5 cm

38. 1.3 cm   **39.** 4.8 cm   **40.** 8.8 cm

LET'S GO METRIC

Repeat the activities on page 194, using a meterstick instead of a yardstick.

SKILLS REFRESHER

			Skill	Page
Multiply.				
1. 14×10 140	**2.** 72×100 7200	**3.** 43×1000 43,000	11	463
4. 20×1000 20,000	**5.** 1.4×10 14	**6.** 1.4×100 140	13	466
7. 0.17×100 17	**8.** 2.1×1000 2100	**9.** 8.16×10 81.6		
Divide.				
10. $\frac{25}{10}$ 2.5	**11.** $\frac{185}{100}$ 1.85	**12.** $\frac{25}{1000}$ 0.025	21	478

5.6 / EQUIVALENT METRIC LENGTHS

Proportions are useful in changing from one metric unit to another. For most metric uses, all you have to remember is the following:

10 millimeters = 1 centimeter   1000 millimeters = 1 meter

100 centimeters = 1 meter   1000 meters = 1 kilometer

Example 1: Change 14 cm to millimeters.

10 mm = 1 cm   **Be sure to list the units**
? mm = 14 cm   **in the same order.**

$\dfrac{10}{n} = \dfrac{1}{14}$ **Let *n* stand for the number of millimeters.**

$10 \times 14 = n \times 1$ **Find the cross products.**
$140 = n$ **Multiply.**

14 cm = 140 mm

Example 2: Change 20 km to meters.

1000 m = 1 km
n m = 20 km

$\dfrac{1000}{n} = \dfrac{1}{20}$

$1000 \times 20 = n \times 1$
$20{,}000 = n$

20 km = 20 000 m
            ↑
Current metric usage recommends space instead of commas in writing measurements with five or more digits.

Example 3: Change 25 mm to centimeters.

10 mm = 1 cm
25 mm = n cm

$\dfrac{10}{25} = \dfrac{1}{n}$

$10 \times n = 25 \times 1$
$10n = 25$

$n = 2.5$ **Divide by 10.**

25 mm = 2.5 cm

Example 4: Change 185 m to kilometers.

1000 m = 1 km
185 m = n km

$\dfrac{1000}{185} = \dfrac{1}{n}$

$1000 \times n = 185 \times 1$
$1000n = 185$

$n = 0.185$

185 m = 0.185 km

EXERCISES

Change each measurement to complete the following:

1. 1 m = $\underset{100}{\underline{\hspace{1cm}}}$ cm

2. 1 m = $\underset{1000}{\underline{\hspace{1cm}}}$ mm

3. 1 km = $\underset{1000}{\underline{\hspace{1cm}}}$ m

4. 1 cm = $\underset{10}{\underline{\hspace{1cm}}}$ mm

5. 10 cm = $\underset{100}{\underline{\hspace{1cm}}}$ mm

6. 50 cm = $\underset{500}{\underline{\hspace{1cm}}}$ mm

7. 8 km = $\underset{8000}{\underline{\hspace{1cm}}}$ m

8. 19 km = $\underset{19\ 000}{\underline{\hspace{1cm}}}$ m

9. 29 m = $\underset{29\ 000}{\underline{\hspace{1cm}}}$ mm

10. 83 m = $\underset{83\ 000}{\underline{\hspace{1cm}}}$ mm

11. 1.8 cm = $\underset{18}{\underline{\hspace{1cm}}}$ mm

12. 2.5 mm = $\underset{0.25}{\underline{\hspace{1cm}}}$ cm

13. 2.6 km = $\underset{2600}{\underline{\hspace{1cm}}}$ m

14. 8.5 km = $\underset{8500}{\underline{\hspace{1cm}}}$ m

15. 80 mm = $\underset{8}{\underline{\hspace{1cm}}}$ cm

16. 150 mm = $\underset{15}{\underline{\hspace{1cm}}}$ cm

17. 5000 m = $\underset{5}{\underline{\hspace{1cm}}}$ km

18. 1000 m = $\underset{1}{\underline{\hspace{1cm}}}$ km

19. 17 mm = $\underset{1.7}{\underline{\hspace{1cm}}}$ cm

20. 125 mm = $\underset{12.5}{\underline{\hspace{1cm}}}$ cm

21. 170 m = $\underset{0.17}{\underline{\hspace{1cm}}}$ km

22. 155 m = $\underset{0.155}{\underline{\hspace{1cm}}}$ km

23. The length of an Olympic-sized pool is 50 meters. In order to swim 1 kilometer, how many lengths would you need to swim? 20 lengths

24. The length of one long-distance race in track is 20 000 meters. How many kilometers is this? 20 km

25. Using an Olympic-sized pool, how many lengths would you have to swim to complete an 800-meter race? 16 lengths

26. The overall length of a sports car was given as 433 centimeters. What is the length of the car in meters? 4.33 m

27. The wheelbase (distance between centers of the front wheel and the rear wheel) of the car in exercise 26 is 245 centimeters. How much greater is the overall length than the wheelbase in meters? 1.88 m

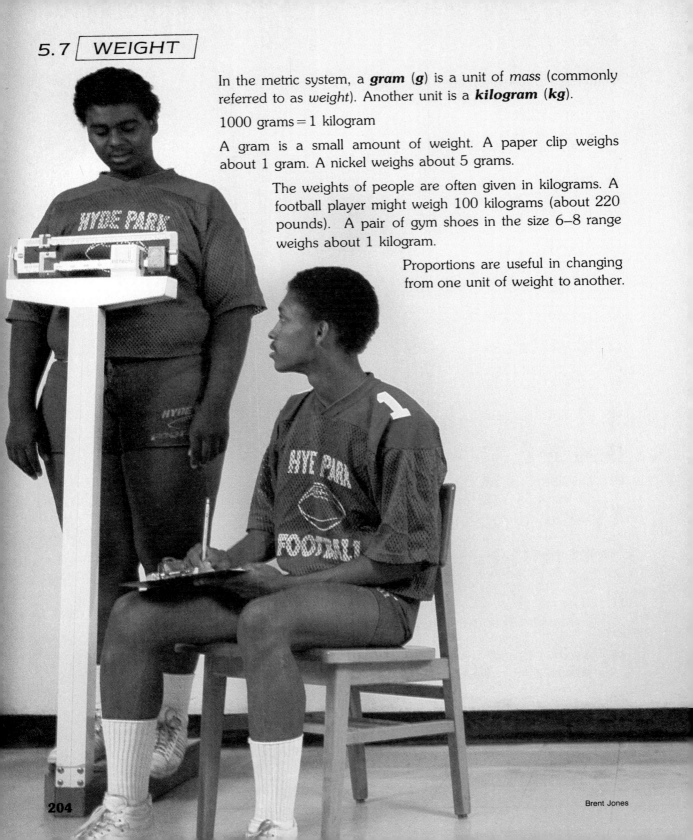

5.7 WEIGHT

In the metric system, a **gram** (**g**) is a unit of *mass* (commonly referred to as *weight*). Another unit is a **kilogram** (**kg**).

1000 grams = 1 kilogram

A gram is a small amount of weight. A paper clip weighs about 1 gram. A nickel weighs about 5 grams.

The weights of people are often given in kilograms. A football player might weigh 100 kilograms (about 220 pounds). A pair of gym shoes in the size 6–8 range weighs about 1 kilogram.

Proportions are useful in changing from one unit of weight to another.

Brent Jones

Example 1:   Change 8.5 kg to grams.

$$1000 \text{ g} = 1 \text{ kg}$$
$$n \text{ g} = 8.5 \text{ kg}$$
$$\frac{1000}{n} = \frac{1}{8.5}$$
$$1000 \times 8.5 = n \times 1$$
$$8500 = n$$

8.5 kg = 8500 g

Example 2:   Change 757 g to kilograms.

$$1000 \text{ g} = 1 \text{ kg}$$
$$757 \text{ g} = n \text{ kg}$$
$$\frac{1000}{757} = \frac{1}{n}$$
$$1000 \times n = 757 \times 1$$
$$1000n = 757$$
$$n = 0.757$$

757 g = 0.757 kg

In the customary system, **pounds** (**lb**) and **ounces** (**oz**) are the most common units of weight.

16 ounces = 1 pound

Example 3:   Change $2\frac{1}{2}$ lb to ounces.

$$16 \text{ oz} = 1 \text{ lb}$$
$$n \text{ oz} = 2\frac{1}{2} \text{ lb}$$
$$\frac{16}{n} = \frac{1}{2\frac{1}{2}}$$
$$16 \times 2\frac{1}{2} = n \times 1$$
$$40 = n$$

$2\frac{1}{2}$ lb = 40 oz

Example 4:   Change 75 oz to pounds.

$$16 \text{ oz} = 1 \text{ lb}$$
$$75 \text{ oz} = n \text{ lb}$$
$$\frac{16}{75} = \frac{1}{n}$$
$$16 \times n = 75 \times 1$$
$$16n = 75$$
$$n = 4\frac{11}{16} \quad \textbf{Divide by 16.}$$

75 oz = $4\frac{11}{16}$ lb

EXERCISES

1. The number of grams in 1 kilogram is 1000.

2. The number of ounces in 1 pound is 16.

3. Would kilograms or would grams be better to measure the weight of an elephant? kilograms

4. Would pounds or would ounces be better to measure the weight of a pencil? ounces

What is a short way to write each unit of measure?

5. gram g

6. kilogram kg

7. pound lb

8. ounce oz

205

Which weight is heavier?

9. 1 pound or <u>17 ounces</u>

10. 999 grams or <u>1 kilogram</u>

Complete the following:

11. 29 kg = $\overset{29\ 000}{\underline{\hspace{1.5em}}}$ g

12. 68 kg = $\overset{68\ 000}{\underline{\hspace{1.5em}}}$ g

13. 127 g = $\overset{0.127}{\underline{\hspace{1.5em}}}$ kg

14. 963 g = $\overset{0.963}{\underline{\hspace{1.5em}}}$ kg

15. 8.3 kg = $\overset{8300}{\underline{\hspace{1.5em}}}$ g

16. 39.2 kg = $\overset{39\ 200}{\underline{\hspace{1.5em}}}$ g

17. 128 lb = $\overset{2048}{\underline{\hspace{1.5em}}}$ oz

18. 102 lb = $\overset{1632}{\underline{\hspace{1.5em}}}$ oz

19. 128 oz = $\overset{8}{\underline{\hspace{1.5em}}}$ lb

20. 1632 oz = $\overset{102}{\underline{\hspace{1.5em}}}$ lb

21. $9\frac{1}{4}$ lb = $\overset{148}{\underline{\hspace{1.5em}}}$ oz

22. $3\frac{1}{2}$ lb = $\overset{56}{\underline{\hspace{1.5em}}}$ oz

23. $\frac{3}{4}$ lb = $\overset{12}{\underline{\hspace{1.5em}}}$ oz

24. $\frac{5}{8}$ lb = $\overset{10}{\underline{\hspace{1.5em}}}$ oz

25. 100 oz = $\overset{6\frac{1}{4}}{\underline{\hspace{1.5em}}}$ lb

26. 10 oz = $\overset{\frac{5}{8}}{\underline{\hspace{1.5em}}}$ lb

27. 24 oz = $\overset{1\frac{1}{2}}{\underline{\hspace{1.5em}}}$ lb

28. 8 oz = $\overset{\frac{1}{2}}{\underline{\hspace{1.5em}}}$ lb

29. 18 g = $\overset{0.018}{\underline{\hspace{1.5em}}}$ kg

30. 7 g = $\overset{0.007}{\underline{\hspace{1.5em}}}$ kg

Another unit of weight in the metric system is a **milligram** (**mg**). (1000 milligrams = 1 gram) Medicines are often measured in milligrams. Complete the following:

31. 125 g = $\overset{125\ 000}{\underline{\hspace{1.5em}}}$ mg

32. 75 mg = $\overset{0.075}{\underline{\hspace{1.5em}}}$ g

33. 1 mg = $\overset{0.001}{\underline{\hspace{1.5em}}}$ g

34. 1085 g = $\overset{1\ 085\ 000}{\underline{\hspace{1.5em}}}$ mg

Jacqueline Durand

Another unit of weight in the customary system is a **ton**. (1 ton = 2000 pounds) The hauling capacity of a truck is often given in tons. Change each weight to pounds.

35. $\frac{1}{2}$ ton   1000 lb

36. $\frac{3}{4}$ ton 1500 lb

37. $1\frac{1}{2}$ tons   3000 lb

38. 2 tons   4000 lb

39. 3.4 tons 6800 lb

40. 0.6 ton 1200 lb

41. Each person on an overseas flight is allowed 20 kilograms of luggage. On a certain flight, the excess baggage cost is $6.50 per kilogram. If a person has 22.3 kilograms of luggage, how much extra will this person pay? $14.95

42. Diamonds are measured by a unit of weight called a *carat*. (142 carats = 1 ounce) Diamonds used for engagement rings range from $\frac{1}{4}$ to 1 carat, in most cases. In 1905 a rough diamond weighing 3106 carats was found in South Africa. How much is this in ounces? $21\frac{62}{71}$ oz

43. The largest animal in the world is the blue whale. In 1931 a blue whale weighing 195 tons was captured. How much is 195 tons in pounds? (2000 pounds = 1 ton)   390,000 lb

44. One of the most expensive substances in the world is a chemical called californium 252. It sells for $100 per tenth of a *microgram*. (1 000 000 micrograms = 1 gram) How much would a gram of californium 252 sell for? $1,000,000,000

FINDING WEIGHTS

Use the scales below to find the weight of each box.

1. box A 146 lb

2. box B 127 lb

3. box C 96 lb

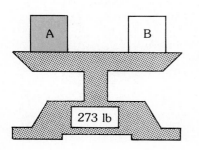

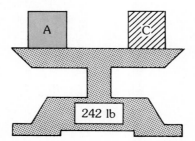

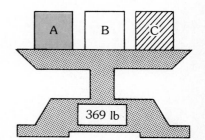

5.8 CAPACITY

The amount a container can hold is called its **capacity.**
Some common units of capacity are given in the table below.

Customary units	Metric units
16 fluid ounces (fl oz) = 1 pint (pt)	1000 milliliters (mL) = 1 liter (L)
2 cups = 1 pt	1000 liters = 1 kiloliter (kL)
2 pt = 1 quart (qt)	
4 qt = 1 gallon (gal)	

1 liter is about 1.06 quarts.

You can use proportions to change from one unit of measure to another.

Example 1: Change 50 qt to gallons.

$$4 \text{ qt} = 1 \text{ gal}$$
$$50 \text{ qt} = n \text{ gal}$$
$$\frac{4}{50} = \frac{1}{n}$$
$$4 \times n = 50 \times 1$$
$$4n = 50$$
$$\frac{4n}{4} = \frac{50}{4}$$
$$n = 12\frac{1}{2}$$

50 qt = $12\frac{1}{2}$ gal

Example 2: Change 3.2 liters to milliliters.

$$1000 \text{ mL} = 1 \text{ liter}$$
$$n \text{ mL} = 3.2 \text{ liters}$$
$$\frac{1000}{n} = \frac{1}{3.2}$$
$$1000 \times 3.2 = n \times 1$$
$$3200 = n$$

3.2 liters = 3200 mL

Paul Conklin

EXERCISES

1. 1 liter = <u>1000</u> milliliters

2. 1 kiloliter = <u>1000</u> liters

3. 1 gallon = <u>4</u> quarts

4. 1 quart = __2__ pints

5. 1 pint = __2__ cups

6. 1 pint = __16__ fluid ounces

7. Which is larger, a liter or a quart?
a liter

8. Which is smaller, a milliliter or a liter?
a milliliter

Grant Heilman

What is a short way to write each unit of measure?

9. fluid ounce fl oz   **10.** pint pt   **11.** quart qt

12. gallon gal   **13.** milliliter mL   **14.** liter L

Complete the following:

15. 2.2 liters = __2200__ mL   **16.** 8.3 liters = __8300__ mL

17. 1500 mL = __1.5__ liters   **18.** 855 mL = __0.855__ liter

19. 18 gal = __72__ qt   **20.** 25 gal = __100__ qt

21. 6 pt = __96__ fl oz   **22.** 15 pt = __240__ fl oz

23. $\frac{1}{4}$ gal = __1__ qt   **24.** $\frac{1}{2}$ gal = __2__ qt

25. 38 qt = __$9\frac{1}{2}$__ gal   **26.** 70 qt = __$17\frac{1}{2}$__ gal

27. 28 qt = __56__ pt   **28.** 16 qt = __32__ pt

29. 9 pt = __$4\frac{1}{2}$__ qt   **30.** 21 pt = __$10\frac{1}{2}$__ qt

31. 80 fl oz = __5__ pt   **32.** 128 fl oz = __8__ pt

33. 456 kL = __456 000__ liters   **34.** 921 kL = __921 000__ liters

35. $2\frac{1}{2}$ pt = __5__ cups   **36.** $5\frac{1}{2}$ pt = __11__ cups

In recipe books, many items are measured in *teaspoons*. There are 3 teaspoons in 1 tablespoon and 16 tablespoons in 1 cup. Complete the following:

37. 1 pt = __96__ teaspoons

38. 1 tablespoon = __$\frac{1}{2}$__ fl oz

39. 1 teaspoon = __$\frac{1}{6}$__ fl oz

40. 1 cup = __48__ teaspoons

41. The engine displacement of a car is often measured in liters.

	Total engine displacement	Number of cylinders
Car A	1.4 liters	4
Car B	2.3 liters	6
Car C	7.5 liters	8

For each car above, find the displacement per cylinder.

Car A, 0.35 L
Car B, 0.383 or about 0.38 L
Car C, 0.9375 L

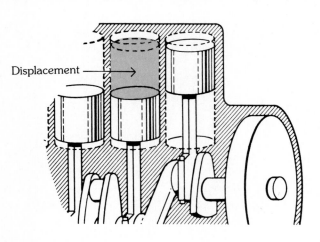

Displacement →

42. One of the most expensive perfumes in the world is called De Berens No. 1. It is made in France and sells for $150 per $\frac{1}{3}$ ounce. How much would 1 quart of that perfume sell for? $14,400

43. A *fifth* is a unit of capacity used to measure liquids. A *fifth* is $\frac{1}{5}$ gallon. 1 fifth = ____ quart. $\frac{4}{5}$

44. A fifth of a certain beverage costs $3.25; a quart costs $3.75. What would a gallon cost at each price? Which is the better buy—a fifth or a quart? $16.25; $15.00; a quart

5.9 | TIME |

When you solve problems involving units of time, it is often necessary to change from one unit of time to another.

60 seconds (sec) = 1 minute (min)

60 minutes (min) = 1 hour (hr or h)

24 hours = 1 day

365 days = 1 year

366 days = 1 leap year

Example 1:

        1

    7 min 23 sec   **Add the seconds.**

+ 58 min 50 sec

66 min 7̶3̶ sec   **Change 73 sec to 1 min 13 sec,**
            13   **since 73 = 60 + 13.**

Add the minutes.

1 hr 6 min 13 sec   **Change 66 min to 1 hr 6 min and remember to include the seconds.**

Example 2:

    5   73

   6̶ hr 1̶3̶ min   **Since you cannot subtract 45**

− 3 hr 45 min   **from 13, change 6 hr 13 min to**

  2 hr 28 min   **5 hr 73 min. Then subtract.**

When using a watch or a clock with a 12-hour dial, we think of a day as being separated into two 12-hour periods—A.M. (before noon) and P.M. (after noon). When a 24-hour dial is used, as in the military services or in spaceflights, there is no need for A.M. and P.M.

Example 3: A bus leaves Milwaukee at 7:45 A.M. and arrives in Chicago at 9:30 A.M. How long does the trip take?

Since both times are A.M. (or when both times are P.M.), you can think about and solve the problem like this:

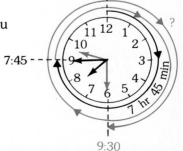

  8   90

  9̶ hr 3̶0̶ min **Since you cannot subtract**

− 7 hr 45 min **45 from 30, change 9 hr**

  1 hr 45 min **30 min to 8 hr 90 min.**

The trip took 1 hr 45 min.

211

Example 4: A car came into a parking lot at 9:10 A.M. and went out at 3:20 P.M. How long was it parked?

Since one time is A.M. and the other P.M., think about the problem as follows:

Amount of time parked

$$
\begin{array}{r}
^{11}\ \ ^{60} \\
\cancel{12}\ \text{hr}\ \ \cancel{0}\ \text{min} \\
-\ \ 9\ \text{hr}\ 10\ \text{min} \\
\hline
2\ \text{hr}\ 50\ \text{min}
\end{array}
\qquad
\begin{array}{l}
^{1} \\
2\ \text{hr}\ 50\ \text{min}\quad \text{before noon} \\
+\ 3\ \text{hr}\ 20\ \text{min}\quad \text{after noon} \\
\hline
6\ \text{hr}\ \cancel{70}\ \text{min} \\
\hspace{3.5em}{}_{10}
\end{array}
$$

The car was parked 6 hr 10 min.

EXERCISES

1. $\underline{365}$ days = 1 year

2. $\underline{3}$ weeks = 21 days

3. $\underline{60}$ min = 1 hr

4. $\underline{60}$ sec = 1 min

5. 1 min $\underline{5}$ sec = 65 sec

6. 1 hr $\underline{40}$ min = 100 min

7. $\underline{85}$ sec = 1 min 25 sec

8. $\underline{63}$ min = 1 hr 3 min

Add or subtract.

9.
$$
\begin{array}{r}
6\ \text{min}\ 15\ \text{sec} \\
+15\ \text{min}\ 32\ \text{sec} \\
\hline
21\ \text{min}\ 47\ \text{sec}
\end{array}
$$

10.
$$
\begin{array}{r}
8\ \text{hr}\ 28\ \text{min} \\
+2\ \text{hr}\ 31\ \text{min} \\
\hline
10\ \text{hr}\ 59\ \text{min}
\end{array}
$$

11.
$$
\begin{array}{r}
28\ \text{min}\ 48\ \text{sec} \\
-12\ \text{min}\ 44\ \text{sec} \\
\hline
16\ \text{min}\ 4\ \text{sec}
\end{array}
$$

12.
$$
\begin{array}{r}
7\ \text{hr}\ 40\ \text{min} \\
-1\ \text{hr}\ 28\ \text{min} \\
\hline
6\ \text{hr}\ 12\ \text{min}
\end{array}
$$

13.
$$
\begin{array}{r}
7\ \text{min}\ 42\ \text{sec} \\
+6\ \text{min}\ 30\ \text{sec} \\
\hline
14\ \text{min}\ 12\ \text{sec}
\end{array}
$$

14.
$$
\begin{array}{r}
4\ \text{hr}\ 10\ \text{min} \\
+3\ \text{hr}\ 80\ \text{min} \\
\hline
8\ \text{hr}\ 30\ \text{min}
\end{array}
$$

15.
$$
\begin{array}{r}
6\ \text{min}\ 28\ \text{sec} \\
-2\ \text{min}\ 42\ \text{sec} \\
\hline
3\ \text{min}\ 46\ \text{sec}
\end{array}
$$

16.
$$
\begin{array}{r}
15\ \text{hr}\ 33\ \text{min} \\
-\ 8\ \text{hr}\ 48\ \text{min} \\
\hline
6\ \text{hr}\ 45\ \text{min}
\end{array}
$$

Tell how long it is from one time to the next.

17. 3:15 P.M. to 7:25 P.M.
    4 hr 10 min

18. 3:04 A.M. to 11:20 A.M.
    8 hr 16 min

19. 5:32 A.M. to 11:50 A.M.
6 hr 18 min

20. 8:22 P.M. to 10:07 P.M.
1 hr 45 min

21. 8:00 A.M. to 2:00 P.M.
6 hr

22. 11:00 A.M. to 5:10 P.M.
6 hr 10 min

23. 7:23 A.M. to 3:40 P.M.
8 hr 17 min

24. 9:05 A.M. to 1:40 P.M.
4 hr 35 min

25. 10:15 P.M. to 6:25 A.M.
8 hr 10 min

26. 11:30 P.M. to 2:14 A.M.
2 hr 44 min

27. Flight 711 was scheduled for takeoff at 11:18 A.M. Due to engine trouble, takeoff was delayed for 1 hour 44 minutes. At what time did Flight 711 take off? 1:02 P.M.

28. It takes 2 hours 12 minutes to load a tank truck. If you start loading the truck at 8:58 A.M., when will the truck be fully loaded? 11:10 A.M.

29. A person punched a time clock at 7:40 A.M. and punched out at 4:20 P.M. How long did the person work?
8 hr 40 min

30. A train leaves Louisville at 3:40 P.M. and arrives at Cincinnati at 5:23 P.M. How long does the trip take?
1 hr 43 min

31. A car parked in a parking garage at 9:10 A.M. and left at 1:32 P.M. How long was the car parked?
4 hr 22 min

32. A boat cruise on Lake Michigan leaves at 10:30 A.M. and returns at 3:15 P.M. How long is the cruise? 4 hr 45 min

James P. Rowan

Application 27 may be used at this time. **213**

Many people plant gardens for enjoyment and to save money.

Seeds for
CUCUMBERS

Days to
harvest: 60

2.5 g   59¢

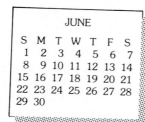

Seeds for
WAX BEANS

Days to
harvest: 53

1.7 oz   99¢

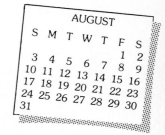

Seeds for
GREEN PEPPERS

Days to
harvest: 75

0.28 oz   55¢

		MAY				
S	M	T	W	T	F	S
				1	2	3
4	5	6	7	8	9	10
11	12	13	14	15	16	17
18	19	20	21	22	23	24
25	26	27	28	29	30	31

		JUNE				
S	M	T	W	T	F	S
1	2	3	4	5	6	7
8	9	10	11	12	13	14
15	16	17	18	19	20	21
22	23	24	25	26	27	28
29	30					

		JULY				
S	M	T	W	T	F	S
		1	2	3	4	5
6	7	8	9	10	11	12
13	14	15	16	17	18	19
20	21	22	23	24	25	26
27	28	29	30	31		

		AUGUST				
S	M	T	W	T	F	S
					1	2
3	4	5	6	7	8	9
10	11	12	13	14	15	16
17	18	19	20	21	22	23
24	25	26	27	28	29	30
31						

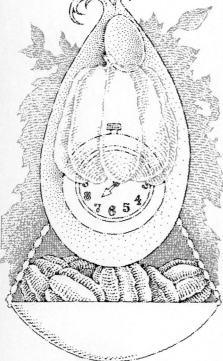

Suppose you plant the seeds from the three packages shown above on May 8. Use the calendar to determine when you may expect to harvest each vegetable.

1. cucumbers
July 7

2. wax beans
June 30

3. green peppers
July 22

4. During a good season, the package of cucumber seeds shown above may yield about 100 pounds of cucumbers. Suppose cucumbers sell for 39¢ per pound. Find the value of the cucumbers that you may be able to harvest. $39

5. During a good season, the weight of a harvest of wax beans may be about 30 times the weight of the seeds in the package. About how many ounces of wax beans may you be able to harvest from the package of seeds shown above? 51 oz

6. During a good season, you may be able to harvest about 5 pounds of tomatoes per plant. Suppose tomatoes sell for 79¢ per pound. Find the value of the tomatoes that you may be able to harvest from 4 tomato plants. $15.80

Draw two straight lines that meet at a point. Mark off 16 points $\frac{1}{4}$ inch apart on each line. Label the points as shown. Then use a ruler to join 1 to 1, 2 to 2, and so on. The resulting "curve" is formed by straight lines.

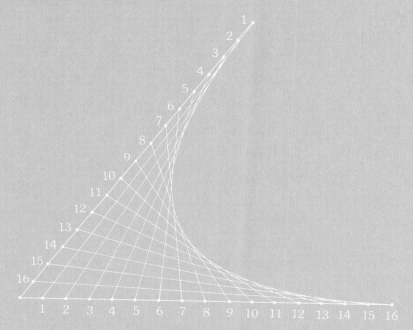

This idea can be used to create many interesting designs. Two examples are shown below. See if you can make up some new ones.

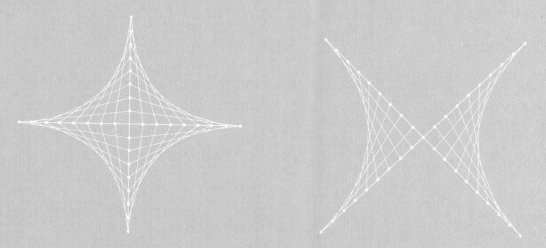

215

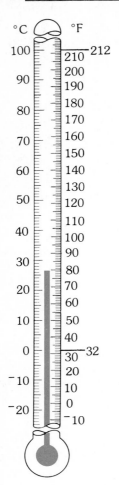

Temperature can be measured with a **Fahrenheit scale** or with a **Celsius scale.** For both scales the symbol ° stands for *degrees.* Some equivalent temperatures are given below.

	Fahrenheit scale	Celsius scale
boiling point of water	212°F	100°C
freezing point of water	32°F	0°C
recommended room-air temperature	68°F	20°C
highest recorded air temperature (Libya)	136°F	58°C
lowest recorded air temperature (Antarctica)	‾127°F*	‾88°C
normal body temperature	98.6°F	37°C
normal January temperature in Chicago, Illinois	26°F	‾3°C
normal January temperature in Miami, Florida	67°F	19°C
normal January temperature in Fairbanks, Alaska	‾11°F	‾24°C

*‾127° means 127° below zero.

EXERCISES

For each temperature below, find an equivalent temperature by using the other scale on the thermometer above.

1. 100°F 38°C

2. 40°F 4°C

3. 20°C 68°F

4. 60°C 140°F

5. 32°F 0°C

6. 212°F 100°C

7. 10°C 50°F

8. 30°C 86°F

9. 0°F ‾18°C

10. 10°F ‾12°C

11. ‾10°C 14°F

12. ‾5°C 23°F

216

For each question, give the answer in both Fahrenheit and Celsius temperatures. Refer to the table on page 216.

13. What is the normal body temperature?
98.6°F; 37°C

14. What is the highest recorded air temperature? 136°F; 58°C

15. What is the lowest recorded air temperature? ⁻127°F; ⁻88°C

16. What is the freezing point of water?
32°F; 0°C

17. What is the difference between the boiling point of water and the freezing point of water? 180°F; 100°C

18. What is the difference between the recommended room-air temperature and the normal body temperature?
30.6°F; 17°C

19. What is the difference between the boiling point of water and the highest recorded air temperature?
76°F; 42°C

20. What is the difference between the normal January temperature in Miami and the freezing point of water?
35°F; 19°C

21. What is the difference between the lowest recorded air temperature and the normal January temperature in Fairbanks? 116°F; 64°C

22. What is the difference between the normal January temperatures in Chicago and Miami? (Notice that on the Celsius scale, one temperature is above zero and the other is below zero.) 41°F; 22°C

23. What is the difference between the highest recorded air temperature and the lowest recorded air temperature?
263°F; 146°C

24. What is the difference between the normal January temperature in Chicago and the lowest recorded temperature in Antarctica? 153°F; 85°C

HOW WARM IS IT?

Use both a Fahrenheit thermometer and a Celsius thermometer to measure the following:
Answers for exercises 1-2 will vary.

1. the temperature of your classroom

2. the temperature of water from a faucet

Angles occur in designs, buildings, and instructions, as shown below. An **angle** has two sides that meet at a point. The sides can extend from their common point as far as necessary.

Norman Prince

Often an angle must be measured. Most of the time, you measure angles with a **protractor.** The unit on the protractor is the **degree.** Many protractors look like the one shown below.

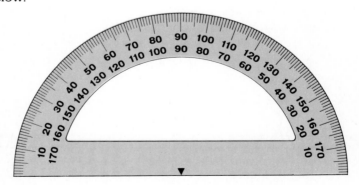

Think of drawing lines from the center of the protractor to each mark on the outer edge. You would draw 180 small angles, side by side. Each of those angles would have a measure of 1 degree (written 1°).

Example 1:   Measure with a protractor.

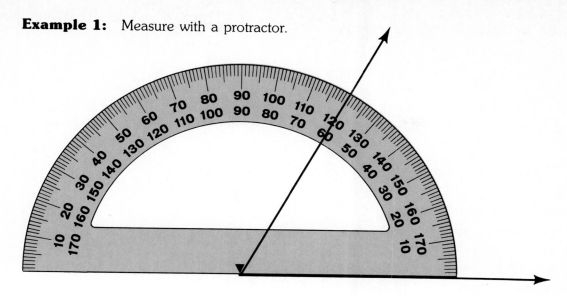

a. Place the center of the protractor at the point where the sides of the angle meet.

b. Lay the bottom edge of the protractor along one side of the angle. Extend the sides of the angle if needed.

c. Read the number of degrees from the scale that has its 0° mark on a side of the angle. The measure of the angle is 60°.   (In some cases, you will read from the other scale, as in the next example.)

In deciding which scale to use, the idea of a **right angle** is useful. The corner of this page forms a right angle. A right angle has a measure of 90°. Therefore an angle that is larger than a right angle has a measure of more than 90°. An angle that is smaller than a right angle has a measure less than 90°.

Example 2:   Measure with a protractor.

The angle is smaller than a right angle. So its measure is less than 90°.

Use the scale that has its 0° mark on a side of the angle. The measure is 36°.

Example 3: Measure with a protractor.

The angle is larger than a right angle. So the measure is more than 90°. The measure is 160°.

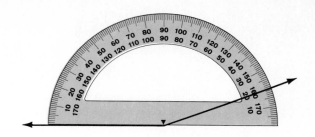

Example 4: Draw an angle with a measure of 35°.

a. First draw the horizontal side of the angle.

b. Place the bottom edge of the protractor on that side so that the center of the protractor is on point A.

c. On the circular edge of the protractor, locate the 35° mark on the scale that has its 0° mark on the horizontal side. Draw a dot at the 35° mark.

d. Draw the other side of the angle from point A through the dot at the 35° mark.

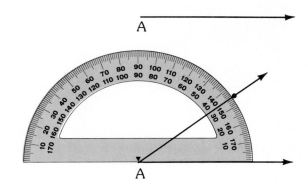

EXERCISES

Complete each sentence.

1. 45° is read ___45 degrees___.

2. An angle has __2__ sides that meet at a point.

3. There are __90__ degrees in a right angle.

4. Angles are measured with an instrument called a __protractor__.

Refer to the angles below.

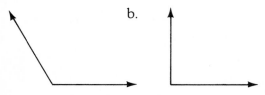
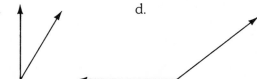

5. Which angle is a right angle? b

6. Which angles are larger than a right angle? a and d

Measure each angle with a protractor.

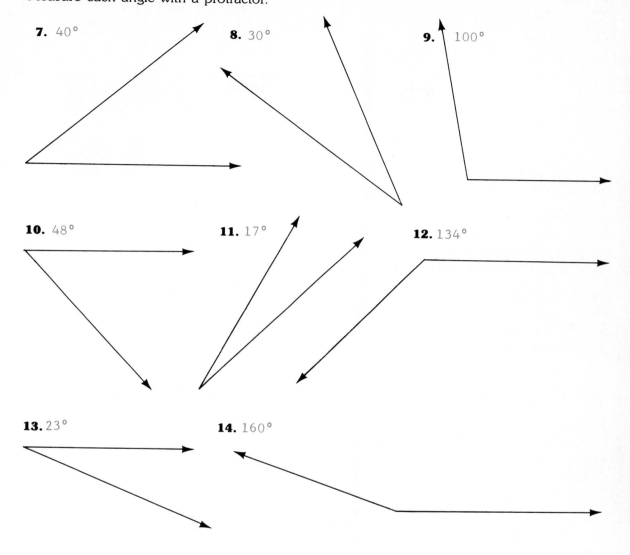

7. 40°   **8.** 30°   **9.** 100°

10. 48°   **11.** 17°   **12.** 134°

13. 23°   **14.** 160°

Draw an angle for each measurement.
See students' drawings.

15. 45°   **16.** 30°   **17.** 120°   **18.** 150°

19. 52°   **20.** 83°   **21.** 163°   **22.** 98°

23. What is the measure of the angle formed by the hands of
a clock at 2:00? At 11:00? At 4:00? At 7:00? 60°; 30°; 120°; 150°

Applications 29–30 may be used at this time.

Name a unit of measure that could be used to measure each of the following: 5.1
Answers for exercises 1-4 will vary.

1. your weight pound

2. your waist measurement inch

3. your age year

4. your body temperature
degree Fahrenheit

Which are standard units of measure?

5. a gram Yes

6. a whole lot No

7. a little while No

8. a mile Yes

Each ancient unit can be described by what other name? 5.2

9. the width of the thumb inch or thumb width

10. the distance between fingertips of outstretched arms fathom

11. the distance from the elbow to the tip of the middle finger cubit

12. the distance from the tip of the nose to the tips of the fingers of an outstretched arm yard

Measure each segment to the nearest $\frac{1}{8}$ inch. 5.3

13. _____ $1\frac{3}{8}$ in.

14. _____ $2\frac{5}{8}$ in.

15. _____
$1\frac{7}{8}$ in.

16. _____ $2\frac{1}{8}$ in.

Change each measurement. 5.4

17. 6 feet to inches 72 in.

18. 7 yards to inches 252 in.

19. 84 inches to feet 7 ft

20. 2 miles to feet 10,560 ft

Draw a segment for each length. 5.5
See students' drawings.

21. 16 cm

22. 88 mm

23–26. Measure each segment in exercises 13–16 to the nearest centimeter.

13. 4 cm; 14. 7 cm; 15. 5 cm; 16. 5 cm

Complete the following:

5.6

27. 2 m = $\overset{2000}{\underline{}}$ mm

28. 18 km = $\overset{18\ 000}{\underline{}}$ m

29. 880 mm = $\overset{88}{\underline{}}$ cm

30. 28 000 m = $\overset{28}{\underline{}}$ km

31. 5 lb = $\overset{80}{\underline{}}$ oz

32. 8 kg = $\overset{8000}{\underline{}}$ g

5.7

33. 48 oz = $\overset{3}{\underline{}}$ lb

34. 5000 g = $\overset{5}{\underline{}}$ kg

35. 3.8 liters = $\overset{3800}{\underline{}}$ mL

36. 8 gal = $\overset{32}{\underline{}}$ qt

5.8

37. 1125 mL = $\overset{1.125}{\underline{}}$ liters

38. 6 qt = $\overset{12}{\underline{}}$ pt

39. 12 qt = $\overset{3}{\underline{}}$ gal

40. 10 pt = $\overset{160}{\underline{}}$ fl oz

Add or subtract.

5.9

41. 3 hr 50 min
    $+$1 hr 15 min
    5 hr 5 min

42. 8 min 35 sec
    $-$6 min 53 sec
    1 min 42 sec

43. 8 hr 10 min
    $-$4 hr 20 min
    3 hr 50 min

44. 3 hr 50 min
    $+$6 hr 30 min
    10 hr 20 min

Use the thermometer on page 216 to change each temperature to the other scale.

5.10

45. 10°C 50°F

46. 90°F 32°C

Measure each angle with a protractor.

5.11

Measurements for exercises 47-48 may vary.

47. 45°

48. 108°

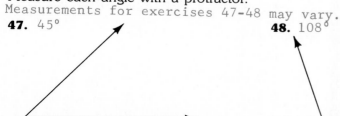

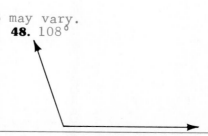

Choose the correct answer.

1. A (<u>meter</u>, pace) is a standard unit of measure.

2. A (<u>fathom</u>, hand) is an ancient unit for the distance between fingertips when the arms are outstretched.

Measure each segment to the nearest $\frac{1}{2}$ inch.

3. ———————————
$1\frac{1}{2}$ in.

4. ———————————
2 in.

Complete the following:

5. 15 feet is 180 inches.

6. 180 inches is 5 yards.

Measure each segment to the nearest centimeter.

7. ——————— 3 cm

8. ————————— 4 cm

Complete the following:

9. 48 cm = 480 mm

10. 8500 m = 8.5 km

11. 160 oz = 10 lb

12. 2.5 kg = 2500 g

13. 12 qt = 3 gal

14. 7 liters = 7000 mL

Add or subtract.

15.   14 min 48 sec
   + 9 min 18 sec
   24 min 6 sec

16.   9 hr 40 min
   − 3 hr 48 min
   5 hr 52 min

17.   8 hr 25 min
   +2 hr 35 min
   11 hr

18. At what Fahrenheit temperature does water freeze? 32°F

Use a protractor to draw an angle for each measurement.
See students' drawings.

19. 68°

20. 125°

1. How many right angles does a rectangle have? 4

2. How many sides does a hexagon have? 6

Find the perimeter of each rectangle.

3. length, 63 m; width, 47 m   220 m

4. each side, $2\frac{1}{2}$ yd   10 yd

Find the area of each rectangle.

5. length, 8.2 cm; width, 2.6 cm
21.32 cm^2

6. each side, $8\frac{1}{4}$ inches $68\frac{1}{16}$ in^2

Complete the following:

7. 6 yd^2 = __54__ ft^2

8. 1440 in^2 = __10__ ft^2

Find the area of each parallelogram.

9. base, 12 ft; height, 9 ft   108 ft^2

10. base, 93 mm; height, 78 mm   7254 mm^2

Find the area of each triangle.

11. base, 36 cm; height, 20 cm
360 cm^2

12. base, 14 m; height, 26 m   182 m^2

13. Find the circumference of a circle with a diameter of 18 feet. Use $\frac{22}{7}$ for π. $56\frac{4}{7}$ ft

14. Find the area of a circle with a radius of 8 meters. Use 3.14 for π.   200.96 m^2

Find the volume of each rectangular solid.

15.

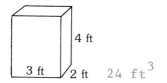

3 ft   2 ft   4 ft   24 ft^3

16.

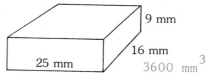

9 mm   16 mm   25 mm   3600 mm^3

Complete the following:

17. 15 yd^3 = __405__ ft^3

18. 810 ft^3 = __30__ yd^3

19. Find the volume of a cylinder whose base has a radius of 5 centimeters. The height of the cylinder is 10 centimeters. Use 3.14 for π.   785 cm^3

225

POLYGONS

The road signs below have shapes that are very common. Each sign has the shape of a **polygon.**

A polygon has three or more sides. All the sides are line segments. Special names are given to polygons according to their number of sides. A few are shown below.

 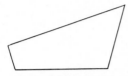

Triangle
(3 sides)

Quadrilateral
(4 sides)

Pentagon
(5 sides)

Hexagon
(6 sides)

Octagon
(8 sides)

Some special kinds of quadrilaterals (4-sided polygons) are shown below.

 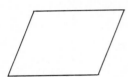 

Trapezoid
(one pair of parallel sides)

Parallelogram
(both pairs of opposite sides parallel)

Rectangle
(parallelogram with four right angles)

Square
(rectangle with all sides the same length)

EXERCISES

How many sides does each polygon have?

1. triangle 3

2. square 4

3. rectangle
4

4. parallelogram 4

5. hexagon 6

6. pentagon
5

How many right angles does each quadrilateral have?

7. rectangle 4

8. square 4

Tell how many sides each traffic sign has. Then name the polygon with that number of sides.

9. stop sign 8; octagon

10. yield sign 3; triangle

11. school-crossing sign 5; pentagon

12. speed-limit sign 4; quadrilateral

For each figure, measure $\overline{AB}$, $\overline{BC}$, $\overline{CD}$, and $\overline{DA}$ to the nearest centimeter.

13.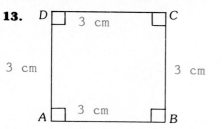

14.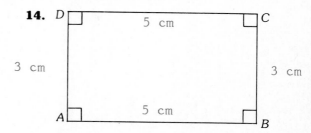

15.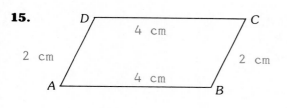

16.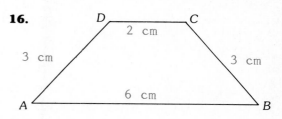

Refer to your measurements from exercises 13–16.

17. Which polygons have opposite sides of equal length?
the polygons in exercises 13, 14, and 15

18. Which polygon has all sides of equal length?
the polygon in exercise 13

Look at the figures in exercises 13–16.

19. For which polygons will opposite sides never meet, no matter how far they are extended? the polygons in exercises 13, 14, and 15

20. For which polygon will one pair of opposite sides meet when extended? the polygon in exercise 16

The following statements are true. Draw a figure to illustrate each statement.
See students' drawings for exercises 21-26.

21. A triangle can have one right angle.

22. The three sides of a triangle can be equal in length.

23. A rectangle can have four sides of equal length.

24. A parallelogram can have four right angles.

25. A parallelogram can have four sides of equal length and no right angles.

26. A parallelogram can have four sides of equal length and four right angles.

27. What kind of polygons do you see in the honeycomb shown at the right? hexagons

28. The building in the picture below is the headquarters of the Department of Defense. The building gets its name from its shape. What do you think its name is?

Pentagon Building

James H. Pickerell   William J. Weber/John D. Cunningham

SKILLS REFRESHER

Add.

		Skill	Page
1. $3\frac{3}{8}+4\frac{1}{4}+5\frac{1}{8}$ $12\frac{3}{4}$	**2.** $2\frac{1}{6}+3\frac{1}{12}+5\frac{1}{2}+1\frac{5}{12}$ $12\frac{1}{6}$	42	510
3. $1.75+3.82+1.47$ 7.04 **4.** $3.72+0.8+6.1+0.124$ 10.744		6	454

Multiply.

			Skill	Page
5. $2(6\frac{1}{4})$ $12\frac{1}{2}$	**6.** $4(3\frac{1}{2})$ 14	**7.** $4(6\frac{1}{4})$ 25	44	514

Solve each proportion.

			Skill	Page
8. $\frac{9}{153}=\frac{1}{n}$ 17	**9.** $\frac{9}{n}=\frac{1}{36}$ 324	**10.** $\frac{144}{864}=\frac{1}{n}$ 6	—	143

228   *Application 31 may be used at this time.*

6.2 PERIMETER

An old quilt is 80 inches long by 70 inches wide. It needs a new border. How many inches of binding tape is needed to border the quilt?

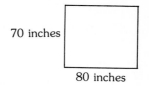

70 inches

80 inches

Karen Tanaka/James H. Pickerell

70 + 80 + 70 + 80 = 300

300 inches of tape is needed.

The quilt problem involved **perimeter**—the distance around a closed figure. You can find the perimeter of a polygon by adding the lengths of the sides.

Examples: Find the perimeter of each polygon. Let *P* stand for the measure of the perimeter.

a.

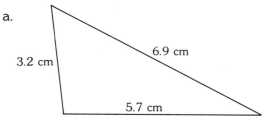

3.2 cm

6.9 cm

5.7 cm

b.

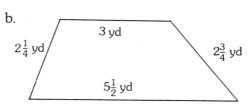

$2\frac{1}{4}$ yd

3 yd

$2\frac{3}{4}$ yd

$5\frac{1}{2}$ yd

$P = 3.2 + 5.7 + 6.9$
$P = 15.8$

The perimeter is 15.8 cm.

$P = 5\frac{1}{2} + 2\frac{1}{4} + 3 + 2\frac{3}{4}$

$P = 13\frac{1}{2}$

The perimeter is $13\frac{1}{2}$ yd.

Formulas are useful for finding perimeters of rectangles and squares.

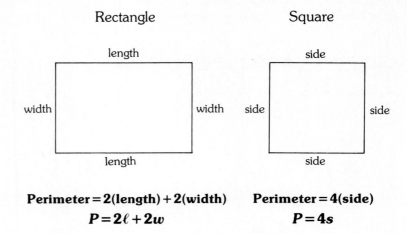

Rectangle	Square

$$Perimeter = 2(length) + 2(width) \qquad Perimeter = 4(side)$$
$$P = 2\ell + 2w \qquad\qquad\qquad P = 4s$$

Examples:

c. What is the perimeter of a rectangle with a length of 6.2 meters and a width of 3.8 meters?

$P = 2\ell + 2w$ **or** $P = 2\ell + 2w$

$P = 2(6.2) + 2(3.8)$ $P = 2(6.2) + 2(3.8)$

$P = 12.4 + 7.6$ **Multiply.** $P = 2(6.2 + 3.8)$

$P = 20.0$ **Add.** $P = 2(10.0)$ **Add.**

                                             $P = 20.0$ **Multiply.**

The perimeter is 20 meters.

d. What is the perimeter of a square with each side $2\frac{3}{4}$ inches long?

$P = 4s$

$P = 4\left(2\frac{3}{4}\right)$

$P = 4\left(\frac{11}{4}\right)$

$P = 11$ **Multiply.**

The perimeter is 11 inches.

EXERCISES

1. What is the formula for the perimeter of a rectangle? $P = 2\ell + 2w$
What does each letter stand for? P: perimeter, ℓ: length, w: width

2. What is the formula for the perimeter of a square? $P = 4s$

Find the perimeter of each polygon.

3.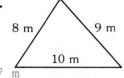
8 m   9 m
10 m
27 m

4.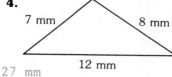
7 mm   8 mm
12 mm
27 mm

5.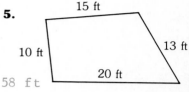
15 ft
10 ft   13 ft
20 ft
58 ft

6.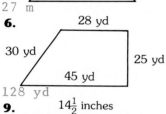
28 yd
30 yd   25 yd
45 yd
128 yd

7.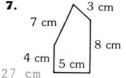
3 cm
7 cm
8 cm
4 cm   5 cm
27 cm

8.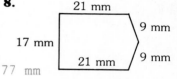
21 mm
9 mm
17 mm
21 mm   9 mm
77 mm

9.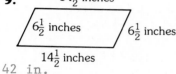
$14\frac{1}{2}$ inches
$6\frac{1}{2}$ inches $6\frac{1}{2}$ inches
$14\frac{1}{2}$ inches
42 in.

10.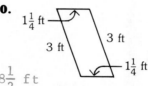
$1\frac{1}{4}$ ft
3 ft   3 ft
$1\frac{1}{4}$ ft
$8\frac{1}{2}$ ft

11.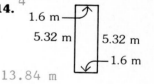
$3\frac{1}{2}$ mi $2\frac{3}{8}$ mi $3\frac{1}{2}$ mi
$3\frac{1}{2}$ mi $2\frac{3}{8}$ mi $3\frac{1}{2}$ mi
$18\frac{3}{4}$ mi

12.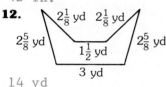
$2\frac{1}{8}$ yd $2\frac{1}{8}$ yd
$2\frac{5}{8}$ yd $2\frac{5}{8}$ yd
$1\frac{1}{2}$ yd
3 yd
14 yd

13.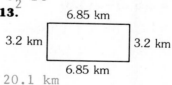
6.85 km
3.2 km   3.2 km
6.85 km
20.1 km

14.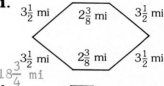
1.6 m
5.32 m   5.32 m
1.6 m
13.84 m

The lengths of the sides of a polygon are given. Find the perimeter.

15. $2\frac{1}{2}$ ft, $3\frac{1}{4}$ ft, 5 ft, $2\frac{1}{2}$ ft, $1\frac{1}{2}$ ft $14\frac{3}{4}$ ft

16. $5\frac{3}{4}$ in., $7\frac{1}{8}$ in., $10\frac{1}{2}$ in., $12\frac{3}{8}$ in. $35\frac{3}{4}$ in.

17. 72.4 cm, 93.7 cm, 11.5 cm, 43.15 cm, 99.4 cm, 84.8 cm   404.95 cm

18. 7.47 mm, 1.3 mm, 8.549 mm, 8.43 mm   25.749 mm

19. $3\frac{1}{12}$ ft, $7\frac{1}{6}$ ft, $8\frac{1}{2}$ ft, $9\frac{5}{12}$ ft $28\frac{1}{6}$ ft

20. $10\frac{1}{2}$ yd, $15\frac{3}{4}$ yd, $21\frac{5}{12}$ yd, $30\frac{1}{3}$ yd   78 yd

Find the perimeter of a rectangle with each given length and width.

21. 28 ft, 23 ft   102 ft

22. 31 cm, 17 cm   96 cm

23. $2\frac{1}{2}$ ft, 3 ft
11 ft

24. 6 in., $4\frac{1}{2}$ in.   21 in.

25. 327 m, 105 m   864 m

26. 5.28 m, 7.39 m
25.34 m

Find the perimeter of a square with each given side.

27. $3\frac{1}{2}$ ft   14 ft

28. $6\frac{1}{4}$ in.   25 in.

29. 747 mm
2988 mm

30. 99.5 m   398 m

31. 87.6 cm   350.4 cm

32. $7\frac{3}{8}$ in. $29\frac{1}{2}$ in.

33. A garden is to be fenced completely with a chain-link fence. The garden is 38.2 meters long by 28.1 meters wide. How many meters of fencing is needed?   132.6 m

34. A square pen is to be built as a rabbit cage. The pen is to be $8\frac{1}{2}$ feet on each side. How many feet of fencing is needed?   34 ft

Paul Light/Lightwave   Artstreet

35. A fringe is to be sewn around the outer edge of a bedspread that measures 80 inches by 60 inches. How many feet of fringe is needed? If fringe sells for $0.98 a yard and is only sold in whole yards, how much will the fringe cost? $23\frac{1}{3}$ ft; $7.84

36. A picture that measures 24 inches by 18 inches is to be framed with a $1\frac{1}{2}$-inch-wide frame. How many inches of frame is needed to surround the picture?   HINT: Find the outside perimeter of the frame.   96 in.

37. A wallpaper border is to be applied around a room that is $20\frac{1}{2}$ feet long by $14\frac{1}{2}$ feet wide. How many feet of border is needed?   70 ft

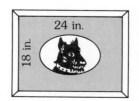

24 in.

18 in.

The **area** of a figure is the amount of surface inside the figure. Area is measured in square units. Two common units of area are shown below. Other common units of area are the square foot (ft²), the square meter (m²), and the square yard (yd²).

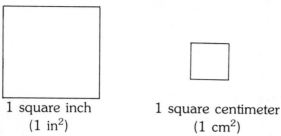

1 square inch
(1 in²)

1 square centimeter
(1 cm²)

Example 1: Find the area of a rectangle that measures 5 centimeters by 3 centimeters.

The dashed lines below show that there are 15 square centimeters inside the rectangle.

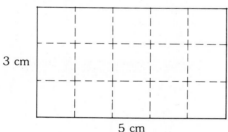

3 cm

5 cm

Note that 3 rows of 5 square centimeters each make 15 square centimeters.

To find the number of squares inside a rectangle, you can multiply the number of rows by the number of squares in each row.

To find the area of a rectangle, multiply the length by the width. (The length and the width must be in the same units.)

Area = length × width

$$A = \ell w$$

width

length

233

Example 2: What is the area of a rectangle having a length of 14 inches and a width of 6 inches?

$A = \ell w$

$A = 14(6)$

$A = 84$ **Multiply.**

The area is 84 square inches.

To find the area of a square, multiply the measure of a side by itself.

Area = side × side

$A = s^2$

side

side

Example 3: What is the area of a square having a side of 7 meters?

$A = s^2$ **s^2 is read "s squared."**

$A = 7^2$ **7^2 is read "7 squared."**

$A = 49$ **$7^2 = 7 \times 7 = 49$**

The area is 49 square meters.

EXERCISES

1. Name five common units of area. Possible answers: in^2, ft^2, cm^2, m^2, yd^2

2. Write the formula for the area of a rectangle. What does each letter stand for? A = ℓw; A: area, ℓ: length, w: width

3. Write the formula for the area of a square. A = s^2

4. If the length and the width of a rectangle are 9 inches and 6 inches, the area is 54 square <u>inches</u>.

5. If the length and the width of a rectangle are 9 centimeters and 6 centimeters, the area is 54 <u>square</u> centimeters.

6. If the side of a square is 4 feet, its area is <u>16</u> square feet.

Find the area of each rectangle.

7.

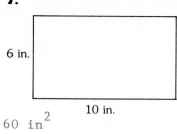

6 in.

10 in.

60 in^2

8.

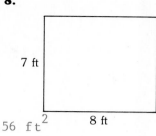

7 ft

8 ft

56 ft^2

9.

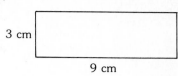

3 cm

9 cm

27 cm^2

10.

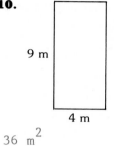

9 m

4 m

36 m^2

11.

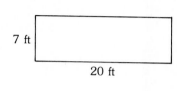

7 ft

20 ft

140 ft^2

12.

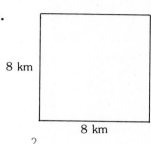

8 km

8 km

64 km^2

Find the area of a rectangle having each given length and width.

13. 16 ft, 15 ft
240 ft^2

14. 25 cm, 13 cm
325 cm^2

15. 14 yd, 18 yd
252 yd^2

16. 17 mm, 36 mm
612 mm^2

17. 783 ft, 125 ft
97,875 ft^2

18. 155 cm, 397 cm
61 535 cm^2

19. 1.5 km, 2.3 km
3.45 km^2

20. 3.2 m, 6.3 m
20.16 m^2

21. $1\frac{1}{2}$ yd, $3\frac{1}{2}$ yd
$5\frac{1}{4}$ yd^2

22. $7\frac{1}{4}$ in., $2\frac{1}{2}$ in.
$18\frac{1}{8}$ in^2

23. $3\frac{1}{4}$ in., $2\frac{1}{4}$ in.
$7\frac{5}{16}$ in^2

24. $8\frac{3}{4}$ in., $6\frac{1}{4}$ in.
$54\frac{11}{16}$ in^2

25. 2.25 mi, 3.5 mi
7.875 mi^2

26. 6.39 m, 7.85 m
50.1615 m^2

27. 75.4 km, 25.3 km
1907.62 km^2

28. 93.9 cm, 79.9 cm
7502.61 cm^2

29. 9.875 m, 1.5 m
14.8125 m^2

30. 4.3 cm, 0.055 cm
0.2365 cm^2

Find the area of a square having each given side.

31. 28 m 784 m^2

32. 87 in. 7569 in^2

33. $2\frac{1}{2}$ ft $6\frac{1}{4}$ ft^2

34. $1\frac{1}{4}$ in. $1\frac{9}{16}$ in^2

35. 7.2 cm 51.84 cm^2

36. 1.8 mm 3.24 mm^2

37. 2.25 m 5.0625 m^2

38. 8.43 km 71.0649 km^2

39. 1.02 in. 1.0404 in^2

Find the area of each figure in square feet. HINT: Each figure can be separated into two rectangles.

40.

9 ft

12 ft

18 ft

8 ft

252 ft^2

41.

28 ft

8 ft

15 ft

20 ft

364 ft^2

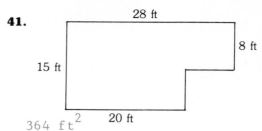

42. Assume that the figure in exercise 41 is the floor plan of a room. The floor is to be covered with tiles that cost $0.98 per square foot. How much will it cost to tile the floor? $356.72

43. A gymnasium floor is to be covered with a sealer that covers 500 square feet per gallon. If the floor measures 80 feet by 125 feet, how many gallons are needed?   20 gallons

44. The drawing at the right shows a wall with a door and a window. What is the area of the window? What is the area of the door? If the wall is to be painted, how many square feet of surface needs to be covered? (The door and the window won't be painted.)

15 ft^2; 21 ft^2; 60 ft^2

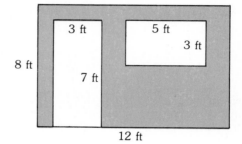

3 ft

5 ft

3 ft

8 ft

7 ft

12 ft

AN EXTRA UNIT?

Use graph paper to make a square like the one below. Cut the square as shown by the dashed lines. Try to fit the pieces together to make a rectangle like the one at the right.

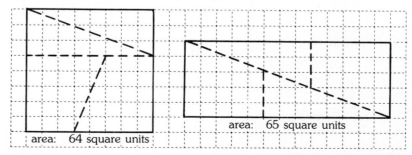

area: 64 square units

area: 65 square units

Why is the area of the rectangle greater than the area of the square?   When the pieces are rearranged, there is a narrow gap along the diagonal line that has an area of 1 square inch.

6.4 EQUIVALENT AREAS

The square below shows a relationship between square feet and square yards.

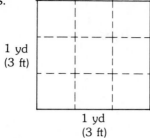

1 yd
(3 ft)

1 yd
(3 ft)

Each side is 3 feet long, so the area is 9 square feet. Each side is also 1 yard long, so the area is also 1 square yard.

9 square feet = 1 square yard

$$9 \text{ ft}^2 = 1 \text{ yd}^2$$

Example 1: Change 198 square feet to square yards.

$9 \text{ ft}^2 = 1 \text{ yd}^2$ **Let n stand for the num-**
$198 \text{ ft}^2 = n \text{ yd}^2$ **ber of square yards.**

$$\frac{9}{198} = \frac{1}{n}$$

$$9 \times n = 198 \times 1$$

$$9n = 198$$

$$\frac{9n}{9} = \frac{198}{9}$$

$$n = 22$$

There are 22 square yards in 198 square feet.

Example 2: Change 25 square yards to square feet.

$9 \text{ ft}^2 = 1 \text{ yd}^2$
$n \text{ ft}^2 = 25 \text{ yd}^2$

$$\frac{9}{n} = \frac{1}{25}$$

$$9 \times 25 = n \times 1$$

$$225 = n$$

There are 225 square feet in 25 square yards.

Sometimes you need to change an area from square feet to square inches. Since a square with an area of 1 square foot has a length of 12 inches and a width of 12 inches, its area is 12×12, or 144, square inches.

$A = s^2$
$A = 12^2$
$A = 144$

12 in. | 1 square foot |

12 in.

144 square inches = 1 square foot
144 in^2 = 1 ft^2

EXERCISES

1. 1 square yard is equivalent to ___9___ square feet.

2. 1 square foot is equivalent to ___144___ square inches.

3. Which covers more area—10 square feet or 1 square yard? 10 square feet

4. Which covers less area—100 square inches or 1 square foot? 100 square inches

Complete the following:

5. 18 ft^2 = ___ yd^2 2

6. 27 ft^2 = ___ yd^2 3

12 **7.** 108 ft^2 = ___ yd^2

8. 228 ft^2 = ___ yd^2 $25\frac{1}{3}$

9. 2 yd^2 = ___ ft^2 18

45 **10.** 5 yd^2 = ___ ft^2

11. 10 yd^2 = ___ ft^2 90

12. 18 yd^2 = ___ ft^2 162

120 **13.** 1080 ft^2 = ___ yd^2

14. 927 ft^2 = ___ yd^2 103

15. $2\frac{1}{2}$ yd^2 = ___ ft^2 $22\frac{1}{2}$

$49\frac{1}{2}$ **16.** $5\frac{1}{2}$ yd^2 = ___ ft^2

17. 100 ft^2 = ___ yd^2 $11\frac{1}{9}$

18. 250 ft^2 = ___ yd^2 $27\frac{7}{9}$

432 **19.** 3 ft^2 = ___ in^2

20. 4 ft^2 = ___ in^2 576

21. 288 in^2 = ___ ft^2 2

5 **22.** 720 in^2 = ___ ft^2

23. $2\frac{1}{2}$ ft^2 = ___ in^2 360

24. $5\frac{1}{2}$ ft^2 = ___ in^2 792

$2\frac{1}{2}$ **25.** 360 in^2 = ___ ft^2

26. A carpet is on sale for $17.55 per square yard. What would be an equivalent price per square foot? $1.95

27. A counter top is 30 inches wide by 96 inches long. How many square feet of material is needed to cover the counter top? 20 ft^2

28. A room is 24 feet long by 12 feet wide. What is its floor area in square feet? In square yards? How much would it cost to carpet the room with carpeting that costs $9.95 per square yard? 288 ft^2; 32 yd^2; $318.40

29. A tabletop is 3 feet long by 2 feet wide. What is its area in square feet? In square inches? How much would it cost to tile the tabletop with tiles that sell for $0.04 per square inch? 6 ft^2; 864 in^2; $34.56

30. How many square inches are in 1 square yard? 1296

31. How many square centimeters are in 1 square meter? 10 000

32. How many square meters are in 1 square kilometer? 1 000 000

33. How many square millimeters are in 1 square meter? 1 000 000

There are 43,560 square feet in an **acre.** For each field whose length and width are given, find the area in square feet. Then tell if the field is larger or smaller than an acre.

34. 300 ft, 180 ft
54,000 ft^2; larger

35. 400 ft, 125 ft
50,000 ft^2; larger

36. 279 ft, 198 ft
55,242 ft^2; larger

MATH FROM THE 1870'S

The following problems appeared in a math book that was published in 1877. Can you do them?

The Bettmann Archive

1. A field 100 rods long and 30 rods wide contains how many acres? (1 acre = 160 square rods)

18.75 acres

2. Upon how many acres of ground can the entire population of the globe stand, supposing that 25000 persons can stand upon one acre, and that the population is 1000000000?

40,000 acres

3. A man purchased a house for 2375 dollars, and expended 340 dollars in repairs; he then sold it for railroad stock worth 867 dollars, and 235 acres of western land valued at 8 dollars an acre; what did he gain by the trade? $32

Farmers work very hard and must take many risks. Such factors as poor weather, high interest rates, and depressed market prices can cause farmers severe hardships. It is also very expensive to raise animals. For example, a cow eats about 150 pounds of grass, grain, and hay per day. Nevertheless, many people enjoy farming because of its life-style and the opportunity to work with nature.

A unit of area used in farming is the **acre.** An acre is 4840 square yards—almost the area covered by a football field, excluding end zones.

1. Seed corn is sold in 50-pound bags that contain about 80,000 seeds each. How many bags of seed corn should a farmer buy to plant 100 acres with 24,000 seeds per acre?

   30 bags

2. A farmer hopes to harvest 120 bushels of shell corn per acre and sell it for $3 per bushel. How much money does the farmer hope to earn from 100 acres? $36,000

3. It costs $2\frac{3}{4}$¢ per bushel per month to store shell corn. How much must a farmer pay to store 12,000 bushels for 6 months? $1980

4. A holstein cow can produce about 90 pounds of milk per day. Suppose the milk is sold to a dairy for $13.25 per 100 pounds. How much money can a farmer receive each day from the milk produced by 80 holstein cows? $954

Linda Ridgeway/Cyr Agency

Dan White/Picture Group

Dominoes are made of two squares and have only one arrangement.

Pentominoes have five squares and twelve arrangements.

1. Use $\frac{1}{2}$-inch squares to draw twelve pentominoes like those above. Then cut them out.

2. The twelve pieces can be fitted together to form a 6×10 rectangle. Try it. Possible answers for exercises 2-3 are given at right.

3. It is also possible to form 5×12, 4×15, and 3×20 rectangles with pentomino pieces. Try to form each one. (Making the 3×20 rectangle is very difficult, since there are only two possible ways to do it.)

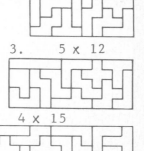

2. 6 x 10

3. 5 x 12

4 x 15

3 x 20

PARALLELOGRAMS

In a parallelogram, as shown at the left below, each pair of opposite sides are parallel. Opposite sides are also the same length.

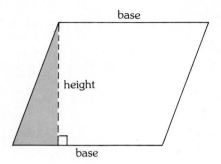

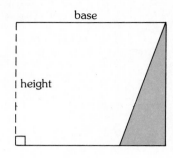

To find the area of the parallelogram, think of cutting along the dashed line and sliding the triangle as shown to form a rectangle.

The length of the rectangle is the length of the base of the parallelogram. The heights of the figures are the same. The area of the rectangle can be found like this:

Area = base × height

Any parallelogram can be made into a rectangle as shown above. If b and h are used to stand for the measures of the base and the height, then $A = bh$.

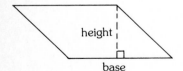

To find the area of a parallelogram, multiply the base by the height.

$A = bh$

Example: Find the area of the parallelogram.

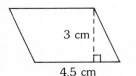

$A = bh$

$A = 4.5(3)$

$A = 13.5$

The area is 13.5 square centimeters.

EXERCISES

1. The distance between the bases of a parallelogram is
called the ___height___.

2. Write the formula for the area of a parallelogram. What
does each letter stand for? $A = bh$; A: area, b: base, h: height

Each square below is 1 square centimeter. Give the following measurements for each parallelogram: base, height, area.

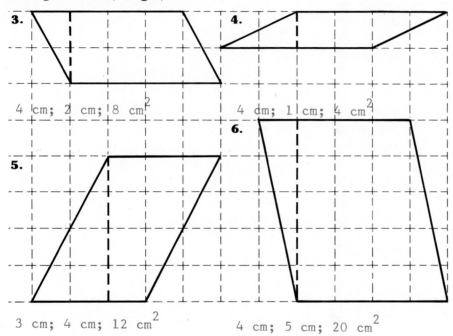

3.

4 cm; 2 cm; 8 cm^2

4.

4 dm; 1 cm; 4 cm^2

5.

3 cm; 4 cm; 12 cm^2

6.

4 cm; 5 cm; 20 cm^2

Find the area of a parallelogram with each given base and height.

7. 7 ft, 9 ft
   63 ft^2

8. 4 cm, 7 cm
   28 cm^2

9. 10 in., 8 in.
   80 in^2

10. 6 m, 8 m
   48 m^2

11. $4\frac{1}{4}$ in., 8 in.
   34 in^2

12. $1\frac{1}{2}$ ft, 5 ft
   $7\frac{1}{2}$ ft^2

13. $2\frac{1}{3}$ yd, $1\frac{1}{2}$ yd
   $3\frac{1}{2}$ yd^2

14. $9\frac{1}{2}$ in., $5\frac{1}{8}$ in.
   $48\frac{11}{16}$ in^2

15. 1.5 cm, 3.5 cm
   5.25 cm^2

16. 8.2 m, 9.3 m
   76.26 m^2

17. 6.33 m, 9.35 m
   59.1855 m^2

18. 7.25 m, 3.4 m
   24.65 m^2

19. 5.47 km, 7.85 km
   42.9395 km^2

20. 788 ft, 567 ft
   446,796 ft^2

21. 885 yd, 520 yd
   460,200 yd^2

Find each area.

22. a parking lot

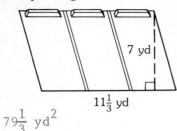

7 yd

$11\frac{1}{3}$ yd

$79\frac{1}{3}$ yd^2

23. a sidewalk between buildings

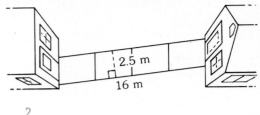

2.5 m

16 m

40 m^2

Estimate the area of each state by finding the area of the parallelogram.

24. Tennessee

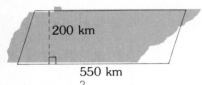

200 km

550 km

110 000 km^2

25. Nebraska

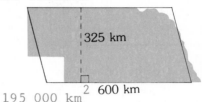

325 km

600 km

195 000 km^2

Trace each parallelogram in exercises 3–6 on another sheet of paper. Cut each parallelogram along the heavy dashed line. Then rearrange the parts to form a rectangle.

26. Find the area of each rectangle (in square centimeters).   3. 8 cm^2 4. 4 cm^2
5. 12 cm^2 6. 20 cm^2

27. In each case, is the area of the rectangle the same as the area of the original parallelogram?   Yes

SKILLS REFRESHER

Multiply.

			Skill	Page
1. $\frac{1}{2}(8)(10)$ 40	**2.** $\frac{1}{2}(11)(5)$ $27\frac{1}{2}$	**3.** $2\times\frac{22}{7}\times21$ 132	33	494
4. $\frac{1}{2}(3\frac{1}{2})(4)$ 7	**5.** $\frac{1}{2}(10)(2\frac{1}{2})$ $12\frac{1}{2}$	**6.** $\frac{1}{2}(6.8)(1.2)$ 4.08	44	514

Find each result.

7. 6^2 36	**8.** 8^2 64	**9.** 10^2 100	25	483
10. 5×3^2 45	**11.** 3.14×4^2 50.24	**12.** $3.14\times(2.5)^2$ 19.625		

244

6.6 TRIANGLES

John D. Cunningham

Jack Corn/Corn's Photo Service

Remember that the area of a parallelogram is the product of the base and the height. The formula is $A = bh$.

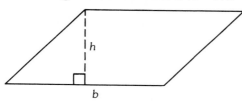

Suppose you have to find the area of a triangle. Think of cutting a parallelogram in half as shown below.

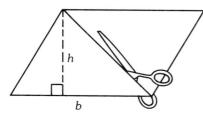 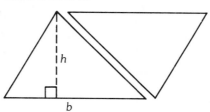

Two triangles of the same size are formed. Each triangle is **half** of the parallelogram. The formula for the area of the parallelogram is $A = bh$. So the formula for the area of one of the triangles is $A = \frac{1}{2}bh$.

To find the area of a triangle, find $\frac{1}{2}$ the product of the base and the height.

Area $= \frac{1}{2} \times$ base $\times$ height

$A = \frac{1}{2}bh$

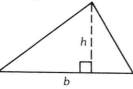

Artstreet

245

Example: Find the area of the triangle.

$A = \frac{1}{2}bh$

$A = \frac{1}{2}(20)(8)$

$A = \frac{20}{2}(8)$

$A = (10)(8)$

$A = 80$

The area is 80 square centimeters.

EXERCISES

1. Write the formula for the area of a triangle. What does each letter stand for? $A = \frac{1}{2}bh$; A: area, b: base, h: height

2. Draw a triangle. Then trace it on another sheet of paper. Cut out both triangles and put them together to form a parallelogram. See students' drawings.

Each square below is 1 square centimeter. Give the following measurements for each triangle: base, height, area.

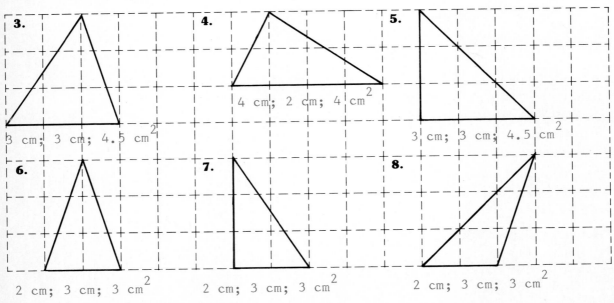

3. 3 cm; 3 cm; 4.5 cm^2

4. 4 cm; 2 cm; 4 cm^2

5. 3 cm; 3 cm; 4.5 cm^2

6. 2 cm; 3 cm; 3 cm^2

7. 2 cm; 3 cm; 3 cm^2

8. 2 cm; 3 cm; 3 cm^2

Find the area of a triangle with each given base and height.

9. 28 in., 18 in. $252\ in^2$

10. 74 cm, 62 cm $2294\ cm^2$

11. 37 ft, 79 ft $1461\frac{1}{2}\ ft^2$

12. 93 mm, 76 mm $3534\ mm^2$

13. $1\frac{1}{2}$ in., 10 in. $7\frac{1}{2}\ in^2$

14. 20 ft, $3\frac{1}{2}$ ft $35\ ft^2$

15. $2\frac{1}{2}$ ft, $2\frac{1}{2}$ ft $3\frac{1}{8}\ ft^2$

16. $1\frac{1}{4}$ in., $1\frac{1}{4}$ in. $\frac{25}{32}\ in^2$

17. 6.8 cm, 30 cm $102\ cm^2$

18. 8.5 m, 42 m $178.5\ m^2$

19. 8.3 m, 7.5 m $31.125\ m^2$

20. 1.2 km, 3.6 km $2.16\ km^2$

21. $3\frac{1}{3}$ yd, $6\frac{1}{2}$ yd $10\frac{5}{6}\ yd^2$

22. $2\frac{1}{2}$ ft, $8\frac{1}{2}$ ft $10\frac{5}{8}\ ft^2$

23. 7.38 km, 5.28 km $19.4832\ km^2$

24. 5.25 m, 3.70 m $9.7125\ m^2$

Find each area shown in color.

25.

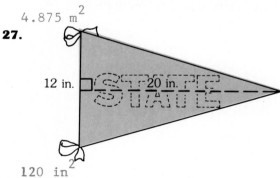

6.5 m

1.5 m

$4.875\ m^2$

26.

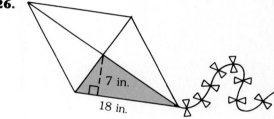

7 in.

18 in.

$63\ in^2$

27.

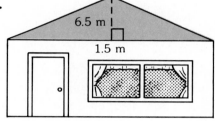

12 in.

20 in.

$120\ in^2$

28.

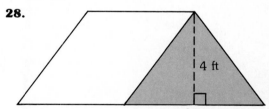

4 ft

6 ft

$12\ ft^2$

29.

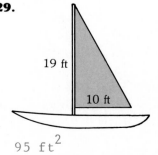

19 ft

10 ft

$95\ ft^2$

30.

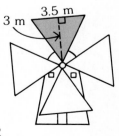

3 m 3.5 m

$5.25\ m^2$

Applications 32–33 may be used at this time. **247**

Circles are common figures in everyday life. You see circles in wheels, jar lids, plates, and many other objects.

Find three circular objects of different sizes. Mark a point on the outer edge of each object. Roll each object along a meter-stick for one complete turn. The distance an object travels in one complete turn is equal to the distance around the object, or its **circumference.** Record the circumferences, to the nearest millimeter, in a table like that shown below.

Find the length of a **diameter** of each object to the nearest millimeter. A diameter of a circle is a line segment passing through the center and joining two points on the circle. Record those lengths in the table.

Answers will vary.

	Circumference	Diameter	$C \div d$
first object	___	___	___
second object	___	___	___
third object	___	___	___

Compute $C \div d$ to the nearest hundredth for each object. You should get about the same number each time. What is it?

3.14

For any circle, $C \div d$ is always the same number. The number is approximately 3.14 or $\frac{22}{7}$. However, since the number cannot be represented exactly by a decimal or a fraction, the Greek letter π (called *pi*) is used.

6.7 | CIRCUMFERENCE

The **circumference** of a circle is the distance around the circle.

A **diameter** of a circle is a line segment that passes through the center and joins two points on the circle.

A **radius** is a line segment that joins the center to any point on the circle.

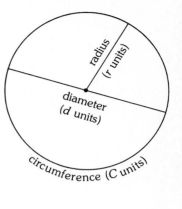

Let C and d stand for the measures of the circumference and a diameter of a circle. For all circles, $C \div d$ is the same number. That number cannot be expressed exactly as a decimal or as a fraction. The number is called *pi* and represented by the symbol π. It is approximately equal to 3.14 or $\frac{22}{7}$.

$$C \div d = \pi \quad \text{or} \quad \frac{C}{d} = \pi$$

$$\frac{C}{d}(d) = \pi d \quad \text{Multiply both sides by } \boldsymbol{d}.$$

$$C = \pi d$$

For all circles, the length of a radius is half the length of a diameter. Let r stand for the measure of a radius.

$$d = 2r$$

If you replace d with $2r$ in the formula $C = \pi d$, you get $C = \pi(2r)$, which can be changed to

$$C = 2\pi r$$

Example 1: Find the circumference of a circle having a diameter of 8 inches. Use 3.14 for π.

$$C = \pi d$$
$$C = (3.14)(8)$$
$$C = 25.12$$

8 in.

The circumference is 25.12 inches.

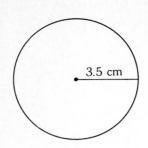

3.5 cm

Example 2: Find the circumference of a circle having a radius of 3.5 centimeters.

$$C = 2\pi r$$
$$C = 2(3.14)(3.5)$$
$$C = 21.98$$

The circumference is 21.98 centimeters.

EXERCISES

1. What number do you get when you divide the measure of a circle's circumference by the measure of its diameter? π

2. A line segment that joins the center of a circle to a point on the circle is called a ___radius___.

3. A diameter of a circle is (twice, half) as long as a radius of that circle.

4. What decimal is approximately equal to π? 3.14

5. What fraction is approximately equal to π? $\frac{22}{7}$

6. Give two different formulas for finding the circumference of a circle. $C = \pi d$, $C = 2\pi r$

The length of a radius is given. Find the length of a diameter.

7. 18 in. 36 in.   8. 25 m 50 m   9. 1.3 m 2.6 m

10. 52 ft 104 ft   11. 41 cm 82 cm   12. 7.5 ft 15 ft

The length of a diameter is given. Find the length of a radius.

13. 28 ft 14 ft   14. 62 cm 31 cm   15. 24.6 m 12.3 m

16. $15\frac{1}{2}$ in. $7\frac{3}{4}$ in.   17. 80 m 40 m   18. 13.2 ft 6.6 ft

The length of a diameter is given. Find the circumference. Use 3.14 for π.

19. 6 in.   18.84 in.　　**20.** 15 ft   47.1 ft

21. 28 cm   87.92 cm　　**22.** 5.9 m   18.526 m

23. 3.63 in.   11.3982 in.　　**24.** 7.28 m   22.8592 m

25. 22.1 mm   69.394 mm　　**26.** 38.5 cm   120.89 cm

The length of a radius is given. Find the circumference. Use $\frac{22}{7}$ for π.

27. 14 ft   88 ft　　**28.** 35 in.   220 in.

29. 28 mm   176 mm　　**30.** 70 m   440 m

31. 21 yd   132 yd　　**32.** 63 cm   396 cm

33. 49.7 cm   312.4 cm　　**34.** 19.6 m   123.2 m

In exercises 35–39, use 3.14 for π.

35. A wheel has a diameter of 28 inches. How far does the wheel roll in one complete turn?   87.92 in.

36. A circular rug is 5 feet in diameter. How many feet of fringe is needed to border it?   15.7 ft

37. A circular pool is to be surrounded by a low fence. If a radius of the pool measures $3\frac{1}{2}$ feet, how many feet of fence is needed?   21.98 ft

38. The famous Big Ben in London has clock faces that are 23 feet across. What is the circumference of each face?   72.22 ft

39. The largest four-faced clock in the world is on the Allen-Bradley Building in Milwaukee, Wisconsin. It has a 20-foot-long minute hand. How far does the tip of the minute hand travel in 1 hour (one complete turn)?   125.6 ft

CALCULATOR SKILL on page 531 may be used at this time.

The British Tourist Authority

Application 34 may be used at this time.   **251**

6.8 AREA OF A CIRCLE

Suppose you draw a square around a circle with a radius measure r as shown below.

Each side of the square has a measure of $2r$. The area of the square is $(2r)(2r)$, or $4r^2$.

So the area of the circle is less than $4r^2$.

Suppose you draw a square inside the circle as shown below.

The area of the triangle shaded red is $\frac{1}{2}(2r)(r)$, or r^2. The area of the square is twice that much, or $2r^2$.

So the area of the circle is more than $2r^2$.

The area of the circle is between $2r^2$ and $4r^2$. The average of the two areas would be a good estimate of the area of the circle.

$$\frac{2r^2 + 4r^2}{2} = \frac{6r^2}{2}, \text{ or } 3r^2$$

By using the method shown above and by doubling the number of sides (8 sides, 16 sides, and so on), mathematicians have found the following formula for the area of a circle:

$$A = \pi r^2$$

Example: Find the area of a circle with a radius 6 centimeters long.

$A = \pi r^2$

$A = 3.14(6)(6)$

$A = 113.04$

The area is 113.04 square centimeters.

EXERCISES

1. Write the formula for the area of a circle. $A = \pi r^2$

2. In the formula $A = \pi r^2$, r^2 means ___r___ × ___r___.

3. If a radius of a circle is 3 inches long, the circle's area is 3.14(3)(3), or 28.26 _____.   square inches

4. If a radius of a circle is 4 feet long, the circle's area is 3.14 × __16__ square feet.

The length of a radius is given. Find the area of the circle. Use 3.14 for π.

5. 5 cm 78.5 cm^2

6. 6 mm 113.04 mm^2

7. 10 ft 314 ft^2

8. 8 yd 200.96 yd^2

9. 20 ft 1256 ft^2

10. 14 in. 615.44 in^2

11. 46 cm 6644.24 cm^2

12. 29 mm 2640.74 mm^2

13. 6.2 in. 120.7016 in^2

14. 3.8 m 45.3416 m^2

15. 1.4 m 6.1544 m^2

16. 2.8 cm 24.6176 cm^2

17. 10.2 cm 326.6856 cm^2

18. 16.1 in. 813.9194 in^2

19. 123 mm $47\ 505.06$ mm^2

The length of a diameter is given. Find the area of the circle. Use $\frac{22}{7}$ for π. Remember, r stands for radius measure.

20. 14 in. 154 in^2

21. 28 ft 616 ft^2

22. 70 cm 3850 cm^2

23. 84 mm 5544 mm^2

24. 142 yd $15{,}843\frac{1}{7}$ yd^2

25. 56 in. 2464 in^2

26. 2.8 cm 6.16 cm^2

27. 8.4 mm 55.44 mm^2

28. 11.2 in. 98.56 in^2

Find the area of each circle. Use 3.14 for π.

29. pizza 113.04 in^2

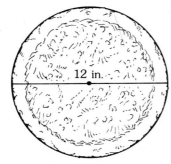

12 in.

30. tray 1256 cm^2

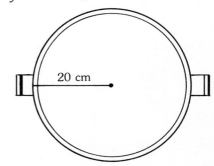

20 cm

31. skillet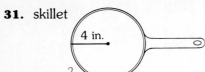

50.24 in^2

32. plate

63.585 in^2

33. fountain

3.14 m^2

34. clock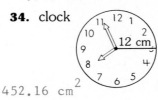

452.16 cm^2

For exercises 35–38, use 3.14 for π.

35. A sewer cover has a diameter of 18 inches. What is its area? 254.34 in^2

36. A jar lid has a radius of 3.5 centimeters. What is its area?

38.465 cm^2

37. A circular windowpane 100 centimeters in diameter is cut from a square piece of glass that is 100 centimeters on a side. How much glass is wasted? 2150 cm^2

38. Six circular discs are cut from a piece of sheet metal that is 30 inches long by 20 inches wide. Each disc is 10 inches in diameter. How much sheet metal is wasted?

129 in^2

SKILLS REFRESHER

Multiply.

			Skill	Page
1. $18 \times 25 \times 15$	**2.** $41.6 \times 24 \times 34$	**3.** $4.8 \times 3.5 \times 15$	13	466
6750	33,945.6	252		

Solve each proportion.

4. $\frac{27}{81} = \frac{1}{n}$ 3	**5.** $\frac{27}{60} = \frac{1}{n}$ $2\frac{2}{9}$	**6.** $\frac{27}{n} = \frac{1}{10}$ 270	—	143

Multiply.

7. $\frac{22}{7} \times 7 \times 1 \times 1$ 22	**8.** $\frac{22}{7} \times 14 \times 2\frac{1}{2} \times 2\frac{1}{2}$ 275	44	514

6.9 | VOLUME |

Plane figures—such as squares, triangles, and circles—are flat. They have only two dimensions. However, **solid figures,** or **solids,** have three dimensions.

The solids shown on this page are **rectangular solids** because each face is a rectangle. The special kind of rectangular solid shown below is a **cube.** All of its faces are squares.

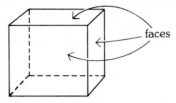

faces

The amount of space that a solid contains is called its **volume.** Volume is measured in **cubic units.**

A cube that is 1 inch long, 1 inch wide, and 1 inch high contains 1 **cubic inch** (in^3). Other common units of volume are the cubic foot (ft^3), the cubic yard (yd^3), the cubic centimeter (cm^3), and the cubic meter (m^3).

Example 1: What is the volume of a rectangular solid that is 5 centimeters long, 3 centimeters wide, and 4 centimeters high?

**number of cubes
in bottom layer: 3 × 5, or 15**

number of layers: 4

total number of cubes: 4 × 15, or 60

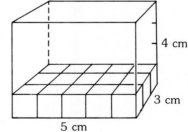

4 cm

3 cm

5 cm

The volume of the rectangular solid is 60 cubic centimeters.

To find the volume of a rectangular solid, multiply the area of the base by the height.

Volume = area of base × height

$$V = Bh$$

Example 2: Find the volume of the rectangular solid. The area of its base is 6 square centimeters.

Since the area of the base is given, all you need to do is multiply that area by the height.

$V=Bh$

$V=6\times5$

$V=30$

5 cm

6 cm^2

The volume is 30 cubic centimeters.

Example 3: A room is 7 meters long, 5.5 meters wide, and 3 meters high. What is its volume?

Since the area of the base is not given, you must find it.

A room is a rectangular solid. So the area of its base is $B=\ell w$.

$V=Bh$ (or $V=\ell wh$)

$V=(7\times5.5)\times3$

$V=115.5$

3 m

5.5 m

7 m

The volume is 115.5 cubic meters.

In Example 3, notice the following:

For any rectangular solid the volume formula $V=Bh$ can also be stated as follows:

$V=\ell wh$

EXERCISES

1. Write the formula for the volume of a rectangular solid.   V = Bh

2. What is another way to state the volume formula $V=Bh$ for a rectangular solid?   V = ℓwh

3. If the length, the width, and the height of a rectangular solid are expressed in feet, its volume will be expressed in ___cubic___ feet.

256

4. If the area of the base of a rectangular solid is 10 square centimeters and the height is 5 centimeters, the volume is 50 cubic _____. centimeters

Find the volume of each rectangular solid, given the area of the base and the height.

5. base, 9 ft^2; height, 6 ft 54 ft^3

6. base, 8 cm^2; height, 4 cm 32 cm^3

7. base, 7 m^2; height, 9 m 63 m^3

8. base, 6 mm^2; height, 2 mm 12 mm^3

Find the area of the base of each rectangular solid. Then find the volume.

9.

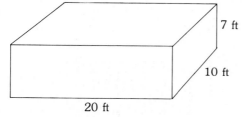

7 ft
10 ft
20 ft

200 ft^2; 1400 ft^3

10.

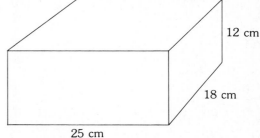

12 cm
18 cm
25 cm

450 cm^2; 5400 cm^3

11.

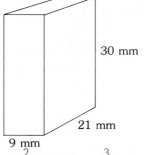

30 mm
21 mm
9 mm

189 mm^2; 5670 mm^3

12.

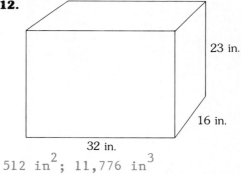

23 in.
16 in.
32 in.

512 in^2; 11,776 in^3

13.

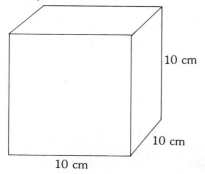

10 cm
10 cm
10 cm

100 cm^2; 1000 cm^3

14.

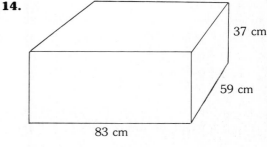

37 cm
59 cm
83 cm

4897 cm^2; 181 189 cm^3

257

15. An aquarium is 12 inches wide, 30 inches long, and 15 inches high. What is its volume?　5400 in^3

16. A contractor is digging a basement that is 20 feet wide, 34 feet long, and 8 feet deep. How many cubic feet of dirt must be removed?　5440 ft^3

17. A driveway is 8 feet wide and 25 feet long. It is covered with a concrete slab that is 6 inches ($\frac{1}{2}$ foot) deep. How many cubic feet of concrete is needed for the driveway?　100 ft^3

18. A classroom is 35 feet long, 20 feet wide, and $9\frac{1}{2}$ feet high. How many cubic feet of space is in the classroom?　6650 ft^3

Find each volume.

19.

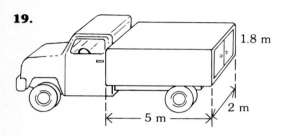

1.8 m

2 m

5 m

18 m^3

20.

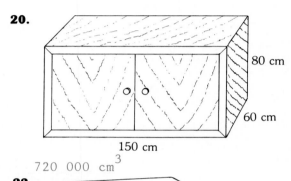

80 cm

60 cm

150 cm

720 000 cm^3

21.

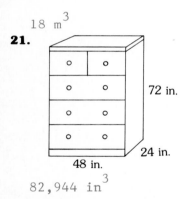

72 in.

24 in.

48 in.

82,944 in^3

22.

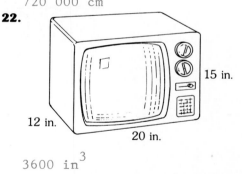

15 in.

12 in.

20 in.

3600 in^3

A factory makes auto parts that are packed in boxes 3 inches by 5 inches by 2 inches. How many boxes would fit into packing crates that have the following dimensions?

23. 36 inches by 20 inches by 24 inches　576

24. 12 inches by 15 inches by 10 inches　60

25. There are 231 cubic inches of water in 1 gallon. How many gallons of water would the aquarium in exercise 15 hold?　about 23.4 gal

26. A gallon of water weighs about 8.3 pounds. How much would enough water to fill the aquarium in exercise 15 weigh?　about 194.22 lb

1. A cube is painted red and cut into 27 smaller cubes as shown. Complete the chart.

Number of smaller
cubes having exactly

5 red faces	0
4 red faces	0
3 red faces	8
2 red faces	12
1 red face	6
0 red faces	1

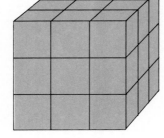

A corner of the cube shown below was sliced off by a plane. The cut left a triangle.

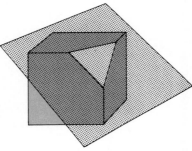

A cube can be sliced in many ways. For each exercise below, tell what figure is left after the cube is sliced by a plane.

2.

rectangle

3.

hexagon

4.

pentagon

5.

(The plane is parallel to the base.)

square

259

A cube with a volume of 1 cubic yard is 3 feet long, 3 feet wide, and 3 feet high. So you can easily find how many cubic feet are in 1 cubic yard.

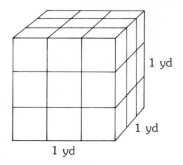

1 yd

1 yd

1 yd

Volume = (length × width) × height

$$V = (3 \times 3) \times 3$$
$$V = 9 \times 3$$
$$V = 27$$

The volume is 27 cubic feet.

27 cubic feet = 1 cubic yard

This fact is useful in finding *equivalent volumes.* Often you need to change a volume from cubic feet to cubic yards (or vice versa).

Example 1:   Change 540 cubic feet to cubic yards.

 27 cubic feet = 1 cubic yard
540 cubic feet = *n* cubic yards

$$\frac{27}{540} = \frac{1}{n}$$

$$27 \times n = 540 \times 1 \quad \textbf{Find the cross-products.}$$

$$27n = 540$$

$$n = \frac{540}{27} \qquad \textbf{Divide by 27.}$$

$$n = 20$$

There are 20 cubic yards in 540 cubic feet.

Concrete is usually sold by the cubic yard. Often it is easier to find a volume in cubic feet. Then you can find the equivalent volume in cubic yards.

Example 2: A concrete driveway is 30 feet long, 20 feet wide, and 6 inches thick. How many *cubic yards* of concrete is needed for the driveway?

First find the volume in cubic feet. Notice that the height (thickness) is given as 6 inches. So change 6 inches to $\frac{1}{2}$ foot.

Volume = (length × width) × height

$$V = (30 \times 20) \times \frac{1}{2}$$

$$V = 600 \times \frac{1}{2}$$

$$V = 300$$

Norma Morrison

The volume is 300 cubic feet. Now change 300 cubic feet to cubic yards.

27 cubic feet = 1 cubic yard
300 cubic feet = n cubic yards

$$\frac{27}{300} = \frac{1}{n}$$

$$27 \times n = 300 \times 1$$

$$27n = 300$$

$$n = \frac{300}{27}$$

$$n = 11\frac{3}{27}, \text{ or } 11\frac{1}{9}$$

So $11\frac{1}{9}$ cubic yards of concrete is needed. (In practice, such a result would be rounded up to the nearest half or full cubic yard of concrete.)

261

EXERCISES

1. A volume of 1 cubic yard is equivalent to __27__ cubic feet.

2. A cube that is 1 foot long, 1 foot wide, and 1 foot high is called a __cubic__ __foot__.

Change each volume to cubic yards.

3. 54 cubic feet 2 yd^3

4. 81 cubic feet 3 yd^3

6. 108 cubic feet 4 yd^3

7. 100 cubic feet $3\frac{19}{27} \text{ yd}^3$

9. 500 cubic feet $18\frac{14}{27} \text{ yd}^3$

10. 750 cubic feet $27\frac{7}{9} \text{ yd}^3$

5. 6 yd^3

8. $5\frac{1}{3} \text{ yd}^3$

11. 1.5 yd^3

5. 162 cubic feet
See above.

8. 144 cubic feet
See above.

11. 40.5 cubic feet
See above.

Change each volume to cubic feet.

12. 6 cubic yards 162 ft^3

13. 8 cubic yards 216 ft^3

14. 10 cubic yards 270 ft^3

15. 14 cubic yards 378 ft^3

16. $2\frac{1}{2}$ cubic yards $67\frac{1}{2} \text{ ft}^3$

17. $3\frac{1}{3}$ cubic yards 90 ft^3

18. $12\frac{1}{2}$ cubic yards $337\frac{1}{2} \text{ ft}^3$

19. $15\frac{1}{4}$ cubic yards $411\frac{3}{4} \text{ ft}^3$

20. 7.4 cubic yards 199.8 ft^3

21. A basement is dug that is 35 feet long, 18 feet wide, and 8 feet deep. How many *cubic yards* of dirt must be removed? $186\frac{2}{3} \text{ yd}^3$

22. A concrete pad to support a heavy machine is poured into a form that is 28 feet long, 16 feet wide, and 1 foot deep. How many *cubic yards* of concrete is needed? $16\frac{16}{27} \text{ yd}^3$

23. A concrete patio is 18 feet long, 10 feet wide, and 6 inches deep. How many *cubic yards* of concrete was needed for the patio? $3\frac{1}{3} \text{ yd}^3$

24. A concrete supporting column has a 1-foot-by-1-foot base and is 10 feet high. What is its volume in cubic feet? If 12 of these columns are to be poured, how many *cubic yards* of concrete is needed? 10 ft^3; $4\frac{4}{9} \text{ yd}^3$

25. Before the concrete for a runway 300 feet wide and 10,000 feet long was poured, the runway was covered with a layer of sand 8 inches thick. How many *cubic yards* of sand was used? $74{,}074\frac{2}{27} \text{ yd}^3$

The total area of all the faces of a solid is called the **surface area.** To find the surface area of a rectangular solid, you must find the areas of six rectangles. For the solid at the right, the lengths of only three edges are labeled. From these, you can determine the lengths of all the other edges.

AB, EF, DC, and *GH* are 16 centimeters.
AD, BC, FH, and *EG* are 20 centimeters.
BF, AE, CH, and *DG* are 12 centimeters.

area of ABFE = 16 × 12, or 192 cm²
area of DCHG = 16 × 12, or 192 cm² — **2 × 192 = 384**

area of BFHC = 12 × 20, or 240 cm²
area of AEGD = 12 × 20, or 240 cm² — **2 × 240 = 480**

area of ABCD = 16 × 20, or 320 cm²
area of EFHG = 16 × 20, or 320 cm² — **2 × 320 = 640**
1504 Add.

The surface area is 1504 cm².

1. How many square inches of paper is needed to wrap a box that is 10 inches long, 8 inches wide, and 6 inches high? (Assume that none of the paper overlaps.) 376 in²

2. How many square feet of chicken wire is needed to cover a rabbit pen 2½ feet wide, 6 feet long, and 3 feet high? 81 ft²

3. A cardboard-box manufacturer wants to make a box with a *volume* of 64 cm³.

a. Show that each box below has the correct volume.
b. Find the surface area of each box. Which box would require the least amount of cardboard? Box 3 requires the least amount of cardboard.

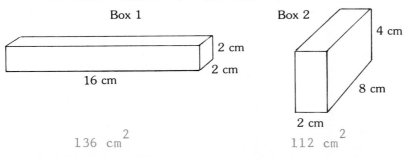

Box 1

16 cm
2 cm
2 cm

136 cm²

Box 2

4 cm
8 cm
2 cm

112 cm²

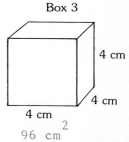

Box 3

4 cm
4 cm
4 cm

96 cm²

It has been proved that there are only five solids with these properties: (1) All edges are the same length. (2) All faces have the same size and shape. (3) The same number of edges meet at each corner. Each solid is pictured below.

Tetrahedron   **Cube**   **Octahedron**   **Dodecahedron**   **Icosahedron**

These solids are called **Platonic solids** (after Plato, a philosopher of ancient Greece). Plato felt that earth, fire, air, water, and the universe had the forms of these solids.

You can construct a model of each Platonic solid by using the following patterns. However, each pattern should be enlarged. Cut on the solid lines; fold on dashed lines.

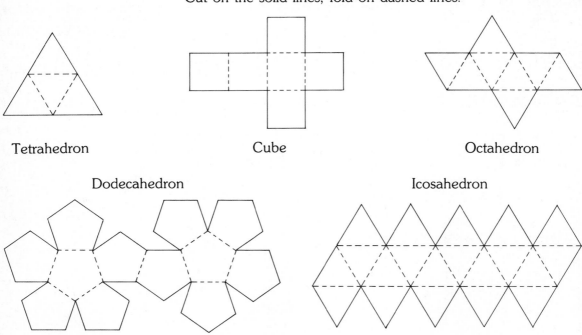

Tetrahedron   Cube   Octahedron

Dodecahedron   Icosahedron

6.11 / CYLINDERS

A common solid figure is a **cylinder.** A tin can is one example. Some other examples are pictured below.

Artstreet

Artstreet

M.L. Dembinsky, Jr.

A cylinder has two circular bases of the same size. To find the volume of a cylinder, you multiply the area of a base by the height.

Volume of cylinder = area of base × height

Let r stand for the radius measure of the base, and let h stand for the height. Since the base is a circle, the area of the base is πr^2.

Then the formula for the volume of a cylinder can be written as follows:

$V = \pi r^2 h$

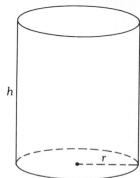

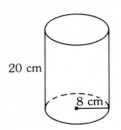

20 cm

8 cm

Example 1: Find the volume of a cylinder whose height is 20 centimeters and whose base has a radius measuring 8 centimeters. Use 3.14 for π.

$$V = \pi r^2 h$$
$$V = 3.14 \times 8 \times 8 \times 20$$
$$V = 4019.2$$

The volume is 4019.2 cubic centimeters.

EXERCISES

1. Write the formula for the volume of a cylinder. $V = \pi r^2 h$

2. In the formula $V = \pi r^2 h$, r^2 means $\underline{}^{\,r} \times \underline{}^{\,r}$.

For each cylinder, the area of the base is given. Find the volume.

3.

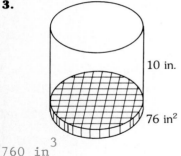

10 in.

76 in²

760 in^3

4.

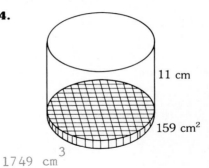

11 cm

159 cm²

1749 cm^3

For each cylinder, the radius measure of the base and the height are given. Find the volume. Use $\frac{22}{7}$ for π.

5.

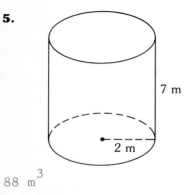

7 m

2 m

88 m^3

6.

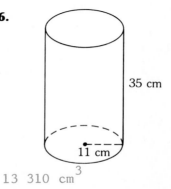

35 cm

11 cm

$13\ 310 \text{ cm}^3$

7.

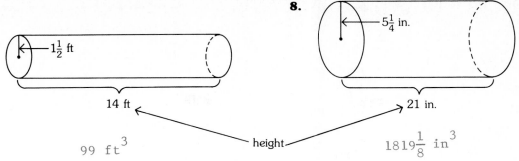

$1\frac{1}{2}$ ft

14 ft

height

99 ft^3

8.

$5\frac{1}{4}$ in.

21 in.

$1819\frac{1}{8} \text{ in}^3$

Find the volume of each cylinder. Use 3.14 for π if necessary.

9. area of base, 18.3 m²; height, 5.2 m 95.16 m^3

10. area of base, 47.2 mm²; height, 31.5 mm 1486.8 mm^3

11. radius of base, 5.1 cm; height, 18 cm 1470.0852 cm^3

12. radius of base, 1.5 m; height, 1 m 7.065 m^3

13. diameter of base, 10 in.; height, 9 in. 706.5 in^3

14. diameter of base, 280 mm; height, 60 mm $3\ 692\ 640 \text{ mm}^3$

Use 3.14 for π.

15. A tin can has a height of 6 inches. A radius of the base is 2 inches long. What is the can's volume? 75.36 in^3

16. An oil drum is 90 centimeters high. A radius of its base is 30 centimeters long. What is the drum's volume? $254\ 340 \text{ cm}^3$

17. An inner radius (AB) of a steel pipe is 2 centimeters. An outer radius (AC) is 2.5 centimeters. If the length of the pipe is 50 centimeters, what is the volume of steel needed to make the pipe? 353.25 cm^3

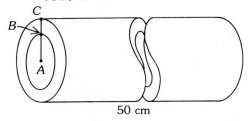

C
B

A

50 cm

18. A concrete tree-container is shaped like a cylinder. An inner radius is 20 inches and an outer radius is 22 inches. What is the volume of concrete needed to make the container if its height is 12 inches? 3165.12 in^3

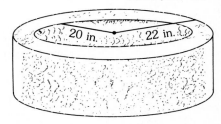

20 in.   22 in.

267

Comparing Volumes

Double the height.

$V = 3.14 \times 2 \times 2 \times 6$
$V = 75.36$

Being familiar with solids and knowing how to find volumes can be helpful when shopping.

Compare the other cans with this one.

Double the radius.

You can find the volume of each can by using the formula $V = \pi r^2 h$.

$V = 3.14 \times 2 \times 2 \times 3$
$V = 37.68$

$V = 3.14 \times 4 \times 4 \times 3$
$V = 150.72$

The can on the left has twice the volume of the can in the middle. But the can on the right has four times the volume of the can in the middle.

In the example below, an edge of the larger package is twice as long as an edge of the smaller package. But the volume of the larger package is 8 times the volume of the smaller.

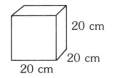

20 cm
20 cm
20 cm

10 cm
10 cm
10 cm

$V = (20 \times 20) \times 20 = 8000$

$V = (10 \times 10) \times 10 = 1000$

1. Find the volume of each cereal box below. 2964 cm^3; 4872 cm^3

2. Observe the weight of the cereal in each box. Which box contains more cereal (and hence less air) per cubic centimeter of space? the 15-ounce box

24 cm
6.5 cm
19 cm

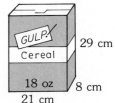

29 cm
8 cm
21 cm

Two solid figures that you may have heard of are the **pyramid** and the **cone.**

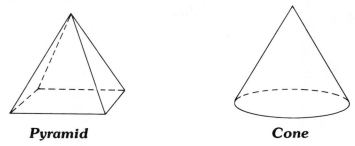

Pyramid   **Cone**

Think of filling each solid with liquid. The pyramid will be emptied into a rectangular solid of equal base and equal height. The cone will be emptied into a cylinder of equal base and equal height.

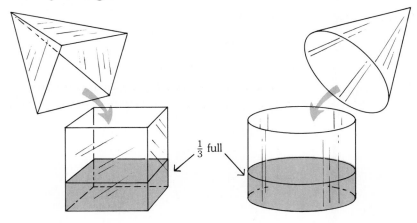

$\frac{1}{3}$ full

For the rectangular solid:

$$V = Bh$$

For the cylinder:

$$V = \pi r^2 h$$

For the pyramid:

$$V = \frac{1}{3}Bh$$

For the cone:

$$V = \frac{1}{3}\pi r^2 h$$

As a project, use plastic models if they are available to show that these formulas are true. If models are not available, you can make models from cardboard and use sand to fill the models.

269

How many sides does each polygon have?   6.1

1. pentagon   5   **2.** quadrilateral   4

For the given polygon are all four sides always equal?

3. square   Yes   **4.** rectangle No

Find the perimeter of each polygon.   6.2

5. square with a side of 16 cen-   **6.** rectangle with a length of $4\frac{1}{2}$
timeters   64 cm   inches and a width of 3 inches
                                                  15 in.

7. triangle with sides of 6.5 cm, 4.2   **8.** pentagon with sides of 18 ft, 19 ft,
cm, and 3.8 cm   14.5 cm   20 ft, 17 ft, and 10 ft   84 ft

Find the area of a rectangle with each given length and width.   6.3

9. 40 ft, 18 ft   720 ft^2 **10.** 17 m, 15 m   255 m^2

Find the area of a square with each given side.

11. 16 inches   256 in^2 **12.** 28 cm 784 cm^2

Complete the following: 6.4

13. 7 yd^2 = _63_ ft^2 **14.** 108 ft^2 = _12_ yd^2

15. 5 ft^2 = _720_ in^2 **16.** 288 in^2 = _2_ ft^2

Find the area of each parallelogram.   6.5

17.   **18.**

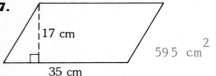

595 cm^2

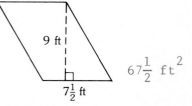

$67\frac{1}{2}$ ft^2

Find the area of a triangle with each given base and height.   6.6

19. 34 in., 10 in.   **20.** 40 mm, 18 mm   **21.** 3.8 m, 2 m   **22.** $2\frac{1}{2}$ ft, 5 ft
170 in^2 360 mm^2 3.8 m^2 $6\frac{1}{4}$ ft^2

Find the circumference of each circle. Use 3.14 for π.

6.7

23.

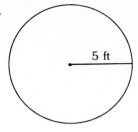

5 ft

31.4 ft

24.

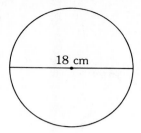

18 cm

56.52 cm

Find the area of each circle. Use $\frac{22}{7}$ for π.

6.8

25. A radius is 35 ft. 3850 ft^2 **26.** A diameter is 42 mm. 1386 mm^2

Find the volume of each rectangular solid.

6.9

27.

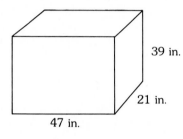

39 in.

21 in.

47 in.

38,493 in^3

28.

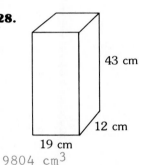

43 cm

12 cm

19 cm

9804 cm^3

Complete the following:

6.10

29. 28 yd^3 = ___ ft^3 756   **30.** $1\frac{1}{3}$ yd^3 = ___ ft^3 36

31. 567 ft^3 = ___ yd^3 21   **32.** 900 ft^3 = ___ yd^3 $33\frac{1}{3}$

Find the volume of each cylinder. Use 3.14 for π.

6.11

33.

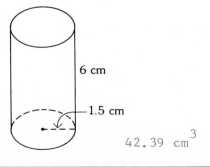

6 cm

1.5 cm

42.39 cm^3

34.

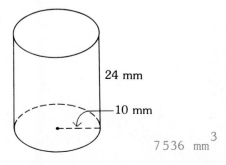

24 mm

10 mm

7536 mm^3

1. How many sides does a parallelogram have? 4

2. How many right angles does a square have? 4

Find the perimeter of each polygon.

3. rectangle with a length of 41 mm and a width of 28 mm
138 mm

4. square with each side $1\frac{1}{4}$ inches
5 in.

Find the area of each polygon.

5. rectangle with a length of 7.3 m and a width of 4.1 m 29.93 m^2

6. square with each side $6\frac{1}{2}$ inches
$42\frac{1}{4} \text{ in}^2$

Complete the following:

7. $5 \text{ yd}^2 = \underline{45} \text{ ft}^2$

8. $432 \text{ in}^2 = \underline{3} \text{ ft}^2$

Find the area of each parallelogram.

9. base, 21 cm; height, 12 cm
252 cm^2

10. base, 15 ft; height, 12 ft
180 ft^2

Find the area of each triangle.

11. base, 28 ft; height, 18 ft
252 ft^2

12. base, 80 m; height, 60 m
2400 m^2

13. A circle has a radius of 6 feet. Find the circumference. Use $\frac{22}{7}$ for π. $37\frac{5}{7} \text{ ft}$

14. Find the area of a circle with a diameter of 10 meters. Use 3.14 for π. 78.5 m^2

Find the volume of each rectangular solid.

15.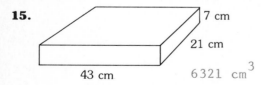
7 cm
21 cm
43 cm
6321 cm^3

16.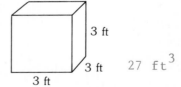
3 ft
3 ft
3 ft
27 ft^3

Complete the following:

17. $21 \text{ yd}^3 = \underline{567} \text{ ft}^3$

18. $162 \text{ ft}^3 = \underline{6} \text{ yd}^3$

19. Find the volume of a cylinder whose base has a radius of 9 centimeters and whose height is 15 centimeters. Use 3.14 for π. 3815.1 cm^3

Name a unit of measure that is commonly used to measure each of the   5.1
following: Possible answers are given for exercises 1-4.

1. your height inch

2. weight of a frog gram

3. time to boil an egg minute

4. length of the Ohio River mile

Is the given unit a standard unit of measure?

5. kilometer Yes

6. glassful No

7. long time No

8. pound Yes

Which ancient unit is about the following length?   5.2

9. 6 feet fathom

10. 18 inches cubit

11. 4 inches hand

12. 8 inches handspan

Measure each segment to the nearest $\frac{1}{8}$ inch.   5.3

13. _____ $1\frac{1}{8}$ in.

14. _____ $\frac{7}{8}$ in.

15. _____ $1\frac{5}{8}$ in.

16. _____ $2\frac{1}{8}$ in.

Change each measurement as follows.   5.4

17. 2 yards to inches 72 in.

18. 4 feet to inches 48 in.

19. 108 inches to feet 9 ft

20. 3 miles to feet 15,840 ft

Draw segments of the following lengths: 5.5
See students' drawings.

21. 21 cm

22. 75 mm

23–26. Measure each segment in exercises 13–16 to the nearest centimeter.
23. 3 cm 24. 2 cm 25. 4 cm 26. 5 cm

Complete the following: 5.6

27. 7 km = ___ m 7000

28. 9 m = ___ mm 9000

29. 14 000 km = ___ m 14 000 000

30. 140 mm = ___ m 0.140

31. 2 kg = ___ g 2000　　　　　**32.** 6 lb = ___ oz 96　　　　　5.7

33. 3000 g = ___ kg 3　　　　　**34.** 80 oz = ___ lb 5

35. 2350 mL = ___ liters 2.350　　**36.** 1.4 liters = ___ mL 1400　　5.8

37. 5 qt = ___ pt 10　　　　　**38.** 5 gal = ___ qt 20

39. 8 pt = ___ fl oz 128　　　　**40.** 16 qt = ___ gal 4

Add or subtract.　　　　　　　　　　　　　　　　　　　　　　5.9

41.　　1 hr 23 min　　　　　　**42.**　　9 min 12 sec
　　　　+4 hr 43 min　　　　　　　　　　−2 min 38 sec
　　　　　6 hr 6 min　　　　　　　　　　　6 min 34 sec
43.　　5 hr 15 min　　　　　　**44.**　　10 hr 0 min
　　　　−3 hr 30 min　　　　　　　　　　− 4 hr 18 min
　　　　　1 hr 45 min　　　　　　　　　　　5 hr 42 min

Use the thermometer on page 216 to change each temperature to the other　　5.10
scale.

45. 25°C 77°F　　　　　　　　**46.** 40°F 4°C

Measurements for exercises 47-48 may vary.
Measure each angle with a protractor.　　　　　　　　　　　　5.11

47.　105°　　　　　　　　　　**48.** 22°

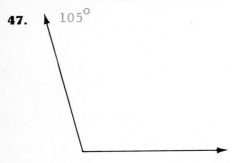

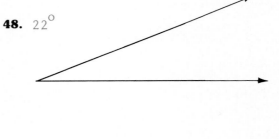

How many sides does each polygon have?　　　　　　　　　　　6.1

49. hexagon 6　　　　　　　**50.** octagon 8

Does the given polygon always have 4 right angles?

51. parallelogram No　　　　**52.** rectangle Yes

274

Find the perimeter of each polygon.

6.2

53. square with a side of 22 inches
                                    88 in.

54. rectangle with a length of 2.5
cm and a width of 3.5 cm   12 cm

55. triangle with sides of 3.8 m, 5.4
m, and 3.6 m   12.8 m

56. pentagon with sides of 28 mm,
42 mm, 17 mm, 34 mm, and
13 mm   134 mm

Find the area of a rectangle with each given length and width.

6.3

57. 73 cm, 41 cm 2993 cm^2

58. 43 inches, 27 inches 1161 in^2

Find the area of a square with each given side.

59. 14 mm 196 mm^2

60. 63 ft 3969 ft^2

Complete the following:

6.4

61. $12 \text{ yd}^2 = \underline{108} \text{ ft}^2$

62. $81 \text{ ft}^2 = \underline{9} \text{ yd}^2$

63. $3 \text{ ft}^2 = \underline{432} \text{ in}^2$

64. $576 \text{ in}^2 = \underline{4} \text{ ft}^2$

Find the area of each parallelogram.

6.5

65.

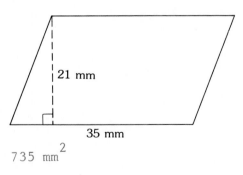

735 mm^2

66.

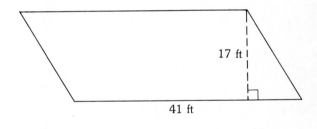

697 ft^2

Find the area of a triangle with each given base and height.

6.6

67. 24 ft, 16 ft 192 ft^2

68. 30 m, 18 m 270 m^2

69. 9.4 mm, 4.2 mm 19.74 mm^2

70. $3\frac{1}{4}$ in., 6 in. $9\frac{3}{4} \text{ in}^2$

Find the circumference of each circle. Use 3.14 for π.   6.7

71.

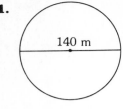

140 m

439.6 m

72.

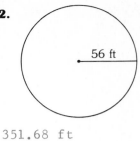

56 ft

351.68 ft

Find the area of each circle. Use $\frac{22}{7}$ for π.   6.8

73. A radius is 21 inches.

1386 in^2

74. A diameter is 49 meters.

1886.5 m^2

Find the volume of each rectangular solid.   6.9

75.

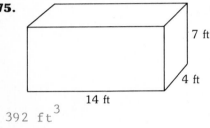

7 ft

4 ft

14 ft

392 ft^3

76.

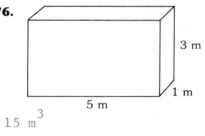

3 m

1 m

5 m

15 m^3

Complete the following: 6.10

77. 17 yd³ = ____ ft³   459

78. $2\frac{2}{3}$ yd³ = ____ ft³   72

79. 108 ft³ = ____ yd³   4

80. 500 ft³ = ____ yd³ $18\frac{14}{27}$

Find the volume of each cylinder. Use 3.14 for π.   6.11

81.

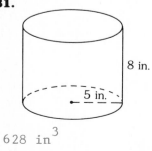

8 in.

5 in.

628 in^3

82.

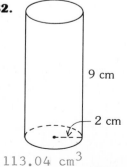

9 cm

2 cm

113.04 cm^3

CUMULATIVE REVIEW

1. A bicycle that regularly sells for $123.99 is on sale for 10% off. Find the sale price. $111.59

2. Ken earns $4.20 an hour. How much does he earn for 33 hours of work? $138.60

3. Jessie is paid $5.25 an hour and time and a half for overtime. How much did she earn for 45 hours of work last week? $249.40 (Answers may vary.)

4. Bill is paid 5¢ for each envelope that he addresses. In one month he addressed 8125 envelopes. How much did he earn that month? $406.25

5. Millie earns $5\frac{1}{2}\%$ commission for selling houses. How much is her commission for selling a house for $68,500? $3767.50

6. Conrad is paid $3.75 an hour, plus a commission of 2% on all sales over $1500 per week. This week he worked $37\frac{1}{2}$ hours and sold $5425 worth of merchandise. How much did he earn this week? $219.13

7. Brian is a hair stylist. He charges $11.25 for a haircut. One day he gave 12 haircuts and received $28.50 in tips. What was his income for that day? $163.50

8. Melody drives a cab. Her wages are one half of the fares she collects. She pays for one half of the gasoline used in her cab. During one week she collected $425 in fares and received $35.75 in tips. The gasoline bill was $74.60. What was her income that week? $210.95

9. Find the weekly net pay if the weekly gross pay is $194 and the following deductions are made:

federal income tax	$22.60	state income tax	$8.73
social security	13.68	medical insurance	5.15
union dues	4.25		$139.59

10. Emily had a taxable income of $13,423 for the year. The amount of income tax due was $1968. During the year, $2145 was withheld from her wages for income tax. Will Emily have to pay more tax or will she get a refund? How much will the amount be? Refund; $177

Correlation

Items	Sec
1	7.2
2–3	7.3
4	7.4
5–6	7.5
7–8	7.6
9	7.7
10	7.8

Sarah was looking for a part-time job. She applied at several different restaurants. At each restaurant she was asked to complete an employment application form. A typical employment application form is shown below.

HAMBURGER EMPORIUM
APPLICATION FOR EMPLOYMENT
AN EQUAL OPPORTUNITY EMPLOYER

PERSONAL

NAME _____
LAST   FIRST   MIDDLE

DATE _____

PRESENT ADDRESS _____
NO. & ST.   CITY   STATE   ZIP CODE

SOC. SEC. NUMBER _____

PHONE NUMBER _____

PREVIOUS ADDRESS _____
NO. & ST.   CITY   STATE   ZIP CODE

ARE YOU AN AMERICAN CITIZEN ☐ YES ☐ NO

DATE AVAILABLE FOR EMPLOYMENT _____

IF NO, STATE TYPE OF VISA _____

JOB INTEREST

POSITION APPLIED FOR _____   SALARY EXPECTED _____ PER _____

HOW WERE YOU REFERRED TO THIS COMPANY? _____

NAMES OF RELATIVES OR FRIENDS EMPLOYED BY THIS COMPANY? _____

EDUCATION

GRADE OR JR. HIGH SCHOOL   CIRCLE LAST GRADE COMPLETED   1 2 3 4 5 6 7 8 9

	NAME	CITY & STATE	MAJOR COURSE	GRADUATED YES — NO	TYPE OF DIPLOMA OR DEGREE
HIGH SCHOOL					
COLLEGE					
BUSINESS OR TRADE SCHOOL					

SCHOOL HONORS _____

EMPLOYMENT HISTORY

PREVIOUS EMPLOYERS (LIST MOST RECENT FIRST) OTHER NAME(S)† IF USED IN PREVIOUS EMPLOYMENT A. NAME OF EMPLOYER B. ADDRESS OF EMPLOYER	TIME EMPLOYED MO. YR.	NATURE OF WORK	SALARY A. STARTING B. ENDING	REASON FOR LEAVING	NAME OF SUPERVISOR
1. A. B.	FROM TO		A. B.		
2. A. B.	FROM TO		A. B.		
3. A. B.	FROM TO		A. B.		

†Note: We request other names used in employment in order to conduct proper, authorized reference checks.

MISC.

IF THERE ARE ANY POSITIONS OR TYPES OF POSITIONS FOR WHICH YOU SHOULD NOT BE CONSIDERED, OR JOB DUTIES YOU CANNOT PERFORM BECAUSE OF A PHYSICAL, MENTAL OR MEDICAL DISABILITY, PLEASE DESCRIBE. _____

STARTING DATE: _____   HOURS YOU WOULD WORK _____

PRE-EMPLOYMENT STATEMENT

I understand and agree that employment with Doubleday & Co., Inc., and its subsidiaries (the "Company") is subject to my passing a physical examination and satisfactory references. Any misrepresentation made by me in this application or during the physical examination may be sufficient cause for cancellation of this application or termination of employment.

SIGNED _____   DATE _____

Mary Elenz Tranter

An application form helps the employer find out about your qualifications. Application forms should be filled out carefully. Answers should be as brief and as neat as possible. Before listing a person's name as a reference, ask the person for permission to do so.

When Sarah returned the application form to the Hamburger Emporium, the manager asked her to stay for an interview. During the interview, Sarah was able to learn more about the job—duties, responsibilities, working conditions, hours, pay, and so on. The manager asked Sarah several questions to find out if her qualifications matched the requirements of the job. Most interviewers pay close attention to applicants' manners, behavior, dress, confidence, and ability to answer questions clearly.

EXERCISES

Answers for exercises 1-4 will vary. Possible answers are given.

1. What kind of information is important to find out about a job? duties, hours, pay

2. What kinds of questions might you be asked during an interview? Have you had other jobs?; What are your grades in school?

3. Why would it be a good idea to tour the place of employment during working hours before accepting a job?
   to check on working conditions

4. What kind of questions might an employer ask the people you listed as references? Is the person reliable?

SKILLS REFRESHER

				Skill	Page
Express each percent as a decimal.					
1. 25% 0.25	**2.** 15% 0.15	**3.** 5% 0.05	**4.** 10% 0.1	46	518
Multiply.					
5. 0.25×4.64 1.16		**6.** 0.15×42.4 6.36		14	468
7. 0.3×15.1 4.53		**8.** 0.5×25 12.5			

Application 37 may be used at this time.   **279**

Example 1: Sean worked as a sales clerk in a toy store. Every item in the store was on sale for 20% off. Sean helped put new price stickers on the items.

What price should Sean mark on a soccer ball that regularly sells for $12.99?

$12.99   Find 20% of $12.99   regular price
× 0.20   sale price.   − 2.60   amount of discount
2.5980   Round to near- $10.39   sale price
         est cent.

Sean should mark the soccer ball to sell for $10.39.

Example 2: Katie worked as a waitress in a small diner. On each check Katie had to compute the cost of the food items and then add the sales tax to find the total. In Katie's state the sales-tax rate was 6%, so she used a table as shown.

6% SALES TAX

Amount of Sales Tax			Amount of Sales Tax		
.00—	.08	.00	7.25—	7.41	.44
.09—	.24	.01	7.42—	7.58	.45
.25—	.41	.02	7.59—	7.74	.46
.42—	.58	.03	7.75—	7.91	.47
.59—	.74	.04	7.92—	8.08	.48
.75—	.91	.05	8.09—	8.24	.49
.92—	1.08	.06	8.25—	8.41	.50
1.09—	1.24	.07	8.42—	8.58	.51
1.25—	1.41	.08	8.59—	8.74	.52
1.42—	1.58	.09	8.75—	8.91	.53
1.59—	1.74	.10	8.92—	9.08	.54
1.75—	1.91	.11	9.09—	9.24	.55
1.92—	2.08	.12	9.25—	9.41	.56
2.09—	2.24	.13	9.42—	9.58	.57
2.25—	2.41	.14	9.59—	9.74	.58
2.42—	2.58	.15	9.75—	9.91	.59
2.59—	2.74	.16	9.92—	10.08	.60
2.75—	2.91	.17	10.09—	10.24	.61
2.92—	3.08	.18	10.25—	10.41	.62
3.09—	3.24	.19	10.42—	10.58	.63
3.25—	3.41	.20	10.59—	10.74	.64
3.42—	3.58	.21	10.75—	10.91	.65
3.59—	3.74	.22	10.92—	11.08	.66
3.75—	3.91	.23	11.09—	11.24	.67
3.92—	4.08	.24	11.25—	11.41	.68
4.09—	4.24	.25	11.42—	11.58	.69
4.25—	4.41	.26	11.59—	11.74	.70
4.42—	4.58	.27	11.75—	11.91	.71
4.59—	4.74	.28	11.92—	12.08	.72
4.75—	4.91	.29	12.09—	12.24	.73
4.92—	5.08	.30	12.25—	12.41	.74
5.09—	5.24	.31	12.42—	12.58	.75
5.25—	5.41	.32	12.59—	12.74	.76
5.42—	5.58	.33	12.75—	12.91	.77
5.59—	5.74	.34	12.92—	13.08	.78
5.75—	5.91	.35	13.09—	13.24	.79
5.92—	6.08	.36	13.25—	13.41	.80
6.09—	6.24	.37	13.42—	13.58	.81
6.25—	6.41	.38	13.59—	13.74	.82
6.42—	6.58	.39	13.75—	13.91	.83
6.59—	6.74	.40	13.92—	14.08	.84
6.75—	6.91	.41	14.09—	14.24	.85
6.92—	7.08	.42	14.25—	14.41	.86
7.09—	7.24	.43	14.42—	14.58	.87

Kenji Kerins

Example 3: Meagan worked as a cashier at a supermarket. Meagan entered the cost of each item and used the register to find the total cost of all items, the amount of sales tax, and the total bill. She then entered the amount of money a customer gave her, and the cash register showed the amount of change she should give the customer.

For example, for a sale that totaled $16.56, the customer gave Meagan a $20 bill. The cash register showed that she should give the customer $3.44 in change. Meagan's supervisor told her the best way to make change is to use as few bills and coins as possible.

Meagan counted out 3 one-dollar bills, 1 quarter, 1 dime, 1 nickel, and 4 pennies.

EXERCISES

Find the sale price of each item.

1. regular price $15.99; 20% off $12.79

2. regular price $8.99; 10% off
$8.09

3. regular price $25.49; 15% off $21.67

4. regular price $65.89; 25% off
$49.42

5. regular price $34.98; 30% off $24.49

6. regular price $128.99; 20% off
$103.19

7. regular price $53.97; 10% off $48.57

8. regular price $135.50; 25% off
$101.62

Copy and complete each of the meal checks. Use the sales-tax table on page 280.

9.

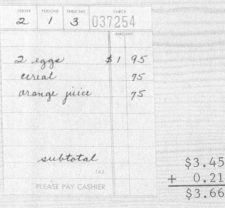

SERVER	PERSONS	TABLE NO.	CHECK
4	2	9	037225

hamburger
platter $3 95
fruit plate 3 50
2 milk 1 00

subtotal $8.45
TAX   +   0.51
PLEASE PAY CASHIER $8.96

10.

SERVER	PERSONS	TABLE NO.	CHECK
2	1	3	037254

2 eggs $1 95
cereal 75
orange juice 75

subtotal $3.45
TAX   +   0.21
PLEASE PAY CASHIER $3.66

281

11.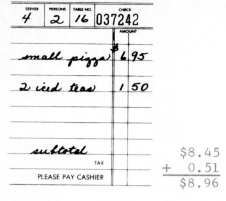

Guest Check

SERVER	PERSONS	TABLE NO.	CHECK
4	2	16	037242

	AMOUNT
small pizza	$6.95
2 iced tea	1.50
subtotal	
TAX	
PLEASE PAY CASHIER	

$8.45
+ 0.51
$8.96

12.

Guest Check

SERVER	PERSONS	TABLE NO.	CHECK
7	2	11	037171

	AMOUNT
soup and sandwich	$2.50
salad bar	2.75
lemonade	75
apple juice	75
subtotal	
TAX	
PLEASE PAY CASHIER	

$6.75
+ 0.41
$7.16

Copy and complete the following chart:

	Total bill	Amount given to clerk	Amount of change	Change 1¢	5¢	10¢	25¢	$1	$5	$10
	$5.95	$10.00	$4.05	0	1	0	0	4	0	0
13.	$15.35	$20.00	$4.65	0	1	1	2	4	0	0
14.	$7.68	$10.00	$2.32	2	1	0	1	2	0	0
15.	$3.99	$20.00	$16.01	1	0	0	0	1	1	1
16.	$12.13	$15.00	$2.87	2	0	1	3	2	0	0
17.	$12.97	$20.02	$7.05	0	1	0	0	2	1	0
18.	$11.08	$20.00	$8.92	2	1	1	3	3	1	0
19.	$15.46	$20.01	$4.55	0	1	0	2	4	0	0
20.	$9.82	$20.02	$10.20	0	0	2	0	0	0	1

SKILLS REFRESHER

Multiply.

			Skill	Page
			13	466

1. 3.75
× 12
45

2. 5.15
× 25
128.75

3. 4.35
× 40
174

4. 6.25
× 15
93.75

5. 10.05
× 20
201

6. 4.60
× 32
147.2

Many supermarkets use electronic cash registers. The clerk no longer has to enter the price of each item but simply has to pass each item over a scanner. The scanner reads the bars and spaces—called the **Universal Product Code,** or UPC—printed on the package. The store's computer receives the message, translates the code into the product name and size, and searches its memory to locate the current price of the item. In an instant that information is sent back to the cash register and automatically printed on the register receipt.

Part of the Universal Product Code is the code for the manufacturer. The rest is the code for the particular product.

Mary Elenz Tranter

Since most packaged goods already have the Universal Product Code printed on the package, store clerks do not have to stamp the prices on individual items. Prices can be posted on store shelves. After each sale the computer automatically reduces the inventory by the number of items sold so that the store manager can be advised of the status of the inventory and of the sales.

How might the customer benefit from the use of the UPC system in a supermarket? Possible answer: faster time at check-out

Visit a store that uses an electronic cash register, talk to the manager or bookkeeper, and make a report on other uses or advantages of such a cash register.

283

Example 1: Daniel is paid $3.35 an hour to operate a dishwasher in a restaurant. He worked 12 hours this week. How much did he earn?

$3.35	**hourly rate**
×12	**hours worked**
$40.20	**amount earned**

By law, employers are required to pay for **overtime** to most employees who work more than 40 hours per week. The hourly rate for overtime is usually **time and a half,** which means $1\frac{1}{2}$, or 1.5, times the hourly rate. The overtime rate for Sundays and holidays is usually **double time,** which means 2 times the hourly rate.

Bryce Flynn/Picture Group

Example 2: Gloria worked 45 hours this week at her job as a word processor. She earns $7.50 an hour and time and a half for overtime. How much did Gloria earn this week?

Gloria's earnings can be found in either of these ways:

a. Gloria is paid $7.50 an hour for the first 40 hours.

7.50 × 40 = 300.00

The overtime rate is 1.5 times the regular rate.

7.50 × 1.5 = 11.25

She is paid for 5 hours of overtime.

11.25 × 5 = 56.25

$300.00	**earnings for 40 hours**
+ 56.25	**earnings for overtime**
$356.25	**weekly earnings**

b. Five hours of overtime is equivalent to 7.5 hours of regular time.

5 × 1.5 = 7.5

So the 45 hours worked is equivalent to 47.5 hours at regular pay.

$7.50	**hourly rate**
×47.5	**number of hours**
$356.25	**weekly earnings**

EXERCISES

Answers may vary for exercises 13 and 16.

Copy and complete the table below. Time and a half is paid for overtime.

Employee	Regular hourly rate	Number of hours worked in 1 week	Regular pay	Overtime pay	Total pay
1. Appleby, J.	$4.15	$37\frac{1}{2}$	$155.63	0	$155.63
2. Baker, L.	$5.45	15	$81.75	0	$81.75
3. Barley, R.	$3.75	24	$90	0	$90
4. Beach, J.	$6.25	40	$250	0	$250
5. Bender, C.	$8.40	35	$294	0	$294
6. Brown, K.	$5.60	$10\frac{1}{2}$	$58.80	0	$58.80
7. Denlinger, D.	$7.10	20	$142	0	$142
8. Hallet, C.	$9.20	42	$368	$27.60	$395.60
9. Kreamer, D.	$4.30	30	$129	0	$129
10. May, D.	$3.55	22	$78.10	0	$78.10
11. O'Boyle, R.	$4.00	$33\frac{1}{4}$	$133	0	$133
12. Sawyer, C.	$7.50	45	$300	$56.25	$356.25
13. Steinruck, J.	$4.85	$43\frac{1}{2}$	$194	$25.48	$219.48
14. Van Aken, T.	$10.00	36	$360	0	$360

15. Chris Moore worked as a ride operator at an amusement park. He worked $7\frac{1}{2}$ hours each day, Monday through Friday. He is paid $3.65 per hour. What was his total pay for the week? $136.88

16. Kim Geib has a job as a computer operator. She is paid $6.75 per hour and time and a half for overtime. This week, Monday through Friday, she worked $8\frac{1}{2}$ hours per day. What was her total pay for the week? $295.33

17. John Deitz worked as a part-time clerk in a hardware store. He worked 3 hours on Monday, 4 hours on Friday, and $8\frac{1}{2}$ hours on Saturday. He is paid $5.25 per hour. What was his total pay for the week? $81.38

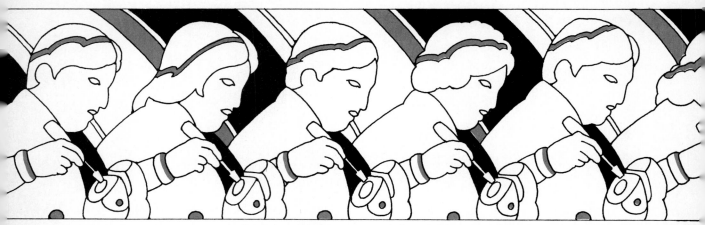

Some workers are paid for each item they complete or produce. This is called **piecework.** The amount a worker earns depends upon the number of items he or she produces.

Example 1: Lee works in a shirt factory and is paid $2.00 for each shirt completed. If Lee averages 5 shirts each hour, how much will he earn in an 8-hour day? How much will he earn in a 5-day week?

$8 \times 5 = 40$ **completed 40 shirts in 1 day**

$2 \times 40 = 80$ **earned $80 per day**

$5 \times 80 = 400$ **earned $400 per week**

Some workers are paid an hourly wage and are expected to make a specified number of items. If a worker's production exceeds that number, a bonus is paid for each additional item produced.

Example 2: Bruce is paid $5.25 per hour for a 35-hour week. If Bruce completes more than 1500 items per week, he is paid 10¢ for each item over 1500. In one week Bruce completed 1835 items. How much did he earn?

$5.25	1835	335	$183.75
×35	−1500	×0.10	+ 33.50
$183.75	335	$33.50	$217.25
regular weekly pay	bonus items	amount of bonus	weekly income

EXERCISES

Find the amount earned for each of the following:

1. 7 hours; 9 items per hour; $0.75 per item $47.25

2. 8 hours; 35 items per hour; $0.25 per item $70

3. 5 days; 275 items per day; $0.35 per item $481.25

4. 5 days; 1800 items per day; $0.05 per item $450

5. $7\frac{1}{2}$ hours; 5 items per minute; $0.03 per item $67.50

6. Joe delivers ads from door to door. He is paid $6\frac{1}{4}$¢ per packet. How many packets must Joe deliver to earn $25?   400 packets

7. Rosa is paid 76¢ for each machine part she assembles. How much does she earn in an 8-hour day if she makes 15 parts per hour? How much can she earn in a 5-day week? $91.20; $456

8. Jo has a carpet-cleaning business. She charges $35.00 to clean an average-size carpet. How much will she earn in 4 days if she can clean 5 average-size carpets per day? $700

9. Adam charges $35 to clean a small office and $55 to clean a large office. In one month he cleaned 25 large offices and 48 small offices. How much did he earn that month? $3055

10. Joan earns extra money by typing reports for college students. She charges $2.00 per page. How much did she earn for typing a paper that had 19 pages? $38

11. Brian sews buttons on shirts. He is paid $4.22 an hour for an 8-hour day. If he sews on more than 1200 buttons per day, he is paid 3¢ for each additional button. How much did he earn in one day if he sewed on 1350 buttons? $38.26

12. Kim packages some game pieces. She earns 8¢ for each of the first 250 packages, $9\frac{1}{2}$¢ for each of the next 250 packages, and 11¢ for each package over 500. How much did she earn if she completed 419 packages? 615 packages? $36.06; $56.40

Commission is the amount of money, usually a percent of the selling price, paid for selling a product or a service. Many salespeople are paid a commission.

Salespeople are usually paid in one of the following ways:

Straight salary—they are paid a specific amount each pay period.

Straight commission—they are paid by commission only. Sometimes the rate of commission increases as sales increase.

Salary plus commission—they are paid a salary plus a commission. Sometimes the commission is only on sales over a specified amount.

James H Pickerell

Example 1: Lynn Chan sells cosmetics. She earns a 35% commission on sales. Last week her sales totaled $258.60. How much did Lynn earn last week?

35% of $258.60

$$\begin{array}{r} \$258.60 \\ \times\,0.35 \\ \hline \$90.5100 \end{array}$$

Lynn earned $90.51 last week.

Example 2: Leon Johnson sells major appliances. He is paid a monthly salary of $900, plus a commission of 10% on his monthly sales over $2000. Find his income for a month having sales of $5819.50.

$$\begin{array}{r} \$5819.50 \\ -\,2000.00 \\ \hline \$3819.50 \end{array} \qquad \begin{array}{r} \$3819.50 \\ \times\,0.10 \\ \hline \$381.950 \end{array} \qquad \begin{array}{r} \$900.00 \\ +\,381.95 \\ \hline \$1281.95 \end{array} \begin{array}{l} \text{salary} \\ \text{commission} \\ \text{monthly income} \end{array}$$

sales over   commission
$2000

Example 3: Ruth Clements sells business machines. She is paid a monthly commission of 5% on the first $2000 of sales and $6\frac{1}{2}\%$ on sales over $2000. Find her monthly income on sales of $15,865.

$15,865 total sales
−   2,000
$13,865

$2000	$13,865	$100.00
×0.05	×0.065	+ 901.23
$100.00	$901.225	$1001.23
commission on sales of $2000	commission on sales over $2000	monthly income

EXERCISES

1. Joan sells real estate. She receives 6% commission for selling a house. How much commission did she receive for selling a house for $74,950? $4497

2. Diego sells furniture. He is paid $210 per week, plus 3.5% commission on all sales. In one week he sold $6894 worth of furniture. Find his income for the week. $451.29

3. Heather sells computers. She earns 10% commission on all sales. Last month her sales were $15,489. Find the amount of commission. $1548.90

4. As a sales representative, Emily earns 10% commission on the first $4500 of sales and 15% on all sales over $4500. Find her income for last month if her sales were $11,865. $1554.75

5. Steve receives a salary of $250 per week, plus a commission of 1.5% on all sales over $1500. Last week he sold $4700 worth of carpeting. Find his income. $298

6. Derrick receives a commission of 5% on all sales up to $2500 and 10% on sales over $2500. How much did he earn last month on sales of $9453? $820.30

7. Jason sells aluminum siding. He earns a monthly salary of $400, plus 15% commission on all sales over $3000. Find his income for the month if he sold $4750 worth of aluminum siding. $662.50

In many service occupations, such as porter, hair stylist, waiter, or waitress, tips make up a major part of income. The Fair Labor Standards Act establishes a minimum wage for most employees in the United States. The law also states that tips can be counted as income to satisfy the minimum-wage requirement.

Example 1: Gene Anderson works as a waiter. He is paid $2.10 per hour. One week he worked 32 hours and received $123.75 in tips. Find his income for that week.

$2.10	$123.75	tips
× 32	+ 67.20	regular pay
$67.20	$190.95	income

Example 2: Francesca drives a taxi. Her wages are two thirds of the fares she collects. She pays for half of the gasoline used. In one week Francesca collected $498 in fares and got $78.50 in tips. The gasoline bill was $81.50. Find her income for the week.

$\frac{2}{3} \times \$498 = \$332$ **wages for the week**

$332.00	wages
+ 78.50	tips
$410.50	receipts

$\frac{1}{2} \times \$81.50 = \$40.75$ **half of gas cost**

$410.50	receipts
− 40.75	cost of gas
$369.75	income

EXERCISES

1. As a porter, Mark is paid $3.75 an hour, plus tips. What was his income for a 35-hour week if he received $235 in tips? $366.25

2. Su-Lynn is a barber. She charges $10.50 for a haircut. One day she gave 15 haircuts and got $25.35 in tips. How much did she earn that day? $182.85

Andy worked as a waiter. He had to complete the following report for his employer. Find his income for the week.

	Day	Hourly rate	Hours worked	Tips	Daily income
3.	Mon.	$2.75	4	$21.50	$32.50
4.	Tue.	$2.75	4	$23.75	$34.75
5.	Fri.	$2.75	$5\frac{1}{2}$	$42.35	$57.48
6.	Sat.	$2.75	$7\frac{1}{2}$	$114.00	$134.63
				total	$259.36

Mikki Ansin/Lightwave

7. Kate is a taxi driver. Her wages are half of the total fares she collects. One week Kate collected $575 in fares and got $78.50 in tips. Find her income for that week. $366

8. As a waitress, Amanda is required to give 25% of her tips to other employees who help her. Amanda is paid $3.15 per hour for a 40-hour week. She got $215 in tips. Find her income for the week. $287.25

9. Chris is a skycap at the airport. He works 40 hours each week at $4.15 per hour. He received $115 in tips. Find his income for the week. $281

SKILLS REFRESHER

Add.

								Skill	Page
1.	15.29 + 3.75 = 19.04	**2.**	26.83 + 9.48 = 36.31	**3.**	2.19 12.74 + 15.41 = 30.34	**4.**	8.49 3.68 + 9.56 = 21.73	6	454

Subtract.

								Skill	Page
5.	103.50 − 13.65 = 89.85	**6.**	75.86 − 14.97 = 60.89	**7.**	152.00 − 19.27 = 132.73	**8.**	200.00 − 48.31 = 151.69	8	458

291

WEEKLY JOB LIST

JOB NUMBER	COMPANY	LOCATION
2159	Al's Fishery	25 W. 57th Ave
42284	Tylor's Pet Shop	10 E. Lop Blvd
81326	Corner Grocery	12 E. Main St.

Suppose you have decided to find a part-time job. There are factors besides salary that you should consider about the job. Several questions you could ask yourself are listed below. You will probably have other questions.

TRANSPORTATION

How far away is the job?

Can I walk or take public transportation, or do I need a car?

HOURS

Do I work the same schedule each week or do the hours and the days vary?

Will I have to work nights? Weekends? Holidays?

Is overtime required?

KIND OF WORK

What type of environment will I be working in? Will it be quiet or noisy? Will I be indoors or outdoors? Will there be dust or fumes?

Is the job related to my career goals?

Is there a possibility that the job could develop into a permanent position?

EXPENSES

Am I required to wear a uniform? If so, is it supplied and cleaned by the employer? If a uniform is not required, do I need a special wardrobe, or will school clothes be acceptable?

Am I required to pay union dues?

Kenji Kerins

When comparing different jobs, you must consider the expenses incurred for each job. It may benefit you to take the lower-paying job if the expenses for that job will be less.

Anne Jones was looking for a part-time job. She wanted to work 4 days a week for a total of 20 hours. She was offered two jobs. One job was as a clerk in a store two blocks from her home, so she could walk to work. The pay was $4.00 per hour.

$$\begin{array}{r} \$4.00 \\ \times 20 \\ \hline \$80.00 \end{array}$$

Anne would earn $80 per week.

The second job was as a checker in a grocery store 3 miles from her home, so she would have to use public transportation. The bus fare was 60¢ each way. The pay was $4.25 per hour, with union dues of $2.15 each week.

$20 \times \$4.25 = \$85.00$

$$\begin{array}{rl} \$85.00 & \text{wages} \\ -\quad 2.15 & \text{union dues} \\ \hline 82.85 & \\ -\quad 4.80 & \text{bus fare (4 round trips)} \\ \hline \$78.05 & \text{weekly income} \end{array}$$

Anne would have an income of $78.05 per week.

If both jobs interested Anne and there were not other circumstances to determine a choice, she should consider taking the lower-paying job—as a clerk in the store 2 blocks from home.

Consider the two jobs described below. Determine how much your income would be for each job if you worked 25 hours.

Job A	Job B
Hourly rate: $3.45	Hourly rate: $3.20
Weekly union dues: $2.05	Weekly uniform expense: $3.20
Transportation cost: $10.00	$76.80
$74.20	

Computer Supplement, Disk 1, Lesson 3, may be used at this time.

Will & Angie Rumpf

Jeff earns $4.10 an hour at his job in the supermarket. This week he worked 40 hours. A copy of his paycheck stub is shown below.

This week Jeff earned $164.00. That amount is called **gross pay.** Notice that deductions were made for the following: federal income tax (F.I.T.), social security tax (F.I.C.A.), state income tax, city income tax, medical insurance, and union dues. The last four deductions may vary from state to state and from company to company.

The **net pay** is found by subtracting the sum of all the deductions from the gross pay. Net pay is often called *take-home pay* since it is the amount you take home.

The amount of federal income tax withheld depends upon the amount of income, the length of the pay period, marital status, and the number of withholding allowances. Withholding allowances are usually you, your spouse, and your dependent children.

No. 10827

EMPLOYEE NUMBER	PERIOD ENDING	HOURS		
		REGULAR	ADDITIONAL REGULAR	OVERTIME
108427	7/29/85	40	0	0

EARNINGS					
REGULAR	ADDITIONAL REGULAR	OVERTIME	OTHER	C D	GROSS PAY
$164.00	0	0	0		$164.00

DEDUCTIONS						
F.I.T.	F.I.C.A.	STATE TAX	CITY TAX	STATE U C TAX	P.S.T.	MEDICAL INSURANCE
$16.30	$11.56	$3.61	$1.64			$3.05

DEDUCTIONS					NET PAY
GROUP LIFE INS.	OTHER INS.	UNION DUES	SUPPLEMENTAL INSURANCE	OTHER	
		$2.50			$125.34

When Jeff began working, his employer asked him to complete a Form W-4. The Form W-4 tells the employer how many withholding allowances Jeff claimed, so that the correct amount of federal income tax can be withheld. The Internal Revenue Service (IRS) provides employers with tables, like those on page 296, to determine the correct amount of federal tax to withhold.

Form **W-4**	Department of the Treasury—Internal Revenue Service **Employee's Withholding Allowance Certificate**	OMB No. 1545-0010

1 Type or print your full name
JEFFREY W. CARRANE

2 Your social security number
111-22-3333

Home address (number and street or rural route)
14023 ANDREW CIRCLE

City or town, State, and ZIP code
ANYTOWN, USA

3 Marital Status
☒ Single ☐ Married
☐ Married, but withhold at higher Single rate
Note: If married, but legally separated, or spouse is a nonresident alien, check the Single box.

4 Total number of allowances you are claiming (from line F of the worksheet on page 2) . . . . /

5 Additional amount, if any, you want deducted from each pay . . . . $

6 I claim exemption from withholding because (see instructions and check boxes below that apply):

a ☐ Last year I did not owe any Federal income tax and had a right to a full refund of **ALL** income tax withheld, **AND**

b ☐ This year I do not expect to owe any Federal income tax and expect to have a right to a full refund of **ALL** income tax withheld. If both a and b apply, enter the year effective and "EXEMPT" here . . ▶ Year

c If you entered "EXEMPT" on line 6b, are you a full-time student? . . . . ☐ Yes ☐ No

Under penalties of perjury, I certify that I am entitled to the number of withholding allowances claimed on this certificate, or if claiming exemption from withholding, that I am entitled to claim the exempt status.

Employee's signature ▶ Jeffrey W. Carrane   Date ▶ _____ , 19____

7 Employer's name and address **(Employer: Complete 7, 8, and 9 only if sending to IRS)**

8 Office code

9 Employer identification number

Jeff's employer also asked him to complete a form for state withholding exemptions.

State Department of Revenue **ST-W-4** EMPLOYEE'S STATE WITHHOLDING EXEMPTION CERTIFICATE	PRINT FULL NAME JEFFREY W. CARRANE HOME ADDRESS 14023 ANDREW CIRCLE SOCIAL SECURITY NO. 111-22-3333

HOW TO CLAIM YOUR STATE WITHHOLDING EXEMPTION

1. Write number of personal and dependency exemptions to which you are ENTITLED on your Federal Income Tax Return (Form 1040 or 1040A) . . . . [/]

2. To claim your full state exemption, enter the amount shown on Line 1. If you elect to reduce the amount of your state exemption for purposes of withholding state income tax, enter a lesser number . . . . [/]

3. I claim exemption from withholding (to be checked only if line 6, Federal Form W-4 is checked) . . . . [ ]

I CERTIFY that the withholding exemption(s) claimed on this certificate does not exceed the amount to which I am entitled on my federal income tax return.

(Date) _____ , 19____ (Signed) Jeffrey W. Carrane

SINGLE Persons—WEEKLY Payroll Period

And the wages are—		And the number of withholding allowances claimed is—				
At least	But less than	0	1	2	3	4
		The amount of income tax to be withheld shall be—				
92	94	8.40	5.60	3.30	1.00	0
94	96	8.70	5.90	3.60	1.20	0
96	98	9.00	6.10	3.80	1.50	0
98	100	9.30	6.40	4.00	1.70	0
100	105	9.80	6.90	4.50	2.10	0
105	110	10.50	7.60	5.10	2.70	.40
110	115	11.30	8.40	5.70	3.30	1.00
115	120	12.00	9.10	6.30	3.90	1.60
120	125	12.80	9.90	7.00	4.50	2.20
125	130	13.50	10.60	7.80	5.10	2.80
130	135	14.30	11.40	8.50	5.70	3.40
135	140	15.00	12.10	9.30	6.40	4.00
140	145	15.80	12.90	10.00	7.10	4.60
145	150	16.50	13.60	10.80	7.90	5.20
150	160	17.70	14.80	11.90	9.00	6.10
160	170	19.20	16.30	13.40	10.50	7.60
170	180	20.70	17.80	14.90	12.00	9.10
180	190	22.20	19.30	16.40	13.50	10.60
190	200	24.10	20.80	17.90	15.00	12.10
200	210	26.00	22.40	19.40	16.50	13.60
210	220	27.90	24.30	20.90	18.00	15.10
220	230	29.80	26.20	22.50	19.50	16.60
230	240	31.70	28.10	24.40	21.00	18.10
240	250	33.60	30.00	26.30	22.70	19.60
250	260	35.50	31.90	28.20	24.60	21.10
260	270	37.40	33.80	30.10	26.50	22.80
270	280	39.30	35.70	32.00	28.40	24.70
280	290	41.70	37.60	33.90	30.30	26.60
290	300	44.20	39.50	35.80	32.20	28.50
300	310	46.70	41.90	37.70	34.10	30.40
310	320	49.20	44.40	39.60	36.00	32.30
320	330	51.70	46.90	42.10	37.90	34.20
330	340	54.20	49.40	44.60	39.80	36.10
340	350	56.70	51.90	47.10	42.30	38.00
350	360	59.20	54.40	49.60	44.80	40.00
360	370	61.70	56.90	52.10	47.30	42.50
370	380	64.20	59.40	54.60	49.80	45.00
380	390	66.70	61.90	57.10	52.30	47.50
390	400	69.20	64.40	59.60	54.80	50.00
400	410	71.70	66.90	62.10	57.30	52.50
410	420	74.20	69.40	64.60	59.80	55.00
420	430	76.80	71.90	67.10	62.30	57.50
430	440	79.80	74.40	69.60	64.80	60.00
440	450	82.80	77.10	72.10	67.30	62.50
450	460	85.80	80.10	74.60	69.80	65.00
460	470	88.80	83.10	77.30	72.30	67.50
470	480	91.80	86.10	80.30	74.80	70.00
480	490	94.80	89.10	83.30	77.50	72.50
490	500	97.80	92.10	86.30	80.50	75.00
500	510	100.80	95.10	89.30	83.50	77.80

MARRIED Persons—WEEKLY Payroll Period

And the wages are—		And the number of withholding allowances claimed is—				
At least	But less than	0	1	2	3	4
		The amount of income tax to be withheld shall be—				
92	94	5.60	3.30	1.00	0	0
94	96	5.90	3.60	1.20	0	0
96	98	6.10	3.80	1.50	0	0
98	100	6.30	4.00	1.70	0	0
100	105	6.80	4.50	2.10	0	0
105	110	7.40	5.10	2.70	.40	0
110	115	8.00	5.70	3.30	1.00	0
115	120	8.60	6.30	3.90	1.60	0
120	125	9.20	6.90	4.50	2.20	0
125	130	9.80	7.50	5.10	2.80	.50
130	135	10.40	8.10	5.70	3.40	1.10
135	140	11.00	8.70	6.30	4.00	1.70
140	145	11.60	9.30	6.90	4.60	2.30
145	150	12.20	9.90	7.50	5.20	2.90
150	160	13.10	10.80	8.40	6.10	3.80
160	170	14.30	12.00	9.60	7.30	5.00
170	180	15.50	13.20	10.80	8.50	6.20
180	190	16.70	14.40	12.00	9.70	7.40
190	200	18.40	15.60	13.20	10.90	8.60
200	210	20.10	16.80	14.40	12.10	9.80
210	220	21.80	18.50	15.60	13.30	11.00
220	230	23.50	20.20	16.90	14.50	12.20
230	240	25.20	21.90	18.60	15.70	13.40
240	250	26.90	23.60	20.30	17.10	14.60
250	260	28.60	25.30	22.00	18.80	15.80
260	270	30.30	27.00	23.70	20.50	17.20
270	280	32.00	28.70	25.40	22.20	18.90
280	290	33.70	30.40	27.10	23.90	20.60
290	300	35.40	32.10	28.80	25.60	22.30
300	310	37.10	33.80	30.50	27.30	24.00
310	320	38.80	35.50	32.20	29.00	25.70
320	330	40.50	37.20	33.90	30.70	27.40
330	340	42.20	38.90	35.60	32.40	29.10
340	350	43.90	40.60	37.30	34.10	30.80
350	360	45.60	42.30	39.00	35.80	32.50
360	370	47.30	44.00	40.70	37.50	34.20
370	380	49.30	45.70	42.40	39.20	35.90
380	390	51.50	47.40	44.10	40.90	37.60
390	400	53.70	49.50	45.80	42.60	39.30
400	410	55.90	51.70	47.50	44.30	41.00
410	420	58.10	53.90	49.60	46.00	42.70
420	430	60.30	56.10	51.80	47.70	44.40
430	440	62.50	58.30	54.00	49.80	46.10
440	450	64.70	60.50	56.20	52.00	47.80
450	460	66.90	62.70	58.40	54.20	50.00
460	470	69.40	64.90	60.60	56.40	52.20
470	480	71.90	67.10	62.80	58.60	54.40
480	490	74.40	69.60	65.00	60.80	56.60
490	500	76.90	72.10	67.30	63.00	58.80
500	510	79.40	74.60	69.80	65.20	61.00

Look at the table at the left. Jeff earned $164. Since Jeff is single and has one withholding allowance, $16.30 was withheld for federal income tax.

In Jeff's state, 2.2% of his income is withheld for state income tax and 1% for city income tax. This amount varies from state to state and from city to city. The F.I.C.A., or social security tax, is 7.05% of his wages. His employer sends Jeff's contribution, plus an equal matching contribution, to the federal government.

Jeff also has $3.05 deducted from each paycheck, or $12.20 each month, for medical insurance. The medical insurance premium is $45.50 per month. Jeff's employer pays the additional $33.30 each month as a benefit to employees.

EXERCISES

Use the appropriate table on page 296 to find the amount of federal income tax withheld.

	Weekly gross pay	Single/Married	Withholding allowances	F.I.T.
1.	$98.50	S	1	$6.40
2.	$310.00	M	3	$29.00
3.	$345.00	S	2	$47.10
4.	$227.38	S	0	$29.80
5.	$274.00	M	4	$18.90
6.	$150.25	M	2	$8.40

Jared Sawyer is a bookkeeper for a small business. He is responsible for calculating each employee's net pay. Copy and complete the chart below. Use the appropriate table on page 296 to determine the amount of federal income tax to withhold. The state income tax rate is 2%, the city tax rate is $1\frac{1}{2}$%, and the social-security tax rate is 7.05%.

	Weekly gross pay	Single/Married	Withholding allowances	F.I.T.	F.I.C.A.	State tax	City tax	Med. ins.	Other	Weekly net pay
7.	$120.00	S	2	$7.00	$8.46	$2.40	$1.80	$8.95	$10.00	$81.39
8.	$225.00	M	2	$16.90	$15.86	$4.50	$3.38	$10.05	$5.00	$169.31
9.	$198.00	M	3	$10.90	$13.96	$3.96	$2.97	$15.50		$150.71
10.	$265.00	M	4	$17.20	$18.68	$5.30	$3.98	$16.75	$15.00	$188.09
11.	$104.50	S	1	$6.90	$7.37	$2.09	$1.57	$5.25	$11.50	$69.82
12.	$247.00	S	1	$30.00	$17.41	$4.94	$3.71	$5.25		$185.69

Computer Supplement, Disk 1, Lesson 4, may be used at this time.

A social security number is required of almost everyone in the United States. Your social security number is required for job applications, income tax forms, savings accounts, credit forms, and so on. In fact, for identification purposes, your social security number is becoming as important as your name. There may be many people with the same name you have, but no one else has your social security number.

If you do not have a social security number, contact a post office or a local social security office for an application. You will be sent a social security card, as shown here, bearing the number assigned to you.

The amount of withholding for social security is set and controlled by Congress. Your employer will match the amount you pay and send both amounts to the federal government. Social security is a pay-as-you-go system—that is, the payroll taxes paid by current employees are paid out in benefits to current retirees, disabled people, and survivors. The money is not invested in an account in your name, but the government does keep a record of how much you pay in over the years.

As shown in the table below, the amount of payroll tax for social security is equal to a percent of a base wage. For example, for 1985, workers pay 7.05% of the first $41,100 of earnings. For 1986, workers pay 7.15% of the first $44,100 of earnings.

Social security taxes

Year	Tax rates (in percent)	Wage base*
1977	5.85%	$16,500
1978	6.05	17,700
1979	6.13	22,900
1980	6.13	25,900
1981	6.65	29,700
1982	6.70	32,400
1983	6.70	35,100
1984	6.70	38,100
1985	7.05	41,100
1986	7.15	44,100
1987	7.15	47,100
1988	7.15	50,100

*Amounts for 1985–88 are based on economic predictions.

Example 1: Find the payroll deduction for social security on a weekly paycheck of $875 in 1985.

$875
×0.0705   7.05%
$61.6875

Payroll deduction is $61.69.

Example 2: Find the withholding for social security tax on an annual income of $45,000 in 1986.

$44,100   **maximum wage base for 1986**
×0.0715   **7.15% rate for 1986**
$3153.1500

The withholding is $3153.15.

Find the payroll tax for social security for each amount of earnings during 1985.

1. $725 $51.11   **2.** $1250 $88.13   **3.** $3515 $247.81   **4.** $52,000
$2897.55

Find the payroll tax for social security for each amount of earnings during 1986.

5. $845 $60.42   **6.** $1525 $109.04   **7.** $6775 $484.41   **8.** $48,500
$3153.15

Possible answers are given for exercises 9-12.
Use the bar graph at the right to answer these questions.

9. The maximum tax in 1988 will be about how many times what it was in 1970? about 9 times

10. Can you give two reasons why the amount of tax increased so rapidly?
inflation; people are living longer

11. The change during 1980–1988 is about how many times the change during 1970–1978? about 3 times

12. If the trend continues, what would you predict for the maximum social security tax in the year 1990? about $4000

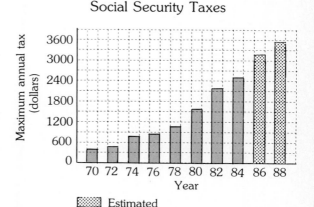

Social Security Taxes

Estimated

299

At the end of each year, employers must provide each employee with a statement showing the total income earned for the year and the amount of taxes withheld. The information is provided on Form W-2. A copy of the Form W-2 must accompany a person's income tax return when it is filed with the Internal Revenue Service.

It is a good idea to save your paycheck stubs throughout the year so that you can be sure the information on Form W-2 is correct.

Jeff Carrane worked about 20 hours each week during the school year and 40 hours each week during the summer at a local supermarket. His Form W-2 for that year is shown below.

Since he earned more than $3300, Jeff must file an income tax return on or before April 15 of the following year. Jeff can use Form 1040EZ. The IRS provides detailed instructions to help you decide which tax form to use.

1 Control number	3 Employer's identification number	4 Employer's State number	Copy B to be filed with employee's FEDERAL tax return
2 Employer's name, address, and ZIP code		W-2 Wage and Tax Statement	This information is being furnished to the Internal Revenue Service.
SHOP & SAVE SUPERMARKET 92484 TYLOR STREET ANYTOWN, USA		5 Stat. em De- Legal 942 Sub- ploye ceased rep. emp. total	Void
		6 Allocated tips	7 Advance EIC payment
8 Employee's social security number 111-22-3333	9 Federal income tax withheld $373.20	10 Wages, tips, other compensation $4920.00	11 Social security tax withheld $346.86
12 Employer's name, address and ZIP code Jeffrey W. Carrane 14023 Andrew Circle Anytown, USA	13 Social security wages		14 Social security tips
	16 *		
	17 State income tax $108.12	18 State wages, tips, etc.	19 Name of State
Department of the Treasury Internal Revenue Service OMB No. 1545-0008	20 Local income tax $49.20	21 Local wages, tips, etc.	22 Name of locality

Form 1040EZ Income Tax Return for
Single filers with no dependents (s)

OMB No. 1545-0675

Name & address

If you don't have a label, please print:

JEFFREY W. CARRANE
Write your name above (first, initial, last)

14023 ANDREW CIRCLE
Present home address (number and street)

ANYTOWN, USA
City, town, or post office, state, and ZIP code

Please write your numbers like this.

1234567890

Social security number

111 22 3333

Presidential Election Campaign Fund
Check box if you want $1 of your tax to go to this fund. ▶

		Dollars	Cents

Figure your tax

1 Wages, salaries, and tips. Attach your W-2 form(s). 1 — 4 920 00

2 Interest income of $400 or less. If more than $400, you cannot use Form 1040EZ. 2 — 15 64

Attach Copy B of Form(s) W-2 here

3 Add line 1 and line 2. This is your adjusted gross income. 3 — 4 935 64

4 Allowable part of your charitable contributions. Complete the worksheet on page 19. Do not write more than $25. 4 — 00 00

5 Subtract line 4 from line 3. 5 — 4 935 64

6 Amount of your personal exemption. 6 — 1 000 00

7 Subtract line 6 from line 5. This is your **taxable income.** 7 — 3 935 64

8 Enter your Federal income tax withheld. This should be shown in Box 9 of your W-2 form(s). 8 — 373 20

9 Use the tax table on pages 29-34 to find the **tax** on your taxable income on line 7. Write the amount of tax. 9 — 196 00

Refund or amount you owe

10 If line 8 is larger than line 9, subtract line 9 from line 8. Enter the amount of your refund. 10 — 177 20

Attach tax payment here

11 If line 9 is larger than line 8, subtract line 8 from line 9. Enter the amount you owe. Attach check or money order for the full amount, payable to "Internal Revenue Service." 11

Sign your return

I have read this return. Under penalties of perjury, I declare that to the best of my knowledge and belief, the return is true, correct, and complete.

Your signature   Date

X Jeffrey W. Carrane   2/12/84

For IRS Use Only—Please do not write in boxes below.

For Privacy Act and Paperwork Reduction Act Notice, see page 38.

Jeff completed Form 1040EZ as shown on page 301. The information on lines 1 and 8 is found on his Form W-2. He received $15.64 interest from the bank. This amount is reported on line 2.

The table below is used to find the tax on the taxable income (line 7). Notice that the taxable income is not the same as the income reported on line 1. Why? *because interest is added and deductions are subtracted*

The amount of tax that is read from the table is recorded on line 9. Note from line 10 that Jeff will receive a refund. If the amount of tax withheld were less than the amount of tax, Jeff would have entered that amount on line 11.

It is required that you sign the form and attach Copy B of Form W-2 when filing your tax return.

If line 37 (taxable income) is—		And you are—			
At least	But less than	Single	Married filing jointly *	Married filing separately	Head of a household
		Your tax is—			
3,000					
3,000	3,050	80	0	151	80
3,050	3,100	85	0	158	85
3,100	3,150	91	0	164	91
3,150	3,200	96	0	171	96
3,200	3,250	102	0	177	102
3,250	3,300	107	0	184	107
3,300	3,350	113	0	190	113
3,350	3,400	118	0	197	118
3,400	3,450	124	c3	203	124
3,450	3,500	131	8	210	129
3,500	3,550	137	14	216	135
3,550	3,600	144	19	223	140
3,600	3,650	150	25	229	146
3,650	3,700	157	30	236	151
3,700	3,750	163	36	242	157
3,750	3,800	170	41	249	162
3,800	3,850	179	47	256	168
3,850	3,900	190	52	263	173
3,900	3,950	196	58	271	179
3,950	4,000	201	63	278	184
4,000					
4,000	4,050	206	69	286	190
4,050	4,100	212	74	293	195
4,100	4,150	217	80	301	201
4,150	4,200	222	85	308	206
4,200	4,250	228	91	316	212
4,250	4,300	235	96	323	217
4,300	4,350	241	102	331	223
4,350	4,400	248	107	338	228
4,400	4,450	255	113	346	234
4,450	4,500	262	118	353	241
4,500	4,550	270	124	361	247
4,550	4,600	277	129	368	254
4,600	4,650	285	135	376	260

If line 37 (taxable income) is—		And you are—			
At least	But less than	Single	Married filing jointly *	Married filing separately	Head of a household
		Your tax is—			
4,650	4,700	292	140	383	267
4,700	4,750	300	146	391	273
4,750	4,800	307	151	398	280
4,800	4,850	315	157	406	286
4,850	4,900	322	162	413	293
4,900	4,950	330	168	421	299
4,950	5,000	337	173	428	306
5,000					
5,000	5,050	345	179	436	312
5,050	5,100	352	184	443	319
5,100	5,150	360	190	451	325
5,150	5,200	367	195	458	332
5,200	5,250	375	201	466	338
5,250	5,300	382	206	473	345
5,300	5,350	390	212	481	351
5,350	5,400	397	217	488	358
5,400	5,450	405	223	496	364
5,450	5,500	412	228	503	371
5,500	5,550	420	234	511	377
5,550	5,600	427	241	518	384
5,600	5,650	435	247	526	390
5,650	5,700	442	254	533	397
5,700	5,750	450	260	541	403
5,750	5,800	457	267	548	410
5,800	5,850	465	273	556	416
5,850	5,900	472	280	563	423
5,900	5,950	480	286	571	429
5,950	6,000	487	293	579	436
6,000					
6,000	6,050	495	299	587	442
6,050	6,100	502	306	596	449
6,100	6,150	510	312	604	455
6,150	6,200	517	319	613	462
6,200	6,250	525	325	621	468
6,250	6,300	532	332	630	475

If line 37 (taxable income) is—		And you are—			
At least	But less than	Single	Married filing jointly *	Married filing separately	Head of a household
		Your tax is—			
6,300	6,350	540	338	638	481
6,350	6,400	547	345	647	488
6,400	6,450	555	351	655	494
6,450	6,500	562	358	664	501
6,500	6,550	570	364	672	508
6,550	6,600	577	371	681	515
6,600	6,650	585	377	689	523
6,650	6,700	592	384	698	530
6,700	6,750	600	390	706	538
6,750	6,800	607	397	715	545
6,800	6,850	615	403	723	553
6,850	6,900	622	410	732	560
6,900	6,950	630	416	740	568
6,950	7,000	637	423	749	575
7,000					
7,000	7,050	645	429	757	583
7,050	7,100	652	436	766	590
7,100	7,150	660	442	774	598
7,150	7,200	667	449	783	605
7,200	7,250	675	455	791	613
7,250	7,300	682	462	800	620
7,300	7,350	690	468	808	628
7,350	7,400	697	475	817	635
7,400	7,450	705	481	825	643
7,450	7,500	712	488	834	650
7,500	7,550	720	494	842	658
7,550	7,600	727	501	851	665
7,600	7,650	735	508	859	673
7,650	7,700	742	515	868	680
7,700	7,750	750	523	876	688
7,750	7,800	757	530	885	695
7,800	7,850	765	538	893	703
7,850	7,900	772	545	902	710
7,900	7,950	780	553	910	718
7,950	8,000	787	560	919	725

If line 37 (taxable income) is—		And you are—				If line 37 (taxable income) is—		And you are—				If line 37 (taxable income) is—		And you are—			
At least	But less than	Single	Married filing jointly *	Married filing separately	Head of a household	At least	But less than	Single	Married filing jointly *	Married filing separately	Head of a household	At least	But less than	Single	Married filing jointly *	Married filing separately	Head of a household
		Your tax is—						Your tax is—						Your tax is—			
8,000						10,750	10,800	1,253	980	1,477	1,208	13,500	13,550	1,787	1,425	2,147	1,720
8,000	8,050	795	568	928	733	10,800	10,850	1,262	988	1,489	1,217	13,550	13,600	1,798	1,434	2,160	1,729
8,050	8,100	802	575	937	740	10,850	10,900	1,271	995	1,500	1,226	13,600	13,650	1,808	1,442	2,173	1,739
8,100	8,150	810	583	947	748	10,900	10,950	1,281	1,003	1,512	1,235	13,650	13,700	1,819	1,451	2,186	1,748
8,150	8,200	817	590	956	755	10,950	11,000	1,290	1,010	1,523	1,244	13,700	13,750	1,829	1,459	2,199	1,758
8,200	8,250	825	598	966	763	**11,000**						13,750	13,800	1,840	1,468	2,212	1,767
8,250	8,300	832	605	975	770	11,000	11,050	1,300	1,018	1,535	1,253	13,800	13,850	1,850	1,476	2,225	1,777
8,300	8,350	840	613	985	778	11,050	11,100	1,309	1,025	1,546	1,262	13,850	13,900	1,861	1,485	2,238	1,786
8,350	8,400	847	620	994	785	11,100	11,150	1,319	1,033	1,558	1,271	13,900	13,950	1,871	1,493	2,251	1,796
8,400	8,450	855	628	1,004	793	11,150	11,200	1,328	1,040	1,569	1,280	13,950	14,000	1,882	1,502	2,264	1,805
8,450	8,500	862	635	1,013	800	11,200	11,250	1,338	1,048	1,581	1,289	**14,000**					
8,500	8,550	870	643	1,023	808	11,250	11,300	1,347	1,055	1,592	1,298	14,000	14,050	1,892	1,510	2,277	1,815
8,550	8,600	879	650	1,032	815	11,300	11,350	1,357	1,063	1,604	1,307	14,050	14,100	1,903	1,519	2,290	1,824
8,600	8,650	887	658	1,042	823	11,350	11,400	1,366	1,070	1,615	1,316	14,100	14,150	1,913	1,527	2,303	1,834
8,650	8,700	896	665	1,051	830	11,400	11,450	1,376	1,078	1,627	1,325	14,150	14,200	1,924	1,536	2,316	1,843
8,700	8,750	904	673	1,061	839	11,450	11,500	1,385	1,085	1,638	1,334	14,200	14,250	1,934	1,544	2,329	1,853
8,750	8,800	913	680	1,070	848	11,500	11,550	1,395	1,093	1,650	1,343	14,250	14,300	1,945	1,553	2,342	1,862
8,800	8,850	921	688	1,080	857	11,550	11,600	1,404	1,100	1,661	1,352	14,300	14,350	1,955	1,561	2,355	1,872
8,850	8,900	930	695	1,089	866	11,600	11,650	1,414	1,108	1,673	1,361	14,350	14,400	1,966	1,570	2,368	1,881
8,900	8,950	938	703	1,099	875	11,650	11,700	1,423	1,115	1,684	1,370	14,400	14,450	1,976	1,578	2,381	1,891
8,950	9,000	947	710	1,108	884	11,700	11,750	1,433	1,123	1,696	1,379	14,450	14,500	1,987	1,587	2,394	1,900
9,000						11,750	11,800	1,442	1,130	1,707	1,388	14,500	14,550	1,997	1,595	2,407	1,910
9,000	9,050	955	718	1,118	893	11,800	11,850	1,452	1,138	1,719	1,397	14,550	14,600	2,008	1,604	2,420	1,919
9,050	9,100	964	725	1,127	902	11,850	11,900	1,461	1,145	1,730	1,406	14,600	14,650	2,018	1,612	2,433	1,929
9,100	9,150	972	733	1,137	911	11,900	11,950	1,471	1,153	1,742	1,416	14,650	14,700	2,029	1,621	2,446	1,938
9,150	9,200	981	740	1,146	920	11,950	12,000	1,480	1,162	1,753	1,425	14,700	14,750	2,039	1,629	2,459	1,948
9,200	9,250	989	748	1,156	929	**12,000**						14,750	14,800	2,050	1,638	2,472	1,957
9,250	9,300	998	755	1,165	938	12,000	12,050	1,490	1,170	1,765	1,435	14,800	14,850	2,060	1,646	2,485	1,967
9,300	9,350	1,006	763	1,175	947	12,050	12,100	1,499	1,179	1,776	1,444	14,850	14,900	2,071	1,655	2,498	1,976
9,350	9,400	1,015	770	1,184	956	12,100	12,150	1,509	1,187	1,788	1,454	14,900	14,950	2,081	1,663	2,511	1,986
9,400	9,450	1,023	778	1,194	965	12,150	12,200	1,518	1,196	1,799	1,463	14,950	15,000	2,092	1,672	2,525	1,995
9,450	9,500	1,032	785	1,203	974	12,200	12,250	1,528	1,204	1,811	1,473	**15,000**					
9,500	9,550	1,040	793	1,213	983	12,250	12,300	1,537	1,213	1,822	1,482	15,000	15,050	2,103	1,680	2,540	2,005
9,550	9,600	1,049	800	1,222	992	12,300	12,350	1,547	1,221	1,835	1,492	15,050	15,100	2,115	1,689	2,555	2,016
9,600	9,650	1,057	808	1,232	1,001	12,350	12,400	1,556	1,230	1,848	1,501	15,100	15,150	2,127	1,697	2,570	2,026
9,650	9,700	1,066	815	1,241	1,010	12,400	12,450	1,566	1,238	1,861	1,511	15,150	15,200	2,139	1,706	2,585	2,037
9,700	9,750	1,074	823	1,251	1,019	12,450	12,500	1,575	1,247	1,874	1,520	15,200	15,250	2,151	1,714	2,600	2,047
9,750	9,800	1,083	830	1,260	1,028	12,500	12,550	1,585	1,255	1,887	1,530	15,250	15,300	2,163	1,723	2,615	2,058
9,800	9,850	1,091	838	1,270	1,037	12,550	12,600	1,594	1,264	1,900	1,539	15,300	15,350	2,175	1,731	2,630	2,068
9,850	9,900	1,100	845	1,279	1,046	12,600	12,650	1,604	1,272	1,913	1,549	15,350	15,400	2,187	1,740	2,645	2,079
9,900	9,950	1,108	853	1,289	1,055	12,650	12,700	1,613	1,281	1,926	1,558	15,400	15,450	2,199	1,748	2,660	2,089
9,950	10,000	1,117	860	1,298	1,064	12,700	12,750	1,623	1,289	1,939	1,568	15,450	15,500	2,211	1,757	2,675	2,100
10,000						12,750	12,800	1,632	1,298	1,952	1,577	15,500	15,550	2,223	1,765	2,690	2,110
10,000	10,050	1,125	868	1,308	1,073	12,800	12,850	1,642	1,306	1,965	1,587	15,550	15,600	2,235	1,774	2,705	2,121
10,050	10,100	1,134	875	1,317	1,082	12,850	12,900	1,651	1,315	1,978	1,596	15,600	15,650	2,247	1,782	2,720	2,131
10,100	10,150	1,142	883	1,328	1,091	12,900	12,950	1,661	1,323	1,991	1,606	15,650	15,700	2,259	1,791	2,735	2,142
10,150	10,200	1,151	890	1,339	1,100	12,950	13,000	1,672	1,332	2,004	1,615	15,700	15,750	2,271	1,799	2,750	2,152
10,200	10,250	1,159	898	1,351	1,109	**13,000**						15,750	15,800	2,283	1,808	2,765	2,163
10,250	10,300	1,168	905	1,362	1,118	13,000	13,050	1,682	1,340	2,017	1,625	15,800	15,850	2,295	1,816	2,780	2,173
10,300	10,350	1,176	913	1,374	1,127	13,050	13,100	1,693	1,349	2,030	1,634	15,850	15,900	2,307	1,825	2,795	2,184
10,350	10,400	1,185	920	1,385	1,136	13,100	13,150	1,703	1,357	2,043	1,644	15,900	15,950	2,319	1,833	2,810	2,194
10,400	10,450	1,193	928	1,397	1,145	13,150	13,200	1,714	1,366	2,056	1,653	15,950	16,000	2,331	1,842	2,825	2,205
10,450	10,500	1,202	935	1,408	1,154	13,200	13,250	1,724	1,374	2,069	1,663	**16,000**					
10,500	10,550	1,210	943	1,420	1,163	13,250	13,300	1,735	1,383	2,082	1,672	16,000	16,050	2,343	1,851	2,840	2,215
10,550	10,600	1,219	950	1,431	1,172	13,300	13,350	1,745	1,391	2,095	1,682	16,050	16,100	2,355	1,860	2,855	2,226
10,600	10,650	1,227	958	1,443	1,181	13,350	13,400	1,756	1,400	2,108	1,691	16,100	16,150	2,367	1,870	2,870	2,236
10,650	10,700	1,236	965	1,454	1,190	13,400	13,450	1,766	1,408	2,121	1,701	16,150	16,200	2,379	1,879	2,885	2,247
10,700	10,750	1,244	973	1,466	1,199	13,450	13,500	1,777	1,417	2,134	1,710	16,200	16,250	2,391	1,889	2,900	2,257

EXERCISES

Use the tax tables on pages 302–303 to find the amount of tax on each of the following. Assume that each of the people is single. Tell whether there is a refund or a balance due.

	Taxable income	Tax withheld	Amount of tax	Refund or Balance due
1.	$6702	$595.25	$600	Balance due
2.	$9879	$1076.40	$1100	Balance due
3.	$4879	$375.00	$322	Refund
4.	$14,325	$1842.00	$1955	Balance due
5.	$8036	$843.55	$795	Refund
6.	$12,433	$1299.20	$1566	Balance due
7.	$9055	$875.00	$964	Balance due
8.	$10,644	$1279.35	$1227	Refund
9.	$15,120	$2088.00	$2127	Balance due
10.	$10,000	$1257.50	$1125	Refund
11.	$13,535	$2335.44	$1787	Refund
12.	$11,062	$1183.20	$1309	Balance due

Use all the information given to complete a Form 1040EZ. Assume that each of the people is single.

13. Kimberly received $34.80 in interest from the bank. Refund of $266.20

1 Control number 000000	3 Employer's identification number 1010	4 Employer's State number 00	Copy B to be filed with employee's FEDERAL tax return
2 Employer's name, address, and ZIP code		W-2 Wage and Tax Statement	This information is being furnished to the Internal Revenue Service
DOUGLAS COMPANY 1016 UNIVERSITY STREET ANY WHERE, USA		5 Stat em De-ployer ceased rep Legal 942 emp Sub-total	Void
		6 Allocated tips	7 Advance EIC payment
8 Employee's social security number 222-11-1111	9 Federal income tax withheld $1383.20	10 Wages, tips, other compensation $10,920.00	11 Social security tax withheld $769.86
12 Employee's name, address and ZIP code	13 Social security wages	14 Social security tips	
Kimberly M. Miller 821 Circle Street Any Where, USA	16 *		
	17 State income tax $273.00	18 State wages, tips, etc	19 Name of State
Department of the Treasury Internal Revenue Service OMB No. 1545-0008	20 Local income tax	21 Local wages, tips, etc	22 Name of locality

W-2 2 WIDE 3 PART

63-CB14

Don Lansu

14. Steve received $25.30 in interest from the bank. Balance due of $175.12

1 Control number	3 Employer's identification number	4 Employer's State number	
1016	131959	00	Copy B to be filed with employee's FEDERAL tax return

2 Employer's name, address, and ZIP code

ACME SUPPLY COMPANY
1225 INDUSTRY DRIVE
ANY CITY, USA

W-2 Wage and Tax Statement

This information is being furnished to the Internal Revenue Service

5 Stat em ployee	De ceased	Legal rep	942 emp	Sub total	Void

6 Allocated tips	7 Advance EIC payment

8 Employee's social security number	9 Federal income tax withheld	10 Wages, tips, other compensation	11 Social security tax withheld
000-11-2222	$1842.88	$15,600.00	$1099.80

12 Employee's name, address and ZIP code

Steve J. Tacushi
5320 South Avenue
Any City, USA

13 Social security wages	14 Social security tips

16 *

17 State income tax	18 State wages, tips, etc	19 Name of State
$343.20		

20 Local income tax	21 Local wages, tips, etc	22 Name of locality
$546.00		

Department of the Treasury Internal Revenue Service   OMB No. 1545-0008

---

15. Jorge received $15.75 in interest from the bank. $393.00

Refund of

1 Control number	3 Employer's identification number	4 Employer's State number	
91757	5862	00	Copy B to be filed with employee's FEDERAL tax return

2 Employer's name, address, and ZIP code

DARP INCORPORATED
121157 ENFANT WAY
ANY CITY, USA

W-2 Wage and Tax Statement

This information is being furnished to the Internal Revenue Service

5 Stat em ployee	De ceased	Legal rep	942 emp	Sub total	Void

6 Allocated tips	7 Advance EIC payment

8 Employee's social security number	9 Federal income tax withheld	10 Wages, tips, other compensation	11 Social security tax withheld
111-11-3333	$925.00	$7236.50	$580.67

12 Employee's name, address and ZIP code

Jorge P. Martinez
120484 Big Day Road
Any Village, USA

13 Social security wages	14 Social security tips

16 *

17 State income tax	18 State wages, tips, etc	19 Name of State
$288.28		

20 Local income tax	21 Local wages, tips, etc	22 Name of locality

Department of the Treasury Internal Revenue Service   OMB No. 1545-0008

---

16. Melinda received $29.85 in interest from the bank. She Refund
also has $7.00 of allowable charitable contributions. of $195.00

1 Control number	3 Employer's identification number	4 Employer's State number	
42284	22448	00	Copy B to be filed with employee's FEDERAL tax return

2 Employer's name, address, and ZIP code

TYLER'S PET SHOP
107 LOP BLVD.
ANY PLACE, USA

W-2 Wage and Tax Statement

This information is being furnished to the Internal Revenue Service

5 Stat em ployee	De ceased	Legal rep	942 emp	Sub total	Void

6 Allocated tips	7 Advance EIC payment

8 Employee's social security number	9 Federal income tax withheld	10 Wages, tips, other compensation	11 Social security tax withheld
333-22-1111	$275.00	$4015.00	$283.06

12 Employee's name, address and ZIP code

Melinda J. Johnson
8 S. Rabbit Circle
Any Place, USA

13 Social security wages	14 Social security tips

16 *

17 State income tax	18 State wages, tips, etc	19 Name of State
$100.38		

20 Local income tax	21 Local wages, tips, etc	22 Name of locality
$60.23		

Department of the Treasury Internal Revenue Service   OMB No. 1545-0008

305

Application 38 may be used at this time.

Not everyone can use tax tables like those shown on pages 302–303 to determine the amount of income tax owed. Some people must use Tax Rate Schedules, like the one shown below for single taxpayers.

Schedule X Single Taxpayers Use this Schedule if you checked **Filing Status Box 1** on Form 1040—	If the amount on Form 1040, line 37 is: Over—	But not over—	Enter on Form 1040, line 38	of the amount over—
	$0	$2,300	—0—	
	2,300	3,400	.......11%	$2,300
	3,400	4,400	$121 + 13%	3,400
	4,400	8,500	251 + 15%	4,400
	8,500	10,800	866 + 17%	8,500
	10,800	12,900	1,257 + 19%	10,800
	12,900	15,000	1,656 + 21%	12,900
	15,000	18,200	2,097 + 24%	15,000
	18,200	23,500	2,865 + 28%	18,200
	23,500	28,800	4,349 + 32%	23,500
	28,800	34,100	6,045 + 36%	28,800
	34,100	41,500	7,953 + 40%	34,100
	41,500	55,300	10,913 + 45%	41,500
	55,300	....	17,123 + 50%	55,300

Example: Find the tax for a taxable income of $11,350.

First, locate the correct line on the Schedule.

$11,350 is over $10,800 but not over $12,900.

The tax is $1,257+19% of the amount over $10,800.

To compute the tax, find the amount over $10,800.

$$\begin{array}{r} \mathbf{\$11,350} \\ -\ \ \mathbf{10,800} \\ \hline \mathbf{\$550} \end{array}$$

The tax is $1,257 + 19% of $550.

$$0.19 \times \$550 = \$104.50$$

$$\begin{array}{r} \mathbf{\$1,257} \\ +\ \ \ \ \mathbf{104.50} \\ \hline \mathbf{\$1,361.50} \end{array}$$

The tax on $11,350 is $1362 to the nearest whole dollar.

Use the Tax Rate Schedule to find the tax owed on each of the following amounts. In computing taxes, you are allowed to round all amounts to the nearest whole dollar.

1. $3600 $147
2. $7800 $761
3. $21,400 $3761
4. $37,800 $9433
5. $15,280 $2164
6. $54,928 $16,956
7. $33,774 $7836
8. $10,250 $1164
9. $18,450 $2935
10. $28,673 $6004
11. $29,000 $6117
12. $40,320 $10,441

Brent Jones

Since income tax laws are sometimes complicated and always changing, many taxpayers use the services of tax consultants. A tax consultant specializes in preparing income tax returns and in advising clients of legal deductions and how to claim such deductions. A tax consultant chooses the income tax form that would permit the client to pay the least taxes.

The work sheet below shows the summary of the itemized deductions for Mr. and Mrs. Reigle.

Line	Work sheet	Itemized Deductions	SCHEDULE A
7	Total medical and dental expenses		0
12	Total taxes		2760 00
16	Total interest expense		5320 00
20	Total contributions		300 00
21	Total casualty and theft losses		
25	Total miscellaneous deductions		0
26	Add lines 7, 12, 16, 20, 21, and 25.		8380 00
27	If you checked Form 1040 filing status box for married, joint, write $3400; for single, write $2300.		3400 00
28	Subtract line 27 from line 26. Write your answer here and on Form 1040, line 34a. (If line 27 is more than line 26, write zero.)		4980 00

Standard deductions of $3400 for married persons filing jointly and $2300 for single persons have already been considered when making the tax tables. Should your itemized deductions exceed the appropriate amount, you are allowed to deduct the excess, as determined for line 28.

Mr. and Mrs. Reigle are married persons filing jointly, so the tax consultant entered $3400 on line 27. As shown on line 28, they will be allowed to deduct $4980.

On a sheet of paper, find the amount of itemized deductions allowed for each exercise.

1.

Line	Work sheet	Itemized Deductions	SCHEDULE A
7	Total medical and dental expenses		125 00
12	Total taxes		876 00
16	Total interest expense		326 00
20	Total contributions		115 00
21	Total casualty and theft losses		
25	Total miscellaneous deductions		498 00
26	Add lines 7, 12, 16, 20, 21, and 25.		
27	If you checked Form 1040 filing status box for married, joint, write $3400; for single, write $2300.		2300 00
28	Subtract line 27 from line 26. Write your answer here and on Form 1040, line 34a. (If line 27 is more than line 26, write zero.)		

line 26: 1940; line 28: 0

2.

Line	Work sheet	Itemized Deductions	SCHEDULE A
7	Total medical and dental expenses		213 00
12	Total taxes		2315 00
16	Total interest expense		3176 00
20	Total contributions		295 00
21	Total casualty and theft losses		
25	Total miscellaneous deductions		0
26	Add lines 7, 12, 16, 20, 21, and 25.		
27	If you checked Form 1040 filing status box for married, joint, write $3400; for single, write $2300.		3400 00
28	Subtract line 27 from line 26. Write your answer here and on Form 1040, line 34a. (If line 27 is more than line 26, write zero.)		

line 26: 5999; line 28: 2599

1. A pair of jeans that regularly sell for $22.95 are on sale for 15% off. Find the sale price. $19.51   7.2

2. Melissa is paid $4.75 an hour. How much did she earn in one week if she worked $37\frac{1}{2}$ hours? $178.13   7.3

3. Michael is paid $5.50 an hour. He is paid time and a half for overtime. How much did he earn for 45 hours in one week? $261.25

4. Kyle packs items into cartons. He is paid 15¢ for each of the first 500 cartons that he packs and $17\frac{1}{2}$¢ for each carton over 500. If he packed 815 cartons, how much did he earn? $130.13   7.4

5. Jerri is paid $3.75 an hour. She also earns 11¢ for each shirt over 300 that she finishes each week. How much would she earn in a 40-hour week if she completed 450 shirts? $166.50

6. Marilyn is paid a 4% commission on all her sales. One week her sales were $5625. Find her commission. $225   7.5

7. Dave sells furniture. He receives $150 a week plus 3.5% commission on sales over $1000. How much did he earn in one week if he sold $4585 worth of furniture? $275.48

Robert is paid $3.15 per hour as a waiter. Copy and complete the chart below.   7.6

Day	Hours worked	Wages	Tips	Total earned
8. Mon.	5	$15.75	$17.65	$33.40
9. Tue.	4	$12.60	$15.20	$27.80
10. Thur.	$5\frac{1}{2}$	$17.33	$22.35	$39.68
11. Fri.	7	$22.05	$31.15	$53.20
12. Sat.	8	$25.20	$42.20	$67.40

Total $221.48

Copy and complete the chart below. Use the appropriate table on page 296 to determine the amount of federal income tax to be withheld. The state income tax rate is 2.5%, the city income tax rate is 2%, and the social security tax rate is 7.05%.

7.7

	Weekly gross pay	Single/ Married	Withholding allowances	F.I.T.	F.I.C.A.	State tax	City tax	Med. ins.	Other	Weekly net pay
13.	$354.00	M	2	$39.00	$24.96	$8.85	$7.08	$11.95	$19.14	$243.02
14.	$372.75	S	1	$59.40	$26.28	$9.32	$7.46	$ 4.15	$20.00	$246.14
15.	$424.50	M	3	$47.70	$29.93	$10.61	$8.49	$13.75	$15.00	$299.02

Use the information on the Form W-2 below to complete a Form 1040EZ. If a Form 1040EZ is not available, use page 301 as a model to do the computation needed through line 11. Assume that each of the people is single.

7.8

16.

1 Control number 81326	3 Employer's identification number 1026	4 Employer's State number 00	Copy B to be filed with employee's FEDERAL tax return

2 Employer's name, address, and ZIP code

L.N.S. INC.
2 WEST TEXAS AVENUE
ANY WHERE, USA

W-2 Wage and Tax Statement

This information is being furnished to the Internal Revenue Service.

5 Stat em De Legal 942 Sub-
ployee ceased rep emp total Void

6 Allocated tips 7 Advance EIC payment

| 8 Employee's social security number 111-00-0000 | 9 Federal income tax withheld $1591.20 | 10 Wages, tips, other compensation $12,437.00 | 11 Social security tax withheld $876.81 |

12 Employee's name, address and ZIP code

Karl Lawrence Anderson
1D East Lily Avenue
Any Where, USA

13 Social security wages 14 Social security tips

16 *

17 State income tax $373.11 18 State wages, tips, etc 19 Name of State

20 Local income tax $124.37 21 Local wages, tips, etc 22 Name of locality

Department of the Treasury Internal Revenue Service OMB No. 1545-0008

Refund of $215.20

17.

1 Control number 21325	3 Employer's identification number 91248	4 Employer's State number 00	Copy B to be filed with employee's FEDERAL tax return

2 Employer's name, address, and ZIP code

JAY'S 4 COMPANY
1656 HERBERT ROAD
ANY PLACE, USA

W-2 Wage and Tax Statement

This information is being furnished to the Internal Revenue Service.

5 Stat em De Legal 942 Sub-
ployee ceased rep emp total Void

6 Allocated tips 7 Advance EIC payment

| 8 Employee's social security number 000-11-0000 | 9 Federal income tax withheld $1990.08 | 10 Wages, tips, other compensation $16,584.00 | 11 Social security tax withheld $1169.17 |

12 Employee's name, address and ZIP code

Nicole Leigh Clavey
42757 Route HAS
Any Place, USA

13 Social security wages 14 Social security tips

16 *

17 State income tax $497.52 18 State wages, tips, etc 19 Name of State

20 Local income tax $165.84 21 Local wages, tips, etc 22 Name of locality

Department of the Treasury Internal Revenue Service OMB No. 1545-0008

Balance due of $244.92

1. Find the sale price of a radio that regularly sells for $25.99 and is on sale for 20% off. $20.79

2. Copy and complete the meal check. Use the sales tax table on page 280.

CHECK		
pizza slice	$1	75
salad bar	2	95
2 apple juice	1	50
Subtotal		
Tax		
TOTAL		

$6.20
+ 0.37
$6.57

3. Jim earns $4.20 an hour and time and a half for overtime. How much did he earn in one week if he worked 42 hours? $180.60

4. Su-Lynn is paid 25¢ for every circuit board she completes. How much did she earn in a 5-day week if she averaged 395 circuit boards per day? $493.75

5. Danielle is paid 6% commission for each house she sells. How much is her commission on a $76,000 house? $4560

6. Steve earns 5% commission on the first $2000 of sales and 8% on all sales over $2000. In one month his sales were $15,985. Find his commission. $1218.80

7. Martha is paid $2.75 an hour as a waitress. Last week she worked 35 hours and received $85 in tips. How much did she earn last week? $181.25

8. Use the table on page 296 to find the amount of federal income tax to withhold from earnings of $232.85. The person is single with one withholding allowance. How much state income tax would be withheld if the tax rate is 3.5%? $28.10; $8.15

9. Use the tax tables on pages 302–303 to complete the following for a single person.

Taxable income	Tax withheld	Amount of tax	Refund or Balance due
$9763.75	$1065.00	$1083	Refund

Correlation	
Items	Sec
1–2	7.2
3	7.3
4	7.4
5–6	7.5
7	7.6
8	7.7
9	7.8

Find each cash-on-hand amount.

	Income	Expense	Cash on hand
			$78.25
1.		$22.65	55.60
2.		9.42	46.18
3.	$18.97		65.15
4.		42.16	22.99

Copy and complete the table.

	Budget category	Amount	Percent
5.	food	$15	25%
6.	clothing	12	20%
7.	savings	6	10%
8.	other	27	45%
	totals	$60	100%

Correlation

Items	Sec
1–4	8.1
5–6	8.2
7–8	8.3
9	8.4
10	8.5
11	8.6
12	8.7
13	8.9
14	8.10
15	8.11

9. Find the amount of money in a checking account after these transactions.

Starting balance: $126.84
$12.13

Check No. 612: A & B Co., $29.60, groceries
613: Tripp's, $42.25, clothing
614: C. Kohn, $225.00, rent
Deposit: $182.14

10. Complete the form at the right to reconcile the account.

Bank balance, $209.63
Check register balance, $151.55
Outstanding checks, $84.28
Outstanding deposit, $25.00
Service charge, $1.20

	Bank balance		
−	Outstanding checks		Check register balance
			− Service charges
+	Outstanding deposits		Corrected balance
	Corrected balance		

209.63
84.28
125.35
25.00
150.35

151.55
1.20
150.35

11. Erica borrowed $500 at 12.5% for 6 months. How much was due at the end of the 6 months?
$531.25

12. You deposit $300 in a savings account at 8% compounded semi-annually. If you make no withdrawals, how much will be in your account at the end of 1 year?
$324.48

13. $c = na - b$

Find the cost of credit (c) if the number of payments (n) is 14, the amount of each payment (a) is $12.50, and the amount borrowed (b) is $160. $15

14. $r = \frac{24c}{b(n+1)}$

Find the annual percentage (r) for the money borrowed in exercise 13. 15%

15. Find the finance charge and the new balance for the following credit-card account if the rate is 1.5% of the average daily balance: June 1: unpaid balance of $175.86
June 15: payment of $50
$2.24; $128.10

MANAGING PERSONAL FINANCES

	INCOME	
1	Salary (Net)	
2	Other	
	TOTAL INCOME	
	OUTGO	
3	Food	
4	Clothing	1
	Laundry, Cleaning, etc.	
	Rent or Mortgage	
	Electricity, Gas	
	ephone	
	ing	
	hold Expense	
	ense	

The first step toward managing your finances is to find how you spend your money. This requires keeping accurate records. One way is to use a chart such as the one below.

Example: High-school student's record of spending for a week

Day	Item	Income	Expense	Cash on hand
	left from last week			$ 4.82
Sun.	allowance	$35.00		39.82
Mon.	bus fare & lunch		$2.50	37.32
	school supplies		0.90	36.42
Tues.	bus fare & lunch		2.75	33.67
Wed.	bus fare & lunch		2.50	31.17
	clothing		8.42	22.75
	earnings	10.00		32.75
Thurs.	bus fare & lunch		2.50	30.25
	phonograph record		8.98	21.27
Fri.	bus fare & lunch		4.00	17.27
	entertainment & food		6.45	10.82
Sat.	movie		4.50	6.32

Each income amount is added to the cash on hand. Each expense is subtracted. The cash-on-hand column tells you how much money you have at any given time.

EXERCISES

1. On the chart, _income_ is added to the cash on hand.

2. On the chart, _expenses_ are subtracted from the cash on hand.

3. What was the total income for the week? $45

4. How much was spent on clothing? $8.42

312

Kenji Kerins

Find each amount of cash on hand.

5.

Day	Item	Income	Expense	Cash on hand
	left from last week			$23.60
Mon.	lunch		$ 1.25	22.35
	bicycle tire repair		6.90	15.45
Tues.	lunch		1.95	13.50
	gift		9.00	4.50
Wed.	lunch		1.27	3.23
	extra earnings	$ 6.00		9.23
Thurs.	lunch		1.98	7.25
Fri.	lunch		2.16	5.09
	paycheck	52.80		57.89
Sat.	deposit to savings		25.00	32.89 ← Checkpoint: If you get the number shown, your work up to this point is correct.
	dentist bill		25.00	7.89

6.

Day	Item	Income	Expense	Cash on hand
	left from last week			$24.05
Fri.	lunch		$ 3.45	20.60
	paycheck	$187.50		208.10
Sat.	groceries		31.18	176.92
	food & entertainment		22.40	154.52
Mon.	lunch		3.95	150.57
Tues.	lunch		4.21	146.36
	deposit to savings		40.00	106.36
Wed.	lunch		4.82	101.54
Thurs.	lunch		4.15	97.39 ← Checkpoint
	telephone bill		22.50	74.89

7. Week	Item	Income	Expense	Cash on hand
	previous month's balance			$589.72
First week	rent		$450.00	139.72
	groceries		96.50	43.22
	gasoline & bus fares		36.00	7.22
	paycheck (two weeks)	$904.50		911.72
	recreation		20.00	891.72
Second week	groceries		112.15	779.57
	clothing		56.89	722.68
	doctor bill		40.00	682.68
	gasoline & bus fares		36.00	646.68
	car payment		156.18	490.50
	personal needs		97.20	393.30 ← Checkpoint

8. Week	Item	Income	Expense	Cash on hand
	left from first two weeks			$393.30
Third week	groceries		$ 98.31	294.99
	gas, electric, telephone		152.65	142.34
	insurance premium		74.90	67.44
	paycheck (two weeks)	$904.50		971.94
	car repairs		62.80	909.14
	gasoline & bus fares		25.00	884.14
Fourth week	groceries		121.60	762.54
	personal needs		59.89	702.65
	gasoline & bus fares		40.00	662.65
	clothing		52.64	610.01
	gifts & recreation		67.38	542.63 ← Checkpoint

Use the charts in exercises 7 and 8.

9. What was the family's income for the whole month? $1809

10. How much did the family spend on clothing for the entire month? $109.53

11. Find the total they spent on groceries. $428.56

12. Find the total they spent on transportation (car payments, gasoline, repairs, bus fares). $355.98

13. How much money did they have at the beginning of the month (previous month's balance)? How much did they have at the end of the month? $589.72; $542.63

14. Did they spend more or less than their income during the month? How much *more* or less? more; $47.09

Possible answers are given for exercises 1-2.

1. Some expenses are fixed—the same each month (such as rent). Other expenses are variable—change from month to month (such as recreation). Look over the expenses on the charts on page 314. Which expenses are fixed and which are variable?

Fixed: rent, car payment, insurance

Variable: groceries, gasoline & bus fares, clothing, recreation, doctor bill, personal needs, utilities, car repairs, gifts

2. If income does not match expenses, something needs to be changed. How might income be changed? How can variable expenses be changed? How can fixed expenses be changed? Income: work overtime, get second job; Variable: reduce unnecessary expenses, look for sales; Fixed: get less expensive housing, buy smaller car

Reduce to lowest terms.

Skill	Page
32	493

1. $\frac{3}{18}$ $\frac{1}{6}$ **2.** $\frac{4}{36}$ $\frac{1}{9}$ **3.** $\frac{4}{14}$ $\frac{2}{7}$ **4.** $\frac{6}{16}$ $\frac{3}{8}$

5. $\frac{8}{18}$ $\frac{4}{9}$ **6.** $\frac{6}{30}$ $\frac{1}{5}$ **7.** $\frac{3}{21}$ $\frac{1}{7}$ **8.** $\frac{10}{25}$ $\frac{2}{5}$

After keeping records for a time, you will notice that most of your expenses fall into certain categories, or areas, such as the following:

Food   groceries, beverages, meals out, etc.
Housing   rent, mortgage payments, property taxes, etc.
Clothing   clothes, cleaning, mending, etc.
Personal   allowances, medical, dental, education, etc.
Transportation   car payments, bus fares, parking, etc.
Recreation   movies, parties, vacations, etc.
Savings   savings accounts or other investments
Other   whatever is not included elsewhere

This is not the only way expenses can be grouped. Different people will spend their money in different ways. But, no matter how you arrange your expenses, the next step is to find how much of your income, *on the average*, is spent on each area. This can be done with percents.

Example: Cathy has an average weekly income of $30. She usually spends her income as shown below. Find the percent of her income she spends on each category.

food	$6
clothing	5
recreation	7
personal	3
savings	6
other	3
total	$30

To find a percent, you can use a proportion.

$6 out of $30 is spent on food. That is the same as how much out of $100?

$$\frac{6}{30} = \frac{x}{100}$$

$600 = 30x$ **Find the cross products.**

$20 = x$ **Divide both sides by 30.**

20% of the total income is spent on food.

The following chart shows all the percents worked out:

Category	Average amount	Proportion used	Percent
food	$6	$\frac{6}{30} = \frac{x}{100}$	20%
clothing	5	$\frac{5}{30} = \frac{x}{100}$	$16\frac{2}{3}\%$
recreation	7	$\frac{7}{30} = \frac{x}{100}$	$23\frac{1}{3}\%$
personal	3	$\frac{3}{30} = \frac{x}{100}$	10%
savings	6	$\frac{6}{30} = \frac{x}{100}$	20%
other	3	$\frac{3}{30} = \frac{x}{100}$	10%
totals	$30		100%

Notice that the sum of the percents is 100%. This is always true and allows you to check your work easily.

Shortcut for solving proportions:

Sometimes you can make a proportion easier to solve by reducing one of the sides.

$$\frac{6}{30} = \frac{x}{100}$$

$\frac{1}{5} = \frac{x}{100}$ **Reduce $\frac{6}{30}$ to $\frac{1}{5}$.**

$100 = 5x$ **Find the cross products.**

$20 = x$ **Divide by 5.**

Compare this solution to the one on the opposite page.

EXERCISES

What proportion can be used to find each percent?

1. $5 out of $20 $\frac{5}{20} = \frac{x}{100}$

2. $9 out of $36 $\frac{9}{36} = \frac{x}{100}$

3. $8 out of $32 $\frac{8}{32} = \frac{x}{100}$

4. $7 out of $35 $\frac{7}{35} = \frac{x}{100}$

5. $12 out of $60 $\frac{12}{60} = \frac{x}{100}$

6. $18 out of $72 $\frac{18}{72} = \frac{x}{100}$

7. $45 out of $225 $\frac{45}{225} = \frac{x}{100}$

8. $84 out of $112 $\frac{84}{112} = \frac{x}{100}$

Find the percent spent out of each income.

9. $14 out of $70 (Use $\frac{14}{70} = \frac{x}{100}$ and reduce $\frac{14}{70}$.) 20%

10. $15 out of $60 (Use $\frac{15}{60} = \frac{x}{100}$ and reduce $\frac{15}{60}$.) 25%

11. $16 out of $80 20%

12. $7 out of $70 10%

13. $125 out of $500 25%

14. $120 out of $600 20%

Copy and complete each chart. Where possible, reduce one side of the proportion to make it easier to solve.

15. High-school student

Category	Amount	Proportion	Percent		
				$\frac{15}{60} = \frac{x}{100}$	
food	$12	$\frac{12}{60} = \frac{x}{100}$	20%		
clothing	15	_____	25%	$\frac{9}{60} = \frac{x}{100}$	
personal	9	_____	15%		
recreation	15	_____	25%	$\frac{15}{60} = \frac{x}{100}$	
savings	6	_____	10%	$\frac{6}{60} = \frac{x}{100}$	
other	3	_____	5%		
totals	$60		100%	$\frac{3}{60} = \frac{x}{100}$	

16. Single working person

Category	Amount	Proportion	Percent		
				$\frac{40}{250} = \frac{x}{100}$	
rent	$75	$\frac{75}{250} = \frac{x}{100}$	30%		
food	40	_____	16%	$\frac{25}{250} = \frac{x}{100}$	
transportation	25	_____	10%		
personal	30	_____	12%	$\frac{30}{250} = \frac{x}{100}$	
recreation	25	_____	10%	$\frac{25}{250} = \frac{x}{100}$	
savings	40	_____	16%		
other	15	_____	6%	$\frac{40}{250} = \frac{x}{100}$	
totals	$250		100%	$\frac{15}{250} = \frac{x}{100}$	

17. Family of three

Category	Amount	Proportion	Percent
rent	$420	_____	30%
food	350	_____	25%
clothing	140	_____	10%
savings	112	_____	8%
recreation	140	_____	10%
personal	70	_____	5%
other	168	_____	12%
totals	$1400		100%

$$\frac{420}{1400} = \frac{x}{100}$$

$$\frac{350}{1400} = \frac{x}{100}$$

$$\frac{140}{1400} = \frac{x}{100}$$

$$\frac{112}{1400} = \frac{x}{100}$$

$$\frac{140}{1400} = \frac{x}{100}$$

$$\frac{70}{1400} = \frac{x}{100}$$

$$\frac{168}{1400} = \frac{x}{100}$$

18. Family of five

Category	Amount	Proportion	Percent
housing	$500	_____	25%
food	500	_____	25%
transportation	360	_____	18%
savings	100	_____	5%
clothing	200	_____	10%
entertainment	140	_____	7%
other	200	_____	10%
totals	$2000		100%

$$\frac{500}{2000} = \frac{x}{100}$$

$$\frac{500}{2000} = \frac{x}{100}$$

$$\frac{360}{2000} = \frac{x}{100}$$

$$\frac{100}{2000} = \frac{x}{100}$$

$$\frac{200}{2000} = \frac{x}{100}$$

$$\frac{140}{2000} = \frac{x}{100}$$

$$\frac{200}{2000} = \frac{x}{100}$$

TALK IT OVER

Possible answers are given for exercises 1-4.

1. Why must records be kept over a period of time to estimate your average expenses? some expenses occur at irregular intervals, prices change

2. Do you suppose that the percent of income spent on each category would change with the amount of income? How? What other factors might determine the part of income that is spent on each category? Yes; percent may decrease for fixed expenses, but may increase for variable expenses; family size and age

3. Is a written plan necessary for good money management? Why? Yes; It helps to control expenses and to plan future income needs.

4. Do you think it is a good idea to save a specified amount each week or month? Why? Yes; for emergencies, for security

Once you have found how much of your income, *on the average,* is spent on each category, you might decide something needs to be changed. Here are some questions you might ask.

Are there some categories on which I should spend a smaller percent, such as clothing or recreation?

Are there some categories on which I should spend a larger percent, such as savings?

Should I make allowance for expenses that come up less often than once a month, such as insurance payments or large purchases (stereos, furniture, etc.)?

Should I make allowance for unexpected expenses, such as repairs or medical expenses?

The answers to these questions may affect your **budget,** your plan for spending your income. The important thing is once you decide how much of your income to spend on each category, stick to it.

Example: After studying the records of spending he had been keeping for a while, Bob decided on the percents shown below. If his weekly income is $150, how much can he spend for food?

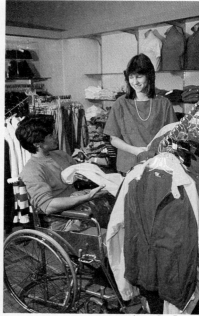
Jacqueline Durand

food	30%
clothing	18%
recreation	20%
personal	12%
savings	6%
other	14%
total	100%

By proportion

$$\frac{x}{150} = \frac{30}{100}$$

$$\frac{x}{150} = \frac{3}{10}$$

$$10x = 450$$

$$x = 45$$

By multiplication

$$30\% = \frac{30}{100} = 0.30$$

$$0.30 \times 150 = 45$$

$45 can be spent on food.

The following chart shows all the amounts worked out:

Category	Budget percent	Amount to be spent
food	30%	$45.00
clothing	18%	27.00
recreation	20%	30.00
personal	12%	18.00
savings	6%	9.00
other	14%	21.00
totals	100%	$150.00

Jacqueline Durand

Notice that the sum of the percents is 100%. That should always be true in a budget.

Notice also that the sum of the amounts is equal to the total income. You can check your work by adding the separate amounts to see if the sum is the total income.

EXERCISES

1. A plan for spending your income is called a <u>budget</u>.

2. A budget shows how much of your income can be spent on each <u>category</u>.

Use the chart at the top of this page.

6. $\frac{x}{150} = \frac{6}{100}$, $\frac{x}{150} = \frac{3}{50}$, $50x = 450$, $x = 9$

3. Show that the recreation amount is $30 by solving a proportion. $\left(\frac{x}{150} = \frac{20}{100}\right)$
$\frac{x}{150} = \frac{1}{5}$, $5x = 150$, $x = 30$

4. Show that the recreation amount is $30 by using multiplication. $(0.20 \times \$150)$
$0.20 \times 150 = 30.00$

5. Show that the clothing amount is $27 by multiplying. $0.18 \times 150 = 27.00$

6. Show that the savings amount is $9 by using a proportion. See answer above.

7. Show that the amount for personal needs is $18 by using a proportion.
$\frac{x}{150} = \frac{12}{100}$, $\frac{x}{150} = \frac{3}{25}$, $25x = 450$, $x = 18$

8. Show that the amount for other expenses is $21 by using multiplication.
$0.14 \times 150 = 21.00$

Copy and complete the chart.

9. A high-school student

Category	Percent	Amount
food	24%	$12
clothing	20%	$10
savings	8%	$ 4
recreation	22%	$11
personal	16%	$ 8
other	10%	$ 5
totals	100%	$50.00

10. A single working person

Category	Percent	Amount
housing	25%	$225
food	25%	$225
entertainment	18%	$162
clothing	15%	$135
other	17%	$153
totals	100%	$900.00

Frank Siteman/Taurus

11. A family of four

Category	Percent	Amount
rent	22%	$308
food	28%	$392
transportation	14%	$196
savings	5%	$ 70
entertainment	8%	$112
personal	5%	$ 70
clothing	14%	$196
other	4%	$ 56
totals	100%	$1400.00

12. A family of three

Category	Percent	Amount
housing	20%	$300
food	22%	$330
savings	10%	$150
clothing	13%	$195
transportation	10%	$150
recreation	12%	$180
personal	5%	$ 75
other	8%	$120
totals	100%	$1500.00

13. Suppose the sum of the percents is less than 100%. Would you be planning to spend less than or more than your total income? less than

14. In exercise 12, suppose you find the amount for "Personal" first. Then what would be an easy way to find the amounts for "housing," "savings," and "transportation"? Multiply by 4 for "housing"; Multiply by 2 for "savings" and "transportation."

15. In exercise 12, how much is 1% of the total amount? Knowing that, what is an easy way to find any of the amounts? $15; Multiply 15 by the number of percent.

16. Name some expenses that you would include under "other." medical, insurance, gifts, etc.

17. What might be some advantages and some disadvantages of an annual budget over a monthly budget?
Advantages: helps with long-term goals, such as buying a car or a home
Disadvantages: doesn't take into account emergency spending or changes in spending

---

TALK IT OVER

Possible answers are given for exercises 1-7.

1. Why is a budget necessary for good money management? because it helps you to plan your expenses and to keep within your income

2. How can budgeting help you to avoid getting into financial difficulties? by helping you avoid overspending and by helping you be sure of enough money for future spending

3. How might the amount of monthly income affect your budget? by affecting the percents allotted to fixed and variable expenses

4. Other than income, what might influence the way you budget your money? age, number and age of children, occupation, area where you live

5. What are some goals a young person might have that could more easily be achieved by using a budgeting plan? education; large purchases such as a car, a stereo

6. What are some goals a young married couple might have to include in their budget? saving for a house, children's education

7. What do you consider the most important rule for successful budgeting? Why? making and following a reasonable budget plan; prevents indebtedness

A check is an order to your bank to pay from your account the amount on the check. When you open a checking account, you are provided with both checks and a check register. The check register is used to keep track of the balance in your account. It works much like the records of expenses in Section 8.1.

Example:

to whom the check is payable

date

check number

amount of money in numerals

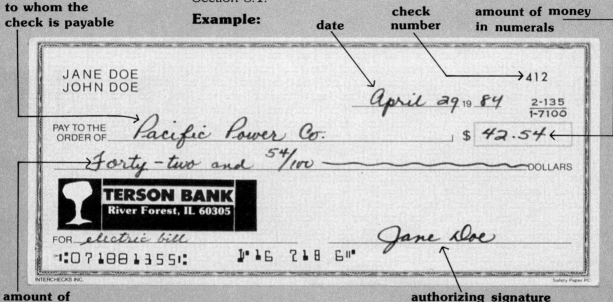

amount of money in words

authorizing signature

Jane Doe wrote the check above to pay an electric bill for $42.54. The check is recorded as the last entry in her check register for the last part of April.

Check No.	Date	Description	Amount (−)		Deposit (+)		Balance	
							440	35
408	4-18	To D & K Management Co.	375	00			-375	00
		For Rent					265	35
409	4-23	To Berg's Dept. Store	56	20			-56	20
		For Clothing					209	15
410	4-23	To Avenue National Bank	148	27			-148	27
		For Car payment					60	88
	4-26	To			450	00	+450	00
		For					510	88
411	4-27	To Hansen's Market	31	18			-31	18
		For Groceries					479	70
412	4-29	To Pacific Power Co.	42	54			-42	54
		For Electric Bill					437	16
		To						
		For						

Ed Hoppe Photography

Notice that the amount of each check is *subtracted from* the balance. Each deposit is *added to* the balance.

EXERCISES

1. In a check register, the amount of a check is ___subtracted___ from the balance.

2. In a check register, a deposit is ___added___ to the balance.

Complete each section of a check register by finding each balance.

3.

Check No.	Date	Description	Amount (−)	Deposit (+)	Balance 40 62	
161	9-22	To Bell Telephone Co.	28 46		−28 46	
		For Telephone bill				
	9-23	To		227 00	+227 00	12.16
		For				239.16
162	9-25	To A + B Garage	49 00		−49 00	
		For Auto repair				190.16
163	9-25	To Safety Insurance Co.	78 21		−78 21	
		For Insurance premium				111.95
164	9-26	To Cash	50 00		−50 00	
		For				61.95
165	9-30	To Olson's Market	26 45		−26 45	
		For Groceries				35.50
166	9-30	To History Magazine	20 00		−20 00	
		For 1-year subscription			15 50	

4.

Check No.	Date	Description	Amount (−)	Deposit (+)	Balance 204 50	
237	3-19	To Consolidated Edison	36 17		−36 17	
		For Electric bill				168.33
238	3-20	To B & G Market	42 58		−42 58	
		For Groceries				125.75
239	3-20	To Peoples Gas Co.	24 80		−24 80	
		For Gas bill				100.95
	3-22	To		556 16	+556 16	
		For				657.11
240	3-24	To Internal Revenue Service	58 00		−58 00	
		For Taxes				599.11
241	3-28	To E. Whitehouse	425 00		−425 00	
		For Rent				174.11
242	3-30	To Sherman St. Garage	70 00		−70 00	
		For Monthly parking			104 11	

```
┌─────────────────────────────────────────────────────────────┐
│                                                             │
│   YOUR NAME                              No. _____    │
│                                                             │
│   PAY                        _____ 19 _____     │
│   TO THE                                                    │
│   ORDER OF _____  $ _____   │
│                                                             │
│   _____ DOLLARS       │
│   YOUR BANK                                                  │
│                                                             │
│                              _____  │
│                                                             │
└─────────────────────────────────────────────────────────────┘
```

For each exercise use 3 copies of the check above and 1 copy of a check register like those on the previous page. Then fill in the checks to pay the bills. Use today's date and your own signature. Finally, fill in the check register and find the final balance.

5. Starting balance: $426.50

  Check No. 511:   Commonwealth Edison, $32.84, electric bill

         512:    R. Young & Co., $36.18, shoes

         513:    Elkhorn Realty Co., $268.00, rent
                      final balance: $89.48

6. Starting balance: $207.18

  Check No. 601:   Mogul Oil Co., $38.54, gasoline credit card

         602:    Bell Telephone Co., $11.56, telephone bill

         603:    Richard J. Wren, D.D.S., $75.00, dentist
                      final balance: $82.08

For each exercise use a copy of a check register and fill it in. Find each final balance.

7. Starting balance: $426.42

  Check No. 739:   Kobelt Travel Agency, $295.37, airline tickets

         740:    North Shore Ski Club, $15.00, club dues

         741:    Wilson's Gift Shop, $8.76, stationery

  Deposit paycheck: $487.15

         742:    Bartok's Appliance Store, $568.14, refrigerator
                      final balance: $26.30

8. Starting balance: $246.50

Check No. 819:   Book-of-the-Month Club, $11.28, books

820:   Bockner's Pharmacy, $5.85, medicine

Deposit: $164.18

821:   State National Bank, $150.00, deposit to savings

822:   Clausen's Market, $46.62, groceries

final balance: $196.93

9. Starting balance: $189.47

Check No. 946:   Columbia Hospital, $65.00, X rays

947:   Neary's Florist Shop, $16.82, plants

948:   Bell Telephone Co., $21.24, telephone bill

949:   March of Dimes, $25.00, donation

Deposit: $212.60

950:   Federal Savings & Loan, $100.00, savings

final balance: $174.01

10. Starting balance: $386.12

Check No. 156:   Marino's Camera Store, $16.95, developing pictures

157:   Arkin's Garage, $24.00, car repair

158:   T. Pace & Co., $206.88, clothing

Deposit: $347.90

159:   Maslak Carpet Co., $168.00, rug

160:   American Realty Co., $220.00, rent

final balance: $98.19

Jacqueline Durand

Don Lansu

Once a month the bank sends you a statement of your checking account. This statement shows the amount of each deposit and the amount paid out of your account for each check. The bank may also return the paid checks, called **canceled checks.**

Each month it is necessary to *reconcile* the account. That is, you must account for any difference between the balance on the bank statement and the balance in your check register.

How can these two balances be different?

The **bank statement** may have items *not* in your check register, such as service charges or charges for an overdrawn account.

Your **check register** may have items *not* on the bank statement, such as checks you have written but which have not yet reached the bank and are therefore not yet subtracted from your balance.

Example: Here is the Does' bank statement for April.

Compare this bank statement to the part of the check register on page 324.

452.04	Beginning balance
953.64	Total checks
1037.50	Total deposits
1.50	Service charge
534.40	Ending balance

TERSON BANK

Account number 1 16 718 6

Date   APRIL 30

JOHN & JANE DOE
123 W. 45TH ST.
CITY, STATE

Look at the dates on the check register and then at the dates for the same checks on the bank statement. It takes time for a check you write to reach the bank.

Notice also that two checks (409 and 412) did not get to the bank by April 30.

CHECKS PAID			DEPOSITS	
NO.	DATE	AMOUNT	DATE	AMOUNT
398	4–02	75.00	4–05	387.50
399	4–03	4.65	4–12	200.00
400	4–06	42.33	4–26	450.00
401	4–06	38.43		
402	4–09	14.12		
403	4–13	106.76		
404	4–16	11.56		
405	4–17	32.18		
406	4–17	50.00		
407	4–21	24.16		
408	4–23	375.00		
410	4–26	148.27		
411	4–30	31.18		

When you compare the bank statement with the check register on page 324, you will see that two checks written toward the end of the month have not yet been paid by the bank. Such checks are called **outstanding checks.**

Find outstanding checks from the check register.

No. 409 **56.20**
No. 412 **42.54**
          98.74 ← total of outstanding checks

To the bank statement:

include whatever is in the check register that is not on the bank statement.
↓

534.40	Bank balance
− 98.74	Subtract total of outstanding checks.
435.66	
+ 0	Add total of outstanding deposits.
435.66	Corrected balance

To the check register:

include whatever is on the bank statement that is not in the check register.
↓

437.16	Check register balance
− 1.50	Subtract any service charges
435.66	Corrected balance

A form like this is usually provided on the back of the bank statement.

Make sure you know where all the information written on it can be found.

The two corrected balances should be the same. If they are not, then either you or the bank has made an error. Report errors made by the bank as soon as possible. Always adjust your check register to show the corrected balance. The Does should subtract 1.50 from the balance in their check register.

EXERCISES

1. Checks paid by the bank from your account and returned to you are called _____ checks. canceled

2. Checks you have written but that do not show as paid on the bank statement are called _____ checks. outstanding

3. The total of outstanding checks should be _____ from the balance shown on the _____. subtracted; bank statement

4. Service charges should be _____ from the balance shown in your _____. subtracted; check register

329

Copy and complete each form to reconcile the account.

5.

264.12	Bank balance
– 98.60	Subtract total of outstanding checks.
165.52	
+ 0	Add total of out-standing deposits.
165.52	Corrected balance

166.72	Check register balance
– 1.20	Subtract any service charges.
165.52	Corrected balance

6.

174.20	Bank balance
– 56.35	Subtract total of outstanding checks.
117.85	
+50.00	Add total of out-standing deposits.
167.85	Corrected balance

170.35	Check register balance
– 2.50	Subtract any service charges.
167.85	Corrected balance

For each exercise make a form like the ones above and use it to reconcile the account.

7. Bank balance: $328.57; check register balance: $207.94; total of outstanding checks:$147.43; service charge: $1.80; total of outstanding deposits: $25.00.

corrected balance:
$206.14

8. Bank balance: $216.90; check register balance: $235.21; total of outstanding checks: $58.19; service charge: $1.50; total of outstanding deposits: $75.00.

corrected balance:
$233.71

9. Bank balance: $278.25; check register balance: $383.66; outstanding checks: $35.00, $14.23, $22.56; service charge: $2.20; outstanding deposit: $175.00.

corrected balance:
$381.46

10. Bank balance: $309.78; check register balance: $287.76; outstanding checks: $14.95, $46.27, $12.50; service charge: $1.70; outstanding deposit: $50.00.

corrected balance:
$286.06

For each exercise make a form like those on the opposite page. Then use the given bank statement and the correct check register on page 325 to find all the information needed to reconcile the account.

11. This bank statement goes with the check register in exercise 3 on page 325.

BANK STATEMENT

		CHECKS PAID			DEPOSITS	
		No.	Date	Amount	Date	Amount
35.46	Beginning balance	155	9–3	8.20	9–5	200.00
400.44	Total checks	156	9–6	14.91	9–7	78.14
505.14	Total deposits	157	9–7	190.00	9–23	227.00
1.20	Service charge	158	9–7	3.12		
		159	9–16	49.60		
138.96	Ending balance	160	9–22	7.15		
		161	9–26	28.46		
		162	9–29	49.00		
		164	9–30	50.00		

corrected balance: $14.30

12. This bank statement goes with the check register in exercise 4 on page 325.

BANK STATEMENT

		CHECKS PAID			DEPOSITS	
		No.	Date	Amount	Date	Amount
219.48	Beginning balance	232	3–4	34.20	3–8	256.16
774.89	Total checks	233	3–5	6.47	3–22	556.16
812.32	Total deposits	234	3–11	108.00		
2.40	Service charge	235	3–14	4.25		
		236	3–15	118.22		
254.51	Ending balance	237	3–27	36.17		
		238	3–27	42.58		
		241	3–31	425.00		

corrected balance: $101.71

Application 39 may be used at this time.

Computer Supplement, Disk 2, may be used at this time.

When you borrow money, you are using someone else's money. When you put money into a savings account, someone else is using your money. **Interest** is money paid for the use of money. The amount of money being used is the ***principal.*** The length of time the money is used is the ***term.***

interest = principal × rate × time (in years)

$$i = p \times r \times t \quad \text{or} \quad i = prt$$

The amount of money at the end of the term is the original principal plus the interest it earned in that term.

amount = principal + interest

$$A = p + i$$

Example 1: Tina borrowed $500 at 12% interest. She agreed to repay the principal plus the interest in 3 months. Find the amount due at that time.

Step 1: Find the interest.

$i = prt$

$i = 500 \times 12\% \times \frac{1}{4}$ 3 months $= \frac{1}{4}$ yr $= 0.25$ yr

$i = 500 \times 0.12 \times 0.25$ 12% $= 0.12$

$i = 15$

The interest is $15.

Step 2: Find the amount due.

$A = p + i$

$A = 500 + 15$

$A = 515$

The amount due is $515.

Example 2: Fred borrowed $420 to buy new appliances. He agreed to repay the loan in 60 days at an interest rate of $12\frac{1}{2}\%$. Find the amount due at that time.

Step 1: Find the interest.

$i = prt$

$i = 420 \times 0.125 \times \dfrac{60}{360}$

$i = 420 \times 0.125 \times \dfrac{1}{6}$

$i = 8.75$

When computing interest, 360 days is usually considered 1 year. So t is $\frac{60}{360}$, or $\frac{1}{6}$. Since $\frac{1}{6}$ cannot be given exactly as a decimal, use $\frac{1}{6}$.

The interest is $8.75.

Step 2: Find the amount due.

$A = p + i$

$A = 420 + 8.75$

$A = 428.75$

The amount due is $428.75.

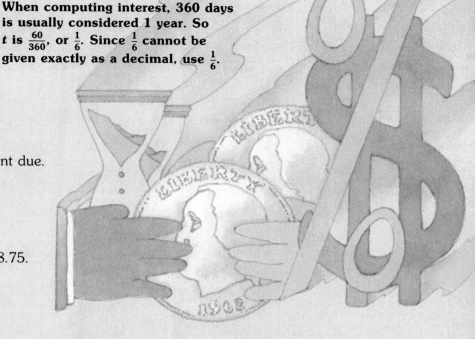

EXERCISES

Copy and complete the table.

	Principal	Interest rate	Term	Interest	Amount due
1.	$600	15%	6 months	$ 45	$ 645
2.	$250	$13\frac{1}{2}\%$	30 days	$ 2.81	$ 252.81
3.	$1200	$11\frac{1}{2}\%$	90 days	$ 34.50	$1234.50
4.	$2500	12%	1 year	$300	$2800
5.	$900	$10\frac{3}{4}\%$	3 months	$ 24.19	$ 924.19
6.	$1500	14%	9 months	$157.50	$1657.50

7. Edward borrowed $550 to purchase audio equipment for his band. He agreed to repay the loan in 45 days with $11\frac{3}{4}\%$ interest. Find the amount due in 45 days. $558.08

8. Susan planned to borrow $1200 to pay for a vacation. She will repay the loan in 6 months with 12.5% interest. Find the amount due in 6 months. $1275

9. Craig wanted to borrow $600 to pay some medical bills. He decided he could repay the loan in 60 days. If the interest rate was $11\frac{1}{2}$%, what was the amount due in 60 days? $611.50

10. Tiffany got a $1500 loan at an interest rate of $12\frac{3}{4}$% for 6 months. Find the amount due in 6 months. $1595.63

11. Laura borrowed $400 to pay a repair bill. She agreed to repay the loan in 30 days with 11% interest. What is the amount due in 30 days? $403.67

12. Kirsten borrowed $1200 to pay for her moving expenses to another city. She agreed to repay the loan in 1 year with 15% interest. What is the amount due in 1 year? $1380

13. Phil borrowed $875 for 90 days at 18% interest. What is the amount due in 90 days? $914.38

14. Tim bought a $300 savings certificate for 6 months at 10.5% interest. Find the amount of money Tim will get for the certificate at the end of 6 months. $315.75

15. Sally had $650 she did not need for another 90 days. So she deposited it in a savings account that paid 6% interest. How much money will be in her account at the end of 90 days? $659.75

16. Greg wanted to borrow $1000. First Bank would loan him the money for 6 months at $17\frac{1}{2}$% interest. Second Bank would loan him the money for 9 months at 16% interest. Which is the better deal for Greg? First Bank

17. Byron borrowed $550 for 30 days. At the end of 30 days he repaid the loan in the amount of $555.50. What was the rate of interest? 12%

8.7 | COMPOUND INTEREST

Juan put $700 in a savings account that paid 8% interest **compounded** quarterly. Find how much Juan had in his account at the end of 1 year.

Compounded quarterly means that interest is paid at the end of each quarter ($\frac{1}{4}$ year). The *amount* in the account at the end of the first quarter—the original principal plus the interest for the first quarter—becomes the *principal* for the second quarter. That process continues until 1 year has elapsed.

Example 1: Solve the problem at the top of the page. To do so, make a table like that below. Round the interest to the nearest cent.

Quarter	Principal	Interest $p \times r \times t$	Amount $p + i$
1	$700	$700 \times 0.08 \times 0.25 = $14	$714
2	$714	$714 \times 0.08 \times 0.25 = $14.28	$728.28
3	$728.28	$728.28 \times 0.08 \times 0.25 = $14.57	$742.85
4	$742.85	$742.85 \times 0.08 \times 0.25 = $14.86	$757.71

At the end of 1 year Juan has $757.71 in his account.

Compounded annually means that interest is paid yearly.

Compounded semiannually means that interest is paid every $\frac{1}{2}$ year.

Compounded quarterly means that interest is paid every $\frac{1}{4}$ year.

Compounded daily means that interest is paid every day.

Example 2: You buy a $450 savings certificate that pays 9.5% interest compounded semiannually. Find the value of the certificate at the end of 18 months.

To solve the problem, make a table. *Semiannually* means every 6 months, or $\frac{1}{2}$ year. So use 0.5 for *t*. Round the interest to the nearest cent.

	Principal	Interest $p \times r \times t$	Amount $p + i$
first 6 months	$450	$450 \times 0.095 \times 0.5 = \$21.38$	$471.38
second 6 months	$471.38	$471.38 \times 0.095 \times 0.5 = \$22.39$	$493.77
third 6 months	$493.77	$493.77 \times 0.095 \times 0.5 = \$23.45$	$517.22

The certificate will be worth $517.22 in 18 months.

EXERCISES

Find the amount for each of the following:

1. $600 at 6% compounded semiannually for 1 year $636.54

2. $1500 at 7.5% compounded annually for 3 years $1863.45

3. $3000 at 8% compounded quarterly for 1 year $3247.29

4. $4500 at 9.2% compounded semiannually for 18 months $5150

5. $2500 at 5.5% compounded annually for 4 years $3097.06

6. $800 at $6\frac{1}{4}$% compounded quarterly for 9 months $838.09

7. $550 at 7% compounded annually for 2 years $629.70

8. $1000 at 10% compounded semiannually for 2 years $1215.51

9. $10,000 at $15\frac{1}{2}$% compounded annually for 4 years $17,796.23

10. $20,000 at $10\frac{3}{4}$% compounded semiannually for 18 months $23,401.45

11. $15,000 at 9.5% compounded quarterly for 1 year $16,476.57

12. $25,000 at 14% compounded semiannually for 2 years $32,769.91

8.8 | COMPOUND INTEREST TABLE

As you learned in the preceding lesson, a lot of computation is needed to find compound interest. For many years, financial institutions have used compound interest tables, as shown below, to make the computation easier. Today, most financial institutions use computers to do the job. In fact, computers made it possible to have interest compounded daily.

COMPOUND INTEREST TABLE

Number of Periods	1.5%	2%	2.5%	3%	3.5%	4%	5%	6%	7%	8%
1	1.0150	1.0200	1.0250	1.0300	1.0350	1.0400	1.0500	1.0600	1.0700	1.0800
2	1.0302	1.0404	1.0506	1.0609	1.0712	1.0816	1.1025	1.1236	1.1449	1.1664
3	1.0457	1.0612	1.0769	1.0927	1.1087	1.1248	1.1576	1.1910	1.2250	1.2597
4	1.0614	1.0824	1.1038	1.1255	1.1475	1.1699	1.2155	1.2625	1.3108	1.3605
5	1.0773	1.1041	1.1314	1.1593	1.1877	1.2167	1.2763	1.3382	1.4026	1.4693
6	1.0934	1.1262	1.1597	1.1941	1.2293	1.2653	1.3401	1.4186	1.5007	1.5869
7	1.1098	1.1487	1.1887	1.2299	1.2723	1.3159	1.4071	1.5036	1.6058	1.7138
8	1.1265	1.1717	1.2184	1.2668	1.3168	1.3686	1.4775	1.5938	1.7182	1.8059
9	1.1434	1.1951	1.2489	1.3048	1.3629	1.4233	1.5513	1.6895	1.8385	1.9990
10	1.1605	1.2190	1.2801	1.3439	1.4106	1.4802	1.6289	1.7908	1.9672	2.1589
11	1.1779	1.2434	1.3121	1.3842	1.4600	1.5395	1.7103	1.8983	2.1049	2.3316
12	1.1956	1.2682	1.3449	1.4258	1.5111	1.6010	1.7959	2.0122	2.2522	2.5182
13	1.2136	1.2936	1.3785	1.4685	1.5640	1.6651	1.8856	2.1329	2.4098	2.7196
14	1.2318	1.3195	1.4130	1.5126	1.6187	1.7317	1.9799	2.2609	2.5785	2.9372
15	1.2502	1.3459	1.4483	1.5580	1.6753	1.8009	2.0789	2.3966	2.7590	3.1722
16	1.2690	1.3728	1.4845	1.6047	1.7340	1.8730	2.1829	2.5404	2.9522	3.4259
17	1.2880	1.4002	1.5216	1.6528	1.7947	1.9479	2.2920	2.6928	3.1588	3.7000
18	1.3073	1.4282	1.5597	1.7024	1.8575	2.0258	2.4066	2.8543	3.3799	3.9960
19	1.3270	1.4568	1.5987	1.7535	1.9225	2.1068	2.5270	3.0256	3.6165	4.3157
20	1.3469	1.4859	1.6386	1.8061	1.9898	2.1911	2.6533	3.2071	3.8697	4.6610

The table shows how much $1 will amount to in n years (periods) at various rates of interest compounded annually.

Example 1: $1 at 6% interest compounded annually will amount to $1.2625, or $1.26, in 4 years. (See red tint on table.)

Example 2: $200 at 6% interest compounded annually will amount to $200 \times \$1.2625$, or $252.50, in 4 years.

The table can also be used to find interest that is compounded more frequently than once a year.

Compounded semiannually: Use $\frac{1}{2}$ the interest rate and twice the number of interest periods.

Compounded quarterly: Use $\frac{1}{4}$ the interest rate and 4 times the number of interest periods.

Example 3: Find the amount for $450 at 8% compounded semiannually for 3 years.

Compounded semiannually
so use $\frac{1}{2}$ of 8%, or 4%
so there will be 6 interest periods in the 3 years

$1 at 4% for 6 periods will amount to $1.2653. (See blue tint in table on page 337.)

So $450 will amount to 450 × $1.2653, or $569.39, to the nearest cent.

EXERCISES

Use the table on page 337 to find the amount for each of the following:

	Principal	Rate	Compounded	Term	
1.	$100	6%	annually	7 years	$150.36
2.	$2000	8%	semiannually	3 years	$2530.60
3.	$1799	10%	quarterly	3 years	$2419.48
4.	$3200	7%	annually	10 years	$6295.04
5.	$850	6%	semiannually	4 years	$1076.78
6.	$1200	12%	quarterly	18 months	$1432.92
7.	$540	8%	quarterly	5 years	$802.39
8.	$3000	7%	annually	11 years	$6314.70
9.	$4000	6%	semiannually	4 years	$5067.20
10.	$900	12%	quarterly	3 years	$1283.22
11.	$6000	8%	annually	15 years	$19,033.20
12.	$750	8%	semiannually	5 years	$1110.15

CALCULATOR SKILL on page 534 may be used at this time.

8.9 | COST OF CREDIT

More and more people are making use of credit, a way to "buy now and pay later." You may already have used credit—borrowing money from a friend is a form of credit. Credit is often used through charge accounts or installment purchases.

Credit is essentially borrowing money—and it costs money to borrow money. So you should expect to pay for credit.

Example 1: Suppose you buy a $300 TV on credit. You agree to pay $27 a month for 12 months. Find the cost of this credit.

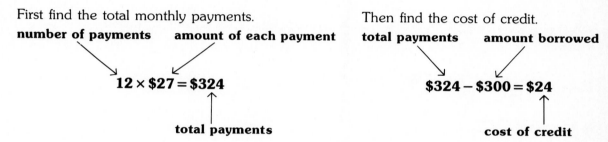

First find the total monthly payments.

number of payments   **amount of each payment**

$$12 \times \$27 = \$324$$

total payments

Then find the cost of credit.

total payments   **amount borrowed**

$$\$324 - \$300 = \$24$$

cost of credit

The work can be simplified by using this formula.

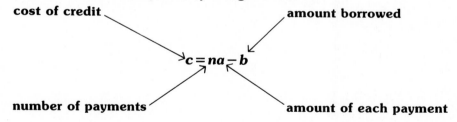

cost of credit   **amount borrowed**

$$c = na - b$$

number of payments   **amount of each payment**

Example 2: Solve the problem in Example 1 with the formula.

$c = na - b$

$c = 12(27) - 300$ **Substitute.**

$c = 324 - 300$ **Multiply.**

$c = 24$ **Subtract.**

The cost of credit is $24. You must pay $24 more to buy the TV on credit than if you paid cash.

Example 3: Suppose you buy the $300 TV under these conditions: a down payment of $60 and 12 monthly payments of $21.60 each. Find the cost of credit.

First find the amount borrowed.

purchase price **down payment**

$$\$300 - \$60 = \$240$$

amount borrowed

Now use the formula.

$$c = na - b$$
$$c = 12(21.60) - 240$$
$$c = 259.20 - 240$$
$$c = 19.20$$

The cost of credit is $19.20.

Notice that the cost of credit is less in this case. This is to be expected since less money is borrowed.

In general, the more money you borrow, the more the cost of credit. Also, the longer you take to pay, the more the credit will cost.

NOTE: By law, the dollar cost of credit, or finance charge, must be stated on all installment contracts. Read the entire installment contract before signing so that you will know what you are signing.

EXERCISES

1. To find the credit cost, multiply the ___ of payments by the ___ of each payment and then subtract the amount ___. number; amount; borrowed

2. Give two common ways in which credit is used. charge accounts and installment purchases

3. Tell what each letter stands for in $c = na - b$.
   See page 339.

4. If you make a down payment on an installment purchase, the amount borrowed is the ___ minus the ___.
   purchase price; down payment

Find the credit cost for each amount borrowed.

	b Amount borrowed	n Number of payments	a Monthly payment	$c = na - b$ Credit cost
5.	$380	6	$68	$ 28
6.	$550	10	$64	$ 90
7.	$490	9	$63	$ 77
8.	$180	6	$33.30	$ 19.80
9.	$400	12	$39.50	$ 74
10.	$500	12	$50.40	$104.80

First find the amount borrowed, then the credit cost.

	p Cash price	d Down payment	$b = p - d$ Amount borrowed	n Number of payments	a Monthly payment	$c = na - b$ Credit cost
11.	$100	$10	$ 90	3	$35.00	$ 15
12.	$150	$40	$110	2	$60.00	$ 10
13.	$375	$55	$320	6	$58.00	$ 28
14.	$375	$85	$290	6	$53.30	$ 29.80
15.	$800	$150	$650	12	$65.00	$130
16.	$800	$100	$700	12	$70.58	$146.96

Solve in the same way as exercises 11–16.

17. A $360 TV is purchased with a down payment of $45 and 12 monthly payments of $28.75. What is the credit cost? $30

18. A bicycle with a cash price of $220 is bought on credit. There is a down payment of $35 and 12 monthly payments of $18.30. Find the credit cost. $34.60

19. The easy-payment plan for a $449 stereo requires a down payment of $65 and 18 payments of $25.75. Find the credit cost. $79.50

20. A $329 sewing machine is bought on the installment plan. There is a down payment of $65 and 18 payments of $16.50. Find the credit cost. $33

21. The down payment on a refrigerator selling for $520 is $70. Then there are 24 payments of $22.50. What is the credit cost? $90

22. A $1980 motorcycle is going for $200 down and 24 monthly installments of $90.48. Find the credit cost. $391.52

SKILLS REFRESHER

Divide. Give answers as decimals.

				Skill	Page
1. $\frac{12}{200}$ 0.06	**2.** $\frac{36}{300}$ 0.12	**3.** $\frac{96}{800}$ 0.12	**4.** $\frac{91}{1300}$ 0.07	20	476

Reduce to lowest terms. Then multiply.

5. $\frac{4(6)}{9(16)}$ $\frac{1}{6}$	**6.** $\frac{10(12)}{16(15)}$ $\frac{1}{2}$	**7.** $\frac{24(12)}{80(15)}$ $\frac{6}{25}$	**8.** $\frac{24(26)}{200(13)}$ $\frac{6}{25}$	34	496

Change to a percent.

9. 0.145	**10.** 0.08	**11.** 0.125	**12.** 1.23	—	168
14.5%	8%	12.5%	123%		

8.10 | ANNUAL PERCENTAGE RATE

You should know the cost of credit for any installment purchase. You should also know the **annual percentage rate,** the annual interest rate for buying on credit.

Suppose you want to find the annual interest rate when buying the $300 TV in Example 1, page 339. Payments were $27 each for 12 months (1 year). The cost of credit was $24.

$24 out of $300 is $\frac{24}{300}$, or $\frac{8}{100}$, or 8% per year. Right?

Not really. If you borrowed $300 and made a single payment of $324 at the end of the year, you would be paying 8% interest. But on this credit purchase you would not have the $300 for a full year. When you make the first $27 payment at the end of the first month, you have the use of only $273. After two months you would have the use of only $246, and so on. So the annual interest rate will be greater than 8%.

You can use the following formula to find the annual percentage rate for any monthly payment plan:

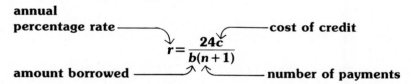

annual percentage rate ⟶   cost of credit

$$r = \frac{24c}{b(n+1)}$$

amount borrowed   **number of payments**

Example 1: Find the annual percentage rate for the TV problem above.

$r = \dfrac{24c}{b(n+1)}$

$r = \dfrac{24(24)}{300(12+1)}$ **Substitute.**

$r = \dfrac{24(24)}{300(13)}$ **Add (in parentheses).**

$r = \dfrac{576}{3900}$ **Multiply.**

$r = 0.148$ **Divide. Round to nearest thousandth.**

The annual percentage rate is 14.8%.

Example 2: A $400 stereo is bought on credit. There are 18 monthly payments. The cost of credit is $57. Find the annual percentage rate.

$$r = \frac{24c}{b(n+1)}$$

$$r = \frac{24(57)}{400(18+1)} \quad \textbf{Substitute.}$$

$$r = \frac{24(57)}{400(19)} \quad \textbf{Add (in parentheses).}$$

$$r = \frac{1368}{7600} \quad \textbf{Multiply.}$$

$$r = 0.18 \quad \textbf{Divide.}$$

The annual percentage rate is 18%.

Another way to solve the equation is to *reduce* before doing the multiplication.

$$r = \frac{24(\overset{3}{\cancel{57}})}{400(\cancel{19})} \quad \textbf{Divide 19 and 57 by 19.}$$

$$r = \frac{\overset{6}{\cancel{24}}(\overset{3}{\cancel{57}})}{\underset{100}{\cancel{400}}(\underset{1}{\cancel{19}})} \quad \textbf{Divide 24 and 400 by 4.}$$

$$r = \frac{18}{100}, \text{ or } 18\%$$

Why are 24 and 400 divided by 4 when it is possible to divide by a larger number? so that the denominator will be 100

NOTE: Like the dollar cost of credit, the annual percentage rate must, by law, be stated on all installment contracts.

EXERCISES

1. The annual percentage rate is the <u>annual</u> interest rate you must pay for credit.

2. Explain how to change a decimal to a percent. Move the decimal point 2 places to the right and insert the % sign.

3. Tell what each letter stands for in $r = \frac{24c}{b(n+1)}$. See page 343.

4. In Section 8.8 you found the cost of credit as an amount of money. In this section you find the cost of credit as a _____. percent

344

Find each annual percentage rate. Reduce whenever possible before multiplying.

	b Amount borrowed	n Number of payments	c Credit cost	$r = \dfrac{24c}{b(n+1)}$ Rate
5.	$200	14	$25	20%
6.	$300	12	$26	16%
7.	$400	12	$39	18%
8.	$500	15	$60	18%

First find the dollar cost of credit as you did in Section 8.9. Then find the annual percentage rate.

	b Amount borrowed	n Number of payments	a Monthly payment	$c = na - b$ Credit cost	$r = \dfrac{24c}{b(n+1)}$ Rate
9.	$300	15	$22	$30	15%
10.	$700	14	$55	$70	16%
11.	$600	12	$53.25	$39	12%
12.	$400	12	$35.50	$26	12%

First find the amount borrowed. Then find the dollar cost of credit. Finally find the annual percentage rate.

	Cash price	Down payment	Amount borrowed	Number of payments	Monthly payment	Credit cost	$r = \dfrac{24c}{b(n+1)}$ Rate
13.	$345	$45	$300	12	$28.25	$39	24%
14.	$459	$59	$400	16	$29.25	$68	24%
15.	$244	$94	$150	15	$11.20	$18	18%
16.	$355	$75	$280	14	$22.00	$28	16%
17.	$528	$48	$480	14	$37.95	$51.30	17.1%

18. A guitar is on sale for $170. If it is bought on the installment plan, there is a down payment of $30 and 14 monthly payments of $11 each. Find the dollar cost of credit and the annual percentage rate. $14; 16%

19. A 10-speed bicycle is on sale for $129. If it is bought on an installment plan, there is a down payment of $29 and 6 monthly payments of $17.60. Find both the dollar cost of credit and the annual percentage rate.
$5.60; 19.2%

Brent Jones

20. Nora bought a pair of skis on credit for $155. She made a down payment of $25 and then paid $15.60 a month for 9 months. What was the cost of credit? What was the annual percentage rate? $10.40; 19.2%

21. Mike bought a $388 amplifier on an easy-payment plan. The down payment was $52 and the 12 monthly payments were each $30.73. What was the cost of credit? What was the annual percentage rate? $32.76; 18%

22. A $339 microwave oven is bought on credit with a $51 down payment. There are 12 monthly payments of $26.47 each. Find both the cost of credit and the annual percentage rate.
$29.64; 19%

23. Rather than use the monthly payment plan in exercise 22, suppose you borrow $288 from a bank at 10% for 1 year. With the $288, and the $51 you have, you can pay cash for the oven. Would this plan save you money? Yes

24. Jean wants to buy a $650 sofa for her living room. She is considering two plans for paying for the sofa.

a. Make a down payment of $150 and 10 monthly payments of $54 each.

b. Borrow $500 from the bank at 12% interest for 10 months. Then pay cash for the sofa.

Which plan is less expensive? How much less will that plan cost? plan a; $10 less

What is the annual percentage rate for plan **a**? (Round to the nearest tenth of a percent.) 17.5%

In primitive times a farmer who had extra grain might trade with a hunter who had extra meat. Then each of them could have some meat and some grain. The farmer might also trade with a potter, giving grain in exchange for clay pots. But what if the potter wanted meat instead of grain? Then the farmer would have to trade more grain with the hunter to get the meat to trade for the pots. Things could become even more complicated if the farmer also wanted goods such as clothing or tools.

To simplify things, some object that everyone valued was needed. The farmer and everyone else could trade one or more of these objects for whatever goods they wanted. Money is such an object.

Today we think of money as metal coins or paper bills. In different societies, "money" has meant objects such as cattle, rings, or fish. Here is a list of other moneys.

Wampum, strings of beads made from polished shells, was used by North American Indians.

Whale teeth were used in the Fiji Islands.

Iron bars, often formed as spearheads or knives, were used in Africa.

Lumps of salt were used to pay Roman soldiers. A soldier who did not earn his pay was "not worth his salt."

Feathers of jungle birds were glued to a rope coil and used in the Santa Cruz Islands.

Coconuts were used in the Nicobar Islands.

Playing cards with the governor's signature on the back were used by early Canadian colonists.

Cowry shells were used in both Africa and the South Pacific.

Japanese tree money had coins on "branches" that could be broken off to make change.

Possible answers are given below.

Below is a list of monetary units. Find where each is used.

Buffalo Museum of Science

Feather coil

The Chase Manhattan Bank

Japanese tree money

kyat	franc	lira	quetzal	schilling
rupee	guilder	mark	rial	yen
zloty	krone	peso	ruble	yuan
Burma	France	Italy	Guatemala	Austria
India	Netherlands	E. Germany	Iran	Japan
Poland	Denmark	Mexico	U.S.S.R.	China

347

Judy White/Berg Associates

A **credit union** is a cooperative organization that makes small loans to its members at low interest rates. Members often have a fixed amount of money deducted from their pay to purchase shares in the union. The more shares a member owns, the more money the member can borrow.

Credit unions must meet government standards and operate under a specified set of regulations. Much of the work of operating a credit union is done by its members on a voluntary basis.

Example: You borrow $240 from your credit union and agree to pay it back in 6 monthly payments of $40 each, plus 1% a month on the unpaid balance. How much interest will be paid?

Month	Principal at start of month	At end of month Paid on principal	At end of month Paid in interest
first	$240	$40	$2.40
second	200	40	2.00
third	160	40	1.60
fourth	120	40	1.20
fifth	80	40	0.80
sixth	40	40	0.40
			$8.40

The total interest will be $8.40.

Solve the following problems:

1. Lisa borrowed $180 from a credit union on March 1. She agreed to pay $20 per month on the principal and $1\frac{1}{2}\%$ per month on the unpaid balance. She was unable to make the $20 payment for May, but she did pay the interest. How much interest did she pay during the term of the loan? $15.90

2. Juan borrowed $120 from his credit union on July 1 and agreed to pay $20 a month. On October 1 he paid $20 and borrowed another $100. He then agreed to pay $60 a month until the total debt was paid. How much interest did Juan pay, at the rate of 1% per month on the unpaid balance? $6.60

8.11 / CREDIT CARDS

Many people use credit cards to buy on credit. Each month the credit-card company sends a statement showing how much is owed. If the full amount is paid, there is no finance charge. If the full amount is not paid, a finance charge must be paid the following month. Credit-card companies use different ways of computing the finance charge. One way is to compute the finance charge on the **average daily balance.** The *average daily balance* is found by dividing the sum of the daily balances by the number of days in the month.

Example 1: On September 1 the unpaid balance on Lisa's account was $235.75. On September 15 a payment of $100 was credited to her account. The finance charge was 1.8% per month on the average daily balance. Find the finance charge and the new balance on September 30.

Joseph A. Di Chello, Jr.

Date	New credit	Payment	Balance
Sept. 1			$235.75
2			235.75
.			.
.			.
.			.
13			235.75
14			235.75
15		$100	135.75
16			135.75
.			.
.			.
.			.
29			135.75
30			135.75
			$5472.50

14 days at $235.75 →

$$\begin{array}{r} \$235.75 \\ \times\,14 \\ \hline \$3300.50 \end{array}$$

16 days at $135.75 →

$$\begin{array}{r} \$135.75 \\ \times\,16 \\ \hline \$2172.00 \end{array}$$

$$\begin{array}{r} \$3300.50 \\ +\ 2172.00 \\ \hline \$5472.50 \end{array}$$

Find the average daily balance.

$$30\overline{)5472.500} \quad 182.41\overline{6}$$

The average daily balance, to the nearest cent, is $182.42.

349

Find the finance charge.

$182.42	average daily balance
×0.018	rate per month
$3.28356	finance charge

Find the new balance.

$235.75	old balance
− 100.00	payment
135.75	
+ 3.28	finance charge
$139.03	new balance

Example 2: Jerome's unpaid balance on July 1 was $142.75. On July 15 a $36.42 charge (new credit) was posted. On July 20 a $75 payment was posted. The finance charge is 1.75% per month on the average daily balance. Find the finance charge for July and the balance as of July 31.

Date	New credit	Payment	Balance
July 1			$142.75
.			.
.			.
.			.
14			142.75
15	$36.42		179.17
.			.
.			.
.			.
19			179.17
20		$75.00	104.17
.			.
.			.
.			.
31			104.17
			$4144.39

14 days at $142.75 →

$142.75	
×14	
$1998.50	

5 days at $179.17 →

$179.17	
×5	
$895.85	

12 days at $104.17 →

$104.17	
×12	
$1250.04	

$1998.50
895.85
+ 1250.04
$4144.39

average daily balance

$$\frac{133.69}{31)\overline{4144.39}}$$

$133.69

finance charge

$133.69
×0.0175
$2.339575

$2.34

new balance

$142.75	old balance
+ 36.42	new credit
179.17	
− 75.00	payment
104.17	
+ 2.34	finance charge
$106.51	new balance

EXERCISES

1. The average daily balance is found by dividing the sum of the daily balances by the number of <u>(days</u>, weeks) in the month.

Copy and complete the tables to find the finance charge and the end-of-month balance.

2. The finance charge is 1.6% of the average daily balance.

Date	New credit	Payment	Balance
Oct. 1			$156.75
.			.
.			.
.			.
7			156.75
8		$75.00	81.75
.			.
.			.
.			.
15			81.75
16		$50.00	31.75
.			.
.			.
.			.
31			31.75
			$2259.25

$156.75	old balance	
− 75.00	payment	
$ 81.75		
− 50.00	payment	
$ 31.75		
+ 1.17	finance charge	
$ 32.92	new balance	

3. The finance charge is 1.5% of the average daily balance.

Date	New credit	Payment	Balance
Sept. 1			$96.80
.			.
.			.
.			.
10			96.80
11		$25.00	71.80
.			.
.			.
.			.
22			71.80
23	$21.30		93.10
.			.
.			.
.			.
30			93.10
			$2574.40

$ 96.80	old balance	
− 25.00	payment	
$ 71.80		
+ 21.30	new credit	
$ 93.10		
+ 1.29	finance charge	
$ 94.39	new balance	

4. The finance charge is 1.75% of the average daily balance.

Date	New credit	Payment	Balance
Jan. 1			$235.65
.			.
.			.
.			.
5			235.65
6	$36.80		272.45
.			.
.			.
.			.
10			272.45
11	21.35	$125.00	168.80
.			.
.			.
.			.
24			168.80
25	$42.25		211.05
.			.
.			.
31			211.05

```
$ 235.65   old balance
+   36.80   new credit
$ 272.45
-  125.00   payment
$ 147.45
+   21.35   new credit
$ 168.80
+   42.25   new credit
$ 211.05
+    3.60   finance charge
$ 214.65   new balance
```

Find the finance charge and the new balance on the last day of the month on each of the following accounts. The finance charge is 1.8% of the average daily balance.

5. March 1: balance of $235.80
20: new credit of $45.20
25: payment of $100.00
$4.15; $185.15

6. Nov. 1: balance of $372.73
10: payment of $120.00
20: payment of $80.00
$4.67; $177.40

Some credit-card companies require a minimum payment each month. For the following problems, assume that the minimum payment is 5% of the balance, rounded to the nearest dollar.

7. The balance on Bill's credit-card statement for April was $215.75. Find the minimum amount he must pay. $11

8. Peggy's credit-card statement for February showed a balance of $305.60. Find the minimum amount she must pay.
$15

For the following problems, assume that the minimum payment is 7.5% of the balance, rounded to the nearest dollar.

9. Susan's credit-card statement for March showed a balance of $217.25. Find the minimum amount she must pay.
$16

10. The balance on Mike's credit-card statement for June was $86.40. Find the minimum amount he must pay. $6

Brad Bower/Picture Group

Steve wants to buy a personal computer system that sells for $2000. He could use any of the following plans to buy the system on credit:

Plan A: Make a down payment of 25% of the purchase price at the store and then make 18 monthly payments of $100 each.

Plan B: Borrow $2000 from a bank for 12 months at 16% interest. (The $2000 plus interest is repaid in one lump sum.)

Plan C: Borrow $2000 from a finance company. Repay the loan with 36 monthly payments of $68.80 each.

Possible answers are given for exercises 5–6.
Answer the following questions:

1. What is the cost of credit for Plan A? $300

2. If Steve chooses Plan C, how much interest will he pay? $476.80

3. Find the annual percentage rate for Plans A and C. 25.3%; 15.5%

4. Under which plan can Steve get the computer system for the least amount of money? Plan A

5. Under what conditions might Steve choose Plan B over Plan A? if he didn't have a down payment

6. Under what conditions might Steve choose Plan C over Plan B? if he wanted to repay the loan in a series of small payments rather than in one large payment

353

Find each cash-on-hand amount.   8.1

	Day	Item	Income	Expense	Cash on hand
		balance			$129.85
1.	Fri.	paycheck	$256.48		386.33
2.		groceries		$ 20.75	365.58
3.	Sat.	rent		145.00	220.58
4.		entertainment		12.60	207.98
5.	Mon.	lunch		3.85	204.13

Find each percent.   Find each amount.   8.2,
                                                                                       8.3

Budget category	Amount	Percent		Budget category	Amount	Percent
6. food	$ 40	25%	**10.** food	$ 56	16%
7. housing	48	30%	**11.** rent	84	24%
8. savings	16	10%	**12.** recreation	87.50	25%
9. other	56	35%	**13.** other	122.50	35%
totals	$160	100%	totals	$350.00	100%

Find the amount in a checking account after these transactions.   8.4

14. Starting balance: $586.25

Check No. 221: Reed Management Co., $375.00, rent
         222: Bell Telephone Co., $20.28, phone bill

Deposit: $78.00

Check No. 223: C & D Garage, $42.63, car repair
         224: B. Dobson & Co., $79.18, clothing $147.16

Make and complete a form as shown at the right to reconcile the account.   8.5

15. Bank balance, $128.91
Check register balance, $118.01
Outstanding checks, $63.40
Outstanding deposits, $50.00
Service charge, $2.50

Bank balance				128.91	118.01
− Outstanding checks		Check register balance		63.40	2.50
		− Service charges		65.51	115.51
+ Outstanding deposits		Corrected balance		50.00	
Corrected balance				115.51	

16. Minerva borrowed $1500 to buy some furniture. She agreed to repay the loan at the end of 2 years at 12% interest. How much was due at the end of the 2 years? $1860

8.6,
8.7

17. James bought an $800 certificate of deposit that matured in 1 year at 8.5% interest compounded quarterly. How much was the certificate worth at the end of the year? $870.20

Find the cost of credit. $c = na - b$

8.9

	b	n	a	c
	Amount borrowed	Number of payments	Monthly payments	Cost of credit
18.	$180.00	12	$16.00	$12
19.	$270.00	14	$21.00	$24
20.	$335.00	15	$24.60	$34
21.	$206.00	12	$18.75	$19

Find the annual percentage rate. $r = \dfrac{24c}{b(n+1)}$

8.10

	b	n	c	r
	Amount borrowed	Number of payments	Cost of credit	Rate
22.	$300.00	12	$26.00	16%
23.	$400.00	12	$39.00	18%
24.	$480.00	24	$85.00	17%
25.	$320.00	14	$40.00	20%

Find the finance charge and the end-of-month balance for the following credit-card account if the rate is 1.6% of the average daily balance.

8.11

26. Dec. 1:   unpaid balance of $88.75
Dec. 7:   new credit of $35.40
Dec. 10:   payment of $50.00 $1.31; $75.46

Find each cash-on-hand amount.

	Income	Expense	Cash on hand
			$64.35
1.	$12.75		77.10
2.		$38.40	38.70
3.		7.50	31.20
4.		9.75	40.95

Copy and complete the table.

Budget category	Amount	Percent
5. food	$15	20%
6. clothing	$24	32%
7. savings	$ 6	8%
8. other	30	40%
totals	$75	100%

9. Find the amount of money in a checking account after making these transactions. $119.39

Starting balance: $157.52
Deposit: $62.50

Check No. 426: Sim's Gift Shop, $22.47, gift
427: State Bank, $50.00, savings
428: A & B Mart, $28.16, food

10. Complete the form at the right to reconcile the account.

Bank balance, $172.81
Check register balance, $96.05
Outstanding checks, $98.26
Outstanding deposits, $20.00
Service charge, $1.50

	Bank balance		Check register balance
−	Outstanding checks		
		−	Service charges
+	Outstanding deposits		Corrected balance

172.81
98.26
74.55
20.00
94.55

96.05
1.50
94.55

11. Frank borrowed $375 to pay a repair bill. He agreed to repay the loan in 90 days with 11% interest. How much was due after 90 days? $385.31

12. You deposit $650 in a savings account at 9% compounded semiannually. If you make no withdrawals, how much will be in your account in 18 months? $741.76

13. $c = na - b$

Find the cost of credit (c) if the number of payments (n) is 12, the amount of each payment (a) is $23.50, and the amount borrowed (b) is $250. $32

14. $r = \dfrac{24c}{b(n+1)}$

Find the annual percentage rate (r) for the money borrowed in exercise 13. 23.6%

15. Find the finance charge and the new balance for the following credit-card account if the rate is 1.6% of the average daily balance: Feb. 1: unpaid balance of $785.29
Feb. 17: new credit of $98.08 $13.24; $896.61
(Answers are based on 28 days in February.)

1. Exercise equipment that regularly sells for $179.50 is on sale for 20% off. Find the sale price. $143.60

7.2

2. Carlos earns $4.25 per hour working at a printing shop. How much does he earn in one week by working 38 hours? $161.50

7.3

3. Mindy is paid $3.95 per hour and time and a half for overtime (over 40 hours per week). How much did she earn last week by working 46 hours? $193.55

4. Peggy is paid 18¢ for each of the first 200 electronic toys that she checks each day and 22¢ for each toy over 200. How much did she earn today by checking 250 toys? $47

7.4

5. Mark is paid $2.10 per hour plus 35¢ for each car he runs through the car wash. How much did he earn by washing 32 cars in 8 hours? $28

6. Emily is paid a 6% commission on all her sales in a department store. One week her sales were $3475. How much did she earn that week? $208.50

7.5

7. Arthur is paid $115 per week plus 4.5% commission on all sales in a paint store. How much did he earn last week by selling $3850 worth of paint? $288.25

8. Judy is paid $3.25 per hour in a beauty salon. Copy and complete the chart to find her total earnings for one week.

7.6

Day	Hours worked	Wages	Tips	Total earned
Tues.	4	$ 13	$9.00	$ 22
Wed.	$6\frac{1}{2}$	$ 21.13	$10.75	$ 31.88
Thurs.	6	$ 19.50	$8.50	$ 28
Fri.	7	$ 22.75	$12.25	$ 35
Sat.	$8\frac{1}{2}$	$ 26	$15.50	$ 41.50
Totals	$31\frac{1}{2}$	$102.38	$56	$158.38

Copy and complete the chart below. Use the appropriate table on page 296 to determine the amount of federal income tax to be withheld. The state income tax rate is 1.5%, the city income tax rate is 0.6%, and the social security tax rate is 7.05%.

	Weekly gross pay	Single Married	Withholding allowances	F.I.T.	F.I.C.A.	State tax	City tax	Med. ins.	Weekly net pay
9.	$265.00	S	1	$33.80	$18.68	$3.98	$1.59	$5.50	$201.45
10.	$387.50	M	2	$44.10	$27.32	$5.81	$2.33	$10.00	$297.94
11.	$415.00	S	2	$64.60	$29.26	$6.23	$2.49	$10.00	$302.42

Use the information on each Form W-2 below to complete a Form 1040EZ for a single person. If a Form 1040EZ is not available, use page 301 as a model to do the computation needed through line 11.

7.8

12.

1 Control number 33438	3 Employer's identification number 4511	4 Employer's State number 00	Copy B to be filed with employee's FEDERAL tax return

Refund of $258.53

2 Employer's name, address, and ZIP code
D.C. PRODUCTS
27 N. Hoyne
ANYDALE, USA

W-2 Wage and Tax Statement

This information is being furnished to the Internal Revenue Service

5 Stat em De- ployee ceased | Legal rep | 942 emp | Sub- total | Void

6 Allocated tips | 7 Advance EIC payment

8 Employee's social security number 333-11-2222	9 Federal income tax withheld $2087.53	10 Wages, tips, other compensation $14,720.00	11 Social security tax withheld $1037.76

12 Employee's name, address and ZIP code
Michelle N. Horton
12484 S. Friberg
ANYDALE, USA

13 Social security wages | 14 Social security tips

16 *
$220.80

17 State income tax | 18 State wages, tips, etc | 19 Name of State

20 Local income tax | 21 Local wages, tips, etc | 22 Name of locality

Department of the Treasury Internal Revenue Service   OMB No. 1545-0008

13.

1 Control number 95355	3 Employer's identification number 3555	4 Employer's State number 00	Copy B to be filed with employee's FEDERAL tax return

Refund of $421.56

2 Employer's name, address, and ZIP code
RAP'S FASHIONS
957 N. YOWSER ROAD
ANYTOWN, USA

W-2 Wage and Tax Statement

This information is being furnished to the Internal Revenue Service.

5 Stat em De- ployee ceased | Legal rep | 942 emp | Sub- total | Void

6 Allocated tips | 7 Advance EIC payment

8 Employee's social security number 222-66-8225	9 Federal income tax withheld $2548.56	10 Wages, tips, other compensation $16,135.00	11 Social security tax withheld $1137.52

12 Employee's name, address and ZIP code
Anthony L. Maxwell
500 N. Carolyn Drive
ANYTOWN, USA

13 Social security wages | 14 Social security tips

16 *

17 State income tax | 18 State wages, tips, etc | 19 Name of State
$242.03

20 Local income tax | 21 Local wages, tips, etc | 22 Name of locality

Department of the Treasury Internal Revenue Service   OMB No. 1545-0008

Find each cash-on-hand amount.   8.1

Day	Item	Income	Expense	Cash on hand
	balance			$116.30
14. Wed.	lunch		$3.56	112.74
15.	clothing		$49.19	63.55
16. Thurs.	gasoline		$8.50	55.05
17.	paycheck	$132.68		187.73
18. Fri.	groceries		$21.56	166.17

Find each percent or each amount to complete the table.   8.2

Budget category	Amount	Percent
19. food	$84	21%
20. rent	$92	23%
21. clothing	$40	10%
22. recreation	$44	11%
23. savings	$32	8%
24. other	$108	27%
totals	$400	100%

8.3

Find the amount in a checking account after these transactions.   8.4

25. Starting balance: $132.58
   Check No. 305: Midtown Bank, $50.00, savings
            306: Cash, $30.00
        Deposit: $46.28
   Check No. 307: Northern Power Co., $34.22, electric bill $64.64

Make and complete a form as shown at the right to reconcile the account.   8.5

26. Bank balance, $106.40
   Check register balance, $131.63
   Outstanding checks, $52.27
   Outstanding deposits, $75.00
   Service charge, $2.50

	Bank balance				106.40	131.63
−	Outstanding checks		Check register balance		52.27	2.50
			−	Service charges	54.13	129.13
+	Outstanding deposits			Corrected balance	75.00	
	Corrected balance				129.13	

Find the interest and the amount due. $i = prt$ 8.6

	Principal	Rate	Term	Interest	Amount due
27.	$700	9%	1 year	$ 63	$ 763
28.	$500	11%	6 months	$ 27.50	$ 527.50
29.	$2500	8%	5 years	$1000	$3500

30. You deposit $1500 in a savings account at 10% interest   8.7
compounded quarterly. How much will be in your ac-
count at the end of 9 months? $1615.34

Find each cost of credit. $c = na - b$ 8.9

	Amount borrowed	Number of payments	Monthly payment	Cost of credit
31.	$90	8	$12	$ 6
32.	$165	12	$15	$15
33.	$470	18	$28	$34

Find the annual percentage rate. $r = \frac{24c}{b(n+1)}$ 8.10

	Amount borrowed	Number of payments	Cost of credit	Rate
34.	$500	15	$60	18%
35.	$200	14	$20	16%
36.	$600	18	$95	20%

Find the finance charge and the end-of-month balance for the following credit-   8.11
card account. The rate is 1.8% of the average daily balance.

37. November 1: unpaid balance $215.50
November 15: payment of $125.00
November 20: new credit of $54.50 $3.04; $148.04

CUMULATIVE REVIEW

1. In a survey of 2400 teenagers, 7% claimed they would like to travel once they have completed school and are working full-time. How many teenagers surveyed claimed they would like to travel? 168

2. You cannot afford to spend more than 30% of your gross monthly pay for rent. Suppose you work 40 hours per week at $6.95 per hour. Can you afford to pay $300 per month for rent? Yes

3. Find the unit price for each item to the nearest tenth of a cent. Then tell which is the better buy.

   16 ounces of fruit cocktail for $0.79 4.9¢

   29 ounces of fruit cocktail for $1.36 4.7¢

4. You order a turkey sandwich for $2.25, a bowl of soup for $0.95, and a glass of milk for $0.75. The rate of sales tax is 7%. Find the total bill. $4.23

5. Joe bought a shirt for $22.95. He wore the shirt 12 times. What was the wearing cost of the shirt? (Round to the nearest cent.) $1.91

6. You and a friend rent a tennis court for 2 hours at $11 per hour. You split the cost equally. How much does each of you pay? $11

7. The sticker on a new compact car lists the base price as $8792, options totaling $1563, and a destination charge of $370. What is the sticker price of the car? $10,725

8. The selling price of a car is $11,967. Ron will borrow $8000 from the bank at 14% interest for 24 months. What is the total cost of the car? (Refer to the table on page 391.) $13,183

9. Leon has a driver-rating factor of 2.20. He has liability insurance for 50,000/100,000/25,000. What is the premium for this coverage? (Refer to the table on page 396.) $106.04

10. Debbie's medical bills totaled $642 last year. Her major medical insurance will pay 80% of these expenses after the annual $150 deductible is met. How much of the bill will Debbie pay? $248.40

Correlation	
Items	Sec
1	9.1
2	9.2
3	9.3
4	9.4
5	9.5
6	9.6
7	9.7
8	9.8
9	9.9
10	9.10

9.1 HOW TEENAGERS SPEND MONEY

Recently about 2400 teenagers were asked, "What particular thing do you look forward to buying or using your money for when you have completed school and are working full-time?" The five things mentioned most frequently are shown in this table.

	Girls	Boys
Car	20%	45%
Living away from home	25%	14%
Clothes	17%	7%
Contributing to family household	10%	9%
Travel	8%	6%

Source: USA TODAY

This chapter concentrates on some of the ways teenagers can use money—and use it wisely.

EXERCISES

For exercises 1–10, refer to the above survey. Assume that 1200 boys and 1200 girls took part in the survey.

1. Which thing was mentioned most frequently by boys? buying a car

2. Which thing was mentioned most frequently by girls? living away from home

3. How many girls surveyed prefer spending money on a car? HINT: Find 20% of 1200. 240

4. How many boys surveyed prefer spending money on a car? 540

5. How many teenagers surveyed prefer spending money on a car? 780

6. About (20%, 33%, 69%) of the teenagers surveyed prefer spending money on a car.

7. How many girls surveyed prefer spending money on living-away expenses? 300

8. How many boys surveyed prefer spending money on living-away expenses? 168

9. How many teenagers surveyed prefer spending money on living-away expenses? 468

10. About (11%, 20%, 39%) of the teenagers surveyed prefer spending money on living-away expenses.

Carmela works full-time and takes home $215 per week. She lives with her parents and pays them $40 per week to help with family expenses.

11. How much money does Carmela have left each week after she pays her parents? $175

12. How much money does Carmela pay her parents in 1 year? (1 year = 52 weeks) $2080

13. If Carmela rented an apartment, it would cost her $360 per month. Find the rent for 1 year. $4320

14. How much money does Carmela save on rent in a year by living at home (apartment rent versus what she pays her parents)? $2240

As an employee in a clothing store, Elizabeth is entitled to a 20% discount on all merchandise she purchases.

15. Suppose she buys an outfit that regularly sells for $71. How much is the discount? $14.20

16. How much will the outfit cost her? $56.80

Myles bought a car. His monthly payments are $190. He must also pay $875 per year for insurance. Ralph uses his parents' car and has no monthly payments to make. He does, however, pay his parents $345 every 6 months for his share of the insurance costs.

17. How much does Myles pay in monthly payments in 1 year? $2280

18. How much does it cost Myles in monthly payments and insurance for 1 year? $3155

19. How much does Ralph pay in 1 year? $690

20. In 1 year, how much less does Ralph pay for car costs than Myles? $2465

SKILLS REFRESHER

			Skill	Page
Should < or > replace each ●?				
1. 508 > 499	**2.** 6.8 > 5.9	**3.** 8.995 < 10.99	3	450
Round.				
4. $6.19 (nearest dollar) $6	**5.** 0.355 (nearest hundredth) 0.36		4	451
Find each quotient to the nearest tenth.				
6. 8)‾158‾ 19.8	**7.** 12)‾89‾ 7.4	**8.** 1.4)‾153‾ 109.3	23	480
9. 3.78)‾220‾ 58.2				

Before you agree to rent an apartment, you should consider *all* of the costs that are involved. **Move-in costs** often include a fee for a credit check, a security deposit (usually one month's rent), the first month's rent (plus the first month's parking fee, if any), and a pet deposit. You should also find out how much the average monthly utility bill is.

When you choose an apartment to rent, you may be asked to sign a **lease.** A lease is a contract between the tenant (the person who rents the apartment) and the landlord (the person who owns or manages the apartment). It specifies such things as how long the tenant will rent the apartment, the monthly rent, the due date of the rent, and rules about breaking the lease.

Suppose you decide to rent a 1-bedroom apartment at The Landings. Before you move in, you must pay $20 for a credit check, a security deposit of one month's rent, and the first month's rent.

Example 1: Find the move-in cost at The Landings.

$$\begin{array}{rl} \$\ 20 & \text{credit check} \\ 325 & \text{security deposit} \\ +\ 325 & \text{first month's rent} \\ \hline \$670 & \end{array}$$

The move-in cost is $670.

THE LANDINGS

1-bedroom apartments
$325 per month
Heat included

Example 2: You decide that you cannot afford to spend more than 30% of your gross monthly pay for rent. Suppose you work 40 hours per week at $7.15 per hour. Can you afford to live at The Landings?

Step 1: Estimate your gross monthly pay.

Since there are about 4 weeks in a month, you work about 4 × 40, or 160, hours per month.

Round your hourly wage to the nearest dollar. $7.15 is about $7.

$$\begin{array}{r} 160 \\ \times \$7 \\ \hline \$1120 \end{array} \quad \text{estimated gross monthly pay}$$

Step 2: Find 30% of the gross monthly pay.

$$\begin{array}{r} \$1120 \\ \times 0.30 \\ \hline \$336.00 \end{array}$$

Since 30% of your gross monthly pay ($336) is more than the monthly rent of $325, you can afford to live at The Landings.

EXERCISES

1. A contract between a tenant and a landlord that specifies such things as the monthly rent is called a (treaty, <u>lease</u>, security deposit).

2. A tenant's move-in cost generally is (less than, the same as, <u>more than</u>) the monthly rent.

Reggie decides to rent a 1-bedroom apartment at Buff Bay. Before moving in, he must pay $20 for a credit check, a security deposit of one month's rent, and the first month's rent. Since he owns a cat, he must also pay a $200 pet deposit. Reggie works 40 hours per week at $7.83 per hour. He does not want to pay more than 30% of his gross monthly pay for rent. Estimates may vary.

> **BUFF BAY**
>
> 1-bedroom apartment
> $370 per month
> Heat included
> Pet deposit required

3. Find Reggie's move-in cost. $960

4. Estimate Reggie's gross monthly pay. $1280

5. Find 30% of Reggie's estimated gross monthly pay. $384

6. Can Reggie afford to live at Buff Bay? Yes

7. Suppose Reggie earned only $6.83 per hour. Could he still afford the rent? No

8. Suppose Reggie's gross yearly income were $15,000. Could he afford to live at Buff Bay? Yes

Reggie found that his average utility bill will be about $35 per month. It will also cost about $9 per month for renter's insurance.

9. How much will Reggie pay each month in rent, utilities, and insurance? $414

10. How much will Reggie pay each year for rent, utilities, and insurance? $4968

Alma decided to rent the apartment described in the ad at the right. Before moving in, she must pay $25 for a credit check, a security deposit of 1.5 times the monthly rent, the first month's rent, and $30 for a parking space. Alma works 40 hours per week at $5.95 per hour. She does not want to pay more than 25% of her gross monthly pay for rent.

> 9901 S. Oglesby
> 1-bedroom apt.
> $290/month
> Parking—$30/month
> No pets

11. How much is the security deposit? $435

12. Find Alma's move-in cost. $780

13. Estimate Alma's gross monthly pay. $960

14. Can Alma afford to rent the apartment? No

You and a friend decide to save money by renting a 2-bedroom apartment at McRoach Plaza. You will share the expenses equally. Before moving in, the following amounts must be paid:

- $44 in credit checks (for both of you)
- one month's rent for a security deposit
- the first month's rent—plus parking for 2 cars

McRoach Plaza
"The Ultimate in Living"
$550/month 2-bedroom apt.
Parking available at $35/month

15. Find the total move-in costs for you and your friend. $1214

16. How much must each of you pay in move-in costs? $607

17. How much must each of you pay in rent each month? $275

18. How much will you save in monthly rent by sharing an apartment at McRoach Plaza instead of renting a 1-bedroom apartment by yourself at Buff Bay (ad on page 365)? $95

19. You work 40 hours per week at $6.25 per hour. You do not want to spend more than 30% of your gross monthly pay for rent. Can you afford to rent an apartment at McRoach Plaza with your friend? Yes

20. Your friend earns $10,660 (gross) per year and does not want to spend more than one week's gross pay for monthly rent. Can your friend afford to rent an apartment with you at McRoach Plaza? No

Judy and Gabrielle would like to share one of the apartments described below. Judy earns $10,800 (gross) per year. Gabrielle earns $250 (gross) per week. Both Judy and Gabrielle do not want to spend more than 30% of their gross monthly pay for rent.

Ming Manor
$690 per month
2-bedroom apt.

Country Club Hills
2-bedroom apartments
$570 per month

908 W. Argyle
$495 per month
2-bedroom apt.

Find how much each would have to pay in monthly rent for each apartment.

21. Ming Manor $345   **22.** Country Club Hills $285   **23.** 908 W. Argyle $247.50

24. Which of the apartments can Judy afford? 908 W. Argyle

25. Which of the apartments can Gabrielle afford? Country Club Hills and 908 W. Argyle

26. Which of the apartments can both of them afford?
908 W. Argyle

9.3 | COMPARISON SHOPPING

One of these brands of peanut butter is the *better buy.* It makes sense to buy the less expensive of two choices if price is the only difference.

One way to find which brand gives more for the money is to determine the price per ounce for each brand. The price per ounce is called a *unit price.*

A **unit price** is a price for one unit of the item, such as one ounce, one gram, or one bar. The brand with the lower unit price is the **better buy.**

Mary Elenz Tranter

Example 1: Which brand of peanut butter is the better buy?

Step 1: Write each price in cents.

$2.49 = 249¢

$2.98 = 298¢

Step 2: Divide each price by the number of ounces to find the unit price. Round each quotient to the nearest tenth.

Dr. Crunch Peanut Butter

$$
\begin{array}{r}
17.78 \rightarrow 17.8¢ \\
14\overline{)249.00} \\
14 \\
\overline{109} \\
98 \\
\overline{11\ 0} \\
9\ 8 \\
\overline{1\ 20} \\
1\ 12 \\
\overline{8}
\end{array}
$$
unit price (to the nearest tenth of a cent)

Carolina Peanut Butter

$$
\begin{array}{r}
18.62 \rightarrow 18.6¢ \\
16\overline{)298.00} \\
16 \\
\overline{138} \\
128 \\
\overline{10\ 0} \\
9\ 6 \\
\overline{40} \\
32 \\
\overline{8}
\end{array}
$$
unit price (to the nearest tenth of a cent)

Step 3: Compare unit prices.

17.8¢ < 18.6¢, so *Dr. Crunch Peanut Butter* costs less per ounce. *Dr. Crunch Peanut Butter* is the better buy.

Mary Elenz Tranter

Example 2: Which size is the better buy?

Generic products are products not protected by trademark registration. They are usually distributed by grocery stores and are generally cheaper than brand-name products.

Step 1: Change to the smaller unit.
That is, change 2 lb 4 oz to ounces.

2 lb 4 oz = 32 oz + 4 oz = 36 oz
2 lb = 2 × 16, or 32, oz

Step 2: Divide each price (in cents) by the number of ounces.

12-oz size

$$\begin{array}{r} 7.75 \longrightarrow 7.8¢ \\ 12\overline{)93.00} \quad \textbf{unit price} \end{array}$$

2-lb-4-oz size

$$\begin{array}{r} 7.19 \longrightarrow 7.2¢ \\ 36\overline{)259.00} \quad \textbf{unit price} \end{array}$$

Step 3: Compare unit prices.
7.2¢ < 7.8¢, so the 2-lb-4-oz size is the better buy.

NOTE: Even if the larger size has a lower unit price, it may not turn out to be the "better buy" if you are unable to use all the contents before spoilage occurs. In the exercises, it will be assumed that no spoilage will occur.

EXERCISES

1. To find the unit price, divide the (price, quantity) by the (price, quantity).

2. If there are no other differences, the better buy is the choice with the (lower, higher) unit price.

Find each unit price to the nearest tenth of a cent.

3. 5 oz for 65¢ 13.0¢

4. 8 oz for 74¢ 9.3¢

5. 3 cans for $0.98 32.7¢

6. 4 rolls for $1.35 33.8¢

7. 14 oz for $1.09 7.8¢

8. 12 oz for $2.39 19.9¢

9. 1 lb 8 oz for $3.00 12.5¢
(Find the price per ounce.)

10. 2 lb 12 oz for $5.99 13.6¢
(Find the price per ounce.)

11. 1.5 kg for $2.00 $1.333

12. 3.78 L for $2.17 57.4¢

368

Find the unit price for each item. Then tell which is the better or best buy. Where necessary, round quotients to the nearest tenth of a cent.

13. 7 oz for 35¢ 5.0¢
12 oz for 48¢ 4.0¢

14. 9 oz for 72¢ 8.0¢
12 oz for 99¢ 8.3¢

15. 3 cans for $1.00 33.3¢
2 cans for $0.69 34.5¢

16. 2 sticks for $1.39 69.5¢
4 sticks for $2.75 68.8¢

17. 4 lb for $5.09 $1.273
5 lb for $6.47 $1.294

18. 10 oz for $1.97 19.7¢
16 oz for $3.10 19.4¢

19. 6 oz for 45¢ 7.5¢
8 oz for 55¢ 6.9¢
12 oz for 84¢ 7.0¢

20. 8 oz for $0.87 10.9¢
10 oz for $1.06 10.6¢
16 oz for $1.58 9.9¢

21. 14 oz for $1.17 8.4¢
1 lb 8 oz for $1.94 8.1¢
(Find the price per ounce.)

22. 16 oz for $0.83 5.2¢
5 lb 4 oz for $3.49 4.2¢
(Find the price per ounce.)

23. 1 qt for $3.69 11.5¢
1 qt 16 fl oz for $5.66 11.8¢
(Find the price per fluid ounce.
1 qt = 32 fl oz)

24. 1 gal for $2.22 55.5¢
1 qt for $0.62 62.0¢
(Find the price per quart.
1 gal = 4 qt)

25. 6.5 oz for $0.99 15.2¢
15.5 oz for $2.20 14.2¢

26. 2.5 kg for $5.00 $2.00
4 kg for $8.27 $2.068

27. 1.89 L for $1.32 69.8¢
3.78 L for $2.44 64.6¢

28. 0.5 L for $1.22 $2.44
1.75 L for $4.08 $2.331

5 lb 4 oz—$3.85

10 pounds—$7.72

49 oz—$2.47

Mary Elenz Tranter

29. Which detergent is the best buy?
generic laundry detergent

30. You can use a discount coupon to lower a unit price. Simply subtract the value of the coupon from the item's price and divide as before. Suppose you have 75¢-off coupons for both *Bright Laundry Detergent* and *Powder Power*. Now which detergent is the best buy? Powder Power

A savings of 0.5¢ per ounce may not seem like much money. But the amount a family saves in a full year by getting the best buys can be a large sum. Copy and complete the chart.

Item and price	Unit price (nearest tenth of a cent)	Average week's supply	Cost of average week's supply	Amount saved by getting the better buy in 1 week	in 1 year
Example: Cereal 16 oz for $1.89 20 oz for $2.18	 11.8¢/oz 10.9¢/oz	36 oz	11.8 10.9 ×36 ×36 424.8 392.4 $4.25 $3.92	$4.25 − 3.92 $0.33	$0.33 ×52 $17.16
31. Frozen orange juice 6 oz for $0.96 12 oz for $1.69	 16.0¢/oz 14.1¢/oz	36 oz	 $5.76 $5.08	$0.68	$35.36
32. Bread 16 oz for 89¢ 20 oz for $1.18	 5.6¢/oz 5.9¢/oz	40 oz	 $2.24 $2.36	$0.12	$6.24
33. Jam 12 oz for $1.19 1 lb 2 oz for $1.50	 9.9¢/oz 8.3¢/oz	12 oz	 $1.19 $1.00	$0.19	$9.88
34. Mouthwash 0.95 L for $3.59 1.42 L for $5.00	 $3.779/L $3.521/L	0.75 L	 $2.83 $2.64	$0.19	$9.88

◢ TALK IT OVER ▭

1. Should you *always* buy the product with the lowest unit price? What factors, other than price, might you consider before buying different kinds of items? No; quality, personal preference, quantity you need, etc.
2. Go to a store and find the best buy from among these items: Answers will vary.

   • brand-name item not on sale   • brand-name item on sale   • either or both of the above items with a discount coupon   • generic item

   Report your findings to the class.

1. By having the pizza sliced into 12 pieces, is the customer in the above cartoon going to get any more pizza? Why or why not? No. The amount of pizza remains the same. The customer is getting more but smaller pieces.

A 10-inch pizza is a circular pizza with a *diameter* of 10 inches. You can find the area of such a pizza by using the formula for the area of a circle.

$$A = \pi r^2$$

Use 3.14 for π. 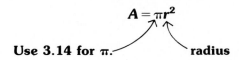 radius

2. The area of a 10-inch pizza is equal to 3.14×5^2, or $\underline{78.5}$, square inches.

3. At Pasquesi's Pizza Parlor, one 14-inch pizza sells for the same price as two 7-inch pizzas.

a. Find the area of one 14-inch pizza. 153.86 in^2

b. Find the total area of two 7-inch pizzas. 76.93 in^2

c. Which gives you more pizza for your money, one 14-inch pizza or two 7-inch pizzas? How much more?
one 14-inch pizza; 76.93 in^2 more

4. At Mr. Anchovy's, a 10-inch pizza sells for $7.95 and a 12-inch pizza sells for $11.05.

a. Find the unit price (price per square inch of pizza) for each pizza. Round to the nearest tenth of a cent. 10-inch pizza: 10.1¢
12-inch pizza: 9.8¢

b. Which pizza is the better buy?
the 12-inch pizza

EATING ECONOMICALLY

Bohdan Hrynewych/Southern Light

The cost and quality of meals can vary, depending upon where they are eaten and how they are prepared. Four common ways to plan a meal are (1) prepare and eat a meal at home, (2) eat convenience foods at home, (3) purchase a carry-out meal, and (4) eat at a restaurant.

If you shop well, preparing and eating a meal at home should be the most economical and nutritious way to plan a meal. However, it is also the most time-consuming way.

Convenience foods are processed and packaged to save you preparation time. They generally come boxed, bagged, bottled, or canned and require little preparation other than heating. The quality can be good, but the cost per serving usually is greater than for food prepared at home.

Carry-out meals are ideal for people "on the run." However, some of what is available could be classified as junk food. Carry-out meals may cost a little more than convenience foods.

Restaurant food can be as nutritious as food prepared at home. However, as with convenience foods and carry-out meals, you do not always know what is in the food you are eating. It is also the most expensive way to plan a meal. Nevertheless, eating out in a restaurant does provide a fun way to eat a wide variety of foods in various atmospheres.

Example 1: You order a roast-beef sandwich, a cup of soup, a medium milk, and fruit. The rate of sales tax is 6.5%. Find the total bill. (Use the menu on page 373.)

$$
\begin{array}{r}
\$4.50 \\
1.10 \\
0.80 \\
+\ 0.40 \\
\hline
\$6.80
\end{array}
\qquad
\begin{array}{r}
\$6.80 \\
\times 0.065 \\
\hline
\$0.442 \longrightarrow \$0.44
\end{array}
\qquad
\begin{array}{l}
\text{sales tax to the} \\
\text{nearest cent}
\end{array}
$$

The total bill is $6.80 + $0.44, or $7.24.

MENU						
Sandwiches				**Beverages**	medium	large
Cheese	$2.75	Roast beef	$4.50	Soft drinks	$0.65	$0.95
Club	$5.25	Corned beef	$4.75	Milk	$0.80	$1.15
Soup				**Desserts**		
cup $1.10;		bowl $1.45		Ice cream $0.90		Fruit $0.40

Example 2: You would like to leave a 15% tip for the meal you ordered in Example 1. Estimate the tip.

Since you do not need to pay a tip on the sales tax, estimate 15% of $6.80 (the total cost of the items).

$$15\% \text{ of } \$6.80 = \underbrace{10\% \text{ of } \$6.80}_{} + \underbrace{\tfrac{1}{2} \text{ of } (10\% \text{ of } \$6.80)}_{}$$

10% of $6.80 = $0.68, or about 70¢

$\tfrac{1}{2}$ **of 70 = 35¢**

The tip should be about 70¢ + 35¢, or $1.05.

Example 3: You order a club sandwich, a bowl of soup, a medium milk, and fruit. Estimate the total cost of the meal, including sales tax and tip.

A quick way to estimate the total cost of a meal is to round up the price of every item to the next dollar. By rounding up the price of *every* item, you will be allowing amounts for the sales tax and tip.

$5.25 → $6
$1.45 → $2
$0.80 → $1
$0.40 → $1
$\overline{\hspace{1.5em}}$
$10

The total estimated cost of the meal is about $10.

Find the actual cost of the meal in Example 3 if the rate of sales tax is 5% and you will leave an estimated 15% tip. Does the estimated total cost of $10 provide a good approximation as to how much money you need to have for the meal?

$7.90 + $0.40 + $1.20 = $9.50; Yes

meal   tax   tip

EXERCISES

For exercises 1–4, answer with one of these ways to plan a meal:

- Prepare and eat a meal at home.
- Eat convenience foods at home.
- Purchase a carry-out meal.
- Eat at a restaurant.

1. Which way is generally the most economical and nutritious? Prepare and eat a meal at home.

2. Which way is least economical? Eat at a restaurant.

3. Which way would be best for people who do not have time to prepare a meal, but who do want to eat a nutritious meal at home? Eat convenience foods at home.

4. Which way provides the greatest control over what is in the food you eat? Prepare and eat a meal at home.

Find the total bill for each of the orders shown below. The rate of sales tax is 5.5%. (Do not include a tip.)

5.

	$2.25
	0.85
Subtotal	3.10
Tax	0.17
Total	$3.27

6.

	$5.50
	0.95
	1.20
Subtotal	7.65
Tax	0.42
Total	$8.07

7.

	$9.75
	$3.20
	$1.50
Subtotal	14.45
Tax	0.79
Total	$15.24

8.

	$2.00
	9.40
	1.90
	8.75
	1.25
Subtotal	23.30
Tax	1.28
Total	$24.58

9.

	$10.20
	0.90
	2.75
	3.00
Subtotal	16.85
Tax	0.93
Total	$17.78

10.

	$6.50
	$6.50
	$1.20
	$1.20
	$0.80
Subtotal	16.20
Tax	0.89
Total	$17.09

Estimates for exercises 11-16 may vary.

11–16. Estimate a 15% tip for each of the orders shown in exercises 5–10. Use the method given in Example 2 on page 373. 11. $0.45; 12. $1.20; 13. $2.25; 14. $3.50; 15. $2.55; 16. $2.40

Estimate the total cost for each of the orders listed in exercises 17–20. Use the method given in Example 3 on page 373.

17. broiled trout (complete luncheon with soup), dinner salad, milk $7

18. roast turkey (a la carte), cup of soup, iced tea, jello $7

19. For 2 people: 2 orders of chopped beef (complete luncheons with salad), bowl of soup, 2 glasses of milk $12

20. For 2 people: broiled trout (a la carte), bowl of soup, dinner salad, rice pudding, roast turkey (complete luncheon), 2 glasses of iced tea $15

Today's Specials		
	a la carte	Complete Luncheon*
Roast Turkey	$3.80	$4.75
Broiled Trout	$3.65	$4.40
Chopped Beef	$2.90	$3.65
Cup of soup $0.75	Bowl of soup	$1.10
Dinner Salad $0.80		
Soft Drinks $0.50	Milk	$0.75
Iced Tea $0.65	Coffee	$0.45
Rice Pudding $0.60	Jello	$0.35
*includes salad or cup of soup and dessert		

Exercises 21–24 show four ways to plan a chicken dinner for two people. For each way, find the total cost for the two people. (Costs involving such things as travel, heating, and sales tax are not included.)

21. *Chicken prepared at home:*

whole chicken and breading	$2.35
coleslaw (ingredients)	$0.65
beverage	$0.25 per person
	$3.50

22. *Packaged chicken heated at home:*

box of frozen chicken	$3.95
coleslaw (from a deli)	$0.69
beverage	$0.25 per person
	$5.14

23. *Carry-out chicken:*

bucket of chicken	$5.69
coleslaw	$0.45 per person
beverage	$0.60 per person
	$7.79

24. *Chicken eaten at a restaurant:*

chicken and coleslaw dinner	$5.69 per person
beverage	$0.75 per person

Include an estimated 15% tip. $14.83

Answers for exercises 24-25 may vary due to the estimated tip.

25. Find the difference in total costs between the most expensive and the least expensive chicken dinners (for two people). $11.33

Application 41 may be used at this time.
Computer Supplement, Disk 3, Lesson 3, may be used at this time. **375**

When you are purchasing clothes, it is important to be selective. Plan a wardrobe that will be practical and that will meet your individual needs. Choose items of clothing that will give you the most for the money you are spending.

Jan is a full-time student and works a part-time job. She has saved some extra money to spend on clothes. After shopping around, Jan narrows down her choices to these two possible outfits. Which outfit would you buy?

$68

$55

Photos by Pam Hasegawa/Taurus

Initially, it looks as if the dress is considerably more expensive than the attractive fad outfit. Before completely ruling out the possibility of buying the dress, consider these questions.

Where could you wear the dress?
Where could you wear the fad outfit?
Which outfit is more versatile?

Basic clothing styles do not frequently change. Skirts of a certain length and ties of a certain width can be worn for several years. On the other hand, **fad clothes** are seasonal. After five or six months you may not feel comfortable wearing them because they are no longer fashionable.

The **wearing cost** of an article of clothing is the amount of money it costs the consumer for each time the item is worn.

Example 1: The dress costs $68 and is worn 35 times in 3 years. Find the wearing cost.

$$\text{times worn} \longrightarrow \overset{\displaystyle 1.942 \longleftarrow \textbf{wearing cost}}{35)\overline{68.000}} \longleftarrow \textbf{cost}$$

Round to the nearest cent: $1.94
It would cost Jan $1.94 for each time she wore the dress.

Example 2: The fad outfit costs $55 and is worn 12 times in 5 months. Find the wearing cost.

$$\text{times worn} \longrightarrow \overset{\displaystyle 4.583 \longleftarrow \textbf{wearing cost}}{12)\overline{55.000}} \longleftarrow \textbf{cost}$$

Round to the nearest cent: $4.58
It would cost Jan $4.58 for each time she wore the fad outfit.

The dress is the better buy. It can be worn more often and costs less per time worn. However, it is up to consumers to decide how to spend their money.

Buying something on sale can save you a considerable amount of money. You can pick up some good buys at end-of-the-season sales, anniversary sales, and grand opening sales. Many stores advertise in the newspaper. Some stores mail out circulars to preferred customers—so get on the mailing list of your favorite stores. Sales provide consumers with an opportunity to buy something they may otherwise not be able to afford.

Which sport coat would you buy? You need to find the sale price of the wool sport coat before you make your decision.

This Weekend Only at **Rap's Fashions**
Name Brand, 100% Wool Sport Coats
REGULAR PRICE $95 NOW 25% OFF

GRAND OPENING SALE
Polyester Blend Sport Coats Just **$70** at **Mickey's**

Example 3: Find the sale price of the wool sport coat.

$95   **Find 25% of the** $95.00   **regular price**
× 0.25   **regular price.**   − 23.75   **discount**
$23.75 $71.25   **sale price**

The sale price of the wool sport coat is $71.25.

Because of the sale, there is very little difference in the prices of the two sport coats. The consumer, in this situation, will not have to buy the less expensive jacket because of a limited budget.

Take the time to do some comparison shopping. Consumers may find the same item or a similar item on sale at different stores. Careful shopping will provide the consumer with the best buys.

Example 4: Which store is selling the shoes for less?

Bradley's sale price:

   $28.95
−   **6.00**
   $22.95

Marcey's sale price:

  $28.95   **$28.95**
× **0.15**   −   **4.34**
 $4.3425   **$24.61**

Round to the nearest cent: $4.34

By doing some comparison shopping, you would get a better buy at Bradley's.

EXERCISES

Find the wearing cost for each article of clothing. Round to the nearest cent.

Item	Cost	Times worn	
1. jeans	$40	48	$0.83
2. fad jeans	$35	20	$1.75
3. tie	$18	11	$1.64
4. fad tie	$12	4	$3.00
5. sweater	$45	38	$1.18
6. fad sweater	$39	15	$2.60

Find the sale price of each of the following. Round to the nearest cent.

Item	Regular price		Percent of discount
7. coat	$132	$99	25%
8. boots	$70	$45.50	35%
9. dress	$43	$36.55	15%
10. shirt	$17	$15.30	10%
11. robe	$34	$27.20	20%
12. slippers	$12	$10.80	10%

13. At Jackie's Boutique, a $35 dress is on sale for 25% off. A discount store is selling the same dress for $27.95. At which store will you get the better buy? at Jackie's Boutique

14. Mark can buy a $25 shirt for 15% off or a similar $28 shirt for 20% off. Which shirt is less expensive? the $25 shirt

15. A $30 sweater at Logo's Department Store is reduced by $5.50. The same sweater sells for $32 at Robin's Department Store and is on sale for 25% off. Which store is selling the sweater for less? Robin's Department Store

16. A $24 pair of pants is on sale at Drew's Department Store for 15% off. A similar pair of pants at Crawford Department Store costs $27 and is on sale for 20% off. Which pair of pants is less expensive? the pants at Drew's Department Store

SKILLS REFRESHER

Multiply.

				Skill	Page
1. 0.85×23	**2.** 0.79×567	**3.** 0.82×2347	**4.** 0.75×6548	13	466
19.55	447.93	1924.54	4911		
5. 0.27×82	**6.** 0.05×63	**7.** 0.02×200	**8.** 0.90×8972		
22.14	3.15	4	8074.8		

Computer Supplement, Disk 3, Lesson 4, may be used at this time.

SPENDING MONEY FOR LEISURE ACTIVITIES

To maintain proper mental and physical health, it is important to participate in leisure activities. The advertisements shown in this lesson describe the costs of some of the recreational activities that are available.

NOW FORMING TEAMS FOR SKYWAY'S BOWLING LEAGUE
33-week season
$8 per week

Includes 3 games/week, trophies, and banquet

PARK FOREST COMMUNITY SWIMMING POOL

Summer Membership Rates:
Individual Membership $75
Family Membership $135
(Members are entitled to unlimited swimming.)

Nonmember Daily Rates:
Weekdays $3.50
Weekends $5.00

FROST TENNIS CLUB

Yearly Membership Fee: $150

Court Time Per Hour (Members only)

	6 A.M.–9 A.M.	9 A.M.–6 P.M.	6 P.M.–10 P.M.
Monday–Thursday	$7	$10	$13
Friday	$7	$10	$18
Saturday	$10	$13	$18
Sunday	$10	$13	$13

EXERCISES

1. Giselle swam 20 times on weekdays and 10 times on weekends during the summer at the Park Forest Community Swimming Pool. Each time she paid the nonmember daily rate.

   a. How much did she pay in all? $120

   b. How much could she have saved if she had purchased an individual membership at the beginning of the summer? $45

2. Tim decides to join Skyway's Bowling League. How much will it cost him for the full 33-week season? $264

3. Tim has a choice. He can rent bowling shoes for 75¢ per week or he can buy a pair of bowling shoes. Suppose he buys a pair for $18.75. Beginning with which week of the bowling season will he be "money ahead" by buying the shoes instead of renting them? week 26

4. Ruby and a friend play tennis at the Frost Tennis Club every Wednesday morning from 7:00 to 8:00. They share the cost for court time equally. How much will each pay for 35 weeks of court time? (Do not include the yearly membership fee.) $122.50

5. You and 3 friends rent a court at Frost Tennis Club on Saturday night from 8:00 to 10:00. You share the cost equally. How much does each of you pay? $9

6. Lois decides to join the Frost Tennis Club. She and a friend plan to play tennis and share the cost every Sunday afternoon from 2:00 to 3:00.

   a. How much will it cost Lois to join the club and play 52 weeks of tennis? $488

   b. How much will it cost Lois to play tennis each of the 52 hours if the membership fee is included as part of the total cost? (Round to the nearest cent.) $9.38

7. There are 8 courts at the Frost Tennis Club. How much money will the Frost Tennis Club take in if all of the courts are rented every hour on a Saturday? $1752

Many people enjoy spending leisure time watching movies at home on a video cassette recorder (VCR).

8. How much would a nonmember have to pay for six 1-day rentals on weekends at Herrera's? $30

9. Suppose you plan to have thirty 1-day rentals on weekends during a year. How much would you save by joining the club rather than by paying nonmember rates? (Consider the membership fee and the free rentals in your computation.) $18

10. Bob is a nonmember and wants to rent a movie for 1 day on Thursday. However, he thinks he may have to return it 3 days late. How much less would it cost him to rent the movie for 4 days than to rent it for 1 day and pay 3 days of late charges? $5.50

Rent Home Movies.

Join
HERRERA'S VIDEO MOVIE CLUB.

1-year Membership—$60
(includes six free 1-day rentals for any day of the week)

Price Schedule (per movie)

	Members	Non-members
1 day (Mon.–Thurs.)	$2.00	$3.00
1 day (Fri.–Sun.)	$3.00	$5.00
4 days	$5.00	$8.00
Late charge per day	$2.00	$3.50

Many people enjoy reading books for pleasure. Since books can be very expensive, some people look for bargains at used-book stores.

11. Suppose you buy 5 books at Briscoe Book Exchange, read them, and then trade them back 2 for 1. Suppose you continue reading and trading until you no longer have 2 books to trade.
   a. How many books will you be able to read on your initial $6 investment? 9
   b. Find the average cost per book read. (Round to the nearest cent.) 67¢

12. Suppose you buy 10 books and continue reading and trading as described in exercise 11.
   a. How many books will you be able to read on your initial $10 investment? 19
   b. Find the average cost per book read. 53¢

BRISCOE BOOK EXCHANGE

Buy and trade used books.

5 used books for $6
10 used books for $10
Trade in 2 books for 1.

Many people enjoy spending leisure time listening to music.

13. Suppose you join the Groovy Record Club and get the 8 albums for 1¢ and buy 8 more albums at the regular price during the next 2 years.
   a. Find the total cost (including shipping and handling) for the 16 albums. $104.24
   b. Find the average cost (including shipping and handling) per album. (Round to the nearest cent.) $6.52

14. A discount record store sells the same 16 albums for only $7.99 each. $127.84
   a. How much would it cost to buy the 16 albums from the discount store?
   b. How much would you save by buying the 16 albums through the club? $23.60

GROOVY RECORD CLUB

8 ALBUMS FOR

1¢*

*plus $3.99 for shipping and handling
Just send us a check for $4.00 (1¢ for the albums and $3.99 for shipping and handling) and we'll send you 8 albums. In exchange, you must agree to buy 8 more albums during the next 2 years at our regular price of $9.98—plus $2.55 per album for shipping and handling.

MUSICAL INTERLUDE

The music below is written in $\frac{4}{4}$ time. The table at the right shows the note values for music written in $\frac{4}{4}$ time.

All music is separated into *measures*. Each measure is separated from the next measure by a vertical line called a *bar line*. When music is written in $\frac{4}{4}$ time, there are four counts to each measure.

Symbol	Name	Note value
o	whole note	4 counts
♩ (half)	half note	2 counts
♩	quarter note	1 count
♪	eighth note	$\frac{1}{2}$ count

Copy the music below. Draw bar lines so that there are four counts to each measure. The first bar line is drawn.

If you enjoy bowling, it is important to know how to keep score. A game of bowling consists of 10 frames. In each frame you throw 2 balls, except when you get a *strike*. A strike occurs when you knock all the pins down with the first ball.

1	2	3	4	5	6	7	8	9	10
6 2	5 —	8 ⟋	7 ⟋	— 4	☒	8 1	☒	☒ 6 2	
8	13	30	40	44	63	72	98	116	124

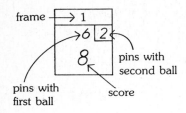

In frame 1, you knocked down 6 pins with the first ball and 2 pins with the second ball. You knocked down 8 pins with both balls. Your score for frame 1 is 8.

In frame 2, you knocked down 5 pins with the first ball and 0 pins (shown by the —) with the second ball. You knocked down 5 pins in frame 2.

To find your score for frame 2, add the number of pins knocked down in frame 2 to the score in frame 1. Your score for frame 2 is $8 + 5$, or 13.

In frame 3, you knocked down 8 pins with the first ball and the rest of the pins with the second ball. Since all the pins were knocked down with 2 balls in the same frame, you got a *spare*. To record a spare, draw a diagonal (/) in the small square.

A **spare** counts for 10 pins, plus the number of pins knocked down with the first ball in the next frame. You can find the score for frame 3 as follows:

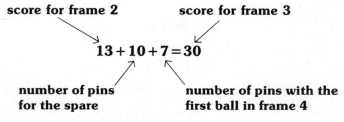

Your score for frame 4 is $30 + 10 + 0$, or 40.

Your score for frame 5 is 40+4, or 44.

In frame 6, you knocked down all the pins with the first ball, so you got a *strike*. To record a strike, draw an X in the small square.

A **strike** counts 10 pins plus the number of pins knocked down with the next two balls. You can find the score for frame 6 as follows:

score for frame 5   **score for frame 6**

$$44 + 10 + 9 = 63$$

number of pins   **number of pins with the next**
for the strike   **two balls after the strike**

Kenji Kerins

Your score for frame 7 is 63+9, or 72.

You got a strike in frame 8. On the next two balls, you got another strike (10 pins) and 6 pins. Your score for frame 8 is 72+10+16, or 98.

Your score for frame 9 is 98+10+8, or 116.

Your score for frame 10 is 116+8, or 124.

Copy and score each game below.

1.

1	2	3	4	5	6	7	8	9	10
16 /	6 1 23	43 ⊠	2 / 62	9 – 71	– / 87	6 3 96	⊠ 113	5 2 120	5 4 129

When you get a spare in frame 10, you get to throw 1 extra ball.

2.

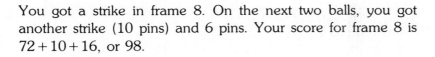

1	2	3	4	5	6	7	8	9	10 ↓
8 1 9	⊠ 26	5 2 33	– / 51	8 / 71	⊠ 91	5 / 102	1 7 110	9 – 119	3 / 8 137

When you get a strike in frame 10, you get to throw 2 extra balls.

3.

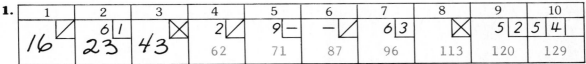

1	2	3	4	5	6	7	8	9	10 ↓ ↓
⊠ 25	⊠ 43	5 3 51	9 / 70	9 / 90	⊠ 102	– 2 104	7 / 114	– 8 122	⊠ 4 5 141

385

Purchasing a car is probably one of the largest investments you will make during your lifetime. Therefore, choose a car that will meet your individual needs and budget. Consumer guides are a reliable source of information. In the privacy of your own home, away from the pressures of a dealership showroom, you might want to research such things as road performance, safety, reliability, fuel economy, depreciation rate, available options, and price.

Bryce Flynn/Picture Group

The **sticker price** on a new car is the price the manufacturer suggests the car be sold for. The sticker price is made up of three parts. The **base price** is the cost of the car with standard equipment. **Options** are extra features, such as air conditioning, a rear-window defogger, or white-sidewall tires, that provide convenience or safety or that enhance the appearance of the car. The **destination charge** is the cost of shipping the car from the factory to the dealer.

However, the **invoice price** (the cost of the car to the dealer) is considerably less than the sticker price. Consumer magazines often report on the percentage markup on the base price and the options. Consumers should take advantage of this information. If you know the invoice price of the car you want to buy before you walk into a dealer showroom, you will have the upper hand in negotiating a price.

Example 1: Find the sticker price of this mid-sized 1984 four-door sedan:

Base price:		**$9520.00**
Options:	**Tinted glass**	110.00
	Power windows	260.00
	Air conditioning	690.00
	Radio	112.00
	Side moldings	55.00
	Power antenna	60.00
Destination charge:		414.00

$9,520.00	base price
1,287.00	total cost of options: (110 + 260 + 690 + 112 + 55 + 60)
+ 414.00	destination charge
$11,221.00	sticker price

Example 2: You read in a consumer magazine that the dealer cost of this car is 87% of the sticker base price and 85% of the cost of the listed options. Find the invoice price of this car:

$8282.40	base price 87% of $9520
1093.95	option price 85% of $1287
+ 414.00	destination charge remains the same
$9790.35	invoice price

Example 3: What is the difference between the sticker price and the invoice price?

$11,221.00	sticker price
− 9,790.35	invoice price
$1,430.65	This is your room for negotiating.

What should you pay for this car? Remember that the dealer will want to make a profit. Keep in mind that the minimum markup on most domestic cars is between $150 and $400. This markup should include both profit for the dealer and overhead costs.

Suppose both you and the salesperson agree on a price of $250 over the cost. You add this to the invoice price and make a firm offer. However, suppose the salesperson claims that your offer is unreasonable, perhaps even below cost. Ask to see the official invoice. An honest salesperson will allow you to confirm your calculations. If your figures are correct, stick to your offer. A sale at a low markup is better than no sale at all.

Example 4: You and the salesperson agree that $250 over the invoice price is a reasonable markup on the car. What is the **selling price** of the car?

$9,790.35	invoice price
+ 250.00	markup
$10,040.35	selling price (There are still more costs to add to this.)

In most states you are required to pay a sales tax. Sales tax will increase the price of the car considerably. The amount of tax varies from state to state.

You will also need to register your car. In order to do this, you must submit a **Certificate of Title** (proof of ownership) to the state. The title gives the state the information needed to complete the registration. Then the state will issue license plates for your car. The charge for registration, license plates, and title will vary from state to state. Your salesperson will offer to process this transaction for you. But, you may opt to handle this matter on your own and avoid dealership charges.

Karen Tanaka

EXERCISES

Find the sticker price.

1. Compact car
Base price: $8745
Options: $1375
Destination charge: $370
$10,490

2. Luxury car
Base price: $15,967
Options: $3159
Destination charge: $500
$19,626

3. Full-sized car
Base price: $9984
Options: $2842
Destination charge: $475
$13,301

Compute the sales tax for each car.

4. Selling price: $8943
Sales tax: 6%
$536.58

5. Selling price: $9275
Sales tax: 7%
$649.25

6. Selling price: $10,380
Sales tax: 5.5%
$570.90

Mr. and Mrs. Vanis want to purchase this new mid-sized car. They read in a consumer magazine that the dealer pays 86% of the base price and 85% of the option price.

Base price:	$9325
Options:	$2476
Destination charge:	$ 414

7. What is the sticker price of this car?
$12,215

8. What is the invoice price of this car?
$10,538.10

9. What is the difference between the sticker price and the invoice price?
$1676.90

10. Mr. and Mrs. Vanis offered $150 over the invoice price. What was their offer?
$10,688.10

11. There is a 6% sales tax in the state where Mr. and Mrs. Vanis live. Their offer is accepted. How much sales tax will they pay? $641.29

12. The state also charges a $3 fee for the title and $45 for car registration and license plates. What is the total cost of the car? $11,377.39

Pat Michaels wants to buy this new compact car. He read in a consumer magazine that the dealer pays 89% of the base price listed on the sticker and 87% of the price of the options.

Base price:	$8823
Options	
Tinted glass:	105
Body trim:	47
Power brakes:	125
Power steering:	210
Air conditioning:	625
Destination charge:	370

13. What is the total cost of the options? $1112

14. What is the sticker price of the car? $10,305

15. What is the invoice price of the car?
$9189.91

16. Pat offered $175 over the invoice price of the car. What was his offer?
$9364.91

17. There is a 5% sales tax in the state where Pat lives. His offer is accepted by the salesperson. How much tax will he pay? $468.25

18. The state where he lives also charges a $2 fee for the title and $39 for car registration and license plates. What is the total cost of the car? $9874.16

Application 43 may be used at this time.   **389**

9.8 | FINANCING A CAR

Rick Doble/Southern Light

Jake is buying a new sports car. The total selling price of the car is $12,000. Since Jake has only $3500 in his savings account, he must borrow money to pay for the car.

Jake shopped around for the lowest interest rate. He found that the local bank where he has a savings account offered a 12% rate of interest but required a down payment of one third of the selling price of the car. A local savings and loan association required a 25% down payment to get a 13% interest rate. Jake found that the dealership charged the highest rate of interest. Jake would like to have the lowest interest rate possible.

Example 1: How much down payment does the bank require?

$$\frac{1}{3} \text{ of } 12{,}000 = \frac{1}{3} \times 12{,}000$$
$$= \frac{1}{3} \times \frac{12{,}000}{1}$$
$$= \frac{12{,}000}{3}$$
$$= 4000$$

The bank requires a $4000 down payment on the loan.

Example 2: How much down payment does the savings and loan association require?

$12,000   Find 25% of $12,000.
$\times 0.25$
$3000.00

The savings and loan association requires a $3000 down payment on the loan.

Since Jake does not have enough money to use as a down payment on a loan from the bank, he decided to borrow money from the savings and loan association for a higher rate of interest.

Artstreet

390

Example 3: How much money did Jake borrow from the savings and loan association (with a $3000 down payment)?

$12,000	**selling price**
− 3,000	**down payment**
$ 9,000	**amount borrowed**

Jake borrowed $9000 from the savings and loan association.

Most people borrow money to buy a car for 36 months or longer. As the table below indicates, the longer the repayment period on the loan, the smaller the monthly payments. However, the longer the repayment period, the more interest you will pay. This table shows approximate monthly payments. Figures are rounded to the nearest dollar; actual amounts may vary slightly.

		Monthly payment		
	Loan amount	24 months	36 months	48 months
	$4,000	$188	$133	$105
	5,000	235	166	132
	6,000	282	199	158
12%	7,000	330	233	184
	8,000	377	266	211
	9,000	424	299	237
	10,000	471	332	263
	$4,000	$190	$135	$107
	5,000	238	168	134
	6,000	285	202	161
13%	7,000	333	236	188
	8,000	380	270	215
	9,000	428	303	241
	10,000	475	337	268
	$4,000	$192	$137	$109
	5,000	240	171	137
	6,000	288	205	164
14%	7,000	336	239	191
	8,000	384	273	219
	9,000	432	308	246
	10,000	480	342	273

Example 4: If Jake takes out a 36-month loan, how much interest will he pay on the $9000 at 13%? (Refer to the table on page 391.)

$303	monthly payment		$10,908	total repayment
×36	no. of months	−	9,000	amount borrowed
$10,908	total repayment		$1,908	interest

The interest on a 36-month loan will be $1908.

Example 5: If Jake takes out a 48-month loan, how much interest will he pay?

$241	monthly payment		$11,568	total repayment
×48	no. of months	−	9,000	amount borrowed
$11,568	total repayment		$2,568	interest

The interest on a 48-month loan will be $2568.

Example 6: How much money will Jake save if he borrows the money for 36 months instead of 48 months?

$2568	interest on the 48-month loan
− 1908	interest on the 36-month loan
$660	savings

Jake will save $660 if he takes out a 36-month loan instead of a 48-month loan. However, he must decide if he can make the higher monthly payment.

Example 7: Suppose Jake decides to take out a loan for 36 months. What will be the total amount paid for the car?

$12,000	selling price
+ 1,908	interest
$13,908	total amount paid for the car

Jake will pay a total of $13,908 for his new car. This is $1908 more than the original cost of the car.

EXERCISES

Find the amount of down payment for each car.

1. Selling price: $9780
Down payment: 30%
$2934

2. Selling price: $7952
Down payment: $\frac{1}{4}$
$1988

3. Selling price: $6052
Down payment: 25%
$1513

The selling price of each car is given. Find the amount of money borrowed if a 20% down payment is made.

4. $9760 $7808

5. $12,505 $10,004

6. $5995 $4796

Lucia is buying a new car for $10,972. She will borrow $7000 at 13% interest from the bank. (Refer to the table on page 391.)

7. What will Lucia's monthly car payment be if she has a 24-month loan? $333

8. What will Lucia's total repayment to the bank be on a 24-month loan? $7992

9. How much interest will Lucia pay on a 24-month loan? $992

10. What will Lucia's monthly car payment be if she has a 36-month loan? $236

11. What will Lucia's total repayment be on a 36-month loan? $8496

12. How much interest will Lucia pay on a 36-month loan? $1496

13. On which loan will Lucia pay less interest? a 24-month loan

14. How much money will Lucia save if she borrows money for 24 months instead of 36 months? $504

Jill bought a new car for $14,893. She borrowed $10,000 for 48 months at 12% interest. (Refer to the table on page 391.)

15. What is Jill's monthly car payment? $263

16. What is her total repayment to the loan company? $12,624

17. How much interest will Jill pay on her loan? $2624

18. What is the total amount Jill paid for her car? $17,517

19. Carl's car costs $6543. He will borrow $4000 at 13% interest for 24 months. What is the total amount Carl paid for the car? $7103

20. Which would be more expensive, an $8000 loan for 36 months at 12% interest or an $8000 loan for 24 months at 13% interest? How much more? the 36-month loan; $456

393

Car owners will tell you how expensive it is to keep a car in good running condition. However, you can do your own routine maintenance and small repairs. This will save you a great deal of money on parts and labor.

Item	Store price
oil filter	$4.27
oil (quart)	$1.19
fuel filter	$2.41

1. Mary's car needs a new fuel filter. The mechanic at a neighborhood service station quoted Mary a price of $4.95 for the filter and $6.00 for labor. How much money will Mary save if she buys the filter and changes it herself? $8.54

2. Bill wants to change the oil in his car. He needs five quarts of oil and an oil filter. The mechanic at the service center will charge $24.95 for this service. How much will Bill save if he does this routine maintenance himself? $14.73

Fredrik D. Bodin/Picture Group

3. The spark plugs on Joan's car need to be changed. Seko's Spark Shop charges $20.60 for the spark plugs and $18.00 for the labor. How much money will Joan save if she pays $8.26 for the plugs at a discount store and changes them herself? $30.34

4. Vito drives 15,000 miles every year. His car gets 25 miles per gallon of gasoline. At the self-service station, Vito pays $1.23 for a gallon of gasoline. At the full-service station, he pays $1.37 for a gallon. How much will Vito save in one year by buying all his gasoline at the self-service station? $84

H. Armstrong Roberts

Many teenagers would like to travel once they graduate from school and are working full-time. One way to combine travel and work is to be a travel agent. Travel agents receive commissions from transportation companies, hotels, and tour operators for trips that they book. Travel agents also are able to take advantage of reduced rates for personal travel.

The most important factors for success as a travel agent are sincere interests in travel and in people. At least two years of college is desired, along with completion of a program at a travel-agency school. Courses in foreign language, mathematics, geography, history, accounting, and business management are helpful. Since a travel agent usually uses a computer extensively, familiarity with computers and good typing skills are also important.

1. Milton Kerr books a $1575 cruise and a $399 round-trip flight through a travel agent. The travel agent will collect a 15% commission from the cruise company for the cruise and a 10% commission from the airline for the flight. Find the total commission. $276.15

2. The Lees plan to stay at a hotel in London and at a hotel in Paris. Their travel agent needs to collect in advance the first night's hotel bill for each hotel. In London the first night's bill is 68 English pounds, and in Paris the first night's bill is 875 French francs. The travel agent must convert each amount to U.S. dollars.

   Suppose the current exchange rates are the following:

   1 English pound = 1.3983 U.S. dollars
   1 French franc = 0.1199 U.S. dollar $95.08
   a. Find the first night's bill in London in U.S. dollars.
   b. Find the first night's bill in Paris in U.S. dollars.
       $104.91

3. Anne has worked as a travel agent for 1 year. She is now entitled to take a trip at 75% off the usual price. Suppose she takes a trip that usually costs $688. How much will she have to pay? $172

395

| CAR INSURANCE |

Artstreet

Automobile accidents often result in serious injuries or extensive property damage. Car insurance will protect a driver against financial losses from accidents. Remember, drivers are legally responsible for any costs that arise from accidents they cause. Therefore, it is strongly recommended that all drivers have insurance.

Some states require that all drivers carry **liability insurance.** Liability insurance includes two types of coverage. **Bodily injury** coverage will pay for medical expenses of someone who was injured by the car you were driving. **Property damage** coverage will pay for damages to someone's property that were caused by an accident that was your fault.

The amount of liability coverage you have is usually expressed in multiples of $5000, as shown in the following example:

100,000/300,000/25,000

Bodily injury limits		Property damage limits
100,000	300,000	25,000
$100,000 maximum to each person you injure	$300,000 maximum to all persons you injure	$25,000 maximum for all property you damage

For each type of insurance coverage you have you must pay an annual **premium.** The amount of the premium depends on a **driver-rating factor** (your age, your sex, where you live, whether you are a full-time or a part-time driver, your marital status, and other information about you as the driver) and a **base rate** for the amount of coverage you want.

Premium = Driver-rating factor × Base rate

Liability Insurance Table

Property damage limits	Bodily injury limits				
	25,000/50,000	50,000/100,000	50,000/200,000	100,000/200,000	100,000/300,000
25,000	43.40	48.20	50.40	53.00	53.80
50,000	44.80	49.40	51.60	54.20	55.20
100,000	46.00	50.80	53.00	55.60	56.40

Example 1: John is 18 years old, unmarried, and has a good driving record. He has liability insurance coverage for 50,000/100,000/25,000. What is the premium for this coverage if John has a driver-rating factor of 2.6? (The base rate is the entry in the table on page 396 that is in the 50,000/100,000 column of the 25,000 row.)

Artstreet

Driver-rating factor × Base rate = Premium
$$2.6 \times 48.20 = 125.32$$

John will pay $125.32 for the liability coverage on his car.

Comprehensive coverage pays for damages to your car caused by fire, theft, vandalism, or an act of God. **Collision coverage** pays for damages to your car if an accident is your fault or if a person that damages your car has no liability insurance. With either of these coverages, you can have a **deductible.** A deductible is the amount you pay before the insurance takes over. A deductible will lessen the premium on a particular coverage. For either of these types of coverage, the base rate is determined by the amount of coverage you want, the age group of your car, and the insurance rating group (size and value of your car). The amount of premium depends on the base rate and the driver-rating factor.

Premium = Driver-rating factor × Base rate

Age group	Insurance rating group						Insurance rating group					
	1–5	6	7	8	9	10	1–5	6	7	8	9	10
	$50 Deductible: comprehensive						$50 Deductible: collision					
1984	9.40	12.20	14.80	19.00	27.00	33.40	43.80	47.20	54.00	60.60	67.40	74.20
1983	8.60	11.20	13.60	17.40	24.80	30.80	40.20	43.40	49.60	55.80	62.00	68.20
1982	8.20	10.80	13.00	16.80	23.80	29.40	38.60	41.60	47.60	53.40	59.40	65.20
1981	7.40	9.60	11.60	14.80	21.00	26.00	34.20	36.80	42.20	47.20	52.60	57.80
	Full coverage: comprehensive						$100 Deductible: collision					
1984	14.80	18.20	21.40	24.80	33.00	39.60	36.80	42.80	49.00	55.00	61.20	67.40
1983	13.60	16.80	19.60	22.80	30.40	36.40	33.80	39.40	45.00	50.60	56.40	62.00
1982	13.00	16.00	18.80	21.80	29.00	34.80	32.40	37.60	43.20	48.40	53.80	59.40
1981	11.60	14.20	16.60	19.40	25.80	30.80	28.80	33.40	38.20	43.00	47.80	52.60

John's car is a 1983 model. He is in insurance rating group 7 and has a driver-rating factor of 2.6.

Example 2: John has a $50 deductible on his comprehensive insurance. What is the premium?

Driver-rating factor × Base rate = Premium

2.6 × 13.60 = 35.36

The premium is $35.36.

Example 3: John has a $50 deductible on his collision insurance. What is the premium?

Driver-rating factor × Base rate = Premium

2.6 × 49.60 = 128.96

The premium is $128.96.

Example 4: What is John's total annual insurance premium?

$$\begin{array}{rl} \$125.32 & \text{liability premium} \\ 35.36 & \text{comprehensive premium} \\ + \ 128.96 & \text{collision premium} \\ \hline \$289.64 & \text{total annual premium} \end{array}$$

John's total annual insurance premium is $289.64.

Medical payment coverage pays for medical expenses for you or your passengers due to an accident. ***Uninsured motorists*** coverage provides payment for bodily injury to you or your passengers if the other driver is responsible but does not have liability insurance. Check with your agent about other types of coverage.

EXERCISES

Marsha has 50,000/100,000/25,000 liability coverage, $50 deductible on collision, full comprehensive coverage, uninsured motorists coverage, and $10,000 medical coverage per person. Determine the type of coverage that would apply in each situation and how much the insurance company would pay.

1. The windshield on Marsha's car is broken by some children playing baseball. It will cost $282 to replace.
comprehensive; $282

2. The accident is Marsha's fault. It will cost $178 to repair the fender on her car. collision; $128

3. Damage worth $440 is done to Marsha's car by a driver who has no insurance.
collision; $390

4. Marsha causes damage worth $550 to someone's car. liability (property damage); $550

5. Marsha's car is stolen. It is worth $6200. comprehensive; $6200

6. liability (property damage); $2600
The accident is Marsha's fault. She causes damage worth $2600 to public property.

7. Marsha is injured in an accident that is her fault. Her medical bills total $3470.
medical payment; $3470

8. Ms. Jay sues Marsha for $75,000 in a bodily injury suit and wins the case.
liability (bodily injury); $50,000

Jason's driver-rating factor is 2.45. His car is a 1982 model and is in insurance rating group 6. He wants the following coverages for his car: $50 deductible on collision, $50 deductible on comprehensive, and 25,000/50,000/50,000 liability coverage. (Refer to the tables on pages 396 and 397.)

9. What is the premium for the comprehensive coverage? $26.46

10. What is the premium for the collision coverage? $101.92

11. What is the liability premium? $109.76

12. What is Jason's total annual insurance premium? $238.14

Joanne Baker has a driver-rating factor of 2.90. Her car is a 1984 model and is in insurance rating group 7. She has $100 deductible on collision, $50 deductible on comprehensive, and 50,000/100,000/50,000 liability coverage. (Refer to the tables on pages 396 and 397.)

13. What is the premium for the comprehensive coverage? $42.92

14. What is the premium for the collision coverage? $142.10

15. What is the liability premium? $143.26

16. What is the total annual premium? $328.28

Joanne found out that when she turns 25 next year, her driver-rating factor will be 1.00. She plans to keep the same car and the same type of insurance coverage.

17. What will her total annual premium be after she turns 25? $113.20

18. How much money will she save on car insurance after she turns 25? $215.08

Montain Jeffery has 50,000/200,000/50,000 liability coverage. His driver-rating factor is 3.10. He decides to pay two semiannual premiums rather than one large annual premium. Each semiannual premium is 50.5% of the annual premium.

19. What is the annual premium for Montain's liability coverage? $159.96

20. To the nearest cent, what is each semiannual premium for this coverage? $80.78

21. How much more will it cost Montain to make two semiannual payments on the liability coverage than one annual payment? $1.60

22. Are there any advantages to making semiannual payments rather than annual payments? Answers will vary.

The cost of medical care is continually rising. To protect yourself from financial hardships caused by serious illness, you should have health insurance.

Most health-insurance plans include two types of coverage: **basic medical** insurance and **major medical** insurance. Basic medical insurance usually includes full or partial coverage for hospital stays, X rays, lab tests, in-hospital physicians' visits, and so on. With some plans, you must meet a deductible before the basic medical coverage goes into effect. You are responsible for all expenses not covered under the basic medical insurance.

Jane had surgery and was hospitalized for five days. After she was released from the hospital, she needed some medication and a private nurse for three days. She has basic medical coverage with an annual $100 deductible. Her bills included the following items and totaled $5495:

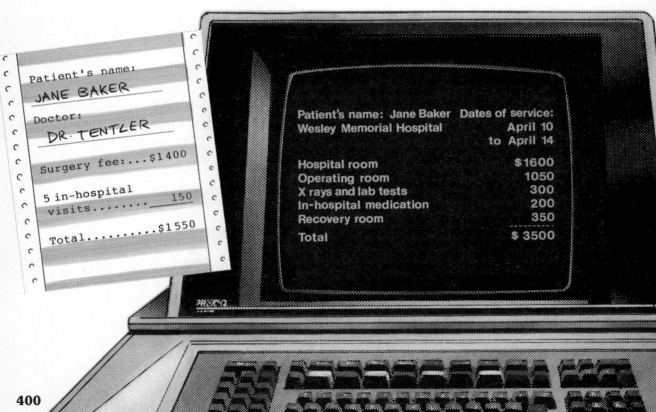

Dale's Drugstore

Patient's name:

Jane Baker

Medication.... $70

Patient's name:
JANE BAKER

Doctor:
DR. TENTLER

Surgery fee:...$1400

5 in-hospital
visits........ 150

Total..........$1550

Patient's name: Jane Baker   Dates of service:
Wesley Memorial Hospital   April 10
                                    to April 14

Hospital room	$1600
Operating room	1050
X rays and lab tests	300
In-hospital medication	200
Recovery room	350
Total	$ 3500

Example 1: Jane's basic medical insurance paid the following:

Basic medical insurance coverage

Hospital room paid at 100%	**$1600**
Operating room paid at 100%	**1050**
X rays and lab tests paid at 100%	**300**
Medication paid at 100%	**200**
Recovery room paid at 100%	**350**
Surgery paid at 80% (80% of $1400)	**1120**
5 in-hospital physician's visits*	**+ 50**
Total eligible amount	**$4670**
Less $100 deductible	**− 100**
Total amount paid by basic medical insurance	**$4570**

*$10 maximum per visit

Major medical insurance coverage pays for expenses not covered by the basic medical coverage or that go beyond the limits of the basic medical coverage. With many plans, major medical will pay only a percent of the remaining expenses after a deductible is met. Remember, each plan is different and provides different coverage.

Example 2: Jane's major medical insurance will pay 80% of all remaining eligible expenses after the $100 deductible is met.

Major medical coverage

Balance of fees from in-hospital physician's visits	**$100**
Private nurse	**375**
Out-of-hospital medication	**+ 70**
Total	**$545**
Less deductible	**− 100**
Major medical pays 80% of this amount	**445**
	×0.80
Amount paid by major medical insurance	**$356**

Patient's name: _Jane Baker_

Nurse: _Ms. T. Burts_

Dates of service: ..... _April 15_ to _April 17_

Total charges.....................$375

Example 3:

How much of her bill will Jane have to pay?

Amount paid by basic medical insurance	**$4570**
Amount paid by major medical insurance	**+ 356**
Total amount paid by insurance:	**$4926**

Total bill:	**$5495**
Total amount paid by insurance:	**− 4926**
Amount Jane will have to pay:	**$569**

Jane will have to pay $569 of her bill.

Most people will have some form of health insurance. Health insurance companies sell individual and group plans. Purchasing individual insurance coverage is much more expensive than obtaining coverage with a group plan.

One benefit many companies offer their employees is group health insurance. The company may pay the entire premium or you may be asked to pay a small portion of it. Group plans may also cover the insured person's spouse and children.

EXERCISES

Your basic medical insurance has no annual deductible. Major medical insurance has an annual deductible of $50 and pays 75% of the remaining expenses. You have the following bills from a recent hospital stay and recovery:

	Charge
Hospital room (paid at 100% by basic medical insurance)	$1125
Intensive care (paid at 100% by basic medical insurance)	1600
Oxygen (paid at 100% by basic medical insurance)	750
Tests (paid at 100% by basic medical insurance)	476
In-hospital medication (paid at 100% by basic medical insurance)	135
9 in-hospital physician's visits ($15 maximum per visit paid by basic medical insurance; balance covered by major medical insurance)	270
Out-of-hospital medication (covered by major medical insurance)	75
Ambulance service (covered by major medical insurance)	+ 50
Total	$4481

1. How much of the bill will your basic medical insurance pay? $4221

2. What is the balance of the bill after the basic medical insurance pays its share? $260

3. How much of the bill is eligible for major medical coverage after the deductible is met? $210

4. How much of this eligible amount will major medical insurance pay? $157.50

5. What is the total amount of the bill paid by the insurance? $4378.50

6. How much of the original bill will you have to pay? $102.50

Your basic medical insurance has no annual deductible and will pay up to $200 per calendar year for diagnostic X rays and tests. Major medical insurance will pay 80% of the unpaid balance after a $50 deductible is met. You have some tests and X rays that total $450.

7. How much of this bill will your basic medical insurance pay? $200

8. What is the balance of the bill after the basic medical insurance pays its share? $250

9. How much of the bill is eligible for major medical coverage after the deductible is met? $200

10. How much of the eligible amount will major medical insurance pay? $160

11. What is the total amount of the bill paid by the insurance? $360

12. How much of the bill will you have to pay? $90

You have made six visits to your doctor's office for treatment of a mild ailment. Each visit costs $30 and the doctor has prescribed medication that totaled $75. Your basic medical insurance will pay the "usual and customary" charges of $25 for each office visit. Major medical insurance will pay 80% of the cost of the medication after a $50 deductible is met.

13. What is the total cost of your visits to the doctor's office? $180

14. What is your total bill for doctor's visits and medication? $255

15. How much will the basic medical insurance pay toward your visits to the doctor's office? $150

16. How much will major medical insurance pay toward the medication? $20

17. What is the total amount your insurance will pay? $170

18. How much of the original bill will you have to pay? $85

CHAPTER REVIEW

1. In a survey of 1200 teenage boys, 7% claimed they would like to buy some new clothes once they have completed school and are working full-time. How many boys surveyed claimed they would like to buy clothes? 84

9.1

2. You decide to rent an apartment in Schindler Estates. Before moving in you must pay $25 for a credit check, a security deposit of one month's rent, and the first month's rent. Find your move-in cost. $775

9.2

> **SCHINDLER ESTATES**
> 1-BDR. Apt.
> $375 per month

3. You work 40 hours per week at $9.05 per hour. You do not want to pay more than 30% of your gross monthly pay for rent. Can you afford to live at Schindler Estates? Yes

Find the unit price for each item to the nearest tenth of a cent. Then tell which is the better buy.

9.3

4. 10 oz for $0.89   8.9¢
   16 oz for $1.35   8.4¢

5. 1.5 kg for $4 $2.667
   2 kg for $5.50 $2.750

You order items at a restaurant that cost $7.90, $7.90, $2.50, $1.75, and $0.90. The rate of sales tax is 8%.

9.4

6. Find the total bill. $22.63

7. Estimate a 15% tip for the above order. $3.15 (Answers may vary.)

8. Donna bought a swimsuit for $39. She wore it 18 times. Find the wearing cost of the swimsuit. (Round to the nearest cent.) $2.17

9.5

9. A $93 sport coat is on sale for 15% off. A similar sport coat sells for $99 and is reduced $15. Which sport coat is less expensive? the $93 sport coat

You join a tape club. You get 5 tapes for a total of $1.50. Later you buy 5 more tapes at $8.99 each—plus $2.45 per tape for shipping and handling.

9.6

10. Find the total cost (including shipping and handling) for the 10 tapes. $58.70

11. Find the average cost (including shipping and handling) per tape. $5.87

The sticker on a new subcompact car lists the base price as $7095, options totaling $1092, and a destination charge of $370. The dealer pays 88% of the base price and 86% of the price of the options.

12. What is the sticker price of the car? $8557

13. What is the invoice price of the car? $7552.72

Diego is buying a new car for $13,956. He will take out a $10,000 loan at 13% interest for 36 months. (Refer to the table on page 391.)

14. How much interest will Diego pay on the loan? $2132

15. What is the total amount Diego paid for his car? $16,088

Julio has a driver-rating factor of 2.75. His car is a 1981 model and is in insurance rating group 9. He has the following insurance coverages: 50,000/ 200,000/100,000 liability, $100 deductible on collision, and $50 deductible on comprehensive coverage. (Refer to the tables on pages 396 and 397.)

16. What is the premium on the liability coverage? $145.75

17. What is the premium on the collision coverage? $131.45

18. What is the premium on the comprehensive coverage? $57.75

19. What is Julio's total annual premium? $334.95

Henry had surgery. His total hospital bill was $3532. The bill from the doctor for surgery and in-hospital visits was $1575. His basic medical insurance pays the entire hospital bill after the $50 deductible is met. Major medical insurance will pay 80% of the doctor bills after the $100 deductible is met.

20. How much of this bill will basic medical insurance pay? $3482

21. How much of this bill will major medical insurance pay? $1180

22. What is the total amount that the insurance will pay? $4662

23. How much of this bill will Henry have to pay? $445

1. In a survey of 1200 teenage girls, 17% claimed they would like to buy some new clothes once they have completed school and are working full-time. How many girls surveyed claimed they would like to buy clothes? 204

2. You cannot afford to spend more than 25% of your gross monthly pay for rent. Suppose you work 40 hours per week at $5.15 per hour. Can you afford to pay $245 per month for rent? No

3. Find the unit price for each item to the nearest tenth of a cent. Then tell which is the better buy.

   32 ounces of fruit juice for $1.05   3.3¢

   46 ounces of fruit juice for $1.39   3.0¢

4. You order items at a restaurant that cost $3.95, $1.65, and $0.75. The rate of sales tax is 5.5%. Find the total bill. $6.70

5. Carmellita bought a pair of boots for $73. She wore the boots 24 times. What was the wearing cost of the boots? (Round to the nearest cent.) $3.04

6. The yearly membership fee at a health club is $250. This includes full use of all facilities. Suppose you join the club and estimate that you will use the facilities about 150 times during the year. Find the average cost per visit. $1.67

7. The sticker on a new full-sized car lists the base price as $9584, options totaling $2563, and a destination charge of $475. What is the sticker price of the car? $12,622

8. Julie is buying a car for $9732. She will borrow $5000 from the bank for 36 months at 14%. What is the total cost of the car? (Refer to the table on page 391.) $10,888

9. Rosa has a driver-rating factor of 1.65. Her car is a 1982 model and is in insurance rating group 9. She wants comprehensive insurance with a $50 deductible. What will her premium be for this coverage? (Refer to the table on page 397.) $39.27

10. Emilia's medical expenses totaled $734. Her major medical insurance will cover 75% of these expenses after the annual $100 deductible is met. How much of this bill will the insurance pay? $475.50

Correlation	
Items	Sec
1	9.1
2	9.2
3	9.3
4	9.4
5	9.5
6	9.6
7	9.7
8	9.8
9	9.9
10	9.10

1. There are 3 red, 4 blue, and 5 white marbles in a bag. You pick one marble without looking. Find the probability of getting a white marble. Express it as a fraction. $\frac{5}{12}$

2. The probability of an outcome that is certain to occur is _____1_____.

3. You have 5 shirts and 3 pairs of pants. How many possible outfits (of shirts and pants) are there? 15 outfits

4. There are 8 blue, 7 black, and 5 green marbles in a bag. You pick one marble without looking. Find the probability of getting a black marble. Express it as a percent. 35%

5. Suppose you flip a coin 30 times. Predict how many times you would expect to get heads. 15 times

Correlation	
Items	Sec
1	10.1
2	10.2
3	10.3
4	10.4
5	10.5
6	10.6
7	10.7
8	10.8
9–10	10.9
11–12	10.10

Choose the correct answer.

6. A machine that can receive, store, process, and display large amounts of data is a (computer, central processing unit).

7. Computers are used in schools to (replace teachers, help students learn).

8. The information that a computer prints is called (output, input).

Find the value of each BASIC expression.

9. 24/8   3

10. 2+6*8   50

Write the output that will be produced when each program is run.

11.
```
10 LET L=5
20 LET W=6
30 LET A=L*W
40 PRINT "THE AREA IS"
50 PRINT A
60 END
```
THE AREA IS
30

12.
```
10 LET X=1
20 PRINT X
30 LET X=X+1
40 IF X<5 THEN GO TO 20
50 END
```
1
2
3
4

Wheel of Luck

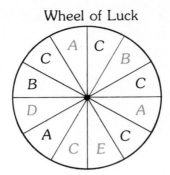

You are to spin the Wheel of Luck once. When it stops, the pointer will be on one of the sections. You would like to know your *chance* or **probability** of getting a C.

Each section is called an **outcome.** There are 12 sections on the wheel, so there are 12 possible outcomes. Since each outcome is as likely to occur as any other outcome, we say that the outcomes are **equally likely.**

How many of the sections are marked C? Since 5 of the 12 outcomes are C, the probability of getting a C can be given by this fraction:

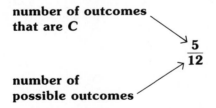

number of outcomes that are C

$\dfrac{5}{12}$

number of possible outcomes

We write **p(C)** to stand for the "probability of getting a C." If all the outcomes are equally likely, we can use the following formula for finding the probability of getting a C:

$$p(C) = \frac{\textbf{number of outcomes that are C}}{\textbf{number of possible outcomes}}$$

Example 1: You spin the wheel once. What is the probability of getting a D?

$$p(D) = \frac{1}{12}$$

Example 2: You spin the wheel once. What is the probability of getting a green letter?

p(a green letter) $= \dfrac{6}{12}$, or $\dfrac{1}{2}$.

When using fractions, give the probability in lowest terms.

EXERCISES

You spin the Wheel of Luck (on page 408) once. Find each probability.

1. p(E) $\dfrac{1}{12}$

2. p(B) $\dfrac{1}{6}$

3. p(A) $\dfrac{1}{4}$

4. p(a black letter) $\dfrac{1}{2}$

5. p(a green A) $\dfrac{1}{6}$

6. p(a black C) $\dfrac{1}{3}$

These slips of paper are put into a hat. You pick one slip without looking.

7. How many possible outcomes are there? 10

8. Are the outcomes equally likely? Yes

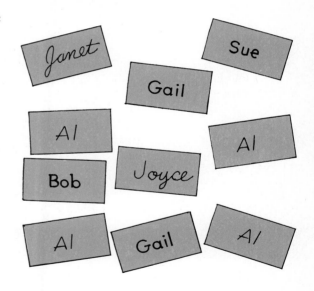

Find each probability.

9. p(Janet) $\dfrac{1}{10}$

10. p(Gail) $\dfrac{1}{5}$

11. p(Al) $\dfrac{2}{5}$

12. p(a male name) $\dfrac{1}{2}$

13. p(a female name) $\dfrac{1}{2}$

14. p(a 3-letter name) $\dfrac{1}{5}$

You pick one marble without looking. Find each probability.

15. p(white) $\dfrac{2}{9}$

16. p(black) $\dfrac{4}{9}$

17. p(blue) $\dfrac{1}{3}$

18. p(not blue) $\dfrac{2}{3}$

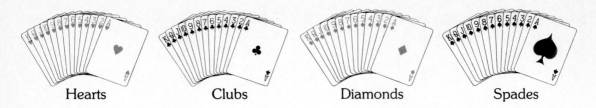

Hearts   Clubs   Diamonds   Spades

The 52 cards in a regular deck of playing cards are shown. Notice that there are 13 cards in each suit—hearts, clubs, diamonds, and spades. The deck is thoroughly shuffled and placed facedown. You draw one card without looking. Find each probability.

19. p(a club) $\frac{1}{4}$ **20.** p(a diamond) $\frac{1}{4}$

21. p(a 10) $\frac{1}{13}$ **22.** p(an ace) $\frac{1}{13}$

23. p(the queen of spades) $\frac{1}{52}$ **24.** p(the 8 of clubs) $\frac{1}{52}$

25. p(a red card) $\frac{1}{2}$ **26.** p(a black card) $\frac{1}{2}$

27. p(a heart) $\frac{1}{4}$ **28.** p(a spade) $\frac{1}{4}$

29. p(a red 3) $\frac{1}{26}$ **30.** p(a black king) $\frac{1}{26}$

31. p(a jack) $\frac{1}{13}$ **32.** p(a 4) $\frac{1}{13}$

A *picture card* is a jack, queen, or king.

33. p(a red picture card) $\frac{3}{26}$ **34.** p(a picture card) $\frac{3}{13}$

Your friend is thinking of a whole number from 1 through 10.
You are to guess the number.

35. Suppose you guess 5. What is the probability that your guess is correct? $\frac{1}{10}$

36. Suppose you guess 8. What is the probability that your guess is too high? $\frac{7}{10}$

37. Suppose you guess 2. What is the probability that your guess is too low? $\frac{4}{5}$

38. Suppose you guess 3 and find out that your guess is wrong. Then you make another guess from the remaining 9 numbers. What is the probability that your second guess is correct? $\frac{1}{9}$

10.2 / 0 AND 1 PROBABILITIES

This coin is "fixed." It has 2 heads and no tails. Thus, if you flip the coin, you are *certain* to get heads. You are also *certain not to* get tails.

The front and back sides
of a "fixed" coin

If the coin is flipped once, there are 2 possible outcomes— both heads. Thus,

$$p(\text{heads}) = \frac{2}{2}, \text{ or } 1.$$

The probability of an outcome that is certain to occur is 1.

None of the outcomes are tails, so

$$p(\text{tails}) = \frac{0}{2}, \text{ or } 0.$$

The probability of an outcome that is certain not to occur is 0.

The probability of any outcome is 0, 1, or between 0 and 1.

EXERCISES

1. A probability can never be greater than __1__.

2. A probability can never be less than __0__.

3. What does a probability of 0 mean?
The outcome is certain not to occur.

4. What does a probability of 1 mean?
The outcome is certain to occur.

The six faces of a die (singular of *dice*) have 1, 2, 3, 4, 5, and 6 dots. You roll a die once. Find each probability.

5. p(5) $\frac{1}{6}$

6. p(7) 0

7. p(a number less than 7) 1

8. p(6) $\frac{1}{6}$

9. p(an even number) $\frac{1}{2}$

10. p(an odd number) $\frac{1}{2}$

11. p(a number greater than 5) $\frac{1}{6}$

12. p(a number less than 6) $\frac{5}{6}$

The table shows how many of each kind of sandwich are in a picnic basket. You select one sandwich without looking.

Kind of sandwich	Number of sandwiches
corned beef	8
bologna	6
salami	1

13. How many possible outcomes are there? 15

14. What is the probability of getting a meat sandwich? 1

15. What is the probability of getting a cheese sandwich? 0

16. What is the probability of getting a salami sandwich? $\frac{1}{15}$

17. What is the probability of not getting a salami sandwich? $\frac{14}{15}$

18. Add the answers you got for exercises 16 and 17. $\frac{1}{15} + \frac{14}{15} = \frac{15}{15}$, or 1

19. Use your answer for exercise 18 to complete this sentence: When you add the probability that something *will* happen and the probability that it *will not* happen, the result is 1.

20. Suppose you select a salami sandwich and eat it. Then you select another sandwich.

a. What is the probability that your second sandwich will be a salami sandwich? 0

b. What is the probability that your second sandwich will not be a salami sandwich? 1

ODDS AND PROBABILITY

Suppose the *odds* for your winning a game are 3 to 2. This means that for *every* 3 times you win a game, you probably will lose 2 times. So in 3+2, or 5, games you should win 3 times. Hence, the *probability* of your winning is $\frac{3}{5}$.

Copy and complete the table below.

Team	Odds for winning	Probability of winning
Bears	4 to 3	$\frac{4}{7}$
Bills	7 to 4	$\frac{7}{11}$
Packers	1 to 1	$\frac{1}{2}$
Broncos	2 to 3	$\frac{2}{5}$

10.3 | SAMPLE SPACES

Suppose you roll a white die and a red die at the same time. The table below shows the different ways the two dice can land.

A list or a table of all possible outcomes is called a **sample space.**

White die

	1	2	3	4	5	6
1	1,1	2,1	3,1	4,1	5,1	6,1
2	1,2	2,2	3,2	4,2	5,2	6,2
3	1,3	2,3	3,3	4,3	5,3	6,3
4	1,4	2,4	3,4	4,4	5,4	6,4
5	1,5	2,5	3,5	4,5	5,5	6,5
6	1,6	2,6	3,6	4,6	5,6	6,6

Red die

There are 36 possible outcomes in the sample space. One of the outcomes is 2,3. So, $p(2,3) = \frac{1}{36}$.

There are 4 outcomes for getting a total of 5 on both dice. They are 1,4; 2,3; 3,2; and 4,1. So, $p(\text{total of } 5) = \frac{4}{36}$, or $\frac{1}{9}$.

EXERCISES

You roll a pair of dice. Find each probability.

1. $p(3,5)$ $\frac{1}{36}$

2. $p(6,6)$ $\frac{1}{36}$

3. $p(\text{total of } 3)$ $\frac{1}{18}$

4. $p(\text{total of } 11)$ $\frac{1}{18}$

5. $p(\text{total of } 7)$ $\frac{1}{6}$

6. $p(\text{total of } 9)$ $\frac{1}{9}$

7. $p(\text{total of } 12)$ $\frac{1}{36}$

8. $p(\text{total of } 2)$ $\frac{1}{36}$

9. $p(\text{same number on both dice})$ $\frac{1}{6}$

10. $p(\text{even number on both dice})$ $\frac{1}{4}$

11. $p(8 \text{ on one die})$ 0

12. $p(\text{total less than } 13)$ 1

13. $p(\text{total less than } 5)$ $\frac{1}{6}$

14. $p(\text{total greater than } 4)$ $\frac{5}{6}$

You are going on a trip. You may depart by bus, train, or plane. You may come home only by bus or plane. The sample space below shows all of the possible ways to travel. (A result of *bus, plane* means you depart by bus and return by plane.)

Depart   Come home   Results

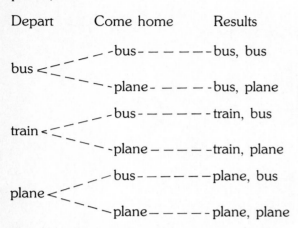

bus <
— bus — — — — — bus, bus
— plane — — — — bus, plane

train <
— bus — — — — — train, bus
— plane — — — — train, plane

plane <
— bus — — — — — plane, bus
— plane — — — — plane, plane

Eric Kroll/Taurus

15. How many possible outcomes (results) are there? 6

16. In 2 of the results you depart by plane. So, p(depart by plane) = ____, or $\frac{1}{3}$. $\frac{2}{6}$

Find each probability.

17. p(bus, plane) $\frac{1}{6}$

18. p(plane, bus) $\frac{1}{6}$

19. p(plane, plane) $\frac{1}{6}$

20. p(train, train) 0

21. p(depart by bus) $\frac{1}{3}$

22. p(come home by plane) $\frac{1}{2}$

23. p(at least one way by bus) $\frac{2}{3}$

24. p(at least one way by train) $\frac{1}{3}$

25. Suppose you have a choice of 3 shirts—one blue, one gray, and one red. You also have a choice of 3 jeans—two blue and one tan. Copy and complete the sample space to show all of the possible outfits. (An outcome of B,t means "blue shirt, tan jeans.")

Shirt

Jeans	blue (B)	gray (G)	red (R)
blue (b)	B,b	G,b	R,b
blue (b)	B,b	G,b	R,b
tan (t)	B,t	G,t	R,t

26. How many possible outcomes (outfits) are there? 9

Use the sample space of outfits from page 414. You choose a shirt and jeans at random. Find each probability.

27. p(B,t) $\frac{1}{9}$

28. p(B,b) $\frac{2}{9}$

29. p(T,t) 0

30. p(R,b) $\frac{2}{9}$

31. p(getting a red shirt) $\frac{1}{3}$

32. p(getting blue jeans) $\frac{2}{3}$

33. Copy and complete the sample space for choosing one dinner and one dessert at random from the menu.

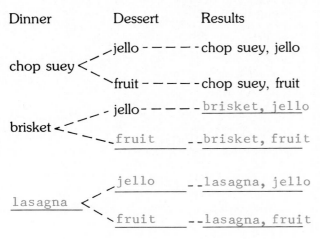

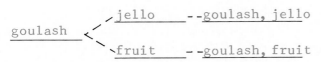

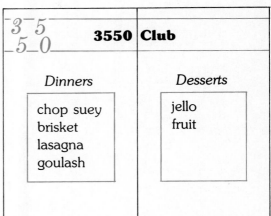

34. How many possible outcomes are there? 8

You choose one dinner and one dessert at random. Find each probability.

35. p(brisket, fruit) $\frac{1}{8}$

36. p(goulash, jello) $\frac{1}{8}$

37. p(getting fruit for dessert) $\frac{1}{2}$

You enter an elevator and press one of the buttons without looking. The probability of getting a number greater than 7 is $\frac{3}{10}$. You can write the probability as a percent by using either of these two ways:

$$\frac{3}{10} = \frac{a}{100}$$

$$300 = 10a$$

$$30 = a$$

$$\begin{array}{r} 0.30 = 30\% \\ 10\overline{)3.00} \\ \underline{3\ 0} \\ 00 \\ \underline{0} \\ 0 \end{array}$$

$$\frac{3}{10} = \frac{30}{100} = 30\%$$

So p(a number greater than 7) = 30%.

The probability of getting a number less than 11 is $\frac{10}{10}$, or 100%.

The probability of an outcome that is certain to occur is 100%.

The probability of pressing number 13 is $\frac{0}{10}$, or 0%.

The probability of an outcome that is certain not to occur is 0%.

The probability of any outcome is 0%, 100%, or between 0% and 100%.

EXERCISES

1. If the probability of an outcome is 100%, then the outcome is (<u>certain</u>, certain not) to occur.

2. If an outcome is certain not to occur, then its probability is (100%, 1%, <u>0%</u>).

You press one of the elevator buttons without looking. Find each probability as a percent.

3. p(5) 10%

4. p(12) 0%

5. p(a number less than 4)
30%

6. p(a number greater than 6)
40%

7. p(an odd number)
50%

8. p(an even number)
50%

The table shows how many of each kind of ticket are in a jar. You select one ticket at random.

Kind of ticket	Number of tickets
grand prize	1
1st prize	2
2nd prize	2
3rd prize	5
4th prize	` 10

9. How many possible outcomes are there? 20

10. How many outcomes are there for *not* getting the grand prize? 19

Find each probability as a percent.

11. p(grand prize) 5%

12. p(not getting the grand prize) 95%

13. p(4th prize) 50%

14. p(not getting a 4th prize) 50%

15. p(2nd prize) 10%

16. p(3rd prize) 25%

17. p(a prize) 100%

18. p(not getting a prize) 0%

One student will be selected at random to represent the school at a special event. The table below shows how many students in each class volunteered to be selected. Each name is written on a slip of paper, and one slip is to be drawn.

	Freshmen	Sophomores	Juniors	Seniors
Males	0	3	10	11
Females	4	8	5	9

19. How many possible outcomes are there? 50

20. How many outcomes are there for getting a female? 26

21. p(female) 52%

22. p(male) 48%

23. p(freshman) 8%

24. p(sophomore) 22%

25. p(junior) 30%

26. p(senior) 40%

27. p(male sophomore) 6%

28. p(female junior) 10%

29. p(female senior) 18%

30. p(male freshman) 0%

You have a penny and a dime. You flip each coin once.

31. Copy and complete the sample space.

Penny   Dime   Results

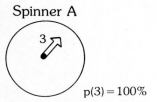

heads <
    heads - - - - heads, heads
    tails _ _ _ heads, tails

tails <
    heads _ _ _ tails, heads
    tails _ _ _ tails, tails

32. How many possible outcomes are there?   4

Find each probability as a percent.

33. p(both coins heads)   25%

34. p(both coins tails)   25%

35. p(penny heads, dime tails)   25%

36. p(one head, one tail)   50%

Spinner A

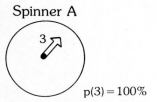

p(3) = 100%

Spinner B

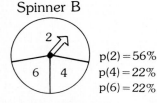

p(2) = 56%
p(4) = 22%
p(6) = 22%

Spinner C

p(1) = 51%
p(5) = 49%

You and a friend each are to pick one of the spinners shown above. You each spin your pointer once, and whoever gets the larger number wins. The probability of getting a particular number is given next to the spinner.

37. Suppose your friend picks spinner C and you pick spinner A. What is the probability that you will win?   51%

38. Suppose your friend picks spinner B and you pick spinner A. What is the probability that you will win?   56%

39. Suppose your friend picks spinner C and you pick spinner B.

  a. Your friend spins first and gets a 1. What is the probability that you will win?   100%

  b. You spin first and get a 2. Now your friend spins. What is the probability that you will lose?   49%

SKILLS REFRESHER

Multiply.

			Skill	Page
1. $\frac{1}{2} \times 14$ 7	**2.** $\frac{3}{4} \times 20$ 15	**3.** $\frac{2}{5} \times 40$ 16	33	494
4. 0.50×50 25	**5.** 0.25×80 20	**6.** 0.04×75 3	13	466

Uses of probability occur in business, insurance, games of chance, and other activities.

1. *Quality control:* When a product is mass-produced, it is often nearly impossible to inspect every item. So most manufacturers use a sampling procedure. For example, a flash-bar factory might randomly pick 200 flash bars out of every 10,000 and inspect them.

   Most manufacturers are willing to accept a small percent of defective items. It would be more costly to try to achieve perfection than to refund the purchase price of or replace a few defective items. Hence, consumers should not be too surprised if they purchase a defective item. On the other hand, consumers should expect the manufacturer to refund the price of or replace such an item.

   Suppose the flash-bar manufacturer finds an average of 4 defective flash bars in every sample of 200 bars. Find, as a percent, the probability that a bar you buy from them will be defective. 2%

2. *Insurance:* In figuring life-insurance rates, companies use tables based on past records. One such table shows that for 16-year-olds, 1.5 deaths per 1000 people occur in a year. The same table shows that for 60-year-olds, the annual death rate is 20 per 1000. Thus, the probability that a 16-year-old will die during next year is $\frac{1.5}{1000} = 0.0015$, or 0.15%.

   Find the probability as a percent that a 60-year-old will die during the next year. Who is more likely to pay a higher premium, a 16-year-old or a 60-year-old? Why? 2%; a 60-year-old; greater chance of dying that year

3. *Lotteries:* Many states conduct lotteries in order to raise money. In one state, 30,000,000 tickets are sold before the grand prize drawing is held. The winner receives one million dollars. If you buy one ticket, what is the probability that you will win one million dollars? How many tickets would you have to buy so that the probability of your winning one million dollars is $\frac{1}{2}$? Do you think buying lottery tickets is a good investment? $\frac{1}{30,000,000}$; 15,000,000; No

419

Bryce Flynn/Picture Group

You roll a die once. What is the probability of getting a 5?

Suppose you roll a die 24 times. You can **predict** how many times you would expect to get a 5 as follows:

probability of   **number of**
getting a 5   **rolls**

$$\frac{1}{6} \times 24 = 4$$

number of times you
would expect to get a 5

Example: A company tests some of the computers it makes and finds that 2% of them are defective. Predict how many computers will be defective if the company makes 4000 computers.

2% of 4000 = 0.02 × 4000 = 80

The company can expect 80 defective computers.

EXERCISES

1. You flip a coin once. What is the probability of getting heads? $\frac{1}{2}$

2. Suppose you flip a coin 20 times. Predict how many times you would expect to get heads. 10

3. Suppose you flip a coin 80 times. Predict how many times you would expect to get tails. 40

4. Suppose you flip a coin 300 times. Predict how many times you would expect to get heads. 150

5. Suppose you do not know the answer to the multiple-choice question at the right, so you guess. What is the probability of guessing the correct answer? $\frac{1}{5}$

Which amendment gave women the right to vote?

a. 16th   **b.** 17th   **c.** 18th

b. 19th   **e.** 20th

6. On a test there are 10 multiple-choice questions like the one shown. You guess at all the questions. Predict how many answers you would expect to guess correctly. 2

7. On a test there are 25 multiple-choice questions like the one shown. You guess at all the questions. Predict how many answers you would expect to guess correctly. 5

100 people were polled to see whom they preferred for mayor. The results are shown below. Use the results to do exercises 8–11.

Candidate	Kempf	Lebovitz	McTavish
Number of votes	53	39	8

8. What percent of those polled prefer Kempf? 53%

9. What percent of those polled prefer McTavish? 8%

10. Suppose 3000 people vote in the general election. Predict how many will vote for Kempf. 1590

11. Suppose 3000 people vote in the general election. Predict how many will vote for McTavish. 240

12. You roll a die once. What is the probability of getting a number less than 5? $\frac{2}{3}$

13. You roll a die 60 times. Predict how many times you would expect to get a number less than 5. 40

14. According to a survey, the probability is 15% that a person will watch the TV show *Benjie-Man*. Predict how many people will watch *Benjie-Man* in a city of 7000. 1050

15. The probability that a person picked at random will have type A+ blood is $\frac{1}{4}$. Suppose there are 80 people in a room. Predict how many of them have type A+ blood. 20

16. A company tests some of the radios it makes and finds that 1.5% of them are defective. Predict how many radios will be defective if the company makes 10,000 radios. 150

17. 50 people were asked to tell the radio station they prefer. WBMS was picked by 18 people. How many people would you expect to pick WBMS in a poll of 600 people? 216

Applications 45–46 may be used at this time.

IT'S IN THE BAG

5 marbles are in the bag. Some are green, and the rest are blue. Predict how many marbles of each color are in the bag by doing this experiment:

Draw one marble from the bag at random. Record its color, and then place it back in the bag. Repeat the procedure until you have made ten draws.

Suppose you get the results shown at the right. Use those results to predict how many green marbles and how many blue marbles are in the bag.

Color	Tally
Green	IIII
Blue	HHI I

2 green; 3 blue

Mary Elenz Tranter

Michael Philip Manheim/
Marilyn Gartman Photo Agency

A *computer* is an electronic machine that can receive large amounts of data, store the data, process the data with amazing speed, and then display the results in a way that is easy to read. Thus, a computer is designed to do four main jobs.

1. **Receive data**   Data put into a computer are called *input.* Input is usually a set of facts and a set of instructions telling the computer what to do with the facts.

2. **Store data**   A computer has a *memory* that can store the data until needed.

3. **Process data**   A main reason for using a computer is to have it do something with the data. This could include such things as performing mathematical calculations or arranging a list of names into alphabetical order. The fastest computers are able to process millions of pieces of data in seconds.

4. **Display processed data**   Information that is produced and displayed by a computer is called *output.*

Computers come in many sizes. The largest, called a *mainframe computer,* is large enough to fill a classroom. A smaller computer, a *minicomputer,* is about the size of a large television set. It can store vast amounts of information, but not nearly as much as a mainframe computer. The smallest computer, a *microcomputer,* can fit on top of a small desk. It is often called a "home" or "personal" computer because many people buy it for home use. It also can store large amounts of information, but not as much as a minicomputer.

Although a calculator can do many of the things that a computer can do, a computer is more powerful because it can store larger amounts of data and can process the data much faster. As a result, computers are able to solve much more complicated problems than calculators can solve.

The mechanical parts of a computer are called **hardware.** Although computers differ greatly in size, all have these basic pieces of hardware:

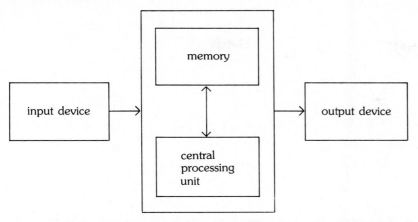

An input device receives the data. There are many types of input devices, such as the keyboard, a disk drive, a cassette recorder, or a "mouse" (a desktop device that enables a person to communicate with a computer by pointing to information on the screen).

The memory stores the data for later use.

The central processing unit (called CPU) processes the data. It performs all calculations and selects the instructions from the memory in their proper order.

An output device displays the processed data. There are many types of output devices, such as a television screen or a high-speed printer.

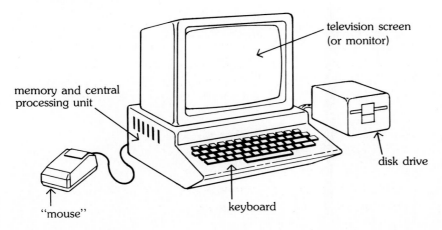

EXERCISES

Choose the correct answer.

1. A machine that can receive, store, process, and display large amounts of data is a (central processing unit, <u>computer</u>).

2. Data put into a computer are called (<u>input</u>, output).

3. The computer that can store the most information is called a (<u>mainframe computer</u>, minicomputer, microcomputer).

4. The mechanical parts of a computer are called (output, <u>hardware</u>).

5. The (memory, <u>central processing unit</u>) performs all calculations.

6. An (input, <u>output</u>) device displays the processed data.

7. The keyboard is an example of an (<u>input</u>, output) device.

8. A "personal" or "home" computer is a (mainframe computer, minicomputer, <u>microcomputer</u>).

9. A computer stores data in its (<u>memory</u>, central processing unit).

10. A computer is superior to a calculator in that it has the ability to (think, <u>store larger amounts of data and process the data faster</u>).

11. Suppose a computer is used to grade a set of papers. Tell which part of the computer (input device, memory, central processing unit, or output device) would do each job.

   a. Receive the ungraded papers and the answer key. input device

   b. Display the results. output device

   c. Store the information from the papers and the answer key. memory

   d. Use the answer key to grade the papers. central processing unit

12. Suppose a computer could make a pizza. Tell which part of the computer (input device, memory, central processing unit, or output device) would do each job.

   a. Mix the ingredients and bake the pizza according to the recipe. central processing unit

   b. Serve the pizza. output device

   c. Receive the ingredients and the recipe. input device

   d. Store the ingredients and the recipe. memory

10.7 | HOW ARE COMPUTERS USED?

Computers affect all of us in our daily lives, so it is important to be aware of where and how they are used. Here are some ways that computers are used.

1. *Government:* The Internal Revenue Service (IRS) uses computers to keep track of more than 120,000,000 tax returns each year. The computers check for errors, print checks to those people who need refunds, and print letters to those people who still owe money. The Federal Bureau of Investigation (FBI) uses computers to store people's fingerprints. This enables the FBI, when necessary, to compare very quickly someone's fingerprints with those stored in the computer's memory.

2. *Industry:* Many factories use computers to operate machines that make products. Those machines, called **robots,** are often used to perform tasks that are dangerous, delicate, or repetitive. Robots can weld, drill, paint, or wrap items almost endlessly without so much as taking a coffee break.

3. *Business:* Banks use computers to keep track of all transactions that are made. Many supermarkets use a computerized checkout system that eliminates the need to ring up the price of each item by hand. The computer also keeps an inventory of each item that is sold. Many publishing companies and newspapers use computers to help them edit manuscript, set type, and fit type on a page. This use of a computer is known as **word processing.** Some companies use computers to print mailing lists and letters, such as those inviting people to enter contests. Often the computer inserts the person's name on the letter to provide a "personal touch."

4. *Education:* Computers are used in schools to help students learn many different subjects. This is known as **computer-assisted instruction** (CAI). Computers are also used in schools to keep track of student progress and to print class schedules and grade reports.

Jacqueline Durand

5. *Medicine:* Case histories of patients are often stored in computers for instant retrieval. Many hospitals use computers to monitor a patient's temperature, heart rate, and blood pressure. The moment there is a problem with a vital sign, an alarm is sounded. Some doctors use computerized X-ray machines that enable them to detect things that would not show up on ordinary X rays.

6. *Home:* Many people have microcomputers in their homes for educational purposes, to keep track of household expenses, and to operate video games. You may have a computer in your home without realizing it. Certain microwave ovens, video recorders, push-button telephones, automobiles, electronic games, and digital watches have computers built into them. These machines can receive, store, process, and display data.

We have just seen how computers can be very useful to us. However, the use and *misuse* of computers can also pose serious problems to society. For example, credit bureaus collect and store detailed information about people so that financial decisions can be made. The computer files that hold this information are called **data banks.** The information could include where a person lives and works, how much money the person earns and owes, and whether or not the person has ever been sued. Unless access to such personal information is controlled, a person's right to privacy may be threatened. Many people fear that data banks contain wrong information about them. Everyone has the right to see what is in his or her file and to make sure that any mistakes are corrected.

Another area of concern is what is known as computer crime. Computer crime usually involves the use of a computer to carry out an illegal act. This could include illegally transferring money from one bank account to another, stealing information that is stored in a computer, or illegally changing information that is stored in a computer. To protect against computer crime, many computers require the use of one or more special passwords. If the correct password is not entered, the computer will not retrieve any information.

EXERCISES

Choose the correct answer.

1. Suppose the FBI used a computer to help investigate a suspect. Which of these tasks would the computer **not** be able to do?
   a. Compare the suspect's fingerprints with those on file.
   b. Display personal information about the suspect.
   c. Determine if the suspect is innocent or guilty.

2. Suppose you are president of a bank. Which of these jobs would you most likely use a computer for?
   a. Answer customer questions about the various types of accounts that are available.
   b. Interview people to be bank tellers.
   c. Print monthly statements for the customers.

3. Which of these items probably has a computer built into it?
   a. a microwave oven with a memory
   b. an electric shaver
   c. an electric pencil sharpener

4. Which of these is **not** a reason for using computers in schools?
   a. Help students learn.
   b. Keep track of student records.
   c. Replace teachers.

5. Computer crime generally refers to
   a. the use of a computer to carry out an illegal act.
   b. the stealing of a computer.
   c. the storing of information in data banks.

6. Which of these is a reason for using computers in medicine?
   a. Replace doctors and nurses.
   b. Provide comfort and counsel to the patient and to the patient's family.
   c. Monitor a patient's vital signs.

7. Publishing companies solve problems involving the manipulation of words by using
   a. word processing.
   b. computer-assisted instruction.
   c. robots.

8. Which of these is **not** true about data banks?
   a. Information is stored in data banks.
   b. Money is deposited in data banks.
   c. Data banks can be used to invade someone's privacy.

9. Which job might be more suitable for a person to do than a robot?
   a. Drill holes into wood on an assembly line.
   b. Examine furniture for defects.
   c. Remove hot metal from a blast furnace.

10. Which of the following do you think an automobile dealer has the right to know before selling you a car on credit?
    a. which charities you give to and how much money you give
    b. how much money you are earning at your present job
    c. your religion

10.8 HOW TO TELL A COMPUTER WHAT TO DO

Although computers can do many things, they do not have the ability to *think*. To perform a task, they must be given a specific set of instructions describing a step-by-step process to follow. A chart that shows a sequence of steps that need to be followed to perform a task is called a ***flowchart.***

Suppose a computer could make a fried egg. This flowchart could be used to tell the computer what to do.

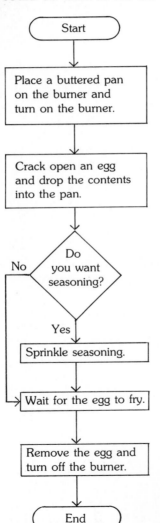

Kenji Kerins

A flowchart begins with the word "Start" enclosed in an oval.

Arrows are used between the steps to show which step is to be done next. Instructions that a computer is told to follow are enclosed in rectangles.

When a decision needs to be made, a question is enclosed in a diamond. The questions are *Yes-No* in nature. (If no seasoning is wanted, the computer skips the step "Sprinkle seasoning" and goes to the step "Wait for the egg to fry.")

A flowchart ends with the word "End" enclosed in an oval. This tells the computer that the task is finished.

This flowchart could be used to tell a computer to print the multiples of 5 from 5 though 25. The information that a computer prints is called **output.**

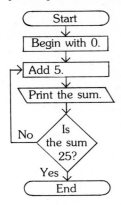

Information that a computer is told to print is enclosed in a parallelogram.

If the sum is 25, the computer goes to the step "End." Otherwise, the computer goes to the step "Add 5."

The output for this flowchart would look like this:

5
10
15
20
25

EXERCISES

1. A chart that shows a sequence of steps that need to be followed to perform a task is called a <u>flowchart</u>.

2. The information that a computer prints is called (input, <u>output</u>).

3. The steps shown below, if placed in the proper order in the flowchart, describe a procedure for getting up in the morning. Copy the flowchart and insert the steps in the correct places.

You are sleeping.

Reset the alarm and go back to sleep.

Get up out of bed.

Are you still sleepy?

The alarm rings, waking you up.

End

Start

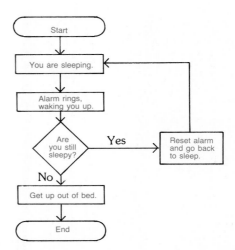

429

4. The steps shown below, if placed in the proper order in the flowchart, describe a procedure for making a telephone call. Copy the flowchart and insert the steps in the correct places.

Is someone else on the line?

Hang up.

Talk.

Pick up the receiver.

Does someone answer the phone?

Dial the number.

Start

End

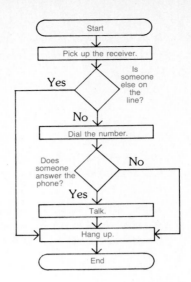

5. This flowchart provides a set of instructions for a robot to go through the maze shown below. Have the robot follow the instructions, and then indicate the letter of the space on which the robot stops. Robot stops on A.

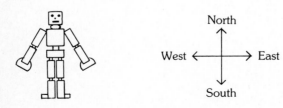

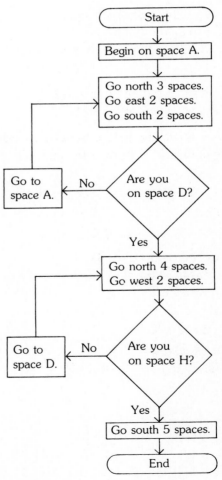

Write the output for each flowchart.

6.

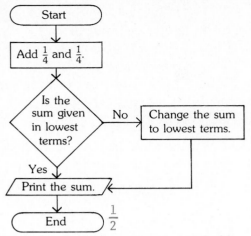

$\frac{1}{2}$

Flowcharts for exercises 8-10 may vary.

7.

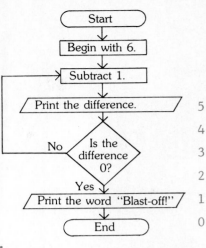

5

4

3

2

1

0

Blast-off!

8. Write a flowchart that describes a procedure for washing some dishes that are in a sink. Include at least one decision that must be made based on a *Yes-No* question.

9. Write a flowchart that describes a procedure for printing the numbers from 1 through 5.

10. Write a flowchart that describes a procedure for printing the multiples of 3 from 3 through 21.

SKILLS REFRESHER

Find each result.

			Skill	Page
1. $26-19+32$ 39	**2.** $6+8\times7$ 62	**3.** $15-8\div2$ 11	—	98
4. $\frac{9}{3}+6$ 9	**5.** $(7-2)\times5$ 25	**6.** $10-(6+4)$ 0		
7. $(6\div6)\times6$ 6	**8.** $24-\frac{8}{2}$ 20	**9.** $12-7+5$ 10		

Replace *n* with 3 and *x* with 4. Then find each answer.

10. nx 12	**11.** $7x$ 28	**12.** $2(x+n)$ 14	—	96
13. $6(x-n)$ 6	**14.** $n(9-x)$ 15	**15.** $x(n+7)$ 40		

James H. Pickerell

A flowchart helps you organize a set of instructions for a computer to follow. However, computers do not understand the English language. They understand computer languages. A computer language widely used with microcomputers is BASIC. (The letters in BASIC stand for **B**eginner's **A**ll-purpose **S**ymbolic **I**nstruction **C**ode.)

Some symbols in BASIC are the same as those used in math; some are different. Study the examples below.

Math symbol	BASIC symbol	Computation in BASIC
+	+	8 + 9 = 17
−	−	12 − 7 = 5
×	*	6*7 = 42
÷	/	15/5 = 3

A computer will follow the rule for the order of operations, as shown below.

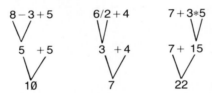

$$8 - 3 + 5 \qquad 6/2 + 4 \qquad 7 + 3*5$$
$$5 + 5 \qquad\quad 3 + 4 \qquad\quad 7 + 15$$
$$10 \qquad\qquad 7 \qquad\qquad 22$$

Many computers put a slash through the digit 0 to emphasize that it's a zero—and not the letter "O."

Parentheses are used in BASIC to indicate which operation to do first.

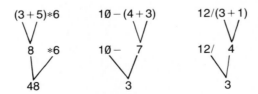

$$(3 + 5)*6 \qquad 10 - (4 + 3) \qquad 12/(3 + 1)$$
$$8 \quad *6 \qquad\quad 10 - \quad 7 \qquad\quad 12/ \quad 4$$
$$48 \qquad\qquad\quad 3 \qquad\qquad\quad 3$$

However, in BASIC parentheses are *not* used to indicate multiplication. The symbol * must always be used to indicate multiplication.

$$5*7 = 35 \qquad 3*(8 - 2) = 18$$

432

When you use the BASIC language to have a computer do math, you need to use the word PRINT. PRINT tells a computer to print the value of an expression—either on the screen or on paper in the printer.

Another word, LET, tells a computer to assign a value to a variable. PRINT is used to tell a computer to print the value of a variable.

Suppose you enter the following BASIC instructions into a computer:	After each instruction is entered, the computer will do the following:
PRINT 8 + 2	Print 10.
PRINT 5*(2 + 6)	Print 40.
LET A = 5	Assign 5 to variable A.
LET B = 7	Assign 7 to variable B.
PRINT A	Print 5.
PRINT B	Print 7.
PRINT A + B	Print 12.
LET C = A*B	Assign 35 to variable C.
PRINT C	Print 35.
PRINT 2*C	Print 70.

EXERCISES

Choose the correct answer.

1. BASIC is a (type of computer, <u>computer language</u>).

2. In BASIC, the symbol * means (add, <u>multiply</u>, divide).

3. In BASIC, the symbol / means (subtract, multiply, <u>divide</u>).

4. In BASIC, parentheses are used to indicate (<u>which operation to do first</u>, multiplication).

5. In BASIC, the word that tells a computer to assign a value to a variable is (<u>LET</u>, PRINT).

6. In BASIC, the instruction PRINT 6 + 3 will cause a computer to (print 6 + 3, <u>print 9</u>, assign 9 to a variable).

Copy and complete the table.

	Math expression	BASIC expression	Result
7.	6×8	6*8	48
8.	$20 \div 5$	20 / 5	4
9.	6 - 5 + 1	6 − 5 + 1	2
10.	$3 + 4 \times 8$	3 + 4 * 8	35
11.	$15 + 8 - 6$	15 + 8 - 6	17
12.	$12 \div 6 + 6$	12/6 + 6	8
13.	$6 - (5 + 1)$	6 - (5 + 1)	0
14.	$(24 \div 6) \div 2$	(24 / 6) / 2	2
15.	8 - 5 X 0	8 − 5*∅	8
16.	$7(9 - 8)$	7 * (9 - 8)	7

Tell what a computer will do after each BASIC instruction is entered.

17.
a. PRINT 16+2   Print 18.
b. PRINT 16−2   Print 14.
c. PRINT 16*2   Print 32.
d. PRINT 16/2   Print 8.
e. PRINT 16*2/2   Print 16.

18.
a. LET A=8   Assign 8 to A.
b. LET B=4   Assign 4 to B.
c. PRINT A   Print 8.
d. PRINT B   Print 4.
e. PRINT A/B   Print 2.

19.
a. LET C=5   Assign 5 to C.
b. LET D=8   Assign 8 to D.
c. LET E=C*D   Assign 40 to E.
d. PRINT E   Print 40.
e. PRINT E+C   Print 45.

20.
a. LET F=12   Assign 12 to F.
b. LET G=4   Assign 4 to G.
c. LET H=F/G   Assign 3 to H.
d. PRINT H   Print 3.
e. PRINT H*G   Print 12.

21.
a. LET J=3   Assign 3 to J.
b. LET K=7   Assign 7 to K.
c. PRINT 5*K   Print 35.
d. PRINT 2*(J+K)   Print 20.
e. PRINT J*(1∅−K)   Print 9.

22.
a. LET L=2   Assign 2 to L.
b. LET M=9   Assign 9 to M.
c. PRINT L*1   Print 2.
d. PRINT 5*(M−L)   Print 35.
e. PRINT M*(2−L)   Print 0.

In the previous lesson you learned how to write instructions in the BASIC language. After each instruction was entered into a computer, the computer followed that instruction. However, it is usually desirable to have a computer follow a sequence of instructions only after *all* of them have been entered into the computer.

A **computer program** is a set of numbered instructions written in a computer language that a computer follows in order. A computer will not follow the instructions until it is told to do so. In BASIC, the command RUN is entered to tell a computer to begin following the instructions. This is known as *running a program*.

An example of a computer program written in BASIC is shown below.

Lambert Studios

Each instruction begins with a *line number*. A computer follows the instructions in the order given by the line numbers. Multiples of 10 usually are used for the line numbers.

RUN is not part of a program; hence, it does not get a line number. When it is entered, it tells a computer to run the program.

```
10 LET X = 25
20 LET Y = 75
30 LET S = X + Y
40 LET A = S/2
50 PRINT "THE MEAN IS"
60 PRINT A
70 END

RUN
THE MEAN IS
50
```

In lesson 10.9 you learned that PRINT tells a computer to print the value of a variable or an expression. It also tells a computer to print the words or symbols contained between quotation marks.

END is used to tell a computer that it has reached the end of the program.

The output is shown below the word RUN.

What did line 30 instruct the computer to do?   Assign 100 to variable S.

What did line 40 instruct the computer to do?   Assign 50 to variable A.

A person who writes a computer program is called a **programmer.** A computer program is called **software.** In fact, any computer manual (including the computer literacy section in this text) is also called software.

Sometimes a programmer would like a computer to repeat a procedure several times. The program below instructs a computer to find the circumference of circles with diameters of 1 (unit), 2 (units), and 3 (units). However, a separate set of instructions for each circle is not needed. Instead, the computer is instructed to go back and use the same sequence of instructions for each circle.

```
10 LET D=1
20 LET C=3.14*D
30 PRINT "WHEN THE DIAMETER IS"
40 PRINT D
50 PRINT "THE CIRCUMFERENCE IS"
60 PRINT C
70 PRINT
80 LET D=D+1
90 If D<4 THEN GO TO 20
100 END
```

Line 70 instructs a computer to print a blank line in the output.

Line 80 instructs a computer to increase the value of D by 1. ⟶

Line 90 instructs a computer to make a decision. If the value of D is less than 4, the computer is sent to line 20. Otherwise the computer goes to the next line, line 100.

```
RUN
WHEN THE DIAMETER IS
1
THE CIRCUMFERENCE IS
3.14
```

This is the output when a computer follows lines 10–60.

```
WHEN THE DIAMETER IS
2
THE CIRCUMFERENCE IS
6.28
```

In line 80, the value of D is increased to 2. Since 2<4, line 90 sends the computer back to line 20. This is the subsequent output (through line 60).

Line 70 instructs the computer to print this blank line.

```
WHEN THE DIAMETER IS
3
THE CIRCUMFERENCE IS
9.42
```

In line 80, the value of D is increased to 3. Since 3<4, line 90 sends the computer back to line 20. This is the subsequent output (through line 60).

In line 80, the value of D is increased to 4. Since 4 is not less than 4 (line 90), the computer goes to line 100.

436

EXERCISES

Choose the correct answer.

8. THE TAX IS
10
THE TOTAL COST IS
210

1. A (flowchart, computer program) is a set of numbered instructions written in a computer language that a computer follows in order.

2. In BASIC, the command (START, RUN) is entered to tell a computer to begin following the instructions in a program.

3. Each instruction in a computer program begins with (a line number, the word LET).

4. In BASIC, the instruction PRINT "THE ANSWER IS" will cause a computer to print ("THE ANSWER IS", THE ANSWER IS).

5. A person who writes a computer program is called a (programmer, robot).

6. Computer programs and manuals are called (software, hardware).

Write the output that will be produced when each program is run.

7.
```
10 LET F=18
20 LET G=37
30 LET H=32
40 LET S=F+G+H
50 LET A=S/3
60 PRINT "THE MEAN IS"
70 PRINT A
80 END
```
THE MEAN IS
29

8.
```
10 LET R=0.05
20 LET P=200
30 LET T=R*P
40 PRINT "THE TAX IS"
50 PRINT T
60 LET C=P+T
70 PRINT "THE TOTAL COST IS"
80 PRINT C
90 END
```
See answer above.

THE TAX IS
10
THE TOTAL COST IS
210

9.
```
10 LET D=6
20 LET D=D-1
30 PRINT D
40 IF D>0 THEN GO TO 20
50 PRINT "BLAST-OFF!"
60 END
```
5
4
3
2
1
0
BLAST-OFF!

10.
```
10 LET S=1
20 LET A=S*S
30 PRINT "A SQUARE WITH SIDE"
40 PRINT S
50 PRINT "HAS AN AREA OF"
60 PRINT A
70 LET S=S+1
80 IF S<3 THEN GO TO 20
90 END
```
See answer above.

A SQUARE WITH SIDE
1
HAS AN AREA OF
1
A SQUARE WITH SIDE
2
HAS AN AREA OF
4

Applications 47–50 may be used at this time.

Computer careers can be put into two categories. Some careers mainly involve working with hardware (the mechanical parts of a computer). Others mainly involve working with software (computer programs and manuals).

Careers With Hardware:

Data-entry clerks type information into computers. They do not have to know much about computers, but they should be good typists.

Computer operators operate computers and monitor them while they are running. A degree from a 2-year college or technical training is usually required.

Service engineers maintain and repair computers. Technical training from a technical school or a community college is required.

Paul Light/Lightwave

Careers With Software:

Programmers write computer programs. Many of them need to know several computer languages. A college degree is required and a background in mathematics is often desired.

Systems analysts plan methods of processing data and handling results. They work with programmers to make sure that the most efficient programs are written to solve a problem. A college degree is required, but often a graduate degree is desired.

Technical writers write manuals that describe how to operate computers, how to write programs, and how to use programs. Their job requires a college degree and good writing skills.

Charles Gupton/Southern Light

Look in the Help Wanted section of a newspaper and cut out ads for computer-related jobs. Bring the ads to class and discuss which jobs mainly involve working with hardware and which mainly involve working with software. Discuss the qualifications for those jobs.

This is a game for three people. There are two players and one person who pretends to be a computer (called The Computer).

The game begins with The Computer thinking of a 3-digit number. The two players take turns guessing the number. The first player to guess the number becomes The Computer for the next round.

After each guess is made, The Computer prints a clue according to these rules:

If the number guessed has exactly	The Computer prints
no correct digits	nothing
1 correct digit, but in the wrong position	☐
2 correct digits, but both in the wrong positions	☐ ☐
3 correct digits, but all 3 in the wrong positions	☐ ☐ ☐
1 correct digit in the correct position	■
1 correct digit in the correct position and 1 correct digit in the wrong position	■ ☐
1 correct digit in the correct position and 2 correct digits in the wrong positions	■ ☐ ☐
2 correct digits in the correct positions	■ ■
3 correct digits in the correct positions	■ ■ ■

Here is a sample round. The Computer is thinking of 548.

Guesses	The Computer prints
Player A: 250	☐
Player B: 260	
Player A: 315	☐
Player B: 587	■ ☐
Player A: 578	■ ■
Player B: 579	■
Player A: 548	■ ■ ■

You pick one marble without looking. Express each probability as a fraction.

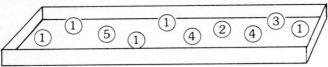

1. p(2) $\frac{1}{10}$ **2.** p(1) $\frac{1}{2}$ **3.** p(4) $\frac{1}{5}$ 10.1

4. p(a number less than 6)   1   **5.** p(6)   0   10.2

You draw one card from each box without looking.

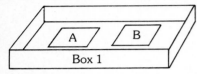   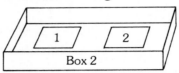

6. Copy and complete the sample space to show the possible results.   10.3

Box 1   Box 2   Results
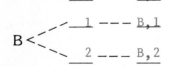

7. How many possible outcomes are there?   4

8. Find p(A,2). $\frac{1}{4}$

9. Find p(B,B).   0

10. Find p(getting A on one card). $\frac{1}{2}$

You pick one score without looking. Express each probability as a percent.   10.4

Scores: 89   72   89   66   100   58   20   100   100   97

11. p(89) 20%   **12.** p(100) 30%   **13.** p(a score greater than 57)   90%

14. 100 people were polled to see which brand of detergent they prefer. Only 30 of them said they prefer *Brand X*. Predict how many people would prefer *Brand X* if 250 people were polled.   75 people   **15.** A company tests some of the watches it makes and finds that 3% of them are defective. Predict how many watches will be defective if the company makes 2000 watches.   60 watches   10.5

16. Suppose a computer could make muffins. Tell which part of the computer (input device, memory, central processing unit, or output device) would do each job.

    a. Serve the muffins. `output device`

    b. Mix the ingredients and bake the muffins. `central processing unit`

    c. Receive the ingredients and the recipe. `input device`

    d. Store the ingredients and the recipe. `memory`

10.6

17. The use of a computer to carry out an illegal act is known as (computer literacy, <u>computer crime</u>).

10.7

18. The steps shown below, if placed in the proper order in the flowchart, describe a procedure for writing a note with a pen. Copy the flowchart and insert the steps in the correct places.

START
END
Write the note.
Throw the pen away.
Find a pen.
Does the pen work?

10.8

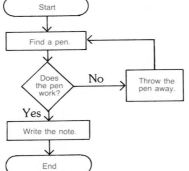

Find the value of each BASIC expression.

10.9

19. 8*(2+6) 64

20. 15−12/3 11

21. Computer programs and manuals are called (<u>software</u>, hardware).

10.10

Write the output that will be produced when each program is run.

22. 10 LET X=30
    20 LET Y=50
    30 LET S=X+Y
    40 LET A=S/2
    50 PRINT "THE MEAN IS"
    60 PRINT A   THE MEAN IS
    70 END   40

23. 10 LET L=3
    20 LET W=4
    30 LET A=L*W
    40 PRINT A
    50 LET L=L+1
    60 IF L<5 THEN GO TO 30 12
    70 END   16

1. There are 5 blue, 8 red, and 2 yellow marbles in a bag. You pick one marble without looking. Find the probability of getting a blue marble. Express it as a fraction. $\frac{1}{3}$

2. The probability of an outcome that is certain not to occur is <u>0</u>.

3. You roll a white die and a red die. How many possible outcomes are in the sample space showing all of the different ways the dice can land? 36

4. 12 students walked to school, 7 came by bus, and 6 drove. Find the probability that a student chosen at random drove to school. Express it as a percent. 24%

5. Suppose you roll a die 30 times. Predict how many times you would expect to get a 2. 5

Correlation	
Items	Sec
1	10.1
2	10.2
3	10.3
4	10.4
5	10.5
6	10.6
7	10.7
8	10.8
9–10	10.9
11–12	10.10

Choose the correct answer.

6. The part of a computer that processes data is the (<u>central processing unit</u>, memory).

7. Many factories use computers to operate (<u>robots</u>, central processing units) to make products.

8. A chart that uses such symbols as rectangles, diamonds, and arrows to show a sequence of steps is called a (computer program, <u>flowchart</u>).

Find the value of each BASIC expression.

9. 6−3/3   5

10. 5*(6+2)   40

Write the output that will be produced when each program is run.

11. 10 LET L=7
    20 LET W=4
    30 LET P=2*(L+W)
    40 PRINT "THE PERIMETER IS"
    50 PRINT P
    60 END   THE PERIMETER IS
                    22

12. 10 LET R=1
    20 LET A=3.14*R*R
    30 PRINT A
    40 LET R=R+1
    50 IF R<3 THEN GO TO 20
    60 END   3.14
                    12.56

1. In a survey of 1200 boys, 9% claimed they would like to contribute to the family household once they have completed school and are working full-time. How many boys surveyed claimed they would like to contribute to the family household? 108 boys

9.1

2.

> REID APARTMENTS
> $340 per month
> 1–BR. APT.

You decide to rent an apartment at Reid Apartments. Before moving in you must pay $20 for a credit check, a security deposit of one month's rent, and the first month's rent. Find your move-in cost. $700

9.2

3. You work 40 hours per week at $7.70 per hour. You do not want to pay more than 30% of your gross monthly pay for rent. Can you afford to live at Reid Apartments? Yes

Find the unit price for each item to the nearest tenth of a cent. Then tell which is the better buy.

9.3

4. 8 oz for 69¢ 8.6¢/oz
  14 oz for $1.15 8.2¢/oz

5. 12 oz for $1.37 11.4¢/oz
  1 lb 4 oz for $2.38 11.9¢/oz
  (Find the price per oz.)

You order items at a restaurant that cost $8.95, $7.50, $1.75, $1.75, and $0.90. The rate of sales tax is 6.5%.

9.4

6. Find the total bill. $22.21

7. Estimate a 15% tip for the above order. $3.15 (Answers may vary.)

8. Bruce bought a jogging suit for $56. He wore the suit 76 times. What was the wearing cost of the jogging suit? (Round to the nearest cent.) 74¢/time worn

9.5

9. At Berkley's Department Store, a $45 sweater is on sale for 15% off. A discount store is selling the same sweater for $30. At which store will you get the better buy? at the discount store

You join a book club. You get 4 books for a total of $0.99. Later you buy 4 more books at $10.75 each—plus $2.50 per book for shipping and handling.

9.6

10. Find the total cost (including shipping and handling) for the 8 books. $53.99

11. Find the average cost (including shipping and handling) per book. (Round to the nearest cent.) $6.75

The sticker on the car Natalie chose lists the base price as $10,942, the cost of options as $2831, and the destination charge as $414. She found that the cost to the dealer is 89% of the base price and 90% of the price of the options.

9.7

12. What is the sticker price of this car? $14,187

13. What is the invoice price of this car? $12,286.28

Bernard is buying a new car for $12,475. He will borrow $10,000 from the savings and loan at 13% interest for 24 months. (Refer to the table on page 391.)

9.8

14. How much interest will Bernard pay on this car loan? $1400

15. What is the total cost of the car? $13,875

16. Helene has a driver-rating factor of 1.45. Her car is a 1984 model and is in insurance rating group 7. She wants her insurance to include the following coverages: liability for 25,000/50,000/50,000, a $50 deductible on collision, and full coverage on comprehensive. What is the total annual premium? (Refer to the tables on pages 396 and 397.) $174.29

9.9

17. Bernie had minor surgery as an outpatient. The total hospital bill was $225 and the doctor's surgery fee was $180. Bernie's basic medical insurance will pay the entire hospital bill after a $100 deductible is met. Major medical will pay 75% of the doctor's bill. How much will the insurance pay in all? $260

9.10

You pick one card from this hand without looking. Express each probability as a fraction.

10.1

18. p(a 3) $\frac{1}{8}$

19. p(an ace) $\frac{1}{4}$

20. p(a spade) $\frac{3}{8}$

21. p(a club) $\frac{5}{8}$

22. p(a black card) 1

23. p(a heart) 0

10.2

You draw one marble from each bowl without looking.

10.3

24. Copy and complete the sample space to show the possible results.

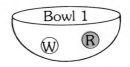 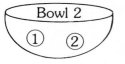

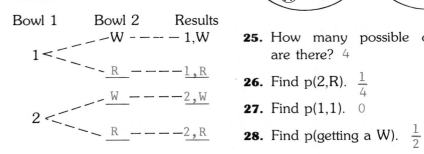

Bowl 1	Bowl 2	Results
1	W	1,W
	R	1,R
2	W	2,W
	R	2,R

25. How many possible outcomes are there? 4

26. Find p(2,R). $\frac{1}{4}$

27. Find p(1,1). 0

28. Find p(getting a W). $\frac{1}{2}$

In playing a game, you are asked to draw one card without looking. Express each probability as a percent.

10.4

Win $500	Win $500	Lose $500	Go back 3 spaces	Go ahead 3 spaces
Win $1000	Lose $1000	Win $500	Win $500	Lose $500

29. p(lose $1000) 10% **30.** p(win $500) 40% **31.** p(win some money) 50%

32. You flip a coin 60 times. Predict how many times you would expect to get heads. 30

10.5

33. A company tests some of the cameras it makes and finds that 2% of them are defective. Predict how many cameras will be defective if the company makes 5000 cameras. 100

34. A machine that can receive, store, process, and display large amounts of data is a (<u>computer</u>, central processing unit).

10.6

35. A computer stores data in its (input device, <u>memory</u>).

36. A "personal" or "home" computer is a (mainframe computer, minicomputer, <u>microcomputer</u>).

37. Computers are used in hospitals to (<u>monitor the vital signs of patients</u>, replace doctors).

10.7

38. The steps shown below, if placed in the proper order in the flowchart, describe a procedure for trying to hit a baseball. Copy the flowchart and insert the steps in the correct places.

10.8

Hold the bat and wait for a pitch.

Swing the bat.

Do not swing the bat.

START

END

Is it a good pitch?

Take a bat to the batter's box.

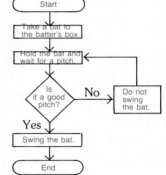

Find the value of each BASIC expression.

10.9

39. 7*(9−1)   56

40. 4+8/4   6

41. A (<u>computer program</u>, flowchart) is a set of numbered instructions written in a computer language that a computer follows in order.

10.10

Write the output that will be produced when each program is run.

42.
```
10 LET R=0.06
20 LET P=150
30 LET T=R*P
40 PRINT "THE TAX IS"
50 PRINT T
60 END
```
THE TAX IS
9

43.
```
10 LET L=3
20 LET W=2
30 LET P=2*(L+W)
40 PRINT P
50 LET L=L+1
60 IF L<5 THEN GO TO 30
70 END
```
10
12

COMPUTING SKILLS REFRESHER

Contents

Periods	Billions			Millions			Thousands			Ones		
Place values	hundred billions	ten billions	billions	hundred millions	ten millions	millions	hundred thousands	ten thousands	thousands	hundreds	tens	ones
Digits			2,	6	0	1,	8	0	0,	0	0	0
Value of each nonzero digit							8	0	0,	0	0	0
						1,	0	0	0,	0	0	0
				6	0	0,	0	0	0,	0	0	0
			2,	0	0	0,	0	0	0,	0	0	0

2,601,800,000 is read

two billion, six hundred one million, eight hundred thousand.

107,008,000,039 is read

one hundred seven billion, eight million, thirty-nine.

10. one million, two hundred forty-nine thousand, six hundred fifty-seven

11. two hundred thirty-four million, two hundred thirty-four thousand

EXERCISES

12. forty-two billion, one hundred twenty-three thousand, seven hundred forty-one

Name the value of each underlined digit.

1. 7̲42   700   **2.** 6̲990   6000   **3.** 9̲70,555   70,000

4. 12,373,005   2,000,000   **5.** 8,7̲35,670,000   700,000,000   **6.** 892,605,010,072   90,000,000,000

9. nine hundred forty-two thousand, thirty-one

Write in words.

7. eight thousand, nine hundred forty-two

7. 8942   **8.** 24,763   **9.** 942,031

8. twenty-four thousand, seven hundred sixty-three

10. 1,249,657   **11.** 234,234,000   **12.** 42,000,123,741

Answers for exercises 10-12 are given above.

13. 20,001   **14.** 702,003,000,500   **15.** 6,905,038,090

twenty thousand, one   seven hundred two billion, three million, five hundred   six billion, nine hundred five million, thirty-eight thousand, ninety

Write each numeral.

16. twenty-seven thousand, one hundred   27,100   **17.** ten million, two hundred ten   10,000,210

18. seventeen billion, two hundred forty-two million, seventy thousand   17,242,070,000

19. one billion, one million, one thousand, one   1,001,001,001

20. three hundred forty billion, three thousand, seven hundred twelve   340,000,003,712

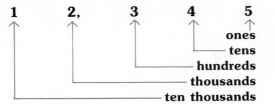
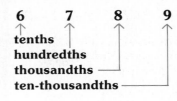

Since the 6 is in the tenths place, its value is 0.6.

The value of the 7 is 0.07.

In decimals for numbers less than 1, a 0 is written in the ones place to call attention to the decimal point.

The value of the 8 is 0.008.

The value of the 9 is 0.0009.

0.008 is read *eight thousandths*.

0.0031 is read *thirty-one ten-thousandths*.

In decimals for numbers greater than 1, the decimal point is read *and*.

27.8 is read *twenty-seven and eight tenths*.

8.16 is read *eight and sixteen hundredths*.

Writing final 0's to the right of the decimal point does not change the value of the decimal.

0.7 = 0.70 = 0.700 = 0.7000   **8 = 8.0 = 8.00 = 8.000**

9. twenty and seventy-six thousandths
10. fifteen ten-thousandths
11. eight hundred forty-two and eight hundred forty thousandths

EXERCISES

12. thirty-one and four thousand two ten-thousandths

Name the value of each underlined digit.

1. 642.8 2   **2.** 123.456 0.05   **3.** 0.0015 0.001   **4.** 3.0402 0.0002

Write in words.

5. four and six tenths   7. four and six thousandths

5. 4.6   **6.** 4.06   **7.** 4.006   **8.** 48.73

6. four and six hundredths   8. forty-eight and seventy-three hundredths

9. 20.076   **10.** 0.0015   **11.** 842.840   **12.** 31.4002

Answers for exercises 9-12 are given above.

Write each of these as a decimal.

13. seven and nine tenths
7.9

14. fourteen and eight hundredths
14.08

15. one hundred thirty-nine thousandths
0.139

16. two and three ten-thousandths
2.0003

Write three decimals that have the same value as each of the given numbers.

Possible answers for exercises 17-19 are given.

17. 0.5 0.50, 0.500, 0.5000   **18.** 1.6 1.60, 1.600, 1.6000   **19.** 9 9.0, 9.00, 9.000

449

The symbols < and > always point to the smaller number.

5 is greater than 3.

5>3

0.68 is less than 1.52.

0.68<1.52

Examples:

To compare two whole numbers, start at the left and compare digits in the same place-value position.

1. Compare 35,027 and 35,019.

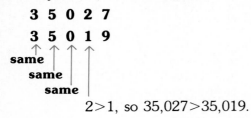

2>1, so 35,027>35,019.

2. Compare 769 and 1024.

```
      7 6 9
    1 0 2 4
    ↑
```
Since 769 does not have a digit in the thousands place, 769<1024.

To compare two decimals, write them so that each has the same number of digits after the decimal point. Then start at the left and compare digits in the same place-value position.

3. Compare 0.58 and 0.569.

0.5 8 0 ⟵ **Write 0.58 as 0.580.**

0.5 6 9

same
same

8>6, so 0.58>0.569.

4. Compare 6 and 6.01.

6.0 0 ⟵ **Write 6 as 6.00.**

6.0 1

same
same

0<1, so 6<6.01.

EXERCISES

Write < or > for each ●.

1. 87 > ●78

2. 599 < ●602

3. 513 < ●531

4. 2680 < ●2681

5. 8500 > ●8055

6. 27,529 < ●27,531

7. 999 < ●1003

8. 55,000 > ●7777

9. 103,423 > ●99,854

10. 3.45 < ●3.54

11. 0.98 < ●1.09

12. 0.01 > ●0.001

13. 22.5 > ●22.47

14. 1.587 < ●15.87

15. 0.48 > ●0.396

16. 6 > ●5.99

17. 7.02 > ●7

18. 0.4 < ●0.4002

When the digit to the right of the place being rounded to
• is less than 5, round down.   • is 5 or more, round up.

Examples:

1. Round to the nearest 10.
Check the ones digit.

7 5 3
Round down to 750.

2. Round to the nearest 100.
Check the tens digit.

8 5 2
Round up to 900.

3. Round to the nearest 1000.
Check the hundreds digit.

7 9 , 9 2 3
Round up to 80,000.

4. Round to the nearest whole number.
Check the tenths digit.

4 0.5 8
Round up to 41.

5. Round to the nearest tenth.
Check the hundredths digit.

3 7.5 4 2
Round down to 37.5.

6. Round to the nearest hundredth (cent).
Check the thousandths digit.

$4.3 4 8
Round up to $4.35.

EXERCISES

Round to the nearest 10.

1. 43 40   **2.** 65 70   **3.** 97 100   **4.** 955 960   **5.** 2004 2000

Round to the nearest 100.

6. 750 800   **7.** 99 100   **8.** 5555 5600   **9.** 70,506 70,500   **10.** 103.5 100

Round to the nearest 1000.

11. 7609 8000   **12.** 5555 6000   **13.** 2099 2000   **14.** 29,255 29,000   **15.** 80,500 81,000

Round to the nearest whole number or to the nearest dollar.

16. 57.1 57   **17.** 1.099 1   **18.** 199.8 200   **19.** $39.57 $40   **20.** $0.622 $1

Round to the nearest tenth.

21. 3.45 3.5   **22.** 0.707 0.7   **23.** 387.52 387.5   **24.** 16.98 17.0   **25.** 0.09 0.1

Round to the nearest hundredth or to the nearest cent.

26. 2.004 2.00   **27.** 3.628 3.63   **28.** 0.8542 0.85   **29.** $0.005 $0.01   **30.** $9.997 $10.00

To add whole numbers:

Step 1:   Align the ones, the tens, the hundreds, and so on.
Step 2:   Add the ones, the tens, the hundreds, and so on.

Examples:

1. $342 + 156$

Add the ones first.
Add the tens next.
Add the hundreds last.

$$
\begin{array}{r}
3\,|\,4\,|\,2 \\
+1\,|\,5\,|\,6 \\
\hline
4\,|\,9\,|\,8
\end{array}
$$
] addends
← sum

2.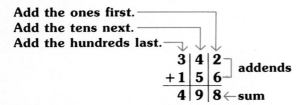

3.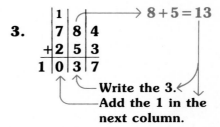

4. To add more than two numbers, add in any order.

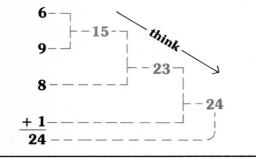

or

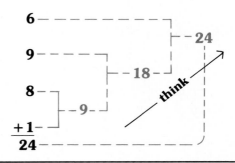

5.

The sum in the tens column is 15. Write the 5. Add the 1 in the next column.

$$
\begin{array}{r}
1\,|\,2 \\
5\,|\,6 \\
3\,|\,1\,|\,3\,|\,9 \\
6\,|\,0\,|\,2\,|\,8 \\
+\,5\,|\,3\,|\,1 \\
\hline
9\,|\,7\,|\,5\,|\,4
\end{array}
$$

The sum in the ones column is 24. Write the 4. Add the 2 in the next column.

EXERCISES

Add.

1. 32 +26 58	**2.** 50 +27 77	**3.** 81 + 9 90	**4.** 256 +102 358	**5.** 934 + 25 959
6. 67 +23 90	**7.** 37 +15 52	**8.** 38 +87 125	**9.** 78 + 9 87	**10.** 7 +56 63
11. 352 +629 981	**12.** 407 + 33 440	**13.** 389 + 6 395	**14.** 650 +250 900	**15.** 346 +571 917
16. 80 +888 968	**17.** 747 +163 910	**18.** 172 +359 531	**19.** 896 + 17 913	**20.** 399 + 8 407
21. 858 +449 1307	**22.** 617 +387 1004	**23.** 897 +498 1395	**24.** 703 +698 1401	**25.** 958 + 42 1000
26. 7051 +2037 9088	**27.** 6208 + 576 6784	**28.** 8381 + 909 9290	**29.** 6745 +2989 9734	**30.** 79,620 +36,880 116,500
31. 438 278 +224 940	**32.** 289 632 +523 1444	**33.** 8742 5631 9214 +7580 31,167	**34.** 9461 8394 2046 +3774 23,675	**35.** 15,674 28,936 16,248 +32,995 93,853
36. 5372 436 95 +3724 9627	**37.** 378 4968 27 +1201 6574	**38.** 56 325 25,100 + 9,519 35,000	**39.** 466 8051 7989 + 78 16,584	**40.** 18,961 770 9 + 1,090 20,830

41. $10 + 20 + 30 + 40$ 100

42. $48 + 49 + 51 + 52$ 200

43. $980 + 970 + 20 + 30$ 2000

44. $135 + 175 + 45 + 65$ 420

45. $7000 + 4 + 30 + 500$ 7534

46. $85,267 + 387 + 143 + 97$ 85,894

47. $151 + 152 + 153 + 15,480$ 15,936

48. $28 + 4388 + 192 + 65,003$ 69,611

To add decimals:

Step 1: Align the decimal points.

Step 2: Add as you would for whole numbers.

Examples:

1. $43.3 + 15.4$

Add first.
Add next.
Add last.

$$\begin{array}{r} 4\,|\,3\,!\,3 \\ +1\,|\,5\,!\,4 \\ \hline 5\,|\,8\,!\,7 \end{array}$$ addends ←— sum

Be sure to align the decimal points.

2. $\rightarrow 8 + 6 = 14$

$$\begin{array}{r} 1\,| \\ 0\,!\,8 \\ +0\,!\,6 \\ \hline 1\,!\,4 \end{array}$$

Write the 4.
Add the 1 in the next column.

3. $\rightarrow 6 + 7 = 13$

$$\begin{array}{r} ||\,1| \\ 8\,|\,3\,.\,4\,|\,6 \\ +2\,|\,3\,!\,1\,|\,7 \\ \hline 1\;0\,|\,6\,!\,6\,|\,3 \end{array}$$

Write the 3.
Add the 1 in the next column.

4. $\rightarrow 9 + 3 = 12$

$$\begin{array}{r} |\,1| \\ 1\,|\,2\,!\,9\,|\,4 \\ +|\,6\,!\,3\,|\,2 \\ \hline 1\,9\,!\,2\,|\,6 \end{array}$$

Write the 2.
Add the 1 in the next column.

5. $0.13 + 23.4 + 1.24 + 15$

Writing zeros ——→ 00.13   . . . or to the right of all other digits
to the left . . .   23.40 ←— does not change the value of a decimal.
                       01.24
                     + 15.00 ←— Here the decimal point
                     ———————   must also be inserted.
                       39.77

EXERCISES

Add.

1. 4.8
  + 5.1
  9.9

2. 0.6
  + 7.3
  7.9

3. 23.3
  + 74.5
  97.8

4. 86.45
  + 1.04
  87.49

5. 7
  + 2.456
  9.456

6. 0.8
  + 0.2
  1.0

7. 0.6
  + 0.7
  1.3

8. 0.9
  + 0.8
  1.7

9. 1.6
  + 3.5
  5.1

10. 42.0
  + 8.9
  50.9

11. 58.6
  + 7.3
  65.9

12. 74.2
  + 7.9
  82.1

13. 59.9
  + 10.3
  70.2

14. 1.08
  + 2.04
  3.12

15. 3.58
  + 0.55
  4.13

16. 1.038
  + 4.698
  5.736

17. 0.6946
  + 0.1398
  0.8344

18. 4.79
  + 6.82
  11.61

19. 19.99
  + 0.01
  20.00

20. 24.63
  + 188.74
  213.37

21. 281.08
  + 87.92
  369.00

22. 8.743
  + 7.999
  16.742

23. 0.5874
  + 0.8357
  1.4231

24. 939.48
  + 85.75
  1025.23

25. 9.288
  + 14.937
  24.225

26. 7.38 + 8.41   15.79

27. 3.32 + 0.53   3.85

28. 7.603 + 1.309   8.912

29. 16 + 9.88   25.88

30. 12.601 + 0.43   13.031

31. 46.97 + 4.697   51.667

32. 1.3
  2.1
  + 6.5
  9.9

33. 4.68
  1.10
  + 3.24
  9.02

34. 28.081
  7.315
  + 3.139
  38.535

35. 0.3104
  1.7092
  + 4.1908
  6.2104

36. 6
  1.305
  + 12.06
  19.365

37. 18.47
  209.1
  + 0.053
  227.623

38. 94
  205.96
  + 0.5
  300.46

39. 5.999
  23
  + 2.01
  31.009

40. 6.805
  90.37
  + 12.006
  109.181

41. 7.89
  0.789
  + 0.0789
  8.7579

42. 6.20 + 3.95 + 1.81 + 5.04   17

43. 21.3 + 8.9 + 112.6 + 13.5   156.3

44. 8.47 + 9 + 2.8 + 0.007   20.277

45. 7.234 + 0.096 + 12 + 137   156.33

455

To subtract whole numbers:

Step 1:   Align the ones, the tens, the hundreds, and so on.

Step 2:   Subtract the ones, the tens, the hundreds, and so on.

Examples:

1. 984 − 351

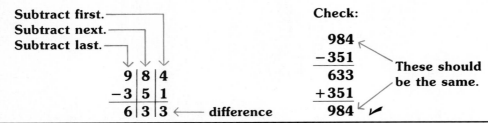

Subtract first.
Subtract next.
Subtract last.

```
  9 | 8 | 4
- 3 | 5 | 1
  6 | 3 | 3   ←— difference
```

Check:

```
  984
− 351
  633
+ 351
  984
```

These should be the same.

---

2.   864
        − 237

Rename 64 as 5 tens and 14 ones. Subtract.

```
      5 | 14
  8 | 6̸ | 4̸
- 2 | 3 | 7
  6 | 2 | 7
```

Check:

```
  864
− 237
  627
+ 237
  864
```

These should be the same.

---

3.   921
        − 375

Rename 21 as 1 ten and 11 ones. Subtract the ones.

```
      1 | 11
  9 | 2̸ | 1̸
- 3 | 7 | 5
          6
```

Rename 9 hundreds and 1 ten as 8 hundreds and 11 tens. Subtract and check.

```
          11
  8 | 1̸ | 11
  9 | 2̸ | 1̸
- 3 | 7 | 5
  5 | 4 | 6
+ 3 | 7 | 5
  9 | 2 | 1
```

These should be the same.

---

4. 5300 − 187

Rename to get some tens.

```
      2 | 10 |
  5 | 3̸ | 0̸ | 0
-     | 1  | 8 | 7
```

Rename to get some ones. Subtract and check.

```
          9 |
      2 | 1̸0 | 10
  5 | 3̸ | 0̸  | 0̸
-     | 1  | 8 | 7
  5 | 1  | 1 | 3
+     | 1  | 8 | 7
  5 | 3  | 0 | 0
```

These should be the same.

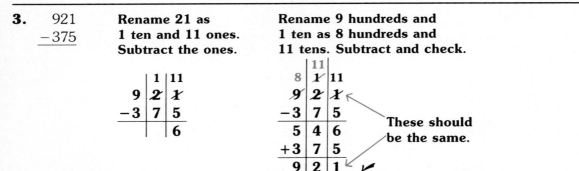

EXERCISES

Subtract. Check by adding.

1. 98
−71
27

2. 54
−14
40

3. 79
− 8
71

4. 986
−700
286

5. 670
− 40
630

6. 82
−19
63

7. 71
− 8
63

8. 286
−147
139

9. 836
−627
209

10. 377
− 48
329

11. 418
− 9
409

12. 975
−382
593

13. 503
−273
230

14. 928
− 30
898

15. 317
−275
42

16. 845
−546
299

17. 217
−138
79

18. 630
−343
287

19. 828
−199
629

20. 555
− 66
489

21. 864
− 98
766

22. 710
− 9
701

23. 607
−607
0

24. 503
−314
189

25. 408
−389
19

26. 500
−126
374

27. 700
−388
312

28. 800
− 97
703

29. 300
−271
29

30. 400
− 8
392

31. 7985
−6431
1554

32. 5864
− 721
5143

33. 6471
−2435
4036

34. 8391
− 72
8319

35. 7406
−5366
2040

36. 8729
−5688
3041

37. 9437
−6501
2936

38. 8341
−7473
868

39. 7431
− 242
7189

40. 8126
−7251
875

41. 9498
−3789
5709

42. 3097
−2168
929

43. 8936
− 947
7989

44. 8103
−2385
5718

45. 5002
− 777
4225

46. 52,439
−38,849
13,590

47. 89,032
−61,423
27,609

48. 72,891
− 3,493
69,398

49. 63,987
−23,998
39,989

50. 20,000
− 2,671
17,329

51. 6431 − 4926 1505

52. 501 − 68 433

53. 1304 − 725 579

54. 1713 − 44 1669

55. 4826 − 510 4316

56. 15,800 − 1492 14,308

To subtract decimals:

Step 1:   Align the decimal points.

Step 2:   Subtract as you would for whole numbers.

Examples:

1. $7.486 - 2.172$

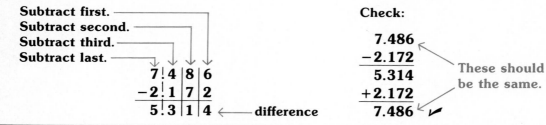

Subtract first.
Subtract second.
Subtract third.
Subtract last.

$$
\begin{array}{c|c|c|c}
7 & 4 & 8 & 6 \\
-2 & 1 & 7 & 2 \\
\hline
5 & 3 & 1 & 4
\end{array}
$$

← difference

Check:

$$
\begin{array}{r}
7.486 \\
-2.172 \\
\hline
5.314 \\
+2.172 \\
\hline
7.486
\end{array}
$$

These should be the same.

---

2. $\begin{array}{r} 87.83 \\ -84.57 \\ \hline \end{array}$

Rename to get more hundredths.

$$
\begin{array}{c|c|c|c}
 & & 7 & 13 \\
8 & 7. & 8 & 3 \\
-8 & 4. & 5 & 7 \\
\hline
\end{array}
$$

Subtract.

$$
\begin{array}{c|c|c|c}
 & & 7 & 13 \\
8 & 7. & 8 & 3 \\
-8 & 4. & 5 & 7 \\
\hline
3. & 2 & 6
\end{array}
$$

---

3. $\begin{array}{r} 185.31 \\ -\ \ 73.59 \\ \hline \end{array}$

Rename to get more hundredths. Subtract the hundredths.

$$
\begin{array}{c|c|c|c|c}
 & & & 2 & 11 \\
1 & 8 & 5. & 3 & 1 \\
- & 7 & 3. & 5 & 9 \\
\hline
 & & & & 2
\end{array}
$$

Rename to get more tenths. Subtract.

$$
\begin{array}{c|c|c|c|c}
 & & & 12 & \\
 & & 4 & 2 & 11 \\
1 & 8 & 5. & 3 & 1 \\
- & 7 & 3. & 5 & 9 \\
\hline
1 & 1 & 1. & 7 & 2
\end{array}
$$

Writing zeros to the right of all other digits does not change the value of a decimal.

4. $4.36 - 2$

$$
\begin{array}{c|c|c}
4. & 3 & 6 \\
-2. & 0 & 0 \\
\hline
2. & 3 & 6
\end{array}
$$

5. $31 - 0.24$

$$
\begin{array}{c|c|c}
3 & 1. & 0 & 0 \\
- & & 0. & 2 & 4 \\
\hline
\end{array}
$$

$$
\begin{array}{c|c|c}
 & & 9 & \\
 & 0 & 10 & 10 \\
3 & 1. & 0 & 0 \\
- & & 0. & 2 & 4 \\
\hline
3 & 0. & 7 & 6
\end{array}
$$

EXERCISES

Subtract.

1. 6.95
−3.21
3.74

2. 7.84
−6.30
1.54

3. 6.652
−5.431
1.221

4. 271.5
− 31.2
240.3

5. 8.649
−0.51
8.139

6. 8.3
−3.4
4.9

7. 0.92
−0.75
0.17

8. 6.91
−5.43
1.48

9. 5.73
−3.29
2.44

10. 28.6
−26.9
1.7

11. 8.36
−6.43
1.93

12. 36.53
−12.63
23.90

13. 3.817
−2.143
1.674

14. 1.57
−0.86
0.71

15. 894.0
−736.1
157.9

16. 6.321
−3.142
3.179

17. 35.437
−21.358
14.079

18. 394.75
−142.87
251.88

19. 15.32
−12.97
2.35

20. 21.67
− 8.76
12.91

21. 821.6
−351.7
469.9

22. 286.78
−175.99
110.79

23. 18.3654
− 6.5865
11.7789

24. 894.71
−156.38
738.33

25. 43.14
− 7
36.14

26. 17.412
−13.646
3.766

27. 194.28
−189.49
4.79

28. 34.731
−33.845
0.886

29. 6.4331
−6.4229
0.0102

30. 0.013
−0.009
0.004

31. 6.00
−0.24
5.76

32. 27.00
− 3.12
23.88

33. 134.00
− 3.71
130.29

34. 253.00
− 23.46
229.54

35. 14.000
− 0.002
13.998

36. 4.203
−0.026
4.177

37. 1.326
−0.248
1.078

38. 30.4
− 2.8
27.6

39. 80.02
− 8.32
71.70

40. 32.496
−18
14.496

41. 76
−56.53
19.47

42. 9
−0.06
8.94

43. 17
− 8.9
8.1

44. 130.2
− 0.98
129.22

45. 15.33
− 7.624
7.706

46. 13.04
− 7.8
5.24

47. 132.65
− 11.68
120.97

48. 46
− 3.71
42.29

49. 827.34
− 98
729.34

50. 0.001
−0.0005
0.0005

51. 189.35 − 6.4 182.95

52. 67.3 − 0.592 66.708

53. 200 − 1.1 198.9

54. 27.32 − 0.21 27.11

55. 186.7 − 8.9 177.8

56. 18.67 − 8.9 9.77

57. 100 − 0.9 99.1

58. 60 − 0.01 59.99

59. 13.46 − 2 11.46

60. 136.2 − 9 127.2

61. 463.25 − 463 0.25

62. 1.1375 − 0.2 0.9375

Add.

1.	34 +55 89	**2.**	30 +67 97	**3.**	8.4 +1.3 9.7	**4.**	219 + 61 280	**5.**	0.3 +0.8 1.1
6.	1820 +4170 5990	**7.**	958 +3047 4005	**8.**	26.17 +42.37 68.54	**9.**	10.28 + 7.15 17.43	**10.**	6 +5.82 11.82
11.	545 + 5 550	**12.**	0.33 +1.73 2.06	**13.**	40.84 + 8.29 49.13	**14.**	3999 + 2 4001	**15.**	7776 + 48 7824
16.	36.9 + 3.8 40.7	**17.**	827 +729 1556	**18.**	5.66 +0.77 6.43	**19.**	75,709 + 2,703 78,412	**20.**	0.07 +0.952 1.022
21.	29.948 + 0.643 30.591	**22.**	75.57 + 9.5 85.07	**23.**	869 +5809 6678	**24.**	2097 +8942 11,039	**25.**	15,000 +35,000 50,000
26.	89.98 +53.02 143.00	**27.**	6.71 +6.30 13.01	**28.**	48,975 +76,395 125,370	**29.**	97.806 + 5.303 103.109	**30.**	0.674 +0.928 1.602

31. $23 + 34 + 12$ 69

32. $5.2 + 0.29 + 1.3$ 6.79

33. $352 + 179 + 7200$ 7731

34. $4.74 + 0.2 + 18.391$ 23.331

35.	13.7 21.25 +98.3 133.25	**36.**	542 68 +206 816	**37.**	12.14 35.216 +17.587 64.943	**38.**	26,170 548 + 3,194 29,912	**39.**	25 2.56 + 0.002 27.562

40. $9 + 7 + 6 + 8$ 30

41. $600 + 6000 + 6 + 60$ 6666

42. $0.5 + 0.13 + 7 + 12.906$ 20.536

43. $58.6 + 0.586 + 5.86 + 586$ 651.046

44.	13.7 70.4 32.1 +91.6 207.8	**45.**	618 126 583 +940 2267	**46.**	4.8 0.27 1.63 +0.526 7.226	**47.**	360 1520 8770 + 910 11,560	**48.**	0.03 10.305 96.08 + 3.685 110.100

49.
```
   15.62
   38.04
   92.61
 + 15.34
  161.61
```

50.
```
   8,261
  80,316
  51,005
 +35,674
 175,256
```

51.
```
  28,303
   1,940
  65,296
 +   830
  96,369
```

52.
```
   0.286
  19.764
  24
 + 0.194
  44.244
```

53.
```
   23.4
   0.012
   0.8
 +98
 122.212
```

Subtract. Check by adding.

54.
```
   95
  −71
   24
```

55.
```
   349
  −101
   248
```

56.
```
   86.8
  − 4.7
   82.1
```

57.
```
   770
  −521
   249
```

58.
```
   9.43
  −0.41
   9.02
```

59.
```
   75
  −56
   19
```

60.
```
   842
  −404
   438
```

61.
```
   39.6
  −17.8
   21.8
```

62.
```
   5.29
  −3.19
   2.10
```

63.
```
   795
  − 86
   709
```

64.
```
   8324
  − 218
   8106
```

65.
```
   478.08
  − 43.31
   434.77
```

66.
```
   9.59
  −0.87
   8.72
```

67.
```
   6.178
  −0.30
   5.878
```

68.
```
   3140
  − 440
   2700
```

69.
```
   363
  − 97
   266
```

70.
```
   465
  −269
   196
```

71.
```
   16.10
  − 4.38
   11.72
```

72.
```
   904.5
  −132.7
   771.8
```

73.
```
   23
  − 7.6
   15.4
```

74.
```
   4200
  −1530
   2670
```

75.
```
   9000
  − 741
   8259
```

76.
```
   1.5
  −1.284
   0.216
```

77.
```
   27
  − 4.94
   22.06
```

78.
```
   0.01
  −0.004
   0.006
```

79.
```
   53,400
  −17,895
   35,505
```

80.
```
   13,250
  −   769
   12,481
```

81.
```
   95.06
  −68.3
   26.76
```

82.
```
   4.232
  −1.784
   2.448
```

83.
```
   80,000
  −79,893
   107
```

84.
```
   8.41
  −3
   5.41
```

85.
```
   18.24
  − 0.63
   17.61
```

86.
```
   9.67
  −0.3
   9.37
```

87.
```
   14
  − 0.27
   13.73
```

88.
```
   4000
  − 98
   3902
```

89. $9225 - 1382$ 7843

90. $16.41 - 8.53$ 7.88

91. $4820 - 835$ 3985

92. $292.3 - 97.61$ 194.69

93. $32.7 - 4.683$ 28.017

94. $12.48 - 4$ 8.48

95. $623.58 - 0.7$ 622.88

96. $92 - 0.375$ 91.625

97. $4623 - 176$ 4447

98. $843.7 - 21.5$ 822.2

99. $2964 - 34.61$ 2929.39

100. $98,000 - 963$ 97,037

101. $68,411 - 9162$ 59,249

102. $400 - 0.725$ 399.275

103. $29.6832 - 0.99$ 28.6932

These all mean *multiply 3 and 4.*

3 × 4	**3(4)**	**4**	**3**
4 × 3	**(4)(3)**	**× 3**	**× 4**

3 × 4 = 12   **(3)(4) = 12**   **4**
↑ ↑ ↑   **× 3**
factors product   **12**

EXERCISES

Multiply.

1. 5 × 2 10   **2.** 1 × 8 8   **3.** 2 × 4 8   **4.** 6 × 1 6   **5.** 3(6) 18

6. 9(4) 36   **7.** 4(6) 24   **8.** 5(8) 40   **9.** (2)(3) 6   **10.** (5)(7) 35

11. (4)(5) 20   **12.** (0)(7) 0   **13.** 6   **14.** 8   **15.** 9
                                                    × 5   × 9   × 6
                                                    ──   ──   ──
                                                    30   72   54

16. 8   **17.** 9 × 0 0   **18.** 7 × 4 28   **19.** 9 × 9 81   **20.** 5 × 9 45
     × 7
     ──
     56

21. 9(7) 63   **22.** 6(7) 42   **23.** 7(7) 49   **24.** 3(8) 24   **25.** 9(3) 27

26. 1(7) 7   **27.** (7)(3) 21   **28.** 2(6) 12   **29.** 8   **30.** 7
                                                                     × 6   × 5
                                                                     ──   ──
                                                                     48   35

31. 3   **32.** 9   **33.** 9 × 5 45   **34.** 6 × 8 48   **35.** 4 × 9 36
     × 8   × 8
     ──   ──
     24   72

36. 7 × 6 42   **37.** 8(8) 64   **38.** 8(4) 32   **39.** 3(5) 15   **40.** 5(6) 30

41. 1   **42.** 7   **43.** 6   **44.** 3   **45.** 4
     × 7   × 9   × 3   × 9   × 8
     ──   ──   ──   ──   ──
     7   63   18   27   32

46. 4   **47.** 7   **48.** 2   **49.** 6 × 9 54   **50.** 8 × 5 40
     × 7   × 3   × 0
     ──   ──   ──
     28   21   0

51. 4 × 3 12   **52.** 7 × 8 56   **53.** 6(6) 36   **54.** 8(0) 0   **55.** (4)(4) 16

56. (6)(4) 24   **57.** 5 × 4 20   **58.** 3 × 3 9   **59.** (7)(2) 14   **60.** 5(5) 25

Examples:

1.
$$10 \times 234 = 2340$$
$$100 \times 234 = 23,400$$
$$1000 \times 234 = 234,000$$

Write **234** followed by the number of zeros in the other factor.

2.
$$10 \times 240 = 2400$$
$$100 \times 240 = 24,000$$
$$1000 \times 240 = 240,000$$

Write **240** followed by the number of zeros in the other factor.

3.

$$\begin{array}{r} 900 \\ \times 3 \\ \hline 2700 \end{array}$$

2 zeros
+0 zeros
2 zeros

Multiply **9** and **3**; then write the zeros.

4.

$$\begin{array}{r} 600 \\ \times 50 \\ \hline 30000 \end{array}$$

2 zeros
+1 zero
3 zeros

Multiply **6** and **5**; then write the zeros.

EXERCISES

Multiply.

1. 10×29
290

2. 10×87
870

3. 100×38
3800

4. 100×47
4700

5. 1000×91
91,000

6. 1000×74
74,000

7. 10×830
8300

8. 100×270
27,000

9. 1000×480
480,000

10. 370×100
37,000

11. 210×10
2100

12. 10×3800
38,000

13. 320×1000
320,000

14. 9100×100
910,000

15. 30×5
150

16. 400×5
2000

17.
$$\begin{array}{r} 100 \\ \times 197 \\ \hline 19,700 \end{array}$$

18.
$$\begin{array}{r} 1000 \\ \times 307 \\ \hline 307,000 \end{array}$$

19.
$$\begin{array}{r} 4634 \\ \times 10 \\ \hline 46,340 \end{array}$$

20.
$$\begin{array}{r} 1000 \\ \times 8245 \\ \hline 8,245,000 \end{array}$$

21.
$$\begin{array}{r} 8960 \\ \times 100 \\ \hline 896,000 \end{array}$$

22.
$$\begin{array}{r} 1000 \\ \times 3240 \\ \hline 3,240,000 \end{array}$$

23.
$$\begin{array}{r} 136 \\ \times 10 \\ \hline 1360 \end{array}$$

24.
$$\begin{array}{r} 142 \\ \times 1000 \\ \hline 142,000 \end{array}$$

25. 3000×5
15,000

26. 5000×9
45,000

27. 9×50
450

28. 8×400
3200

29. 6×700
4200

30. 7×7000
49,000

31. 6000×5
30,000

32. 800×7
5600

33. 80×60
4800

34. 800×60
48,000

35. 80×600
48,000

36. 8000×600
4,800,000

37. 80×500
40,000

38. 700×40
28,000

39. 600×600
360,000

40. 5000×40
200,000

Examples:

1.
```
    32
   × 4
   128
```
4 × 30 ⌐⌐ 4 × 2

2.
```
   1
  32
  × 6
  192
```
The 1 of 12 may be written here to remind you to add it to the next product.

6 × 2 = 12. Write the 2; then add the 1 to 6 × 3.

3.

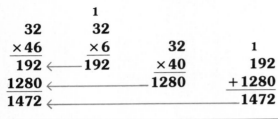

```
              1
  32         32
 × 46        × 6        32          1
  192  ←──── 192       × 40        192
 1280  ←──────────────1280       + 1280
 1472  ←──────────────────────── 1472
```

4.

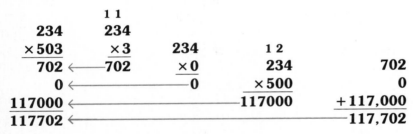

```
                1 1
   234         234
  × 503        × 3        234                 1 2
   702  ←───── 702       × 0          234          702
     0  ←───────────────── 0         234            0
117000  ←─────────────────────── 117000      × 500     + 117,000
117702  ←───────────────────────────────117000      117,702
```

With more than two factors, multiply in any order or grouping.

5.

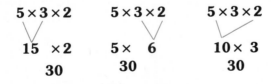

```
5 × 3 × 2    5 × 3 × 2    5 × 3 × 2    5 × 3 × 2
               15  × 2    5 ×   6     10 × 3
                  30        30          30
```

---

6. 3 × 4 × 5 × 6 = 360

(3 × 4) × (5 × 6)

[3 × (4 × 5)] × 6

[(3 × 4) × 5] × 6

3 × [4 × (5 × 6)]

These are only a few of the ways to group the factors. The *order* of the factors can also be changed. However, the result will always be 360.

EXERCISES

Multiply.

1. 42 $\times 3$ 126	**2.** 84 $\times 2$ 168	**3.** 70 $\times 8$ 560	**4.** 21 $\times 9$ 189
5. 410 $\times 6$ 2460	**6.** 824 $\times 2$ 1648	**7.** 721 $\times 4$ 2884	**8.** 932 $\times 3$ 2796
9. 134 $\times 22$ 2948	**10.** 943 $\times 12$ 11,316	**11.** 834 $\times 21$ 17,514	**12.** 701 $\times 19$ 13,319
13. 623 $\times 32$ 19,936	**14.** 503 $\times 23$ 11,569	**15.** 311 $\times 89$ 27,679	**16.** 412 $\times 34$ 14,008
17. 28 $\times 3$ 84	**18.** 34 $\times 4$ 136	**19.** 48 $\times 3$ 144	**20.** 36 $\times 7$ 252
21. 54 $\times 8$ 432	**22.** 93 $\times 7$ 651	**23.** 89 $\times 8$ 712	**24.** 73 $\times 7$ 511
25. 46 $\times 24$ 1104	**26.** 38 $\times 14$ 532	**27.** 74 $\times 26$ 1924	**28.** 84 $\times 32$ 2688
29. 83 $\times 41$ 3403	**30.** 37 $\times 91$ 3367	**31.** 85 $\times 31$ 2635	**32.** 78 $\times 35$ 2730
33. 321 $\times 63$ 20,223	**34.** 821 $\times 37$ 30,377	**35.** 621 $\times 87$ 54,027	**36.** 531 $\times 98$ 52,038
37. 248 $\times 72$ 17,856	**38.** 506 $\times 83$ 41,998	**39.** 138 $\times 35$ 4830	**40.** 507 $\times 65$ 32,955
41. 823 $\times 87$ 71,601	**42.** 935 $\times 65$ 60,775	**43.** 805 $\times 78$ 62,790	**44.** 345 $\times 65$ 22,425
45. 876 $\times 302$ 264,552	**46.** 623 $\times 304$ 189,392	**47.** 965 $\times 806$ 777,790	**48.** 480 $\times 701$ 336,480

49. $5 \times 12 \times 8$ 480

50. $4 \times 17 \times 5$ 340

51. $7 \times 5 \times 2 \times 5$ 350

52. $3 \times 15 \times 4 \times 11$ 1980

To multiply a whole number and a decimal:

Step 1:   Multiply as you would for whole numbers.

Step 2:   Place the decimal point in the product. The number of digits to the right of the decimal point in the product is equal to the number of digits to the right of the decimal point in the decimal factor.

Examples:

1.
$$\begin{array}{r} 32 \\ \times\,0.1 \\ \hline 3.2 \end{array}$$
←1 digit to the right of the decimal point

2.
$$\begin{array}{r} 721 \\ \times\,0.34 \\ \hline 28\ 84 \\ 216\ 3 \\ \hline 245.14 \end{array}$$
←2 digits to the right of the decimal point

3.
$$\begin{array}{r} 0.632 \\ \times\,23 \\ \hline 1\ 896 \\ 12\ 64 \\ \hline 14.536 \end{array}$$
←3 digits to the right of the decimal point

---

4. Use this shortcut to multiply by 10, 100, 1000, and so on.

To multiply by	move the decimal point	Example:	
10	1 place to the *right*	$10 \times 0.75 = 07.5 = 7.5$	If the product is a whole number, no decimal point is needed.
100	2 places to the *right*	$100 \times 2.46 = 246$	
1000	3 places to the *right*	$1000 \times 1.2 = 1200$	Insert 0's as needed.

---

5. Use this shortcut to multiply by 0.1, 0.01, 0.001, and so on.

To multiply by	move the decimal point	Example:	
0.1	1 place to the *left*	$0.1 \times 40 = 4.0 = 4$	
0.01	2 places to the *left*	$0.01 \times 2 = 0.02$	Insert 0's as needed.
0.001	3 places to the *left*	$0.001 \times 6 = 0.006$	

EXERCISES

Copy each exercise and place the decimal point in the product.

1. $\begin{array}{r} 42 \\ \times 0.6 \\ \hline 252 \\ {\scriptstyle\wedge} \end{array}$ **2.** $\begin{array}{r} 306 \\ \times 0.08 \\ \hline 2448 \\ {\scriptstyle\wedge} \end{array}$ **3.** $\begin{array}{r} 5.063 \\ \times 9 \\ \hline 45567 \\ {\scriptstyle\wedge} \end{array}$ **4.** $\begin{array}{r} 0.814 \\ \times 40 \\ \hline 32560 \\ {\scriptstyle\wedge} \end{array}$

5. $10 \times 5.41 = 541$ **6.** $0.096(100) = 96$

7. $0.1 \times 549 = 549$ **8.** $(4261)(0.001) = 4261$

Multiply.

9. 579×0.5 $\quad 289.5$ **10.** 579×0.05 $\quad 28.95$ **11.** 579×0.005 $\quad 2.895$

12. 73.49×3 $\quad 220.47$ **13.** 10×5.6 $\quad 56$ **14.** 0.833×10 $\quad 8.33$

15. 0.1×54 $\quad 5.4$ **16.** 86×0.1 $\quad 8.6$ **17.** 1628×2.3 $\quad 3744.4$

18. $10(9.03)$ $\quad 90.3$ **19.** $(0.1)(1246)$ $\quad 124.6$ **20.** $450(0.01)$ $\quad 4.5$

21. 843×0.61 $\quad 514.23$ **22.** 16.3×12 $\quad 195.6$ **23.** 1000×5.946 $\quad 5946$

24. 0.7×10 $\quad 7$ **25.** 100×0.7 $\quad 70$ **26.** 0.7×1000 $\quad 700$

27. 6×0.1 $\quad 0.6$ **28.** 0.01×6 $\quad 0.06$ **29.** 6×0.001 $\quad 0.006$

30. $6.34(123)$ $\quad 779.82$ **31.** $(6.864)(5)$ $\quad 34.32$ **32.** $(702.5)8$ $\quad 5620$

33. 100×52.8 $\quad 5280$ **34.** 0.001×28 $\quad 0.028$ **35.** 10×0.1 $\quad 1$

36. $3.62(87)$ $\quad 314.94$ **37.** $(60)(58.5)$ $\quad 3510$ **38.** $(0.99)1000$ $\quad 990$

39. 1.06×80 $\quad 84.8$ **40.** 1000×0.001 $\quad 1$ **41.** 550×0.028 $\quad 15.4$

42. $\begin{array}{r} 62 \\ \times 0.01 \\ \hline 0.62 \end{array}$ **43.** $\begin{array}{r} 6.2 \\ \times 100 \\ \hline 620 \end{array}$ **44.** $\begin{array}{r} 0.015 \\ \times 2000 \\ \hline 30 \end{array}$ **45.** $\begin{array}{r} 62.72 \\ \times 25 \\ \hline 1568 \end{array}$

46. $\begin{array}{r} 0.0575 \\ \times 450 \\ \hline 25.875 \end{array}$ **47.** $\begin{array}{r} 0.001 \\ \times 999 \\ \hline 0.999 \end{array}$ **48.** $\begin{array}{r} 3000 \\ \times 0.06 \\ \hline 180 \end{array}$ **49.** $\begin{array}{r} 0.05 \\ \times 40000 \\ \hline 2000 \end{array}$

To multiply decimals:

Step 1: Multiply as you would for whole numbers.

Step 2: Place the decimal point in the product. The number of digits to the right of the decimal point in the product is equal to the total number of digits to the right of the decimal points in the factors.

Examples:

1.			2.		
	4.3	1 digit		36.82	2 digits
	×0.1	+1 digit		×0.401	+3 digits
	0.43	2 digits		3682	
				0000	
				14 728	
				14.76482	5 digits

EXERCISES

Copy each exercise and place the decimal point in the product.

1.	92.3	2.	6.25	3.	10.003	4.	0.942
	×6.2		×0.04		×0.086		×0.103
	57226		02500		0860258		0097026

5.	3.786	6.	38.14	7.	0.0004	8.	1.626
	×4.1		×0.002		×275.1		×0.05
	155226		007628		011004		008130

Multiply.

9.	10.5	10.	8.37	11.	4.17	12.	2.831
	×7.6		×0.42		×2.8		×4.2
	79.8		3.5154		11.676		11.8902

13.	0.731	14.	0.4321	15.	18.73	16.	0.1563
	×0.86		×0.8		×9.20		×1.606
	0.62866		0.34568		172.316		0.2510178

17.	32.83	18.	3.016	19.	88.01	20.	147.6
	×0.009		×0.07		×0.005		×0.0004
	0.29547		0.21112		0.44005		0.05904

21. 12.65(3.11)
39.3415

22. 2.8×0.0093
0.02604

23. 153.6×6.04
927.744

24. (4.021)(2)(9.6)
77.2032

25. (10)(0.0008)(52.36)
0.41888

26. (99.9)(5)(1.11)
554.445

Multiply.

1. 383×10 3830
2. 726×100 72,600
3. 21×1000 21,000

4. 10×2983 29,830
5. 100×45 4500
6. 1000×684 684,000

7.
$$\begin{array}{r} 42 \\ \times 3 \\ \hline 126 \end{array}$$

8.
$$\begin{array}{r} 31 \\ \times 8 \\ \hline 248 \end{array}$$

9.
$$\begin{array}{r} 63 \\ \times 2 \\ \hline 126 \end{array}$$

10.
$$\begin{array}{r} 13 \\ \times 4 \\ \hline 52 \end{array}$$

11.
$$\begin{array}{r} 34 \\ \times 12 \\ \hline 408 \end{array}$$

12.
$$\begin{array}{r} 97 \\ \times 11 \\ \hline 1067 \end{array}$$

13.
$$\begin{array}{r} 21 \\ \times 67 \\ \hline 1407 \end{array}$$

14.
$$\begin{array}{r} 43 \\ \times 22 \\ \hline 946 \end{array}$$

15.
$$\begin{array}{r} 73 \\ \times 9 \\ \hline 657 \end{array}$$

16.
$$\begin{array}{r} 85 \\ \times 6 \\ \hline 510 \end{array}$$

17.
$$\begin{array}{r} 38 \\ \times 7 \\ \hline 266 \end{array}$$

18.
$$\begin{array}{r} 56 \\ \times 4 \\ \hline 224 \end{array}$$

19.
$$\begin{array}{r} 63 \\ \times 27 \\ \hline 1701 \end{array}$$

20.
$$\begin{array}{r} 59 \\ \times 83 \\ \hline 4897 \end{array}$$

21.
$$\begin{array}{r} 47 \\ \times 53 \\ \hline 2491 \end{array}$$

22.
$$\begin{array}{r} 68 \\ \times 35 \\ \hline 2380 \end{array}$$

23.
$$\begin{array}{r} 422 \\ \times 304 \\ \hline 128,288 \end{array}$$

24.
$$\begin{array}{r} 542 \\ \times 103 \\ \hline 55,826 \end{array}$$

25.
$$\begin{array}{r} 723 \\ \times 309 \\ \hline 223,407 \end{array}$$

26.
$$\begin{array}{r} 586 \\ \times 24 \\ \hline 14,064 \end{array}$$

27.
$$\begin{array}{r} 368 \\ \times 2.1 \\ \hline 772.8 \end{array}$$

28.
$$\begin{array}{r} 465 \\ \times 8.6 \\ \hline 3999 \end{array}$$

29.
$$\begin{array}{r} 78.4 \\ \times 10 \\ \hline 784 \end{array}$$

30.
$$\begin{array}{r} 1.27 \\ \times 0.1 \\ \hline 0.127 \end{array}$$

31. $73.4(100)$ 7340
32. 10×3.87 38.7
33. 0.68×1000 680

34. 691×0.6 414.6
35. $(0.01)(7)$ 0.07
36. 59.6×0.001 0.0596

37.
$$\begin{array}{r} 6.9 \\ \times 0.2 \\ \hline 1.38 \end{array}$$

38.
$$\begin{array}{r} 3.27 \\ \times 0.6 \\ \hline 1.962 \end{array}$$

39.
$$\begin{array}{r} 51.4 \\ \times 0.32 \\ \hline 16.448 \end{array}$$

40.
$$\begin{array}{r} 96.23 \\ \times 1.26 \\ \hline 121.2498 \end{array}$$

41.
$$\begin{array}{r} 0.681 \\ \times 2.14 \\ \hline 1.45734 \end{array}$$

42.
$$\begin{array}{r} 0.962 \\ \times 0.103 \\ \hline 0.099086 \end{array}$$

43.
$$\begin{array}{r} 6.003 \\ \times 28.6 \\ \hline 171.6858 \end{array}$$

44.
$$\begin{array}{r} 820.4 \\ \times 0.0006 \\ \hline 0.49224 \end{array}$$

45.
$$\begin{array}{r} 8008 \\ \times 0.003 \\ \hline 24.024 \end{array}$$

46.
$$\begin{array}{r} 0.1111 \\ \times 4.4 \\ \hline 0.48884 \end{array}$$

47.
$$\begin{array}{r} 9823 \\ \times 0.2232 \\ \hline 2192.4936 \end{array}$$

48.
$$\begin{array}{r} 426 \\ \times 0.999 \\ \hline 425.574 \end{array}$$

49. $7 \times 2 \times 4 \times 11$ 616
50. $6 \times 3.2 \times 20$ 384

51. $2 \times 4.2 \times 5 \times 3.1$ 130.2
52. $10.3 \times 3 \times 2.5$ 77.25

These all mean *divide 12 by 3*.

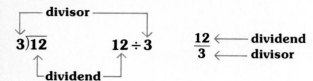

If you know the multiplication facts, then you should also know the division facts. Since $4 \times 3 = 12$, $12 \div 3 = 4$. Multiplication is used to check division.

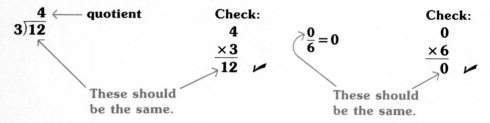

EXERCISES

Divide and check.

1. $8\overline{)40}$ 5   **2.** $3\overline{)27}$ 9   **3.** $6\overline{)24}$ 4   **4.** $5\overline{)20}$ 4   **5.** $7\overline{)0}$ 0

6. $21 \div 3$ 7   **7.** $8 \div 2$ 4   **8.** $8 \div 4$ 2   **9.** $36 \div 4$ 9   **10.** $6 \div 6$ 1

11. $\dfrac{14}{2}$ 7   **12.** $\dfrac{30}{5}$ 6   **13.** $\dfrac{28}{4}$ 7   **14.** $\dfrac{8}{8}$ 1   **15.** $\dfrac{35}{7}$ 5

16. $18 \div 6$ 3   **17.** $64 \div 8$ 8   **18.** $0 \div 8$ 0   **19.** $42 \div 6$ 7   **20.** $36 \div 9$ 4

21. $5\overline{)15}$ 3   **22.** $2\overline{)16}$ 8   **23.** $4\overline{)16}$ 4   **24.** $3\overline{)24}$ 8   **25.** $8\overline{)24}$ 3

26. $1 \div 1$ 1   **27.** $12 \div 4$ 3   **28.** $28 \div 7$ 4   **29.** $63 \div 9$ 7   **30.** $45 \div 9$ 5

31. $6\overline{)36}$ 6   **32.** $9\overline{)0}$ 0   **33.** $6\overline{)30}$ 5   **34.** $7\overline{)56}$ 8   **35.** $9\overline{)9}$ 1

36. $\dfrac{9}{1}$ 9   **37.** $\dfrac{45}{5}$ 9   **38.** $\dfrac{32}{8}$ 4   **39.** $\dfrac{15}{3}$ 5   **40.** $\dfrac{48}{6}$ 8

41. $56 \div 8$ 7   **42.** $48 \div 8$ 6   **43.** $54 \div 9$ 6   **44.** $7 \div 1$ 7   **45.** $72 \div 9$ 8

46. $\dfrac{63}{7}$ 9   **47.** $\dfrac{21}{7}$ 3   **48.** $\dfrac{40}{5}$ 8   **49.** $\dfrac{81}{9}$ 9   **50.** $\dfrac{0}{5}$ 0

51. $7\overline{)49}$ 7   **52.** $9\overline{)27}$ 3   **53.** $7\overline{)42}$ 6   **54.** $8\overline{)72}$ 9   **55.** $6\overline{)54}$ 9

Example: 53 ÷ 6

Think: 6 × 8 = 48, so 53 ÷ 6 is more than 8.
6 × 9 = 54, so 53 ÷ 9 is less than 9.

Therefore, 53 ÷ 6 is between 8 and 9. Use 8 as the ones digit.

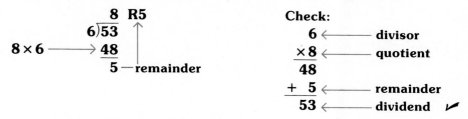

Check:

6	← divisor
× 8	← quotient
48	
+ 5	← remainder
53	← dividend ✔

The remainder is *always* less than the divisor.

Here is another way to show 53 ÷ 6.

$$8\frac{5}{6}$$
$$6\overline{)53}$$
$$\underline{48}$$
$$5$$

The remainder 5 can also be written $\frac{5}{6}$.

EXERCISES

Divide. Check your answers.

1. $3\overline{)29}$ 9 R2 **2.** $5\overline{)38}$ 7 R3 **3.** $6\overline{)43}$ 7 R1 **4.** $3\overline{)11}$ 3 R2 **5.** $8\overline{)60}$ 7 R4

6. 39 ÷ 4 9 R3 **7.** 27 ÷ 6 4 R3 **8.** 10 ÷ 4 2 R2 **9.** 15 ÷ 4 3 R3 **10.** 23 ÷ 5 4 R3

11. $\frac{32}{7}$ 4 R4 **12.** $\frac{17}{5}$ 3 R2 **13.** $\frac{19}{7}$ 2 R5 **14.** $\frac{22}{3}$ 7 R1 **15.** $\frac{34}{6}$ 5 R4

16. $8\overline{)19}$ 2 R3 **17.** $2\overline{)15}$ 7 R1 **18.** $7\overline{)24}$ 3 R3 **19.** $9\overline{)57}$ 6 R3 **20.** $5\overline{)49}$ 9 R4

21. 11 ÷ 5 2 R1 **22.** 29 ÷ 4 7 R1 **23.** 17 ÷ 2 8 R1 **24.** 30 ÷ 8 3 R6 **25.** 16 ÷ 6 2 R4

26. $\frac{20}{9}$ 2 R2 **27.** $\frac{37}{7}$ 5 R2 **28.** $\frac{35}{8}$ 4 R3 **29.** $\frac{51}{6}$ 8 R3 **30.** $\frac{23}{6}$ 3 R5

31. $5\overline{)41}$ 8 R1 **32.** $8\overline{)50}$ 6 R2 **33.** $9\overline{)31}$ 3 R4 **34.** $3\overline{)26}$ 8 R2 **35.** $6\overline{)59}$ 9 R5

36. 19 ÷ 2 9 R1 **37.** 70 ÷ 8 8 R6 **38.** 34 ÷ 4 8 R2 **39.** 89 ÷ 9 9 R8 **40.** 50 ÷ 9 5 R5

Examples:

1. $86 \div 2$

$$\begin{array}{r} 43 \\ 2\overline{)86} \end{array}$$

$4 \times 2 \longrightarrow \underline{8}$

$ 6$

$3 \times 2 \longrightarrow \underline{6}$

$ 0$

Think: $2\overline{)8}^{\,4}$

Think: $2\overline{)6}^{\,3}$

Check:

$$\begin{array}{r} 43 \\ \times 2 \\ \hline 86 \end{array} \text{✔}$$

2. $128 \div 8$

$$\begin{array}{r} 16 \\ 8\overline{)128} \end{array}$$

$1 \times 8 \longrightarrow \underline{8}$

$ 48$

$6 \times 8 \longrightarrow \underline{48}$

$ 0$

Think: $8\overline{)12}^{\,1}$

Think: $8\overline{)48}^{\,6}$

Check:

$$\begin{array}{r} 4 \\ 16 \\ \times 8 \\ \hline 128 \end{array} \text{✔}$$

---

3. $816 \div 4$

$$\begin{array}{r} 204 \\ 4\overline{)816} \end{array}$$

$2 \times 4 \longrightarrow \underline{8}$

$ 1$

$0 \times 4 \longrightarrow \underline{0}$

$ 16$

$4 \times 4 \longrightarrow \underline{16}$

$ 0$

Think: $4\overline{)8}^{\,2}$

Think: $4\overline{)1}^{\,0}$

Think: $4\overline{)16}^{\,4}$

Check:

$$\begin{array}{r} 1 \\ 204 \\ \times 4 \\ \hline 816 \end{array} \text{✔}$$

4. $2509 \div 6$

$$\begin{array}{r} 418 \text{ R1} \\ 6\overline{)2509} \end{array}$$

$4 \times 6 \longrightarrow \underline{24}$

$ 10$

$1 \times 6 \longrightarrow \underline{6}$

$ 49$

$8 \times 6 \longrightarrow \underline{48}$

$ 1$

Think: $6\overline{)25}^{\,4}$

Think: $6\overline{)10}^{\,1}$

Think: $6\overline{)49}^{\,8}$

Check:

$$\begin{array}{r} 14 \\ 418 \\ \times 6 \\ \hline 2508 \\ + 1 \\ \hline 2509 \end{array} \text{✔}$$

The quotient can also be written $418\frac{1}{6}$.

EXERCISES

Divide. Check your answers.

1. $\dfrac{24}{2\overline{)48}}$ 2. $\dfrac{32}{3\overline{)96}}$ 3. $\dfrac{21}{4\overline{)84}}$ 4. $\dfrac{11}{5\overline{)55}}$

5. $\dfrac{122}{4\overline{)488}}$ 6. $\dfrac{213}{3\overline{)639}}$ 7. $\dfrac{324}{2\overline{)648}}$ 8. $\dfrac{2112}{4\overline{)8448}}$

9. $\dfrac{301}{3\overline{)903}}$ 10. $\dfrac{110}{5\overline{)550}}$ 11. $\dfrac{2012}{4\overline{)8048}}$ 12. $\dfrac{3104}{2\overline{)6208}}$

13. $\dfrac{51}{5\overline{)255}}$ 14. $\dfrac{52}{3\overline{)156}}$ 15. $\dfrac{211}{8\overline{)1688}}$ 16. $\dfrac{41}{7\overline{)287}}$

17. $\dfrac{91}{6\overline{)546}}$ 18. $\dfrac{82}{4\overline{)328}}$ 19. $\dfrac{923}{2\overline{)1846}}$ 20. $\dfrac{832}{3\overline{)2496}}$

21. $\dfrac{701}{5\overline{)3505}}$ 22. $\dfrac{903}{3\overline{)2709}}$ 23. $\dfrac{701}{4\overline{)2804}}$ 24. $\dfrac{903}{2\overline{)1806}}$

25. $\dfrac{309}{3\overline{)927}}$ 26. $\dfrac{105}{5\overline{)525}}$ 27. $\dfrac{108}{7\overline{)756}}$ 28. $\dfrac{207}{4\overline{)828}}$

29. $\dfrac{108}{6\overline{)648}}$ 30. $\dfrac{2093}{2\overline{)4186}}$ 31. $\dfrac{3206}{3\overline{)9618}}$ 32. $\dfrac{2106}{4\overline{)8424}}$

33. $\dfrac{208}{6\overline{)1248}}$ 34. $\dfrac{408}{8\overline{)3264}}$ 35. $\dfrac{509}{7\overline{)3563}}$ 36. $\dfrac{609}{5\overline{)3045}}$

37. $\dfrac{24}{3\overline{)72}}$ 38. $\dfrac{17}{4\overline{)68}}$ 39. $\dfrac{16}{6\overline{)96}}$ 40. $\dfrac{151}{5\overline{)755}}$

41. $\dfrac{467}{2\overline{)934}}$ 42. $\dfrac{284}{3\overline{)852}}$ 43. $\dfrac{136}{7\overline{)952}}$ 44. $\dfrac{146}{4\overline{)584}}$

45. $\dfrac{442}{9\overline{)3978}}$ 46. $\dfrac{847}{8\overline{)6776}}$ 47. $\dfrac{441}{6\overline{)2646}}$ 48. $\dfrac{7303}{5\overline{)36515}}$

49. $\dfrac{542\ R5}{7\overline{)3799}}$ 50. $\dfrac{562\ R3}{4\overline{)2251}}$ 51. $\dfrac{663\ R7}{9\overline{)5974}}$ 52. $\dfrac{387\ R2}{5\overline{)1937}}$

53. $\dfrac{762\ R6}{8\overline{)6102}}$ 54. $\dfrac{2753\ R2}{6\overline{)16520}}$ 55. $\dfrac{4832\ R2}{3\overline{)14498}}$ 56. $\dfrac{865\ R1}{2\overline{)1731}}$

57. $\dfrac{864\ R1}{7\overline{)6049}}$ 58. $\dfrac{461\ R2}{5\overline{)2307}}$ 59. $\dfrac{1837\ R2}{4\overline{)7350}}$ 60. $\dfrac{575\ R2}{8\overline{)4602}}$

Examples:

1. 25)72

$$
\begin{array}{r}
2 \ \text{R22} \\
25\overline{)72} \\
2 \times 25 \longrightarrow 50 \\
\hline
22
\end{array}
$$

Think: 25)72 → 2

Check:
$$
\begin{array}{r}
1 \\
25 \\
\times 2 \\
\hline
50 \\
+22 \\
\hline
72 \ \checkmark
\end{array}
$$

The quotient can also be written $2\frac{22}{25}$.

---

2. 15)326

$$
\begin{array}{r}
21 \ \text{R11} \\
15\overline{)326} \\
2 \times 15 \longrightarrow 30 \\
\hline
26 \\
1 \times 15 \longrightarrow 15 \\
\hline
11
\end{array}
$$

Think: 15)32 → 2

Think: 15)26 → 1

Check:
$$
\begin{array}{r}
15 \\
\times 21 \\
\hline
15 \\
300 \\
\hline
315 \\
+ \ 11 \\
\hline
326 \ \checkmark
\end{array}
$$

The quotient can also be written $21\frac{11}{15}$.

---

3. 231)47124

$$
\begin{array}{r}
204 \\
231\overline{)47124} \\
2 \times 231 \longrightarrow 462 \\
\hline
92 \\
0 \times 231 \longrightarrow 0 \\
\hline
924 \\
4 \times 231 \longrightarrow 924 \\
\hline
0
\end{array}
$$

Think: 231)471 → 2

Think: 231)92 → 0

Think: 231)924 → 4

Check:
$$
\begin{array}{r}
1 \\
231 \\
\times 204 \\
\hline
924 \\
0 \\
+46200 \\
\hline
47124 \ \checkmark
\end{array}
$$

EXERCISES

Divide. Check your answers.

1. 38)76 → 2

2. 52)83 → 1 R31

3. 26)78 → 3

4. 34)87 → 2 R19

5. 59)654 → 11 R5

6. 32)755 → 23 R19

7. 23)740 → 32 R4

8. 37)825 → 22 R11

9. 42)5316 → 126 R24

10. 56)7060 → 126 R4

11. 35)7735 → 221

12. 24)3192 → 133

13. 34)93 → 2 R25

14. 28)65 → 2 R9

15. 37)72 → 1 R35

16. 43)85 → 1 R42

17. 27)972 → 36

18. 31)605 → 19 R16

19. 46)845 → 18 R17

20. 21)819 → 39

21. 33)754 → 22 R28

22. 54)694 → 12 R46

23. 24)786 → 32 R18

24. 36)816 → 22 R24

25. 23)646 → 28 R2

26. 39)928 → 23 R31

27. 47)831 → 17 R32

28. 29)659 → 22 R21

29. 75)3825 → 51

30. 43)2630 → 61 R7

31. 87)1224 → 14 R6

32. 54)4523 → 83 R41

33. 38)2946 → 77 R20

34. 82)84542 → 1031

35. 32)96634 → 3019 R26

36. 25)76990 → 3079 R15

37. 682)9604 → 14 R56

38. 157)1803 → 11 R76

39. 538)7532 → 14

40. 324)75684 → 233 R192

41. 241)98936 → 410 R126

42. 423)93891 → 221 R408

43. 583)626142 → 1074

44. 364)556992 → 1530 R72

45. 142)642266 → 4523

46. 471)30256 → 64 R112

47. 506)25234 → 49 R440

48. 283)10471 → 37

49. 327)185082 → 566

50. 252)199332 → 791

51. 299)301099 → 1007 R6

To divide a decimal by a whole number:

Step 1: Write the decimal point in the quotient directly above the decimal point in the dividend.

Step 2: Divide as you would for whole numbers.

Examples:

1.

$$\begin{array}{r} 0.2 \\ 3\overline{)0.6} \end{array}$$

$0 \times 3 \longrightarrow 0$
$ 6$
$2 \times 3 \longrightarrow \underline{6}$
$ 0$

Think: $3\overline{)0}$ → 0

Think: $3\overline{)6}$ → 2

Check:
$$\begin{array}{r} 0.2 \\ \times 3 \\ \hline 0.6 \end{array}$$ ✔

2.

$$\begin{array}{r} 0.05 \\ 7\overline{)0.35} \end{array}$$

$0 \times 7 \longrightarrow 0$
$ 3$
$0 \times 7 \longrightarrow 0$
$ 35$
$5 \times 7 \longrightarrow \underline{35}$
$ 0$

Think: $7\overline{)0}$ → 0

Think: $7\overline{)3}$ → 0

Think: $7\overline{)35}$ → 5

3.

$$\begin{array}{r} 0.802 \\ 8\overline{)6.416} \end{array}$$

$0 \times 8 \longrightarrow 0$
$ 6\,4$
$8 \times 8 \longrightarrow 6\,4$
$ 1$
$0 \times 8 \longrightarrow 0$
$ 16$
$2 \times 8 \longrightarrow \underline{16}$
$ 0$

Think: $8\overline{)6}$ → 0

Think: $8\overline{)64}$ → 8

Think: $8\overline{)1}$ → 0

Think: $8\overline{)16}$ → 2

4. Divide 39 by 6 until there is a 0 remainder. Write a decimal point in the quotient.

$$\begin{array}{r} 6 \\ 6\overline{)39} \\ \underline{36} \\ 3 \end{array}$$

Write 39 as 39.0 and continue dividing.

$$\begin{array}{r} 6.5 \\ 6\overline{)39.0} \\ \underline{36} \\ 3\,0 \\ \underline{3\,0} \\ 0 \end{array}$$

Check:
$$\begin{array}{r} 6.5 \\ \times 6 \\ \hline 39.0 \end{array}$$
$(39.0 = 39)$ ✔

5. Divide 0.5 by 4 until there is a 0 remainder. Check by multiplying.

$$\begin{array}{r} 0.1 \\ 4\overline{)0.5} \\ \underline{0\,4} \\ 1 \end{array}$$

Write 0.5 as 0.50 and continue dividing.

$$\begin{array}{r} 0.12 \\ 4\overline{)0.50} \\ \underline{0\,4} \\ 10 \\ \underline{8} \\ 2 \end{array}$$

Write 0.50 as 0.500 and continue dividing. (Use as many 0's after the digits to the right of the decimal point in the dividend as necessary.)

$$\begin{array}{r} 0.125 \\ 4\overline{)0.500} \\ \underline{0\,4} \\ 10 \\ \underline{8} \\ 20 \\ \underline{20} \\ 0 \end{array}$$

EXERCISES

Divide. Check your answers.

1. $\overset{0.3}{3\overline{)0.9}}$ 2. $\overset{0.4}{2\overline{)0.8}}$ 3. $\overset{0.1}{5\overline{)0.5}}$ 4. $\overset{0.2}{4\overline{)0.8}}$

5. $\overset{0.08}{2\overline{)0.16}}$ 6. $\overset{0.09}{3\overline{)0.27}}$ 7. $\overset{0.08}{6\overline{)0.48}}$ 8. $\overset{0.07}{9\overline{)0.63}}$

9. $\overset{0.08}{7\overline{)0.56}}$ 10. $\overset{0.09}{5\overline{)0.45}}$ 11. $\overset{0.08}{4\overline{)0.32}}$ 12. $\overset{0.09}{8\overline{)0.72}}$

13. $\overset{0.41}{6\overline{)2.46}}$ 14. $\overset{0.602}{7\overline{)4.214}}$ 15. $\overset{0.403}{5\overline{)2.015}}$ 16. $\overset{0.61}{9\overline{)5.49}}$

17. $\overset{3.11}{7\overline{)21.77}}$ 18. $\overset{6.32}{3\overline{)18.96}}$ 19. $\overset{7.21}{4\overline{)28.84}}$ 20. $\overset{6.02}{6\overline{)36.12}}$

21. $\overset{3.15}{27\overline{)85.05}}$ 22. $\overset{2.68}{35\overline{)93.80}}$ 23. $\overset{6.24}{12\overline{)74.88}}$ 24. $\overset{0.532}{40\overline{)21.280}}$

25. $\overset{6.27}{34\overline{)213.18}}$ 26. $\overset{3.68}{52\overline{)191.36}}$ 27. $\overset{5.28}{43\overline{)227.04}}$ 28. $\overset{5.24}{68\overline{)356.32}}$

Divide until there is a 0 remainder. Check.

29. $\overset{0.505}{92\overline{)46.46}}$ 30. $\overset{0.654}{25\overline{)16.35}}$ 31. $\overset{8.65}{34\overline{)294.1}}$ 32. $\overset{41.66}{15\overline{)624.9}}$

33. $\overset{0.00735}{46\overline{)0.3381}}$ 34. $\overset{0.055}{18\overline{)0.99}}$ 35. $\overset{0.915}{64\overline{)58.56}}$ 36. $\overset{9.35}{88\overline{)822.8}}$

37. $\overset{0.0325}{68\overline{)2.21}}$ 38. $\overset{0.0825}{76\overline{)6.27}}$ 39. $\overset{0.248}{25\overline{)6.2}}$ 40. $\overset{0.00325}{16\overline{)0.052}}$

41. $\overset{0.3375}{28\overline{)9.45}}$ 42. $\overset{0.002}{300\overline{)0.6}}$ 43. $\overset{0.528}{25\overline{)13.2}}$ 44. $\overset{0.0625}{12\overline{)0.75}}$

45. $\overset{0.0266}{500\overline{)13.3}}$ 46. $\overset{0.0625}{8\overline{)0.5}}$ 47. $\overset{0.0375}{40\overline{)1.5}}$ 48. $\overset{0.80625}{8\overline{)6.45}}$

49. $\overset{39.5}{2\overline{)79}}$ 50. $\overset{7.6}{5\overline{)38}}$ 51. $\overset{31.5}{6\overline{)189}}$ 52. $\overset{14.75}{4\overline{)59}}$

53. $\overset{23.375}{8\overline{)187}}$ 54. $\overset{0.0875}{80\overline{)7}}$ 55. $\overset{32.875}{16\overline{)526}}$ 56. $\overset{53.625}{8\overline{)429}}$

Use this shortcut to divide by 10, 100, 1000, and so on.

To divide by	move the decimal point	Example:
10	1 place to the *left*	$73 \div 10 = 7.3$
100	2 places to the *left*	$5.82 \div 100 = 0.0582$ **Insert 0's as needed.**
1000	3 places to the *left*	$0.158 \div 1000 = 0.000158$

EXERCISES

Copy each exercise and place the decimal point in the quotient.

1. $740 \div 10 = 740$

2. $250 \div 1000 = 0250$

3. $823.34 \div 100 = 82334$

4. $96 \div 1000 = 0096$

5. $64.8 \div 100 = 0648$

6. $0.1 \div 1000 = 00001$

7. $10\overline{)43.89}$ 4389

8. $100\overline{)6}$ 00060

9. $1000\overline{)6074.1}$ 60741

10. $\frac{6.59}{10} = 0659$

11. $\frac{560.8}{100} = 5608$

12. $\frac{6500}{1000} = 6500$

Divide.

13. $752 \div 10$ 75.2

14. $7 \div 10$ 0.7

15. $0.9 \div 10$ 0.09

16. $80.4 \div 10$ 8.04

17. $2000 \div 10$ 200

18. $0.003 \div 10$ 0.0003

19. $3271 \div 100$ 32.71

20. $42 \div 100$ 0.42

21. $7.46 \div 100$ 0.0746

22. $0.653 \div 100$ 0.00653

23. $0.0094 \div 100$ 0.000094

24. $8500 \div 100$ 85

25. $8000 \div 1000$ 8

26. $29,342 \div 1000$ 29.342

27. $12 \div 1000$ 0.012

28. $0.56 \div 1000$ 0.00056

29. $12.28 \div 1000$ 0.01228

30. $0.007 \div 1000$ 0.000007

31. $10\overline{)95}$ 9.5

32. $100\overline{)100.6}$ 1.006

33. $1000\overline{)899}$ 0.899

34. $\frac{0.1}{10}$ 0.01

35. $\frac{2}{100}$ 0.02

36. $\frac{1.08}{1000}$ 0.00108

Multiplying a divisor and a dividend by the same nonzero number does not change the quotient. This idea is very useful when dividing by a decimal.

Examples:

1. $0.2\overline{)48}$

Step 1: Multiply 0.2 by 10 to get a whole number. Multiply 48 by 10 so that the quotient is not changed.

$0.2\overline{)48\,0}$ Insert 0's as needed.

Step 2: Divide.

$$240$$
$$2\overline{)480}$$

Check: Multiply the quotient by the *original* divisor. Compare the product with the *original* dividend. ✔

$$240$$
$$\times\,0.2$$
$$48.0$$ ⟵ These should be the same.

$0.2\overline{)48}$

---

2. $0.042\overline{)3.6582}$

Step 1: Multiply the divisor and the dividend by 1000.

$0.042\overline{)3.6582}$

Step 2: Write the decimal point in the quotient. Divide.

$$87.1$$
$$42\overline{)3658.2}$$

Check:

$$87.1$$
$$\times\,0.042$$
$$3.6582$$ ✔

$0.042\overline{)3.6582}$

These should be the same.

EXERCISES

What is the smallest number (10, 100, or 1000) that you could multiply both numbers by to get a whole-number divisor?

1. $0.4\overline{)4.8}$ 10

2. $6.4\overline{)33.28}$ 10

3. $0.002\overline{)10}$ 1000

4. $3.46\overline{)27.68}$ 100

5–8. Find each quotient in exercises 1–4.

5. 12

6. 5.2

7. 5000

8. 8

Divide.

9. $486.5 \div 0.7$ 695

10. $3120 \div 1.5$ 2080

11. $7608 \div 0.8$ 9510

12. $6.46 \div 3.8$ 1.7

13. $0.07\overline{)0.35}$ 5

14. $0.08\overline{)0.064}$ 0.8

15. $0.74\overline{)4.8248}$ 6.52

16. $1.6\overline{)6.1664}$ 3.854

17. $0.003\overline{)0.27}$ 90

18. $0.064\overline{)0.7872}$ 12.3

19. $0.005\overline{)0.0225}$ 4.5

20. $0.32\overline{)10.944}$ 34.2

21. $164.4 \div 2.4$ 68.5

22. $42 \div 0.06$ 700

23. $1736 \div 0.031$ 56,000

24. $40.044 \div 0.47$ 85.2

25. $0.23\overline{)21.2888}$ 92.56

26. $0.023\overline{)2.12888}$ 92.56

27. $0.68\overline{)0.021828}$ 0.0321

28. $2.06\overline{)98.88}$ 48

Examples:

1. Find $9.98 \div 4$ to the nearest *whole number*.

**To round to this place,
this digit is needed.**

$$2.4 \leftarrow \text{Stop dividing.}$$

$$
\begin{array}{r}
2.4 \\
4\overline{)9.9\ 8} \\
\underline{8} \\
1\ 9 \\
\underline{1\ 6} \\
3
\end{array}
$$

Round 2.4 to the nearest whole number.
Check the tenths digit.

$$2.\overset{\downarrow}{4}$$

less than 5, so
round down to 2

The quotient to the nearest whole number is 2.

---

2. Find $7.0068 \div 0.3$ to the nearest *tenth*.

**To round to this place,
this digit is needed.**

$$2\ 3.3\ 5 \leftarrow \text{Stop dividing.}$$

$$0.3\overline{)7.0068} \qquad 3\overline{)7\ 0.0\ 6\ 8}$$

Round 23.35 to the nearest tenth.
Check the hundredths digit.

$$2\ 3.3\ 5$$

equal to 5, so
round up to 23.4

The quotient to the nearest tenth is 23.4.

---

3. Find $4 \div 1.3$ to the nearest *hundredth*.

**To round to this place,
this digit is needed.**

$$3.0\ 7\ 6 \leftarrow \text{Stop dividing.}$$

$$1.3\overline{)4.0} \longrightarrow 13\overline{)4\ 0.0\ 0\ 0}$$

Insert 0's   Insert 0's
as needed.   as needed.

Round 3.076 to the nearest hundredth.
Check the thousandths digit.

$$3.0\ 7\ 6$$

more than 5, so
round up to 3.08

The quotient to the nearest hundredth is 3.08.

4. Find $0.16 \div 0.033$ to the nearest *thousandth*.

**To round to this place,
this digit is needed.**

$$4.8\ 4\ 8\ 4 \leftarrow \text{Stop dividing.}$$

$$0.033\overline{)0.160}\qquad 33\overline{)1\ 6\ 0.0\ 0\ 0\ 0}$$

**Insert 0's
as needed.**   **Insert 0's
as needed.**

The quotient to the nearest thousandth is 4.848.

EXERCISES

Find each quotient to the nearest whole number.

1. $3\overline{)5.67}$ 2 **2.** $7\overline{)10.23}$ 1 **3.** $12\overline{)13.99}$ 1 **4.** $50\overline{)43.05}$ 1

5. $0.1\overline{)0.85}$ 9 **6.** $0.4\overline{)9.75}$ 24 **7.** $0.05\overline{)0.08}$ 2 **8.** $5.8\overline{)40}$ 7

9. $31 \div 4$ 8 **10.** $43 \div 6$ 7 **11.** $49 \div 4.3$ 11 **12.** $11.1 \div 0.09$
                                                                                                     123

Find each quotient to the nearest tenth.

13. $6\overline{)8.82}$ $\overset{1.5}{}$ **14.** $5\overline{)25.30}$ $\overset{5.1}{}$ **15.** $3\overline{)96.318}$ $\overset{32.1}{}$ **16.** $23\overline{)138.92}$ $\overset{6.0}{}$

17. $3.4\overline{)21.532}$ $\overset{6.3}{}$ **18.** $0.47\overline{)3.8822}$ $\overset{8.3}{}$ **19.** $0.5\overline{)312.4}$ $\overset{6.248}{}$ **20.** $0.024\overline{)12.09}$ $\overset{503.8}{}$

21. $81 \div 5$ 16.2 **22.** $63 \div 4$ 15.8 **23.** $87 \div 0.9$ 96.7 **24.** $26.1 \div 2.6$
                                                                                                     10.0

Find each quotient to the nearest hundredth.

25. $4\overline{)2.536}$ $\overset{0.63}{}$ **26.** $6\overline{)4.962}$ $\overset{0.83}{}$ **27.** $9\overline{)48.06}$ $\overset{5.34}{}$ **28.** $75\overline{)244.55}$ $\overset{3.26}{}$

29. $3.4\overline{)2.1532}$ $\overset{0.63}{}$ **30.** $16.2\overline{)21.6755}$ $\overset{1.34}{}$ **31.** $0.7\overline{)82}$ $\overset{117.14}{}$ **32.** $0.58\overline{)9.4}$ $\overset{16.21}{}$

33. $17 \div 8$ 2.13 **34.** $8 \div 17$ 0.47 **35.** $18 \div 6.8$ 2.65 **36.** $0.3149 \div 0.05$
                                                                                                     6.3

Find each quotient to the nearest thousandth.

37. $3\overline{)4.7003}$ $\overset{1.567}{}$ **38.** $5\overline{)8.9999}$ $\overset{1.800}{}$ **39.** $72\overline{)9.84}$ $\overset{0.137}{}$ **40.** $30\overline{)0.058}$ $\overset{0.002}{}$

41. $0.54\overline{)0.09846}$ $\overset{0.182}{}$ **42.** $0.25\overline{)15.658}$ $\overset{62.632}{}$ **43.** $0.063\overline{)8.12}$ $\overset{128.889}{}$ **44.** $1.7\overline{)8}$ $\overset{4.706}{}$

45. $12 \div 7$ 1.714 **46.** $7 \div 12$ 0.583 **47.** $83 \div 0.032$ 2766.667 **48.** $6.8 \div 0.007$
                                                                                                     971.429

Divide. Use remainder notation where necessary. Check.

1. 72 ÷ 8 9

2. 54 ÷ 7 7 R5

3. 84 ÷ 4 21

4. 65 ÷ 9 7 R2

5. 3)963 321

6. 4)840 210

7. 2)1608 804

8. 6)1266 211

9. 7)1421 203

10. 5)525 105

11. 9)1818 202

12. 3)921 307

13. 6)312 52

14. 8)184 23

15. 4)228 57

16. 7)574 82

17. 6)3228 538

18. 8)4416 552

19. 9)7569 841

20. 4)2788 697

21. 698 ÷ 5 139 R3

22. 397 ÷ 4 99 R1

23. 489 ÷ 6 81 R3

24. 658 ÷ 3 219 R1

25. $\frac{4499}{6}$ 749 R5

26. $\frac{4128}{7}$ 589 R5

27. $\frac{3913}{5}$ 782 R3

28. $\frac{2188}{6}$ 364 R4

29. 24)7824 326

30. 32)7712 241

31. 43)5339 124 R7

32. 53)6533 123 R14

33. 37)9472 256

34. 58)36934 636 R46

35. 322)65688 204

36. 431)143186 332 R94

Divide until there is a 0 remainder. Check.

37. 9)63.18 7.02

38. 7)2.177 0.311

39. 24)86.4 3.6

40. 31)176.7 5.7

41. 12)42 3.5

42. 65)150.8 2.32

43. 28)91.7 3.275

44. 48)996 20.75

45. 84 ÷ 10 8.4

46. 37.2 ÷ 100 0.372

47. 0.08 ÷ 100 0.0008

48. 2 ÷ 1000 0.002

49. 0.4)4.8 12

50. 0.25)0.815 3.26

51. 5.7)11.685 2.05

52. 0.008)0.01 1.25

53. 0.03)2.442 81.4

54. 0.011)0.0715 6.5

55. 3.4)0.272 0.08

56. 2.5)20 8

Find each quotient to the nearest hundredth.

57. 7)8.80 1.26

58. 0.7)1.3 1.86

59. 0.007)0.1 14.29

60. 11 ÷ 14 0.79

The product	can be written like this	and is read like this:
3×3	3^2	*three squared* or *three to the second power*
$3 \times 3 \times 3$	3^3	*three cubed* or *three to the third power*
$3 \times 3 \times 3 \times 3$	3^4	*three to the fourth power*

exponent

3^2

base

An exponent tells the number of times the base is used as a factor.

Examples:

1. $3^2 = 3 \times 3$
    $= 9$

2. $2^4 = 2 \times 2 \times 2 \times 2$
    $= 4 \times 4$
    $= 16$

3. $(2.3)^2 = 2.3 \times 2.3$
    $= 5.29$

4. exponent 2 $10^2 = 10 \times 10 = 1\,00$ 2 zeros

exponent 3 $10^3 = 10 \times 10 \times 10 = 1000$ 3 zeros

exponent 4 $10^4 = 10 \times 10 \times 10 \times 10 = 10,000$ 4 zeros

5. $3^3 \times (0.2)^2 \times 5 = 3 \times 3 \times 3 \times 0.2 \times 0.2 \times 5$

   $= \quad 27 \quad \times \quad 0.04 \quad \times 5$

   $= \quad 27 \quad \times \quad\quad 0.2$

   $= \quad\quad\quad 5.4$

EXERCISES

Express in words.

   four squared   one to the fourth power   three to the sixth power

1. 4^2 **2.** 5^3 **3.** 1^4 **4.** 6^2 **5.** 3^6 **6.** 12^3

      five cubed   six squared   twelve cubed

Find the result.

7. 5^2 25   **8.** 4^2 16   **9.** 1^4 1   **10.** 3^3 27   **11.** 10^5 100,000 **12.** 3^4 81

13. 4^3 64   **14.** 10^6 **15.** 2^5 32   **16.** 0^3 0   **17.** $(1.2)^2$ 1.44 **18.** $(0.05)^2$ 0.0025

      1,000,000

19. $5^2 \times 10^2$ 2500   **20.** $2^3 \times 10^4$ 80,000   **21.** 12×3^3 324

22. $9^2 \times 3^4 \times 0^3$ 0   **23.** $4 \times 6^2 \times 2^3$ 1152   **24.** $3 \times 5^2 \times (0.1)^2$ 0.75

There are 4 parts the same size.
3 of the parts are shaded red.
$\frac{3}{4}$ of the figure is shaded red.

× × × ○ ×
○ × ○ × ×

There are 10 objects.
7 of the objects are X's.
$\frac{7}{10}$ of the set are X's.

numerator ⟶ **3**
denominator ⟶ **4**

These *fractions* are
read this way.

7 ⟵ numerator
10 ⟵ denominator

three fourths ⟵ ⟶ *seven tenths*

A fraction whose numerator is less than its denominator
names a number less than 1.

EXERCISES

Use a fraction to tell how much is in red.

1. $\frac{5}{6}$

2. 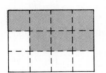 $\frac{7}{12}$

3. $\frac{2}{3}$

4. $\frac{1}{4}$

5.  $\frac{7}{9}$

6. × × × × × × × $\frac{4}{7}$

7. $\frac{5}{8}$

8. $\frac{5}{9}$

9. $\frac{3}{3}$, or 1

10. 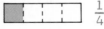 $\frac{7}{12}$

11. $\frac{0}{4}$

12.  $\frac{3}{10}$

13. × × × × × × × × × $\frac{4}{9}$

14.  $\frac{3}{5}$

15. $\frac{6}{11}$

16.  $\frac{2}{8}$, or $\frac{1}{4}$

17. 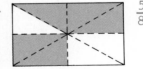 $\frac{2}{6}$, or $\frac{1}{3}$

18. $\frac{2}{4}$, or $\frac{1}{2}$

Express in words.

19. $\frac{1}{2}$
one
half

20. $\frac{1}{3}$
one
third

21. $\frac{1}{4}$
one
fourth

22. $\frac{3}{8}$
three
eighths

23. $\frac{1}{16}$
one
sixteenth

24. $\frac{2}{5}$
two
fifths

25. $\frac{2}{3}$
two
thirds

26. $\frac{6}{8}$
six
eighths

27. $\frac{7}{12}$
seven
twelfths

28. $\frac{3}{20}$
three
twentieths

29. $\frac{6}{50}$
six
fiftieths

30. $\frac{4}{100}$
four
hundredths

31. $\frac{5}{9}$
five
ninths

32. $\frac{9}{17}$
nine
seventeenths

33. $\frac{3}{31}$
three
thirty-firsts

34. $\frac{15}{16}$
fifteen
sixteenths

35. $\frac{3}{3}$
three
thirds

36. $\frac{17}{22}$
seventeen
twenty-seconds

37. $\frac{0}{5}$
zero
fifths

38. $\frac{7}{1000}$
seven
thousandths

Draw a figure like the one shown. Then shade the amount indicated by the fraction.
See student's drawings.

39. $\frac{3}{5}$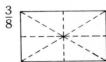

40. $\frac{5}{12}$

41. $\frac{4}{9}$

42. $\frac{4}{4}$

43. $\frac{3}{8}$

44. $\frac{9}{14}$

45. $\frac{2}{5}$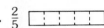

46. $\frac{0}{6}$

47. $\frac{3}{7}$

48. $\frac{1}{2}$

49. $\frac{3}{4}$

50. $\frac{1}{3}$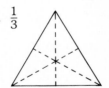

Draw the figure described. Separate it into parts and shade the amount indicated by the fraction. Possible answers are given below.

51. square; $\frac{2}{4}$

52. circle; $\frac{7}{8}$

53. rectangle; $\frac{1}{10}$

54. triangle; $\frac{5}{6}$

55. square; $\frac{2}{3}$

56. circle; $\frac{2}{6}$

485

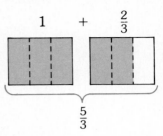

1   + $\frac{2}{3}$

$\frac{5}{3}$

$$1+\frac{2}{3}=\frac{3}{3}+\frac{2}{3}$$
$$=\frac{5}{3}$$

15. twelve and one half

$1+\frac{2}{3}$ can also be written as the **mixed number** $1\frac{2}{3}$. It is read *one and two thirds.*

16. twenty-seven and three fifths

A *mixed number* stands for the *sum* of a *whole number* and a *fraction.*

17. nine and seven tenths

A fraction whose numerator and denominator are equal (but not 0) names the number 1. A fraction whose numerator is greater than its denominator names a number greater than 1.

18. thirty-six and twenty-one hundredths

EXERCISES

Use a mixed number to tell how much is in red.

1. $1\frac{3}{4}$

$3\frac{5}{7}$ 2.

3. $2\frac{3}{5}$

4. $2\frac{3}{8}$

5. $1\frac{1}{3}$

6. $1\frac{1}{2}$

Write each sum as a mixed number.

7. $5+\frac{3}{8}$ $5\frac{3}{8}$ **8.** $4+\frac{3}{4}$ $4\frac{3}{4}$ **9.** $\frac{2}{5}+3$ $3\frac{2}{5}$ **10.** $\frac{7}{8}+8$ $8\frac{7}{8}$

11. $\frac{7}{1}+\frac{3}{7}$ $7\frac{3}{7}$ **12.** $\frac{3}{10}+\frac{6}{1}$ $6\frac{3}{10}$ **13.** $\frac{4}{4}+\frac{1}{2}$ $1\frac{1}{2}$ **14.** $\frac{5}{6}+\frac{6}{6}$ $1\frac{5}{6}$

Write in words.
Answers for exercises 15-18 are given above.

15. $12\frac{1}{2}$ **16.** $27\frac{3}{5}$ **17.** $9\frac{7}{10}$ **18.** $36\frac{21}{100}$

19. eight and six sevenths   21. nine and five twenty-seconds

19. $8\frac{6}{7}$ **20.** $3\frac{2}{3}$ **21.** $9\frac{5}{22}$ **22.** $15\frac{3}{50}$

20. three and two thirds   22. fifteen and three fiftieths

Examples:

1. Change $3\frac{5}{8}$ to a fraction.

Step 1: To find the numerator of the fraction, multiply the denominator by the whole number and add the numerator.

Step 2: Use the same denominator.

$$3\frac{5}{8} = \frac{(8 \times 3) + 5}{8}$$

$$= \frac{24 + 5}{8}$$

$$= \frac{29}{8}$$

---

2. Change $\frac{30}{7}$ to a mixed number.

Step 1: Divide the numerator by the denominator to get a whole number quotient and a remainder.

Step 2: Write the whole number, followed by a fraction made up of the remainder over the divisor.

$$\frac{30}{7} \longrightarrow 7\overline{)30} \quad \begin{array}{r} 4 \\ \underline{28} \\ 2 \end{array}$$

So $\dfrac{30}{7} = 4\dfrac{2}{7}$. $\longleftarrow$ remainder
$\longleftarrow$ divisor

---

3. Change $\frac{36}{3}$ to a whole number.

$$\frac{36}{3} \longrightarrow 3\overline{)36} \quad \begin{array}{r} 12 \\ \underline{3} \\ 6 \\ \underline{6} \\ 0 \end{array}$$

So $\dfrac{36}{3} = 12$.

EXERCISES

Change each mixed number to a fraction.

1. $1\frac{7}{8}$ $\frac{15}{8}$

2. $4\frac{3}{5}$ $\frac{23}{5}$

3. $2\frac{1}{6}$ $\frac{13}{6}$

4. $3\frac{3}{4}$ $\frac{15}{4}$

5. $7\frac{1}{2}$ $\frac{15}{2}$

6. $8\frac{3}{5}$ $\frac{43}{5}$

7. $4\frac{3}{10}$ $\frac{43}{10}$

8. $2\frac{3}{100}$ $\frac{203}{100}$

9. $5\frac{4}{5}$ $\frac{29}{5}$

10. $8\frac{7}{10}$ $\frac{87}{10}$

11. $2\frac{4}{9}$ $\frac{22}{9}$

12. $6\frac{4}{7}$ $\frac{46}{7}$

13. $6\frac{2}{3}$ $\frac{20}{3}$

14. $9\frac{1}{5}$ $\frac{46}{5}$

15. $1\frac{3}{4}$ $\frac{7}{4}$

16. $1\frac{43}{50}$ $\frac{93}{50}$

17. $2\frac{1}{7}$ $\frac{15}{7}$

18. $4\frac{2}{9}$ $\frac{38}{9}$

19. $7\frac{1}{4}$ $\frac{29}{4}$

20. $3\frac{6}{7}$ $\frac{27}{7}$

21. $5\frac{7}{9}$ $\frac{52}{9}$

22. $6\frac{9}{10}$ $\frac{69}{10}$

23. $9\frac{1}{3}$ $\frac{28}{3}$

24. $7\frac{2}{5}$ $\frac{37}{5}$

25. $5\frac{5}{6}$ $\frac{35}{6}$

26. $5\frac{5}{7}$ $\frac{40}{7}$

27. $4\frac{3}{8}$ $\frac{35}{8}$

28. $6\frac{8}{9}$ $\frac{62}{9}$

29. $1\frac{3}{7}$ $\frac{10}{7}$

30. $3\frac{5}{9}$ $\frac{32}{9}$

31. $10\frac{2}{7}$ $\frac{72}{7}$

32. $11\frac{1}{8}$ $\frac{89}{8}$

Change each fraction to a mixed number or a whole number.

33. $\frac{17}{2}$ $8\frac{1}{2}$

34. $\frac{19}{4}$ $4\frac{3}{4}$

35. $\frac{37}{37}$ 1

36. $\frac{9}{1}$ 9

37. $\frac{25}{4}$ $6\frac{1}{4}$

38. $\frac{16}{7}$ $2\frac{2}{7}$

39. $\frac{43}{2}$ $21\frac{1}{2}$

40. $\frac{59}{6}$ $9\frac{5}{6}$

41. $\frac{37}{4}$ $9\frac{1}{4}$

42. $\frac{18}{6}$ 3

43. $\frac{21}{10}$ $2\frac{1}{10}$

44. $\frac{25}{6}$ $4\frac{1}{6}$

45. $\frac{38}{9}$ $4\frac{2}{9}$

46. $\frac{63}{8}$ $7\frac{7}{8}$

47. $\frac{91}{9}$ $10\frac{1}{9}$

48. $\frac{23}{7}$ $3\frac{2}{7}$

49. $\frac{68}{8}$ $8\frac{1}{2}$

50. $\frac{93}{5}$ $18\frac{3}{5}$

51. $\frac{68}{5}$ $13\frac{3}{5}$

52. $\frac{85}{3}$ $28\frac{1}{3}$

53. $\frac{108}{5}$ $21\frac{3}{5}$

54. $\frac{17}{5}$ $3\frac{2}{5}$

55. $\frac{79}{3}$ $26\frac{1}{3}$

56. $\frac{99}{8}$ $12\frac{3}{8}$

57. $\frac{25}{3}$ $8\frac{1}{3}$

58. $\frac{87}{3}$ 29

59. $\frac{95}{95}$ 1

60. $\frac{69}{8}$ $8\frac{5}{8}$

61. $\frac{17}{8}$ $2\frac{1}{8}$

62. $\frac{23}{8}$ $2\frac{7}{8}$

63. $\frac{25}{9}$ $2\frac{7}{9}$

64. $\frac{37}{8}$ $4\frac{5}{8}$

The same amount is shaded in each square.

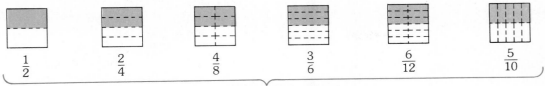

$$\frac{1}{2} \qquad \frac{2}{4} \qquad \frac{4}{8} \qquad \frac{3}{6} \qquad \frac{6}{12} \qquad \frac{5}{10}$$

equivalent fractions

Fractions that name the same number are *equivalent fractions*.

Equivalent fractions have equal *cross products*.

Examples:

1. $16 \xleftarrow{\hspace{1em}} \frac{2}{4} \times\hspace{-0.3em}\frac{4}{8} \xrightarrow{\hspace{1em}} 16$

$16 = 16$, so $\frac{2}{4}$ and $\frac{4}{8}$ are equivalent.
That is, $\frac{2}{4} = \frac{4}{8}$.

2. $28 \xleftarrow{\hspace{1em}} \frac{7}{8} \times\hspace{-0.3em}\frac{3}{4} \xrightarrow{\hspace{1em}} 24$

28 does not equal 24, so $\frac{7}{8}$ and $\frac{3}{4}$ are NOT equivalent.

To find a fraction equivalent to a given fraction, multiply or divide both the numerator and the denominator by the same number (but not 0).

3. $\dfrac{1}{2} = \dfrac{1 \times 5}{2 \times 5} = \dfrac{5}{10}$

4. $\dfrac{6}{15} = \dfrac{6 \div 3}{15 \div 3} = \dfrac{2}{5}$

5. $\dfrac{2}{7} = \dfrac{\boxed{?}}{21}$ $\times 3$

Think: $\dfrac{2 \times 3}{7 \times 3} = \dfrac{6}{21}$

So $\frac{2}{7} = \frac{6}{21}$.

6. $\dfrac{2}{4} = \dfrac{\boxed{?}}{10}$ **Since there is no whole number such that $4 \times \boxed{?} = 10$, the method above does not work.**

Think: $20 \xleftarrow{\hspace{1em}} \frac{2}{4} \times\hspace{-0.3em}\frac{\boxed{?}}{10} \xrightarrow{\hspace{1em}} 4 \times \boxed{?}$ **Find the cross products.**

So $20 = 4 \times \boxed{?}$; but $20 = 4 \times 5$, so $\frac{2}{4} = \frac{5}{10}$.

489

EXERCISES

Use cross products to determine whether or not the fractions are equivalent.

1. $\frac{2}{3}, \frac{8}{12}$ Yes

2. $\frac{4}{5}, \frac{8}{11}$ No

3. $\frac{4}{3}, \frac{12}{9}$ Yes

4. $\frac{12}{18}, \frac{2}{3}$ Yes

5. $\frac{3}{3}, \frac{5}{5}$ Yes

6. $\frac{3}{1}, \frac{6}{2}$ Yes

7. $\frac{7}{8}, \frac{14}{15}$ No

8. $\frac{9}{2}, \frac{11}{4}$ No

9. $\frac{0}{8}, \frac{0}{12}$ Yes

10. $\frac{7}{3}, \frac{21}{9}$ Yes

11. $\frac{9}{16}, \frac{19}{32}$ No

12. $\frac{45}{100}, \frac{23}{50}$ No

Multiply the numerator and the denominator of each fraction by the given number to find an equivalent fraction.

13. $\frac{2}{3}, 2 \quad \frac{4}{6}$

14. $\frac{3}{4}, 4 \quad \frac{12}{16}$

15. $\frac{3}{5}, 7 \quad \frac{21}{35}$

16. $\frac{1}{5}, 8 \quad \frac{8}{40}$

17. $\frac{2}{2}, 6 \quad \frac{12}{12}$

18. $\frac{0}{2}, 7 \quad \frac{0}{14}$

19. $\frac{4}{3}, 5 \quad \frac{20}{15}$

20. $\frac{7}{6}, 3 \quad \frac{21}{18}$

Divide the numerator and the denominator of each fraction by the given number to find an equivalent fraction.

21. $\frac{18}{24}, 3 \quad \frac{6}{8}$

22. $\frac{15}{15}, 5 \quad \frac{3}{3}$

23. $\frac{18}{12}, 6 \quad \frac{3}{2}$

24. $\frac{0}{4}, 2 \quad \frac{0}{2}$

25. $\frac{42}{56}, 7 \quad \frac{6}{8}$

26. $\frac{90}{50}, 10 \quad \frac{9}{5}$

27. $\frac{25}{75}, 5 \quad \frac{5}{15}$

28. $\frac{36}{16}, 4 \quad \frac{9}{4}$

Replace $?$ with a number that will make the fractions equivalent.

29. $\frac{2}{3} = \frac{?}{9}$ 6

30. $\frac{3}{5} = \frac{?}{10}$ 6

31. $\frac{3}{4} = \frac{15}{?}$ 20

32. $\frac{8}{5} = \frac{16}{?}$ 10

33. $\frac{?}{36} = \frac{5}{12}$ 15

34. $\frac{?}{100} = \frac{7}{10}$ 70

35. $\frac{2}{?} = \frac{8}{8}$ 2

36. $\frac{2}{8} = \frac{?}{12}$ 3

37. $\frac{2}{10} = \frac{5}{?}$ 25

38. $\frac{14}{?} = \frac{21}{6}$ 4

39. $\frac{10}{?} = \frac{15}{24}$ 16

40. $\frac{?}{4} = \frac{21}{6}$ 14

490

An easy way to compare two fractions is to use cross products.

Examples:

1.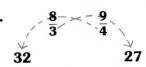

   Since 12>10, $\frac{4}{5}>\frac{2}{3}$.

2.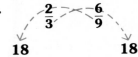

   Since 8<15, $\frac{2}{5}<\frac{3}{4}$.

3.
$$\frac{8}{3} \times \frac{9}{4}$$
   32   27

   Since 32>27, $\frac{8}{3}>\frac{9}{4}$.

4.
$$\frac{2}{3} \times \frac{6}{9}$$
   18   18

   Since 18=18, $\frac{2}{3}=\frac{6}{9}$.

   ($\frac{2}{3}$ and $\frac{6}{9}$ are *equivalent fractions.*)

EXERCISES

Replace ● with <, >, or = to make each sentence true.

1. $\frac{1}{2}$ ● $\frac{1}{3}$ >

2. $\frac{2}{5}$ ● $\frac{2}{9}$ >

3. $\frac{1}{7}$ ● $\frac{2}{7}$ <

4. $\frac{5}{9}$ ● $\frac{4}{9}$ >

5. $\frac{0}{6}$ ● $\frac{0}{7}$ =

6. $\frac{4}{5}$ ● $\frac{5}{6}$ <

7. $\frac{2}{3}$ ● $\frac{3}{4}$ <

8. $\frac{3}{8}$ ● $\frac{2}{7}$ >

9. $\frac{4}{9}$ ● $\frac{5}{8}$ <

10. $\frac{5}{5}$ ● $\frac{3}{3}$ =

11. $\frac{3}{10}$ ● $\frac{2}{9}$ >

12. $\frac{7}{5}$ ● $\frac{8}{9}$ >

13. $\frac{4}{7}$ ● $\frac{3}{2}$ <

14. $\frac{5}{6}$ ● $\frac{7}{8}$ <

15. $\frac{2}{5}$ ● $\frac{6}{15}$ =

16. $\frac{3}{2}$ ● $\frac{5}{4}$ >

17. $\frac{4}{1}$ ● $\frac{3}{1}$ >

18. $\frac{5}{3}$ ● $\frac{7}{2}$ <

19. $\frac{7}{3}$ ● $\frac{6}{5}$ >

20. $\frac{5}{9}$ ● $\frac{7}{12}$ <

21. $\frac{7}{9}$ ● $\frac{9}{10}$ <

22. $\frac{7}{2}$ ● $\frac{8}{3}$ >

23. $\frac{4}{5}$ ● $\frac{12}{15}$ =

24. $\frac{7}{5}$ ● $\frac{8}{7}$ >

The **greatest common factor** (GCF) of two or more numbers is the largest number that is a factor of each number. You will need to know the factors of 24, 36, 49, and 50 to do the examples below.

Factors of 24	Factors of 36	Factors of 49	Factors of 50
$1 \times 24 = 24$	$1 \times 36 = 36$	$1 \times 49 = 49$	$1 \times 50 = 50$
$2 \times 12 = 24$	$2 \times 18 = 36$	$7 \times 7 = 49$	$2 \times 25 = 50$
$3 \times 8 = 24$	$3 \times 12 = 36$		$5 \times 10 = 50$
$4 \times 6 = 24$	$4 \times 9 = 36$		
	$6 \times 6 = 36$		

Examples:

1. Find the greatest common factor of 24 and 36.

Factors of 24:   1, 2, 3, 4, 6, 8, 12, and 24

Factors of 36:   1, 2, 3, 4, 6, 9, 12, 18, and 36

Common factors: 1, 2, 3, 4, 6, 12

Greatest common factor: 12

---

2. Find the greatest common factor of 49 and 50.

Factors of 49:   1, 7, and 49

Factors of 50:   1, 2, 5, 10, 25, and 50

Common factor: 1

Greatest common factor: 1

EXERCISES

Find the greatest common factor of each set of numbers.

1. 4 and 10   2   **2.** 9 and 12   3   **3.** 5 and 10   5   **4.** 3 and 9   3

5. 5 and 7   1   **6.** 8 and 9   1   **7.** 12 and 28   4   **8.** 20 and 30   10

9. 9 and 45   9   **10.** 20 and 21   1   **11.** 18 and 27   9   **12.** 40 and 100   20

A fraction is reduced to **lowest terms** when the greatest common factor of the numerator and the denominator is 1.

To reduce a fraction to lowest terms:

Step 1: Find the greatest common factor of the numerator and the denominator.

Step 2: Divide the numerator and the denominator by their greatest common factor.

Examples:

1. Reduce $\frac{8}{20}$ to lowest terms.

common factors of 8 and 20

factors of 8: **1, 2, 4, 8**   factors of 20: **1, 2, 4, 5, 10, 20**

greatest common factor of 8 and 20

$$\frac{8}{20} = \frac{8 \div 4}{20 \div 4} = \frac{2}{5}$$ Check: $40 \; \frac{8}{20} \! \times \! \frac{2}{5} \; 40$ **The cross products are equal, so the fractions are equivalent.** ✔

2. Reduce $\frac{45}{10}$ to lowest terms.

common factors of 45 and 10

factors of 45: **1, 3, 5, 9, 15, 45**   factors of 10: **1, 2, 5, 10**

greatest common factor of 45 and 10

$$\frac{45}{10} = \frac{45 \div 5}{10 \div 5} = \frac{9}{2}$$ Check: $90 \; \frac{45}{10} \! \times \! \frac{9}{2} \; 90$ **The cross products are equal, so the fractions are equivalent.** ✔

EXERCISES

Reduce each fraction to lowest terms.

1. $\frac{6}{9}$ $\frac{2}{3}$ **2.** $\frac{4}{10}$ $\frac{2}{5}$ **3.** $\frac{6}{18}$ $\frac{1}{3}$ **4.** $\frac{10}{12}$ $\frac{5}{6}$ **5.** $\frac{10}{6}$ $\frac{5}{3}$

6. $\frac{56}{7}$ 8 **7.** $\frac{18}{24}$ $\frac{3}{4}$ **8.** $\frac{9}{45}$ $\frac{1}{5}$ **9.** $\frac{36}{24}$ $\frac{3}{2}$ **10.** $\frac{30}{36}$ $\frac{5}{6}$

11. $\frac{50}{80}$ $\frac{5}{8}$ **12.** $\frac{40}{100}$ $\frac{2}{5}$ **13.** $\frac{15}{60}$ $\frac{1}{4}$ **14.** $\frac{12}{9}$ $\frac{4}{3}$ **15.** $\frac{12}{28}$ $\frac{3}{7}$

493

$\frac{1}{3} \times \frac{2}{5}$ means $\begin{cases} \frac{1}{3} \text{ times } \frac{2}{5} \\ \\ \frac{1}{3} \text{ of } \frac{2}{5} \end{cases}$

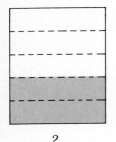

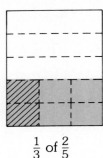

$\frac{2}{5}$ $\frac{1}{3}$ of $\frac{2}{5}$ $\frac{1}{3}$ of $\frac{2}{5} = \frac{2}{15}$

Examples:

1. $\frac{1}{3} \times \frac{2}{5} = \frac{1 \times 2}{3 \times 5}$ ⟵── **Multiply the numerators.**

                    ⟵── **Multiply the denominators.**

        $= \frac{2}{15}$

---

2. $\frac{6}{4} \times \frac{3}{5} \times \frac{3}{2} = \frac{6 \times 3 \times 3}{4 \times 5 \times 2}$

         $= \frac{54}{40}$ **Divide the numerator and the denominator**
                  by their greatest common factor, 2, to
         $= \frac{27}{20}$ **reduce the fraction to lowest terms.**

         $= 1\frac{7}{20}$ **Change the fraction**
                  to a mixed number.

---

3. $\frac{3}{8} \times 16 = \frac{3}{8} \times \frac{16}{1}$ **Name the whole number**
                          as a fraction.

         $= \frac{3 \times 16}{8 \times 1}$

         $= \frac{48}{8}$

                  Change the fraction
         $= 6$ **to a whole number.**

EXERCISES

Write the product as a whole number, as a fraction in lowest terms, or as a mixed number whenever possible.

1. $\frac{1}{3} \times \frac{4}{5}$ $\frac{4}{15}$

2. $\frac{2}{3} \times \frac{2}{5}$ $\frac{4}{15}$

3. $\frac{1}{4} \times \frac{5}{6}$ $\frac{5}{24}$

4. $\frac{3}{5} \times \frac{2}{4}$ $\frac{3}{10}$

5. $\frac{3}{4} \times \frac{5}{2}$ $1\frac{7}{8}$

6. $\frac{5}{3} \times \frac{1}{2}$ $\frac{5}{6}$

7. $\frac{3}{2} \times \frac{3}{5}$ $\frac{9}{10}$

8. $\frac{7}{5} \times \frac{3}{4}$ $1\frac{1}{20}$

9. $\frac{7}{3} \times \frac{3}{5}$ $1\frac{2}{5}$

10. $\frac{5}{2} \times \frac{4}{7}$ $1\frac{3}{7}$

11. $\frac{2}{8} \times \frac{8}{3}$ $\frac{2}{3}$

12. $\frac{1}{3} \times \frac{7}{9}$ $\frac{7}{27}$

13. $\frac{5}{2} \times \frac{5}{2}$ $\cdot 6\frac{1}{4}$

14. $\frac{8}{2} \times \frac{3}{2}$ 6

15. $5 \times \frac{3}{4}$ $3\frac{3}{4}$

16. $9 \times \frac{5}{6}$ $7\frac{1}{2}$

17. $\frac{9}{8} \times \frac{4}{3}$ $1\frac{1}{2}$

18. $5 \times \frac{1}{4}$ $1\frac{1}{4}$

19. $7 \times \frac{2}{5}$ $2\frac{4}{5}$

20. $\frac{9}{7} \times \frac{7}{9}$ 1

21. $\frac{6}{10} \times \frac{5}{3}$ 1

22. $\frac{1}{25} \times 25$ 1

23. $\frac{4}{7} \times \frac{7}{4}$ 1

24. $0 \times \frac{1}{3}$ 0

25. $6 \times \frac{5}{12}$ $2\frac{1}{2}$

26. $10 \times \frac{1}{2}$ 5

27. $\frac{7}{7} \times 4$ 4

28. $27 \times \frac{1}{3}$ 9

29. $\frac{2}{5} \times 10$ 4

30. $\frac{2}{9} \times \frac{3}{8}$ $\frac{1}{12}$

31. $\frac{1}{4} \times \frac{3}{5} \times \frac{7}{2}$ $\frac{21}{40}$

32. $\frac{1}{2} \times \frac{1}{3} \times \frac{1}{4}$ $\frac{1}{24}$

33. $\frac{2}{3} \times \frac{3}{5} \times \frac{1}{4}$ $\frac{1}{10}$

34. $\frac{1}{4} \times 3 \times \frac{3}{5}$ $\frac{9}{20}$

35. $2 \times \frac{1}{2} \times \frac{1}{8}$ $\frac{1}{8}$

36. $2 \times 3 \times \frac{1}{8}$ $\frac{3}{4}$

37. $\frac{1}{2} \times 4 \times 6 \times 6$ 72

38. $\frac{3}{4} \times 6 \times \frac{1}{3} \times 2$ 3

39. $\frac{1}{2} \times \frac{3}{2} \times \frac{3}{2} \times \frac{4}{4}$ $1\frac{1}{8}$

Examples:

1. $\dfrac{2}{3} \times \dfrac{1}{4} = \dfrac{2 \times 1}{3 \times 4}$ Multiply.

$= \dfrac{2}{12}$

$= \dfrac{2 \div 2}{12 \div 2}$ Reduce to lowest terms.

$= \dfrac{1}{6}$ lowest terms

Examples 2–4 show a *shortcut* for multiplying fractions.

2. $\dfrac{2}{3} \times \dfrac{1}{4} = \dfrac{\overset{1}{\cancel{2}} \times 1}{3 \times \underset{2}{\cancel{4}}}$ Divide numerator and denominator by 2 *before* multiplying.

$= \dfrac{1}{6}$ lowest terms

Another way to find the product is given below.

$\dfrac{\overset{1}{\cancel{2}}}{3} \times \dfrac{1}{\underset{2}{\cancel{4}}} = \dfrac{1}{6}$

---

3. $\dfrac{3}{5} \times \dfrac{10}{3} = \dfrac{\overset{1}{\cancel{3}} \times \overset{2}{\cancel{10}}}{\underset{1}{\cancel{5}} \times \underset{1}{\cancel{3}}}$ Divide numerator and denominator by 3 and then by 5.

$= \dfrac{2}{1}$

$= 2$ Change the fraction to a whole number.

---

4. $\dfrac{\overset{3}{\cancel{21}}}{\underset{1}{\cancel{5}}} \times \dfrac{\overset{3}{\cancel{9}}}{\underset{2}{\cancel{14}}} \times \dfrac{\overset{1}{\cancel{5}}}{\underset{2}{\cancel{6}}} = \dfrac{9}{4}$ Divide numerator and denominator by 7, by 3, and by 5.

$= 2\dfrac{1}{4}$ Change the fraction to a mixed number.

EXERCISES

Write each product as a whole number, as a fraction in lowest terms, or as a mixed number whenever possible.

1. $\frac{4}{5} \times \frac{1}{4}$ $\frac{1}{5}$

2. $\frac{1}{3} \times \frac{3}{4}$ $\frac{1}{4}$

3. $\frac{7}{5} \times \frac{1}{7}$ $\frac{1}{5}$

4. $\frac{2}{21} \times \frac{14}{9}$ $\frac{4}{27}$

5. $\frac{3}{16} \times \frac{12}{7}$ $\frac{9}{28}$

6. $\frac{1}{2} \times \frac{4}{7}$ $\frac{2}{7}$

7. $\frac{3}{4} \times \frac{5}{6}$ $\frac{5}{8}$

8. $\frac{18}{4} \times \frac{4}{9}$ 2

9. $\frac{9}{4} \times \frac{14}{15}$ $2\frac{1}{10}$

10. $\frac{3}{16} \times \frac{4}{7}$ $\frac{3}{28}$

11. $\frac{4}{15} \times \frac{9}{10}$ $\frac{6}{25}$

12. $\frac{1}{5} \times \frac{15}{2}$ $1\frac{1}{2}$

13. $\frac{3}{4} \times \frac{4}{9}$ $\frac{1}{3}$

14. $\frac{4}{25} \times \frac{5}{8}$ $\frac{1}{10}$

15. $\frac{5}{8} \times 6$ $3\frac{3}{4}$

16. $\frac{3}{4} \times \frac{4}{3}$ 1

17. $\frac{3}{10} \times 15$ $4\frac{1}{2}$

18. $\frac{3}{2} \times \frac{4}{9}$ $\frac{2}{3}$

19. $\frac{4}{15} \times \frac{5}{8}$ $\frac{1}{6}$

20. $\frac{9}{4} \times \frac{8}{3}$ 6

21. $\frac{9}{25} \times \frac{20}{21}$ $\frac{12}{35}$

22. $\frac{16}{27} \times \frac{21}{20}$ $\frac{28}{45}$

23. $\frac{18}{25} \times \frac{5}{9}$ $\frac{2}{5}$

24. $\frac{12}{5} \times \frac{10}{6}$ 4

25. $\frac{1}{2} \times \frac{4}{5} \times \frac{1}{3}$ $\frac{2}{15}$

26. $\frac{3}{4} \times \frac{1}{2} \times \frac{5}{6}$ $\frac{5}{16}$

27. $\frac{7}{8} \times \frac{4}{5} \times \frac{1}{3}$ $\frac{7}{30}$

28. $\frac{5}{9} \times \frac{7}{10} \times \frac{3}{2}$ $\frac{7}{12}$

29. $\frac{7}{8} \times \frac{4}{5} \times \frac{3}{7}$ $\frac{3}{10}$

30. $\frac{4}{9} \times \frac{3}{8} \times \frac{6}{5}$ $\frac{1}{5}$

31. $\frac{2}{5} \times \frac{1}{4} \times \frac{10}{3}$ $\frac{1}{3}$

32. $\frac{4}{3} \times \frac{5}{6} \times \frac{9}{16}$ $\frac{5}{8}$

33. $\frac{3}{4} \times \frac{8}{5} \times \frac{1}{6}$ $\frac{1}{5}$

34. $\frac{7}{8} \times 12 \times \frac{3}{14}$ $2\frac{1}{4}$

35. $\frac{21}{100} \times \frac{4}{7} \times 50$ 6

36. $\frac{5}{4} \times 32 \times \frac{1}{16}$ $2\frac{1}{2}$

37. $\frac{8}{3} \times \frac{27}{100} \times \frac{1}{2}$ $\frac{9}{25}$

38. $\frac{5}{12} \times \frac{3}{10} \times \frac{0}{3}$ 0

39. $\frac{1}{7} \times \frac{14}{15} \times \frac{5}{6}$ $\frac{1}{9}$

40. $\frac{7}{10} \times \frac{15}{14} \times \frac{4}{3} \times 6$ 6

41. $\frac{5}{4} \times \frac{5}{9} \times \frac{24}{25} \times 10$ $6\frac{2}{3}$

42. $\frac{7}{11} \times \frac{22}{21} \times \frac{6}{5} \times 20$ 16

43. $\frac{6}{5} \times \frac{10}{9} \times 12$ 16

44. $\frac{21}{2} \times \frac{1}{7} \times 0$ 0

45. $\frac{15}{32} \times \frac{4}{21} \times 28$ $2\frac{1}{2}$

46. $\frac{2}{3} \times \frac{7}{5} \times \frac{3}{2}$ $1\frac{2}{5}$

47. $\frac{3}{4} \times \frac{22}{9} \times \frac{6}{5}$ $2\frac{1}{5}$

48. $\frac{11}{3} \times \frac{9}{22} \times \frac{7}{6}$ $1\frac{3}{4}$

49. $\frac{22}{7} \times 14 \times 5$ 220

50. $\frac{25}{3} \times \frac{9}{5} \times \frac{7}{10}$ $10\frac{1}{2}$

51. $\frac{4}{5} \times \frac{35}{6} \times \frac{11}{7}$ $7\frac{1}{3}$

If the product of two numbers is 1, the numbers are *reciprocals* of each other.

Examples:

1. $\frac{2}{5} \times \frac{5}{2} = 1$ $\frac{2}{5}$ and $\frac{5}{2}$ are reciprocals.

---

2. $6 \times \frac{1}{6} = \frac{6}{1} \times \frac{1}{6} = 1$ 6 and $\frac{1}{6}$ are reciprocals.

---

3. $1 \times 1 = 1$ **1 is its own reciprocal.**

---

4. $\boxed{?} \times 0 = 1$ **The product of any number and 0 is always 0. Therefore, 0 has no reciprocal.**

To divide by a fraction, multiply by its reciprocal.

Multiply by the reciprocal.

5. $\frac{1}{2} \div \frac{3}{4} = \frac{1}{2} \times \frac{4}{3} = \frac{1}{\cancel{2}} \times \frac{\cancel{4}^{2}}{3} = \frac{1 \times 2}{1 \times 3} = \frac{2}{3}$

---

6. $5 \div \frac{2}{3} = \frac{5}{1} \div \frac{2}{3}$ **Name 5 as a fraction.**

$= \frac{5}{1} \times \frac{3}{2}$ **Multiply by the reciprocal of the divisor.**

$= \frac{15}{2}$

$= 7\frac{1}{2}$ **Change the fraction to a mixed number.**

---

7. $\frac{1}{5} \div 3 = \frac{1}{5} \div \frac{3}{1}$ **Name 3 as a fraction.**

$= \frac{1}{5} \times \frac{1}{3}$ **Multiply by the reciprocal of the divisor.**

$= \frac{1}{15}$

---

8. $\frac{2}{3} \div 0$ **0 has no reciprocal; therefore, *you cannot divide by 0*. This problem has *no solution*.**

EXERCISES

Name the reciprocal.

1. $\frac{3}{5}$ $\frac{5}{3}$ **2.** $\frac{1}{4}$ $\frac{4}{1}$ **3.** $\frac{7}{8}$ $\frac{8}{7}$ **4.** $\frac{9}{2}$ $\frac{2}{9}$ **5.** 3 $\frac{1}{3}$

6. $\frac{3}{3}$ $\frac{3}{3}$ **7.** 12 $\frac{1}{12}$ **8.** $\frac{1}{2}$ $\frac{2}{1}$ **9.** $\frac{2}{4}$ $\frac{4}{2}$ **10.** $\frac{6}{9}$ $\frac{9}{6}$

Write the quotient as a whole number, as a fraction in lowest terms, or as a mixed number whenever possible.

11. $\frac{1}{4} \div \frac{3}{5}$ $\frac{5}{12}$ **12.** $\frac{3}{5} \div \frac{1}{4}$ $2\frac{2}{5}$ **13.** $\frac{2}{3} \div \frac{7}{8}$ $\frac{16}{21}$ **14.** $2 \div \frac{9}{2}$ $\frac{4}{9}$

15. $4 \div \frac{3}{5}$ $6\frac{2}{3}$ **16.** $5 \div \frac{1}{4}$ 20 **17.** $\frac{1}{2} \div 6$ $\frac{1}{12}$ **18.** $\frac{3}{5} \div 4$ $\frac{3}{20}$

19. $\frac{2}{3} \div 5$ $\frac{2}{15}$ **20.** $\frac{3}{4} \div \frac{4}{3}$ $\frac{9}{16}$ **21.** $\frac{3}{4} \div \frac{3}{5}$ $1\frac{1}{4}$ **22.** $\frac{3}{8} \div \frac{5}{4}$ $\frac{3}{10}$

23. $\frac{4}{9} \div \frac{4}{9}$ 1 **24.** $\frac{6}{7} \div \frac{3}{4}$ $1\frac{1}{7}$ **25.** $\frac{1}{8} \div \frac{7}{8}$ $\frac{1}{7}$ **26.** $\frac{3}{3} \div 4$ $\frac{1}{4}$

27. $\frac{5}{9} \div \frac{2}{3}$ $\frac{5}{6}$ **28.** $\frac{2}{5} \div \frac{3}{10}$ $1\frac{1}{3}$ **29.** $6 \div \frac{3}{7}$ 14 **30.** $\frac{21}{100} \div 7$ $\frac{3}{100}$

31. $\frac{3}{5} \div \frac{4}{5}$ $\frac{3}{4}$ **32.** $\frac{2}{3} \div \frac{3}{2}$ $\frac{4}{9}$ **33.** $\frac{3}{5} \div \frac{3}{4}$ $\frac{4}{5}$ **34.** $\frac{4}{7} \div 2$ $\frac{2}{7}$

35. $\frac{2}{3} \div \frac{4}{6}$ 1 **36.** $5 \div \frac{10}{3}$ $1\frac{1}{2}$ **37.** $\frac{3}{5} \div \frac{1}{8}$ $4\frac{4}{5}$ **38.** $\frac{1}{3} \div \frac{2}{3}$ $\frac{1}{2}$

39. $\frac{5}{8} \div \frac{5}{6}$ $\frac{3}{4}$ **40.** $\frac{7}{9} \div \frac{2}{3}$ $1\frac{1}{6}$ **41.** $\frac{4}{5} \div 3$ $\frac{4}{15}$ **42.** $\frac{5}{8} \div 6$ $\frac{5}{48}$

43. $\frac{2}{3} \div 9$ $\frac{2}{27}$ **44.** $\frac{3}{4} \div 4$ $\frac{3}{16}$ **45.** $5 \div \frac{3}{2}$ $3\frac{1}{3}$ **46.** $10 \div \frac{2}{3}$ 15

47. $2 \div \frac{5}{2}$ $\frac{4}{5}$ **48.** $\frac{4}{9} \div 6$ $\frac{2}{27}$ **49.** $0 \div \frac{3}{4}$ 0 **50.** $\frac{5}{8} \div 0$ no solution

Write the product as a whole number, as a fraction in lowest terms, or as a mixed number whenever possible.

1. $\frac{2}{3} \times \frac{5}{9}$ $\frac{10}{27}$

2. $\frac{4}{5} \times \frac{3}{5}$ $\frac{12}{25}$

3. $\frac{1}{4} \times \frac{7}{8}$ $\frac{7}{32}$

4. $\frac{7}{8} \times \frac{4}{5}$ $\frac{7}{10}$

5. $\frac{7}{9} \times \frac{1}{5}$ $\frac{7}{45}$

6. $\frac{3}{4} \times \frac{5}{9}$ $\frac{5}{12}$

7. $\frac{5}{6} \times \frac{1}{2}$ $\frac{5}{12}$

8. $\frac{5}{8} \times \frac{8}{5}$ 1

9. $\frac{5}{2} \times \frac{8}{3}$ $6\frac{2}{3}$

10. $\frac{5}{8} \times \frac{12}{25}$ $\frac{3}{10}$

11. $\frac{3}{4} \times \frac{3}{5}$ $\frac{9}{20}$

12. $\frac{5}{12} \times 8$ $3\frac{1}{3}$

13. $\frac{9}{10} \times \frac{4}{15}$ $\frac{6}{25}$

14. $15 \times \frac{3}{5}$ 9

15. $\frac{4}{5} \times \frac{2}{3}$ $\frac{8}{15}$

16. $\frac{3}{14} \times 7$ $1\frac{1}{2}$

17. $\frac{4}{5} \times \frac{10}{11}$ $\frac{8}{11}$

18. $\frac{1}{7} \times 7$ 1

19. $\frac{3}{4} \times \frac{16}{21}$ $\frac{4}{7}$

20. $\frac{8}{3} \times \frac{9}{2}$ 12

21. $\frac{1}{6} \times \frac{12}{13}$ $\frac{2}{13}$

22. $\frac{2}{9} \times \frac{18}{4}$ 1

23. $\frac{4}{15} \times \frac{3}{8}$ $\frac{1}{10}$

24. $\frac{5}{9} \times \frac{3}{15}$ $\frac{1}{9}$

25. $\frac{5}{9} \times \frac{9}{5}$ 1

26. $\frac{8}{27} \times \frac{9}{2}$ $1\frac{1}{3}$

27. $\frac{2}{3} \times 24$ 16

28. $\frac{12}{7} \times \frac{7}{18}$ $\frac{2}{3}$

29. $\frac{3}{10} \times 0$ 0

30. $\frac{12}{5} \times \frac{15}{24}$ $1\frac{1}{2}$

31. $\frac{4}{5} \times \frac{25}{32}$ $\frac{5}{8}$

32. $\frac{0}{2} \times \frac{4}{3}$ 0

33. $8 \times \frac{7}{2}$ 28

34. $\frac{7}{8} \times 1$ $\frac{7}{8}$

35. $\frac{11}{5} \times \frac{7}{22}$ $\frac{7}{10}$

36. $\frac{1}{20} \times 15$ $\frac{3}{4}$

37. $\frac{3}{4} \times \frac{8}{15} \times \frac{7}{3}$ $\frac{14}{15}$

38. $\frac{7}{12} \times \frac{4}{5} \times \frac{3}{14}$ $\frac{1}{10}$

39. $\frac{5}{9} \times \frac{7}{50} \times \frac{27}{14}$ $\frac{3}{20}$

40. $\frac{7}{8} \times \frac{8}{7} \times \frac{3}{2}$ $1\frac{1}{2}$

41. $\frac{12}{5} \times \frac{15}{16} \times \frac{4}{9}$ 1

42. $\frac{121}{13} \times \frac{39}{11} \times \frac{3}{44}$ $2\frac{1}{4}$

43. $\frac{8}{9} \times \frac{0}{4} \times \frac{3}{2}$ 0

44. $\frac{5}{8} \times 4 \times \frac{3}{25}$ $\frac{3}{10}$

45. $\frac{5}{6} \times 4 \times 4$ $13\frac{1}{3}$

46. $6 \times \frac{7}{8} \times 2 \times 2$ 21

47. $\frac{3}{4} \times \frac{1}{8} \times 10 \times 10$ $9\frac{3}{8}$

48. $\frac{7}{54} \times 3 \times 3 \times 6$ 7

49. $\frac{5}{12} \times \frac{1}{2} \times 6 \times 6 \times 3$ $22\frac{1}{2}$

50. $\frac{3}{8} \times 3 \times \frac{4}{9} \times 7 \times 7$ $24\frac{1}{2}$

Write the quotient as a whole number, as a fraction in lowest terms, or as a mixed number whenever possible.

51. $\frac{2}{3} \div \frac{3}{4}$ $\frac{8}{9}$

52. $\frac{5}{8} \div \frac{2}{3}$ $\frac{15}{16}$

53. $\frac{3}{5} \div \frac{5}{6}$ $\frac{18}{25}$

54. $\frac{1}{2} \div \frac{2}{3}$ $\frac{3}{4}$

55. $\frac{1}{3} \div \frac{3}{2}$ $\frac{2}{9}$

56. $\frac{3}{4} \div \frac{2}{5}$ $1\frac{7}{8}$

57. $\frac{4}{7} \div \frac{1}{4}$ $2\frac{2}{7}$

58. $\frac{5}{6} \div \frac{5}{9}$ $1\frac{1}{2}$

59. $\frac{9}{10} \div \frac{3}{5}$ $1\frac{1}{2}$

60. $\frac{4}{9} \div \frac{2}{7}$ $1\frac{5}{9}$

61. $\frac{5}{12} \div \frac{10}{21}$ $\frac{7}{8}$

62. $\frac{7}{8} \div \frac{1}{4}$ $3\frac{1}{2}$

63. $\frac{0}{7} \div \frac{2}{3}$ 0

64. $\frac{8}{15} \div \frac{2}{3}$ $\frac{4}{5}$

65. $\frac{9}{20} \div \frac{3}{5}$ $\frac{3}{4}$

66. $\frac{8}{9} \div \frac{4}{6}$ $1\frac{1}{3}$

67. $\frac{1}{6} \div \frac{5}{6}$ $\frac{1}{5}$

68. $\frac{2}{5} \div \frac{4}{15}$ $1\frac{1}{2}$

69. $\frac{1}{4} \div \frac{3}{16}$ $1\frac{1}{3}$

70. $1 \div \frac{9}{5}$ $\frac{5}{9}$

71. $\frac{3}{10} \div \frac{7}{20}$ $\frac{6}{7}$

72. $\frac{8}{9} \div \frac{8}{9}$ 1

73. $\frac{7}{12} \div \frac{21}{36}$ 1

74. $\frac{3}{8} \div \frac{1}{6}$ $2\frac{1}{4}$

75. $\frac{8}{8} \div \frac{3}{2}$ $\frac{2}{3}$

76. $\frac{7}{10} \div \frac{14}{15}$ $\frac{3}{4}$

77. $\frac{3}{7} \div \frac{7}{3}$ $\frac{9}{49}$

78. $\frac{8}{11} \div \frac{4}{3}$ $\frac{6}{11}$

79. $0 \div \frac{3}{5}$ 0

80. $\frac{9}{14} \div \frac{3}{7}$ $1\frac{1}{2}$

81. $\frac{15}{16} \div \frac{5}{12}$ $2\frac{1}{4}$

82. $\frac{5}{18} \div \frac{25}{27}$ $\frac{3}{10}$

83. $\frac{8}{9} \div 4$ $\frac{2}{9}$

84. $\frac{4}{7} \div \frac{3}{3}$ $\frac{4}{7}$

85. $\frac{27}{100} \div \frac{3}{10}$ $\frac{9}{10}$

86. $\frac{14}{25} \div \frac{7}{10}$ $\frac{4}{5}$

87. $\frac{4}{15} \div \frac{4}{5}$ $\frac{1}{3}$

88. $9 \div \frac{3}{4}$ 12

89. $\frac{1}{10} \div 10$ $\frac{1}{100}$

90. $8 \div \frac{4}{5}$ 10

91. $\frac{8}{8} \div \frac{4}{5}$ $1\frac{1}{4}$

92. $\frac{9}{10} \div 15$ $\frac{3}{50}$

93. $5 \div \frac{3}{2}$ $3\frac{1}{3}$

94. $\frac{3}{5} \div \frac{5}{5}$ $\frac{3}{5}$

95. $\frac{7}{8} \div \frac{3}{4}$ $1\frac{1}{6}$

96. $\frac{13}{15} \div \frac{3}{10}$ $2\frac{8}{9}$

97. $\frac{7}{3} \div \frac{10}{3}$ $\frac{7}{10}$

98. $\frac{5}{11} \div \frac{5}{6}$ $\frac{6}{11}$

99. $\frac{4}{15} \div \frac{6}{25}$ $1\frac{1}{9}$

100. $\frac{21}{15} \div \frac{7}{12}$ $2\frac{2}{5}$

101. $\frac{4}{5} \div 0$ no solution

102. $\frac{0}{6} \div \frac{7}{3}$ 0

103. $\frac{15}{14} \div \frac{25}{28}$ $1\frac{1}{5}$

104. $0 \div \frac{4}{5}$ 0

105. $\frac{8}{15} \div 6$ $\frac{4}{45}$

106. $10 \div 6$ $1\frac{2}{3}$

Examples:

1.
$$\frac{2}{4} \qquad \frac{1}{4}$$

$$\frac{3}{4}$$

$$\frac{2}{4} + \frac{1}{4} = \frac{3}{4}$$

2.

$$\begin{array}{r} \frac{4}{7} \\ + \frac{5}{7} \\ \hline \frac{9}{7} \end{array}$$

or $1\frac{2}{7}$

To add fractions that have the same denominator:

Step 1: Add the numerators.

Step 2: Use the same denominator.

Step 3: If necessary, change the sum to lowest terms.

3. $\dfrac{2}{6} + \dfrac{3}{6} = \dfrac{2+3}{6} = \dfrac{5}{6}$

---

4. $\dfrac{3}{16} + \dfrac{5}{16} + \dfrac{1}{16} + \dfrac{3}{16} = \dfrac{3+5+1+3}{16}$

$= \dfrac{\overset{3}{\cancel{12}}}{\underset{4}{\cancel{16}}}$ **Reduce to lowest terms.**

$= \dfrac{3}{4}$

5. $\dfrac{5}{8} + \dfrac{3}{8} + \dfrac{7}{8} + \dfrac{1}{8} = \dfrac{5+3+7+1}{8}$

$= \dfrac{16}{8}$

$= 2$ **Change the fraction to a whole number.**

---

6. $\dfrac{2}{9} + \dfrac{4}{9} + \dfrac{10}{9} = \dfrac{2+4+10}{9}$

$= \dfrac{16}{9}$

$= 1\dfrac{7}{9}$ **Change the fraction to a mixed number.**

7. $\dfrac{7}{12} + \dfrac{5}{12} + \dfrac{4}{12} = \dfrac{7+5+4}{12}$

$= \dfrac{\overset{4}{\cancel{16}}}{\underset{3}{\cancel{12}}}$ **Reduce to lowest terms.**

$= \dfrac{4}{3}$

$= 1\dfrac{1}{3}$ **Change the fraction to a mixed number.**

EXERCISES

Write the sum as a whole number, as a fraction in lowest terms, or as a mixed number whenever possible.

1. $\frac{1}{3}+\frac{1}{3}$ $\frac{2}{3}$

2. $\frac{3}{5}+\frac{1}{5}$ $\frac{4}{5}$

3. $\frac{5}{8}+\frac{2}{8}$ $\frac{7}{8}$

4. $\frac{3}{2}+\frac{5}{2}$ 4

5. $\frac{3}{4}+\frac{2}{4}$ $1\frac{1}{4}$

6. $\frac{3}{5}+\frac{4}{5}$ $1\frac{2}{5}$

7. $\frac{3}{10}+\frac{0}{10}$ $\frac{3}{10}$

8. $\frac{3}{7}+\frac{4}{7}$ 1

9. $\frac{5}{12}$
$+\frac{6}{12}$ $\frac{11}{12}$

10. $\frac{2}{9}$
$+\frac{8}{9}$ $1\frac{1}{9}$

11. $\frac{2}{7}$
$+\frac{6}{7}$ $1\frac{1}{7}$

12. $\frac{8}{3}$
$+\frac{1}{3}$ 3

13. $\frac{1}{4}+\frac{1}{4}$ $\frac{1}{2}$

14. $\frac{1}{8}+\frac{5}{8}$ $\frac{3}{4}$

15. $\frac{2}{10}+\frac{3}{10}$ $\frac{1}{2}$

16. $\frac{1}{9}+\frac{2}{9}$ $\frac{1}{3}$

17. $\frac{9}{12}+\frac{6}{12}$ $1\frac{1}{4}$

18. $\frac{1}{6}+\frac{5}{6}$ 1

19. $\frac{8}{15}+\frac{12}{15}$ $1\frac{1}{3}$

20. $\frac{5}{12}+\frac{1}{12}$ $\frac{1}{2}$

21. $\frac{14}{9}+\frac{4}{9}$ 2

22. $\frac{6}{20}+\frac{18}{20}$ $1\frac{1}{5}$

23. $\frac{6}{6}+\frac{5}{6}$ $1\frac{5}{6}$

24. $\frac{0}{6}+\frac{2}{6}$ $\frac{1}{3}$

25. $\frac{4}{13}+\frac{7}{13}$ $\frac{11}{13}$

26. $\frac{2}{5}+\frac{7}{5}$ $1\frac{4}{5}$

27. $\frac{3}{8}+\frac{3}{8}$ $\frac{3}{4}$

28. $\frac{5}{7}+\frac{5}{7}$ $1\frac{3}{7}$

29. $\frac{3}{10}+\frac{6}{10}$ $\frac{9}{10}$

30. $\frac{7}{15}+\frac{6}{15}$ $\frac{13}{15}$

31. $\frac{2}{12}+\frac{9}{12}$ $\frac{11}{12}$

32. $\frac{6}{11}+\frac{4}{11}$ $\frac{10}{11}$

33. $\frac{4}{15}+\frac{3}{15}+\frac{7}{15}$ $\frac{14}{15}$

34. $\frac{9}{10}+\frac{2}{10}+\frac{7}{10}$ $1\frac{4}{5}$

35. $\frac{4}{9}+\frac{1}{9}+\frac{3}{9}$ $\frac{8}{9}$

36. $\frac{5}{11}+\frac{0}{11}+\frac{3}{11}$ $\frac{8}{11}$

37. $\frac{4}{9}+\frac{9}{9}+\frac{7}{9}$ $2\frac{2}{9}$

38. $\frac{6}{6}+\frac{5}{6}+\frac{1}{6}$ 2

39. $\frac{1}{10}+\frac{3}{10}+\frac{3}{10}$ $\frac{7}{10}$

40. $\frac{6}{7}+\frac{4}{7}+\frac{3}{7}$ $1\frac{6}{7}$

41. $\frac{3}{7}+\frac{1}{7}+\frac{2}{7}$ $\frac{6}{7}$

42. $\frac{8}{9}+\frac{3}{9}+\frac{11}{9}+\frac{5}{9}$ 3

43. $\frac{4}{19}+\frac{8}{19}+\frac{5}{19}$ $\frac{17}{19}$

44. $\frac{0}{15}+\frac{2}{15}+\frac{3}{15}$ $\frac{1}{3}$

45. $\frac{6}{16}+\frac{3}{16}+\frac{7}{16}$ 1

46. $\frac{12}{7}+\frac{4}{7}+\frac{3}{7}+\frac{5}{7}$ $3\frac{3}{7}$

47. $\frac{13}{8}+\frac{3}{8}+\frac{7}{8}+\frac{1}{8}$ 3

Tell what number the ? stands for.

48. $\frac{5}{12}+\frac{?}{12}=\frac{7}{12}$ 2

49. $\frac{?}{11}+\frac{4}{11}=\frac{8}{11}$ 4

50. $\frac{4}{5}+\frac{?}{5}=\frac{12}{5}$ 8

51. $\frac{?}{8}+\frac{7}{8}=\frac{11}{8}$ 4

52. $\frac{10}{7}+\frac{?}{7}=\frac{12}{7}$ 2

53. $\frac{?}{5}+\frac{6}{5}=\frac{14}{5}$ 8

To subtract fractions that have the same denominator:

Step 1:   Subtract the numerators.

Step 2:   Use the same denominator.

Step 3:   If necessary, change the difference to lowest terms.

Examples:

1. $\dfrac{13}{10} - \dfrac{8}{10} = \dfrac{13-8}{10}$

$\qquad\qquad = \dfrac{5}{10}$

$\qquad\qquad = \dfrac{1}{2}$ **lowest terms**

2. $\dfrac{15}{4} - \dfrac{5}{4} = \dfrac{15-5}{4}$

$\qquad\qquad = \dfrac{10}{4}$

$\qquad\qquad = \dfrac{5}{2}$ **lowest terms**

$\qquad\qquad = 2\dfrac{1}{2}$ **Change to a mixed number.**

EXERCISES

Write the difference as a whole number, as a fraction in lowest terms, or as a mixed number whenever possible.

1. $\dfrac{2}{3} - \dfrac{1}{3}$ $\dfrac{1}{3}$ **2.** $\dfrac{4}{5} - \dfrac{2}{5}$ $\dfrac{2}{5}$ **3.** $\dfrac{6}{7} - \dfrac{2}{7}$ $\dfrac{4}{7}$ **4.** $\dfrac{3}{4} - \dfrac{2}{4}$ $\dfrac{1}{4}$ **5.** $\dfrac{3}{2} - \dfrac{2}{2}$ $\dfrac{1}{2}$

6. $\dfrac{8}{9} - \dfrac{6}{9}$ $\dfrac{2}{9}$ **7.** $\dfrac{9}{5} - \dfrac{3}{5}$ $1\dfrac{1}{5}$ **8.** $\dfrac{7}{3} - \dfrac{5}{3}$ $\dfrac{2}{3}$ **9.** $\dfrac{7}{8} - \dfrac{7}{8}$ 0 **10.** $\dfrac{4}{5} - \dfrac{3}{5}$ $\dfrac{1}{5}$

11. $\dfrac{15}{6} - \dfrac{1}{6}$ $2\dfrac{1}{3}$ **12.** $\dfrac{7}{10} - \dfrac{4}{10}$ $\dfrac{3}{10}$ **13.** $\dfrac{3}{4} - \dfrac{1}{4}$ $\dfrac{1}{2}$ **14.** $\dfrac{6}{10} - \dfrac{1}{10}$ $\dfrac{1}{2}$ **15.** $\dfrac{7}{8} - \dfrac{3}{8}$ $\dfrac{1}{2}$

16. $\dfrac{5}{6} - \dfrac{3}{6}$ $\dfrac{1}{3}$ **17.** $\dfrac{9}{8} - \dfrac{7}{8}$ $\dfrac{1}{4}$ **18.** $\dfrac{9}{10} - \dfrac{7}{10}$ $\dfrac{1}{5}$ **19.** $\dfrac{4}{9} - \dfrac{1}{9}$ $\dfrac{1}{3}$ **20.** $\dfrac{5}{7} - \dfrac{2}{7}$ $\dfrac{3}{7}$

21. $\dfrac{9}{2} - \dfrac{5}{2}$ 2 **22.** $\dfrac{8}{13} - \dfrac{3}{13}$ $\dfrac{5}{13}$ **23.** $\dfrac{14}{25} - \dfrac{7}{25}$ $\dfrac{7}{25}$ **24.** $\dfrac{11}{14} - \dfrac{4}{14}$ $\dfrac{1}{2}$ **25.** $\dfrac{12}{7} - \dfrac{3}{7}$ $1\dfrac{2}{7}$

26. $\dfrac{14}{11} - \dfrac{2}{11}$ $1\dfrac{1}{11}$ **27.** $\dfrac{11}{12} - \dfrac{5}{12}$ $\dfrac{1}{2}$ **28.** $\dfrac{37}{100} - \dfrac{13}{100}$ $\dfrac{6}{25}$ **29.** $\dfrac{27}{20} - \dfrac{5}{20}$ $1\dfrac{1}{10}$ **30.** $\dfrac{49}{50} - \dfrac{48}{50}$ $\dfrac{1}{50}$

The **least common multiple** of two or more numbers is the smallest nonzero number that is a multiple of each number.

Examples:

1. Find the least common multiple of 4 and 6.

×	1	2	3	4	5	6	7	8	9	10	11	12
Multiples of 4	4	8	12	16	20	24	28	32	36	40	44	48
Multiples of 6	6	12	18	24	30	36	42	48	54	60	66	72

common multiples

The least common multiple of 4 and 6 is 12.

2. Find the least common multiple of 7, 14, and 21.

×	1	2	3	4	5	6	7	8	9	10	11	12
Multiples of 7	7	14	21	28	35	42	49	56	63	70	77	84
Multiples of 14	14	28	42	56	70	84	98	112	126	140	154	168
Multiples of 21	21	42	63	84	105	126	147	168	189	210	231	252

common multiples

The least common multiple of 7, 14, and 21 is 42.

EXERCISES

Find the least common multiple of each set of numbers.

1. 4 and 7   28

2. 6 and 7   42

3. 3 and 9   9

4. 5 and 15   15

5. 3 and 5   15

6. 4 and 10   20

7. 6 and 24   24

8. 10 and 30   30

9. 7 and 21   21

10. 7 and 8   56

11. 10 and 15   30

12. 8 and 12   24

13. 3, 4, and 12   12

14. 2, 3, and 18   18

15. 1, 4, and 6   12

16. 4, 5, and 10   20

To add or subtract fractions that have different denominators:

Step 1: Change to fractions that have the same denominator. (Use the least common multiple of the denominators.)

Step 2: Then add or subtract. Give the answer in lowest terms.

Examples:

1. $\dfrac{1}{2} + \dfrac{2}{3}$ **different denominators**

$\dfrac{1 \times 3}{2 \times 3} \quad \dfrac{2 \times 2}{3 \times 2}$ **The least common multiple of 2 and 3 is 6.**

$\dfrac{3}{6} + \dfrac{4}{6} = \dfrac{7}{6}$ **same denominator**

$= 1\dfrac{1}{6}$ **Change to a mixed number.**

---

2. $\dfrac{5}{12} + \dfrac{2}{3} + \dfrac{3}{4}$ **different denominators**

$\dfrac{5 \times 1}{12 \times 1} \quad \dfrac{2 \times 4}{3 \times 4} \quad \dfrac{3 \times 3}{4 \times 3}$ **The least common multiple of 12, 3, and 4 is 12.**

$\dfrac{5}{12} + \dfrac{8}{12} + \dfrac{9}{12} = \dfrac{22}{12}$ **same denominator**

$= \dfrac{11}{6}$ **lowest terms**

$= 1\dfrac{5}{6}$ **Change to a mixed number.**

---

3. $\dfrac{5}{6} - \dfrac{5}{8}$ **different denominators**

$\dfrac{5 \times 4}{6 \times 4} \quad \dfrac{5 \times 3}{8 \times 3}$ **The least common denominator of 6 and 8 is 24.**

$\dfrac{20}{24} - \dfrac{15}{24} = \dfrac{5}{24}$ **same denominator**

EXERCISES

Write the sum as a whole number, as a fraction in lowest terms, or as a mixed number whenever possible.

1. $\frac{2}{3}+\frac{3}{4}$ $1\frac{5}{12}$

2. $\frac{3}{8}+\frac{5}{12}$ $\frac{19}{24}$

3. $\frac{2}{3}+\frac{5}{9}$ $1\frac{2}{9}$

4. $\frac{2}{5}+\frac{1}{3}$ $\frac{11}{15}$

5. $\frac{7}{15}+\frac{3}{10}$ $\frac{23}{30}$

6. $\frac{3}{8}+\frac{5}{7}$ $1\frac{5}{56}$

7. $\frac{9}{8}+\frac{5}{32}$ $1\frac{9}{32}$

8. $\frac{3}{14}+\frac{2}{7}$ $\frac{1}{2}$

9. $\frac{1}{2}+\frac{5}{6}+\frac{3}{8}$ $1\frac{17}{24}$

10. $\frac{2}{3}+\frac{1}{4}+\frac{4}{5}$ $1\frac{43}{60}$

11. $\frac{0}{3}+\frac{5}{4}$ $1\frac{1}{4}$

12. $\frac{1}{8}+\frac{3}{5}+\frac{1}{20}$ $\frac{31}{40}$

13. $\frac{5}{8}+\frac{12}{12}$ $1\frac{5}{8}$

14. $\frac{1}{30}+\frac{1}{40}$ $\frac{7}{120}$

15. $\frac{8}{7}+\frac{7}{8}$ $2\frac{1}{56}$

16. $\frac{2}{5}+\frac{1}{6}+\frac{1}{3}$ $\frac{9}{10}$

17. $\frac{5}{4}+\frac{1}{10}+\frac{2}{5}$ $1\frac{3}{4}$

18. $\frac{1}{16}+\frac{5}{8}+\frac{7}{2}$ $4\frac{3}{16}$

19. $\frac{7}{3}+\frac{3}{4}+\frac{5}{6}$ $3\frac{11}{12}$

20. $\frac{5}{3}+\frac{6}{5}+\frac{1}{30}$ $2\frac{9}{10}$

Write the difference as a whole number, as a fraction in lowest terms, or as a mixed number whenever possible.

21. $\frac{3}{4}-\frac{2}{3}$ $\frac{1}{12}$

22. $\frac{5}{12}-\frac{3}{8}$ $\frac{1}{24}$

23. $\frac{2}{3}-\frac{5}{9}$ $\frac{1}{9}$

24. $\frac{5}{5}-\frac{2}{2}$ 0

25. $\frac{7}{15}-\frac{3}{10}$ $\frac{1}{6}$

26. $\frac{5}{7}-\frac{3}{8}$ $\frac{19}{56}$

27. $\frac{9}{8}-\frac{5}{32}$ $\frac{31}{32}$

28. $\frac{7}{8}-\frac{1}{10}$ $\frac{31}{40}$

29. $\frac{5}{4}-\frac{0}{3}$ $1\frac{1}{4}$

30. $\frac{12}{12}-\frac{5}{8}$ $\frac{3}{8}$

31. $\frac{1}{30}-\frac{1}{40}$ $\frac{1}{120}$

32. $\frac{3}{5}-\frac{2}{7}$ $\frac{11}{35}$

33. $\frac{8}{7}-\frac{7}{8}$ $\frac{15}{56}$

34. $\frac{2}{3}-\frac{1}{4}$ $\frac{5}{12}$

35. $\frac{4}{5}-\frac{2}{4}$ $\frac{3}{10}$

36. $\frac{7}{3}-\frac{1}{8}$ $2\frac{5}{24}$

37. $\frac{6}{5}-\frac{2}{3}$ $\frac{8}{15}$

38. $\frac{5}{2}-\frac{1}{3}$ $2\frac{1}{6}$

39. $\frac{3}{5}-\frac{9}{15}$ 0

40. $\frac{11}{5}-\frac{1}{3}$ $1\frac{13}{15}$

41. $\frac{3}{4}-\frac{2}{7}$ $\frac{13}{28}$

42. $\frac{5}{9}-\frac{1}{3}$ $\frac{2}{9}$

43. $\frac{3}{4}-\frac{1}{3}$ $\frac{5}{12}$

44. $\frac{7}{3}-\frac{1}{6}$ $2\frac{1}{6}$

Write the sum as a whole number, as a fraction in lowest terms, or as a mixed number whenever possible.

1. $\frac{3}{8} + \frac{2}{8}$ $\frac{5}{8}$ 2. $\frac{4}{3} + \frac{1}{3}$ $1\frac{2}{3}$ 3. $\frac{6}{11} + \frac{1}{11}$ $\frac{7}{11}$ 4. $\frac{1}{3} + \frac{3}{4}$ $1\frac{1}{12}$

5. $\frac{2}{3} + \frac{3}{5}$ $1\frac{4}{15}$ 6. $\frac{5}{8} + \frac{3}{2}$ $2\frac{1}{8}$ 7. $\frac{1}{9} + \frac{7}{9}$ $\frac{8}{9}$ 8. $\frac{2}{5} + \frac{4}{4}$ $1\frac{2}{5}$

9. $\frac{2}{5} + \frac{3}{4}$ $1\frac{3}{20}$ 10. $\frac{1}{7} + \frac{7}{8}$ $1\frac{1}{56}$ 11. $\frac{1}{9} + \frac{1}{10}$ $\frac{19}{90}$ 12. $\frac{5}{12} + \frac{1}{12}$ $\frac{1}{2}$

13. $\frac{7}{10} + \frac{2}{3}$ $1\frac{11}{30}$ 14. $\frac{4}{4} + \frac{3}{3}$ 2 15. $\frac{8}{3} + \frac{2}{3} + \frac{5}{3}$ 5

16. $\frac{2}{5} + \frac{1}{8}$ $\frac{21}{40}$ 17. $\frac{1}{2} + \frac{2}{5} + \frac{2}{3}$ $1\frac{17}{30}$ 18. $\frac{7}{10} + \frac{4}{5} + \frac{1}{2}$ 2

19. $\frac{8}{5} + \frac{2}{5}$ 2 20. $\frac{4}{7} + \frac{2}{3} + \frac{5}{21}$ $1\frac{10}{21}$ 21. $\frac{5}{7} + \frac{5}{7}$ $1\frac{3}{7}$

22. $\frac{3}{7} + \frac{1}{2} + \frac{5}{2}$ $3\frac{3}{7}$ 23. $\frac{3}{6} + \frac{1}{6}$ $\frac{2}{3}$ 24. $\frac{2}{5} + \frac{1}{5} + \frac{2}{5}$ 1

25. $\frac{3}{5} + \frac{3}{3} + \frac{1}{2}$ $2\frac{1}{10}$ 26. $\frac{5}{3} + \frac{1}{6} + \frac{5}{9}$ $2\frac{7}{18}$ 27. $\frac{7}{15} + \frac{3}{15}$ $\frac{2}{3}$

28. $\frac{5}{6} + \frac{1}{2} + \frac{3}{4}$ $2\frac{1}{12}$ 29. $\frac{5}{6} + \frac{4}{6}$ $1\frac{1}{2}$ 30. $\frac{1}{3} + \frac{3}{5} + \frac{1}{4}$ $1\frac{11}{60}$

31. $\begin{array}{r}\frac{7}{12}\\+\frac{7}{12}\\\hline\end{array}$ $1\frac{1}{6}$ 32. $\begin{array}{r}\frac{7}{10}\\+\frac{3}{10}\\\hline\end{array}$ 1 33. $\begin{array}{r}\frac{5}{6}\\+\frac{3}{8}\\\hline\end{array}$ $1\frac{5}{24}$ 34. $\begin{array}{r}\frac{9}{5}\\+\frac{2}{7}\\\hline\end{array}$ $2\frac{3}{35}$ 35. $\begin{array}{r}\frac{7}{4}\\+\frac{4}{7}\\\hline\end{array}$ $2\frac{9}{28}$

36. $\begin{array}{r}\frac{3}{4}\\+\frac{1}{4}\\\hline\end{array}$ 1 37. $\begin{array}{r}\frac{1}{7}\\+\frac{2}{5}\\\hline\end{array}$ $\frac{19}{35}$ 38. $\begin{array}{r}\frac{7}{4}\\+\frac{3}{4}\\\hline\end{array}$ $2\frac{1}{2}$ 39. $\begin{array}{r}\frac{1}{10}\\+\frac{7}{10}\\\hline\end{array}$ $\frac{4}{5}$ 40. $\begin{array}{r}\frac{7}{20}\\+\frac{3}{5}\\\hline\end{array}$ $\frac{19}{20}$

41. $\begin{array}{r}\frac{4}{3}\\+\frac{2}{5}\\\hline\end{array}$ $1\frac{11}{15}$ 42. $\begin{array}{r}\frac{11}{3}\\+\frac{4}{3}\\\hline\end{array}$ 5 43. $\begin{array}{r}\frac{7}{6}\\+\frac{13}{16}\\\hline\end{array}$ $1\frac{47}{48}$ 44. $\begin{array}{r}\frac{9}{2}\\+\frac{7}{3}\\\hline\end{array}$ $6\frac{5}{6}$ 45. $\begin{array}{r}\frac{1}{2}\\+\frac{5}{2}\\\hline\end{array}$ 3

46. $\begin{array}{r}\frac{19}{25}\\+\frac{4}{5}\\\hline\end{array}$ $1\frac{14}{25}$ 47. $\begin{array}{r}\frac{13}{6}\\+\frac{5}{8}\\\hline\end{array}$ $2\frac{19}{24}$ 48. $\begin{array}{r}\frac{3}{10}\\+\frac{17}{100}\\\hline\end{array}$ $\frac{47}{100}$ 49. $\begin{array}{r}\frac{1}{12}\\+\frac{3}{16}\\\hline\end{array}$ $\frac{13}{48}$ 50. $\begin{array}{r}\frac{3}{8}\\+\frac{7}{8}\\\hline\end{array}$ $1\frac{1}{4}$

Write the difference as a whole number, as a fraction in lowest terms, or as a mixed number whenever possible.

51. $\frac{6}{7} - \frac{4}{7}$ $\frac{2}{7}$

52. $\frac{4}{3} - \frac{2}{3}$ $\frac{2}{3}$

53. $\frac{6}{8} - \frac{3}{8}$ $\frac{3}{8}$

54. $\frac{1}{3} - \frac{1}{4}$ $\frac{1}{12}$

55. $\frac{3}{4} - \frac{1}{6}$ $\frac{7}{12}$

56. $\frac{5}{9} - \frac{4}{9}$ $\frac{1}{9}$

57. $\frac{1}{2} - \frac{1}{3}$ $\frac{1}{6}$

58. $\frac{11}{11} - \frac{2}{11}$ $\frac{9}{11}$

59. $\frac{2}{3} - \frac{1}{2}$ $\frac{1}{6}$

60. $\frac{5}{6} - \frac{3}{8}$ $\frac{11}{24}$

61. $\frac{5}{6} - \frac{2}{3}$ $\frac{1}{6}$

62. $\frac{5}{2} - \frac{3}{2}$ 1

63. $\frac{8}{11} - \frac{5}{11}$ $\frac{3}{11}$

64. $\frac{3}{7} - \frac{1}{3}$ $\frac{2}{21}$

65. $\frac{7}{3} - \frac{1}{2}$ $1\frac{5}{6}$

66. $\frac{3}{5} - \frac{1}{2}$ $\frac{1}{10}$

67. $\frac{13}{15} - \frac{4}{15}$ $\frac{3}{5}$

68. $\frac{4}{4} - \frac{4}{4}$ 0

69. $\frac{7}{8} - \frac{2}{3}$ $\frac{5}{24}$

70. $\frac{9}{10} - \frac{3}{5}$ $\frac{3}{10}$

71. $\frac{12}{5} - \frac{4}{10}$ 2

72. $\frac{13}{4} - \frac{2}{3}$ $2\frac{7}{12}$

73. $\frac{11}{10} - \frac{3}{3}$ $\frac{1}{10}$

74. $\frac{7}{10} - \frac{2}{10}$ $\frac{1}{2}$

75. $\frac{7}{8} - \frac{5}{16}$ $\frac{9}{16}$

76. $\frac{9}{10} - \frac{4}{10}$ $\frac{1}{2}$

77. $\frac{7}{11} - \frac{0}{11}$ $\frac{7}{11}$

78. $\frac{10}{13} - \frac{4}{13}$ $\frac{6}{13}$

79. $\frac{9}{2} - \frac{6}{7}$ $3\frac{9}{14}$

80. $\frac{6}{7} - \frac{3}{5}$ $\frac{9}{35}$

81. $\begin{array}{r} \frac{2}{5} \\ -\frac{1}{10} \end{array}$ $\frac{3}{10}$

82. $\begin{array}{r} \frac{13}{9} \\ -\frac{7}{9} \end{array}$ $\frac{2}{3}$

83. $\begin{array}{r} \frac{8}{20} \\ -\frac{2}{5} \end{array}$ 0

84. $\begin{array}{r} \frac{8}{5} \\ -\frac{3}{2} \end{array}$ $\frac{1}{10}$

85. $\begin{array}{r} \frac{6}{7} \\ -\frac{3}{4} \end{array}$ $\frac{3}{28}$

86. $\begin{array}{r} \frac{7}{20} \\ -\frac{3}{20} \end{array}$ $\frac{1}{5}$

87. $\begin{array}{r} \frac{5}{9} \\ -\frac{2}{5} \end{array}$ $\frac{7}{45}$

88. $\begin{array}{r} \frac{13}{12} \\ -\frac{7}{12} \end{array}$ $\frac{1}{2}$

89. $\begin{array}{r} \frac{11}{6} \\ -\frac{4}{3} \end{array}$ $\frac{1}{2}$

90. $\begin{array}{r} \frac{9}{2} \\ -\frac{7}{5} \end{array}$ $3\frac{1}{10}$

91. $\begin{array}{r} \frac{7}{8} \\ -\frac{1}{8} \end{array}$ $\frac{3}{4}$

92. $\begin{array}{r} \frac{5}{8} \\ -\frac{3}{8} \end{array}$ $\frac{1}{4}$

93. $\begin{array}{r} \frac{7}{12} \\ -\frac{1}{4} \end{array}$ $\frac{1}{3}$

94. $\begin{array}{r} \frac{17}{25} \\ -\frac{7}{25} \end{array}$ $\frac{2}{5}$

95. $\begin{array}{r} \frac{19}{20} \\ -\frac{1}{5} \end{array}$ $\frac{3}{4}$

96. $\begin{array}{r} \frac{9}{4} \\ -\frac{1}{4} \end{array}$ 2

97. $\begin{array}{r} \frac{11}{12} \\ -\frac{7}{12} \end{array}$ $\frac{1}{3}$

98. $\begin{array}{r} \frac{5}{6} \\ -\frac{7}{18} \end{array}$ $\frac{4}{9}$

99. $\begin{array}{r} \frac{12}{7} \\ -\frac{5}{7} \end{array}$ 1

100. $\begin{array}{r} \frac{3}{12} \\ -\frac{4}{16} \end{array}$ 0

To add mixed numbers:

Step 1:   Add the fractions.

Step 2:   Add the whole numbers.

Step 3:   Give the answer in lowest terms. (A mixed number is in *lowest terms* when the fraction is less than 1 and is in lowest terms.)

Examples:

1.
$$3\tfrac{3}{8}$$
$$+4\tfrac{1}{8}$$
$$7\tfrac{4}{8}=7\tfrac{1}{2}\quad\text{lowest terms}$$

2.
$$5$$
$$+3\tfrac{2}{3}$$
$$8\tfrac{2}{3}$$

3.

$$2\tfrac{1}{2}\qquad \tfrac{1}{2}=\tfrac{1\times 3}{2\times 3}=\tfrac{3}{6}\qquad 2\tfrac{3}{6}$$

$$+3\tfrac{1}{3}\qquad \tfrac{1}{3}=\tfrac{1\times 2}{3\times 2}=\tfrac{2}{6}\qquad +3\tfrac{2}{6}$$

$$5\tfrac{5}{6}$$

Rename the fractions so that the denominators are the same.

4.

$$7\tfrac{4}{5}$$
$$+2\tfrac{3}{5}$$
$$9\tfrac{7}{5}\quad\text{Rename }9\tfrac{7}{5}\text{ so the fraction is less than 1.}$$

$$9+\tfrac{7}{5}=9+1\tfrac{2}{5}=9+1+\tfrac{2}{5}=10\tfrac{2}{5}$$

5.

$$\tfrac{5}{12}\qquad \tfrac{5}{12}=\tfrac{5\times 5}{12\times 5}=\tfrac{25}{60}\qquad \tfrac{25}{60}$$

$$+3\tfrac{1}{5}\qquad \tfrac{1}{5}=\tfrac{1\times 12}{5\times 12}=\tfrac{12}{60}\qquad +3\tfrac{12}{60}$$

$$3\tfrac{37}{60}$$

Rename the fractions so that the denominators are the same.

EXERCISES

Write the sum in lowest terms.

1. $3\frac{1}{3}$
$+7\frac{1}{3}$ $10\frac{2}{3}$

2. $9\frac{2}{7}$
$+3\frac{3}{7}$ $12\frac{5}{7}$

3. $4\frac{2}{9}$
$+7\frac{5}{9}$ $11\frac{7}{9}$

4. $2\frac{1}{8}$
$+3\frac{5}{8}$ $5\frac{3}{4}$

5. $7\frac{3}{10}$
$+2\frac{1}{10}$ $9\frac{2}{5}$

6. $5\frac{4}{9}$
$+2\frac{2}{9}$ $7\frac{2}{3}$

7. $2\frac{1}{2}$
$+5\frac{1}{2}$ 8

8. $8\frac{2}{3}$
$+3\frac{1}{3}$ 12

9. $2\frac{4}{7}$
$+9\frac{3}{7}$ 12

10. $2\frac{7}{9}$
$+3\frac{7}{9}$ $6\frac{5}{9}$

11. $6\frac{3}{4}$
$+2\frac{3}{4}$ $9\frac{1}{2}$

12. $4\frac{7}{8}$
$+3\frac{5}{8}$ $8\frac{1}{2}$

13. $4\frac{1}{8}+3\frac{1}{4}$ $7\frac{3}{8}$

14. $5\frac{1}{6}+7\frac{2}{3}$ $12\frac{5}{6}$

15. $2\frac{1}{4}+3\frac{1}{3}$ $5\frac{7}{12}$

16. $2\frac{3}{4}+3\frac{1}{2}$ $6\frac{1}{4}$

17. $3\frac{5}{6}+5\frac{2}{3}$ $9\frac{1}{2}$

18. $2\frac{7}{8}+5\frac{1}{4}$ $8\frac{1}{8}$

19. $2\frac{2}{5}+7\frac{3}{4}$ $10\frac{3}{20}$

20. $10\frac{2}{3}+3\frac{3}{4}$ $14\frac{5}{12}$

21. $4\frac{2}{3}+2\frac{4}{5}$ $7\frac{7}{15}$

22. $\frac{1}{3}+2\frac{1}{6}$ $2\frac{1}{2}$

23. $5\frac{3}{10}+\frac{7}{8}$ $6\frac{7}{40}$

24. $\frac{7}{9}+3\frac{5}{6}$ $4\frac{11}{18}$

25. $9+3\frac{3}{8}$ $12\frac{3}{8}$

26. $4\frac{1}{6}+5$ $9\frac{1}{6}$

27. $13+21\frac{3}{4}$ $34\frac{3}{4}$

28. $6\frac{3}{10}+4\frac{1}{10}+3\frac{3}{10}$ $13\frac{7}{10}$

29. $5\frac{1}{8}+2\frac{3}{8}+9\frac{3}{8}$ $16\frac{7}{8}$

30. $10\frac{1}{9}+1\frac{5}{9}+5\frac{2}{9}$ $16\frac{8}{9}$

31. $5\frac{1}{6}+4\frac{1}{3}+2\frac{1}{12}$ $11\frac{7}{12}$

32. $1\frac{1}{16}+3\frac{1}{8}+2\frac{1}{4}$ $6\frac{7}{16}$

33. $5\frac{1}{2}+3\frac{1}{4}+6\frac{1}{8}$ $14\frac{7}{8}$

34. $12\frac{1}{4}+2\frac{3}{8}+1\frac{13}{16}$ $16\frac{7}{16}$

35. $7\frac{3}{10}+8\frac{9}{10}+11\frac{1}{10}$ $27\frac{3}{10}$

36. $2\frac{3}{8}+4\frac{1}{2}+9\frac{3}{4}$ $16\frac{5}{8}$

37. $4\frac{1}{3}+2\frac{5}{6}+1\frac{1}{2}$ $8\frac{2}{3}$

38. $6\frac{1}{3}+7\frac{1}{2}+3\frac{2}{3}$ $17\frac{1}{2}$

39. $11\frac{3}{5}+5\frac{7}{10}+1\frac{1}{5}$ $18\frac{1}{2}$

40. $6\frac{2}{5}+1\frac{1}{4}+9\frac{2}{3}$ $17\frac{19}{60}$

41. $8\frac{1}{2}+3\frac{7}{10}+2\frac{1}{5}$ $14\frac{2}{5}$

42. $12\frac{1}{3}+7\frac{5}{12}+4\frac{3}{5}$ $24\frac{7}{20}$

43. $8\frac{1}{2}+\frac{2}{3}+3\frac{1}{6}$ $12\frac{1}{3}$

44. $4\frac{1}{4}+7+3\frac{1}{3}$ $14\frac{7}{12}$

45. $5\frac{2}{3}+\frac{7}{8}+9\frac{1}{2}$ $16\frac{1}{24}$

To subtract mixed numbers:

Step 1:   Subtract the fractions.

Step 2:   Subtract the whole numbers.

Step 3:   Give the answer in lowest terms.

Examples:

1. $7\frac{5}{9}$

$-4\frac{4}{9}$

$3\frac{1}{9}$

2. $5\frac{5}{6}$

$-4\frac{1}{6}$

$1\frac{4}{6}=1\frac{2}{3}$

3.

$5\frac{3}{5}$ $\frac{3}{5}=\frac{3\times2}{5\times2}=\frac{6}{10}$ $5\frac{6}{10}$ **Rename the fractions so that the denominators are the same.**

$-2\frac{1}{2}$ $\frac{1}{2}=\frac{1\times5}{2\times5}=\frac{5}{10}$ $-2\frac{5}{10}$

$3\frac{1}{10}$

4. $\frac{1}{3}$ **is less than** $\frac{2}{3}$. **Rename** $3\frac{1}{3}$.

$3\frac{1}{3}$ $3\frac{1}{3}=2+1+\frac{1}{3}=2+\frac{3}{3}+\frac{1}{3}=2+\frac{4}{3}=2\frac{4}{3}$ $2\frac{4}{3}$

$-1\frac{2}{3}$ $-1\frac{2}{3}$

$1\frac{2}{3}$

5.

5 $5=4+1=4+\frac{2}{2}=4\frac{2}{2}$ $4\frac{2}{2}$ **Rename 5 as a mixed number so that the fractions have the same denominator.**

$-3\frac{1}{2}$ $-3\frac{1}{2}$ **Same denominator**

$1\frac{1}{2}$

512

EXERCISES

Write the difference in lowest terms.

1. $4\frac{7}{9}$
$-2\frac{3}{9}$ $2\frac{4}{9}$

2. $6\frac{4}{5}$
$-5\frac{2}{5}$ $1\frac{2}{5}$

3. $7\frac{6}{7}$
$-5\frac{3}{7}$ $2\frac{3}{7}$

4. $9\frac{8}{9}$
$-2\frac{7}{9}$ $7\frac{1}{9}$

5. $3\frac{4}{5}$
$-1\frac{1}{6}$ $2\frac{19}{30}$

6. $7\frac{3}{5}$
$-5\frac{3}{10}$ $2\frac{3}{10}$

7. $8\frac{4}{7}$
$-5\frac{1}{5}$ $3\frac{13}{35}$

8. $8\frac{3}{4}$
$-2\frac{1}{8}$ $6\frac{5}{8}$

9. $6\frac{7}{8}$
$-2\frac{1}{4}$ $4\frac{5}{8}$

10. $5\frac{1}{2}$
$-3\frac{4}{11}$ $2\frac{3}{22}$

11. $7\frac{3}{10}$
$-2\frac{3}{20}$ $5\frac{3}{20}$

12. $12\frac{1}{3}$
$-7\frac{2}{5}$ $4\frac{14}{15}$

13. $4\frac{1}{2}$
$-2\frac{2}{9}$ $2\frac{5}{18}$

14. $6\frac{3}{4}$
$-5\frac{2}{5}$ $1\frac{7}{20}$

15. $7\frac{2}{3}$
$-5\frac{2}{7}$ $2\frac{8}{21}$

16. $9\frac{1}{3}$
$-2\frac{2}{7}$ $7\frac{1}{21}$

17. $5\frac{5}{6}$
$-4\frac{5}{8}$ $1\frac{5}{24}$

18. $8\frac{3}{4}$
$-6\frac{1}{2}$ $2\frac{1}{4}$

19. $7\frac{7}{8}$
$-3\frac{1}{4}$ $4\frac{5}{8}$

20. $6\frac{4}{5}$
$-5\frac{3}{10}$ $1\frac{1}{2}$

21. $7\frac{1}{3}-4\frac{1}{6}$ $3\frac{1}{6}$

22. $8\frac{5}{9}-2\frac{1}{3}$ $6\frac{2}{9}$

23. $12\frac{5}{6}-3\frac{5}{9}$ $9\frac{5}{18}$

24. $9\frac{1}{6}-2\frac{5}{6}$ $6\frac{1}{3}$

25. $11\frac{1}{5}-7\frac{3}{5}$ $3\frac{3}{5}$

26. $9\frac{3}{10}-7\frac{7}{10}$ $1\frac{3}{5}$

27. $3\frac{1}{4}-1\frac{3}{4}$ $1\frac{1}{2}$

28. $7\frac{1}{8}-3\frac{5}{8}$ $3\frac{1}{2}$

29. $4\frac{1}{3}-3\frac{2}{3}$ $\frac{2}{3}$

30. $12\frac{2}{3}-7$ $5\frac{2}{3}$

31. $4\frac{5}{8}-3\frac{5}{12}$ $1\frac{5}{24}$

32. $7\frac{3}{5}-5$ $2\frac{3}{5}$

33. $5\frac{1}{2}-3\frac{5}{8}$ $1\frac{7}{8}$

34. $4\frac{1}{10}-2\frac{3}{5}$ $1\frac{1}{2}$

35. $12\frac{1}{6}-7\frac{2}{3}$ $4\frac{1}{2}$

36. $8\frac{3}{8}-4\frac{3}{4}$ $3\frac{5}{8}$

37. $5\frac{1}{4}-3\frac{1}{2}$ $1\frac{3}{4}$

38. $7\frac{1}{6}-3\frac{2}{9}$ $3\frac{17}{18}$

39. $6-3\frac{1}{2}$ $2\frac{1}{2}$

40. $7-5\frac{3}{8}$ $1\frac{5}{8}$

41. $9-5\frac{8}{10}$ $3\frac{1}{5}$

42. $5-\frac{3}{16}$ $4\frac{13}{16}$

43. $8-\frac{5}{12}$ $7\frac{7}{12}$

44. $13-\frac{3}{7}$ $12\frac{4}{7}$

45. $9\frac{1}{2}-4\frac{1}{2}$ 5

46. $12\frac{3}{5}-7\frac{6}{10}$ 5

47. $8\frac{90}{100}-5\frac{9}{10}$ 3

48. $2\frac{1}{2}-2\frac{3}{6}$ 0

49. $13\frac{1}{2}-4$ $9\frac{1}{2}$

50. $12-11\frac{1}{5}$ $\frac{4}{5}$

51. $4\frac{3}{8}-4\frac{1}{4}$ $\frac{1}{8}$

52. $10\frac{3}{5}-\frac{2}{5}$ $10\frac{1}{5}$

To multiply (or to divide) with mixed numbers:

Step 1: Change the mixed numbers to fractions.

Step 2: Multiply (or divide); write the product (or the quotient) as a whole number, as a fraction in lowest terms, or as a mixed number whenever possible.

Examples:

1. $2\frac{1}{4} \times 4\frac{3}{5} = \frac{9}{4} \times \frac{23}{5}$

$= \frac{9 \times 23}{4 \times 5}$

$= \frac{207}{20}$

$= 10\frac{7}{20}$

2. $3\frac{1}{2} \div 2\frac{2}{5} = \frac{7}{2} \div \frac{12}{5}$

$= \frac{7}{2} \times \frac{5}{12}$

$= \frac{35}{24}$

$= 1\frac{11}{24}$

3. $4\frac{3}{4} \times \frac{4}{5} = \frac{19}{\cancel{4}_1} \times \frac{\cancel{4}^1}{5}$

$= \frac{19}{5}$

$= 3\frac{4}{5}$

4. $\frac{3}{4} \div 3\frac{1}{2} = \frac{3}{4} \div \frac{7}{2}$

$= \frac{3}{\cancel{4}_2} \times \frac{\cancel{2}^1}{7}$

$= \frac{3}{14}$

5. $1\frac{2}{5} \times 4 = \frac{7}{5} \times \frac{4}{1}$

$= \frac{28}{5}$

$= 5\frac{3}{5}$

6. $2 \div 1\frac{3}{4} = \frac{2}{1} \div \frac{7}{4}$

$= \frac{2}{1} \times \frac{4}{7}$

$= \frac{8}{7}$

$= 1\frac{1}{7}$

The form in which you write the result usually depends on what the result is to be used for. Fractions in the final results should be in lowest terms.

EXERCISES

Write the product as a whole number, as a fraction in lowest terms, or as a mixed number whenever possible.

1. $3\frac{1}{2} \times 2\frac{1}{4}$ $7\frac{7}{8}$

2. $2\frac{3}{4} \times 1\frac{1}{2}$ $4\frac{1}{8}$

3. $2\frac{1}{8} \times 3\frac{1}{2}$ $7\frac{7}{16}$

4. $3\frac{1}{8} \times \frac{2}{5}$ $1\frac{1}{4}$

5. $3\frac{2}{3} \times 1\frac{2}{5}$ $5\frac{2}{15}$

6. $3\frac{3}{5} \times 2\frac{1}{3}$ $8\frac{2}{5}$

7. $3\frac{2}{3} \times 5\frac{4}{5}$ $21\frac{4}{15}$

8. $1\frac{1}{2} \times 2\frac{3}{8}$ $3\frac{9}{16}$

9. $6\frac{1}{8} \times 5\frac{1}{2}$ $33\frac{11}{16}$

10. $2\frac{3}{4} \times 2\frac{2}{5}$ $6\frac{3}{5}$

11. $5\frac{3}{4} \times \frac{1}{8}$ $\frac{23}{32}$

12. $3\frac{1}{3} \times 2\frac{3}{4}$ $9\frac{1}{6}$

13. $6\frac{5}{8} \times 1\frac{2}{3}$ $11\frac{1}{24}$

14. $6\frac{1}{3} \times 2\frac{4}{5}$ $17\frac{11}{15}$

15. $2 \times 3\frac{2}{7}$ $6\frac{4}{7}$

16. $7\frac{2}{3} \times \frac{4}{5}$ $6\frac{2}{15}$

17. $8\frac{1}{2} \times \frac{2}{3}$ $5\frac{2}{3}$

18. $4 \times 3\frac{1}{8}$ $12\frac{1}{2}$

19. $\frac{5}{12} \times 4\frac{2}{3}$ $1\frac{17}{18}$

20. $\frac{5}{8} \times 1\frac{3}{5}$ 1

21. $5\frac{1}{5} \times \frac{5}{11}$ $2\frac{4}{11}$

22. $6\frac{7}{8} \times \frac{3}{3}$ $6\frac{7}{8}$

23. $6\frac{2}{3} \times \frac{3}{2}$ 10

24. $3\frac{2}{9} \times \frac{9}{11}$ $2\frac{7}{11}$

25. $2\frac{1}{3} \times 5 \times 1\frac{2}{7}$ 15

26. $7 \times 5\frac{1}{2} \times \frac{3}{7}$ $16\frac{1}{2}$

27. $1\frac{2}{9} \times 3 \times 2\frac{2}{3}$ $9\frac{7}{9}$

28. $\frac{0}{2} \times 3 \times \frac{1}{6}$ 0

Write the quotient as a whole number, as a fraction in lowest terms, or as a mixed number whenever possible.

29. $4\frac{1}{2} \div 2\frac{1}{2}$ $1\frac{4}{5}$

30. $6\frac{2}{5} \div 3\frac{4}{5}$ $1\frac{13}{19}$

31. $3 \div 2\frac{1}{5}$ $1\frac{4}{11}$

32. $2\frac{1}{2} \div 3\frac{3}{4}$ $\frac{2}{3}$

33. $6\frac{3}{8} \div 2\frac{3}{4}$ $2\frac{7}{22}$

34. $4\frac{1}{5} \div 6$ $\frac{7}{10}$

35. $2\frac{1}{2} \div 4\frac{3}{4}$ $\frac{10}{19}$

36. $2\frac{3}{8} \div 6\frac{1}{2}$ $\frac{19}{52}$

37. $5\frac{2}{3} \div 3\frac{1}{4}$ $1\frac{29}{39}$

38. $4\frac{1}{5} \div 2\frac{1}{3}$ $1\frac{4}{5}$

39. $2\frac{3}{6} \div 2\frac{1}{2}$ 1

40. $6\frac{1}{5} \div 2$ $3\frac{1}{10}$

41. $5\frac{1}{5} \div \frac{4}{5}$ $6\frac{1}{2}$

42. $\frac{4}{5} \div 2\frac{2}{3}$ $\frac{3}{10}$

43. $6\frac{7}{8} \div \frac{5}{5}$ $6\frac{7}{8}$

44. $\frac{2}{3} \div 2\frac{1}{6}$ $\frac{4}{13}$

45. $\frac{16}{5} \div 3\frac{1}{5}$ 1

46. $4\frac{5}{6} \div \frac{2}{3}$ $7\frac{1}{4}$

47. $\frac{7}{8} \div 3\frac{1}{4}$ $\frac{7}{26}$

48. $5\frac{1}{8} \div 2\frac{3}{4}$ $1\frac{19}{22}$

49. $7\frac{2}{3} \div \frac{1}{3}$ 23

50. $4\frac{4}{5} \div 6$ $\frac{4}{5}$

51. $8 \div 2\frac{3}{8}$ $3\frac{7}{19}$

52. $3\frac{2}{7} \div \frac{3}{14}$ $15\frac{1}{3}$

53. $1 \div 5\frac{1}{2}$ $\frac{2}{11}$

54. $3\frac{5}{9} \div 32$ $\frac{1}{9}$

55. $0 \div 12\frac{1}{3}$ 0

56. $8 \div 1\frac{3}{5}$ 5

Write the sum as a whole number or as a mixed number.

1. $2\frac{2}{3}+5\frac{2}{3}$ $8\frac{1}{3}$ **2.** $9\frac{5}{8}+3\frac{1}{8}$ $12\frac{3}{4}$ **3.** $4\frac{5}{12}+3\frac{1}{12}$ $7\frac{1}{2}$ **4.** $3\frac{2}{3}+2\frac{1}{3}$ 6

5. $7\frac{7}{8}+3\frac{1}{8}$ 11 **6.** $8\frac{1}{4}+2\frac{7}{12}$ $10\frac{5}{6}$ **7.** $4\frac{5}{6}+2\frac{2}{9}$ $7\frac{1}{18}$ **8.** $4\frac{3}{4}+5\frac{1}{6}$ $9\frac{11}{12}$

9. $2\frac{5}{6}+7\frac{3}{8}$ $10\frac{5}{24}$ **10.** $4\frac{7}{8}+7\frac{5}{12}$ $12\frac{7}{24}$ **11.** $9\frac{3}{5}+5\frac{3}{4}$ $15\frac{7}{20}$ **12.** $5\frac{1}{2}+6\frac{3}{5}$ $12\frac{1}{10}$

13. $9\frac{3}{7}+4\frac{2}{5}$ $13\frac{29}{35}$ **14.** $7\frac{1}{6}+5\frac{2}{7}$ $12\frac{19}{42}$ **15.** $3\frac{1}{2}+6\frac{2}{3}$ $10\frac{1}{6}$ **16.** $5\frac{3}{4}+3\frac{2}{3}$ $9\frac{5}{12}$

17. $6\frac{3}{5}+7\frac{1}{6}$ $13\frac{23}{30}$ **18.** $5\frac{5}{6}+8\frac{3}{10}$ $14\frac{2}{15}$ **19.** $6\frac{1}{2}+4\frac{3}{7}$ $10\frac{13}{14}$ **20.** $8\frac{7}{10}+6\frac{3}{8}$ $15\frac{3}{40}$

21. $3\frac{4}{5}+\frac{3}{8}$ $4\frac{7}{40}$ **22.** $7\frac{3}{5}+27$ $34\frac{3}{5}$ **23.** $3\frac{2}{3}+8\frac{4}{5}$ $12\frac{7}{15}$ **24.** $\frac{5}{12}+8\frac{4}{9}$ $8\frac{31}{36}$

25. $6\frac{2}{3}+2\frac{5}{8}$ $9\frac{7}{24}$ **26.** $5+8\frac{3}{4}$ $13\frac{3}{4}$ **27.** $4\frac{7}{10}+11\frac{4}{15}$ $15\frac{29}{30}$

28. $4\frac{1}{7}+1\frac{2}{7}+9\frac{3}{7}$ $14\frac{6}{7}$ **29.** $6\frac{2}{3}+1\frac{2}{3}+8\frac{1}{3}$ $16\frac{2}{3}$ **30.** $4\frac{1}{10}+9\frac{7}{10}+13\frac{3}{10}$ $27\frac{1}{10}$

31. $3\frac{1}{8}+9\frac{3}{4}+2\frac{1}{12}$ $14\frac{23}{24}$ **32.** $7+5\frac{7}{11}+12$ $24\frac{7}{11}$ **33.** $4\frac{2}{3}+11\frac{1}{6}+2\frac{5}{8}$ $18\frac{11}{24}$

34. $7\frac{2}{3}+1\frac{1}{4}+3\frac{1}{2}$ $12\frac{5}{12}$ **35.** $4\frac{1}{6}+8+\frac{7}{9}$ $12\frac{17}{18}$ **36.** $9\frac{1}{2}+2\frac{3}{5}+\frac{3}{4}$ $12\frac{17}{20}$

Write the difference as a whole number, as a fraction in lowest terms, or as a mixed number whenever possible.

37. $9\frac{5}{7}-3\frac{1}{7}$ $6\frac{4}{7}$ **38.** $12\frac{4}{5}-7\frac{2}{5}$ $5\frac{2}{5}$ **39.** $4\frac{7}{9}-3\frac{5}{9}$ $1\frac{2}{9}$ **40.** $8\frac{7}{8}-2\frac{5}{8}$ $6\frac{1}{4}$

41. $6\frac{3}{10}-4\frac{9}{10}$ $1\frac{2}{5}$ **42.** $11\frac{5}{12}-7\frac{7}{12}$ $3\frac{5}{6}$ **43.** $5\frac{3}{4}-4\frac{3}{4}$ 1 **44.** $8\frac{1}{2}-3\frac{1}{2}$ 5

45. $7\frac{7}{8}-7\frac{2}{3}$ $\frac{5}{24}$ **46.** $7\frac{6}{10}-6\frac{4}{5}$ $\frac{4}{5}$ **47.** $7\frac{1}{3}-4\frac{3}{4}$ $2\frac{7}{12}$ **48.** $4\frac{3}{8}-\frac{5}{16}$ $4\frac{1}{16}$

49. $10-6\frac{2}{3}$ $3\frac{1}{3}$ **50.** $8\frac{5}{9}-3\frac{5}{6}$ $4\frac{13}{18}$ **51.** $12\frac{8}{15}-\frac{4}{5}$ $11\frac{11}{15}$ **52.** $11\frac{1}{5}-7\frac{7}{10}$ $3\frac{1}{2}$

53. $5\frac{8}{11}-3$ $2\frac{8}{11}$ **54.** $7\frac{1}{8}-1\frac{5}{12}$ $5\frac{17}{24}$ **55.** $8-4\frac{3}{16}$ $3\frac{13}{16}$ **56.** $5\frac{1}{2}-2\frac{3}{5}$ $2\frac{9}{10}$

57. $7 - \frac{3}{4}$ $6\frac{1}{4}$ **58.** $12\frac{5}{6} - 6\frac{7}{8}$ $5\frac{23}{24}$ **59.** $9\frac{2}{3} - \frac{5}{6}$ $8\frac{5}{6}$ **60.** $4\frac{3}{7} - 1\frac{1}{10}$ $3\frac{23}{70}$

61. $6 - \frac{4}{9}$ $5\frac{5}{9}$ **62.** $12\frac{5}{9} - 8\frac{7}{12}$ $3\frac{35}{36}$ **63.** $13\frac{9}{10} - 4\frac{1}{6}$ $9\frac{11}{15}$ **64.** $3\frac{1}{12} - 3\frac{1}{18}$ $\frac{1}{36}$

65. $9\frac{5}{8} - \frac{0}{6}$ $9\frac{5}{8}$ **66.** $21 - 5\frac{5}{9}$ $15\frac{4}{9}$ **67.** $4\frac{3}{8} - 1\frac{5}{6}$ $2\frac{13}{24}$ **68.** $4\frac{1}{6} - 3\frac{5}{9}$ $\frac{11}{18}$

69. $13 - \frac{3}{14}$ $12\frac{11}{14}$ **70.** $8\frac{3}{4} - 5\frac{7}{12}$ $3\frac{1}{6}$ **71.** $23\frac{1}{10} - 4\frac{1}{8}$ $18\frac{39}{40}$ **72.** $8\frac{3}{16} - 5\frac{7}{12}$ $2\frac{29}{48}$

Write the product as a whole number or as a mixed number.

73. $1\frac{3}{4} \times 2\frac{1}{2}$ $4\frac{3}{8}$ **74.** $2\frac{2}{3} \times 3\frac{1}{4}$ $8\frac{2}{3}$ **75.** $3\frac{2}{5} \times 1\frac{1}{3}$ $4\frac{8}{15}$ **76.** $2\frac{5}{8} \times 1\frac{1}{4}$ $3\frac{9}{32}$

77. $5\frac{1}{2} \times 3$ $16\frac{1}{2}$ **78.** $1\frac{7}{8} \times 2\frac{1}{2}$ $4\frac{11}{16}$ **79.** $4\frac{1}{3} \times 1\frac{2}{7}$ $5\frac{4}{7}$ **80.** $2\frac{1}{8} \times 1\frac{1}{5}$ $2\frac{11}{20}$

81. $2\frac{3}{7} \times 3\frac{1}{2}$ $8\frac{1}{2}$ **82.** $1\frac{4}{5} \times 4\frac{1}{2}$ $8\frac{1}{10}$ **83.** $4 \times 2\frac{1}{6}$ $8\frac{2}{3}$ **84.** $2\frac{2}{5} \times 2\frac{1}{6}$ $5\frac{1}{5}$

85. $\frac{4}{9} \times 3\frac{1}{4}$ $1\frac{4}{9}$ **86.** $2\frac{3}{4} \times 1\frac{1}{7}$ $3\frac{1}{7}$ **87.** $\frac{3}{4} \times 2\frac{1}{6}$ $1\frac{5}{8}$ **88.** $3\frac{1}{6} \times 2\frac{1}{2}$ $7\frac{11}{12}$

89. $7\frac{2}{3} \times \frac{1}{4}$ $1\frac{11}{12}$ **90.** $2\frac{1}{3} \times 3\frac{1}{6}$ $7\frac{7}{18}$ **91.** $3\frac{1}{4} \times 3$ $9\frac{3}{4}$ **92.** $1\frac{3}{4} \times 1\frac{1}{7}$ 2

93. $1\frac{3}{5} \times 1\frac{2}{7}$ $2\frac{2}{35}$ **94.** $5\frac{1}{2} \times 1\frac{1}{3} \times 2$ $14\frac{2}{3}$ **95.** $2\frac{1}{4} \times \frac{2}{5} \times 3$ $2\frac{7}{10}$ **96.** $3\frac{2}{3} \times 1\frac{3}{4} \times \frac{1}{2}$ $3\frac{5}{24}$

Write the quotient as a whole number, as a fraction in lowest terms, or as a mixed number whenever possible.

97. $2\frac{1}{2} \div 3\frac{1}{4}$ $\frac{10}{13}$ **98.** $3\frac{2}{5} \div 2\frac{1}{6}$ $1\frac{37}{65}$ **99.** $3\frac{1}{2} \div 2\frac{2}{3}$ $1\frac{5}{16}$ **100.** $1\frac{2}{7} \div 1\frac{1}{5}$ $1\frac{1}{14}$

101. $4\frac{1}{3} \div 2\frac{1}{2}$ $1\frac{11}{15}$ **102.** $1\frac{3}{4} \div 2\frac{1}{6}$ $\frac{21}{26}$ **103.** $4\frac{1}{2} \div 1\frac{3}{5}$ $2\frac{13}{16}$ **104.** $1\frac{1}{7} \div \frac{3}{4}$ $1\frac{11}{21}$

105. $3\frac{1}{6} \div 2\frac{5}{8}$ $1\frac{13}{63}$ **106.** $1\frac{1}{4} \div 3$ $\frac{5}{12}$ **107.** $\frac{4}{9} \div 2\frac{1}{3}$ $\frac{4}{21}$ **108.** $\frac{0}{5} \div 1\frac{2}{7}$ 0

109. $2 \div 2\frac{1}{2}$ $\frac{4}{5}$ **110.** $2\frac{2}{3} \div 3\frac{1}{6}$ $\frac{16}{19}$ **111.** $7\frac{2}{3} \div 2\frac{2}{5}$ $3\frac{7}{36}$ **112.** $3\frac{1}{4} \div 1\frac{3}{8}$ $2\frac{4}{11}$

113. $2\frac{4}{5} \div 3\frac{1}{4}$ $\frac{56}{65}$ **114.** $2\frac{1}{6} \div 5\frac{1}{2}$ $\frac{13}{33}$ **115.** $4\frac{2}{3} \div 2\frac{1}{4}$ $2\frac{2}{27}$ **116.** $1\frac{3}{4} \div 2\frac{1}{3}$ $\frac{3}{4}$

117. $7\frac{1}{2} \div 3\frac{1}{2}$ $2\frac{1}{7}$ **118.** $8 \div 1\frac{3}{10}$ $6\frac{2}{13}$ **119.** $3\frac{1}{2} \div 4\frac{1}{6}$ $\frac{21}{25}$ **120.** $2\frac{3}{4} \div 1\frac{2}{5}$ $1\frac{27}{28}$

$\frac{3}{4}$ means $3 \div 4$ or $4\overline{)3}$.

To change a fraction to a decimal, divide the numerator by the denominator.

Examples:

1.
$$\frac{3}{4} = 4\overline{)\begin{matrix}0.75\\3.00\end{matrix}} \qquad \text{So } \frac{3}{4} = 0.75.$$
$$\begin{matrix}2\ 8\\\overline{20}\\\underline{20}\\0 \quad \text{remainder}\end{matrix}$$

2.
$$\frac{7}{4} = 4\overline{)\begin{matrix}1.75\\7.00\end{matrix}} \qquad \text{So } \frac{7}{4} = 1.75.$$
$$\begin{matrix}4\\\overline{3\ 0}\\2\ 8\\\overline{20}\\\underline{20}\\0 \quad \text{remainder}\end{matrix}$$

Notice that the remainder in each of the above division examples is 0. When that happens, the resulting decimal is called a *terminating decimal.*

3.
$$\frac{2}{11} = 11\overline{)\begin{matrix}0.181818\\2.000000\end{matrix}}$$
$$\begin{matrix}1\ 1\\\rightarrow9\ 0\\88\\\rightarrow 2\ 0\\11\\\rightarrow9\ 0\\88\\\rightarrow 2\ 0\\11\\\rightarrow9\ 0\\88\\\rightarrow 2\end{matrix}$$

Remainders repeat.

You could continue dividing indefinitely. The remainders 2 and 9 would keep repeating, and the digits 1 and 8 would keep repeating in the quotient.

You could write: $\quad \frac{2}{11} = 0.\overline{18}.$

The bar over 18 indicates that these digits continually repeat.

4.

$$\frac{13}{3} = 3\overline{)13.0000} \quad \begin{array}{r} 4.3333 \\ \hline \end{array}$$

$$\begin{array}{r} \underline{12} \\ 1\ 0 \\ \underline{9} \\ 10 \\ \underline{9} \\ 10 \\ \underline{9} \\ 10 \\ \underline{9} \\ 1 \end{array}$$

Remainder repeats.

The division process will continue indefinitely, repeating the remainder of 1.

You could write: $\dfrac{13}{3} = 4.\overline{3}.$

In Examples 3 and 4 a digit or digits continually repeat in the quotient. When that happens, the resulting decimal is called a **repeating decimal.**

EXERCISES

Change each fraction to a decimal. Tell whether the decimal is a terminating decimal or a repeating decimal.

1. $\frac{1}{4}$ 0.25
terminating

2. $\frac{1}{8}$ 0.125
terminating

3. $\frac{7}{10}$ 0.7
terminating

4. $\frac{5}{8}$ 0.625
terminating

5. $\frac{9}{2}$ 4.5
terminating

6. $\frac{11}{4}$ 2.75
terminating

7. $\frac{12}{10}$ 1.2
terminating

8. $\frac{37}{10}$ 3.7
terminating

9. $\frac{7}{8}$ 0.875
terminating

10. $\frac{3}{5}$ 0.6
terminating

11. $\frac{31}{20}$ 1.55
terminating

12. $\frac{2}{3}$ 0.$\overline{6}$
repeating

13. $\frac{5}{9}$ 0.$\overline{5}$
repeating

14. $\frac{19}{16}$ 1.1875
terminating

15. $\frac{2}{5}$ 0.4
terminating

16. $\frac{1}{16}$ 0.0625
terminating

17. $\frac{7}{25}$ 0.28
terminating

18. $\frac{13}{20}$ 0.65
terminating

19. $\frac{93}{4}$ 23.25
terminating

20. $\frac{3}{7}$ 0.$\overline{428571}$
repeating

21. $\frac{21}{8}$ 2.625
terminating

22. $\frac{17}{2}$ 8.5
terminating

23. $\frac{5}{12}$ 0.41$\overline{6}$
repeating

24. $\frac{7}{20}$ 0.35
terminating

25. $\frac{7}{25}$ 0.28
terminating

26. $\frac{8}{13}$ 0.$\overline{615384}$
repeating

27. $\frac{47}{1000}$ 0.047
terminating

28. $\frac{3}{50}$ 0.06
terminating

29. $\frac{5}{4}$ 1.25
terminating

30. $\frac{14}{11}$ 1.$\overline{27}$
repeating

To change a mixed number to a decimal:

Step 1: Change the fraction to a decimal.

Step 2: Add the whole number and the decimal.

Examples:

1. Change $4\frac{7}{8}$ to a decimal.

2. Change $5\frac{1}{6}$ to a decimal.

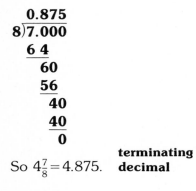

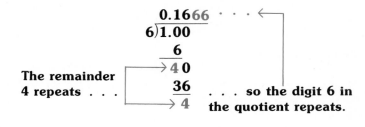

So $4\frac{7}{8} = 4.875$.   **terminating decimal**

So $\frac{1}{6} = 0.1\overline{6}$ and $5\frac{1}{6} = 5.1\overline{6}$.   **repeating decimal**

EXERCISES

Change each mixed number to a decimal. Tell whether the decimal is a terminating decimal or a repeating decimal.

1. $2\frac{1}{2}$ 2.5
terminating

2. $7\frac{1}{5}$ 7.2
terminating

3. $12\frac{3}{10}$ 12.3
terminating

4. $9\frac{1}{4}$ 9.25
terminating

5. $5\frac{1}{8}$ 5.125
terminating

6. $1\frac{3}{16}$ 1.1875
terminating

7. $4\frac{3}{5}$ 4.6
terminating

8. $5\frac{5}{6}$ 5.8$\overline{3}$
repeating

9. $13\frac{4}{25}$ 13.16
terminating

10. $6\frac{7}{20}$ 6.35
terminating

11. $14\frac{2}{3}$ 14.$\overline{6}$
repeating

12. $8\frac{21}{50}$ 8.42
terminating

13. $16\frac{33}{100}$ 16.33
terminating

14. $8\frac{1}{3}$ 8.$\overline{3}$
repeating

15. $2\frac{5}{9}$ 2.$\overline{5}$
repeating

16. $3\frac{2}{9}$ 3.$\overline{2}$
repeating

17. $4\frac{9}{11}$ 4.$\overline{81}$
repeating

18. $5\frac{8}{33}$ 5.$\overline{24}$
repeating

19. $2\frac{7}{9}$ 2.$\overline{7}$
repeating

20. $4\frac{5}{33}$ 4.$\overline{15}$
repeating

21. $5\frac{8}{11}$ 5.$\overline{72}$
repeating

22. $7\frac{4}{5}$ 7.8
terminating

23. $7\frac{5}{12}$ 7.41$\overline{6}$
repeating

24. $13\frac{3}{4}$ 13.75
terminating

In words	Decimal	Fraction
three tenths	0.3	$\dfrac{3}{10}$
forty-three hundredths	0.43	$\dfrac{43}{100}$
twenty-nine thousandths	0.029	$\dfrac{29}{1000}$

If a decimal names a number less than 1, you can change it to a fraction as follows:

Examples:

1. $0.7 = \dfrac{7}{10}$

1 decimal → 1 zero place

2. $0.13 = \dfrac{13}{100}$

2 decimal → 2 zeros places

---

3. $0.242 = \dfrac{242}{1000} = \dfrac{\overset{121}{\cancel{242}}}{\underset{500}{\cancel{1000}}} = \dfrac{121}{500}$ **lowest terms**

3 decimal → 3 zeros places

If a decimal names a number greater than 1, you can change it to a mixed number as follows:

Step 1: Change the part of the decimal to the right of the decimal point to a fraction in lowest terms.

Step 2: Add that fraction to the whole number.

4. 35.25

$\dfrac{25}{100} = \dfrac{1}{4}$

$35.25 = 35\dfrac{1}{4}$

5. 2.072

$\dfrac{72}{1000} = \dfrac{9}{125}$

$2.072 = 2\dfrac{9}{125}$

521

EXERCISES

Change each decimal to a fraction in lowest terms.

1. 0.9 $\frac{9}{10}$

2. 0.99 $\frac{99}{100}$

3. 0.999 $\frac{999}{1000}$

4. 0.3 $\frac{3}{10}$

5. 0.03 $\frac{3}{100}$

6. 0.003 $\frac{3}{1000}$

7. 0.71 $\frac{71}{100}$

8. 0.023 $\frac{23}{1000}$

9. 0.149 $\frac{149}{1000}$

10. 0.5 $\frac{1}{2}$

11. 0.75 $\frac{3}{4}$

12. 0.025 $\frac{1}{40}$

13. 0.125 $\frac{1}{8}$

14. 0.625 $\frac{5}{8}$

15. 0.6 $\frac{3}{5}$

16. 0.84 $\frac{21}{25}$

17. 0.12 $\frac{3}{25}$

18. 0.072 $\frac{9}{125}$

19. 0.004 $\frac{1}{250}$

20. 0.124 $\frac{31}{250}$

21. 0.02 $\frac{1}{50}$

22. 0.109 $\frac{109}{1000}$

23. 0.704 $\frac{88}{125}$

24. 0.16 $\frac{4}{25}$

25. 0.8 $\frac{4}{5}$

26. 0.08 $\frac{2}{25}$

27. 0.11 $\frac{11}{100}$

28. 0.27 $\frac{27}{100}$

29. 0.333 $\frac{333}{1000}$

30. 0.666 $\frac{333}{500}$

Change each decimal to a mixed number in lowest terms.

31. 5.7 $5\frac{7}{10}$

32. 3.4 $3\frac{2}{5}$

33. 9.75 $9\frac{3}{4}$

34. 13.8 $13\frac{4}{5}$

35. 1.1 $1\frac{1}{10}$

36. 2.125 $2\frac{1}{8}$

37. 6.9 $6\frac{9}{10}$

38. 19.25 $19\frac{1}{4}$

39. 4.625 $4\frac{5}{8}$

40. 7.375 $7\frac{3}{8}$

41. 20.512 $20\frac{64}{125}$

42. 12.3125 $12\frac{5}{16}$

43. 323.378 $323\frac{189}{500}$

44. 29.299 $29\frac{299}{1000}$

45. 8.0625 $8\frac{1}{16}$

46. 67.275 $67\frac{11}{40}$

47. 89.63 $89\frac{63}{100}$

48. 9.725 $9\frac{29}{40}$

49. 15.45 $15\frac{9}{20}$

50. 3.382 $3\frac{191}{500}$

51. 2.22 $2\frac{11}{50}$

Contents

Introduction

The primary purpose of this section is to provide instruction and practice in the use of a hand-held calculator. The skills in this section can be developed by using a typical inexpensive calculator having a keyboard similar to that shown below.

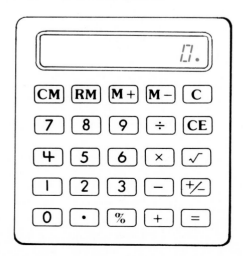

The instructions on the following pages are appropriate for a calculator that has the following features:

1. Operation keys ($+$ $-$ $\times$ $\div$) having only one symbol each, and a separate $=$ key that must be pressed to display the final answer. Should your calculator have keys labeled $+=$ and $-=$, consult the instruction manual that came with your calculator, since the sequences of pressing keys for adding and subtracting will be different from those given in this section.

2. A % key

3. A memory (Memory keys usually bear the letter M with some other symbol, such as CM MR $M+$ $M-$.)

4. A floating decimal—a feature that automatically places the decimal point correctly in the final answer. Some calculators have a fixed decimal point—usually to show hundredths—and are suitable for adding and subtracting amounts of money.

   Add 5.264 and 2.4108 on your calculator. If it shows the answer 7.6748, which is the correct answer, the calculator has a floating decimal. If it shows a different answer, either you have made an error or the calculator has a fixed decimal.

If the labeling of the keys or the sequences of numbers displayed on your calculator are different from those shown in the examples on the following pages, consult the instruction manual that came with your calculator.

Addition and subtraction can be done from left to right.

Example: 89.9 + 217 − 67.54

ENTER	DISPLAY	
C	*0.*	clears calculator
89.9	*89.9*	first number
+	*89.9*	
317	*317.*	incorrect second number
CE	*0.*	clears incorrect entry
217	*217.*	correct second number
−	*306.9*	sum of 89.9 and 217
67.54	*67.54*	number to subtract
=	*239.35*	answer

If your calculator has no CE key, press the C key once, and only once, to clear an incorrect entry (number).

EXERCISES

Use a calculator to find each result.

1. 416.5 + 39.27 − 283.9   171.87

2. 176 + 49.62 − 82.98   142.64

3. 346.2 − 72.7 − 53.4   220.1

4. 10.29 − 7.67 − 1.83   0.79

5. 96.38 + 187.16 − 47.5   236.04

6. 2.401 + 0.992 − 1.706   1.687

7. 255 + 78.2 − 19.77   313.43

8. 72 + 688 − 497   263

9. 7.38 + 2.86 − 4.37   5.87

10. 32.07 − 19.84 + 6.28   18.51

11. 0.945 + 2.362 − 1.706   1.601

12. 64.1 + 32.6 − 27.8   68.9

13. 372 − 269 + 58   161

14. 7.38 − 3.29 − 1.46   2.63

Example: In four games Maria bowled 116, 97, 141, and 109. To find her total score for the four games, find the following sum:

116 + 97 + 141 + 109

ENTER	DISPLAY	
[C]	*0.*	clears calculator
116	*116.*	first number
[+]	*116.*	
97	*97.*	second number
[+]	*213.*	sum of 116 and 97
141	*141.*	third number
[+]	*354.*	sum of 116, 97, and 141
109	*109.*	fourth number
[=]	*463.*	sum of all the numbers

EXERCISES

Use a calculator to find each sum.

1. 321 + 48 + 112 + 247 728

2. 2421 + 3807 + 1926 8154

3. 3.7 + 8.2 + 5.6 + 1.9 19.4

4. 12 + 27 + 31 + 49 + 56 175

5. 17.301 + 39.657 + 74.078 131.036

6. 2.6 + 8.1 + 3.9 + 5.5 + 4.7 24.8

7. 29.4 + 31.7 + 66.5 + 47.2 174.8

8. 1706 + 347 + 2342 + 876 5271

9. 312 + 57.2 + 21.3 + 148 538.5

10. 0.3 + 0.7 + 0.8 + 0.6 + 0.9 3.3

11. 57 + 34 + 22 + 67 180

12. 82 + 31 + 47 + 12 + 95 267

13. 11.09 + 13.8 + 105.99 + 99.009 + 39 268,889

14. 32,580 + 21,498 + 79 + 8888 + 0 63,045

15. 7.955 + 0.089 + 20,469 + 8.80 + 8.6 20,494.444

16. 456.99 + 2.97 + 3008.5 + 0.95 3469.41

Many problems are solved by multiplying two numbers or by dividing one number by another.

Example: 57×31.4

ENTER	DISPLAY	
C	$0.$	clears calculator
57	$57.$	first number
×	$57.$	
31.4	31.4	second number
=	1789.8	product

Example: $201.26 \div 5.8$

ENTER	DISPLAY	
C	$0.$	clears calculator
201.26	201.26	dividend
÷	201.26	
5.8	5.8	divisor
=	34.7	quotient

EXERCISES

Use a calculator to find each result.

1. 79×12.4 979.6

2. 5.72×81.3 465.036

3. 346×6.08 2103.68

4. 207×586 121,302

5. 47.3×9.8 463.54

6. 0.126×0.09 0.01134

7. $319.6 \div 3.4$ 94

8. $4394.5 \div 85$ 51.7

9. $4144 \div 56$ 74

10. $18.72 \div 3.9$ 4.8

11. $27 \div 0.36$ 75

12. $37.68 \div 3.14$ 12

Example: Bert priced a 20-pound bag of lawn fertilizer in three stores. The prices were $5.88, $7.16, and $6.49. To find the mean price, add the numbers and then divide by the number of addends.

$$\frac{5.88 + 7.16 + 6.49}{3}$$

ENTER	DISPLAY	
C	0.	clears calculator
5.88	5.88	first addend
+	5.88	
7.16	7.16	second addend
+	13.04	sum of first two numbers
6.49	6.49	third addend
=	19.53	sum of the three numbers
÷	19.53	
3	3.	number of addends
=	6.51	mean

EXERCISES

Use a calculator to find the mean of each set.

1. 4.3, 8.8, 6.7   6.6

2. 31, 29, 42, 51, 32   37

3. 2.7, 186, 209, 192   147.425

4. 7.8, 6.4, 5.9, 7.3, 8.1   7.1

5. 0.8, 0.7, 1.2, 0.9   0.9

6. 47.22, 39.08, 40.57, 43.67   42.635

7. 2305, 2674, 3103   2694

8. 7, 9, 6, 8, 10, 7, 9   8

9. 5302.17, 4086.85   4694.51

10. 89, 92, 103, 96, 94, 0   79

11. 5.62, 6.03, 4.96, 5.83   5.61

12. 0.56, 0.72, 0.65, 0.59   0.63

CALCULATOR

Example: Find the mean for the frequency table at the right.

Number	Frequency
19	2
21	5
24	3
total	10

ENTER	DISPLAY	
C	$0.$	clears calculator
CM	$0.$	clears memory
19 × 2 =	$38.$	product
M+	$38.$	stores 38 in memory
21 × 5 =	$105.$	product
M+	$105.$	adds 105 to 38 in memory
24 × 3 =	$72.$	product
M+	$72.$	adds 72 to sum in memory
RM	$215.$	recalls sum from memory
÷ 10 =	21.5	divides 215 by 10

The mean is 21.5.

EXERCISES

Use a calculator to find the mean for each frequency table.

1.
Number	Frequency
5	4
6	5
8	8
10	3
total	20 7.2

2.
Number	Frequency
70	5
80	4
90	4
100	2
total	15 82

3.
Number	Frequency
10	4
12	3
16	2
20	3
total	12 14

4.
Number	Frequency
33	2
34	2
37	2
38	1
39	2
total	9; 36

5.
Number	Frequency
55	8
56	9
57	12
58	10
59	11
total	50; 57.14

6.
Number	Frequency
21	14
22	24
23	21
24	12
25	9
total	80; 22.725

One use of ( ) is to indicate which operation to do first. In $(5 \times 3.4) + 2.6$, the multiplication should be done first. However, in $5 \times (3.4 + 2.6)$, the addition should be done first.

Example: $(5 \times 3.4) + 2.6$

ENTER	DISPLAY	
C	0.	clears calculator
5	5.	first factor
×	5.	
3.4	3.4	second factor
= +	17.	product of 5 and 3.4
2.6	2.6	number to add
=	19.6	answer

Example: $5 \times (3.4 + 2.6)$

ENTER	DISPLAY	
C	0.	clears calculator
CM	0.	clears memory
3.4	3.4	first addend
+	3.4	
2.6	2.6	second addend
=	6.	sum of 3.4 and 2.6
M +	6.	stores the sum, 6, in memory
5	5.	first factor
×	5.	
RM	6.	recalls 6 from memory
=	30.	answer

EXERCISES

Use a calculator to find each result.

1. $(27+8) \times 4$ 140

2. $81 \div (24-15)$ 9

3. $128 - (5.6 \times 15)$ 44

4. $(32 \div 4) \times 31.3$ 250.4

5. $(32.6 + 29.8) \div 3$ 20.8

6. $529.7 + (17.8 \times 34)$ 1134.9

7. $7.04 - (13.68 \div 2.4)$ 1.34

8. $(7580 \times 1.08) - 3600$ 4586.4

9. $(25.6 + 71.3) \div 0.3$ 323

10. $8.04 - (20.72 \div 5.6)$ 4.34

11. $218.36 \div (32.7 + 8.5)$ 5.3

12. $(504.3 - 297.6) \times 1.75$ 361.725

13. $(16.4 \times 22.6) + 57.13$ 427.77

14. $400 + (0.26 \times 375)$ 497.5

When two sets of parentheses are used, you can use the following procedure to find the result:

Do this first and store in memory.

$$(14+28) - (52 \div 20) = 39.4$$

Then do this, and subtract the number recalled from memory.

Use a calculator to find each result.

15. $(14+28) \times (52-17)$ 1470

16. $(17 \times 8) \div (28.4 \div 7.1)$ 34

17. $(107 - 58) \div (35 - 28)$ 7

18. $(46 - 27) + (19 \times 7)$ 152

19. $(2436 \div 6) + (18 \times 12)$ 622

20. $(9.7 \times 6.3) - (4.6 + 8.7)$ 47.81

21. $(57.3 - 14.8) \times (8.72 + 12.03)$ 881.875

22. $(23.45 \div 3.5) \times (84.5 - 76.8)$ 51.59

23. $(117.04 + 12.6) - (8.7 \times 10.4)$ 39.16

24. $(8.6 + 7.9) \div (23.2 - 17.5)$ 3

Example: The radius of a circle is 4.3 centimeters long. To find the circumference of that circle, use the following formula:

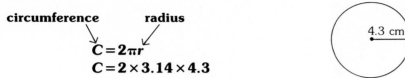

circumference   radius

$$C = 2\pi r$$
$$C = 2 \times 3.14 \times 4.3$$

4.3 cm

ENTER	DISPLAY	
[C]	*0.*	clears calculator
2	*2.*	first number
[×]	*2.*	
3.14	*3.14*	second number
[×]	*6.28*	product of first two numbers
4.3	*4.3*	third number
[=]	*27.004*	product

The circumference is 27.004 centimeters.

EXERCISES

Use a calculator to find each product.

1. $4 \times 3.14 \times 12$ 150.72

2. $5 \times 12 \times 9 \times 17$ 9180

3. $3.7 \times 0.5 \times 23$ 42.55

4. $7 \times 8 \times 7 \times 6 \times 5$ 11,760

5. $5.12 \times 8 \times 3.4$ 139.264

6. $124 \times 32.4 \times 6.6$ 26,516.16

7. $6 \times 5.3 \times 2.05$ 65.19

8. $1.5 \times 72.5 \times 65 \times 4.3$ 30,395.625

9. $23.4 \times 0.35 \times 500$ 4095

10. $8.7 \times 62 \times 4.1 \times 17.2$ 38,038.488

11. $7.5 \times 14 \times 7.5$ 787.5

12. $33 \times 8.46 \times 6.5 \times 0.7$ 1270.269

13. $2.05 \times 3.15 \times 4.2$ 27.1215

14. $0.14 \times 30 \times 1.26 \times 8$ 42.336

If you use the $\boxed{\%}$ key, you eliminate the need to convert a percent (like 8.9%) to a decimal (0.089).

Example: To find 15% of 25, calculate $25 \times 15\%$.

ENTER	DISPLAY	
$\boxed{C}$	$0.$	clears calculator
25	$25.$	first number
$\boxed{\times}$	$25.$	
15	$15.$	number of percent
$\boxed{\%}$	3.75	answer

On some calculators you will need to press the $\boxed{=}$ key as a final step in order to get the answer.

Example: You deposit $5250 in a savings account at 8.9% annual interest. To find how much interest will be earned in the first 3 months, use the interest formula.

First express the amount of time in years as a decimal.
3 months $= \frac{1}{4}$ year $= 0.25$ year

interest principal rate time (years)
$$i = p \times r \times t$$
$$i = 5250 \times 8.9\% \times 0.25$$

ENTER	DISPLAY	
$\boxed{C}$	$0.$	clears calculator
5250	$5250.$	principal
$\boxed{\times}$	$5250.$	
8.9	8.9	number of percent
$\boxed{\%}$	467.25	principal × rate
$\boxed{\times}$	467.25	
0.25	0.25	time
$\boxed{=}$	116.8125	interest

To the nearest cent, $116.81 will be earned in 3 months.

532

EXERCISES

Use a calculator to find each product.

1. $82 \times 6\%$ 4.92

2. $426 \times 10.5\%$ 44.73

3. $15.6 \times 8.5\%$ 1.326

4. $536 \times 75\%$ 402

5. $16,000 \times 12.5\%$ 2000

6. $840 \times 0.75\%$ 6.3

7. $96.8 \times 125\%$ 121

8. $54 \times 2.8\%$ 1.512

9. $1750 \times 110\%$ 1925

10. 5% of 85 4.25

11. 12% of 256 30.72

12. 4.5% of 36 1.62

13. 8.25% of 140 11.55

14. 82% of 315 258.3

15. 6.25% of 3500 218.75

16. 150% of 74 111

17. 11.05% of 25,000 2762.5

18. 125% of 12.4 15.5

Use a calculator to find each product. Round each answer to the nearest hundredth.

19. $1650 \times 9.5\% \times 5$ 783.75

20. $3275 \times 10.5\% \times 0.5$ 171.94

21. $4725 \times 8.25\% \times 3$ 1169.44

22. $10,000 \times 9.85\% \times 0.25$ 246.25

23. $5500 \times 11.25\% \times 2.5$ 1546.88

24. $750 \times 5.75\% \times 1.25$ 53.91

25. $150 \times 10.65\% \times 4$ 63.90

26. $20,000 \times 9.3\% \times 2.75$ 5115.00

27. $15,000 \times 6.7\% \times 3.5$ 3517.50

28. $8050 \times 8.25\% \times 6.5$ 4316.81

Use the interest formula and a calculator to find the amount of interest. Round each answer to the nearest cent.

29. $5400 at 7.5% for 4 years $1620

30. $20,500 at 9.2% for 1.5 years $2829

31. $8050 at 10.4% for 6 months $418.60

32. $6750 at 8.25% for 18 months $835.31

33. $100,000 at 12.75% for 3 months $3187.50

34. $3550.28 at 9.06% for 1 year and 9 months $562.90

Example: You deposit $3000 in a savings account at 8% compounded semiannually. To find how much you will have in the account at the end of the first year, you can apply the interest formula, $i = prt$, twice (once for each six months' interest). You can use the memory to keep a running total of the amount in the account.

Since the interest is being compounded semiannually, the time t in the formula will be $\frac{1}{2}$ year, or 0.5 year.

ENTER	DISPLAY	
$\boxed{C}$	$0.$	clears calculator
$\boxed{CM}$	$0.$	clears memory
3000	$3000.$	principal
$\boxed{M+}$	$3000.$	stores 3000 in memory
$\times 8\% \times 0.5 =$	$120.$	interest for first 6 months
$\boxed{M+}$	$120.$	adds 120 to 3000 in memory
$\boxed{RM}$	$3120.$	recalls sum from memory
$\times 8\% \times 0.5 =$	124.8	interest for second 6 months
$\boxed{M+}$	124.8	adds 124.8 to 3120 in memory
$\boxed{RM}$	3244.8	recalls total from memory

At the end of the first year there will be $3244.8, or $3244.80, in the account.

EXERCISES

Find the amount (to the nearest cent) in each account at the end of 1 year if the interest is compounded semiannually.

1. $2000 at 10% $2205
2. $2500 at 8% $2704
3. $5000 at 8.5% $5434.03

4. $3000 at 6% $3182.70
5. $3500 at 9% $3822.09
6. $8000 at 7.2% $8586.37

Find the amount (to the nearest cent) in each account at the end of 1 year if the interest is compounded quarterly. Remember to use $\frac{1}{4}$, or 0.25, for t in the formula.

7. $2000 at 10% $2207.63
8. $2500 at 8% $2706.08
9. $6000 at 7.2% $6443.80

You can think of $\frac{5}{8}$ as $5 \div 8$.

You can think of any fraction $\frac{a}{b}$ as $a \div b$.

To change a fraction to a decimal, divide the numerator by the denominator.

Example: Change $\frac{5}{8}$ to a decimal.

ENTER	DISPLAY	
C	0.	clears calculator
5	5.	numerator
÷	5.	
8	8.	denominator
=	0.625	decimal for $\frac{5}{8}$

The decimal 0.625 is called a *terminating* decimal, or a decimal that ends. Some other fractions that can be changed to terminating decimals are

$$\frac{1}{2} = 0.5 \qquad \frac{3}{4} = 0.75 \qquad \frac{7}{10} = 0.7 \qquad \frac{19}{100} = 0.19 \qquad \frac{57}{16} = 3.5625$$

Example: Change $\frac{7}{11}$ to a decimal.

ENTER	DISPLAY	
C	0.	clears calculator
7	7.	numerator
÷	7.	
11	11.	denominator
=	0.6363636	decimal for $\frac{7}{11}$

0.6363636 is called a *repeating* decimal. It repeats every two digits, 0.63 63 63 63 $\cdots$, and never ends. We write such a decimal by drawing a bar over the digits that repeat: $\frac{7}{11} = 0.\overline{63}$. Some other fractions that can be changed to repeating decimals are

$$\frac{1}{3} = 0.\overline{3} \qquad \frac{5}{6} = 0.8\overline{3} \qquad \frac{3}{7} = 0.\overline{428571} \qquad \frac{4}{9} = 0.\overline{4} \qquad \frac{25}{11} = 2.\overline{27}$$

EXERCISES

Use a calculator to change each fraction to a decimal.

1. $\frac{1}{4}$ 0.25   **2.** $\frac{2}{5}$ 0.40   **3.** $\frac{5}{6}$ 0.8$\overline{3}$ **4.** $\frac{2}{3}$ 0.$\overline{6}$

5. $\frac{7}{8}$ 0.875   **6.** $\frac{5}{16}$ 0.3125   **7.** $\frac{9}{11}$ 0.$\overline{81}$ **8.** $\frac{4}{9}$ 0.$\overline{4}$

9. $\frac{11}{25}$ 0.44   **10.** $\frac{17}{40}$ 0.425   **11.** $\frac{3}{16}$ 0.1875   **12.** $\frac{3}{8}$ 0.375

13. $\frac{4}{5}$ 0.8   **14.** $\frac{1}{6}$ 0.1$\overline{6}$ **15.** $\frac{3}{22}$ 0.1$\overline{36}$ **16.** $\frac{7}{20}$ 0.35

17. $\frac{13}{5}$ 2.6   **18.** $\frac{9}{4}$ 2.25   **19.** $\frac{7}{3}$ 2.$\overline{3}$ **20.** $\frac{17}{2}$ 8.5

Find decimals for the first three fractions below. Guess decimals for the rest. Then check your guesses with a calculator.

21. $\frac{1}{11}$ 0.$\overline{09}$ **22.** $\frac{2}{11}$ 0.$\overline{18}$ **23.** $\frac{3}{11}$ 0.$\overline{27}$ **24.** $\frac{4}{11}$ 0.$\overline{36}$

25. $\frac{5}{11}$ 0.$\overline{45}$ **26.** $\frac{6}{11}$ 0.$\overline{54}$ **27.** $\frac{7}{11}$ 0.$\overline{63}$ **28.** $\frac{8}{11}$ 0.$\overline{72}$

To change a mixed number to a decimal, change the fraction to a decimal and add the result to the whole number.

Examples: $16\frac{2}{5} = 16.4$ $23\frac{2}{3} = 23.\overline{6}$

Use a calculator to change each mixed number to a decimal.

29. $31\frac{7}{8}$ 31.875   **30.** $205\frac{1}{3}$ 205.$\overline{3}$ **31.** $83\frac{7}{10}$ 83.7   **32.** $67\frac{4}{5}$ 67.8

33. $10\frac{1}{6}$ 10.1$\overline{6}$ **34.** $73\frac{9}{16}$ 73.5625   **35.** $49\frac{5}{12}$ 49.41$\overline{6}$ **36.** $19\frac{1}{9}$ 19.$\overline{1}$

GLOSSARY

angle A figure such as any of the following:

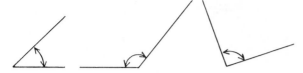

annual percentage rate The annual rate of interest for buying on credit or for earning interest on savings accounts.

area The amount of surface inside a figure.

average daily balance The average of the daily balances for a month (when buying on credit).

bank statement A statement of all transactions made on a bank account for a month.

bar graph A graph that uses bars to represent ordered pairs.

BASIC A computer language (**B**eginner's **A**ll-purpose **S**ymbolic **I**nstruction **C**ode).

budget A plan for coordinating income and expenditures.

Celsius scale A temperature scale on which water boils at 100° and freezes at 0°.

centimeter One hundredth meter.

check register A record of the date, payee, amount, and purpose of each check written.

circle A set of points in a plane that are all the same distance from a point called the center.

circle graph A graph in which the information is represented by parts of the interior of a circle.

circumference The distance around a circle.

commission An amount of money, usually a percentage of the selling price, paid for selling goods or services.

compound interest The interest earned when the principal for each period is the sum of the principal and interest for the preceding period.

computer An electronic machine that receives, stores, processes, and displays data.

computer program A set of numbered instructions written in a computer language, which a computer will follow in order.

coordinates The ordered pairs of numbers that name points in a plane.

cubic unit A unit used to measure volume—a rectangular solid all of whose faces are squares of a specific size (such as cubic inch, cubic foot, cubic centimeter).

customary (measurement) system A system of measurement that has units such as foot, inch, pound, and gallon.

cylinder A solid figure formed by two circular bases of the same size and the tubular surface joining them.

data Facts or information.

diameter A line segment that passes through the center of a circle and joins two points on the circle.

discount The amount of money by which original price is reduced.

equally likely Outcomes are equally likely if one outcome is as likely to occur as another.

equation A mathematical sentence containing an equal sign (=).

equivalent fractions Fractions that name the same number.

equivalent lengths Two or more measurements with different units for the same length.

equivalent ratios Different ratios for the same comparison.

estimate A result obtained by rounding a number or by mentally computing with rounded numbers rather than with actual values.

exponent A number that tells the number of times the base is used as a factor.

$$\text{exponent} \longrightarrow \overset{\downarrow}{2^3} = 2 \times 2 \times 2$$
$$\text{base} \longrightarrow$$

Fahrenheit scale A temperature scale on which water boils at 212° and freezes at 32°.

flowchart A chart that shows a sequence of steps that need to be followed to perform a task.

formula A general rule or principle written as a mathematical sentence.

frequency table A table that shows how many times each item (number, score, etc.) occurs in a set of data.

gram A unit of mass in the metric system.

greatest common factor The greatest whole number that is a factor of each of two or more numbers.

gross pay The total wages earned before deductions.

hexagon A polygon with 6 sides.

interest Money paid for the use of money.

kilogram One thousand grams.

kiloliter One thousand liters.

kilometer One thousand meters.

lease A contract between a tenant and the owner of the property to be rented.

least common multiple The smallest nonzero number that is a multiple of each of two or more numbers.

line graph A graph on which the points that represent ordered pairs are connected by line segments.

liter A unit of capacity in the metric system.

lowest terms A fraction is in lowest terms when the greatest common factor of the numerator and the denominator is 1. A mixed number is in lowest terms when the fraction is in lowest terms and is less than 1.

mean An average found by adding the numbers and dividing by how many numbers there are.

median The middle number when the numbers in a set are listed in order.

meter The basic unit of length in the metric system.

metric (measurement) system A system of measurement that has units such as centimeter, meter, liter, gram, and kilogram.

milligram One thousandth gram.

milliliter One thousandth liter.

millimeter One thousandth meter.

mixed number The sum of a whole number and a fraction—for example $3\frac{4}{5}$.

mode The item or items that occur most often in a list.

net pay The amount of money after all payroll deductions are made.

octagon A polygon with 8 sides.

open sentence A mathematical sentence that contains a variable and is neither true nor false.

order of operations When there are no parentheses to indicate order of operations, multiply and divide from left to right and then add and subtract from left to right.

origin The point at which the x-axis and the y-axis intersect.

outcome One of the possible results or ways that something can occur in an experiment.

overtime The time worked beyond a specified number of hours (usually 40 hours) per week.

parallelogram A quadrilateral with opposite sides parallel.

pentagon A polygon with 5 sides.

percent A ratio of some number to 100.

perimeter The distance around a figure.

pi (π) The ratio of the circumference to the measure of a diameter of the same circle—approximately equal to 3.14, or $\frac{22}{7}$.

piecework Work that is paid for according to the number of pieces completed or produced.

polygon A plane figure formed by three or more line segments having common endpoints and only one interior.

principal The amount of money that is earning interest.

probability The chance that a given outcome, or result, will occur.

proportion A sentence stating that two ratios are equivalent.

protractor An instrument for measuring angles.

quadrilateral A polygon with 4 sides.

radius A line segment that joins the center of a circle to any point on the circle.

range The difference between the highest and lowest scores in a set of scores.

ratio A comparison of two numbers by division.

reciprocals Two numbers are reciprocals of each other if their product is 1.

rectangle A parallelogram with all right angles.

rectangular solid A solid figure with all (6) rectanglar faces.

repeating decimal A decimal in which a digit or digits continuously repeat without end, such as 0.333 · · · or 5.$\overline{18}$.

right angle An angle with a measurement of 90°.

sample space A list or table of all possible outcomes of an experiment.

scale drawing A drawing that represents a real object—the drawing may be a reduction, the same size, or an enlargement.

schematic A diagram that shows how the parts of a system or an object fit together.

similar figures Geometric figures that have the same shape but not necessarily the same size.

solid figures (solids) Three-dimensional figures—figures that enclose space.

solve an equation To find a number or numbers that can replace a variable and make a sentence true.

square A quadrilateral that has all right angles and all sides the same length.

square unit A unit used to measure area—a square of a specified size and its interior (such as square foot, square inch, square meter, square centimeter).

standard units of measure Units of measure with constant sizes, agreed upon by the people who use them.

statistics A branch of mathematics that deals with collecting, organizing, and interpreting data.

terminating decimal A decimal that terminates, or ends, such as 0.12 or 5.682.

trapezoid A quadrilateral with only one pair of opposite sides parallel.

triangle A polygon with 3 sides.

unit price The price, or cost, of 1 unit, such as 1 gram, 1 pound, 1 foot, or 1 bar. (Divide the total cost by the quantity.)

variable A symbol that can be replaced with a number.

volume The amount of space inside a solid figure.

x-axis The horizontal scale of a graph, on which values of x are represented.

y-axis The vertical scale of a graph, on which values of y are represented.

INDEX